D1523326

A

Philip E. Lilienthal (signature)

■   ■   ■

B O O K

The Philip E. Lilienthal imprint
honors special books
in commemoration of a man whose work
at University of California Press from 1954 to 1979
was marked by dedication to young authors
and to high standards in the field of Asian Studies.
Friends, family, authors, and foundations have together
endowed the Lilienthal Fund, which enables UC Press
to publish under this imprint selected books
in a way that reflects the taste and judgment
of a great and beloved editor.

The publisher gratefully acknowledges the generous support of the Philip E. Lilienthal Asian Studies Endowment Fund of the University of California Press Foundation, which was established by a major gift from Sally Lilienthal.

RACE FOR EMPIRE

ASIA PACIFIC MODERN

Takashi Fujitani, Series Editor

T. Fujitani   ·   RACE FOR EMPIRE

Koreans as Japanese and Japanese
as Americans during World War II

University of California Press

Berkeley   Los Angeles   London

University of California Press, one of the most
distinguished university presses in the United States,
enriches lives around the world by advancing scholarship in the humanities, social sciences, and natural
sciences. Its activities are supported by the UC Press
Foundation and by philanthropic contributions from
individuals and institutions. For more information, visit
www.ucpress.edu.

University of California Press
Berkeley and Los Angeles, California

University of California Press, Ltd.
London, England

Library of Congress Cataloging-in-Publication Data

Fujitani, Takashi.
  Race for empire : Koreans as Japanese and Japanese
as Americans during World War II / T. Fujitani.—1
      p. cm.—(Asia Pacific modern ; 7)
  Includes bibliographical references and index.
  ISBN 978-0-520-26223-2 (hardback)
  1. World War, 1939–1945—Participation, Japanese
American. 2. World War, 1939–1945—Participation,
Korean. 3. World War, 1939–1945—Social aspects—
United States. 4. World War, 1939–1945—Social
aspects—Japan. 5. Nationalism—United States—
History—20th century. 6. Nationalism—Japan—
History—20th century. 7. Racism—United States—
History—20th century. 8. Racism—Japan—
History—20th century. I. Title.
  D769.8.A6F798 011
  940.53089'956073—dc23   2011019924

Manufactured in the United States of America

20 19 18 17 16 15 14 13 12
10 9 8 7 6 5 4 3 2

In keeping with a commitment to support environmentally
responsible and sustainable printing practices, UC Press
has printed this book on Rolland Enviro100, a 100% post-
consumer fiber paper that is FSC certified, deinked, processed chlorine-free, and manufactured with renewable
biogas energy. It is acid-free and EcoLogo certified.

CONTENTS

ILLUSTRATIONS

FIGURES

TABLES

MAPS

PREFACE AND
ACKNOWLEDGMENTS

Many years ago I began to write a book on the military and its effects in modern Japan that would have had much less to say about race than does this volume. While this book reflects some of the concerns I had at that time, the racial politics of the mid- to late 1990s derailed that project, at least for a while. In the United States and especially in California, where I have taught for many years, the anti-immigrant movement, the widespread attack on affirmative action, and the steadily growing rant against considerations of race in opening opportunities for historically underrepresented minorities in employment, education, and other arenas of life pushed me to rethink my research agenda. Above all, I was most struck and offended by the virulence and self-righteousness of a type of racism that presented itself as its opposite— namely, as antiracist. Using slogans such as "reverse racism" and pegging as racist even the most modest policies intended to help rectify the effects of centuries of racial discrimination, the movement obviously has a longer history (including within the period that concerns this book) and certainly continues into the present in our post-Obama age—an age that some mistakenly or disingenuously regard as "post-racial." But in the mid- to late 1990s, the movement's hysteria reached a peak.

At such a time I wanted to learn more about the modern histories of racism and its varieties in the United States, initially less as a scholarly pursuit than as a means to better engage in discussions and activism around the ongoing problem of racial justice. An unexpected opportunity to write on the topic emerged in conversations with Geoffrey M. White and Lisa Yoneyama as we planned a major international conference on memories of the Second World War in the Asia-Pacific. Having grown up in California, I had long been struck by the discourse on Japanese American war heroes, both in the mainstream media and in Japanese American communities. I had intense memories of aging and often frail Japanese American men donning clothing, insignia, and caps from the U.S. Army uniforms that they had originally worn as much as half a century earlier, even when the occasion had no immediately apparent relationship to war, nationalism, or military commemoration. Since I wanted to know more about the history of these veterans and to understand how in the politics of race the figure of the Japanese American soldier had come to achieve such visibility in mainstream and Japanese American memories of the war, I decided to research this area for our conference. It seemed a way for me to approach the momentous subject of race in America from an angle with which I already had some organic familiarity, even though at the time I had no idea that I would pursue the topic beyond the conference paper.

In the paper I explored the connections between Japanese American military service, the World War II disavowal of racial discrimination even in the context of Japanese American internment, the inextricable relationship between racism and nationalism, the construction of Japanese Americans as the foremost model minority, the postwar emergence of Japan as what I began to call the model minority nation, and scholarship in Japanese studies. Eventually this paper was published in the volume *Perilous Memories: The Asia Pacific War(s)*, which I co-edited with my conference co-organizers.[1] The ideas that I first sketched out there can be found in various places throughout this book, but especially in chapter 5. I would like to thank Geoff and Lisa first of all, for the collaborative thinking that we did for the conference and volume. So many of my perspectives began to take shape through our intense discussions.

During and soon after the conference many individuals offered criticism and encouragement on the paper, as well as on subsequent presentations based on the essay. I want to mention in particular George Lipsitz, the late Yuji Ichioka, and Lisa Lowe. George helped allay my hesitation to cross over from Asian into American studies and brought me up to speed on the emerging scholarship, including his own, concerning African American engagements with imperial Japan. I am convinced that the sensitivity that he and Ishmael Reed (in a brief conversation) gave me on the ties between African American and Japanese history helped me understand the significance of archival documents that I subsequently discovered concerning wartime fears of a global alliance of the "darker races" with the Japanese, and how such a race panic contributed to the wartime decision first to suspend Japanese Americans from military service, and then to begin accepting them as volunteers. I met Yuji for the first time with some trepidation, since as a pioneer in Asian American studies he had devoted a lifetime of research to Japanese American history while I was admittedly somewhat of an "undocumented worker" in his field. But in addition to offering encouragement he "schooled me," as he might have put it, on thinking about World War II propaganda. Not only have I learned tremendously from Lisa's now classic book, *Immigrant Acts*,[2] and her multiple recent projects, but I have through many years been the beneficiary of her rare intelligence, generosity, commitment to social justice, encouragement, and friendship.

I had known for some time that minorities and colonials had also served in the modern Japanese military, and in the book mentioned in the opening of this preface I had planned to consider the late nineteenth- and early twentieth-century inclusion of national minorities within the military. But as I explored this topic with regard to Japan, it gradually became evident that a study of Korean soldiers in the Japanese military during World War II could be paired with one on Japanese Americans in the U.S. Army. I began to think that a comparative and transnational perspective on these "soldiers of color" might contribute in some way to larger discussions about race, nationalism, colonialism, gender, total war, and more on both sides of the Pacific. I also felt that I had neglected researching such questions in Japanese history for far too long, especially considering the ongoing neo-nationalism, sexism, anti-immigrant movements, and (more or less) veiled racism in Japan that were no less offensive to me than what was going on in what Lipsitz called "California, the Mississippi of the 1990s."[3]

I thank the National Museum of Ethnology in Senri, Japan, which offered me, at the Taniguchi Symposium in late 1997, one of my first opportunities to present some thoughts on the wartime discourse on Korean soldiers in the Japanese army. There I focused on the issue of gender and particularly masculinity in wartime literary and cinematic representations of Korean soldiering, a problematic that runs through several sections of this book (especially chapter 8).[4] At the same time, I did encounter some obstacles and resistance. The conventional disciplines of history and area studies—with their tendencies to limit the boundaries of research to those that fit neatly into nation-states—tend to militate against a transnational project such as mine. In fact, one colleague chided me for "dabbling" in U.S. history. What, after all, was a historian of modern Japan doing speaking and writing on race in America as more than an avocation? On another occasion an eminent Japanese studies professor at a major U.S. university fiercely condemned me in public for suggesting that there was any likeness between Japan and the United States during the war.

But many other individuals as well as colleagues in collaborative projects pushed me to explore the possibilities of the comparative and transnational book that I was only beginning to consider. They also seemed persuaded by one of my central arguments—namely, that while we tend to think of the U.S. and Japanese total war regimes as opposites, they in fact shared many common features, including their heightened disavowal of racial discrimination and simultaneous shift toward an inclusionary form of racism. I need to mention here the encouragement and guidance I received over many years from members of the Nichibei Kyōdō Kenkyūkai (the Japan/U.S. Joint Research Group), headed by Hirota Masaki and Carol Gluck; most of these scholars were also engaged in postnationalist studies of Japan. I want to especially thank Narita Ryūichi, who has played a central role in the transnational circulation of cutting-edge scholarship on Japan, and Naoki Sakai, whose critical works have inspired so many and whose friendship and guidance over the years have been invaluable to me. In 1998–99 the Institute for Research in the Humanities, Kyoto University, supported my research. Affiliation at the Institute first made it possible for me to conduct extended archival research on Koreans in the Japanese military. Not only could I utilize the fantastic resources available at the Institute and Kyoto University, but the Institute's support enabled me to explore numerous archives and libraries in Japan and Korea, to interview several Korean veterans, and to learn from Japanese scholarship on colonialism. Most of all, I want to thank Mizuno Naoki for being as much a teacher as a friend, and for generously sharing rare materials from his personal library.

In 1999 and 2000 funding from the Humanities Center and the Academic Senate at the University of California, San Diego made it possible for me to take multiple trips to conduct research at the Library of Congress and in the National Archives in Washington, D.C., and College Park, Maryland. Through a stroke of luck, on my first day of research in College Park I discovered a document titled "Memorandum on Policy towards Japan," which had been authored by Edwin O. Reischauer in September 1942. The memorandum was something of a smoking gun in that it showed that almost three years before the conflict would come to an end, Reischauer—one of the preeminent architects of postwar Japanese studies as well as U.S. ambassador to Japan from 1961 to 1966—had crafted a plan to maintain the Japanese emperor as a "puppet" in postwar Japan. But just as suggestive for my project, his plan called for the mobilization of Japanese Americans as soldiers as part of a global strategy for managing what he called the "yellow and brown peoples" of Asia. The document demonstrated, among other things, that policy makers and their advisers such as Reischauer always understood the necessity of seeing connections between domestic and global politics, as well as of forging policies for Japan from a broader global vision that explicitly included considerations of race. Because of the historical and contemporary importance of this find, I quickly wrote an article focusing on the document and its contexts for the Japanese journal *Sekai;* the piece was then translated into Korean in *Silch'ŏn munhak,* and I subsequently revised and expanded it into an article in *Critical Asian Studies.* I thank the publishers of these journals for providing opportunities to share my analyses with multiple audiences, and I am also grateful to the many scholars who commented on various versions of the piece.[5]

I could not have written this book without the support and the often constructive skepticism of other scholars and institutions whose work focuses primarily on Korea or on Koreans in Japan. Early in my research on Korean soldiering Higuchi Yūichi and I traded some of our archival findings, but I benefited far more from the exchange, for he has been the pioneer on the topic and he provided much-needed guidance. Im Jon-hye, a trailblazer in the study of literature written in Japanese by Koreans in Japan, graciously shared her knowledge of the literary aspects of Korean soldiering. In 2001 I had the good fortune of participating in a conference at the University of Michigan, "Between Colonialism and Nationalism: Power and Subjectivity in Korea, 1931–1950." A number of participants at the conference, including its organizer, Henry Em, brought to our discussions perspectives that challenged nationalist historiography and helped invigorate my scholarship. I thank the conference participants, but especially Henry, Jin-kyung Lee, and Kim Chul— all of whom have continued to contribute to my thinking on Japanese colonialism in Korea.

In my investigations, I soon discovered that a surprisingly large number of feature films had been made on the theme of Koreans in the Japanese military and that a good number had many elements in common with Hollywood movies. Although I had already been speaking and writing about this topic, in 2003 I had a very fortunate opportunity to present some of my thoughts on these late colonial films to specialists on Korean film at the symposium "Aesthetics and Historical Imagination of Korean Cinema," which was sponsored by the Institute of Media Art (Yonsei University) and the Goethe Institute.[6] I thank the organizers of that symposium and especially Baek Moon Im, who has continued to offer constructive criticism of my work on colonial cinema. I am also indebted to Han Suk-jung, who invited me to present a version of this paper at Dong-a University in Pusan and who shared many of his ideas with me, and to Im Sŏng-mo, who provided useful comments on that occasion. When I first began to analyze colonial films, almost no scholarly work on them existed and it was nearly impossible to view them. I was able to locate only three relevant films housed in the U.S. Library of Congress. Recently, more scholars have begun to research and write on colonial cinema, and much of this new wave of investigation has been enabled by the highly capable staff of the Korean Film Archive, who have rediscovered a number of films produced in the colonial period and made several of them available online and in DVD format. On a more personal note, I am very grateful to the Archive's staff for inviting me to participate in a 2008 international symposium, "Repatriation or Sharing of Film Heritage." Not only did I receive valuable feedback on my presentation at the symposium, but the staff also facilitated my research in their state-of-the-art archive and made it possible for me to reproduce several stills that are included in this book.

I regret that owing to my poor Korean language skills, I have been able to read and employ only a very limited number of primary and secondary texts written in that language. But what I have managed to accomplish in Korean has been enabled by a grant from the Japan Program at the Social Science Research Council and the tutors whom the grant allowed me to hire (and exhaust): most importantly, Moonhwan Choi, "Okky" Choi, Ji Hee Jung, and Su Yun Kim. I have read the Korean texts cited in this book and translations are my own, but I asked Ji Hee to check almost all of my readings for accuracy. I thank my tutors and the Council.

I am likewise deeply indebted to the Japanese American and Korean individuals who shared their Second World War and postwar memories with me. While I have cited only a few of them in the book, their stories and their generosity in meeting with me have served as constant reminders of the ongoing stakes involved in my project and the need to constantly reflect on the ethical and political implications of my research. Among the Japanese American veterans, draft resisters, and community activists of that generation with whom I have communicated over the years, I am especially grateful to Cedrick Shimo, Frank Emi, and Paul Tsuneishi. I have marveled at their unique perspectives and their commitment to producing alternative histories of Japanese American wartime experiences. I have likewise benefited from long conversations with several Korean veterans of World War II, especially Kim Sŏng-su; Mr. Chang, along with his wife Mrs. Yun (pseudonyms), in the Pacific Northwest; and Chŏn Sang-yŏp. Their resilience and honesty have helped me write narratives that I believe are both truer and more complex than the ones I would probably have written had I had access only to written and visual documents from the colonial period.

The difficulty of conducting research in multiple countries and of developing a method and framework for this project has considerably lengthened the process of completing this book. Without multiple small grants from the Academic Senate of the University of California, San Diego as well as several major fellowships that enabled me to take time off from teaching, I would have taken far longer to finish the book. In addition to the already-mentioned sponsorships, I received generous fellowships from the John S. Guggenheim Foundation, the American Council of Learning Societies, the National Endowment for the Humanities (summer stipend), and the Stanford Humanities Center (SHC). I spent a luxurious year under the competent and generous care of the staff of the SHC, where my only obligations were to spend time with brilliant colleagues from multiple disciplines and to devote myself to the book. I want to single out John Bender, the Center's director at the time, for our extended discussions about several philosophers and theorists who have informed my work, and my colleague at the Center, Gordon Chang, for thought-provoking conversations on Asian American history and other topics. While I was visiting at Stanford, Gi-Wook Shin, Kären Wigen, and members of the Asian America's Workshop invited me to several academic and social occasions, allowing me to learn from them and helping me to feel a part of the wider Stanford community.

I have been the beneficiary of an extraordinarily large number of opportunities to conduct research or present my work in Japan, Korea, the United States, Canada, Australia, the United Kingdom, and continental Europe. So many institutions and individuals in these places have assisted me in such a variety of ways that it is impossible to name them all. But in addition to those already acknowledged, I want to especially thank (in alphabetical order) Eiichiro Azuma, Dani Botsman, Leo Ching, Carter J. Eckert, Jonathan Hall, Jeff Hanes, Im Chong Myŏng, Itagaki Ryūta, Kim Jae-yong, Kim Kyŏng-nam, Kitahara Megumi, Komagome Takeshi, Eisei Kurimoto, Colleen Lye, Ethan Mark, Achille Mbembe, Moon-Ho Jung, Nishikawa Nagao, Nishikawa Shin, Ōsawa Masachi, Ōta Osamu, Vince Rafael, Chandan Reddy, Andre Schmid, Shu-mei Shih, the late Miriam Silverberg, Stephanie Smallwood, Serk-Bae Suh, Takagi Hiroshi, Alan Tansman, Tomiyama Ichirō, Sandra Wilson, Sam Yamashita, and Jun Yoo. At UC, San Diego, many colleagues gave me the gift of camaraderie, welcomed the unconventional, and demanded rigor and relevance: most especially, Luis Alvarez, Jody Blanco, Fatima El-Tayeb, Yen Espiritu, Rosemary George, David Gutierrez, Todd Henry, Sara Johnson, Curtis Marez, Roddey Reid, Nayan Shah, Shelley Streeby, Stefan Tanaka, and Danny Widener. This is a rare group of scholars, all of whom work across national boundaries and conventional disciplinary formations. For many years I've subjected numerous cohorts of graduate students in history, literature, ethnic studies, and several other departments at UCSD to repeated explanations of my understanding of history, theory, and much else. I'm grateful that they have responded not only with apparent interest and questions but also by alerting me to additional materials and insights I might incorporate into the book. Andrew Barshay, Bruce Cumings, Harry Harootunian, Tessa Morris-Suzuki, and David Palumbo-Liu all read the penultimate version of the entire, very long manuscript, and provided a host of useful suggestions for revision.

Although none of the chapters in this book is a reprint of earlier publications, I thank the many publishers in Japan, Korea, and the United States who have allowed me to publish pieces of my research along the way and who have permitted me to include materials from these publications in this book. In addition to the publishers already cited, I want to express my gratitude to Iwanami Shoten and especially the editors Kojima Kiyoshi, Baba Kimihiko, and Hara Ikuko for their long-term support of my projects and for publishing my work in *Sekai* as well as in two of their lecture series.[7] At the University of California Press, Reed Malcolm, Kalicia Pivirotto, and Emily Park provided the type of excellent guidance and encouragement that I have grown accustomed to as editor of the series in which this book appears. Alice Falk did another superb job of copyediting for me. I also thank Ryan Moran for skillfully compiling the index.

From the above it is obvious that I could not have written this book without the support and input of a myriad of individuals and institutions located throughout the world, but I've reserved my final message of gratitude for those who have lived most closely with me (literally, figuratively, or both) through many years. To my friends in the East Bay, thanks for always uplifting me with humor and even for ridiculing me when I've been unable to convince you that what I do is real work. Although my parents must have wondered why it takes so long for me to write books, they've always taken an interest in my career; my father at the age of eighty-seven even "googles" me to find out what I've been up to when I haven't been filial enough to tell them myself. They also managed to feed me with the most amazing local foods in their hometown every time I visited, even after my mother's declining health slowed her down from her glory days of cooking. Thank you many times over. To Mari, Kenji, and Yuri, thanks for many years of helping me become more than a brother. Toshiko and the late Toshinao Yoneyama have been as much friends and advisers as in-laws. Thank you for the fun and excitement. Although En has sometimes only pretended to take an interest in my work, I'm grateful for the constant interest he has always manifested in me, and for his ability to entice me away from my desk. Most of all, I cannot begin to adequately thank Lisa, my partner of more than a quarter of a century, whose ideas, support, activism, and constructive criticisms have sustained me throughout. I'm sure that she and others will accuse me of stealing her ideas, and I will have to admit to each and every charge and more. No mere academic citations can amply credit her for the ways that this book and my life have benefited from her companionship and our learning to think together.

As I bring this preface and my acknowledgments to a close, I will repeat the cliché that all errors and clumsy interpretations are my own. But I will add that as much as I am convinced that I am overturning some conventional historical interpretations and methods, I have built on a remarkable local and translocal community of scholarship and support. I can only hope that readers will find something of value in these pages that is remotely worthy of the embarrassment of riches I have been privileged to receive.

NOTE ON ROMANIZATION
AND NAMING

Personal names of those who reside or have resided primarily in China, Japan, or Korea are written with the surname preceding the given name, while the reverse order is followed for all others. In romanizing Korean and Japanese, I follow the McCune-Reischauer and modified Hepburn system (as used in Kenkyūsha's dictionaries), respectively. Exceptions have been made for proper nouns for which there are standard renderings in English (for example, Tokyo, Seoul, Pak Chung Hee), as well as when individuals have indicated that they prefer other romanizations.

I have tried to exercise sensitivity toward the politics of naming and transliteration, but have not avoided the terms or practices in common usage in the places and during the periods studied. With regard to the Japanese American camps, many activists and scholars have long emphasized that the term "relocation center" as applied to the ten main sites is a euphemism that obscures the coercion and violence of evacuation and internment. I agree with this criticism. However, since one of the arguments of this book is that from the government's point of view the camps were supposed to embody the values of liberalism, I rarely use the term "concentration camp" to refer to them. Also, although I believe that the Nazi concentration camps and the U.S. camps for Japanese Americans emerged out of a shared modern political rationality, they should not be conflated, because, as I will argue, the former led directly to extermination of the confined and the latter to assimilation of the segregated into white America, at least in principle and despite targeted expressions or threats of violence. In most cases I therefore employ either the official terms

designating specific types of camps—thus, "assembly center or camp," "relocation center or camp," "segregation center," and so on—or the more generic term
"internment camp" to refer to the various types of wartime camps that confined Japanese Americans. The reader should not assume that I in any way condone the official namings.

How one names Koreans and Korean places is an extremely sensitive political
issue. Not only did the Japanese colonial government attempt to force all Koreans
to adopt "Japanized" names, but the Japanese government continued to pressure
resident Koreans to do the same after the war. However, consistent with my decision to critically examine the most common naming practices of the relevant periods and places rather than substitute anachronistic terms that seem preferable
today, I use the contemporary appellations in the following ways. (1) I privilege the
Korean readings of Korean names whenever possible. (2) When the names are voiced
in films, I have given them as heard, whether in Korean or Japanese. In late colonial
films Koreans were commonly called by the Japanized voicings of the kanji characters making up the Korean names. When this is the case, I have rendered this pronunciation but also included the Korean version in parentheses, at least on its first
appearance, if possible. (3) When Korean names exist only in written texts, I have
generally privileged the Korean pronunciation even though it is quite possible that
Japanese readers may have voiced the kanji in Japanese. (4) In some cases—Korean
assimilationist writers, for example—it is quite likely that authors referred to themselves by the Japanized reading of their names. When I know or have conjectured
that this would be the case, I have followed their practice, because such a transliteration best captures the subject position that they were trying to constitute for
themselves as Japanese from Korea. Thus, for example, I most commonly refer to
the Korean writer Chang Hyŏk-chu as Chō Kakuchū when he writes as a Japanese
author. In addition, when Korean authors identified themselves with their adopted
Japanese names and used them regularly in their writings, I have not altered the
name.

COMMONLY USED
ACRONYMS

For abbreviations used in the notes,
see the bibliography.

AC OF S   assistant chief of staff

ASW   assistant secretary of war

CIG   Counter Intelligence Group

GGK   Government-General of Korea

IR   infantry regiment

JAB   Japanese-American Branch

JACL   Japanese American Citizens League

JAJB   Japanese-American Joint Board

MID   Military Intelligence Division

MIS   Military Intelligence Service

ONI   Office of Naval Intelligence

OPMG   Office of the Provost Marshal General

OWI   Office of War Information

WDC   Western Defense Command

WRA   War Relocation Authority

Ethnic and Colonial Soldiers
and the Politics of Disavowal

> I think there was considerable feeling [among Koreans]
> that it would be better [than seeking independence] to
> join up with Japan, to become Japanese and blend in—
> that becoming truly Japanese might be better for the
> happiness of the Korean people. . . . This is certainly not
> an unreasonable thought. Even thinking about second-
> generation Japanese in Hawaii, you know that with
> respect to Japan, although it was their mother country,
> they swore their allegiance to America. This was a
> tremendous thing. The Hawaii Nisei.
>
> TANAKA TAKEO (former vice governor-general of
> Korea), roundtable discussion, "Koiso sōtoku jidai no
> gaikan—Tanaka Takeo seimu sōkan ni kiku" (1959)

RACISM AND ITS DISAVOWAL IN TOTAL WAR REGIMES

Reflecting on her childhood years in early postwar Japan, the pioneering historian
and activist Utsumi Aiko wrote in her 1991 contribution to the popular Iwanami
Booklet series that she could recall no public memory from that time of the Korean
and Taiwanese men who had fought for Japan as soldiers and sailors during the Asia-
Pacific War. While she remembered those around her struggling to piece together
their lives in the immediate aftermath of the war, or simply getting by from day to
day, she had no childhood memories of these ethnic and colonial soldiers. "Thus,
although the 'War' remained in our daily lives," she wrote, "I had no way of knowing that the Japanese military had drafted soldiers from colonized countries such as
Korea and Taiwan. I never imagined that North and South Koreans such as Kim
Chae-ch'ang, who had been unilaterally stripped of their Japanese citizenship by
the postwar Japanese government and [thereby] had no relief benefits at all, were
among those wounded soldiers that [I noticed] in the streets." While she imagined
retrospectively that there must have been Korean soldiers among the wounded or

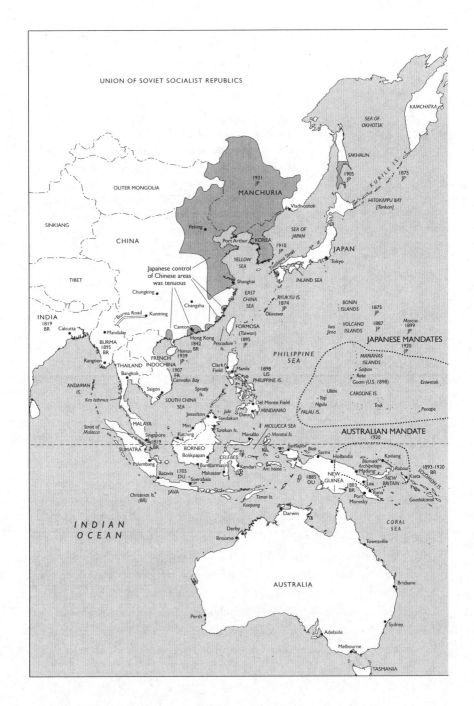

MAP 1.

The Far East and the Pacific: The Imperial Powers, 1 September 1939.
Redrawn in grayscale from the original color map (ca. 1941), courtesy
of the Department of History, United States Military Academy.
Although they might be legitimately contested by various parties today,

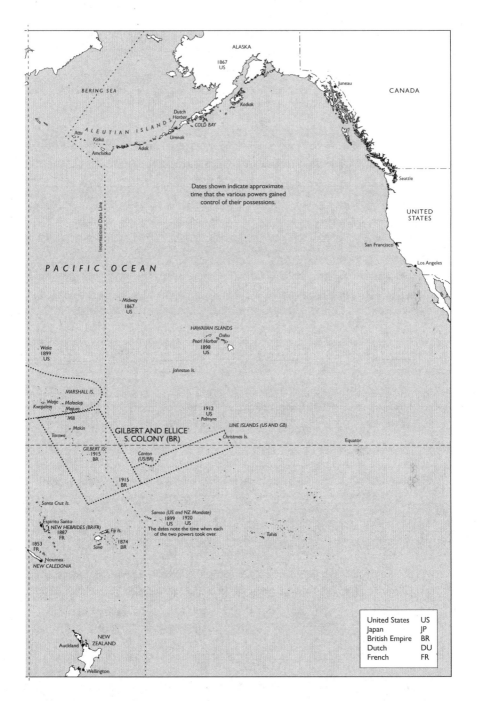

ALASKA

1867
US

BERING SEA

Juneau

CANADA

Kodiak

Dutch
Harbor

COLD BAY

ALEUTIAN ISLANDS

Attu

Kiska

Umnak

Amchitka

Adak

Seattle

Dates shown indicate approximate
time that the various powers gained
control of their possessions.

UNITED
STATES

San Francisco

PACIFIC OCEAN

Los Angeles

Midway
1867
US

HAWAIIAN ISLANDS

Oahu

Pearl Harbor
1898
US

Wake
1899
US

Johnston Is.

MARSHALL IS.

Watje Maloelap

Kwajalein   Majuro

Mili

Makin

Tarawa

1912
US
Palmyra

LINE ISLANDS (US AND GB)

GILBERT AND ELLICE
S. COLONY (BR)

Christmas Is.

Equator

GILBERT IS.
1915
BR

Canton
(US/BR)

1915
BR

Santa Cruz Is.

Espiritu Santo

NEW HEBRIDES (BR/FR)
1887
FR

Fiji Is.

Suva

1874
BR

1853
FR

Noumea
NEW CALEDONIA

Samoa (US and NZ Mandate)
1899   1920
US   US
The dates note the time when each
of the two powers took over.

Tahiti

NEW
ZEALAND

Auckland

Wellington

United States	US
Japan	JP
British Empire	BR
Dutch	DU
French	FR

all notations, dates, spelling, and place-names reproduce the original
to reflect the U.S. Military Academy's understanding of the Asia-
Pacific War as a struggle among empires that had established "control
of their possessions" throughout the region. The exception is the legend,
which has been changed to accommodate grayscale reproduction.

disabled that she had seen in the streets of her war-torn city, to her they were, as she put it, "invisible."[1] Similarly, the well-known filmmaker Ōshima Nagisa has written that when he began preliminary research for a television documentary on Korean veterans in the Japanese military that aired in August 1963, he was shocked to discover that in fact, "all of the white-robed disabled veterans begging in the streets of Japan [were] Korean."[2] Even as late as the mid-1990s, when many Asia-Pacific War memories that had been marginalized began to reemerge in the mainstream media and public debates with the thawing of the Cold War, the historian Kang Duk-sang (Tŏk-sang) lamented that in the flood of publications and TV specials in Japan commemorating the fiftieth anniversary of the recruitment of students into the Japanese military, he had not seen even one reference to Koreans who had been mobilized for this purpose, even though by his calculations about one in every twenty student soldiers had been Korean.[3]

Moreover, ethnic and colonial soldiers remain remarkably absent from the postwar public discourse around Yasukuni Shrine, the national site that is dedicated to the souls of all those who have lost their lives in military service for Japan. Each visit of a postwar prime minister or other high-ranking Japanese official to Yasukuni has sparked strong and fairly predictable outcries from leftists within Japan and from the international community. These critics understand that Yasukuni is a symbol of Japanese militarism and imperialism and that visits to that site represent both a lack of remorse about the past and a renunciation of responsibilities in the present. Rarely do these critics fail to mention that such convicted war criminals as Tōjō Hideki have been deified in this war memorial. And yet regardless of the fact that by official (under)count, 21,181 Korean and 28,863 Taiwanese war dead have also been enshrined at Yasukuni—an uncomfortable reminder that Japan not only waged a war of invasion against its neighbors but was also a multiethnic colonial empire and nation—a conspicuous silence about these ethnic and colonial soldiers remains.[4] Even on Okinawa's Cornerstone of Peace, a sprawling monument on which its builders have attempted to list every participant killed in the Battle of Okinawa—man or woman, enemy or ally, civilian or serviceman—there is a noticeable paucity of Koreans, either with Korean or with "Japanized" names. In many cases, it seems, postcolonial conditions in Korea and the specter of the label "collaborator" have made many Koreans wish to suppress memories of family members who had been Korean servicemen or civilian employees of the Japanese military.[5]

In contrast, it would be hard to deny that in the United States, soldiers of Japanese ancestry have achieved the status of American war heroes. To be sure, not all who live in the United States today have heard about the military exploits of the

100th Infantry Battalion or the 442nd Regimental Combat Team, the two segregated units whose members—nearly all Japanese American—were, as the legend goes, the most highly decorated group of soldiers in U.S. history. Still less known are the thousands of Japanese Americans who joined the war effort in the Pacific as translators and interpreters. Moreover, not all Americans have welcomed this relative abundance of Japanese American war memorials and commemorations. For example, in 2004 vandals defaced the "Go for Broke Monument" in Los Angeles' Little Tokyo with star etchings scraped into the monument's pillars. The commemorative site had been built in 1999 to honor the patriotism of Japanese American soldiers during World War II and to remind the public of the Constitution's guarantees of civil liberties for all Americans.[6]

Yet the failure of some Americans to remember the World War II valor of Japanese Americans, coupled with the force of ongoing anti-Japanese and anti-Asian sentiments, continues to push Japanese American veterans, their children, and their admirers toward more retellings and commemorations of Nisei heroism. Reunions and celebrations of Japanese American veterans of World War II continue to be held throughout the country; highways in California have been named for the 100th, for the 442nd, and for Japanese Americans who served in military intelligence; and the Japanese American National Museum in Los Angeles has prominently featured the story of Japanese American soldiers in its permanent displays and a special exhibit.[7]

In the critical period of the 1980s, the discourse on Japanese American military heroism gained even more prominence in public discussions and served as a powerful catalyst for the American Civil Liberties Act of 1988. As is well-known, the act provided $20,000 in individual payments to former internees and established a $1.25 billion fund for education about the internment of Japanese Americans. The House version of the bill, H.R. 442, carried the name of the 442nd Regimental Combat Team.[8]

Through the 1990s and into the current millennium, mainstream narratives of the war, whether voiced by leaders in government or carried in the popular media, with some regularity at least mention Japanese American internment and military service. For example, during the fiftieth anniversary commemorations of Pearl Harbor, President George H. W. Bush narrativized these Japanese American experiences in his commemoration speeches. The *New York Times* reported that "as he did at every place he spoke, the President lauded the Japanese-Americans who fought in the American armed forces during the war and expressed regrets to those interned 'innocent victims who committed no offense.'" "This ground," he said in one of his speeches in Honolulu, "embraces many American veterans whose love of country was put to the test unfairly by our own authorities. These and other natural-born American citizens faced wartime internment and they committed no crime. They were sent to internment camps simply because their ancestors were Japanese."[9] More recently, his son, President George W. Bush, proclaimed May 2006 as Asian/Pacific American Heritage Month while calling on his fellow citizens to learn about their history—a history that included "the many Asian/Pacific Americans who have courageously answered the call to defend freedom as members of our Armed Forces."[10]

But perhaps the National Japanese American Memorial to Patriotism, dedicated in November 2000 and erected in Washington, D.C., just three blocks away from the Capitol, best testifies to the incorporation of Japanese American internment and military heroism into mainstream U.S. memories of the war. A bronze sculpture at the site's center depicts two cranes struggling to free themselves from the barbed wire that holds them in bondage, while one of the granite walls carries the names of more than 800 Japanese American soldiers who died fighting for their nation. The memorial's point is unambiguous: Japanese Americans, both in battle and on the home front, remained loyal to the United States despite infringements on their civil rights and forced relocation to internment camps. An epigraph attributed to President Truman honors Nisei soldiers by proclaiming: "You fought not only the enemy but you fought prejudice—and you have won. Keep up that fight and we continue to win to make this great Republic stand for just what the Constitution says it stands for[:] the welfare of all the people all the time."[11] In short, despite violent periodic reminders of the persistence of anti-Asian racism and despite haunting memories about the wartime treatment of Japanese Americans that still resist public representation and even individual recollection, the narrative of Japanese American soldiers fighting heroically for freedom at home and abroad, even in the face of racism and incarceration in camps, has achieved a notable if not always comfortable place in mainstream narratives and memories of the war.[12]

Although the world tends to remember or forget these U.S. and Japanese ethnic and colonial soldiers so differently, this book aims to show that during the Second World War their positions, as well as the respective regimes that called them national subjects and then mobilized them into service, were surprisingly similar. My purpose is less to detail the heroic or tragic stories of the soldiers, a task that several scholars have already taken up, than to utilize the two sites of soldiering as optics through which to examine the larger operations and structures of the two changing empires, which were based on the nation-state form, as they struggled to manage racialized populations within the larger demands of conducting total war. While I do not wish to trivialize or minimize the intrinsic importance of telling straightforward histories of the soldiers—and I hope that my book makes some contributions in this regard—I seek to show how discussions about, policies concerning, and representations of these soldiers tell us a great deal about the characteristics of wartime racism, nationalism, imperialism, colonialism, capitalism, gender politics, the family, and related issues on both sides of the Pacific that go well beyond the Japanese American and Korean Japanese soldiers themselves. With regard to one of the primary concerns of this book, I hope that a detailed study of these "soldiers of color"— placed within their larger social, cultural, political, and economic contexts—will help illuminate the dramatic wartime shift in the type of racism that characterized these two regimes: namely, toward an inclusionary rather than exclusionary form, and thus away from what I will be calling "vulgar racism," and toward a more refined and, at least in appearance, often less overtly violent "polite racism."

One of the book's main arguments is that the material and ideational demands of waging total war effected parallel and mutually constitutive changes in the political rationalities of the two colonial empires and nations, producing very similar adjustments to the ways that the regimes managed racialized colonial subjects and national minorities. Most importantly, both the U.S. and Japanese total war regimes shifted decisively toward the strategy of disavowing racism and including despised populations within their national communities. This contrasted with the Nazi regime's solution for managing populations in the conduct of total war— namely, through aggressive territorial expansion and inclusion of those viewed as German within an explicitly articulated and biologically conceived "racial welfare state," coupled with the extermination of undesirable populations or their use as forced laborers, whether they resided inside or outside the Reich's geographical borders.[13]

At the same time, the U.S. and Japanese regimes experimented with new postcolonial models of imperialism—the Greater East Asia Co-Prosperity Sphere and the Atlantic Charter, with its rejection of territorial "aggrandizement"—that operated on the principle of the right to self-determination of all peoples and that therefore fit well with declarations of racial equality. The Japanese regime's expanding and tightening grip over its primary colonies in the late wartime years does not contradict this interpretation, for as we will see, it increasingly incorporated Taiwan and Korea into an enlarged concept of the Japanese nation (put differently, it decolonized by nationalizing) at the same time that it made strenuous efforts to give the appearance that other regions under Japanese imperial domination were in fact self-determining, or at least almost ready to be so. Thus, we must recognize Japan's

1932 establishment of the "puppet regime" of Manchukuo as a formally independent nation-state and the 1934 Tydings-McDuffie Act (Philippine Independence Act)
as parallel experiments in setting up postcolonial client states, a strategy that the
United States perfected after the war but that Japan was forced to abandon.[14] I will
consequently be arguing that the disavowal of racism served the aspirations of the
Japanese and U.S. total war regimes in two complementary and mutually constitutive projects—namely, to achieve global or at least regional hegemony and to unify
internally diverse populations.

I thus write against the grain of most academic writings and everyday common
sense, in that (with some significant exceptions) these tend to distinguish Japan and
the United States during the war as two incommensurable political formations—
the one post–New Deal, liberal-democratic, egalitarian, and a country with few colonial possessions; the other fascist, ultranationalist or totalitarian, a proponent of
racial supremacy, the oppressor of its colonial subjects, and an expansionist empire
that brutalized peoples throughout the Asia-Pacific region and that launched an
illegitimate war against the United States. In the United States, the Second World
War has come unequivocally to represent the "good war" against powers such as
Japan that have threatened freedom and democracy.

Contrary to this dominant view, I attempt to highlight historical convergences
in the characteristics of these two wartime regimes, with special attention to their
treatments of and discourses on colonial and racialized subjects.[15] I hope to make it
clear that the racial common sense of the majority populations in both wartime nations began to shift in roughly "comparable" ways. In both regimes, it became increasingly difficult to sustain policies founded on explicit doctrines of racial or ethnic inequality and for state leaders to make public statements espousing such views.
This does not mean that the United States and Japan moved easily in tandem toward the steady elimination of racism, or that it is difficult to identify many individuals, organizations, and even government agencies of the most vulgar racist kind.
Moreover, I do not mean to suggest that the disavowal of racism precluded systemic
racialized violence. Rather, what I propose is that it is precisely during the Second
World War—when we find some of the most horrific and racially motivated atrocities of the twentieth century committed by Germany, Japan, and the United States
(and many other nations)—that we discover equally vigorous denunciations of
racism by the Japanese and U.S. regimes. It is this uneasy compatibility of racism
and its disavowal in the United States and Japan that I analyze in this book and that
I maintain is part of the legacy of the war years that remains with us today.

Frantz Fanon's astute reflections on the changing character of racism, delivered in Paris in the context of Algeria's struggle for independence and in the wake of the Nazi Holocaust, eloquently capture a moment that I believe the United States and Japan had already reached during the Second World War as they worked out designs for imperialisms that would be viable in a postcolonial world. This was a stage in their racisms when, as Fanon noted, "vulgar racism in its biological form" needed at least to be veiled because of changes in forms of economic exploitation and the corresponding need for "collaborators." Thus,

> It is therefore not as a result of the evolution of people's minds that racism loses its virulence. No inner revolution can explain this necessity for racism to seek more subtle forms, to evolve. . . .
>
> At this stage racism no longer dares appear without disguise. It is unsure of itself. In an ever greater number of circumstances the racist takes to cover. He who claimed to "sense," to "see through" those others, finds himself to be a target, looked at, judged. The racist's purpose has become a purpose haunted by bad conscience.

And while "[f]or a time it looked as though racism had disappeared," that appearance was an illusion: "This soul-soothing, unreal impression was simply the consequence of the evolution of forms of exploitation. . . . The need to appeal to various degrees of approval and support, to the native's cooperation, modified relations in a less crude, more subtle, more 'cultivated' direction. It was not rare, in fact, to see a 'democratic and humane' ideology at this stage." Moreover, as Fanon further noted (anticipating more recent theorists such as Etienne Balibar), this was a stage in the transformation of racism into a subtler form when culture might stand in for race, when what he called "cultural racism" achieved a new dominance. And under these circumstances the "rather unexpected" would even occur—namely, "the racist group points accusingly to a manifestation of racism among the oppressed."[16]

Two critical material factors, not "the evolution of people's minds," propelled the American and Japanese total war regimes toward vigorous campaigns in which each presented itself as the authentic defender of freedom, equality, and anti-imperialism while pointing to the other as not only the true racist power and oppressor but also as duplicitous in its denunciations of racism. First, as total war regimes, both sought to rationally manage and maximize every available human and material resource. Without at least a formal denunciation of racism, they could not hope to successfully mobilize their diverse populations as civilian and military labor power, especially if they wanted to gain some degree of active cooperation from those populations rather than using them only as slave labor. Japan's formal colonies seemed to offer vast reservoirs of human resources for the war effort. With roughly 23.55 million inhabitants in 1940 and 25.1 million in 1944, Korea alone had a population almost one-third the size of Japan proper.[17] Similarly, given its limited human resources the U.S. total war regime could not afford to ignore even its most abjected populations. Not long after the forced evacuation of Japanese Americans from the West Coast, U.S. government agencies, business and agricultural interests, and the army came to recognize that Japanese Americans who had been confined in camps, and who were thereby initially removed from the labor market and from military service, were valuable sources of labor.

Furthermore, the model of each total war regime throughout the world strengthening itself by mobilizing colonial subjects and racialized minorities stimulated the others to follow, resulting in a global system of mutual and multidirectional agitation and emulation. When enemies observed each other effectively utilizing such populations in their war machines, the stakes obviously seemed to rise even higher. The leaderships of almost all of these regimes could not allow their enemies to grow stronger through policies of inclusion and denunciations of racist discrimination even as they witnessed the steady exhaustion of their own racially exclusivist pools of civilian and military labor. For example, in March 1944 Assistant Secretary of War John J. McCloy cited the practices of other nations in urging that more African Americans should be sent into combat. He reasoned that "with so large a portion of our population colored, with the example before us of the effective use of colored troops (of a much lower order of intelligence) by other nations, and with the imponderables that are connected with the situation, we must, I think, be more affirmative about the use of our negro troops."[18] Similarly, in a document prepared in anticipation of questions that the Privy Council might ask regarding a proposal for the voluntary induction of Koreans into the Japanese army, the Government-General of Korea (GGK) cited one of its supporters among the Korean elite, who had a global vision: "From early on the British empire put a system of military service into operation in India, and the effects of recruiting Indians and sending them out into the battlefront have been enormous. Despite the far greater geographical and military importance of Korea for Japan, compared to India for Britain, it is deplorable that no voluntary military system has been implemented [here]."[19]

A very explicit statement on the history, structure, and characteristics of total war and the need for total war empires to emulate one another can be found in one of the Japanese empire's most famous and widely circulated declarations of its vision for a New Order in East Asia—namely, the Japanese Ministry of Education's July 1941 publication, "The Way of Subjects." The text especially emphasizes the qualitative difference between wars fought prior to and after World War I. Earlier wars had been strictly "wars of armaments" (*buryokusen*), in which national defense had been equated with strength in arms. However, from World War I onward, wars became conflicts that mobilized total aggregated strength (*sōryokusen*). In total wars all activities become inextricably intertwined. The consumption of massive amounts of war materials stimulates domestic production while the battlefield and home front become an integrated whole. Struggles in all domains—including diplomacy, the economy, thought, and science—all combine with the "war of armaments" to participate in "wars of total national aggregate strength" (*kokka sōryokusen*). In such circumstances the distinctions between the battlefield and home front collapse, as the totality of the national people joins the war effort. Even the temporal distinction between peacetime and wartime blurs, because it is always necessary to be prepared for war. Furthermore, the text describes the mutual competition in total war preparedness between the powers at war:

> Since the outbreak of the present Great European War, all powers have been struggling with and emulating each other to adopt and strengthen their total war regimes. Britain, the United States, and other democracies are also rushing to prepare their advanced national defense states. As the leader of the Greater East Asia Co-Prosperity Sphere, and while fundamentally reflecting on the mission of reconstructing the world based on moral principles, our nation must rapidly complete its own total war regime, thereby advancing toward the realization of national policies.[20]

The other specific factor driving the United States and Japan toward the disavowal of racism was their common strategy of mobilizing "allies of color" to win the war and to gain their support for the longer-term goal of establishing postwar global, or at least regional, hegemony. In the case of Japan, its leadership could not sustain the design for empire in the multiethnic Asia-Pacific on the exclusionary ideology of the pure Yamato race alone. While it is still not uncommon to assume that the Japanese regime, like that of the Nazis, promoted an uncomplicated ideology of racial purity and superiority, Oguma Eiji, Tessa Morris-Suzuki, and Naoki Sakai, among other scholars, have already made abundantly clear that twentieth-century Japanese discourses on race were multiple, often contradictory, and considerably more complex. Komagome Takeshi also rightly observed some time ago that Japanese colonial policies and discourse were always internally contradictory and inconsistent.[21]

Morris-Suzuki, nicely summarizing and expanding on 1990s scholarship on this topic, has identified at least three major lines of thought in modern Japan concerning race or ethnicity, two of which she derives from Oguma's framework. One of these strands stressed the homogeneous, pure, and superior quality of the ethnos (a discourse that has usually stood for *the* Japanese discourse on race); the other, much like the Latin American and particularly Mexican idea of a "cosmic race," maintained that the strength of the Japanese people emanated precisely from its character as an alloyed race made up of a diversity of racial/ethnic elements. The third strand—which is of a type that critics of universalism such as Naoki Sakai and Etienne Balibar have also scrutinized—stressed Japan's superiority as the center of human progress, a logic that both universalized humanity and created hierarchies indexed to putative distance from the universal and most progressive center.[22] My book resonates with these insights into Japanese understandings of race in modern Japan, in that I will be arguing that Japan's ambition for a postcolonial, multiethnic nation-state and empire was one key factor forcing into retreat the discourse on the Japanese people as a pure race (recall Fanon), while official discourses increasingly emphasized shared racial lineages with others, especially with Koreans, or even rejected explicit racial thinking and the symbolism of blood altogether.

Paralleling and incited by the Japanese empire's strategic disavowal of racism, U.S. leadership increasingly came to denounce racism out of an awareness that such gestures were necessary to further U.S. interests in regions inhabited by those they often called the "yellow and brown peoples." Such a perspective is compatible with the early insights of scholars such as Akira Iriye, and more recently Gerald Horne, who have made the insufficiently appreciated point that the white Allied powers, including the United States and Britain, had to present themselves as committed to racial equality in response to Japanese appeals for the collaborative resistance of non-white peoples to white, racist imperialism in the Asia-Pacific.[23] It is also commonly known that the U.S. Congress in 1943 rescinded the legal exclusion of Chinese from immigration and granted Chinese the possibility of naturalization—a right that had been reserved for those considered white or of African descent—in large part to counter Japanese propaganda claiming "Asia for the Asiatics," to strengthen the U.S.-China alliance in particular, and to lay the groundwork for close postwar economic ties between China and the United States.[24]

Yet I want to complicate this general point by arguing that even as the United

States fought its brutal war against Japan and incarcerated Japanese Americans in camps, its leaders and the media were increasingly compelled to make great efforts to show that its killing of the enemy population (even of children and civilians) and its incarceration of the U.S. minority identified with this enemy population (even of orphaned infants) were not racially motivated. In fact, precisely because of the wartime hypervisibility of Japanese Americans and their internment, it became ever more urgent to demonstrate to racialized minorities at home and to nonwhite peoples throughout the world (especially in Asia) that the United States did not practice racism against even this enemy race. Thus the common view of Asian racialized minorities during the Second World War—that Chinese, Filipinos, and South Asians living in the United States tended to be identified with their countries of origin and thereby benefited from their association with the Allied powers, while Japanese Americans suffered from their conflation with the enemy—is not entirely accurate.

The fate of all U.S. minorities, including Japanese Americans, was tied to a larger propaganda campaign that tried to represent the United States as a nation that did not discriminate against any racial or ethnic minority. In this sense, the McCarren-Walter Act, which allowed the naturalization of Japanese in 1952, was not a simple reversal of a racist wartime policy that had discriminated against those identified with the enemy nation. Instead, like the measures to make Chinese eligible for naturalization in 1943, as well as Filipinos and Asian Indians in 1946, the act was part of a drive that crossed over the 1945 divide: its purpose was to mobilize an ever-greater diversity and number of people for national projects, and to win allies of color. Of course, racist killing and discrimination continued through the war and beyond, but the point I want to make is that even if many racists may not have been "haunted by bad conscience," as Fanon would have it, those directing the total war regime were troubled by the fear that the Japanese propaganda machine could seize on discrimination against domestic minorities, including Japanese Americans, to present Japan as the true liberator of nonwhite peoples throughout the world. In the midst of war, high officials in the U.S. government and military had to begin insisting retrospectively that even the blatantly racist act of removing Japanese Americans from the West Coast had been motivated only by military concerns, not by racism. In the transwar years—by which I mean the period from the Second World War through the peak of the Cold War—even the use of weapons of mass destruction eventually had to be legitimated by the logic of military necessity, rather than viewed simply as a means to exterminate an enemy cast as nonhuman.

Although the argument that Japan and the United States became increasingly alike during the Second World War is out of step with most scholarly and commonsense understandings of the war, there are a few significant exceptions. Perhaps the work most relevant to this book is John W. Dower's classic, *War without Mercy*.[25] Not only does it make a powerful argument about the force of racism in the outbreak, conduct, and aftereffects of the Second World War in the Asia-Pacific region, but through its superbly researched and detailed interrogations of both Japanese and white American racism it also refuses to allow either side to take the moral high ground. Furthermore, although Dower's rhetorical strategy is to show by example rather than to explicitly theorize about historical method, he broke out of the conventional mold of national history writing, and his transnational perspective enables us to see how the histories of the two countries have been and continue to be inextricably intertwined. He made it possible to understand, for instance, that the racism practiced in the United States against African Americans, Native Americans, and Asian Americans served as an alibi for Japanese justifications of their own expansionism; conversely, Japanese propaganda about the seamless unity of their people, their "hearts beating as one" in loyal service to the nation and emperor, reemerged in the United States as racial stereotypes about the herdlike or insectlike mentality of the enemy. Yet precisely because his text is one of the most important works we have on the Second World War, because it is such an important model for transpacific history writing, and because of its enormous impact in the classroom and on scholarly writing, it is necessary to register my discomfort with two aspects of the book and my efforts to go beyond it.

First, despite Dower's many perceptive criticisms of wartime cultural anthropologists such as Ruth Benedict who were engaged in cross-cultural studies of "culture and personality" and "national character," he all too often shares their reliance on ahistorical understandings of "Japanese culture" in order to explain wartime and postwar events. The Japanese concern for "purity and pollution," their partiality toward the color white, their propensity to place themselves and others in their "proper places" in a hierarchical scheme—for Dower, these are all ancient and perduring cultural codes that help explain the uniqueness of Japanese perceptions of themselves and their others during the twentieth century. He explains that these "Japanese modes of perception" originate in a past that he identifies with "ancient times," the "traditional," or "over the centuries," and in "folk religion"[26]—the latter serving Dower as a chronotope that conflates the past with the location of the folk. Most unconvincingly, Dower insists that Japanese comprehended their American enemies during the Second World War and after through originally folk understandings of "strangers" or "outsiders." The Japanese imagined these others to have both malevolent and benevolent qualities, just like the stranger gods (*marebito*) that they believed had visited them from time immemorial. Since the "outsiders" were both malevolent and benevolent, it was easy to reimagine the formerly "bestial" or "deranged" Americans as benefactors once the Occupation forces arrived.

This ahistorical culturalist analysis—much influenced by structural anthropology and Japanese nativist ethnography—is problematic in several ways. Most importantly, it obstructs the real possibility of fully disclosing racism as a problem common to modernity and hence to modern nation-states, societies, and empires. Despite Dower's formidable attempt to critique twentieth-century Japanese and American racisms, in the end he presents the Japanese version as a curious outgrowth of a peculiarly Japanese understanding of otherness that seems hardly to have changed throughout the course of history. The archaic obsession with pollution, the early modern Japanese representations of Europeans as beings with doglike feet and oddly shaped penises, and the twentieth-century imagination of Roosevelt and Churchill as devilish humans—somehow all these disparate and historically discontinuous cases of understanding human difference appear in *War without Mercy* as just so many manifestations of the same root culture.

Such a perspective is problematic because it assumes the coherence of a national culture (as did Benedict and her colleagues) before "Japan" even existed as a widespread concept, ignores cultural differences within Japan, and assumes that culture basically does not change. But perhaps most significantly, despite Dower's effectiveness in critiquing racism and sometimes drawing our attention to resemblances between the American and Japanese versions of this phenomenon, he ultimately reproduces modern Japan as an enigma that can be deciphered only by recourse to broad generalizations about "Japanese culture." Even as *War without Mercy* invited us to think about the United States and Japan as comparable modern nations, his recourse to what we might describe as "culture in the last instance" reinstated the otherness of Japan to America's modernity. In short, Dower reproduced Japan and white America as two incommensurable cultural units, unwittingly putting into practice a method introduced by the very anthropologists of the "national character" school that he criticized. At its worst, to paraphrase Balibar, such an understanding of culture as immutable can function much like biological race to naturalize difference.[27]

Second, I take the unintended effects of American and Japanese propaganda much more seriously than does Dower. While I do not ignore the *intentions* of policy makers, I consider the *effects* of individuals and agencies that acted *as if* the United States and Japan were nations and empires that did not practice racist discrimination. Just as acting *as if* race is grounded in biology carries with it real force, so too acting *as if* we do not practice racism has real-life consequences, in particular making it necessary to adjust the most blatant forms of racial discrimination.[28] Thus, although Dower perceptively shows how contradictions emerged in the United States between practicing racism at home and waging a war that required Asian allies, I want to take the analysis of both Japan's and America's disavowals of racism much further. In particular, I hope to demonstrate that while these disavowals may have begun with the very utilitarian purposes of mobilizing ethnic and colonial soldiers and gaining general cooperation from diverse populations in the United States and the Asia-Pacific region, they had other effects: once such official denunciations of racist discrimination became central components of state ideology at such sites as soldiering, it became increasingly difficult to sustain discriminatory policies and practices in the forms then prevalent. This was as true in the Japanese case as it was in the United States. Therefore, though Dower insists that the Japanese war machine was propelled by a racial ideology advancing the supremacy of the pure Yamato race, such an ideology was fading in most parts of the empire in the last years of the war, especially in the metropole, its formal colonies of Korea and Taiwan, Micronesia, and the Manchukuo client state.

I do not wish to argue that all traces of the discourse on the pure Yamato race disappeared from public view, let alone from inner circles of the military, government leaders, and the bureaucracy. Still, I will maintain that discourses and concrete policies could not simply discriminate against Koreans and other colonial subjects and exclude them from the national community once the utilitarian and material demands of total war accelerated the need for them to cooperate and be included in the war effort. This shift can clearly be seen in the late wartime fate of one of the key texts that Dower cites to substantiate his argument that the Japanese viewed themselves as members of a superior race and that they believed in the urgent necessity of preserving their racial purity. As he explains, the relevant text, *Yamato minzoku o chūkaku to suru sekai seisaku no kentō* (*An Investigation of Global Policy with the Yamato Race as Nucleus*, hereafter *Yamato minzoku*), was completed no later than 1 July 1943; it constituted the bulk of a massive study produced by a team of researchers associated with the Population and Race Section of the Ministry of Health and Welfare's Research Bureau. While Dower readily admits that "there is no reason to believe it [*Yamato minzoku*] was especially influential at the time," he devotes an entire chapter to the document, primarily because he believes it explicitly and concretely articulated many widespread yet "cryptically" expressed assumptions of the period.[29]

To be sure, Dower convincingly demonstrates that the text's authors and Nazi ideologues shared some concerns, including a belief that racial groups are bound by blood, history, political forms, and culture and that superior races must maintain their purity. In the case of the Japanese researchers, this translated into affirming Japan's position at the top of the hierarchy of peoples within the Greater East Asia Co-Prosperity Sphere, as well as strident advocacy of policies aimed to protect the Japanese people from contamination by inferior peoples. However, Dower's analysis of the text is incomplete and to some extent misleading in that the metropolitan and colonial governments ignored several of the study's most important policy recommendations having to do with preserving the Yamato race. Most tellingly for my book, though *Yamato minzoku* warned against excessive contacts between Japanese and their colonial subjects from Korea and Taiwan, including interethnic marriages and mixing in the military, the numbers of Koreans and Taiwanese mobilized as soldiers and sailors only increased. In fact, the Japanese cabinet had already formally approved the decision to begin military conscription of Koreans more than a year earlier, in May 1942, and enormous efforts had already been made to prepare Korea for implementing a draft system beginning in 1944. Only two months after *Yamato minzoku*'s completion, in September 1943 the cabinet announced that Taiwanese would also be drafted in 1945. Moreover, these colonial soldiers and sailors came to serve not in segregated but integrated units.

Also, unlike most other colonial governments in the late colonial years—and indeed unlike the United States, where state antimiscegenation laws were the rule and not the exception—the GGK officially promoted the intermarriage of Koreans and metropolitan Japanese. The details of how this contradiction between racist thinking and its denunciation was negotiated will become clearer in later chapters, but for the time being I will simply point out that as powerful as the discourse on the pure Yamato race may have been in the minds of many within the elite (and outside it), the exigencies of war made it increasingly necessary to disavow racist discrimination and to demonstrate the sincerity of this denunciation through concrete policies. This need was especially strong with regard to official discourses and policies concerning Koreans and Taiwanese, who were, it was repeatedly affirmed, genuinely Japanese.

WHY JAPANESE AMERICAN AND KOREAN JAPANESE SOLDIERS?

The soldiering of Japanese Americans and Koreans within the expanding concept of "Japan" offers particularly revealing and compelling sites from which to consider the changing regulation of racial or ethnic difference in the United States and

Japan, for the pressing matters of recruiting these soldiers to fill military manpower needs as well as performing the disavowal of racism on a global stage forced both regimes to confront actually existing discrimination in unprecedented ways, both within and outside the military. Furthermore, the question of military manpower was usually considered together with overall human resource needs, exacerbating fears of shortfalls in both civilian and military labor. Why would these soldiers fight for regimes in which they and their communities were considered only objects of derision and brutal exploitation? Wouldn't it be necessary to at least present a strong appearance of equal opportunity and merit-based criteria for advancement in rank? Wouldn't the wider Japanese minority in the United States and Korean subjects in the Japanese colonial empire need to be given some concrete signs that the two regimes did not practice racism? How else could the military ensure that these ethnic and colonial soldiers would not turn their weapons in the wrong direction or sabotage efficiency by distrusting, fighting with, or refusing to cooperate with the majority Japanese or white soldiers and officers? Since one of the purposes of recruiting these "soldiers of color" was to demonstrate to the world that the respective regimes believed in racial equality, wouldn't it be necessary to preempt demonstrations of resistance to racism by taking some significant steps toward eliminating discriminatory policies? Otherwise, mutinies, absconding, draft evasion, interethnic or interracial conflicts within the military, and so on might arise and would undermine both military efficiency and the propaganda scheme. Moreover, as we will see, such necessities forced military and civilian leaders, their bureaucracies, and the legions who supported them—writers, filmmakers, social scientists, and those in the media—to exert enormous and concerted efforts in order to demonstrate not just to the negatively racialized populations and potential allies of color throughout the world, but to the majority populations in the two metropoles as well, that their nations were committed to racial equality. Unless they did so, the entire imaginary of Japanese as Americans or Koreans as Japanese would appear to be merely lies.

Because Korea was Japan's largest formal colony and by far the most significant nonmetropolitan source of civilian and military labor, the need to manage Korean ethnic difference in the interests of the war effort may be obvious. As we will see in much greater detail in chapter 1, more than 214,000 Koreans served in the Japanese army and navy beginning in 1938, the year that the army inaugurated a special voluntary system for Koreans. This figure includes about 190,000 Koreans conscripted in 1944 and 1945. The navy and army dispersed these men throughout the armed forces, with most soldiers first entering the army stationed in Korea (Chōsengun), and then transferring out as needed. In addition, the Japanese military had more than 150,000 Korean civilian employees. Broadly referred to in Japanese as *gunzoku,* these were drivers, interpreters, guides, laborers, construction workers, and prison guards—many of whom labored under conditions that were as dangerous as those faced by regular soldiers and sailors.[30] All told, more than 360,000 Koreans served as military and civilian employees in the Japanese Imperial Forces from 1938 to 1945, a figure that makes the relative paucity of postwar memories about them even more striking. To put this number into perspective, in 1939 only about 458,000 men served in the entire U.S. military.[31]

In comparison, the number of Japanese Americans from Hawaii and the mainland United States who served in the army during World War II might seem rather small. Although official and unofficial histories have often put the sum of all Japanese Americans who served in the army during the war at "approximately 33,300," this figure includes all those inducted from 1 July 1940 to 30 November 1946. For the narrower period starting with the attack on Pearl Harbor to the war's end in August 1945, the total of Japanese Americans in the military was roughly 23,500.[32] Yet as we will see in chapter 2, the total war logic of optimizing human resources compelled military and civilian leaders not to discount the labor potential of even relatively small groups such as Japanese Americans. Indeed, the populations of Japanese Americans in the mainland United States (126,947) and the colony of Hawaii (157,905) were not insignificant in wartime; they represented tens of thousands of potential workers who could be placed in key military units and in workplaces vital to the wartime economy.[33]

Furthermore, given the high visibility of Japanese American evacuation and internment on the mainland, the government's handling of this minority became one of the nation's most sensitive and conspicuous barometers of the sincerity of its disavowal of racism. For a state that sought to manage the diversity of its domestic population and to further its political and economic interests throughout the nonwhite world, racism against Japanese Americans became an extreme embarrassment that had to be countered by highly visible demonstrations of America's inclusion of them—most dramatically in the military—even as the camps continued to function (they did not completely close until after the war). Indeed, as I will show in chapter 2, the decisive short-term consideration in reversing the War Department's policy of excluding Japanese Americans from the military—they were included through a volunteer program from early February 1943 on—was the desire to display to the world loyal Japanese Americans who appeared to truly believe in and embody the American principles of freedom and the equality of all regardless of race, national origin, religion, or other signs of difference.

To give just one example, in an early April 1944 memo to Secretary of the Interior Harold L. Ickes, Dillon Myer, the director of the War Relocation Authority (WRA, the civilian agency responsible for managing Japanese Americans removed from the West Coast), argued that following the steps already taken to permit the induction of Japanese Americans into special units of the army, the branches within the army that remained closed to them as well as the navy, from which they were still completely excluded, should be opened to these men. He reasoned that signs of racial discrimination compromised unity at home and the propaganda war abroad.

> It should be pointed out that discrimination on the basis of race tends to undermine the loyalty of the racial minority groups and strikes at the national unity. Further, there is no question that the enemy has effectively charged, in its propaganda broadcasts to neutral or non-belligerent countries in South America and in the Pacific areas, that the United States is a Nation which preaches democracy and practices discrimination. One result of the propaganda efforts of the enemy may be seen in recent news dispatches from India to the effect that Indian troops are fighting on the side of the Japanese in the current efforts to invade India.[34]

Moreover, as surprising as it may be today, the official racial categories used by the Census Bureau in 1940 classified Japanese as the third-largest "non-white race" in the continental United States after "Negroes" and "[American] Indians," in part because "Hispanics" were counted as white.[35] The enormous significance of Japanese Americans during the war in the overall imagination and management of races is evidenced not only by the large volume of the archival record on them and their soldiers but also by their prominence in wartime and immediate postwar publications on American race issues. In popular media representations, of course, but also in supposedly objective data such as census tables that fashioned social reality as much as they reflected it, the Japanese in America stood out in contradictory ways as a high-profile threat, a significant manpower resource, and a linchpin in the handling of America's racial diversity. For example, in a postwar evaluation of "special groups" within the military, by which it meant "color minority groups," the Selective Service considered the cases of "The American Indian," "The Negro," "The Chinese American," "The Japanese American," "The Filipino," "The Puerto Rican," and "Other Races." However, of all these groups it stressed that during the period of the report's central concern (namely, 1940–47), the problem of discrimination within the military was "probably the most acute in every way for Negroes and Japanese Americans." It dedicated a separate chapter to Japanese Americans alone, something it did not do for either African Americans or American Indians, and emphasized overall that "as an American race problem, their situation has been complex and in consequence magnified and distorted."[36]

FROM EXCLUSIONARY TO INCLUSIVE PRACTICES, OR FROM VULGAR TO POLITE RACISM

Our images of Japanese rule over Korea as well as of Japanese American internment are dominated by signs of the negative operations of power: sex and labor under direct coercion, barbed wire, segregation, physical violence, policing, surveillance, expulsion from the national community, unfreedom, and death. These images are not unwarranted, because such practices and displays of power were part of the Japanese and American systems of racialized population management. Yet they reveal only one cluster in the arsenal of technologies available for managing these people during wartime. While I do not mean to ignore ongoing practices of brutality and necropolitics[37]—a violence often without concern for life or law that continued into the period of total war—I want to insist that such spaces or explosions of brutality and repression existed alongside and in fact supplemented another project: one of welcoming newly constituted national subjects such as Japanese Americans and Korean Japanese into the nation, with promises and practices of health, education, sustenance, security, and even greater access to political rights.

Of course, the accelerating wartime movement to include despised minorities and colonial populations within the American and Japanese wartime regimes was not completely unprecedented. Over the past fifteen years, scholars of late nineteenth- and twentieth-century Asian America such as Lisa Lowe and David Palumbo-Liu have shown with great insight and theoretical sophistication how the contradictory demands of capitalism and the U.S. nation-state formation—to secure Asian laborers for domestic production, to advance economic and strategic interests in Asia, to fight wars in Asia, and to sustain a certain type of homogeneity around race, language, and culture—worked both to generate assimilatory discourses and practices of Asian inclusion into America and to dissimilate Asians through racialization. In Lowe's apt formulation, Asian Americans have been "fundamental to the construction of the nation as a simulacrum of inclusiveness," even as they are perpetually imagined as the "foreigner-within." For Palumbo-Liu, the notation "Asian/American," like the construction "and/or," signifies the simultaneously inclusionary and exclusionary relation between the "Asian" and the "American"—the solidus marking at the same time the distinction between the two terms and the possibility that one may slide into the other.[38]

Similarly, we know that the colonial annexation of Korea and the need for Korean laborers as well as elite collaborators in the metropole and throughout the empire had already produced discourses and practices of both inclusiveness and racialized exclusion. On the one hand, along with everyday forms of racist economic exploitation that included differential wage scales and disproportionate opportunities for capital investment in the colonial economy by Japanese, we find extreme moments of violence such as in the colonial state's repression of the March 1 (1919) Independence Movement and the massacre of thousands of Koreans in the Tokyo region after the Great Kanto Earthquake of 1923. Japanese writers helped sustain such treatment of Koreans by producing a discourse on them as uncivilized, backward, unclean, and generally lacking in a modern work ethic.[39]

On the other hand, it is widely accepted that after the March 1 Movement, Japanese colonial policy started to shift from violent rule through suppression (*budan seiji*) toward a softer and culturalist type of rule (*bunka seiji*) that we might think of as hegemonic in the Gramscian sense—a strategy that increasingly sought to rule through the mobilization and control of consent even as the colonial police network expanded.[40] And even earlier, the economic and political incorporation of Korea into Japan produced another related discourse on them as essentially if not actually the same as Japanese in the metropole. Today it is fairly commonly accepted that in the late nineteenth and twentieth centuries, the scholarly and public discourses on the "common ancestry of Japanese and Koreans" (*Nissen dōsoron*), as well as on the "unity of the Mainland and Korea" (*Naisen ittairon*), became powerful discursive means by which to legitimate Japanese domination over and colonial rule in Korea. While there are a few scattered references to such ideas in Tokugawa period (1600–1868) texts, from the late nineteenth century through the prewar and wartime years scholars working in the modern human sciences—primarily historians, linguists, and anthropologists—produced a massive archive of knowledge that lent credence to the idea that the inhabitants of the Japanese archipelago and the Korean Peninsula were descendents of the same ancestors and that they shared many cultural attributes.[41]

In the interwar years scholars, ideologues, and journalists commonly went so far as to note blood ties between Korean royalty and the Japanese aristocracy, and even the imperial household. For example, a 1928 Ministry of Education publication meant for wide distribution throughout Japan identified Empress Jingū's roots in the Korean kingdom of Silla and explained that Emperor Kammu's mother had descended from Koreans. Komatsu Midori, a high official in the Korean colonial government, had already expressed similar ideas in 1916, as did the Romantic philosopher and literary critic Yasuda Yojūro in 1938 and the well-known Korean writer Yi Kwang-su in 1941.[42] No less a figure than the famous right-wing theorist Kita Ikki forthrightly maintained in his 1923 publication, "Plan for the Renovation of Japan," that Koreans and Japanese did not constitute distinct races of people. Not only did the Japanese ethnos contain a strong admixture of Korean blood, but the "nobility of the Nara and Heian periods" had carried the greatest quantity of "pure Korean blood." This was the reason, he explained, why the facial features of most members of the peerage in his day resembled those of Koreans (*"menbō ōku Chōsenjin ni nitaru"*). Moreover, since the nobility of the Nara and Heian periods constituted a privileged class linked by blood to the imperial household, the blood of Koreans flowed within the emperor himself. Finally, on the basis of this history he reasoned that the 1920 political marriage between the Japanese princess Nashimoto Masako and the Korean prince Yi Ŭn had not been without precedent.[43]

Such an inclusionary discourse is usually dismissed as propaganda intended to legitimate Japan's military takeover of Korea. Yet even if we acknowledge this intention, it is difficult to deny the unintended or unavoidable consequences of officially expounding on the sameness of metropolitan Japanese and Koreans. For example, while few have seriously analyzed the political rights seized by colonials in the metropole, empirical research by such scholars as Matsuda Toshihiko make it clear that because the colonial and metropolitan governments repeatedly proclaimed the unity of metropolitan Japan with Korea and Taiwan, they could not foreclose the possibility of Korean participation in Japanese metropolitan politics.[44] Though Japan's Household Registration Law would be used after the war to exclude former colonial subjects living in Japan from voting and holding public office, in the colonial period the law did not prohibit Koreans residing in metropolitan Japan from participating in elections. Prewar and wartime election laws and regulations provided only that among other qualifications, voters and candidates for public office had to be "male subjects of the empire" (*teikoku shinmin taru danshi*) who had resided in the same voting district in metropolitan Japan for a set period of time.

Minimum tax requirements made it impossible for all but the most fortunate colonials to vote prior to 1925, but passage of universal manhood suffrage in that year turned thousands of Korean men into voters and potential officeholders. It also meant that gender complicated the simple colony-metropole split in that at least with regard to voting, metropolitan Japanese women could occupy the subaltern position vis-à-vis Korean men residing in the metropole. Of course, not all Koreans living in Japan acquired the right to vote. The requirement that one had to be a resident in the same voting district for one year made it difficult for Koreans—who often migrated as laborers in construction and mining—to qualify. Also, the minimum age requirement, twenty-five, disqualified a large segment of the population. Therefore, only 9.3 percent of the Korean population in Japan was eligible to vote in the 1928 election, as compared to 20 percent of the metropolitan Japanese. Language barriers also made it difficult for Koreans in Japan to exercise their right to participate in elections. However, the Home Ministry's 1930 decision to recognize votes using the Korean hangul syllabary and the 1934 revision to the Lower House Election Law (*shūgiin giin senkyohō*), which shortened the residency requirement to six months, lessened some of these impediments. In fact, 21 percent of Koreans who participated in the 1930 Lower House election cast their votes in hangul. In some areas, particularly in western Japan, Koreans came to form a significant component of the constituency, and Matsuda informs us that the Christian Socialist Kagawa Toyohiko used placards in hangul during his campaign for the 1930 general election. Although he was the only successful Korean candidate for the Lower House during all of the colonial period, Pak Ch'ung-gŭm—who, we will see, was an active proponent of opening military service to Koreans—was elected to the Diet twice, once in 1932 and again in 1937.

In short, even before the establishment of their total war systems (beginning in July 1937 for Japan and December 1941 for the United States), the relationship of states and dominant metropolitan majorities in the United States and Japan to Japanese Americans and Koreans, respectively, had a complex and contradictory character that conjoined racialized exclusion and universalizing inclusion. We could consider such a racism that works through the inclusion of hierarchized peoples— what Etienne Balibar calls an " 'inclusive' racism," as opposed to an " 'exclusive' racism" that operates through extermination or elimination—a logical outcome of most modern nationalisms; almost all such nationalisms have been founded on the theoretical if not always practical movement toward the formal rejection of difference, most prototypically in the disestablishment of social estates. The Japanese parallel to the paradigmatic French case is the post–Meiji Revolution (1868) abolition of the four-tiered status system, the formal "liberation" of the *buraku* outcaste groups, and the social and political categorization of Okinawans, Ainu, Koreans, and Taiwanese as Japanese nationals (*kokumin*). In a very general sense, we may consider these historical examples as evidence of what Balibar has theorized as the reciprocal or even supplementary relationships of racism with nationalism and universalism (and hence humanism), in which we find the simultaneous presence of racism and its disavowal. As he puts it: "Racist organizations most often refuse to be designated as such, laying claim instead to the title of *nationalist* and claiming that the two notions cannot be equated. Is this merely a tactical ploy or the symptom of a fear of words inherent in the racist attitude? In fact the discourses of race and nation are never far apart, if only in the form of disavowal."[45]

Yet I hope to better historicize Balibar's theorization by showing that the "inclusive" or "inclusionary" character of racisms in the United States and Japan intensified as they mutated in competition with each other into total war regimes, moving toward the greater incorporation of populations that had been despised and were still in many ways excluded from their respective national communities. In the cases to be explored in this book, we witness unprecedented and remarkably similar movements in this direction: on the one side the U.S. nation pulling Japanese Americans into the national community, even out of internment camps; on the other, the Japanese nation increasingly subsuming the entire Korean population into the nation. But for each, these populations were also marked as somehow different, usually with an emphasis on pathological culture and lagging development or assimilation.

The wartime shift toward inclusionary practices entailed a complex recalibration of strategies for managing racialized minority and colonial subjects that may be understood as a transition from what I will call "vulgar" to "polite" racism.[46] The former was more exclusionary, particularistic, inhumane, naturalistic in its understanding of difference, antihistoricist in its denial of the possibility of assimilation (that is, the racialized were outside of history), relatively unconcerned about the health and well-being of marginalized peoples (except insofar as diseases among the abjected had to be controlled to prevent their spread to the racialized core population), and collectivist and ascriptive in racializing groups of individuals without recognizing, or with minimum concern about constituting, individual subjects. In contrast, the latter racism was inclusionary, more but not exclusively universalist, humane, relativist and more culturalist in its understanding of difference, historicist in its affirmation of the possibility of assimilation (that is, the racialized were inside history, but lagging or culturally pathological), at least minimally concerned about fostering the health and well-being of marginalized peoples, and collectivist like vulgar racism in racializing subpopulations, but different in its close attention to the systematic subjectification of individuals making up the aggregated population sets. On the last point, I mean that the strategy shifted from treating these populations as simply objects of rule, without significant interiority, to attempting to constitute them as self-reflexive and knowledgeable subjects who would participate at least to some extent in their own regulation.

All of this is not to deny that real differences existed between the Japanese and American cases. For example, the discourse on assimilation had always been much stronger, and claims about the influence of culture and history complicated the naturalistic view of difference from much earlier in Japan than in the United States. Moreover, because the racialized history of Japan in relation to its neighbors (including Korea) was in large part an effect of Euro-American discourses on racial difference that clustered the diversity of the peoples in the place named as Asia into the category of Asians, discourses of racial affinity such as "the common ancestry of Japanese and Koreans" were mobilized alongside humanistic universalism to disavow differences within the nation and among allies. "White" imperialists, who could not deploy such a strategy of highlighting racial contiguity with the "yellow and brown peoples," tended to rely more strictly on humanistic universalism, not because they were more idealistic or progressive but precisely because Western discourses on race had already naturalized the "races of man" as almost fixed categories. Despite these differences in emphases, I will be arguing that a distinct shift from one type of racism to the other occurred during the wartime and immediate postwar years, and that the American and Japanese cases are roughly comparable, even when we recognize their singularities.

In charting this wartime transformation from vulgar to polite racism, the Foucauldian concepts of "bio-power" and "governmentality" will be particularly useful. While I will defer a fuller explication of these concepts and their applicability to the Japanese and American cases to the chapters that follow, I argue (especially in part I) that prior to the period of total war, Japanese Americans and Korean colonials were more outside than inside the American and Japanese bio-political regimes, respectively. By this I mean that the two nation-states for the most part excluded these groups from the category of populations in need of life sustenance. Under vulgar racism they were not objects of a political rationality that worked through the logic of making people live so that they might be utilized by the state. Instead, power operated on them primarily through the negative logic of repression, exclusions, and the right to exterminate those considered dangerous to society. Under the polite racism of the total war regimes, however, these individuals and subpopulations came to be targeted as worthy of life, education, health, and even to some degree happiness, precisely because these systems came to regard the health and development of even abjected populations as useful for the regime's survival, prosperity, and victory in war. In other words, the stimulation of welfare by warfare affected not only dominant populations but these racialized nationals as well. Of course, since this apparently kind, nurturing, and even pro-natalist treatment of these populations emerged out of an understanding of their utility, when necessary their lives could easily be sacrificed, particularly as soldiers, coerced laborers, and sexual slaves.

The usefulness to this book of the concept of modern governmentality, which complements and overlaps with that of bio-power, is manifold; but before proceeding it may be useful to mention at least one more of its aspects that is crucial to the proposed notion of polite racism. In theorizing and historicizing modern governmentality, Foucault emphasized that in addition to educating and caring for the lives of aggregated populations, power in this way of conceptualizing governing seeks to mobilize the conduct of individuals and groups toward desired ends through their active participation as self-reflexive subjects. In other words, Foucault's understanding of governing under this modality is that it operates through the governing of self-governing: it aims to constitute formally free and responsible subjects while guiding them toward normative choices. Individuals are supposed to experience themselves as acting of their own desire and will, rather than in response to force. In this book such a positive operation of power appears most paradigmatically in the fairly well-known but underanalyzed political ritual carried out in the Japanese American camps in February and March 1943, when the total war regime compelled every adult internee to respond to questionnaires in which they were to profess loyalty and willingness to take up arms in defense of the nation. This was a ritual of free consent in that it presumed the agency of subjects of self-knowledge, yet at the same time civilian administrators and military personnel attempted to guide every internee toward the right choices.

The Japanese total war regime also highlighted acts of Korean voluntary participation in the war effort, particularly as volunteer soldiers and sailors. Only by acknowledging this transmutation in the modality of power from treating colonial subjects simply as objects of force to considering them active subjects of self-knowledge and reflection can we also understand why so many Korean intellectuals in the late 1930s and through the war years renounced their earlier demands for independence and argued that they might find their own self-determination and happiness by becoming Japanese nationalists. It will be quite illuminating to see that much like Japanese American leaders such as Mike Masaoka—who proposed not only that the U.S. military should be opened to Japanese Americans but that they should be formed into a suicide battalion to prove their loyalty—Korean writers and film makers as renowned as Yi Kwang-su (canonized as Korea's first modern novelist), Chang Hyŏk-chu (one of the Japanese empire's most prolific writers), and the filmmaker Hŏ Yŏng (who participated in the Japanese assault on Java as a member of a propaganda corps attached to the Sixteenth Army) explicitly and repeatedly tried to show in their works that becoming Japanese through such acts as soldiering offered the surest avenue for self-determination and happiness.

Such cultural producers, I will argue, were not simply responding to Japanese colonial discourse. We should not regard these Koreans as passive receptors of an already-completed Japanese discourse. The weak term "collaborator" is insufficient for naming subjects so actively involved in figuring the contours of Japanese national/colonial discourse. Instead, they participated in its production, pushing the universalist or at least inclusionary dimension of Japanese nationalism as far as they could in order to locate themselves solidly within it. A similar point could be made about U.S. domestic minorities, who in rebelling against an exclusionary and racially particularistic American nationalism emerged in the wartime and immediate postwar years more inside than outside the national community. One further example of the participation of Koreans in this modality of power is their increased voluntary participation in politics in the metropole. In 1942 no fewer than 6 ethnic Korean candidates ran for the Lower House of the Diet and 108 ran for local elections. It matters less that the 6 who ran for national office all lost, or that only 38 won in local elections, than that from the late 1930s it became possible for many Koreans to more realistically than ever imagine new opportunities for themselves as Japanese.[47]

Furthermore, this book suggests that under both regimes the "governing of self-governing" operated not only at the level of the individual but also in plans for achieving global hegemony in the postcolonial world through the consent of nominally self-determining nation-states. In other words, the workings of power that were supposed to operate through individuals within the nation (including for Japan, Korea, and Taiwan) and on allies outside the nation (including Manchukuo, the Wang Ching-wei government in China, and the Philippines) were homological and mutually supplementary. Perhaps most incredibly, we will see in chapter 2 that by the late summer of 1942, if not earlier, U.S. officials and their advisers were already laying plans to set this mode of power into operation on the enemy people. According to this scheme, which would in fact come to fruition under the U.S. Occupation, the United States would liberate the Japanese people from their military masters' enslavement while reviving the people and their government as a formally self-determining nation-state under a (puppet) emperor, with every attempt made to direct Japan's leaders toward conduct that would further U.S. interests in the region. The people of Japan, in turn, were supposed to experience themselves as participating in self-government, acting not at the behest of the United States but in their own interests and toward the pursuit of universal ideals such as peace, democracy, and liberty. In short, Japan and its people were to be for the United States what the nominally independent Manchukuo and its multiethnic people had earlier been for Japan.

The transnational and comparative method adopted in this book is a product of the view—which I share with a growing number of other scholars—that American studies (including American ethnic studies such as Asian American studies) and other area and national studies must be in better dialogue.[48] This perspective departs significantly from those employed in pioneering studies in English, Japanese, and Korean on the two sets of soldiering that are the subjects of this book. For as informative and important as these works have been on the discrete histories of these two distinct groups of soldiers—and my citations will show how indebted I am to several of them in some important ways—they have framed each of their histories as sui generis stories. The histories of Japanese American soldiers have primarily focused on their wartime heroism in the face of American racism. The purpose, explicit or not, has been to show how Japanese in America have earned the right to be considered full-fledged Americans and citizens.[49] Such a perspective is understandable, for so much writing about U.S. ethnic history—often unwittingly replicating immigration laws by subdividing according to national origin—has had to bear the burden of showing how each ethnic or racialized group deserves inclusion or affirmation as Americans because of their unique contributions to the national community. At the same time, the histories of Koreans in the Japanese Imperial Forces have been largely about the Japanese empire's exploitation of them as military manpower.[50] Here too I cannot dismiss the seriousness and value of such a perspective on Japanese colonialism, for empirical studies of the burdens placed on the Korean people and the atrocities committed against them have been necessary to counteract forgetfulness and denials of colonial responsibilities.

Yet this type of ethnic and national history writing has also distracted us from seeing the transnational linkages between histories that merely appear to be unique and discrete, while they discourage us from noting comparable situations from nation to nation and empire to empire—observations that could enable political and intellectual associations across narrower identities. It will become clear that the civil and military leaders of the United States and Japan were much more cognizant of such global connections and comparabilities than are most conventional historians, and acted accordingly. Moreover, the convergences in the histories of the two nations during World War II are not just ironies of the particular moment of that war. They are also culminations of the intersections and shared characteristics of the United States and Japan as they alternatively cooperated and competed with each other for hegemony in the modern Asia-Pacific. At a minimum, we can note that they have both been based on capitalist economies, are both among the most spectacular success stories of modern nationalism and the nation-state form, were both relatively small to midsize colonial empires that started to experiment with decolonization in the 1930s, both produced the idea that some within their diverse populations could be considered a majority population while others were minorities, both privileged men over women, and so on. And yet the blinders of American and of Japanese exceptionalism have complemented each other to prevent us from adequately engaging with these likenesses. If we are going to continue pursuing disciplinary knowledge formations such as "American studies" or "Japanese studies," I would prefer to think of them as overlapping and interlaced fields that must be attentive to the mutually constitutive and imbricated histories of the nation-states on which they focus, all the while looking beyond such binaries. This book, I hope, will demonstrate that much can be learned by transgressing the conventional boundaries that still sequester the histories of Japan and the United States from one another, as well as the wall that continues to separate the writing of Asian from Asian American history.

This is not to deny differences between the Second World War's total war regimes—no simple litany of comparable examples can substitute for writing that is attentive to the deep singularity and situated meaningfulness of histories with a narrower focus. Thus even as I draw attention to comparabilities or similarities, I do not suggest that the experiences of ethnic and colonial soldiers in the American and Japanese empires were the same or that we can fully comprehend one regime by examining the other. Instead, I use the terms "comparable" or "comparabilities" with the very specific intent of enabling us to consider the similarities between the United States and Japan during wartime, as well as the many ways in which these two apparently discrete histories became increasingly intertwined, without reducing them to an absolute sameness.

The organization of this book reflects this perspective. Part I seeks to bring the wartime histories of the United States and Japan into conversation, pointing to the common requirements of fighting in the Asia-Pacific that led to comparable efforts to incorporate racialized subjects into each of the respective political—and, more broadly, bio-political—regimes. Part II deepens the focus on Japanese American soldiering through an analysis of a range of disparate texts that includes government and military documents, media representations, literature, and film, while part III does the same for Korean soldiering. However, the particular context of soldiering in part II is Japanese American internment. The major task of its chapters is to show how the movement from vulgar to polite racism was worked out in a setting where the reality of incarceration clashed so obviously with the nation's claims that it stood for freedom, democracy, security, welfare, and the preservation of the happiness of all Americans, including those of Japanese descent. Part II also differs slightly in temporal coverage from part III in that it spills over into the period of the Cold War. Such expansion is necessary to highlight the continuity between the wartime and postwar for Japanese Americans (hence the utility of the concept of the "transwar"), insofar as their incorporation into the nation under inclusionary racism began during the war but was realized only during the Cold War years. In other words, this periodization makes it possible to see how the representation of Japanese Americans as the nation's model minority ironically began during the war itself, when the great majority of them were still imprisoned in camps. It also underscores how that representation was further elaborated in a more multiculturalist (in contrast to assimilationist) direction as a result of the Cold War project of mobilizing minorities for national goals, in which Japanese Americans (including the figure of the Japanese American soldier) proved particularly useful in efforts to achieve postcolonial hegemony in the Asia-Pacific.

In contrast, the context for part III is the changing position of Korea during wartime, clearly within the empire but ambiguously caught somewhere between being a colony and being a part of the Japanese nation. Its chapters and the epilogue show that during the war, the colonial relationship was increasingly being refigured into a relation between an expanded concept of the nation and its regions, in which nationalization extended beyond politics in a narrow sense to bio-political attempts to make Koreans live and to reconfigure gender relations and family structures. These attempts resonate in some crucial ways with liberal governmentality. However, unlike the nationalization of Japanese Americans that continued through the war's end, the nationalization of Koreans as Japanese came to an abrupt halt with Japan's defeat. In the postwar era the United States replaced Japan as the major decolonizing/nationalizing power in East Asia, and it operated in many ways much as the Japanese empire had functioned during the period of total war. The postwar/post-"liberation" U.S. occupations in East Asia would work likewise both through continued violence (including by carrying on the work of Japan as the major anticommunist military and police power in the region) and through mobilization of the subtler imperialism of the "government of self-government." The latter, ironically, had been precisely the strategy that Japan had already been working out vis-à-vis its allies in the Greater East Asia Co-Prosperity Sphere.

PART ONE · FROM VULGAR
TO POLITE RACISM

CHAPTER ONE

Right to Kill,
Right to Make Live

Koreans as Japanese

> Go get slaughtered and we promise you a long
> and pleasant life.
>
> MICHEL FOUCAULT, *"The Political Technology
> of Individuals"* (1988)

TOTAL WAR AND THE POPULATION PROBLEM

In its official history of thirty years of Japanese rule in Korea, the Government-General of Korea noted that a fundamental transformation in the state's understanding of "population" had taken place since the beginning of the Sino-Japanese War in 1937. Previously, the population problem had been understood as a matter of an excess—that is, concerned with such issues as the imbalance between a surplus population, on the one hand, and available food and employment on the other. However, because of the wartime need for "human resources" and future demands for "limitless [population] growth," this worry had been totally reversed. "In this way," the history stated, "now the weight of the population problem has shifted from what has been a surplus population problem to its complete opposite, a problem of population deficit."[1]

Although the Government-General's description of the state's new notion is deceptively simple—we formerly had too many people, and now we do not have enough—this reconceptualization of the Korean people as an object of study and intervention had profound and in some ways ironic repercussions that may be appreciated by first considering what Michel Foucault has called "bio-power" and "governmentality."[2] According to Foucault, a fundamental transformation in the exercise of power over the lives and deaths of populations emerged in the eighteenth century and then took hold in the nineteenth. In an older historical moment, as typified by the rule of a transcendent sovereign, power over life and death had operated primarily through a negativity. The sovereign exercised his power through the right to kill—or, put the other way, by allowing subjects to live. But particularly from the nineteenth century on, this old right came to be complemented by one with exactly the opposite character. In contrast to the negative logic of the right to take life, the new mode of power, which Foucault called bio-power, is exercised by making others live—by a productive or positive logic. This bio-power is a "power that exerts a positive influence on life, that endeavors to administer, optimize and multiply it, subjecting it to precise controls and comprehensive regulations."[3] Thus power comes to be concerned with matters such as mortality rates and the ratio of births to deaths. It targets living human beings, gathers knowledge about them, constitutes them in their aggregate as populations, and then seeks to enhance their health, sanitation, birthrate, longevity, and so on. It makes them live and prosper through such measures as public hygiene, charitable institutions, welfare funds, old age pensions, insurance, urban planning, and more. Population became a political problem and a target of regulation.

Similarly, for Foucault it is precisely the discovery of the population as the ultimate end of government that characterizes what he calls governmentality, or how governing is thought about and how power is exercised in the modern period. Here it is not the rationality of government in and of itself that is of primary importance "but the welfare of the population, the improvement of its condition, the increase of its wealth, longevity, health, etc.; and the means that the government uses to attain these ends are themselves all in some sense immanent to the population; it is the population itself on which government will act either directly or through large-scale campaigns, or indirectly through techniques that will make possible, without the full awareness of the people, the stimulation of birth rates, the directing of the flow of population into certain regions or activities, etc."[4] Under this regime of governmentality, three modes of power—sovereignty (operating primarily through laws and achieving its paradigmatic form in the transcendent king), discipline (as constituted through schools, armies, factories, and so on), and government—operate together to manage and make the population prosper in aggregate. However, within this triangular ensemble of power it is above all "government"—in its broad sense of guiding conduct through a vast and deep assemblage of authorities, technologies, and knowledges and of operating through the mobilization of desires and interests—that becomes preeminent. To further clarify, when Foucault says that "government" operates through positive techniques of the "conduct of conduct," he means that government "consists in guiding the possibility of conduct and putting in order the possible outcome."[5]

But how are these sweeping Foucauldian claims about bio-power and govern-mentality relevant to analyzing the understanding of population under the Japanese wartime regime? On the one hand, we must recognize that from early on in Japa-nese rule, the colonial government manifested some concern, albeit with limited scope, to enhance the lives of the colonized population and to discipline them through such means as education and the distribution of medical knowledge and care. In fact, in recent years scholars of colonial Korea have produced excellent work demon-strating how modern understandings of the body, health, medicine, reproduction, and sanitation in Korea were produced and circulated—understandings that could have led to policies designed to nurture and expand the Korean population.[6] More generally, scholars in Korea, Japan, and the Anglophone world have pointed to the "developmental" or, following Foucault, "governmental" or "disciplinary" aspects of Japanese colonial rule in Korea and elsewhere within the Japanese colonial em-pire. Such interventions have been a welcome addition to the long-dominant view that Japanese colonialism worked only through a modality of power characterized by sheer brutality, repression, exploitation, and negativity.[7]

On the other hand, such measures proceeded fitfully and unevenly, at least until the 1930s. As some skeptics of the concept of colonial modernity have already ar-gued, under Japanese colonialism the great masses of the Korean people were more excluded from than incorporated into those apparatuses and institutions that have been identified with modernity, disciplinization, and government, beginning with schools, factories, hospitals, prisons, and so on.[8] Along these lines we can note that even as late as 1941, one researcher found in his study of some rural villages that "[a]pproximately 42.7 percent of women had given birth on their own without the assistance of midwives[;] . . . 31.7 percent of all births were stillbirths, and 35 per-cent of babies died before age one." The Government-General determined that in 1930, only 1.3 midwives were available to serve every 10,000 Korean women, while the comparable figure for women in the Japanese metropole was 18.7.[9] Similarly, a 1926 directory of physicians practicing in Korea lists just 1,212, of whom a mere 40 specialized in gynecology.[10] Moreover, researchers have long noted the GGK's only half-hearted attempts to establish a variety of social and welfare services for Kore-ans during the colonial period.[11] The education of the Korean people as Japanese national subjects was at such a low level that in 1936, only about 8 percent of the to-tal population had any competence in the Japanese language; not until 1938 did the GGK announce a plan to begin universal elementary school education for Koreans (in 1946).[12]

Furthermore, while prior to the 1930s there had been surveys of the Korean people and their customs, reports on laborers, examinations of limited numbers of Korean bodies, and so on, even as late as the final years of the war the colonial government still found itself scrambling to put Korean household registers in order. In other words, the colonial state had not established one of the first foundations for constituting the population into the foremost object of government—namely, a technology to account for it, to know it. The state could not even determine the precise number and whereabouts of Korean people living in the colony, let alone in Manchuria, metropolitan Japan, China, and elsewhere.

Such facts and figures, and many more that could be cited here, indicate that while there may have been some ambiguity about whether the Korean people were understood as a population worthy of education, life, health, reproduction, and happiness, for most of the colonial period the great masses of the Korean people were more outside than inside the regime of governmentality and bio-power. Or, put differently, they were included in the sense of being largely placed in the zone of exclusion. In practice, power was still exercised primarily in its negativity—by the power to take life and by a strategy of limiting or suppressing the activities of those deemed dangerous, such as communists and ethnic nationalists. Through most of the colonial period, Japanese colonialism operated primarily through the racialized exclusionary logic of colonial difference; at best, it allowed what might be called "zones of indifference" or "undecidability," in which Koreans might be allowed to languish, starve, or even die—or, conversely, through which a few might pass into the inside.[13] Here it is also important to keep in mind that, as Foucault explains, "killing" does not "mean simply murder as such, but also every form of indirect murder: the fact of exposing someone to death, increasing the risk of death for some people, or, quite simply, political death, expulsion, rejection, and so on":[14] in other words, acts deducting from life.

With regard to these "zones of indifference" or "undecidability," my point is that ambivalence about the necessity of nurturing a native educated elite and a reliable pool of laborers led to uneven and limited incorporations of specifically targeted segments and individuals within the Korean population into the apparatuses and institutions associated with modern governmentality. But the Korean people as a whole was not constituted as a "population" in the Foucauldian sense—that is, as an entire population whose individual and aggregated lives could be considered objects of positive intervention and regulation.

However, once the logic of total war transformed the population problem into one of lack, the policies of the metropolitan and colonial governments toward their colonial subjects in Korea began to shift dramatically. Now, like "metropolitan Japanese" (*Naichijin*), Koreans were to be made to live. They were to be targeted as living human beings and constituted in their aggregate as a major subpopulation, and the purpose of government would be to enhance their health, sanitation, birthrate, longevity, education, and general well-being. I do not mean to suggest that the efforts to enhance the lives of Koreans made by the colonial authorities equaled the measures taken for the metropolitan Japanese population. And of course various social services offered them, including medical care, were on the whole far inferior to those available in the metropole. Nor did this transformation result in the disappearance of sheer power in its negativity—that is, the right to take life, as exercised directly by the emperor's officials, the police, and laws.

Nevertheless, what we can perceive in an abundance of official documents and policies of the period, especially from 1937 on, is a new commitment to improve the health, education, and welfare of the Korean people. Whether the intentions of colonial administrators and others serving in unofficial organizations supporting the state were noble or sincere does not concern me here. For now, it is enough to note that they acted as if their charge was to work harder to nurture the lives of the Korean people and that when they noted improvements in indices measuring the health, wealth, and happiness of the Korean people, they argued for the necessity of doing more.

And what about the matter of racism or discrimination? Foucault is again suggestive. Under the bio-political regime, racism—understood both narrowly and most broadly as discrimination against all those considered inferior in a normalizing society—operates in the determination of who must live and who must die. It creates caesuras as it fragments the biological field of the human to identify threats to the population, whether internal or external. It distinguishes between those who will foster the life and welfare of the population, and therefore must be made to live, and those who hinder the life and welfare of the population and must be made to die. It necessitates the killing or expulsion of those considered threats so that the population can thrive. In the face of war, a determination had to be made about how to locate Koreans in relation to the Japanese metropolitan population. Were they to be considered a threatening Other that had to be kept apart from the metropolitan core of the Japanese population, treated like slaves and exposed to death, or even exterminated in the manner of the Nazi Holocaust? Or were Koreans to be reconstituted as a subpopulation worthy of being made to live because they could help foster the life and welfare of the metropolitan Japanese population?

There was no absolute resolution of this problem, but as the population shortage in Japan and its colonies came to be felt with increasing acuity through the war years, the ruling elite accelerated the demand that Koreans be made to live and prosper as a part of the Japanese population. The war years, in other words, were a transitional moment in the passage of Koreans from the outside to the inside of the "Japanese" population, a shift managed by the logics and technologies of bio-power and governmentality. Hence as the war progressed it became increasingly imperative to disavow racist feelings toward Koreans. And paralleling this passage from the outside to the inside we find a transformation in the type of racist discrimination against Koreans—that is, a movement from an unabashed and exclusionary "vulgar racism" to a new type of inclusionary and "polite racism" that denied itself to be racist even as it operated as such.

MILITARY SERVICE

The military provides a particularly compelling site from which to witness this passage, since the more the Japanese empire came to depend on the Korean population for soldiers and sailors, the more difficult it became to exclude them from the nation—in both the conventional meaning of a political community and in Foucault's bio-political sense of a population. According to a late November 1937 Korean Army document signed by its chief of staff, Kunō Seiichi, the Korean Army had carefully considered the question of Korean participation in the military since at least 1932. Yoshida Toshiguma, who was at one time head of conscription for the Korean Army, also indicated in his insider's history of Koreans in the Japanese military that in April 1937 Kawagishi Bunzaburō, commander of the Twentieth Division (under the Korean Army), communicated his views on the matter to Koiso Kuniaki, commander of the Korean Army (later governor-general of Korea and then prime minister). According to Kawagishi, conferral of the military obligation upon Koreans could contribute to their formation into good "imperial subjects." This statement was followed in May of the same year by an informal inquiry from the War Ministry's Military Preparations Section (chōboka). Then, in June 1937, the central authorities asked the Korean Army to draft an opinion on this matter and it did so the following month, recommending that Koreans be allowed to volunteer on a trial basis. The Government-General (headed by Minami Jirō) also enthusiastically supported the volunteer system, because it believed that such a move would facilitate its administration of the colony. Thus, according to these sources, serious consideration of Korean military service had begun shortly after the massive invasion of Manchuria in September 1931 (the "Manchurian Incident" or the beginning of what historians sometimes call the "Fifteen-Year War"). However, actual establishment of the volunteer system had been sparked by an inquiry from the War Ministry just before the 7 July 1937 escalation of all-out war with China (the "China Incident"), and concrete policy had been formulated around that time through communications among the Korean Army, the War Ministry, and the Government-General.[15]

According to Yoshida, even after July 1937 War Ministry officials still overwhelmingly believed that the recruitment of Koreans was premature. However, considerable efforts on the part of the Korean Army's high officers and the Government-General alleviated their fears. For example, Commander Koiso sent officers on his staff to Tokyo on multiple occasions to report on the Korean situation and invited War Ministry officials to visit Korea to observe the actual conditions of various social classes. By Yoshida's account, Pak Yŏng-ch'ŏl—a wealthy Korean businessman and the honorary consul-general of Manchuria, who had graduated from the Japanese Military Academy and served in the Japanese Imperial Guard Cavalry—was recruited as local guide for at least one War Ministry official.[16]

In fact, in the period shortly before and after July 1937, Japanese military officers in the Korean Army and GGK officials worked energetically to convince the military and government authorities in the metropole that allowing Koreans into the military would have a positive effect on the sentiments of the Korean people and that Korean males were qualified to serve. Their reasoning fell roughly along the following lines.[17] First, military service would be conducive to enhancing Korean patriotism concerning Japan, because the highest patriotism could be asked only of those given responsibility for national defense.[18] Second, while the authorities worried about the low educational level of Koreans and what they regarded as deficiencies in their spiritual and Japanese-language training, they presented evidence of recent improvements in these areas and projections of further progress. For example, the Government-General noted that military drills (kyōren) had been established with much success in Korea in 1926, just one year after they had begun in the metropole, and that by 1938 sixty-six schools practiced military drills, most led by officers in active service. Young Men's Training Centers (seinen kunrensho) had also been founded in Korea, and by 1937 more than 2,000 metropolitan Japanese and 1,500 Koreans were attending some eight-four centers. Similarly, while the Government-General estimated that as of 1937 the percentage of Koreans seventeen to twenty years of age "able to freely engage in normal conversation in the national (Japanese) language" was only 5.85 percent (97,033 out of 1,657,385 men and women), it cast a positive light on even this dismal figure by predicting a vastly improved situation in the future. Reminding us that in early 1938 the need for military manpower was not as urgent as it would become after the Pearl Harbor attack and that the end of Japanese colonial rule was nowhere in sight, the Government-General projected the language competency of Koreans in this age group as far into the future as 1966. It estimated that by that time more than 1.2 million (45.82 percent) Koreans ages seventeen to twenty would have the desired level of language proficiency.[19]

Third, these military officers and GGK officials claimed that ever since the Manchurian invasion of 18 September 1931—which led immediately to the Japanese takeover of Manchuria and the establishment of Manchukuo as Japan's client state in the following year—the Korean people had become increasingly patriotic in their attitudes toward Japan. The evidence included the impressive number of those who had recanted their former anti-Japanese ethnic nationalism, the engagement in patriotic activities of members of formerly antigovernment religions or of what were routinely called "pseudo-religious" groups, the support of the Korean-language media for national policy, the considerable amounts of money and blood donated for national defense, the tremendous increase in numbers of worshippers at Shinto shrines, and the frequency of Korean-sponsored festivals to pray for or report on war victories. Perhaps most spectacularly, these authorities noted that following the "China Incident" Koreans had shown a remarkable eagerness to join directly in military efforts. In Shanghai, a former hotbed of Korean anti-Japanese activists, more than two hundred youths had volunteered to work at various tasks under the Japanese military. Three of these volunteers had been killed and seven were severely wounded. In Tianjin, Koreans had also formed a "righteous army" and served on the front lines, transporting munitions as well as sick and injured Japanese soldiers. In addition, in the space of a little more than a month following the "China Incident," 105 Koreans had volunteered to serve with the military, some even signing blood oaths.[20]

Fourth, these authorities recounted the longer history of Koreans who had rendered military or police service for Japan. The Korean Army refuted the assumption that the new recruits' inferior abilities might harm the overall fighting performance of Japanese troops if field divisions were integrated. It pointed out that Koreans had served in the Auxiliary Military Police (*kenpei hojo* or, after August 1919, *kenpeiho*) and as Korean police officers (*Chōsen keisatsukan*) and had proven themselves in campaigns to put down anti-Japanese "bandits" (*hizoku*). The Korean Army assured doubters that if given the proper guidance, Koreans would perform as the equals of their metropolitan Japanese peers.[21] One detailed report indicated that the Auxiliary Military Police system for Korean recruits had been established in Korea in June 1908 in conjunction with the general expansion of the military police in Korea. By the following month, Korean auxiliaries totaled some 4,100 men and outnumbered Japanese in the military police by more than two to one. Koreans continued to serve in the Auxiliary Military Police in large numbers after the 1910 annexation, averaging about 4,700 men between 1914 and 1919. During the period 1906–11 alone, there had been 1,109 clashes between MPs and insurgents, with Korean auxiliaries helping to exterminate some 3,600 of the latter. Although reorganizations of the military police in 1919 and of the military more generally in 1925 had drastically reduced the number of Korean auxiliaries, the report emphasized their continuing service, with the main force stationed along the northern national (that is, Korean) border. Overall, the report stressed that the Korean auxiliaries equaled metropolitan Japanese MPs in every way, even though they were technically classified as civilian military employees (*gunzoku*) rather than as military personnel. They had great pride in themselves as "model Koreans" (*Senjin no gihyō*) and had performed with special distinction after the Manchurian invasion, especially in Manchuria and Shanghai. One Korean auxiliary had received the Order of the Golden Kite (an award given for military bravery or leadership), while not even one officer had mutinied or deserted. To a man, the Koreans had performed dutifully.[22]

The same report also commended Koreans for their service with the police. The Government-General, realizing the obvious utility of employing men who shared the same language and "thoughts" as the common Korean people, had employed a large number of Korean policemen (*junsa*). As of October 1937, Koreans numbered 7,203 out of 17,067 policemen in Korea.[23] It admitted that because of the limited term of their training (four months) and their "traditional living environment" (*seikatsu kankyō*), these policemen did not meet metropolitan Japanese standards of self-discipline, responsibility, and active engagement in their duties. However, it also noted recent improvements in their performance—so dramatic that some had been awarded the "highest honor available to policemen, the Distinguished Service Medal."

The report noted that on the other side of the border, Koreans had served with distinction in the Manchurian military. Relying on its principle of the "harmony of the five ethnic groups" (*gozoku kyōwa:* that is, Japanese, Han Chinese, Manchus, Mongols, and Koreans), the Manchukuo state had recruited officers and servicemen from among its one million resident Koreans. These men had been organized into three border surveillance regiments (*kokkyō kanshitai*), placed strategically in Dongning and Hunchun Districts. Korean service in these units had not been entirely without incident. In the summer of 1936, members of one company in Dongning, dissatisfied with their treatment by a Japanese officer, had revolted and fled to Russian territory. Confidence in these soldiers then collapsed, and the recruitment of

Koreans in Jiandao Province was halted. However, the report concluded on a positive note about the potential of Koreans as soldiers, observing that an investigation had revealed that the incident could not be blamed on Koreans alone. Moreover, the remaining Korean soldiers had performed well, particularly in skirmishes with the Russians. Recognition of the value of these Koreans was on the rise, and plans were being made for a further increase in their number.[24]

Thus, by the end of 1937, support for the voluntary soldier system had overcome remaining resistance from some of the central military authorities, leading to the War Ministry's 15 January 1938 announcement that the army would be opened to Korean volunteers. The Army Special Volunteer System Law (*rikugun tokubetsu shiganheirei*) was promulgated as an imperial ordinance (No. 95) on 22 February 1938, and went into effect on 3 April 1938, thus making it possible for Korean "male imperial subjects seventeen years and older" to volunteer for service in the army.[25] Taiwanese became eligible to volunteer for the army from April 1942 on.[26] The military did not accept Korean or Taiwanese volunteers into the navy until the Navy Special Volunteer Law (Imperial Ordinance No. 608) went into effect on 1 August 1943. This law enabled males sixteen to twenty years of age from both colonies to volunteer for most but not all positions within the navy.[27] Kondō Masami has argued that two factors help explain the general reluctance of the navy to accept volunteers until 1943. In comparison to the army, the navy did not have as great a manpower need until this late date. And, interestingly, like the U.S. military, which resisted allowing Japanese Americans to serve in the navy, the Japanese navy was concerned about the ease with which only a few untrustworthy elements could sabotage entire ships.[28] While the Japanese navy overcame this reservation, the U.S. Navy continued to be closed to Japanese Americans through the entire war.

Because the military authorities inaugurated the new system on a trial basis, the number of Korean volunteers initially accepted was very small; its subsequent growth reflected both increased confidence in them and expanding manpower needs. Starting with just 400 and 600 volunteers accepted in 1938 and 1939, respectively, by 1943 the army had enrolled a total of 16,830 Korean volunteers. In the first two years these volunteers were enrolled only in the Korean Army (Nineteenth and Twentieth Divisions); but from 1940 on they also began serving in the Kwantung Army, and from 1942 in the North China Army. In 1943, the final year of the special voluntary system, the army distributed them throughout the service without restriction. Similarly, while they had initially been limited to infantry, transport (*shichōhei*), and anti-aircraft artillery (*kōsha hōhei*) units, from 1941 the army placed them in the field and mountain artillery (*yasan hōhei*) as well, and from 1942 they entered all types of units. In addition, under its special volunteer system the navy took in a total of at least 3,000 Korean volunteers.[29]

The army's voluntary system had been instituted in Korea with the intent of possibly extending military conscription to the colony at some time in the distant future, but the Pearl Harbor attack accelerated these efforts. On 8 May 1942, the Japanese cabinet passed a resolution approving extension of the military draft to Korea, and through Law No. 4 (which was promulgated 1 March 1943 and went into effect on 1 August 1943) the government revised the Military Service Law (*heieki-hō*) to make enforcement of conscription in Korea possible.[30] The decision to implement military conscription in Taiwan followed soon thereafter, as the cabinet approved this resolution in September 1943.[31] As a result, the Japanese military began to conscript Koreans beginning in 1944, and Taiwanese in 1945.

In the most detailed empirical study of the Japanese conscription system in Korea to date, Higuchi Yūichi has estimated that at least 190,000 Korean conscripts served in the army and navy in the last two years of the war. For each of the years 1944 and 1945, these included 55,000 conscripts directly enrolled into active service (*gen'ekihei;* 45,000 to the army and 10,000 to the navy per year), 29,000 conscripts called up by the army after being placed for a time in the reserves (*hojūhei*), and 11,000 conscripts who served in "special duty units" (*tokubetsu kinmutai*). The latter were essentially labor units, and some companies within them probably were not armed.[32] Of those enrolled directly into active service, the military initially attached most to the Korean Army, with a much smaller number joining the Kwantung Army. The Korean Army then distributed Korean conscripts throughout the other armies. A Korean Army document shows that out of 45,000 conscripts put into active service in 1944, it planned to allot the greatest numbers to the China Expeditionary Army (10,445), followed by the Kwantung (9,925) and Southern Armies (7,647), with the remainder placed throughout. Though Korean conscripts served in all types of units, the majority were assigned to the infantry.[33] While official policy dictated that there should be no discrimination against Koreans per se with regard to their assignments, one account notes that "owing to their educational level and technical skill level," few served in technical units (*gijutsu butai*) while a great many were assigned to duty or noncombatant units (*kinmu butai*). This same source claims that the military normally limited the percentage of Koreans serving in any unit—20 percent in frontline units, 40 percent in rearline units, and 80 percent in duty or noncombatant units—although there is evidence that these limits were not strictly observed.[34]

One other relatively small but significant group of Korean and Taiwanese soldiers should be mentioned—namely, "student soldiers." In October 1943 the Japanese government (through Imperial Ordinance No. 755) suspended student deferments for conscription, primarily as a measure to increase the pool of potential military officers. Exceptions continued to be made for those studying in fields deemed essential to the military effort, such as medicine, science, and engineering, but students in the faculties of law and letters could no longer have their service deferred.[35] Korean and Taiwanese students were not subject to this change in the law; and in order to mobilize them for the same purpose, the War Ministry implemented the Army Special Volunteers Extraordinary Induction Regulations (*rikugun tokubetsu shiganhei saiyō kisoku*). Promulgated and put into effect on 20 October 1943, these regulations legally enabled Korean and Taiwanese students enrolled in higher education to volunteer for the army. Most would otherwise have fallen into a gap, as the earlier Army Special Volunteer System was closing down and they exceeded the age requirement (twenty) for the upcoming draft. Under these regulations the Government-General accepted volunteers from 25 October to 20 November of the same year, and those deemed acceptable entered the army on 20 January 1944. About 70 percent (4,385 out of 6,203) of those eligible under these regulations joined.[36] No comparable path existed for colonial students to volunteer for the navy.

Thus, from modest beginnings in the first years of the Army Special Volunteer System to the enforcement of conscription in 1944 and 1945, Korean male youths came to play an extraordinarily large role in the Japanese war effort. By the end of the conflict they were serving in almost all types of units in both the army and navy; and based on the numbers given above—16,830 army volunteers, 3,000 navy volunteers, 190,000 army and navy conscripts, and 4,385 student army volunteers—it is possible to arrive at a rough estimate of more than 214,000 Korean men who served as military personnel in the Japanese armed forces between 1938 and 1945.

CONTRADICTIONS OF MILITARY SERVICE

Scholars tend to agree that the colonial government conceived of the volunteer system not only as of direct importance, in providing military manpower, but also as part of a broader spiritual campaign known as "imperial subjectivization" (*kōminka*), which was intended to constitute the Korean people into loyal subjects of the Japanese emperor.[37] The *kōminka* campaign centered on four major reform programs: religious reforms that sought to replace other religions with Shinto, educational reforms that emphasized Japanization of the spirit and Japanese-language education, the coerced replacement of Korean and Taiwanese names with Japanized ones, and the inclusion of colonial subjects in the military forces. In general, this campaign of assimilation to Japaneseness is usually understood as seeking to extinguish the unique cultural life and traditions of the colonized peoples—or in the often-used expression, to "obliterate the [Korean] ethnos" (*minzoku massatsu*). And within this context, the policy of enlisting colonial subjects into the military is generally explained as an attempt to demonstrate to Koreans and Taiwanese that the Japanese regarded them as their equals, even when they did not.

Given the extreme gap between the actual conditions in which most of the Korean people lived and the extent of the military's as well as the central and colonial government's apparently outrageous claims that Koreans were completely equal to the metropolitan Japanese, it is not difficult to understand why scholars and many others have dismissed the Japanese rulers' pronouncements as simply duplicitous. However, what we might call the "argument of obvious duplicity" is insufficient in at least two respects. First, it posits an unchanging Japanese racism that is immune to transformations in the historical conditions of which it was a part. Second, such a limited view does not take into consideration the unintended effects of issuing pronouncements on equality, even if such a campaign might have begun with purely utilitarian and duplicitous purposes. For instance, the military, central, and colonial authorities determined that in order to make the campaign for the inclusion of Koreans into the military a success, not only would they need to convince the Korean people that the emperor and the nation regarded them as their equals, but it would also be necessary to impress upon the metropolitan Japanese that the Koreans were a trustworthy and loyal people. Between 1938 and 1945, the military authorities and their counterparts in the colonial and central governments targeted their propaganda at Japanese officials throughout the civil and military bureaucracies, and at the great masses of Japanese people scattered throughout the empire, just as much as at the Korean people.

As we will see more fully in later chapters, in addition to propaganda intended for Koreans, mainstream Japanese newspapers, magazines, radio, literature, and even movies conveyed the veracity of Korean and metropolitan Japanese equality to the metropolitan Japanese. Even as the ruling elite may have been duplicitous—in the sense that it most surely maintained discriminatory attitudes toward Koreans while deploying a language and programs of equality—it also became caught up in the discourse of equality it promoted. As some of the most interesting recent literature on European colonialism has argued,[38] even as the Japanese metropole sought to remake its colonies, it was constantly being remade by those same imperial projects.

Colonial policies that deployed the discourse of equality may have begun with utilitarian intent; but that discourse could not be neatly contained so as to make it both believable to the colonial subjects and a transparent lie to the colonizers.

Similarly, after the decision to draft Koreans had been made and preparations were under way for its implementation, the Government-General of Korea sent all the governors of the Korean provinces instructions for guiding public opinion about the new conscription system. In its summary of those instructions, the GGK explained that public opinion should be directed toward the idea that the conscription of Koreans was based on "the principles of the national entity" (*kokutai no hongi*).[39] This phrase most likely referred directly to the Ministry of Education's widely distributed book *Principles of the National Entity* (1937), which, as Tessa Morris-Suzuki has pointed out, never referred to biological race and left ambiguous the question of whether Japanese were supposed to be considered a homogeneous race.[40]

In fact, in its instructions on guiding public opinion the Government-General suggested that Japan was not a racially homogeneous nation and that the conscription of Koreans was based on the "unity of metropolitan Japan and Korea" (*Naisen ittai*) and the "equality of all beneath the emperor's benevolent gaze" (*isshi dōjin*). It also stressed that the spirit and organization of the Imperial Forces were fundamentally different from those of other nations and that the Japanese military would not be organized along the lines of a colonial army—by which it most likely meant that there would be no segregated units. Perhaps most germane to my point, the Government-General indicated that the targets of such efforts at molding public opinion should first include the metropolitan Japanese themselves, especially those residing in Korea.[41]

A considerably different reality from that offered by the argument of obvious duplicity will emerge as we reframe our problematic, moving attention away from the question of the sincerity of *intentions* and toward the *effects* of the disavowal of racist discrimination. More than ever before, especially in the post-1937 era, the conditions of total war released a set of contradictory discourses and practices regarding race or ethnicity that enveloped colonizers and colonized alike, both those who considered themselves unproblematically Japanese and those who sought to become Japanese. Once the official position of the national and colonial regimes dramatically shifted for practical reasons to that of the fundamental equality of Koreans and Japanese, the authorities had no choice but to act *as if* they truly believed in the discourse of equality. This acting *as if* had real-life effects, including pressure to enact concrete changes in policies regarding the management of Koreans—not only in the military but throughout the empire. In the end, the ruling elite contributed to the production and circulation of an emerging racial common sense that made it increasingly difficult to openly espouse vulgar racist views, to appear unconcerned about the health and welfare of the Korean people, and to ignore Korean desires for greater political rights.

FROM THE OUTSIDE TO THE INSIDE
OF THE JAPANESE POPULATION

To be sure, both before and after the mobilization of Koreans as soldiers, many officials continued to resist treating them as equals and harbored anxieties about the consequences of practices that seemed to break down the distinction between the two peoples. Even after the volunteer system had been in place for several years, Japanese military and government officials still often discussed Koreans as aliens. For example, in its immediate post–Pearl Harbor study of "national strength in human resources," the Ministry of War's Military Preparations Section continued to write about the Japanese people in terms of the Yamato ethnos and about others within the colonial empire as "outside peoples" (*gaichi minzoku*). In arguing that Japan's military manpower and civilian labor needs could not be met by the Yamato ethnos alone, it clearly considered the Korean people and other colonial subjects as ethnic groups external to the core Japanese population, or on the outside of what it called "our people" (*waga minzoku*).[42] Koreans and other outside peoples had to be mobilized, it said, but it did not suggest that the Koreans themselves might be considered part of the population worthy of life and security.

One of the most unequivocal official statements of the absolute necessity of maintaining the rigid line of separation between the Japanese people and their colonial subjects can be found in the 1943 study that I touched on briefly in my introduction: namely, *An Investigation of Global Policy with the Yamato Ethnos as Nucleus* (*Yamato minzoku*).[43] The authors of the study displayed their extreme anxiety about the tension between the need to mobilize the empire's human resources for the war effort and the desire to keep the different groups apart. With regard to Koreans and Taiwanese—not unlike U.S. eugenics discourse then current, in which fears of the Other's hyperfecundity exacerbated anxieties about racial contamination—the report claimed that these people not only were unassimilated but also reproduced at an alarmingly rapid rate. Taiwan and Korea occupied important positions as "supply bases" (*heitan kichi*), but they had to be prevented from becoming like "parasites within a lion" (*shishi shinchū no mushi*), meaning that they should not be allowed to bring harm to their mighty host.

The study proposed five rubrics under which to manage Koreans and Taiwanese. First, it should be made clear that Koreans in metropolitan Japan would be sent back to Korea after the war. Second, because of the Russian threat, Koreans living in the border area between northern Korea and eastern Manchuria should be moved elsewhere and replaced with metropolitan Japanese. Third, Koreans should be sent to barren areas such as New Guinea to reclaim the land. Fourth, arrangements should be made so that metropolitan Japanese would constitute 10 percent of the population resident in Korea and Taiwan. Finally, the study listed the numerous ways in which it felt that excesses in the administrative policy of "unifying metropolitan Japan and Korean" had ironically resulted in the oppression of the metropolitan Japanese by the Koreans. Most of the items listed were integral parts of the colonial government's assimilationist campaign—that is, the movement to Japanize names, coeducation, military conscription, voting rights in the metropole (including approval to use Korean hangul when voting), and intermarriage. In short, the eugenically minded researchers in the Ministry of Health and Welfare worried that the colonial empire's assimilationist program, necessitated by the war, threatened to obliterate the boundaries around the core Japanese population. They wanted to keep Koreans as workers, but at a safe distance—residentially, socially, culturally, politically, and sexually.[44]

Another section of the report dealt specifically with the detrimental effects of sex and of marriage between Koreans and metropolitan Japanese, and especially warned of the dangers of the large number of Korean men coupling with Japanese women in the metropole. Citing a study of marriages between African American men and white American women, the report concluded that interracial couplings attracted only the lowest social elements on both sides and should be avoided. Such a finding, it said, had been confirmed by another study of intermarriages between Korean males and metropolitan Japanese females in several areas of metropolitan Japan. But apparently just as troubling for the report's author(s) was that contrary to the usual principle of domination, whereby men of the leading or conquering race took the women of the follower or conquered race as their wives, in the metropole the situation had been reversed: an overwhelming percentage of intermarriages consisted of Korean men taking metropolitan women as their mates. Anticipating Frantz Fanon's well-known psychological argument about black males under white colonialism, the report held that the anomaly of so many Korean males entering into sexual relationships through marriage with women of the "leading race" could be partly explained by the Korean male's wish to "satisfy his desire for conquest" (*seifukukan o manzoku*) of the conqueror. But it also blamed the "excessive discourse on the unification of Koreans and metropolitan Japanese" and the campaign to change names. In the absence of any distinction between Japanese and Korean names, it said, guileless Japanese women in the metropole often misrecognized Koreans as metropolitan Japanese or fell prey to their pleasant conversation. Focusing more on character rather than on physiology, it noted that while no remarkable differences in intellect and physical strength distinguished "mixed blood children" from their metropolitan Japanese counterparts, "as expected, there are many with distorted personalities who do not know shame and whose national spirit is weak."[45]

For most of the war years, even those military and government officials who used the language of equality and who argued for the desirability of including Koreans in the military emphasized that they wanted to maintain the line excluding the Korean people from the metropolitan Japanese political community. For example, in its June 1937 recommendations for implementing the volunteer soldier system, the Korean Army Headquarters (Chōsengun shireibu) warned that Koreans would assuredly seek privileges once the military was opened to them, and strongly cautioned against "catering to the enthusiasm of Koreans for equal rights."[46] Similarly, in its materials prepared in anticipation of questions that the Privy Council would likely ask about the Special Volunteer System, the Government-General stressed that "the question of the right to vote and hold office is inherently a matter that should be considered separately," and it even claimed that the volunteer system was not necessarily a prelude to incorporating Koreans into the conscription system.[47]

Such warnings continued to circulate in military and civilian official circles around the time of the cabinet's formal decision on 8 May 1942 to impose conscription in Korea. A special committee within the Korean Army Headquarters charged with deliberating on the draft in the colony stressed that "military service is a sublime duty of imperial subjects" and that "the rights to vote and hold office should not be given in compensation for implementation of the conscription system in Korea."[48] Similarly, while the explanation of conscription in Korea prepared for the cabinet by the colonial minister (takumu daijin) gave numerous examples in support of the new policy, it also condemned the idea that "the right to vote and hold office should be given in exchange for implementation of the conscription system."[49] A draft of the war minister's views on Korean conscription used the same language of "sublime duty" to reject the notion that political rights could be exchanged for Korean military service. Moreover, while it emphasized that Japan's military needs could be met only by mobilizing Koreans and Taiwanese as military manpower, and lauded the advancements of the Korean people, it insisted that "of course the Yamato race will occupy the center in the defense of Greater East Asia."[50]

Nevertheless, military and colonial officials concluded that the mobilization of Koreans would be effective only if carried out on the basis of an official stance of equality—otherwise, why would Koreans agree to fight and die for Japan and how could interethnic conflicts among the troops be avoided? Once they began campaigning for the incorporation of Koreans into the military by arguing that the colonizers and the colonized were fundamentally the same, it became impossible to block the trajectory toward the increasing inclusion of Koreans within the national community—a community in the senses of a bio-politically targeted and racially united population, and eventually a population allowed to vote and hold public office. Glimmerings of this trajectory are visible even in the June 1937 source, cited above, authored by the Korean Army Headquarters. Although the headquarters urged the Government-General to emphasize the military duty of Koreans and to stifle any demands for expansion of their political rights, the strength of its recommendation to promote the complete identity of the two peoples clearly invited erosion of at least the formal distinctions between metropolitan Japanese and Koreans. The headquarters stressed that the purpose of the amalgamation had been to "truly reveal the reason why it is necessary to make the Koreans, who are of the same race and same ethnos (*dōshu dōzoku*), into one and the same body with us as the true heavenly ethnos." Moreover, it warned that Japanese residents in Korea could not simply expect Koreans to become Japanese without demonstrating reciprocity. Japanese residents in Korea should treat Korea as their native place—literally, as the "site of their ancestral graves" (*funbo no chi*). And they should be magnanimous enough to think of themselves as "Koreans (*Chōsenjin*) who hold firmly to the spirit of the Imperial Nation." For if Koreans were expected to think of themselves as Japanese without "metropolitan Japanese" in Korea considering themselves "Koreans," the policy would fail, since it would "in the end appear to be a unilateral measure." The Korean Army Headquarters even recommended extension of the Household Registration Law (*kosekihō*) to the colony.[51]

It is important to keep in mind that this document and others like it were not intended to serve as propaganda but were recommendations for setting policies. Clearly, whether they personally held racist views or not, the authorities were persuaded both by sheer logic and by such experiences as the 1936 revolt against the Manchurian Army's discriminatory treatment of Koreans, mentioned above, that unless they made genuine efforts to put egalitarian policies into practice, the mass mobilization of Koreans for the war effort would end in failure. For the volunteer soldier system to succeed, they had no choice but to uphold a policy of nondiscrimination, beginning with the treatment of Koreans within the military itself. Thus, unlike the U.S. military, which did not abandon its policy of racial segregation until after the war, the Japanese military explicitly rejected such a policy before it implemented the volunteer system for Koreans. A Korean Army document explained that discriminating against Koreans by placing them in special units would contradict the spirit of national unity and would reduce the efficiency of the special volunteer system by half.[52] The Korean Army Headquarters emphasized the policy of nondiscrimination in no uncertain terms: "insofar as adoption of the volunteer soldier system is recognized and implemented, the treatment of Koreans after their induction must necessarily be based upon the fundamental principle of making metropolitan Japanese and Koreans uniform and equal. Any discriminatory attitude in dealing with this matter, stemming from some trifling reason, must be absolutely eliminated. Otherwise, adoption of this system will end in harm rather than benefit."[53]

Echoing such sentiments, the Government-General stressed in its November 1937 outline of procedures for carrying out the Korean volunteer soldier system that after a rigorous process of selecting appropriate volunteers for enlistment, "in principle the current system should be applied without discrimination between metropolitan Japanese and Koreans. In other words, education, reenlistment, volunteering to become a noncommissioned officer, salary, etc.—in all these things metropolitan Japanese and Koreans should be treated in the same manner."[54]

After the May 1942 announcement that Koreans would become subject to conscription, and especially after concrete preparations began, it became increasingly difficult to maintain the strict line of exclusion between Koreans and metropolitan Japanese by ethnicity, by worthiness of life and welfare, and even in terms of political rights. And in direct contrast to the exclusionary notion cited earlier that Koreans might be mobilized for the military as an "outside people," official documents increasingly included the Korean people as "leaders of the Greater East Asia Co-Prosperity Sphere" (daitōa kyōeiken no shidōsha) and placed them within the concept of the empire's "core leadership" (chūkakuteki shidōsha).[55]

To be sure, even as it denounced discrimination and claimed to recognize Korean inclusion in the core Japanese population, the emerging discourse on Koreans as a part of the Japanese people tended to describe the Korean people as still lagging behind the metropolitan Japanese. While it predicted that all distinctions between Koreans and the metropolitan Japanese would eventually fade away, in the meantime Koreans were to be treated as essentially but not yet actually equals. This was a kind of historicist logic that, as Dipesh Chakrabarty has put it for another context, consigned others to "an imaginary waiting room" of history. In other words, it was a way of telling the Korean people "not yet"[56]—and it resulted not in the disappearance of racism but in the constitution of a new kind of discrimination that reproduced hierarchies through a discourse on cultural character and catching up, even as it strongly denounced ethnic or racial discrimination and gestured toward inclusion. Yet, as we will also see, the very logic of historicism opened up an avenue for increasing numbers of exemplary individuals to slip out of the waiting room and to claim themselves ready to be treated as full-fledged Japanese. And the incessant pressure of meeting the demands of total war led to the piecemeal, if far from complete, dismantling of the waiting room itself.

INCLUSIONARY RACISM AND TRAINING SOLDIERS FROM KOREA

The logic of inclusionary or polite racism, with its simultaneous disavowal and reproduction of racism through a reasoning that was cultural and historicist rather than strictly biological and essentialist, is succinctly expressed in a text that directly affected the treatment of Koreans in the army—namely, *Chōsen shusshinhei no kyōiku sankō shiryō* (*Reference Materials for the Education of Soldiers from Korea*, hereafter *Soldiers from Korea* or "the manual"). Authored by the Inspectorate General of Military Training (Kyōiku Sōkanbu), the highest body providing guidance on army educational matters (with the exception of the Army Air Service), *Soldiers from Korea* appeared in two compact volumes in 1944. Its extensive bibliographic references as well as its contents reveal that its authors had based their generalizations on the vast reservoir of Japanese Orientalist knowledge about the Korean people and their history, and that it served as a manual for Japanese officers charged with training Korean soldiers.[57]

The text begins with a dramatic prologue that emphasized, as the official slogan went, "the equality of all under the emperor's benevolent gaze" (*isshi dōjin*), the rising self-consciousness of Koreans as imperial subjects, and the possibility that these Koreans might have a special mission in making Greater East Asia a reality. While it is often assumed today that the "Japanese" reserved the leading place in East Asia for themselves alone, with other imperial subjects having a "proper place" below them, the prologue declared that these soldiers from Korea should be allowed to fulfill their weighty mission "*as members of the leading race of Greater East Asia*" (*Daitōa no shidō minzoku no ichiin toshite;* emphasis added).

Whether the Koreans would do so, however, depended on the "discernment and passion of [their] educators." The manual warned these educators not to discriminate against Korean soldiers. While instructors must "have sufficient recognition and grasp of [Korean] ethnic characteristics and current conditions in Korea," they should avoid "being slaves to unfounded prejudices or to immediately judging individuals by general tendencies." Furthermore, the manual warned that while it might appear to focus excessively on the faults in the "character, thought, and moral fiber" of Koreans, the same shortcomings could be widely found among individual metropolitan Japanese.[58]

Summarizing the scholarship of anthropologists, folklorists, historians, linguists, and economists as well as studies conducted by various governmental agencies, *Soldiers from Korea* outlined the characteristics that its authors believed distinguished Koreans from their metropolitan Japanese counterparts. In doing so, however, it maintained that these differences were not suprahistorical but rather products of specific geopolitical factors and concrete historical experiences. It explained that although the Korea Peninsula had from ancient times sustained intimate sanguineous, cultural, and political relationships with the Japanese mainland, history had pulled the two regions apart and stamped the Korean people with their particularity. Following the long line of scholarly thought on "the unity of metropolitan Japan and Korea" and the "common ancestry of Japanese and Koreans," the manual supposed an original sameness from which it claimed that the Koreans had degenerated through history. Korea's geographical location next to the great powers—the Chinese, the Manchus, and the Mongols—had been unfortunate, for it had led to unrelenting threats from these powers and only semi-independent status. This situation cultivated an attitude of excessive submissiveness toward the powerful, a kind of clever opportunism vis-à-vis the strong that extended beyond dealings with foreigners. The manual called the resulting Korean character the "diplomatic personality" (*gaikōteki seikaku*) type.[59]

During the Yi dynasty, domestic political instability and the court's failure to win over the people fostered a way of thinking and a character that prized "self-preservation and fixated on the individual family." Moreover, factional strife spread through political life and led to a "chronic ethnic disease" (*minzokuteki koshitsu*)— namely, the tendency to prioritize self-defense above all else, and a personality type notable for its extreme suspiciousness. Members of the political and social elite, the *yangban* and *chungin*, knew only self-interest. Moreover, they tried to line their pockets in public office because factionalism made them constantly insecure about their employment. At the same time, they exacted large profits from the common people. As for the latter, most of them were deeply impoverished peasants who lived in an "extremely primitive" subsistence economy. Unable to rely on the *yangban* elite, the commoners had no choice but to devise strategies for their self-protection. But rather than carve out their own destinies, the illiterate peasantry succumbed to fatalism and conventional beliefs in demons and spirits.[60]

Soldiers from Korea thus portrayed Koreans as a people that history had made backward, and it justified Japan's seizure of Korea through a discourse of protection and benevolence. But if precolonial history had been responsible for their backwardness, Koreans' modern history as part of the Japanese empire was scripted as a story of progress whose yet unrealized telos would be complete assimilation as "members of the leading nation of the Greater East Asia Co-Prosperity Sphere." The history of the "New Korea" (*Shin Chōsen*) was only beginning, and its establishment required the reform of Korean "thought, beliefs, character, and custom" (*shisō, shinkō, seikaku, fūshū*). In other words, if history had created Korean differences, it could also produce sameness as Japanese.

Like so many other writings on Koreans and Korean soldiers, *Soldiers from Korea* also attributed the following characteristics to these colonials and their customs and habits. First, the manual utilized Murayama Chijun's massive ethnographic studies, which had been published by the Government-General, to denigrate Korean religions and beliefs as backward. It held that Korean Confucianism, which had been the dominant belief system under the Yi dynasty, had placed excessive weight on filial piety and thereby trivialized the loyalty of the subject toward the king. As for what it called "pseudo-religions" (*ruiji shūkyō*), a category into which it put such groups as the Tonghak: these were said to be superstitious schools that obstructed the "work ethic" while fomenting social movements and Korean ethnic consciousness. Similarly, the manual disparaged Korean folk religion as primitive, fatalistic, and immature, consisting only of "beliefs in vulgar superstitions" such as demons and spirits, geomancy, and divination. Thus, using a logic and language remarkably similar to Weberian theories of development and modernization, which likewise denigrated superstition and fatalism while valorizing rationalization and "disenchantment of the world,"[61] *Soldiers from Korea* concluded that Korean religion and beliefs contained little of value. Instead, the Japanese spirit should continue to displace these to provide a genuine spiritual foundation for the people of the peninsula, while the spirit of modern science would destroy superstition.

The manual recognized that the "Korean character" possessed some strengths, but it highlighted what its writers regarded as the deficiencies that history had produced. It alleged that Koreans were selfish and had difficulty acting in unison. They had a tendency to scheme, to be inconsistent, to be insincere, and they had little sense of responsibility. On this last point, the manual ironically prefigured Ruth Benedict's classic justification for the United States' paternalistic stance toward the Japanese after the war—namely, that the Japanese national character lacked internalized standards for conduct. Put differently, both the Japanese colonial and later U.S. occupations justified their hegemony by representing the dominated as lacking the modern responsible subject assumed to be necessary for self-governance.[62]

The manual held that the Koreans were obsequious toward the strong and contemptuous of the weak. As a consequence of their long relationship with China, they merely mimicked others and lacked creativity. Even the Tonghak religion was but an eclectic and imitative blend of Confucianism, Buddhism, and Taoism. Confucianism had bred a respect for the literary but not military arts, and therefore Koreans had become effeminate (*bunjaku*). Koreans had grown relatively resigned to poverty, but this tolerance coupled with poor scientific knowledge had lowered their sensitivity to both "filth" (*fuketsu*) and beauty. Though they were talkative and prone to clowning and argumentativeness, most of their arguments remained strictly verbal, since they had little inclination for taking action.

Soldiers from Korea used "scientific" studies of the mental and physical capacities of Koreans to conclude that while Koreans scored slightly below Mainlanders on intelligence tests, the cause was probably educational and environmental disadvantages. Koreans appeared less competent in "complex thought" (*fukuzatsu naru shikōryoku*), but they possessed a strong faculty of memory. Only self-interest could prod them into persistent ambition or volition. Observations of those who had already enlisted indicated that Korean soldiers had good physiques and physical strength and were generally not inferior to the metropolitan Japanese.

The next section of *Soldiers from Korea* is a detailed description of Korean customs, manners, and language. While it is not necessary to summarize all this ethnographic data, it should be noted that even as the manual scorned cultural differences and urged assimilation, it encouraged metropolitan Japanese to practice patience and sensitivity. Thus they should not be offended by such habits as the apparently rude omission of the honorific prefix "*o*" when Koreans spoke in Japanese. They could not be blamed, for no comparable prefix existed in the Korean language. Likewise, metropolitan Japanese should understand that Koreans consider it rude for those in lower social positions to address those in higher positions without first being addressed, so silence should not be understood as lack of affability or good will. "After receiving things, it is customary [for Koreans] not to express thanks"—and so on. In summing up this section on customs and manners, the manual concluded that while "there are not a few cases in which common Korean customs seem extremely rude from the perspective of the customs of metropolitan Japanese," uninformed judgments should not be made and no offense should be taken. Instead, "it is necessary to patiently and earnestly (*junjun toshite*) teach [them] our nation's customs—to reform and guide."[63]

The manual's final section described the behavior of Koreans who were presently, or who had already served, in the Imperial Army. It remarked that the Koreans' overall service record was very good, that they were performing with distinction on the battlefield, and that many had died heroically. An appendix also described their gallantry. Nevertheless, the manual continued to stress that the Korean traits of these soldiers needed to be reformed and it called special attention to behavior within the military that could be attributed to these flaws. For example, the Korean overvaluation of filial piety and individual self-interest posed a problem in handling Korean soldiers, because when they learned of a sick parent they would often do anything necessary to secure leave, including arranging for fictitious telegrams to be sent to them. Moreover, their overzealousness in private affairs fostered a lackadaisical attitude about service in their units. While individual acts of Korean heroism had been observed, the long Korean tradition of disparaging the military arts had resulted in reluctance to perform bold acts of courage, an inability to tolerate horrific battlefield conditions, cowardice at the sight of blood, and excessive demonstrations of pain or exhaustion.

Finally, the manual called attention to differences in everyday sanitation practices that would have been familiar from the discriminatory cultural knowledge about Koreans that had been a part of racial common sense since the late nineteenth century. Especially from around the turn of the century onward, Japanese visitors to Korea had constructed an image of Korea as not only backward and uncivilized but also as a land of filth. Seoul, one writer remarked in a 1905 publication, was the "shit capital" of the world, and Korea's "seven major products" were "shit, tobacco, lice, *kaesang* (courtesans), tigers, pigs and flies."[64] *Soldiers from Korea* drew from this discourse on sanitation, as well as the already-mentioned argument that Korean insensitivity to filthiness was a result of poverty, to explain the Korean soldiers' allegedly coarse eating habits and their "extremely poor sense of sanitation." They poured soup over their rice, ate gluttonously, and spilled rice, the manual said. They customarily used the same containers—whether tin cans, washbowls, or buckets—for eating, for washing their faces, and as mop buckets, and they employed the same rags for wiping floors and tables. They did not like bathing, laundering, or cleaning, and showed no reluctance to spit out phlegm or blow their noses into their hands in public. Flies and lice did not bother them.

It is important to note again, however, that although these characterizations of the Korean soldiers may strike us as extremely derogatory and racist, they were supposed to be counterbalanced by the idea that history and not biology had produced these Korean customs, habits, and consciousness—and that the Korean people could and should be reformed. In this sense, *Soldiers from Korea* shares much more with the U.S. military's policies toward the training of racial minorities than one might expect. While I have not been able to locate a manual for the training of Japanese Americans, the U.S. War Department's *Command of Negro Troops* provides a good comparative text.

Published for restricted internal use in exactly the same month as volume 1 of *Soldiers from Korea*, and for the similar purpose of "help[ing] officers command their troops more effectively by giving them information which will increase their understanding of their men," this manual prominently denounced racism while calling attention to actually existing differences between the African American soldier and his white counterpart. It therefore boldly stated at the outset that the "Selective Service Act requires that there will be no racial discrimination in the selection and training of men for military duty. The same methods of discipline, training, and leadership apply to Negro troops that have proved successful with any other troops." Nevertheless, it noted that the "Negro in the Army has special problems"— problems, it claimed, that had been produced by "the fact that the Negro group has had a history materially different from that of the majority in the Army. Its average schooling has been inferior; its work has been generally less skilled than that of the white man; and its role in the life of the Nation has been limited." Thus, like *Soldiers from Korea*, the American manual denied any biological difference between the racialized minority and the dominant group and instead introduced history as the factor that had produced dissimilarities. It denied "inborn difference," but simultaneously highlighted various "facts," such as those from testing, that seemed to demonstrate the generally poorer aptitude of "Negroes." It rejected the common idea that African Americans possessed an inherent capacity for music and dancing, and yet affirmed that this talent existed and had been born out of "their history and life, not in their race."[65]

The American text mirrored *Soldiers from Korea*'s view of Koreans and its instructions for their Japanese instructors, insisting that lower test results meant not that "Negroes" were "unteachable" but that instructors needed to use "extra patience, skill, and understanding." It invoked the slogan "Good soldiers are made, not born" to highlight the incorrect assumption that inherent deficiencies made

African Americans unreliable in battle. "In all the vast number of studies by psychologists and other scientists during the past two or three decades," it concluded, "there is not one piece of research which proves that Negroes are, as a group, mentally or emotionally defective by heredity."[66] Logically, then, racial theories like those advocated by the Germans had to be rejected, if only in the interests of effective manpower utilization.

We should not assume that either *Command of Negro Troops* or *Soldiers from Korea* necessarily changed the vulgar racist attitudes of the instructors who read them or eliminated racial discrimination from the army. Instead, these texts reflected and advanced the transition to a new inclusionary and ostensibly polite form of racism that insisted upon the illegitimacy of formal racial discrimination, even as it reproduced a racist logic through a discourse of differential histories, lagging development, and culture. Official pronouncements on Koreans and Korean soldiers even commonly came to assert that those with a strong sense of Korean ethnic consciousness who refused assimilationist ideals were the real practitioners of discrimination, not the metropolitan Japanese. In other words, Korean ethnic nationalists could be accused of practicing what some today would call "reverse discrimination," because of their assertion of ethnic difference.[67]

Yet I want to push this point even further to argue that the contradictions inherent in this logic had an almost irrepressible power to unleash changes in an ostensibly egalitarian direction that not even advocates of this new discourse could have foreseen or desired. For example, members of the Kyōchōkai—the semiofficial think tank made up of bureaucrats and business leaders who were charged with researching social conditions, advising the government on social policy, and "harmonizing" the relationship between labor and capital—found themselves in 1944 almost unable to do anything other than recommend a liberal and inclusionary posture vis-à-vis Koreans. To be sure, their August 1944 report, "Question of the Peninsulars [Koreans]" (*Hantōjin mondai*), remarked on the Koreans' generally fine physiques and "particularly their good teeth and eyes," thus suggesting that the culturally based polite racism could never completely severe its ties with biologism. And yet the report also emphasized the high academic aptitude of some Koreans, the increasing difficulty of differentiating Koreans educated in primary school from their Japanese counterparts (even their facial movements were becoming the same, it was said), the effectiveness of educating Koreans, and the need to continue these efforts. After approvingly commenting on all these indications of the Koreans' increasing assimilation to the metropolitan way of life (*Naichi seikatsu*), the report recommended that therefore "good people" (*ii hito*) among the Koreans should be placed in leadership positions. Furthermore, taking special note of the draft's impact, it concluded that "now that the decision has been made to implement military conscription in Korea, in the future we have no choice but to place our fullest trust in the Peninsulars."[68]

Indeed, the contradictions exposed by the mobilization of Koreans for the war effort continued to press the colonial government to reform some of its most obviously discriminatory policies toward Koreans. In the Government-General's compilation of materials collected in anticipation of the eighty-sixth session of the Imperial Diet, its General Affairs Bureau (Sōmukyoku) remarked that in 1944 the "most epoch-making matter from the point of view of (colonial) administration" had been implementation of the military conscription system. And the compilation itself devoted considerable attention to how the colonial government intended to "turn all of Korea's human and material elements into war power (senryokka)," while also making progress in educating, caring for, and eliminating signs of discrimination against the Korean people. The General Affairs Bureau feared that particularly in the wake of independence for the Philippines and Burma, the establishment of Free India (or Azad Hind, the provisional Indian government in exile that was committed to freeing India from British rule), and the promise that Indonesia would become independent, some Koreans, owing to a "narrow-minded ethnic view" (shōjōteki minzoku ishiki), would push for Korean autonomy. In order to forestall such an outcome, it emphasized that such elements had to be made to recognize themselves as "people of the leading great nation of Greater East Asia." This could be accomplished only by responding to the Korean people's wartime contributions with corresponding measures to "reform various aspects of their treatment." Using a variant of what we will soon see was by then an official slogan of the Japanese government, "reform of the treatment of Koreans and Taiwanese," the bureau concluded that "we must realize that there are many matters in need of reform, which can be ascertained through investigations ranging across each and every institution of society and to the smallest details of customary practices, etc."[69]

The Government-General's officials paid special attention to securing the cooperation of Korea's educated elite by eliminating or at least reforming discriminatory policies that specifically affected them. They did so not only because they understood that they needed the elite to staff all the major apparatuses of colonial rule—including the bureaucracy, the police, the military, the media, and businesses—but also because they realized that they could successfully mobilize the Korean masses only with the native elite's assistance. Thus in the last years of the war the colonial government responded with some substance to one of the educated elite's most often heard complaints—namely, that the different salaries paid to Korean and Japanese bureaucrats was a form of discrimination that had to be eliminated.

As early as April 1910, several months before Japan's formal annexation of Korea, the Japanese government's Imperial Ordinance No. 137 had established the legal foundation for permitting salary differentials between metropolitan Japanese and native colonial (*gaichi*) officials by providing that hardship allowances could be given to the former. Two other laws specific to Korea that went into effect on 1 October 1910—GGK Ordinance No. 15 and Imperial Ordinance No. 403—stipulated, for example, that those in the higher civil service (*kōtōkan*) would receive a 40 percent salary supplement while junior officials above rank 5 (*hanninkan gokyū*) would qualify for a 60 percent allowance. In response to charges of discrimination and as a gesture toward the formal policy of metropolitan and colonial equality, the government could have simply abolished the hardship allowance system. Instead, Imperial Ordinance No. 230 (effective 1 April 1944) removed language in the earlier ordinance specifically targeting metropolitan Japanese (*naichijin taru*) for this benefit, thereby making it possible in principle for native colonials throughout the empire to boost their pay to that of their counterparts. The GGK's Ordinance No. 168 and General Directive No. 31 (both effective 10 April 1944) subsequently indicated that Korean officials from the highest-ranking ones in the higher civil service to principals of public middle schools and national elementary schools, as well as village district and township heads, would also become eligible for the allowances.[70]

Speaking in March 1944—that is, just before these legal changes went into effect—Mizuta Naomasa, head of the GGK's Treasury Bureau (*zaimukyokuchō*), explained that the measures to begin eliminating salary differentials constituted part of the larger principle of unifying Korea and metropolitan Japan. With implementation of military conscription drawing near and compulsory primary education only three years away, the inequality produced by the system of special allowances for metropolitan Japanese alone could not be left unresolved. Of course, as Mizuta understood, the 1944 changes still left out the multitude of Koreans working as lower-ranking colonial employees. Yet he justified this exclusion as perfectly in keeping with the ideal of equality in that it restricted the allowance to the ranks of Korean officials who had become completely like metropolitan Japanese, both "materially and spiritually."

In other words, the colonial government would eliminate salary differentials only for those who had become Japanese in their interiority and whose "economic circumstances, lifestyle, and so on, did not differ in any respects from metropolitan

Japanese." For Mizuta, such a limitation did not alter what mattered most—namely, that a fundamental transformation in the principle of determining eligibility would soon occur. As he put it, the allowance would be given "without regard to whether a bureaucrat or the equivalent is metropolitan Japanese, Taiwanese, or whatever, and irrespective of whether he takes one step overseas, as long as he is engaged in colonial administration." In his reasoning, native colonials could no longer be treated differently just because they were not metropolitan Japanese. If they were the equal of metropolitan Japanese in every way, then they would be treated and paid as such. Since Koreans at the top of the bureaucracy were most likely to have assimilated, they would become eligible for the allowances. As we have seen so often, Mizuta's reasoning betrays the way in which cultural racism might continue under the logic of equality. Nevertheless, Mizuta was correct that a fundamental legal principle based on the a priori, ascriptive assumption of difference between Koreans and metropolitan Japanese had been overturned.[71] Moreover, although too late to have been carried out with any significant effect prior to the war's ending, in April 1945 GGK's Ordinance No. 75 eliminated all salary distinctions between metropolitan Japanese and Korean native officials.[72]

Similarly, the GGK's leaders praised themselves for increasing the number of Koreans at the highest levels of the police and colonial bureaucracy. These included the much-heralded appointment to Hwanghae Province of the colony's first provincial Korean Police Bureau chief, Isaka Kazuo (Korean name, Yun Chong-hwa), in 1944, as well as the selection of Koreans to head Kangwŏn Province's Higher Police Department (*kōtō kachō*—that is, the province's "thought police") and Kyŏnggi Province's Criminal Affairs Department. As of late 1944, Koreans held five out of thirteen provincial governorships and they served until the end of the war. The GGK even claimed to be practicing what in today's U.S. English would be called a kind of "affirmative action" for highly educated Koreans. It reported that a particularly large number of Koreans, no fewer than thirty-seven, had passed the higher civil service exam for administration in 1943. "Through the especially cooperative auspices of the central government's authorities," it boasted, "twelve of them had been formally selected for employment in ministries of the central government, thus opening up an unprecedented avenue." Of the remainder, twenty-one took positions in the offices of the GGK, two became students, and one worked in the Manchukuo bureaucracy, with only one failing to find employment. The Government-General also pointed out that in 1943 a member of the Yi family had taken a seat in the Imperial Diet's House of Peers by imperial nomination, and that Han Sang-nyong, a councillor in the Chūsūin advisory body to the governor-general, had been appointed director general (*jimukyoku sōsai*) of the Korea Federation for Total National Mobilization (Chōsen Sōryoku Chōsen Renmei).[73] The latter was the important extra-governmental organization that combined the efforts of bureaucrats, the military, and private individuals to mobilize Koreans for the war effort.

THE POLITICS AND BIO-POLITICS OF INCLUSION

On 22 July 1944, General Koiso Kuniaki succeeded Tōjō Hideki as prime minister of Japan. Koiso had been Korea's governor-general (29 May 1942—22 July 1944) and as such had presided over the introduction of military conscription to the colony. Earlier, as commander of the Korean Army (2 December 1935—15 July 1938), he had also played a major role in establishing Korea's Army Special Volunteer System. In his September 1944 policy speech before the eighty-fifth session of the Imperial Diet, Koiso made it clear to the peoples of the Japanese empire, and in fact to the entire world,[74] that the nation needed to improve its treatment of Koreans and Taiwanese. As he put it,

> As important parts of the imperial nation, Korea and Taiwan are each
> exercising the special characteristics of their regions to contribute to its
> prosperity and the realization of war objectives. They have previously
> produced excellent results as Army Special Volunteer Soldiers and now we
> have come to witness implementation of the military conscription system.
> From the perspective of the nation, the fact that so many compatriots have
> demonstrated the sincerity of their willingness to serve on the sacred battlefield
> is cause for celebration. At the same time, I believe that it is necessary to fully
> reconsider their treatment.[75]

With this speech Koiso set in motion the process by which some version of the slogan "Betterment of the treatment of Korean and Taiwanese compatriots" (*Chōsen oyobi Taiwan dōhō ni taisuru shogū kaizen*) became the Japanese government's official policy—a position that also circulated in public discourse through the media. This campaign unfolded on two fronts. One, explicitly categorized as "political treatment" (*seiji shogū*), centered on the effort to give Koreans and Taiwanese representation in the national Diet. The other, labeled "general treatment" (*ippan shogū*), focused on a range of practices that were supposed to enhance the general welfare and happiness of the Korean and Taiwanese colonial subjects.[76] The latter cluster therefore fits well into Foucault's broader concept of "government."

In its May 1942 study of procedures for recruiting Koreans under the conscription system, the Government-General had been prescient in acknowledging that the issue of political rights would haunt the decision to draft Koreans into the military. "It is as clear as the light of day that like a shadow that follows its object," it said, "a discussion of the rights to vote and hold office will arise in conjunction with the problem of making Koreans subject to the military conscription system."[77] But by late 1944 it was no longer possible to delink conscription as well as the general mobilization of the Korean population for the war effort from this question. As Tanaka Takeo—who had served under Koiso as both his vice governor-general and subsequently his chief cabinet secretary at the time when formal deliberations on Koreans' political rights took place—recalled in a postwar roundtable, the decision to "send them [the Koreans] out as soldiers" (*hei ni dasu*) had been the foremost impetus for "seriously considering the matter of the rights to hold office and vote."[78]

In November of that year, the cabinet passed a resolution to establish the Research Commission on the Political Treatment of the Residents of Korea and Taiwan (Chōsen oyobi Taiwan Zaijūmin Seiji Shogū Chōsakai), and its subsequent regulations (approved 23 December, promulgated 26 December) gave Koiso nearly complete control over its direction and membership. Koiso headed the commission, and he appointed to it some of the leading figures in the government and bureaucracy, including his state and home ministers and members of the Diet. A number of men who occupied or had earlier held high-ranking positions in the colonial governments also sat on the commission, beginning with the vice governors-general of Korea and Taiwan at the time, as well as Tanaka Takeo. However, no Korean or Taiwanese was appointed.

It has been noted that in general the metropolitan government and bureaucracy, fearing the erosion of metropolitan Japanese privilege in the colonies and at home, tended to be passive about or even resistant to granting Koreans and Taiwanese rights to participate in the national Diet—while representatives of the War Ministry, the Government-General, and Koiso himself aggressively promoted the move.[79] In this sense, the fall of the Tōjō cabinet and Koiso's subsequent appointment to the premiership might appear to have been the fortuitous events that enabled eventual passage of the laws granting Taiwanese and Koreans rights to participate in the Imperial Diet. As Tanaka Takeo and a number of other high-ranking former officials of the Government-General recalled in their fascinating postwar recollections on the process by which these legal changes occurred, Koiso had vigorously advocated these rights for Koreans and Taiwanese while serving as Korea's governor-general. The army and navy shared his views. However, Tōjō and officials in the Ministry of Home

Affairs were just as adamantly opposed. Thus, as long as Tōjō remained in power there seemed little hope of passing the requisite legal changes. Conversely, once his cabinet had resigned, it became possible for Koiso to assume power and to push his agenda. While he faced considerable resistance at times, Koiso's strong position and the military's aggressive support of the new policy ensured their ultimate passage.[80]

Although Koiso and supporters such as Tanaka Takeo no doubt played key roles in passing the new legislation, the movement toward further political inclusion of Korea in the nation had begun at the beginning of the total war years. In terms of the colonial empire's administrative structure, the extension of some form of national political rights to the colonies coincided with the larger trend toward the "unification of domestic and colonial administration." This move was given a major institutional boost with the November 1942 abolition of the Colonial Ministry (Takumushō) and the transfer of its jurisdiction over Korea's and Taiwan's governments-general and the Karafuto Agency to the Home Ministry's new Bureau of Administration (Kanrikyoku). In contrast, the relative political outsideness of Kantōshū (Kwantung Leased Territory) and Nan'yō (the Micronesian islands under Japanese mandate) was reflected in the shift of their supervision to the newly established Greater East Asia Ministry (Daitōashō). It might also be noted that in March 1945, the Diet's Lower House accepted a petition abolishing use of the term *gaichi*, "outer territories," to refer to Japanese possessions outside of metropolitan Japan.[81] Even more importantly, as Koiso's speech suggested and as former colonial officials agreed in their recollections, the new promises for greater political inclusiveness emerged as effects of the Japanese empire's mobilization of Korean and Taiwanese in the war effort.[82]

Koreans and Taiwanese received the rights to vote for and send representatives to the national Diet through two laws promulgated on 1 April 1945. Law No. 34 provided that all male imperial subjects residing in Korea and Taiwan who were twenty-five years of age and above and who also paid a minimum of fifteen yen in direct national taxes could vote in elections for representatives to the Diet's Lower House. Korea was allotted twenty-three Lower House representatives; Taiwan, five. To be sure, as Okamoto Makiko has shown, this law with its high minimum tax requirement was calculated to place a limit on the number of eligible Korean and Taiwanese voters in the colonies. Moreover, no election under the new law ever took place, since the war ended before it went into effect.

Limitations aside, Law No. 34 represented a radical reenvisioning of the political relationship between the metropole and its two largest colonies. In the late 1950s Akiyama Shōhei, who had been among those assigned to study the political rights issue around the time of the law's passage, recalled that he and some of his colleagues had not worried a great deal about the implications of this legislation for the wartime period, in large measure because the Imperial Rule Assistance Association's domination of mass politics in Japan would have precluded the colonial vote from having a significant impact. Instead, Akiyama and his colleagues feared that granting Taiwanese and Korean voters rights to participate in the Imperial Diet could have enormous repercussions in the postwar period—and here we should remember that despite the Cairo Declaration's 1943 promise to end Japanese rule over Taiwan and Korea, their immediate liberation was by no means guaranteed. If Korea remained a part of Japan, such a change might have allowed colonials to have the decisive or "casting vote" on critical issues.[83]

Similarly, former Vice Governor General Tanaka Takeo and another former colonial official, Hozumi Shinrokurō, recounted that all Japanese politicians, "big and small," had been very much concerned that granting political rights to Koreans might lead to difficulties similar to Britain's "Irish problem." Hozumi stressed that ever since the late nineteenth century, Irish MPs had held the casting vote at critical times. This resulted eventually in the successes of the Irish National Party, the rise of Sinn Fein, and eventually the split between the independent Republic of Ireland and British-ruled Northern Ireland. Hozumi described the Japanese politicians, who knew how Irish inclusion in British parliamentary politics had stirred up such troubles, as having been "extremely nervous about the casting vote."[84]

Tanaka recalled three general sources of apprehension about Korean representation in the Diet. First, with the Tōjō cabinet's fall, the Diet had once again become an important arena for debate, and Japanese politicians feared that colonial representatives might have a significant impact in such discussions. Second, given that the nation's leaders still did not consider defeat an inevitability, they worried that they might be compelled to fulfill any promises about expanded political rights in the postwar era. Finally, those discussing the matter understood that representation in the Diet and conferral on the colonials of what might be the casting vote opened up the possibility of Korean and Taiwanese independence. In short, these former colonial officials testified that they had genuinely believed that despite the risks involved, it had become necessary to meet some of the colonial demands for enhanced political rights and better overall treatment. They had arrived at this conclusion because of the mobilization of Koreans and Taiwanese for the war effort, not because they assumed that they were about to lose the war and that their promises would become meaningless.[85]

The second law concerned the House of Peers, to which, since 1932, three Koreans and one Taiwanese had received lifetime appointments, under provisions of the then-existing law. In 1945 Imperial Ordinance No. 193 opened up a more substantial avenue for selection of Koreans and Taiwanese to the House of Peers: it stipulated that ten male residents of Korea or Taiwan, each at least thirty years of age, would serve for seven years in the House as direct imperial appointees. In keeping with the empire's formal principle of nondiscrimination, the law did not exclude metropolitan Japanese residents of these colonies from consideration. However, everyone implicitly understood that appointees would be Korean or Taiwanese and that their appointments would be determined by the recommendations of the governments-general. As a result, seven Koreans and three Taiwanese joined the one surviving earlier Korean appointee in the House of Peers. As an eerie reminder of this late wartime moment in which Korea was increasingly becoming a part of the Japanese nation, the names of the new colonial appointees remained on the official registry of Diet members until 4 July 1946. The earlier appointee, a member of the Korean royal family, was still on the official Diet registry when the House of Peers was abolished in May 1947.[86]

Beyond their inclusion in the national political system, wartime mobilization of Koreans also led directly to their constitution into a population worthy of life, health, reproduction, and happiness—in other words, to their inclusion in the regime of governmentality and bio-power. As in all modern nation-states, one of the basic requirements for enabling the state to intervene in the lives and deaths of the people in these ways was to establish an accurate and comprehensive administrative technology by which the population could be identified and monitored. In Japan proper this had been accomplished in the late nineteenth century by putting the previously highly inaccurate household registers (*koseki*) in order. The immediate impetus for doing so had been the introduction of military conscription in the 1870s. The new military recruitment system required a method for locating young men subject to the draft.[87]

In Korea, a similar process unfolded during the war years. There had certainly been earlier attempts, some even predating formal Japanese rule, to turn household registers into instruments through which to efficiently chart and manage the Korean population,[88] but the colonial state succeeded in carrying out a comprehensive campaign to put the household registers in good order only when it began preparing to implement the military conscription system in the colony. Prior to the May 1942 announcement that conscription would begin in 1944, the Korean household registers were in shambles and the authorities knew it. Koreans frequently neglected to set up independent registers when establishing new households; many registers did not include women and children; and many individuals were listed in more than one registry, or, in contrast, households that perished were not removed from the records, resulting in "ghost registers" (*yūrei koseki*). Moreover, household registers often inaccurately noted the age of individuals and in many cases did not give their sex. The very mobile character of the population, especially men of working age, also exacerbated the situation. Although many individuals regularly changed their domiciles, both to other locations within Korea and to places as far off as metropolitan Japan, Manchuria, and North China, most did not bother to submit temporary domicile notices (*kiryū todoke*).[89]

According to an official document prepared for the purpose of estimating the enormous budget and number of personnel required to register all unregistered Koreans and to process the required temporary domicile notifications, more than 1.1 million people in Korea remained unregistered, while just over 6 million (6,001,991) needed to submit temporary domicile notices because they lived in places other than the location given in their household registers. More than 5.2 million of the 6 million figure were Korean. Presumably, almost all of the 1.1 million unregistered were Korean, since all Japanese would have had been accounted for in the metropole. Further, the report estimated that an additional 2.2 million temporary domicile forms needed to be processed for Koreans living outside of Korea. Thus, out of a total population of some 25,154,560 Koreans residing inside and outside of Korea, almost 7.5 million (7,447,497) needed to submit temporary domicile forms. The document further estimated that high percentages of those living in the various administrative units—about 40 percent of those living in municipalities (J. *fu*, K. *pu*), 30 percent of those in townships (J. *yū*, K. *ŭp*), and 20 percent in village districts (J. *men*, K. *myŏn*)—needed to submit temporary domicile notices. Thus even the accurate notation of age and sex in the household registers did not guarantee that the state could actually locate individuals. For all practical purposes, a large, fluid segment of the population remained invisible to the state.[90]

In order to effectively carry out the military draft as well as to mobilize the population for labor, the Government-General of Korea enacted the Korea Temporary Domicile Notification Ordinance (*Chōsen kiryū todoke rei*) in September 1942 and soon thereafter started a concerted effort to keep an accurate record of those residing in areas outside their native places. The ordinance required those residing for ninety days or longer in locations other than their place of household registration to submit notifications of temporary domicile. Also, primarily in order to conduct the military draft, the Government-General in February 1943 launched a massive effort to eliminate inaccuracies in household registers. While the GGK never succeeded in completely monitoring the population, the combined effects of forcing the population to submit temporary domicile notifications and of working more intensely to put all household registers in order enabled the state for the first time to know and regulate almost the entirety of the populace. According to one official source, by the end of 1943 about 80 percent of Korean household registers were considered accurate. Although this fairly successful attempt to make the population visible to the state might at first appear unconnected to bio-power and governmentality in the ways that I've described earlier—that is, as a technology to make the population live—it is relevant to note that one of the factors contributing to the relative success of the effort was the colonial state's attempt to make proper registration a condition for receiving wartime rations. By using such slogans as "From temporary domicile notifications, also [get your] ration tickets," the authorities turned the effort to register and monitor the people into a means both of sustaining their lives and of mobilizing them for death (conscription).[91]

Similar to the situation in the Japanese metropole and many other industrialized nations during the war years,[92] in the colony social welfare measures especially targeted that segment of the population in which the promotion of life was most directly linked to the demand for death. Korean military personnel and their families became recipients of aid under Japan's Military Assistance Law (*gunji fujohō*, 1937). As the Government-General's officials stated in 1944, prior to 1943 the beneficiaries of the law in Korea had been metropolitan Japanese settlers and the small number of families of Koreans who had entered the army through the Special Volunteer Soldier system. However, with the new enrollment of Korean student soldiers, including new officers, and the massive influx of conscripts from 1944, the Government-General predicted that the number of Korean beneficiaries of the law would continue to increase sharply. This was especially likely since the majority of conscripts came from poor farming households.

In order to cope with the projected scale of such aid to Koreans, in 1944 the Government-General took over administration of these benefits from the metropolitan government's Ministry of Health and Welfare and appropriated nearly one million yen (949,657) for military assistance. In addition, although the total amount is not impressive, in 1944 it earmarked funds from the national treasury to pay two-thirds of the costs of benefits to dependents not covered under the law, such as common-law wives, children born out of wedlock, uncles, parents, nieces, and nephews. Officials determined that as of the end of July 1944, 22 percent of almost 45,000 military families required some form of military aid and that the prolonged massive induction of conscripts would continue to push the total number of such families sharply upward. Similarly, they noted that between the beginning of the Sino-Japanese War in 1937 and the end of June 1944, 3,775 households made up of 11,784 individuals had received livelihood aid (*seikatsu fujo*), while there had been 805 cases of assistance for medical care, childbirth, burials, and occupational assistance. The Government-General also offered some assistance to *gunʐoku*, civilian employees of the military who were not covered under the Military Assistance Law. For instance, as of June 1944 it claimed to have paid out funds received from the national treasury to the 1,932 households of *gunʐoku* who had died while in service to the army and navy.[93]

In addition to providing direct monetary aid, the colonial authorities noted that the government had established various institutions to care for veterans and survivors. For example, it described the founding of a sanitarium for veterans afflicted with tuberculosis or pleurisy in Southern Kyŏngsang Province in February 1941, a policy for treating such patients in specialized hospitals and clinics in metropolitan Japan and Korea, efforts to educate veterans released from hospitals to facilitate their reemployment, ten local guidance counselors for wounded veterans, and special privileges for wounded veterans such as free or reduced train fare. Programs and facilities for widows and other survivors included job training and employment offices, established in major cities such as Seoul (Keijō), Taegu, and Pusan; guidance clinics (*gunji engo sōdanjo*) to assist with various matters including the management of family businesses and the arbitration of labor grievances; educational scholarships; and home visitations of guidance counselors.

The network of provincial and more local groups organized under the Korean Headquarters of the Military Assistance Association—which had originally been formed in December 1938, two months after its parent organization had been established as a foundation in metropolitan Japan—joined with the GGK to facilitate these assistance efforts. Moreover, these groups engaged in other activities designed to build Korean support for the military, such as disseminating knowledge about the concept of military assistance, promoting send-off and welcoming home celebrations for soldiers and sailors, encouraging the populace to send letters and gifts to military men, undertaking condolence activities for the fallen, and so on.[94]

In addition, throughout the period of the Asia-Pacific War, but particularly in the war's last years, the colonial state as well as extra-governmental organizations closely tied to the state increasingly targeted the Korean population at large for expanded social services and social welfare. For example, during these years tens of thousands of communal day care centers (*kyōdō takujisho*) were opened to enable the increasing mobilization of women workers. The Korean Disaster Relief Foundation Ordinance (*Chōsen risai kyūjo kikinrei*), promulgated in August 1938, facilitated the collection of funds for disaster victims. Enactment of the Korea Relief and Protection Ordinance (*Chōsen kyūgorei*) on 1 March 1944, although more limited and coming some twelve years after a similar ordinance was passed in metropolitan Japan, marked the high point of legal efforts to increase aid and protection for the elderly, children, pregnant and nursing mothers, and the mentally and physically ill or handicapped.[95]

Administratively, paralleling the establishment of the Ministry of Health and Welfare (Kōseishō) in the metropole in 1938, the Government-General set up its own Bureau of Health and Welfare (Kōseikyoku) in November 1941. As Vice Governor-General Ōno Rokuichirō explained, this independent bureau was established to administer matters concerning labor mobilization and "health, hygiene, and the improvement of physical strength, as well as various types of social and welfare institutions—in short, the various ad hoc and permanent measures concerning the basic cultivation of human resources." Without going into all the details, it may be noted that the Bureau of Health and Welfare was made up of four sections—social, labor, hygiene, and health—and dealt with matters as diverse as physical fitness, maternity, infants and young children, public health issues such as contagious diseases and medical personnel, food and water, labor and unemployment, social and medical relief disaster aid, housing, military relief, and juvenile reformatories.[96]

This does not mean that all Koreans benefited, and many were assuredly exposed to death, but it does explain why many Koreans received support to live and why colonial officials could boast that in some important statistical respects the aggregate population was prospering. For example, in its compilation of materials prepared in anticipation of the eighty-fifth session of the Diet (September 1944), the Government-General stressed that in the three years and seven months that had elapsed between the 1940 national census and the May 1944 population census, the Korean population had dramatically increased. By its calculations, the Korean population in Korea (that is, the population in Korea excluding metropolitan Japanese, other colonials, and foreigners) had grown from 23,546,932 to 25,133,351. Moreover, the colonial government claimed that over the five-year period from 1938 to 1942 (inclusive), the Korean population had experienced an average natural growth (births minus deaths) of 417,638 per year, or an average annual increase of 17.18 per 1,000. The latter far exceeded metropolitan Japan's rate of 12.03 for the same years.[97]

Other scholars have researched this new attention to social services and social welfare in Korea (and I have relied on them heavily here), but they have tended to dismiss these projects as disingenuous, intended only to prevent social discontent and to benefit the Japanese state and war program. Relief efforts for the poor, for example, are said to have not been "pure poor relief " (*junsui na kyūmin*). Moreover, they have tended to focus on the deficiencies in these types of programs and particularly the disparities between efforts in Korea and those in metropolitan Japan.[98] However, I have been suggesting that there is no such thing as "pure poor relief " or social welfare that is independent of power. The history of social services and social welfare throughout the world, including metropolitan Japan, should ultimately be understood as a history of nurturing the life of populations to turn them into efficient workers and soldiers and to preempt social discord, although it would also be ludicrous to deny their obvious benefits to those not called upon to die.[99]

This leads us to the second aspect of the movement toward the "betterment of the treatment of Korean and Taiwanese compatriots," which was announced in Koiso's July 1944 speech—namely, improvement of their "general treatment." Toward the end of 1944, Koiso Kuniaki's cabinet adopted a proposal drafted by the Home Ministry called "On the Improvement of the Treatment of Koreans and Taiwanese" (*Chōsen oyobi Taiwan dōhō ni taisuru kaizen ni kansuru ken*).[100] The proposal consisted of three sections: (1) "items concerning improved treatment of Korean compatriots residing in the metropole," (2) "items concerning improved treatment of Taiwanese compatriots residing in the metropole," and (3) "improvement of treatment within Korea and Taiwan."

The document provided considerable detail only for section 1. The eight items under this section concerned with Koreans in the metropole were (1) "edification of metropolitan Japanese (*Naichijin*) in general" so that they would improve their "everyday treatment" of Koreans; (2) "removal of the system of barriers to travel" between Korea and metropolitan Japan for Koreans; (3) "improvement of treatment by police," in order "to prevent feelings of discrimination from arising"; (4) "improvement of labor management" to ensure that "Korean laborers will feel secure in their area of work and fulfilled in life"; (5) "renovation of welfare services"; (6) "guidance in educational advancement," meaning that Korean children should be treated the same as their metropolitan Japanese counterparts with regard to their education, thereby facilitating the advancement of Koreans into metropolitan Japan's technical colleges and beyond, and appropriate measures should be taken to provide Korean students with financial assistance; (7) "assistance in finding employment"; and (8) "opening up a path to transfer permanent household registers to metropolitan Japan."

Scholars have long known of this proposal. However, they have tended to read it with great skepticism—dismissing it altogether, challenging its authors' sincerity, or minimizing the extent of its significance and effects. They have noted its lack of concrete detail on key recommendations, the absence of any legally binding language, and conversely its utility as propaganda that was intended to give the appearance of Japan's commitment to equality. For instance, neither the proposal nor its more detailed attachment gave any indication of how or when freedom of travel to and from the metropole would be realized, and details were similarly absent regarding the possibility of moving permanent household registries to the metropole. Indeed, as Okamoto Makiko points out, restrictions on travel from the colony to the metropole remained in place through the end of the war, and avenues to transfer household registries never materialized. The latter would have eliminated all legal distinctions between metropolitan Japanese and Koreans, and hence removed the foundation in law for what amounted to discrimination against Koreans by blood.[101] Furthermore, through a meticulous reading of numerous drafts of the proposal, Okamoto convincingly shows that the scope of its specific recommendations gradually narrowed. While early drafts considered measures for all Koreans and Taiwanese within the larger empire, the final draft limited its most extensive and concrete recommendations to Korean residents in Japan. In sum, scholars have tended to minimize the genuine significance of this document and emphasized its shortcomings in improving the situation of Koreans under Japanese colonialism.

Regardless of the limitations of this proposal, however, it must be understood within the larger context of the wartime transition toward inclusion of Koreans both inside and outside of metropolitan Japan in the newly forming multiethnic nation and regime of governmentality. As even Okamoto points out, Koreans residing in Japan were coming to occupy a position as a kind of "minority within metropolitan Japanese society,"[102] rather than simply as colonial subjects. She remarks that particularly because of the late wartime need to efficiently manage Korean laborers in Japan, the Home Ministry and the Health and Welfare Ministry made fairly detailed prescriptions for and budgetary allocations to expand social services, employing in particular the Central Harmonization Society (Chūō Kyōwakai). And I would add that in November 1944, the name of this society—which had been established out of less-centralized organizations in 1939 to manage and assimilate the Korean population in metropolitan Japan—was changed to the Central Society for the Promotion of Welfare (Chūō Kōseikai), a phrase obviously suggesting that the organization's main purpose was to promote life.[103]

Thus it matters less that the cabinet proposal was not fully implemented than that as the war drew to a close, the Japanese discourse on equality and the need to protect and nurture the Koreans both inside and outside the metropole was becoming dominant in official circles. As we have seen, the sweeping measures to include Koreans in the Japanese bio-political and political regimes were so wide-ranging and dramatic that to merely fixate on the limitations of inclusion and the force of ongoing discrimination can only lead to misrecognition of the late wartime transition. Such a misfocus prevents us from recognizing the fundamental shift toward a new form of racism that was beginning to operate precisely through the inclusion of those who had been despised, through the disavowal of racism, through the right to make live, and through the expansion of possible ways in which Koreans might be made to imagine and even sometimes realize their prosperity and happiness as Japanese.

．　　　．　　　．

Shortly after Japan's defeat and faced with the grim prospect of Korea's estrangement from Japan, Yoshida Toshiguma, who had been head of conscription for the Korean Army, closed his insider's history of Koreans in the Japanese army with sentimental praise not only for the Koreans who had fought for Japan but also for what he imagined to have been the Japanese system of absolute equality. "The billowing waves of the Genkai Sea [between metropolitan Japan and Korea] are stormy," he said,

> and once again we face the day when Japan and Korea are estranged from one another. But the military life that the [soldiers] experienced through conscription—one that they sought to the end, and one that practiced complete equality and impartiality and upheld meritocracy as its first principle—this military life planted seeds in their breasts that will certainly become the driving force of the newly rising Korea. And someday in the warm light of spring, the buds from these seeds will surely bloom into flowers of mutual love and respect, coming to fruition in the spirit of a mutual accord.[104]

Yoshida appears to have been completely convinced that in its last years the Japanese empire had overcome racism, practiced equality, and genuinely welcomed Koreans into the nation. He described a mutuality of love and respect in which patriotic Koreans fought and often gave their lives for Japan, while the Japanese system treated them with total impartiality. Yet as striking as the apparent sincerity with which Yoshida expressed his feelings was the gap between such a phantasmic view of Japan's relations with the Korean people and the coercion and violence that so many of them had experienced under colonial rule. Yoshida even chose to ignore the obvious force imposed on young men subjected to the draft during what he himself called the "period of continuous desertions," when recent conscripts had absconded in such great numbers that it had been necessary to increase night watches, spies, and sentries, and even to repair and strengthen iron fences to prevent their escape.[105]

Yoshida's blindness to his own hypocrisy and the regime's brutality should not be understood as simply an individual lapse. Instead, it is but one manifestation of the way in which the polite and inclusionary form of racism of late wartime Japan concealed its own vulgarity through the language of equality and the disavowal of discrimination. But here we might probe even further: if the Japanese regime began to include these previously despised populations within its nation in unprecedented ways, even considering them as part of the national populations in need of life, welfare, and happiness, and if there was indeed a shift from "vulgar" to "polite" racism, and from the "right to kill" to the "right to make live," why then did the Korean people experience so much death and brutality? How can we explain the inhumane treatment accorded to the hundreds of thousands of Korean men forced to labor under horrific and often dangerous conditions with inordinately high mortality and injury rates, or the subjection of tens of thousands of Korean women, if not more, to sexual slavery as "comfort women"? How indeed, when we know that the most gruesome and large-scale wielding of systematic physical and sexual violence against Koreans took place precisely during the turn toward polite racism?[106]

Such questions can be addressed in two ways. First, it is important to recognize that in Foucault's formulation, under the bio-political regime the right to demand death is the flip side of the "right to make live." Foucault reminds us that the emergence of systematic state programs for public health in the late eighteenth century coincided with the development of mass armies and military technologies that resulted in mass death. From the point of view of the bio-political state, the individual is significant only insofar as she or he affects the strength of the state, either positively or negatively: "sometimes what he has to do for the state is to live, to work, to produce, to consume; and sometimes what he has to do is to die." Foucault also reminds us that this conjunction of apparent opposites reaches a climax in the Second World War, when we find both unprecedented butchery and the institutionalization of massive programs of "welfare, public health, and medical assistance." As Foucault explains, "Since population is nothing more than what the state takes care of for its own sake, of course, the state is entitled to slaughter it, if necessary. So the reverse of biopolitics is thanatopolitics." And with even more irony, he says: "One could symbolize such a coincidence by a slogan: Go get slaughtered and we promise you a long and pleasant life."[107]

The wartime instrumentalization of life meant that Japanese and Korean lives could be both nurtured and put up for slaughter in the interests of preserving the core population. However, Koreans in the Japanese empire and, as we will see in the next chapter, Japanese in the U.S. empire had been only very incompletely constituted as populations worthy of the positive workings of government prior to the Asia-Pacific War. Thus, before they could be asked to die in order to defend society, they had to be welcomed into the nation and enticed to enjoy the benefits of their inclusion. So in the case of these two subpopulations during the war, I would have to add a prefatory clause to Foucault's slogan: *"Welcome to the nation,* go get slaughtered and we promise you a long and pleasant life."

Second, as Foucault recognized and as Giorgio Agamben and Achille Mbembe have further theorized, despite the advance of bio-power in modern times, a pure necropolitics—or the sovereign power to take life without regard for life or law—has never disappeared.[108] In the case of Japan's and America's minorities and colonial subjects during the war years, even as they entered into the mainstream populations in some important respects, they continued to be marked as somehow different, usually through discourses of cultural difference. Inclusionary racism made it possible for the two regimes to separate out these subpopulations as a whole, or at least segments of them, and then to constitute them permanently or in moments of crisis into indeterminate states or zones of exception in which power could operate through sheer negativity. The racialized difference was complicated, of course, by markers of class and sex. Thus the wartime constitution of Koreans as newly reawakened Japanese both allowed unprecedented opportunities for some, especially the Korean elite, and also resegmented some—such as poor men mobilized as forced laborers and poor women coerced into sexual slavery—within an expanding imaginary of "Japan." These latter were the exceptions to the positivity of bio-politics, sacrificed for the population at large.

CHAPTER TWO · "Very Useful and
Very Dangerous"
*The Global Politics of Life,
Death, and Race*

> Do not sell this mission short. Though the Japanese
> are but 1/10th of one percent of the population, they
> are potentially very useful and very dangerous.
>
> > "Do's and Don'ts" for staff in the Provost Marshal
> > General Office evaluating Japanese American loyalty
> > questionnaires (ca. March 1943)

> After 15 months at Arizona's vast Poston Relocation
> Center as a social analyst, Commander Leighton
> concluded that many an American simply fails to
> remember that U.S. Japanese are human beings.
>
> > "Japs Are Human," *Time*, 25 June 1945

Perhaps it goes without saying that in the aftermath of Pearl Harbor, even the feeble signs that some Japanese Americans were becoming full-fledged members of the national community rapidly collapsed.[1] Throughout the prewar years the Japanese minority had been more outside than inside the national community. And technologies of human accounting, such as the census, had operated as much to exclude them from society, in fact to defend society from them, as it had worked to include them within the nation. It might be said that they had been incorporated within the larger American bio-political regime, but in large part as a means to exclude them from the liberal benefits of governmentality.

This outsideness had been sustained symbolically as well as administratively and juridically by bureaucratic practices of population management and the well-known web of federal and state laws that had not only shut off the flow of Japanese immigration to the United States but also kept those who had already immigrated and their children at a distance from the properly (and propertied) white civic population. With regard to these juridical mechanisms, I have in mind the Immigration Act of 1924, which effectively ended almost all Japanese immigration until passage of the McCarran-Walter Act in 1952; naturalization laws that allowed only "free white persons" and those of African descent to become naturalized citizens; state-level alien land laws that prohibited those ineligible to become naturalized citizens from owning land; the numerous state antimiscegenation laws; and the like.

In terms of technologies of population management, the 1940 census, which was used to facilitate the evacuation of Japanese from the West Coast, accounted for the Japanese population in a way that was completely different from how it treated those of European ancestry, including those of German and Italian background. While the Census Bureau employed the concepts "German" and "Italian" only to signify countries of birth, the term "Japanese" indicated both a birth country and a race of people. Put differently, according to the census Japanese Americans remained conceptually "Japanese" regardless of their birth in the United States, while German Americans and Italian Americans did not remain "Germans" and "Italians." This meant that almost immediately after the Pearl Harbor attack, the Census Bureau could and did produce tabulations concerning Japanese in the United States based on the race item, but could not do the same for their European counterparts. The bureau provided data to the military that showed the number of Japanese living in very small areas, in some cities down to city blocks. Such information could assist the military in determining if the total number of Japanese had been evacuated.[2]

Moreover, recent work on public health practices and discourses regarding Chinese and Japanese in the United States makes it plain that even the extremely limited state measures to improve the health of these groups were almost exclusively intended to segregate and sanitize them so that they could not medically and racially "contaminate" white communities. Natalia Molina has shown, for example, that even during the 1920s, when public health officials in Los Angeles began to provide a modicum of health care for Mexicans, including well baby clinics, they almost totally excluded Japanese from such measures. The difference in medical practices toward these two communities stemmed from the fact that in the twenties, large-scale white employers no longer considered Japanese a major source of cheap labor. In contrast, since employers viewed the Mexican population as constituting such a pool, its members were provided with a minimum of health care. To be sure, Los Angeles public health officials collected vital statistics about the Japanese, including data on births and deaths. But as Molina demonstrates, they were less concerned to improve the health and extend the lives of Japanese than to monitor their birth rates out of fear of their hyperfecundity and, by extension, the "race suicide" of whites. Similarly, some time ago Roger Daniels showed that New Deal relief agencies had "very little direct impact on Japanese Americans." One Los Angeles country supervisor reported that out of a Japanese American population of some 37,000 in the county, only about 25 had been on relief prior to the war.[3] In short, in the prewar years legal, racial, cultural, social, and medical discourses and practices became complicit in expressing and sustaining the essential outsideness of the Japanese in America. The mass removal of Japanese from the West Coast that began in March 1942 both reflected and reinforced these exclusionary practices.

The civil and military authorities as well as the general white population that actively or tacitly approved of this state racism were sustained at least in part by their ability to regard the Japanese in the United States as not completely human. On the eve of the final decision to evacuate Japanese Americans from the West Coast, for example, the *Los Angeles Times* famously opined that "a viper is a viper wherever the egg is hatched—so a Japanese American, born of Japanese parents—grows up to be a Japanese, not an American."[4] In May 1942 the governor of Idaho advised that all the Japanese in his state be sent back to Japan and that the island should then be sunk. His reason: "they live like rats, breed like rats and act like rats."[5] Such statements reflect the vulgar racist belief that the differences that warranted maintaining the Japanese on the outside of America were of a natural or biological kind; and we can see the easy slippage from metaphor to state practice in the first phase of the evacuation, before the permanent internment camps had been constructed, when Japanese Americans were often housed in quarters that had just been used by livestock. At the "assembly centers" established at the former Tanforan and Santa Anita race tracks, for example, from the spring to fall of 1942 Japanese Americans lived in converted horse stables, and in Portland in the Pacific International Livestock Exposition Pavilion.[6] Animality, as Achille Mbembe suggests, fostered the view of the other as having "no freedom, no history, no individuality in any real sense."[7]

But it is precisely during the period of total war, when contempt for Japanese Americans had risen to such a level that they had been forcibly expelled from the West Coast and then penned in camps like animals, that we witness a rather unexpected turn of events: namely, an unprecedented effort from early 1943 on to include this despised population in the American nation. While many continued to use the animal metaphors—though now arguing that the sheep could be separated from the goats and that they even possessed history and individuality—it became increasingly difficult in public circles and in state policy to sustain the vulgar racists' line of exclusion. During this period the state and its officers were compelled to claim that they did not practice racism; that they would make available to these people the benefits of life, health, education and happiness; and that since America did not practice discrimination, it would also allow the young men of this population to die for the national community.

One of the most decisive forces propelling the new inclusion of the Japanese American population into the nation was the total war logic of manpower utility. It might be thought that the utilization or nonutilization of Japanese Americans as civilian and military manpower was not a major issue for the wartime regime, since the total number of Japanese Americans in the mainland United States (126,947) and the colony of Hawaii (157,905) was very small in relation to the total population of the continental United States (131,669,275) and its colonial empire around the time of the Pearl Harbor attack.[8] However, under conditions of total war the logic of manpower utilization did not operate in such casual fashion. In fact, it is important to note that the beginning of Japanese American internment and therefore the withdrawal from the potential labor pool of tens of thousands of adults coincided exactly with a crisis in national manpower availability. In the spring of 1942, California farmers warned of a labor shortfall for the autumn harvest resulting from military conscription, leading to the inauguration of the "Bracero Program" later that year. This program brought tens of thousands of mostly Mexican workers to the United States annually during the war years and even greater numbers after the war.[9] It is known that by early April 1942—that is, only days after the army began to systematically force Japanese Americans to evacuate from their homes on the West Coast—agricultural interests were already requesting the release of evacuees so that they could provide farm labor. Sugar beet interests called the most loudly for Japanese American workers, and their voices could not be ignored—with almost all foreign supplies of sugar cut off owing to the war, a severe sugar shortfall seemed imminent. In May an agricultural leave program began, and by mid-October 1942 about 10,000 evacuees were at work on seasonal leave. In fact, effective 1 October an elaborate set of rules allowed various types of leave, including extended leave for an indefinite period of time. By the end of the year, the War Relocation Authority (WRA) had committed itself to a policy of leaves and resettlements of evacuees in communities outside of the camps.[10]

The total war logic of manpower utilization extended to the military as well, further pushing the government and the Roosevelt administration to denounce racism and eventually to reject the mass confinement of Japanese Americans. When faced with the need to mobilize all human and material resources to wage war, the American state chose not to leave even the Japanese American camps untouched by the rational necessity of nurturing the life, health, welfare, and education of its inmates. Population accounting in this historical moment meant not just making these aggregations and the individuals constituting them visible to the state so that they could be segregated, as may have been the case when the U.S. military initially rounded up and evacuated the Japanese from the West Coast. Instead, it meant nurturing individual lives, even promoting their freedom and happiness, if only to prepare them ultimately for death.

In this sense the American "relocation centers" with their schools, libraries, hospitals, gymnasiums, baseball fields, community councils, town meetings, elections, nominal freedom of speech and religion, newspapers, gardens, beauty pageants, Boy Scouts, Girl Scouts, Campfire Girls, YMCA, YWCA, and even a showcase orphanage in Manzanar called "Children's Village"—these were constructed so as to replicate (although they did so pathetically) what were regarded as the best features of liberal society.[11] Through the space and mechanisms of the camp, Japanese Americans became constituted as a subpopulation worthy of life and sustenance, even as the barbed wire continued to mark them as a danger. While obviously not exactly the same—most glaringly in the racialized makeup of the internees and the severely compromised conditions for maintaining nuclear families and domestic privacy— in many ways the camp was the liberal nation-state writ small; and in the same way that we have traced the "governmentalization of Korea" as a Japanese colony, it is possible to identity what we might call the "governmentalization of the American internment camps."

Yet there was another factor leading to America's disavowal of vulgar racism and turn to its more polite form that Foucault's general framework for bio-politics and thanatopolitics does not allow us to see. The questions of who should live and who should die, of who should count (or more precisely, be counted) so as to receive the material and spiritual benefits of liberal democracy and the nation, including the right to die as soldiers—the answers to such questions as they relate to Japanese Americans can be fathomed only by examining the concrete historical and transnational contingencies that made Japanese in the United States into Americans during World War II. As we will see, the story of the Japanese American movement to the inside of the American regime of governmentality had as much to do with American wartime and postwar aspirations for hegemony over Japan, Asia, and more generally the "yellow and brown peoples" of the world as with wartime manpower mobilization.

This chapter traces the processes and contingencies by which the racist state's civil and military officers first determined that Japanese Americans should be ex-

cluded from military service, then by the fall of 1942 completely reversed this earlier decision, and then in January 1943 began aggressively recruiting Japanese Americans to become soldiers. As in the previous chapter, I focus primarily on the question of soldiering, because this was the site through which not only the soldiers
themselves but also the racialized communities that they represented passed most
paradigmatically and dramatically from the outside to the inside of the national
community. The complicity of the WRA and the War Department in linking the
recruitment drive for army volunteers to a general program to determine the loyalty of all adult internees, both male and female, calls our attention to the overwhelming symbolic importance of the citizen-soldier as the normative citizen.
Moreover, I pay considerable attention to how discussions and policies regarding
Japanese American soldiering were always interlaced with the larger questions of
how to govern the Japanese American population in general, the nation as a whole,
and the world. As a consequence of these considerations, the regime would promise Japanese Americans the abundant benefits of citizenship while sending many
of them off to die or to suffer injuries with a frequency out of all proportion to
their numbers.

VULGAR RACISM AND FEARS OF A
GLOBAL ALLIANCE OF COLOR

At the time of the Pearl Harbor attack there were around 5,000 Americans of Japanese descent serving in the U.S. Army,[12] the majority of whom had been drafted.
According to a history compiled by the Office of the Provost Marshal General, the
Selective Service System did not discriminate by national origin or race but inducted
"all nationalities alike" and "drew into the Army all nationalities regardless of the
increasing probability of war with the Axis powers." Apparently, very little thought
had been given to controversies that might arise around the induction of Americans of Japanese, Italian, or German descent.[13] However, opportunities for Japanese Americans to serve in the military rapidly diminished after Pearl Harbor. While
hundreds of Japanese Americans continued to receive draft notices and report to
local draft boards after the attack, many already in the army were released without
explanation. As early as mid-January 1942, Major Karl R. Bendetsen, writing on behalf of the provost marshal general, recommended that "no person of Japanese extraction be assigned or transferred" to such particularly vulnerable branches of the
military as "the Air Corps, Signal Corps, Armored Forces, or Chemical Warfare
Service." Instead, he advised that they be placed in "units or installations in the Zone

of the Interior."[14] In late March 1942, Brigadier General James K. Wharton, director of military personnel, noted that a recommendation to cease "induction or enlistment of men of Japanese extraction" had been made on 27 March 1942. He further advised that the estimated 5,000 Japanese Americans then in the army be "absorbed and dispersed in small numbers throughout the interior of the United States." In addition, Wharton urged that those "whose loyalty is seriously doubted" be placed in labor units.[15] By the end of the month, the army had ceased all inductions of Japanese Americans.[16]

Paralleling this rapid cessation of Japanese American inductions and their containment in what were deemed to be areas and units with lower security risks, the War Department swiftly moved to dismiss its Japanese American civilian employees, despite the possible charge of "Why Japs—not Germans & Italians."[17] The contradictions between this policy and the War Department's and government's official stance that it did not discriminate on the basis of race were all too obvious to the relevant employees themselves, who sometimes gained the sympathy of their superiors. For instance, an employee who had been suspended from employment— a U.S. citizen of mixed parentage with a "Japanese" father, a mother who was a British national, and an "American" husband—protested her dismissal and pointed out that the War Department's policy seemed out of line with the very principles "of a country that is Democratic, that stands for fair play and justice." "How can children of a family who have participated and wholeheartedly contributed in everything our country stands for, be suddenly discriminated upon and deprived of their very livilihood [sic]," she demanded, "when they have done nothing to warrant such unfairness?" Finally, rehearsing an argument that would be an important factor in breaking down the vulgar racism that characterized this moment in the exclusion of Japanese Americans from the national community, she asked how the same War Department that had inducted her brother into the army only ten months previously could prevent his sister from "doing her bit by working as a clerk for the Finance Office." Perhaps this "Junior-Clerk typist" did not fully realize how aggressively the War Department was closing the doors on all military employment even as she wrote, and that it would be governed by a strict logic of racial exclusion and containment until the late fall. As the assistant chief of the air staff had put it on New Year's Day 1942, "in time of peace there should be no discrimination because of race or creed. In time of war this government must protect itself from possible enemies."[18]

Indeed, in June 1942 the War Department explicitly declared all Japanese ineligible for induction, regardless of citizenship. As Secretary of War Henry L. Stimson unequivocally informed the Selective Service director, "except as may be specifically authorized in exceptional cases, the War Department will not accept for service with the armed forces, Japanese, or persons of Japanese extraction, regardless of citizenship status or other factors." Selective Service also reclassified all Japanese American registrants, whether citizens or noncitizens, as 4-C, or "nonacceptable alien." Finally, on 14 September 1942 the Board of Officers within the Office of the Army Chief of Staff recommended against further utilization of Japanese Americans. The only exceptions to this general exclusion of Japanese Americans from the military existed within military intelligence, where they were needed as interpreters and translators, and in Hawaii.[19]

In the latter territory, ethnic Japanese made up such a large and important part of the labor force that the commanding general of the Hawaii Department, Delos C. Emmons, resisted the War Department's February 1942 order to dismiss the army's Japanese civilian employees. And even more importantly, he obstructed, albeit somewhat inconsistently, what became aborted plans to evacuate the Japanese population en masse from Hawaii. Again, concerns about a labor shortage and its impact on wartime economic productivity prevailed. Moreover, cognizant of the utility of Nisei as military manpower, Emmons fought back the War Department's plans to release Nisei military personnel in Hawaii from active duty. He proposed instead formation of a special Nisei battalion, a plan that materialized with the 100th Battalion. The latter was a special unit made up of the Hawaiian Nisei who had been separated from their non-Japanese fellow Hawaiian recruits in the Hawaii National Guard just days after Pearl Harbor. This Nisei unit began training on the mainland in June 1942.[20] In short, in Hawaii the more pressing material necessity of utilizing the Japanese American population led to somewhat less exclusionary results, at least locally and with regard to their use as civilian and military workers.

Despite the Hawaii exceptions, by September 1942 it appeared that Japanese Americans would no longer be accepted as military personnel and that the camps would physically and symbolically embody their exclusion from the national community. After much study, however, and in consultation with representatives of various military and civilian agencies within the government as well as other advisers, in January 1943 the War Department declared that it would begin allowing Japanese American citizens to volunteer for the army. In making this decision, the military and civilian authorities fully realized that they had completely reversed the War Department's policies regarding Japanese American military service in the first year or so after Pearl Harbor; and in general they suppressed circulation of detailed knowledge about how exclusionary and clearly racist those policies had been. For instance, when WRA Director Dillon Myer asked in February 1943 to see a copy of the secretary of war's 26 September 1942 letter that had directed all service commands to summarily discharge Japanese Americans from the Enlisted Reserve Corps for no other reason than their ancestry, he acknowledged that it was a "secret document and not for general release." The General Staff Executive Colonel William F. Scobey provided Myer with a copy of the letter, but with the warning that "the directive is confidential and is not to be distributed. The policy announced in the directive is not consistent with the present attitude of the War Department, and steps are now being taken to revise it."[21]

This was an understatement, for by January the military establishment and the executive branch had not only decided to begin readmitting eligible Nisei into the army and placing them in an all–Japanese American special combat team; they had also launched an effort to turn these men and their unit into icons of the nation's categorical denunciation of racist discrimination. As President Franklin D. Roosevelt put it in his now famous words of 1 February 1943 recognizing the formation of the all–Japanese American 442nd Regimental Combat Team:

> No loyal citizen of the United States should be denied the democratic right to exercise the responsibilities of his citizenship, regardless of his ancestry. The principle on which this country was founded and by which it has always been governed is that Americanism is a matter of the mind and heart; Americanism is not, and never was, a matter of race or ancestry. A good American is one who is loyal to this country and to our creed of liberty and democracy. Every loyal American citizen should be given the opportunity to serve this country wherever his skills will make the greatest contribution—whether it be in the ranks of our armed forces, war production, agriculture, government service, or other work essential to the war effort.[22]

In keeping with this inclusionary policy, Japanese Americans once again became subject to the draft from January 1944 on; and in September of that year, the War Department determined that even noncitizen Japanese would be allowed to volunteer for army service.[23] Paralleling these developments, on 3 May 1943 a directive enabled Japanese Americans to once again work as civilian employees in the army.[24]

So what were the considerations that weighed so heavily on the June and September 1942 decisions to exclude Japanese Americans from the military, and by extension the nation? And in early 1943, what factors led to the complete repudiation of the original decision? Why did the War Department and the government more generally change policy from complete exclusion of all Japanese, regardless of citizenship, to acceptance even of Japanese volunteers who were not U.S. citizens?

The original disqualification of Japanese Americans as full-fledged citizen-soldiers was in large part the result of an uncomplicated and vulgar racism. This "naturalistic" vision[25] of Japanese racial difference saw Japanese Americans as so fixed in their physicality and temperament that they seemed outside of history and the possibility of assimilation to white America. A report (approved by the secretary of war on 14 September 1942) of the Board of Officers within the Office of the Army Chief of Staff—appointed by order of the secretary of war to "meet at the call of the president for the purpose of studying and submitting recommendations on the question of military utilization of United States citizens of Japanese ancestry"[26]—makes very clear that this modality of racism outweighed any consideration of their potential as military or civilian labor.

Confirming that any decision about mobilizing minorities as civilian or military labor power under conditions of total war would have to begin by calculating their bio-political utility, the board scoured the data available from sources such as the Selective Service, the Immigration Service, the Adjutant General's Office, the 1940 census, and the War Relocation Authority to arrive at the following figures. It found that about 36,000 male Japanese American citizens were of military age, that about half of these "would be acceptable for induction," and that since about 4,000 were already in the military, there were roughly 14,000 Japanese American male citizens who could potentially be inducted. However, the board indicated that despite their potential and its hope that "an appropriate placement may be found for such a distinctive class of individuals [in the war effort]," this group was "so marked by racial appearance, characteristics and background, that they are particularly repulsive to the military establishment at large and the civilian population of the United States." Along the same lines, it also concluded: "the lone fact that these individuals are of Japanese ancestry tends to place them in a most questionable light as to their loyalty to the United States."

Furthermore, the board stated that the commanding generals of the Services of Supply and the Army Ground Forces—in other words, two major commands under which such soldiers might serve—had indicated that they did "not favor the unrestricted military use of United States citizens of Japanese ancestry, either as combat troops in active theaters or as organized units for other purposes." To be more precise, in his 12 August 1942 letter to the Board, Major L. Duenweg, writing on behalf of Army Ground Forces' commanding general, Leslie J. McNair, recommended that "the employment of United States citizens of Japanese ancestry in the military forces be avoided," and that if avoidance was impossible, "this personnel [should] be assigned to non-critical installations in the Zone of Interior." Duenweg reasoned in ways that would be echoed in the Board of Officers' final report, for he worried that the "adherence of the Japanese to their national customs, language and schools aggravates a natural distrust of all of their race in the present conflict," making it difficult to employ them in the military because other troops would not want to work with them. He also maintained that the physical features of the Japanese— "the characteristic color and features of the Japanese race"—made them both so recognizable as a group and so indistinguishable from one another that it would be unwise to utilize them. Because they could be spotted as group members but not as individuals, excluding them altogether would "facilitate the apprehension of any disloyal individuals who might attempt subversive acts." Presumably, allowing them to mix in would make it impossible to weed out the loyal from the disloyal. Duenweg also mentioned "social complications" and evidence that "Japanese residents of this country are promoting anti-white sentiment among the Negroes," a curious point to which I will return in a moment.[27] Through the enclosure of a memorandum that McNair had written on 26 March 1942, Duenweg also made the board aware that at least since late March, the commanding general had sought not only to "discontinue the induction of soldiers of Japanese ancestry" but "also to discharge those already in the service or place them in work camps."[28]

The commanding general of the Services of Supply had been less categorical in opposing military utilization of Japanese Americans. Through his assistant chief of staff for operations, he informed the board that the absorption of large numbers of Japanese American soldiers into the units under his command was "impracticable," but he left open the possibility that newly inducted Japanese Americans might replace those transferred to other units. He went so far as to suggest that Japanese Americans could be employed as combat or service troops, but also explicitly warned that they should be excluded from the Air Corps, Signal Corps, Armored Force, and Chemical Warfare Service. In addition, he recommended that they not be stationed in Central or South America, nor the Pacific or the Caribbean, while he was open to the idea that they could be used as "combat or service troops in Iceland, Africa, or even the Brisish [sic] Isles."[29] Colonel Martin J. Hans, whose opinion was valued because of his three months of contact with Japanese American citizens during the evacuation process, also weighed in against the possibility of employing Japanese American citizens in the military, simply stating "that he did not trust them."[30]

The Board had also solicited the opinions of Lieutenant General John L. DeWitt, commanding general of the Western Defense Command, who had played a leading role in the mass evacuation of Japanese Americans. Like most of the others,

DeWitt understood that the situation of total war made it necessary to seriously consider employing Japanese Americans as military labor, despite his complete distrust of them. "Failure to utilize the considerable number of American male citizens of Japanese ancestry in the United States, would constitute failure to make use of all available manpower." Therefore, he recommended Nisei military employment, but with many precautions and limitations. He advocated restricting their use to interior service commands in the continental United States, their exclusion from areas where sabotage might "interfere with the war effort," and their placement in "service units only, unarmed." He also recognized that Japanese American interpreters and translators could be employed in the Military Intelligence Division (MID) wherever necessary.[31]

DeWitt's remarkable recommendations may be read for the starkness with which they show that the need to mobilize all possible sources of manpower in the total war effort put tremendous pressure on the military to end its exclusionary practices. Even he—so thoroughly contemptuous of Japanese Americans that he consistently maintained that no test of their loyalty could ever be trusted—even he granted that the U.S. military could not allow Japanese American labor power to be wasted. But unlike the (polite racist) liberals whose views would become dominant in later months, he did not understand that it would be impossible to simply make use of Japanese American labor without formally admitting them into the national community as loyal Americans. His plan unabashedly called for their sheer exploitation under grossly discriminatory conditions without any compensatory benefits to the soldiers or their communities. Put differently, he would have exploited Japanese Americans for their labor without liberal guilt—without bringing them into the American regime of governmentality. In fact, echoing the vulgar racist views of Japanese colonial and military officials before the dominance of polite racism, he explicitly ended his statement with the proviso that the question of future citizenship for Japanese Americans should be delinked from whatever policy the military adopted regarding these people.

Against this generally negative view, the board also heard the more liberal opinions of the WRA's Thomas Holland (who represented Director Dillon Myer) and two colonels, Moses W. Pettigrew and Rufus S. Bratten, both of whom had been trained in the Japanese language and were believed to have expert knowledge of the Japanese people. Holland reported on his conversations with interned Japanese American citizens, saying that "except for a very small percentage" he found them loyal and desirous of "an opportunity to enter combat service and prove their loyalty by actual duty." The military men concurred that the Japanese American (male) citizens represented a "considerable quantity of very good man power" that should not be wasted and that they were on the whole a very loyal group of Americans.[32] The views of these liberals on the "Japanese problem" would not prevail at this time, however.

But here we must also consider a very important secondary factor, complementing vulgar racism, that influenced the board's recommendation to discontinue military inductions of Japanese Americans. This component in the decision-making process does not appear in its short report; but a strong paper trail among the documents collected by the board in its deliberations, as well as other relevant documents, suggests that this element had a deep impact on at least one of the board's advisers, General McNair, and in all likelihood had a far more expansive reach. It was the fear that the Japanese in the United States were busily mobilizing African Americans in a global movement against white privilege and that if they were allowed into the military they would expand their efforts in this campaign. This is what McNair meant when, in the statement quoted above by Duenweg, he alluded to evidence that "Japanese residents of this country are promoting anti-white sentiment among the Negroes."

Because McNair held the powerful position of commanding general of the Army Ground Forces, he had been kept apprised of alleged Japanese agitation among African Americans in the United States since at least March 1942. At that time Congressman D. D. Terry of Arkansas first alerted him to rumors of Japanese subversive activities around Camp Robinson in Little Rock, Arkansas, where a large number of Japanese American soldiers were in training.[33] These Japanese American soldiers had been inducted into the military either before Pearl Harbor or in the short time after the attack when there was still considerable uncertainty about the military eligibility of Japanese Americans.

A Little Rock committee of citizens had first raised such concerns with Congressman Terry as well as the commanding officer of Camp Robinson, Brigadier General F. B. Mallon. According to Mallon's report and a letter penned by Hodson Lewis, one of the leaders of the citizens' committee and the secretary of the local Chamber of Commerce, the locals worried that Japanese American soldiers were "infiltrating into colored areas in Little Rock, and making social contacts therein." They feared that "any equality shown to the Japanese by white people may result in the negroes in this vicinity increasing their demands."[34] Furthermore, Lewis seemed particularly alarmed by the specter of Japanese American soldiers mixing with local women, both white and black. "One of the reasons for our asking you to very strenuously [sic] place our objections before the War Department is the fact that there are very grave social problems arising which are not only embarrassing but can become quite dangerous." His anxieties crystallized around interracial sex: "We are getting reports, founded on good authority, of the co-mingling of Japanese soldiers and negro women, which is causing rather a serious situation among the negro men, which as you know may lead to considerable trouble. Quite a few of the Jap. soldiers are attending the U.S.O. dances at the Auditorium, and while so far our girls have endeavored to be good sports, we do not believe they are going to continue to do so and to dance with these boys without restrictions."[35]

In short, in their race panic the leading citizens of Little Rock betrayed their fears that their conventional world of white supremacy over the black population might be challenged by the sudden presence of an unexpected third race, the Japanese. Moreover, when they expressed their distress they did so in a way that conflated the social and the political with the sexual. The specter of Japanese penetrating into the black and white communities to foment racial unrest melded seamlessly into visions of Japanese sexual intimacy with black and white women.

That such a conflation of social, political and sexual alarm extended far beyond Little Rock can be gauged from other intelligence reports on supposed Japanese subversive activities among African Americans. For example, a report by the MID's Counter-Intelligence Group (CIG) on a "Japanese-Negro" organization called Development of Our Own seemed as concerned about the fact that the group's founder Satakata Takahashi (alias Naka Nakane) had a black wife named Pearl Sherrod— a woman it described as an active participant in the organization and a "huge negress"—as it was impressed by the size of the organization's following (in Detroit alone, some 18,000 followers in 1933 and 83,000 in April 1942) and by the stridency of its calls for an alliance of "the dark races of America with the dark races of Japan in the forcible overthrow of the white race's control of America."[36] One of President Roosevelt's aides remarked that the coupling of Japanese nationals with "Negresses" was a "fifth column move on the part of the Japanese in creating such marriages to build good will and sympathy."[37]

In April 1942 the CIG further fueled the race panic throughout the military and intelligence communities by widely distributing "Japanese Racial Agitation among American Negroes," a study specifically on this issue. The CIG circulated it not only to the Army Ground Forces under McNair's command but also to the First, Second, Third, and Fourth Armies, the Western Defense Command, the Army Air Forces, Services of Supply, the Office of Naval Intelligence, the FBI, the Psychological Warfare Branch, and elsewhere.[38] This report claimed that Japanese subversives were agitating among "American Negroes" to "foster race riots and organized revolt against the United States government and authority" (p. 7). But it also emphasized that the danger of these activities could not be fully appreciated without a more global perspective through which it could be seen that the Japanese attempt to foment racial unrest in the United States was linked to a much larger movement to overthrow the white man. This movement was said to stretch across the globe, from East Asia and the Co-Prosperity Sphere through places such as China and Manchuria to Russian Turkestan; from Burma and South Asia and then on to the Middle East; and across the Atlantic to the West Indies and from there to the cities of America. The report stressed that Japanese propaganda tried to connect American blacks with anti-American and anti-British groups throughout the world, especially emphasizing ties of religion ("particularly the Moslem, as opposed to the Christian"), race ("an artificial grouping of non-white versus the white"), and economy ("the 'have-nots' versus the 'haves' "). The "most common point of origin for organizers and agitators who arouse the Negro organizations," it said, was the British West Indies—precisely because the British empire epitomized the intersection (or as the report put it, the "cross-roads") of the Muslim religion and the "Negro Race." It warned that the British West Indies not only contained a "violently anti-British element" but since the war's outbreak had "become anti-American" (p. 17).

With regard to religion, the report observed quite accurately that Japanese propagandists had been trying to present the Japanese as the "champions of the Mohammedans" against Christianity and white imperialism (p. 4). It remarked on the ties that Japanese agents had forged with Muslim refugees to their country from Russian Turkestan, the great mosques that had been built in Kobe and Tokyo in the 1930s, Japanese printings of the Koran, Japanese efforts to foment independence movements in places such as the Dutch East Indies and South Asia, and so on. The report brought home this panic about a Japanese alignment with Muslims by observing that Japanese agents were also exploiting the "Asiatic religion" to win over "Negroes" and those of "West Indian extraction" in the United States (p. 8). Cautioning that the Muslim population in the Western Hemisphere was far larger than usually estimated, and fearful that West Indian marriages with American blacks were spreading "this religious belief among a wide body of the Negroes" (pp. 8–9), it created a scenario of a global Muslim and "darker skinned" alliance against white privilege—an alliance led by the Japanese.

The report warned that the Japanese strategy to win "Negro support for the Japanese fighting forces" was disarmingly simple: "Japan aims to drive the white man out of Asia and to help the underprivileged and exploited natives to throw off the yoke of the white man's imperialism. The Negroes are underprivileged and exploited victims of the white man. Therefore the Negro should rally to the Japanese cause." Though the report's authors advised some circumspection about their sometimes "over-emphatic" source, it cited a 1940 study that had found that "between eighty and ninety percent of the American colored population who had any views on the subject, at all, were pro-Japanese. Even a drastic revision of these figures, based on the occasional alarmist tendencies of their origin, leaves evidence that intensive Japanese propaganda among this racial group has had considerable effect" (p. 8). And in a section devoted to specific dangers confronting the military, it stressed that the "confirmed objective of underground Japanese practice among Negroes is to promote subversion of Negro troops in the United States Army." It went on:

> One of the leaders, since interned, of the Ethiopian Pacific Movement, is reported to have stated before a meeting of this society that he was going to register next month and "if they give me a gun and send me to Asia or Africa, I will use my own discretion." Upon seeing a soldier in the audience, this leader advised him, "Go back to your outfit and start the whispering campaign; when they tell you to remember Pearl Harbor, you reply, 'Remember Africa.'" (p. 9)

The report added that "there have been recent reports of Japanese-Negro front organizations encouraging Negroes to resist or to evade the draft" (p. 10).

"Japanese-Negro front organizations" included the Emmanual Gospel Mission, "reportedly connected with the Japanese Buddhist Church in San Francisco"; the Afro-Asiatic League, which "advocated a racial war"; the Universal Improvement Association, whose organizer Marcus Garvey had said in 1918 that the "next war would be between Negroes and Whites, and that with Japan's assistance, the Negro would win": the Jamaica Progressive League, which was affiliated with the Peoples National Party, "a very radical, anti-British, and now violently anti-American organization"; the Ethiopian Pacific Movement, whose leader was Robert O. Jordan, "a Negro of West Indian origin who claimed membership in the [Japanese ultranationalist] Black Dragon Society, and support of the German-American Fund"; the Islam Movement, which emphasized "race equality" and claimed that the "origin of the Negro is in Asia, rather than Africa"; the Pacific Movement of the Eastern World, about which more will be said in a moment; the Onward Movement, which had been sponsored by the Japanese and whose speakers told their membership that "with Japanese victory over the United States, the Negroes will hold government offices and be equal with the white people"; and a number of other groups (pp. 11–16).

In the midst of this race panic, McNair received a memo from the adjutant general (dated 29 May 1942), by order of the secretary of war, concerning a situation that he already knew something about—namely, alleged Japanese agitation among blacks in Little Rock, Arkansas. The memo warned McNair that

a. On April 23, 1942, the Commanding General, Seventh Corps Area, his Assistant Chief of Staff, G-1, and his Assistant Chief of Staff, G-2, expressed to an officer from the War Department, who had occasion to visit the Headquarters, Eleventh Corps Area, their concern over the serious situation in Little Rock Arkansas, as it affected Negro and Japanese personnel, both civilian and enlisted. The corps Area Commander considered the situation dangerous and suggested that no more Negro or Japanese troops be sent there.

b. The Corps Area Commander and his Assistant Chief of Staff, G-2, concurred in the opinion of people familiar with the situation that the Negroes are being organized and incited by the Japanese. Indications had been observed of the activities of the "Pacific Movement of the Eastern World," an organization set up by the Japanese to promote anti-white sentiment and the "league of dark races" idea among Negroes. The Negroes of Little Rock were also found to possess more arms than is usual among people of their race.[39]

CIG's "Japanese Racial Agitation among American Negroes" had identified the Pacific Movement of the Eastern World as a "Japanese Negro Front Organization" that had been organized by one Ashima Takis. It indicated that the Pacific Movement's core strength was in the Midwest and that its doctrine was that "Negroes have no stake in America and would be better off if Japan won the war because Japanese, too, are a dark people oppressed by the whites" (pp. 14–15).

In many respects this memo speaks for itself, but I want to end this section by reiterating that while what I have been calling vulgar racism was the primary factor blocking further inductions of Japanese American citizens into the army, fears of a Japanese-led "league of dark races" bent on overthrowing white privilege in places as remote as Egypt and India, and as near as Little Rock and Detroit, exacerbated general anxieties about the Japanese being allowed to roam freely in society at large, let alone within the military.

Furthermore, the connection between the decision to discontinue Japanese American military inductions and anxieties about the radical league of Japanese and African Americans is not limited to the strong paper trail described above. Excellent research by other scholars has already shown that from just after Pearl Harbor through at least September of the following year, fears of subversive activities conducted by Japanese among African Americans reached a high point, leading to the summertime arrests of prominent individual suspects in this movement.[40] To be sure, U.S. counterintelligence had been sensitive to this matter from at least the late 1930s on,[41] but the war's outbreak brought these worries to an unprecedented level. In short, the War Department moved steadily toward its decision to exclude Japanese Americans from the U.S. military precisely during the period of most widespread and intense anxiety about the Japanese as a "Champion of the Darker Races."

It was thus more than coincidence that on 14 September 1942, the exact day that the secretary of war approved the Board of Officers' final report barring Japanese Americans from the military, U.S. District Attorney for the Southern District of New York Matthias Correa announced the arrest of Leonard Robert Jordan and a number of his associates for sedition.[42] A later CIG report on the Ethiopian Pacific Movement—an organization founded in Harlem in 1935, allegedly by Jordan along with a Filipino named Memo de Guzman, a Cherokee Indian by the name of Chief Moon Nelson, and one Jacob Samuel—noted that the group showed "all the tribal markings of the Japanese-Negro propaganda network, and has, from its very beginning, been pro-Japanese in its sympathies." The CIG indicated that Jordan was by birth a British West Indian who had actually served in the Japanese merchant marine. After Pearl Harbor he reportedly took a strong pro-Japanese stance and "told the Harlem Negroes that they would obtain their independent homeland in Africa under the leadership of Japan, and that the Japanese were members of the darker race and friends of the Negroes." According to the CIG, Jordan avowed that "he would be ashamed to wear a United States uniform," and he "repeatedly advised his audience that he would refuse to fight for the United States until the lynching of Negroes and race discrimination had been abolished."[43]

In such a time of hysteria about Japanese provocation among African Americans throughout the country, it did not seem to matter that F. B. Mallon, commanding officer of Camp Robinson, had conducted a "thorough investigation" of "reports that the [Japanese American] soldiers in question were infiltrating into colored areas in Little Rock and making social contacts therein" and determined on 20 March 1942 that "these reports were without foundation."[44] Despite Mallon's conclusion that no such activities were taking place in Little Rock, on 6 July 1942 Major Duenweg, writing on behalf of McNair, recommended that "definite steps be taken by the War Department to stamp out subversive Japanese activities in the vicinity of that station." In fact the fear of further racial unrest in the area around Camp Robinson should Japanese Americans be utilized in the military continued to spread even more widely

among highly placed military officers. For example, in response to the recommendation by Admiral Chester W. Nimitz (commander in chief, U.S. Fleet) to induct
approximately 10,000 Japanese Americans in Hawaii, Major General Thomas T.
Handy, the assistant chief of staff, felt compelled to cite "serious difficulties bor-
dering on riot" at Camp Robinson as one of the chief reasons for maintaining that
the War Department's policy of "not enlisting individuals of Japanese extraction
is sound." The acting army chief of staff himself concurred in this assessment. Likewise, it was apparently irrelevant that after an even more thorough study of the situation, Richard Donovan, the commanding general of the Service Command con-
trolling Arkansas (and therefore Camp Robinson), had concluded by 9 September
1942 that "there is no indication that subversive activities have been either directly
or indirectly concerned with any such disturbances in the past, nor is there any indication that subversive elements are at work among the colored people of this Service Command."[45]

Such findings had no influence on the board's final decision, which recommended
that "in general, the military potential of United States citizens of Japanese ancestry be considered negative because of the universal distrust in which they are held."
The only exception to this exclusionary policy would be their possible use for "intelligence or for [unnamed] specialized purposes."[46] Thus in the short run, not even
the pressure to mobilize all possible sources of human power for the war effort could
break down the vulgar racists' resistance to Japanese American participation in the
military. This was a view fully in keeping with the U.S. government's and the War
Department's general attitude and policy toward Japanese Americans at the time—
namely, that they were an untrustworthy race, perhaps colluding with the "darker
races" to take down the white man, that needed to be confined in concentration camps
and should be completely expelled from the national community. Yet the civil and
military leadership would soon come to regard this vulgar racist stance toward the
Japanese in America, as well as the military's rejection of their utility in the armed
forces, as a dangerous impediment to American national interests.

POLITE RACISM AND AMERICAN HEGEMONY IN ASIA

In October 1942, opinion within and around the War Department swung against
the Board of Officers' recommendation to end the use of Japanese in the military.
While the logic of Japanese Americans' utility as military and civilian manpower
continued to push the state in this direction, in the short term the perception that
Japanese American soldiers might have enormous value in a global propaganda war

emerged as the decisive factor. To be sure, some within the military and civilian leadership mentioned the rights of Japanese Americans as citizens, but this was not the determining element.

On 2 October 1942, Director of the Office of War Information (OWI) Elmer Davis wrote to President Roosevelt, saying that by using loyal "American-citizen Japanese" in the army and navy it would be possible to counter Japanese propaganda in Asia that insisted that the war was a racial conflict. While Davis thought that the morale of "American citizen Japanese" could be improved by allowing them to voluntarily enlist in the U.S. military, he emphasized that such an action would be of great aid to the OWI in its counterpropaganda campaign in the "Philippines, Burma, and elsewhere." He also asked the president to come out with a "public statement . . . in behalf of the loyal American citizens." On 13 October M. S. Eisenhower, the OWI's associate director, wrote to Assistant Secretary of War John J. McCloy concurring with Davis. Then on 15 October McCloy sent a memorandum to Secretary of War Henry Stimson, endorsing Davis's opinion and stating that he believed that Japanese Americans should be allowed to "enlist in special units of the Army and Navy." "I believe," he said, "the propaganda value of such a step would be great and I believe they would make good troops." Moreover, he explicitly remarked on his disagreement with the Board of Officers' earlier recommendation against military utilization of Japanese Americans. Most tellingly, to support his affirmative response to Eisenhower's 13 October communication, McCloy said only: "The propaganda value of the use of Japanese troops would, I think, be of great value throughout the Far East."[47]

On 28 October an unidentified but obviously highly placed official in the War Department, perhaps McCloy, drafted a memorandum to the secretary of war in which he argued that a program for the voluntary enlistment of Japanese American citizens, exclusive of the untrustworthy Nisei who had been partly educated in Japan (*kibei*), should be initiated. He began by reaffirming the instrumentalist argument that all human resources needed to be employed in the war effort, warning that if Japanese Americans in the camps were not given an opportunity to serve in the military, they might come under the sway of dissidents and "their future value as useful citizens may be seriously impaired." While he further mentioned the "fundamental rights of citizens to serve their country" despite the special problems of assimilation for Japanese Americans due to "racial characteristics," he took pains to explain why a segregated voluntary special unit would most effectively achieve the aim of the program. A voluntary as opposed to a compulsory induction system, he stressed, would be most desirable "from the viewpoint of propaganda advantage," presumably because it could demonstrate the free desire of these men to fight for the United States. Moreover, a segregated group would "enable the unit to manifest en masse its loyalty to the United States, and this manifestation would provide the propaganda effect desired."[48]

In mid-November 1942 Colonel Pettigrew, chief of the Far Eastern Group within the War Department's Military Intelligence Service (MIS), wrote a fairly detailed study on the matter for McCloy. As we have seen, in September 1942 the special Board of Officers had rejected Pettigrew's positive views on Japanese American military service; but now, only about two months later, his views had come to represent the War Department's prevailing opinion in most respects. Pettigrew repeated the by then common rationale that the wartime situation required total manpower utilization and that to prevent Japanese Americans from serving in the military was "a total waste of a very considerable and potentially valuable manpower." But his main point was that "the tremendous psychological and moral value to be gained by the formation of a special combat unit" outweighed "all other advantages." As he put it, "This psychological value would obtain not only throughout the world, but upon our own American population, and would unquestionably very greatly improve the post-war conditions of the entire Japanese-American population." In short, Pettigrew suggested that an all–Japanese American unit would have great propaganda value at home and abroad and would also facilitate the return of Japanese Americans back into mainstream society.[49]

Finally, at a 2 January 1943 conference in the assistant secretary of war's office, John J. McCloy himself announced to various high-ranking officers within the War Department and the Office of Naval Intelligence (ONI) that the decision had been made to use "Japanese as combat troops." Again pointing to the factors of manpower utility and propaganda, especially in Asia, he noted that three points had weighed most heavily in the decision: "(1) their fighting qualifications; (2) the propaganda value; and (3) the impact on Asia." According to the firsthand account of W. N. Crist (Military Intelligence), the conference participants still argued about whether the Japanese American troops should be limited to volunteers or if draftees could be included. But Crist's account makes clear that by this time, less than a year after the decision had been made to remove and incarcerate the entire West Coast's Japanese American population, the War Department had reached the new conclusion that the national interest demanded that the loyalty of individual Japanese Americans be assessed so that those deemed eligible could be released from the camps into mainstream society, inducted into the military, or both.[50]

It should be noted, however, that such arguments concerning the value of Japanese American military enlistment were not without precedent. As early as January 1942, John Embree, the noted anthropologist of Japan and Japanese in Hawaii, had argued that Hawaiian Nisei should be actively utilized in the war effort. He appears to have sincerely believed in the loyalty of Hawaiian Nisei, and as a strong liberal nationalist he wrote that entrusting the Hawaiian Nisei with responsibilities and duties would have the double advantage of bolstering the morale of the Japanese communities in Hawaii and the mainland and of more generally countering Axis propaganda about American racism. Reflecting the understanding that national unity had to be maintained to effectively conduct total war, he stressed the importance of keeping up Nisei morale, because "a united nation can only exist when made up of united communities. Any area of indifferent or disaffected individuals is a danger spot in national defense especially in such strategic areas as Hawaii and California." At the same time, assigning the Nisei important tasks "would serve as a valuable preventative against Axis propaganda aimed at weakening the civilian solidarity of areas like Hawaii by appeals to race differences and allegations of race discrimination." In short, Japanese in Hawaii could have utility in the national disavowal of racism by unifying the diverse nation and countering Axis attempts to disrupt that unity. While not going so far as to recommend their total mobilization into the army and navy, Embree rather fantastically suggested two possible deployments for the Nisei. First, individuals well-respected within their communities could be placed in positions of great responsibility, such as "air warden duty." The second was "to have chosen from a group of volunteer selectees or commissioned officers a few of Japanese ancestry to carry out some important military mission—to bomb a Japanese warship for instance. If this were done, the man's name should be published and his Japanese ancestry noted as evidence that in spite of his ancestry he is a loyal American citizen."[51]

Furthermore, during the spring and late summer of 1942, even as the War Department moved steadily toward the exclusion of Japanese Americans from the military, some individuals directly involved in U.S. policy making were already arguing that Japanese American soldiers could play an important propaganda role. It is known that as early as May 1942 Assistant Secretary of War McCloy had expressed support for the military utilization of Japanese Americans.[52] But even more substantially, general propaganda plans drafted in May 1942 under the leadership and signature of Colonel Oscar N. Solbert, head of the Psychological Warfare Branch of the War Department's MIS, proposed that African Americans and Japanese Americans could be employed to show domestic and global audiences that the United States denounced racism.[53] Solbert asserted that efforts should be made in the United

States to "lessen the strong racial prejudices existing in white Americans toward colored races, including the Negro," so that racism in the United States did not give "unwitting aid to the Japanese propaganda attempt to convert the Pacific war into a racialist, Pan Asia war" (p. 34). Like many others, Solbert was most concerned to perform America's disavowal of racism as a means to win the war rather than to abolish racism as an intrinsically important end. While he did not mention Japanese American internment, let alone its discontinuance, he noted that "publicity could be given to valuable work being done by Americans of Japanese ancestry" (p. 34) and that "action taken within this country to improve the conditions of the American Japanese would correlate admirably with propaganda into Japan" (p. 8). The first draft of Solbert's plan even included a recommendation to "recruit, uniform, and equip a Free Japanese Corps of Japanese subjects (coordinate with the Japanese corps in Free China) within the United States," and then baldly stated that these Japanese in America would be mobilized "nominally for combat but actually for symbolic use in propaganda" (p. 18).

The revised version of Solbert's propaganda plan omitted the idea that a military unit made up of Japanese in the United States could serve a useful propaganda function, possibly because the War Department at that time was moving away from utilization of Japanese Americans; but the idea continued to circulate among other individuals involved in policy making. Milton S. Eisenhower's role in the decision-making process appears to have been critical. It should be pointed out that Eisenhower, the youngest brother of the future president, was uniquely positioned to make the connection between Japanese Americans and propaganda: before moving to OWI, he had been the first director of the WRA, the civilian agency charged with managing the evacuated Japanese Americans. Eisenhower had written a detailed letter to McCloy in August 1942 in which he explained why OWI—an agency that had been established in June 1942 to keep the world at home and abroad informed about the status and aims of the war effort through "the press, radio, motion picture, and other facilities," and which became increasingly concerned over time with propaganda and psychological warfare abroad[54]—was particularly concerned about the matter. He began by noting that he understood that the War Department was then in the midst of considering whether to reverse its earlier decision to no longer use Japanese Americans in the military. After stating the need to mobilize all possible manpower resources for the war effort and vouching for the loyalty of "most Japanese born and educated in this country," Eisenhower pointed out that the exclusion of Japanese Americans from the military had made the race card available to the enemy in its propaganda war. Arguing for the necessity of making Japanese Americans subject to the draft, like their German American and Italian American counterparts, he warned that "the decision not to draft Japanese therefore invariably raises the racial issue—a thing we are anxious not to do particularly in the face of the enemy's eagerness to use the divide and conquer technique against us." Summing up, Eisenhower reasoned that if loyal Japanese were to be drafted, the morale of the Nisei's parents would be uplifted; "the enemy could no longer claim that we are discriminating against this minority; and we could press a vigorous story of Japanese-American participation to the enemy, laying the groundwork for a Free Japan movement when the time is ripe."[55]

One of the most well-developed and explicit arguments for the propaganda value of Japanese Americans and Japanese American soldiers was written by Edwin O. Reischauer.[56] On 14 September 1942, the same day that the secretary of war approved the Board of Officers' recommendation against the military utilization of Japanese American citizens, Reischauer completed a memorandum in which he took positions completely at odds with those of the board and most of its advisers. As is well known, Reischauer was to become one of the founding fathers of East Asian and especially Japanese studies in the postwar United States, and was ambassador to Japan from 1961 to 1966. Through his scholarly writings, popular books, and diplomatic efforts he would become one of the central architects of the Cold War U.S.-Japan relationship. No other figure has so completely exemplified the politics of knowledge production in postwar area studies in the Japan field.[57] However, in 1942 Reischauer was undoubtedly not a man of great power in either academia or government. To be sure, during the summer of 1941 he had worked for the State Department and written memos to the ambassador to Japan, Joseph Grew. In the summer of 1942, Assistant Secretary of War McCloy also personally arranged for Reischauer to establish a school in the Washington area for training army translators and cryptanalysts. In other words, while certainly known in Washington at the time that he wrote the memorandum, he was not a major actor in military or political circles. Instead, he was a thirty-one-year-old recent Ph.D. and an aspiring East Asian studies scholar at Harvard, who was sometimes sought out by the State and War Departments as a Japan expert, and whose ideas may have swayed those with more power.[58]

Yet putting aside for the moment the question of Reischauer's stature and personal influence as of September 1942, his memo is worth considering in some detail because it so neatly encapsulates the transnational logic by which those in power and their advisers linked the question of Japanese American admissibility into the military, and by extension the nation, with plans for winning the war and eventually achieving U.S. hegemony in Asia and beyond. Already at this early date, Reischuaer reasoned that while it was important to first win the war, the United States needed to prepare for "winning the peace" that would eventually come. On the basis of his acceptance of a logic of racial sameness between Japanese and Japanese Americans rather than difference by citizenship, he forcefully laid out a plan for winning this peace that linked and in some key respects conflated the two distinct matters of postwar policy toward Japan and the treatment of Japanese Americans. On the one hand, he unabashedly advocated establishment of a postwar "puppet regime," with Hirohito as "puppet." On the other hand, he also argued that Japanese Americans should be mobilized for enlistment into the United States armed forces and that the advantages of such a policy would be even more important in the postwar than in the wartime years.

In the first part of the memorandum, Reischauer explained why it was necessary to retain the Japanese emperor. He reasoned that while it would be imperative to "win the Japanese over to our system after this war," it would be difficult to do so because Japan had no "suitable scapegoats," unlike Germany and Italy, which had Nazi and fascist parties as well as Hitler and Mussolini. When the war ended in Allied victory, Reischauer believed, Germans and Italians could convince themselves that their "evil leaders" had been at fault and would readily come over to the U.S. side. In contrast, the Japanese people had no easy targets: "There is no party to be blamed, and there are few, if any, prominent individuals who could serve as scapegoats." This is where the emperor could play a positive role:

> A first step would naturally be to win over to our side a group willing to cooperate. Such a group, if it represented the minority of the Japanese people, would be in a sense a puppet regime. Japan has used the strategem [*sic*] of puppet governments extensively but with no great success because of the inadequacy of the puppets. But Japan itself has created the best possible puppet for our purposes, a puppet who not only could be won over to our side but who would carry with him a tremendous weight of authority, which Japan's puppets in China have always lacked. I mean, of course, the Japanese Emperor.

Reischauer showed no qualms about establishing and manipulating a puppet regime, even explicitly endorsing the possibility that such a regime might rest on the support of only a minority of the Japanese people. Ironically, Reischauer advised the U.S. leadership to emulate and even improve on Japan's wartime strategy in Manchukuo and with Wang Jingwei's collaborationist regime ("Japan's puppets"), by establishing a new puppet regime in Japan headed by the emperor. In other words, Reischauer proposed that the United States should properly do in Japan what Japan had done ineffectively in China. Put differently: if, as Prasenjit Duara has evocatively argued, Manchukuo was more like Japan's client state than a colony in the post–World War I years—a period when the spread of the ideology of self-determination and rising local nationalisms made direct colonial rule increasingly difficult as a practical strategy of domination—then Manchukuo and the Wang Jingwei regime ought to be considered prefigurations of postwar Asian states, beginning with Japan, under U.S. neo-imperialism.[59] Of course there are differences, but it is striking how Reischauer unabashedly turned Japan's wartime imperialist strategy toward Asia into a handy model for postwar U.S. policy in the same region. Reischauer further elaborated on the perfect puppet that Japan had already produced:

as things are measured in Japan, he [the emperor] is a liberal and a man of peace at heart. It is not improbable that he could be won over to a policy of co-operation with the United Nations far more easily than the vast majority of his subjects. He, and possibly he alone, could influence his people to repudiate their present military leadership. If he proves to have the potentialities of a real leader like his grandfather, so much the better. If he proves to be no more able than his *half-demented father*, his value as a symbol of cooperation and good will can still be extremely valuable. (emphasis added)

Reischauer's recommendations for the treatment of the emperor and his image came with his full recognition that as of September 1942, the U.S. media was not averse to portraying Hirohito as a nearly demonic character and that the U.S. populace tended to associate him with the Japanese military's savagery. Within this context Reischauer stressed that if the United States wished to mobilize the emperor to win the peace, it would be necessary to dissuade the media from circulating such representations.

To keep the Emperor available as a valuable ally or puppet in the post-war ideological battle we must keep him unsullied by the present war. In other words, we cannot allow him to be portrayed to the American people as the counterpart of Hitler and Mussolini in Asia or as the personification of the Japanese brand of totalitarianism. General reviling of the Emperor by our press or radio can easily ruin his utility to us in the post-war world. It would make the American people unprepared to cooperate with him or even to accept him as a tool, and naturally it would make the Emperor himself and the men who surround him less ready to cooperate with our government.

Thus, he concluded his section on the emperor:

During the past several months there has been considerable use of the name Hirohito as a symbol of the evil Japanese system. *With the post-war problem in mind, it would be highly advisable for the government to induce the news-disseminating organs of this country to avoid reference to the Emperor as far as possible and to use individuals, such as Tojo or Yamamoto or even a mythical tooth-some Mr. Moto (in uniform!) as personifications of the Japan we are fighting.* (emphasis added)

The meaning of this statement is perhaps clear enough, but it may be well worth highlighting Reischauer's casual suggestion that as long as Hirohito could be protected from vilification by the media, the "news-disseminating organs" might even use the culturally racist stereotype of "Mr. Moto" to personify Japan. Mr. Moto, it will be remembered, was a fictional "Japanese" figure in U.S. popular culture with a reputation for being sly, seemingly invincible, and potentially duplicitous—first as a spy in novels and then later in films as the sneaky and inscrutable detective who practiced "jūjutsu" and often pretended to befriend white peoples.

The second "and more important" part of the memorandum concerned the propaganda role that Japanese Americans and especially Japanese American soldiers could play in winning the war and the peace. Reischauer warned that Japan was attempting to turn the war into a "holy crusade of the yellow and brown peoples for freedom from the white race," and he feared that "the Japanese might well be able to transform the struggle in Asia in reality into a full-scale racial war." Reischauer introduced the Japanese American issue only in connection with his desire to counter Japanese propaganda that represented the Allies as racists. He expressed no sympathy toward the interned Japanese Americans. Indeed, he justified their confinement as a military necessity and even blamed them for burdening the government with the costs of their surveillance and relocation. He unabashedly employed a language of human accounting that was widespread among military and civilian officials concerned about the "Japanese problem" in the United States: "*Up to the present the Americans of Japanese ancestry have been a sheer liability* to our cause, on the one hand presenting a major problem of population relocation and military surveillance in this country and on the other hand affording the Japanese in Asia with a trump propaganda card. We should reverse this situation and *make of these American citizens a major asset in our ideological war in Asia*" (emphasis added).

Japanese Americans, he asserted, could be used in a global propaganda campaign to prove that the war was not a "racial war to preserve white privilege in Asia, but a war to establish a better world order for all, regardless of race, and when the military victory is achieved, these American citizens of Japanese ancestry could serve as an opening wedge into the minds and hearts of the Japanese people." He suggested that while Japanese Americans might contribute to the war effort in many ways, one of the most effective would be for them to join the armed forces. By fighting enthusiastically for the United States, they could show that the nation did not practice racism, and such a demonstration would be important in winning not only the war but also the peace. Most importantly, he imagined that if Japanese American soldiers could participate in the postwar occupation, the Japanese people would be more willing to cooperate with the victorious nations. He concluded, "The enthusiastic and active participation of 100,000 Japanese Americans and of these Japanese American troops in the cause of the United Nations could be made into a tremendous strategical advantage in the great struggle to win the peace in Asia."

To be sure, Reischauer may not have been the first to suggest that the United States should manipulate the imperial symbol for its own ends rather than criticize the institution. In his propaganda plans of May 1942, cited above, Colonel Oscar N. Solbert, like Reischauer, had argued that the emperor could have great utility in rehabilitating Japan into a peaceful nation. Solbert explained that propaganda efforts toward Japan should seek to insert a wedge between the military and the emperor. The Japanese people should be told that their military government represented neither their interests nor the "desires of the present emperor" (p. 10). Solbert implied no particular liking or sympathy for the emperor, even proposing that "occasional attacks on the Emperor might be requested from the Chinese. . . . Such attacks— allegations, for example, that the Emperor is nothing but a plain, rather stupid human being—would come better from a Far Eastern people than from Westerners" (p. 33). But as a strategy to further U.S. national interests, he felt that respect for the emperor should be given and "he should be presented as a unhappy friend of peace and constitutionalism." By dissociating the emperor from the military, Solbert maintained, the emperor could be transformed from a symbol of war into one of peace. As his May 23 draft put it, "since the Emperor is the focus of Emperor-worship, he is a symbol which can be used to justify political and military action. In the past, the military leaders of Japan have exploited the symbolic aspect of the Emperor for their militaristic schemes. Nevertheless, it is possible to use the Emperor-symbol (not his name) in justifying criticism of the military authority, and in strengthening the case for a return to peace" (p. 33).[60]

Nevertheless, a great deal of evidence suggests that Reischauer and his memo exerted considerable influence among key propaganda strategists and postwar planners, including Solbert himself. For example, echoing the points that Reischauer's memo had made about the need to protect Hirohito's name from attack by the media while scapegoating other Japanese leaders, the 3 November 1942 minutes of the OWI's Board of War Information indicate that it supported "a recommendation from the Bureau of Intelligence [within the OWI] to the effect that the information policy against the use of the name 'Hirohito' as a symbol for the Japanese enemy should be rigidly enforced and, secondly, that OWI ought to devise and popularize the use of some other symbol for the Japanese enemy. . . . With respect to the use of the name 'Hirohito' in official governmental speeches, Mr. Cowles [director of the Domestic Branch within OWI] agreed to call the attention of the Bureau of Publications and Graphics to the established policy in the matter."[61] Elmer Davis, the director of the OWI, associated his agency's policy explicitly with Reischauer in a letter sent to Ralph Barton Perry, the eminent Harvard professor who had originally passed on the Reischauer memorandum to Undersecretary of War Robert P. Patterson. In this 7 November 1942 communication he acknowledged: "Our propaganda to Japan has thus far followed the lines indicated by Dr. Reischauer in the memo you were kind enough to send me on September 17 [that is, Reischauer's memo of 14 September 1942]. Perhaps you will be interested to know that we are trying to arrange to borrow the services of Dr. Reischauer for a number of hours each week." Furthermore, in a handwritten note to Elmer Davis, Solbert (who was on detail from the army to OWI) summarized the main points of Reischauer's memo, jotted down some brief information concerning how the memo had been routed and commented on, and then stated that "Reischauer's recommenda[tion] been in our plans for propag vs Japan from beginning."[62]

To further appreciate the precocity of Reischauer's stance on the emperor, it would be good to recall that according to Nakamura Masanori's study of Joseph Grew and Grew's pivotal role in producing the postwar "symbolic emperor system," it was not until March 1943, a full half year after Reischauer's memo, that Grew most likely began to place his hopes on Hirohito and the so-called moderate element in Japan.[63] This was around the time that other State Department officials began giving serious attention to the imperial question.[64] Reischauer did not necessarily characterize the Japanese people as fanatics. Nor did he resort to the insect metaphor employed by Grew, who later likened the Japanese people to bees whose hive would disintegrate if they lost their queen bee, the emperor.[65] Nevertheless, this man who has been known to the world primarily as a Japanophile and great friend of the Japanese people showed remarkable disregard for the Japanese people themselves and gross condescension toward the very imperial institution that he wished to preserve. For him, even a "half-demented" emperor would do. Furthermore, unlike Grew, who sought to protect the imperial institution but never argued that Hirohito himself should remain on the throne, Reischauer proposed precisely this postwar plan at a time when it was impossible to determine when the war would end or what Hirohito's ultimate role and responsibilities in the war would be.

Similarly, while it is not possible to prove the direct influence of Reischauer's memo on the reversal of the Board of Officers' recommendation against Japanese American soldiering, it is the earliest document in a cluster of key documents put together by the War Department's Organization and Training Division (General Staff) under the label "Enlistment of loyal American citizens of Japanese descent into the Army and Navy." These materials show that at the critical moment in the debate on Japanese Americans in the military, Reischauer's memo found its way into the office of Assistant Secretary of War John J. McCloy through the American Defense Harvard Group, a patriotic organization headed by Ralph Barton Perry. The memo initially went from Perry to Undersecretary of War Patterson, who then forwarded it to McCloy with the comment that "the attached paper concerning American citizens of Japanese descent suggests that they could be usefully employed in the Army."[66]

Reischauer's direct impact on policy concerning the Japanese emperor and Japanese Americans was thus neither decisive nor inconsequential. Yet for my purposes, it is less important to dwell on his influence than to analyze his ideas for what they tell us about a structure of thought that went far beyond one individual. Indeed, what the above contextualization of Reischauer's memorandum suggests is that his formulation of strategies was symptomatic of an emerging elite (and, needless to say, white) American instrumentalist understanding of Japan and Japanese Americans that persisted through the war years and then became a part of common sense in the postwar United States. In his proposal to establish what I will call a "puppet emperor system" in Japan, Reischauer showed little concern for the conditions of the common Japanese people, or even, for that matter, the emperor. Nevertheless, the puppet emperor system was eventually realized when the political and military elite in the United States and Japan, as well as Hirohito himself, collaborated after the war to refashion the monarchy as the core of the so-called symbolic emperor system. While they shielded the emperor from public criticism as well as prosecution at the International Military Tribunal for the Far East, they targeted Tōjō and a limited number of "militarists" for scapegoating, just as Reischauer had advised only nine months after the Pearl Harbor attack and almost three years before the war's end.[67]

Furthermore, just as Reischauer had advised, Japanese Americans not only came to serve in the military during the war but also participated in large numbers in the U.S. Occupation of Japan. Yet in sharp contrast to public statements made by the wartime state and its highest officials—including President Roosevelt, who claimed that the decision to accept Japanese into the military was based on democratic principles and the rejection of racism—the Reischauer memorandum and other documents analyzed here make it clear that nothing mattered more to policy makers and their advisers than the utility of Japanese Americans in the strategic imperative of launching a psychological war against the Japanese and providing material to counter Japanese propaganda in Asia. The question of Japanese Americans' rights as citizens and of redress for racist acts against them, beginning with their mass incarceration, was not a major consideration. The memo and its context also demonstrate how the transwar (meaning the period encompassing the hot and cold wars) passage of the Japanese in America from the outside to the inside of the national community and the turn away from "vulgar racism" cannot be completely understood within the narrow frame of national history. This is not to suggest that international factors outweighed domestic ones, but to insist that the fate of Japanese Americans was overdetermined by global and national forces.

THE PASSAGE FROM THE OUTSIDE TO THE INSIDE OF THE U.S. POPULATION

On 23 January 1943, ten teams of American soldiers reported to Washington, D.C., for a ten-day training program conducted by the provost marshal general. Each team consisted of a white officer and three sergeants, two white and the other Japanese American. The program's purpose was to prepare these men for the task of determining the loyalty of each of the American adult citizens of Japanese ancestry who were then confined in ten internment camps. The training program had become necessary because, as we have seen, the War Department had just reversed its earlier policy following the Pearl Harbor attack of severely limiting Japanese American military service, and also because a labor shortage had pressured the government to release internees for work outside the camps. After they completed the program, the trainees would depart for the camps, where one of their primary tasks would be to take the lead in determining individual loyalty through interviews and questionnaires so that those deemed loyal could, if they wished, join the army or work in the civilian sector.

During the training program the teams' members heard a number of speakers, including representatives from the WRA, ONI, and various offices and agencies within the War Department. Collectively, the speakers revealed that a massive shift had taken place throughout the civilian and military bureaucracies with regard to the official view on the Japanese in America. The entire premise of the mass evacuation of Japanese Americans from the West Coast had been that they were racially different, that they were unassimilable, and that no individual determinations of loyalty to the United States could be made. As the Japanese-American Branch of the Office of the Provost Marshal General described this logic even immediately after the war, "[N]ever had a minority group of this country been subjected to so positive and definite a mass, though justifiable, discrimination."[68] However, these speakers now tried to reverse this logic and convince the team members that except in some very superficial ways Japanese Americans were not biologically different from whites, that they were in most cases loyal to the United States, and that they were not all alike. They stressed that every Japanese American was an individual and that therefore loyalty could be assessed on a case-by-case basis. Those deemed loyal would then be allowed to join the military, work in mainstream society, and live among the white population. Some speakers went even further to emphasize the importance of caring for the lives and welfare of Japanese Americans. Paralleling the wartime movement of Koreans from the outside to the inside of the Japanese population, Japanese in America ironically found themselves transported from the outside to the inside of the American population, only shortly after being removed from the West Coast and put into camps.

In his introductory remarks to the team members, Colonel A. C. Miller, who had been charged with conducting the program, explained that Japanese American citizens were on the whole loyal and that "it is foolish for loyal United States citizens to be deprived of the opportunity to render useful service in winning this war."[69] Colonel William P. Scobey, from the Office of the Assistant Secretary of War, further emphasized that "a great many, virtually all, Nissei [sic] or American-born Japanese, have had the same cultural background as you and I. Their color and their eyes are a little different but they attended the same universities, ate at the same soda fountains, played the same games." He told his listeners that he felt confident about the loyalty of most Japanese Americans and that he wanted some of them to serve in the military and thereby help him realize his desire to "march down the burning streets of Tokyo."[70]

Perhaps the most enthusiastic denunciation of vulgar and biological racism came from Lieutenant Commander Cecil H. Coggins of the ONI, whom military and civilian government leaders regarded as an expert on Japanese and Japanese Americans. Coggins argued that Japanese Americans were no different from any other Americans: "It is a very fundamental mistake in the United States that because a man is a descendant of Japanese that he thinks as Japanese do. That is entirely wrong. A Nissei [sic] thinks like any other American boy who has lived in the same environment exactly. There is nothing in his brain cells or in his cerebral contributions which make him think along oriental lines, none whatever."[71]

During the January 1943 training program, the ironic wartime incorporation of Japanese Americans into the welfare state was most explicitly expressed by E. R. Fryer, deputy director of the WRA, and Calvert L. Dedrick, chief economist in the Office of the Assistant Secretary of War. Fryer first informed the teams that the "hysteria of Pearl Harbor" had died down and that the "growing demand in the country for manpower" had led to some significant changes in "public attitude." And then he went on to explain that camp internees were being provided with what he called "community services," including schools, elected community councils, hospitals, nursing services, and various types of "curative and preventive medicine, all things having to do with sanitation, sanitation inspection and so forth."[72]

With the cold rationality of a man dedicated to employing statistics to monitor and control populations, Dedrick informed the program participants about the U.S. Japanese population's characteristics and how the Census Bureau had used this knowledge in the swift evacuation of this group from the West Coast. He was certainly in a position to know: as one of the most senior of the Census Bureau's technical staff, he had been sent to San Francisco in late February 1942 to assist the army's Western Defense Command in the evacuation and internment of Japanese Americans. Dedrick explained how knowledge compiled by the Census Bureau had been used to locate, assemble, and evacuate this group en masse with no intention of assessing the loyalty of any individual. "Our first step was to set up an area. We split this area of the West Coast into 108 evacuation units, averaging approximately 1,000 persons per unit. We evacuated all together about 110,500 people in the 108 units." Dedrick described how the Japanese families in each evacuation unit had been registered and one representative from each family had been interviewed. He explained that these interviews were very simple and that there had been no attempt to determine individual loyalty.[73]

At the same time that Dedrick's lecture showed how cold, calculating, rational, and unconcerned with the question of loyalty the military and civilian authorities had been at the time of the evacuation, he also called attention to the medical and health services eventually provided to the evacuees. From basic medical services to women's prenatal care, hospitalization, food, clothing, and counseling with social welfare workers—all these, he noted, had been provided at government expense. In addition, each evacuee had been given a medical inspection at the assembly centers, and those suspected of having contagious diseases were isolated. Finally, after pointing to the presence of hospitals both in the assembly centers, which were the first places where the evacuees were housed, and at the ten permanent "relocation centers" that were used through the rest of the war years, he again stated as a matter of plain fact: "as far as I have been able to determine by statistics, there were fewer deaths out of the Japanese population from March to November (1942) than during the past. There were fewer Japanese who died before reaching a proper age. There was a general prolongation of life."[74]

It would be naive to believe that the military and civilian authorities had prioritized the "general prolongation of life" of the Japanese Americans at the time of the evacuation. To be sure, the authorities clearly wished to prevent the spread of communicable diseases and toward that end had administered medical examinations and inoculations. But this was not for the benefit solely of the evacuees, since epidemics could spread to communities outside the assembly centers and camps. Moreover, the authorities obviously had little initial regard for the health of evacuees, who were placed in extremely crowded and unsanitary conditions in the assembly centers—most of which had been converted out of public facilities for animals. In his analysis of why so many individuals in the central Utah "relocation center" had resented the registration program and its loyalty questionnaire, the anthropologist and community analyst John F. Embree identified the past experience of horrific conditions in the assembly centers as one extremely important factor. As he put it: "The psychological wounds of the evacuation period, especially the bitter experiences of Tanforan under wretched social and physical conditions, cannot be underestimated. (E.g., racially biased administrators and housing in stables not properly cleaned of old manure.)"[75] Reports by the United States Public Health Service as well as the army similarly admitted as much.[76]

The locations for the ten permanent relocation centers had likewise not been selected with a concern for the health of the internees. As is well-known, the army had built the camps in extremely inhospitable conditions—in the desert, high plains, or swampland—which presented special health problems, beyond crowding, that few Japanese Americans would have faced had they remained in their communities. These included extreme heat leading to infant deaths, food and water contamination, dust-related illnesses, and malaria.[77] In other words, from the spring to fall of 1942 while Japanese Americans were being evacuated, confined in assembly centers, and then transferred to more permanent relocation centers, the military and civilian authorities had in fact exposed this population to many new health challenges.

What Dedrick's statement on the "prolongation" of Japanese American lives nonetheless reveals is that at least by January 1943, with the WRA clearly responding to civilian manpower needs and with the decision firmly made to open the army to Japanese American volunteers, the military and civilian authorities and bureaucrats were in a position to boast that their treatment of the evacuees had led not just to their successful segregation and confinement but to the enhancement of their life and welfare. The policy of universal access to health care for internees, which had begun in the assembly centers, was now ironically to develop in tandem with managing the relocation centers. For example, according to one nurse at the Granada camp, the medical staff kept files on all babies and preschool children, providing "well baby care" as well as education for mothers (see figure 1).[78] The internees even received dental care, a form of medical attention that many Japanese Americans had gone without before internment, or had resorted to only in emergencies. While certainly far from comprehensive for all inmates at the assembly centers, this service was so improved in the internment camps that a number of camps had more dentists than were needed, leaving some idle.[79] Moreover, under legislative provisions that allowed special welfare assistance for those displaced by the government who were in need, throughout 1943 and 1944 the Social Security Board provided such aid to hundreds of internees who had been resettled in communities outside the camps.[80] For those who remained in the camps, a social welfare staff assisted in resolving family problems and difficulties involving the old, sick, orphans, and delinquent children.[81] Shortly after closing the camps, the WRA issued reports indicating that the internees had been provided with excellent health care, even noting that they had better overall survival rates than the U.S. population at large.[82]

The limited if pioneering empirical scholarship on health care for Japanese Americans in the assembly centers and internment camps has been divided between those who have given the health services in these places relatively high marks and those who have emphasized their deficiencies.[83] However, in framing my problematic I ask not whether health services were adequate but how the neglect of and then relative increase in concern with the health and welfare of interned Japanese Ameri-

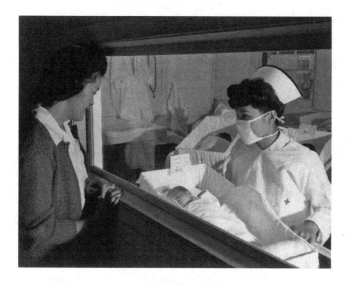

FIGURE 1.
Pro-natalist, bio-political inclusion in the American welfare state.
"Woman looking through window at baby being held by nurse
in maternity ward." Manzanar Relocation Center. Ansel Adams,
photographer. Courtesy of the Library of Congress, Prints and
Photographs Division.

cans might be related to the shift from vulgar to polite racism. Clearly, these spaces of confinement were established as manifestations of a vulgar racism that had conflated the treatment of Japanese Americans with animals and given little thought to their health. The point was to segregate and confine them—to defend society against them—even if it meant evacuating them to extremely harsh environments that were both physically and psychologically challenging. However, paralleling the shift toward the incorporation of those deemed loyal into the civilian and military labor force and the global propaganda campaign to demonstrate that the United States condemned racism, the government's agencies increasingly sought to respond to internees' health needs. As the war against Japan progressed, the state made an unprecedented commitment to make the Japanese in America live and to welcome them into the nation. Ironically, most of this pastoral activity, in the Foucauldian sense of nurturing lives and guiding conduct, took place in the very spaces of confinement that the army had constructed in order to segregate and confine this despised minority. In other words, the wartime inclusion of Japanese into the political and bio-political nation took place in precisely the sites that had originally symbolized their exclusion from the national community.

To be sure, many white Americans refused to accept the Japanese into the national community or to treat them as fully human. The WRA campaign to governmentalize the camps so that they might become mini-Americas and then to release the loyal back into mainstream society drew a severe backlash in the vulgar racist mode. In January 1943, under pressure to transfer administration of the camps away from the WRA to the War Department, a subcommittee of the Senate Committee on Military Affairs launched an investigation into the civilian agency. At one of its hearings to consider a bill to authorize such a change, Senator Monrad C. Wallgren of Washington, who had introduced the bill, voiced his distrust of all Japanese, saying that "a Jap would be an awfully good dog right up to the point that he can pull something." At a later hearing his colleague Senator Chan Gurney of South Dakota did not use an animal metaphor but bluntly pointed out that because the Japanese "are of a different race than most of us in this country," they "should report regularly on their whereabouts if released under the WRA's leave program."[84]

Reflecting the tension between the vulgar racism still entrenched in the general population and the WRA's emphasis on sustaining human lives, many of the complaints concerned food. Especially through early 1944, politicians, the press, and the populace at large often charged that the inmates in the "Jap camps" were being treated too humanely, and then claimed that the "Japs" had too much to eat, including "fancy food items" and baby food. After Congressman J. Parnell Thomas (of New Jersey) visited the West Coast in May 1943 as a member of the Dies Committee (more formally, the Special Committee on Un-American Activities, the forerunner of the infamous House Un-American Activities Committee), he "accused WRA of pampering and overfeeding the evacuees" and also called for immediately ending the "WRA policy of releasing disloyal Japs."[85] One post of the Veterans of Foreign Wars located in Ogden, Utah, passed a resolution on 1 September 1943 in which it not only criticized the government's policy of allowing released Japanese Americans to "move freely throughout the State of Utah," fill the jobs of "American Labor," and be inducted into the military; it also demanded that all Japanese regardless of citizenship be treated as prisoners of war and "legislation be initiated immediately to remove all Japanese from the United States within six months following the close of the war."[86]

In his history of the WRA and his role as its director, Dillon Myer commented on the virulence of this reactionary onslaught from such quarters as the American Legion, the Hearst press, the *Los Angeles Times*, the Committee on Military Affairs of the Senate, the Dies Committee of the House, and other lesser forces and categorized them as "race-baiters" and "racist groups." Despite scholarly works that have placed Myer himself within a long history of U.S. racism,[87] Myer's assessment of others as racists and himself and most of his WRA colleagues as presumably free of racism ought to be understood less as disingenuous than as representative of the new kind of racism that I have been describing. Myer embodied the evolving character of racism in the United States, moving away from the crudeness of those against whom Myer fought as defender of the WRA to his polite brand of racism, which disavowed its own discriminatory assumptions and practices even as it continued to contain Japanese American freedoms behind barbed wire.[88]

In January–February and July 1943, when Dillon Myer went before the Chandler Subcommittee of the Senate Committee on Military Affairs and the Costello Subcommittee of the Dies Committee, respectively, he defended what he regarded as the WRA's humane treatment of camp internees and its position that loyal Japanese Americans should be resettled in outside communities. To the senators Myer emphasized that the Japanese population in America had to be "absorbed" or assimilated into mainstream (white) communities as quickly as possible, while the war was still being fought. Otherwise, after the war the United States would be saddled with a racial problem not unlike that presented by "Indian reservations." He preferred that as many as possible of these Japanese relocate to areas other than the West Coast, so as to "dispose of a racial problem." Myer insisted that the management of this population would have global repercussions, for "the Japanese militaristic government has been trying to prove for some time that this is a racial war, that it is the orientals against the whites. I don't think that we should contribute to their theory by making this a racial issue."[89]

Similarly, at the July House hearing he stressed that the WRA program was being watched not only in Japan but also in "China, India, Thailand, Burma, and many other countries whose collaboration we need if we are to defeat our enemies with a minimum loss of life." And one of his central and most strenuously argued points was that criticisms of the WRA's humane administrative practices had the effect of "providing the enemy with material which can be used to convince the peoples of the Orient that the United States is undemocratic and is fighting a racial war."[90]

In their history published immediately after the war, *WRA: A Story of Human Conservation*, WRA staff likewise cited an official Japanese radio broadcast made at "the height of the congressional investigation of the WRA program" to imply that the Japanese had used Congress's attacks on the WRA to paint the United States as hypocritical on the race issue. "The Anglo-Saxon race feels superior to the Asiatics," the broadcaster had said. "Latest happenings [in the United States] show that their slogan, equal rights for all the people, is nothing but a lie." The WRA's writers had worried about reprisals against American POWs if the Japanese Americans were not well treated. But more importantly, they claimed that in order to win the support of "vast millions of people" in the "Orient" as well as other "non-white people" in "Latin America, Africa, and the South Pacific islands," it had been of vital necessity to keep the humanitarian WRA program on track. "[I]f the program had taken a different turn at some of its crucial stages," they insisted, "the repercussions might have been felt thousands of miles away and for many years to come." In short, U.S. leadership needed to act as if it did not countenance racism—it had to act as if Japanese Americans were entitled to treatment as humans—because the whole world was watching.[91]

Thus despite the resistance of the vulgar racist reactionaries to the "decent" treatment of Japanese Americans, global and domestic conditions came together to usher in the dominance of Myer's brand of polite racism and passage of Japanese Americans into the political and bio-political nation. In fact, the discourse on Japanese American loyalty and military service—especially the possibility of their deaths—made it extremely difficult for critics of the WRA's supposedly overindulgent treatment of the internees to succeed in their efforts to bring back the harsher and more parsimonious rule of the vulgar racists. When on 28 January 1943 the Bureau of Public Relations announced the War Department's intention to form an all–Japanese American army unit, the chairman of the Senate subcommittee, Albert B. Chandler of Kentucky, had little choice but to patriotically read the bureau's press release into the official record.

Titled "Loyal Americans of Japanese ancestry to compose special unit in Army," the bureau's announcement indicated that the unit was being formed not for propaganda purposes but because of the "many earnest requests by loyal American citizens of Japanese extraction for the organization of a special unit of the Army in which they could have their share in the fight against the Nation's enemies." The release also included a statement from Secretary of War Henry Stimson, insisting that the military did not tolerate racist discrimination. "It is the inherent right of every faithful citizen, regardless of ancestry," he had said, "to bear arms in the Nation's battles." Concluding his reading of the release, Chairman Chandler could only comment: "That speaks for itself." And Senator Joseph C. O'Mahoney of Wyoming summed up what seems to have been the prevailing sentiment in the room after several days of testimony: "The principles for which we are fighting the war can be felt and acted upon by peoples of all nationalities and of all races. If we really believe in democracy we believe that the Japanese and the Germans alike can develop those principles, and I think our policy should be to encourage them whenever possible."[92]

Similarly, at the end of the hearing on 11 February 1943, after Myer had summarized the WRA's avowedly anti-racist position, Senator Mahoney asked that President Roosevelt's 1 February letter to Stimson approving the special Japanese American combat team and denouncing racism be entered into the record.[93] In April and May, far from recommending passage of the bill to take the camps out of the WRA's liberal hands, Senator Chandler's subcommittee drew conclusions that essentially supported the WRA and even went beyond the War Department by suggesting that the Selective Service Act should again apply to loyal Japanese Americans.[94]

Even the WRA's foremost detractors on the Costello Subcommittee, including its chair, gradually shifted their position. As Assistant Secretary of War McCloy put it in a telephone conversation, "[T]hey started to lacerate Dillon Myer but they ended up by listening to him."[95] And in their final report of 30 September 1943, the subcommittee sided with the WRA by recommending segregation of disloyal from loyal internees, establishment of a board to investigate those who sought release from camps, and a program of Americanization for those who remained.[96]

Camp administrators continued to portray themselves as the defenders of democracy, equality, freedom, and Japanese American welfare. Accordingly, WRA personnel titled their short history of the agency *WRA: A Story of Human Conservation,* as if to say that their main purpose had been to conserve liberty and human life. Standing in for the state, they arrogated to themselves the right to make the internees live, although the flip side of that right was the demand that Japanese American men expose themselves to death in military service. As the highest WRA embodiment of this sovereign power, Director Myer struggled against the "race-baiters" to nurture Japanese American lives, but at the same time he celebrated their military service and sacrifice, even sending a personalized letter of condolence to every mother in the camps who lost a son on the battlefield.

. . .

In this chapter I have argued that the debate over inclusion of Japanese Americans in the military was really a discussion about whether they should be treated as American citizens located at the core of the bio-political regime, and made to live, or remain segregated, without aid, and exempt from the apparent benefits of liberal society. During these debates about Japanese American admissibility as citizens and as soldiers, the necessity of mobilizing all human and material resources to carry out total war placed incessant pressure on those enamored of old-fashioned vulgar racism—and in the end, they were forced to retreat, if not disappear. The material exigencies of total war pressed the racist state and its leaders to disavow racism and bring Japanese Americans inside the U.S. regime of governmentality—but not without one last victory of the vulgar racists in the September 1942 Board of Officers' decision to discontinue Japanese American military inductions and a reactionary backlash in civil society that lasted in its most intense form until at least early 1944 and, I would suggest, continues as an undercurrent into the present.

I have also tried to show that while the imperative of total human mobilization continued to impress the military and civilian political elite, the decision about whether to welcome Japanese Americans into the army, and by extension the nation, was ultimately also tied to perceptions of how the treatment of the Japanese American minority would affect the state's ability to manage race far beyond the limited issue of Japanese Americans. In the period when U.S. counterintelligence spread a race panic about a Japanese-led global movement of the "darker races" against white supremacy, not even the imperative for manpower mobilization could overcome the perceived necessity of containing Japanese Americans and segregating them not only from whites but from African Americans as well. Such a logic was coupled with a determination to exterminate the Japanese "over there" and pre-empt their drive for empire.

From the fall of 1942 into the following winter, however, a massive shift took place in the domestic and global strategy for managing race in the interests of national strength and empire. As exemplified in the Reischauer memo and the statements of so many other military and civilian officials, U.S. leadership came to be dominated by the view that the continued exclusion of Japanese Americans from the national community threatened to undermine America's ability to win the war and the peace that would follow, because such a stance would make it impossible to capture allies of color—or, as Reischauer put it, the "yellow and brown peoples." Power then shifted away from its more negative form—the exclusion and confinement of those ascribed by race as dangerous, and the separation of people of color not only from the white majority but from each other as well—to a positive logic of inclusion, assimilation, the disavowal of racism, and incorporation of people of color, either as members of the national community or as citizens of allied nations. In the postwar era, as Reischauer recommended, this order would include even Japan and its people.

Therefore, Reischauer's memo and its more general context suggest that the war itself was not simply the moment when the United States sought to destroy Japan in what John W. Dower once described as a "war without mercy,"[97] not simply a time when racism against Japanese Americans led solely to their incarceration and exclusion from white America. Instead, it was also ironically the period during which plans were laid, and in some ways put into practice, for the incorporation of Japan, its emperor, and Japanese Americans into a new U.S. global hegemony, with America now cast as inclusive of Asians. These plans for the preservation of whatever might be useful for "winning the peace" were as much a part of the war as the nuclear destructions of Hiroshima and Nagasaki, the firebombings of Japan's major cities, the killing of at least 100,000 civilians in the Battle of Okinawa, and the trauma imposed on Japanese Americans by the experience of evacuation and incarceration.

State strategies toward Japanese Americans, on the one hand, and Japan, on the other, were thus homological and shifted together. The denunciation of vulgar racism toward Japanese Americans meshed with the denial that the war against Japan was a race war. The inclusion of Japanese Americans into the national community was coupled to the imperial ambition to incorporate Japan and Asia into a new postwar U.S. hegemony in the Asia-Pacific region. Paralleling the new idea that loyal Japanese Americans could be distinguished from the disloyal, it seemed now that the vast majority of the Japanese people and their emperor were essentially (if imperfectly) decent human beings who could be distinguished from the evil military clique.

However, the instrumentalist considerations leading to these shifts virtually guaranteed that even as Japanese Americans would be welcomed into the new regime of governmentality, and even as statesmen and bureaucrats laid plans to reconstitute the Japanese into America's closest allies in the region, racism would not miraculously evaporate. We have seen that the Japanese Americans' utility as labor as well as their role as performers in the national disavowal of racism, not their rights as citizens or the impulse to redress racist acts against them, had most influenced the political and military elite. At base, Reischauer's unabashed and calculating ability to propose policies that would affect the lives and deaths of millions of Japanese and hundreds of thousands of Japanese Americans in Hawaii and the mainland United States stemmed from his otherization of both and his inclusionary hierarchization of the "yellow and brown" peoples within the "we" of both the national and global communities. From his understanding that he and others like him were the privileged subject-citizens of the United States, and that the United States was the privileged subject of global politics, Reischauer easily linked together the problems of Japan's emperor system and of the Japanese minority in the United States.

Reischauer's instrumentalist understanding of minorities would reappear in yet another problematic form in the early postwar years when he dismissed the intrinsic importance of resolving the postcolonial issue of Koreans in Japan. Ignoring the facts that some two million Koreans had been displaced to the Japanese metropole alone during the prewar and wartime years, that many had died attempting to return to Korea, that all Koreans had been unilaterally stripped of their status as Japanese nationals and thereby became ineligible for almost all forms of relief or benefits from the Japanese government, that they faced continuing discrimination and violence in Japan—ignoring all of these harsh realities and more, Reischauer wrote in the May 1951 preface to a pioneering study of Koreans in Japan that "the minority problems of Northeast Asia are not as serious as those of some areas." While he expressed no concern about the plight of the Korean minority in Japan, he made it clear that he worried about them because of their apparent sympathies with communism. He complained that "the Koreans in postwar Japan have created many annoying complications for the American occupation forces," and he criticized them for being "an unassimilable minority" and "a source of irritation and embarrassment to American groups in Japan and to the United Nations forces in Korea."[98] Here it is tempting to conclude that Reischauer's wartime racial thinking and instrumentalist appropriation of minorities melded easily with a rabid postwar anticommunism.

Moreover, even as America's leaders and their liberal advisers came to explain human differences as matters of culture rather than nature, they continued to employ images of Japanese and Japanese American as animals. To be sure, with some important exceptions, they tended not to use those representations of the Japanese as the lesser primates, reptiles, mice, rats, cockroaches, lice, and the like that the popular press and the military mobilized during wartime to dehumanize and enable the killing of the Japanese enemy, or to normalize the confinement of Japanese Americans in assembly centers and then relocation camps.[99] Instead, the highest men in government and the military routinely and without embarrassment continued to refer to loyal Japanese as sheep and the suspect ones as goats. When he was called in by the Chandler Subcommittee as an expert on Japan and the Japanese, for example, Joseph Grew testified that the government's main task regarding Japanese Americans was "separating the goats from the sheep." Nisei loyalty had nothing to do with "Japanese blood," he maintained, and he thought it vital not to alienate these elements by ascribing disloyalty to the Japanese Americans as a race.[100]

Sheep served as perfect metaphors for a liberalized racism, for they invite the desire not for extermination but for a relationship of what might be called "conviviality,"[101] or literally a living together. For these are not beasts, vermin, or pests but domesticated animals with whom humans might live in an intimate, caregiving, and useful relationship, with of course complete clarity about who should guide conduct and who actualized the sovereign power over life and death. Nevertheless, liberal racism's animal talk also strongly intimated that Japanese Americans were still somehow almost naturally a flock different from the majority white population. Here again we see how culture could stand in for nature in separating and giving an almost biological reason for making these good sheep the object of continuing special surveillance and suspicion.

Finally, the newly reformed polite racists could easily slip back into more menacing metaphors of animality. As we have already seen, despite his liberal view that the majority of Japanese Americans were loyal and could be separated from the disloyal, Joseph Grew did not hesitate to refer to the Japanese in Japan as like a swarm of bees that would rage out of control without their queen bee-like monarch. And even as Lieutenant Commander Cecil H. Coggins of the ONI praised the past record of Japanese Americans, criticized biological racism, and argued that the problem of troublemakers in the camps could be blamed almost entirely on the institution of the camps themselves, he equated the recalcitrant with flies on manure: "Any effort to solve this problem [of malcontents within the camps] such as is without dissolving those camps is like sitting on a pile of manure with a fly swatter trying to dispose of the flies. I think you are breeding your own trouble in these camps. The sooner we get rid of them the better."[102]

In fact, the system of Japanese American internment would operate not through the immediate closure of the camps, but through an elaborate structure of exclusions and spaces of confinement that would separate the unredeemable from those believed to make up a loyal flock of Japanese American sheep. This system for managing freedom in a multiracialized nation, especially as regulated through the discourse on soldiering or willingness to bear arms for the nation, is the subject of the next chapter.

PART TWO · JAPANESE AS AMERICANS

CHAPTER THREE

Subject to Choice,
Labyrinth of (Un)freedom

> [F]reedom may very well appear as the condition for the
> exercise of power.
>
> MICHEL FOUCAULT, *"The Subject and Power"* (1982)

> When the Son of man comes in his glory, and all the
> angels with him, then he will sit on his glorious throne.
> Before him will be gathered all the nations, and he will
> separate them one from another as a shepherd separates
> the sheep from the goats, and he will place the sheep at
> his right hand, but the goats at the left. Then the King
> will say to those at his right hand, *Come, O blessed of
> my Father, inherit the kingdom prepared for you from the
> foundation of the world*[.] ... Then he will say to those
> at his left hand, *Depart from me, you cursed, into the
> eternal fire prepared for the devil and his angels*[.]
> (emphasis added)
>
> MATTHEW 25:31–41 (RSV)

The analogy of separating Japanese American goats from sheep that circulated
so widely among civilian and military administrators points to another aspect of the
shift from "vulgar" to "polite" racism that I have touched on but not adequately
analyzed in the previous chapters: namely, that the new modality of governing this
minority could no longer operate through repressive or negative means alone but
needed in addition to urge them in a positive way and guide them toward making
voluntary choices, including the decision to enlist in the military. The new political
rationality would deploy an assemblage of positive practices that Foucault has identified with modern governmentality and, most tellingly, the pastoral relationship of
power upon which modern governmentality is grounded. As Foucault pointed out,
in the pastoral relationship the shepherd or pastor must know not only the flock as

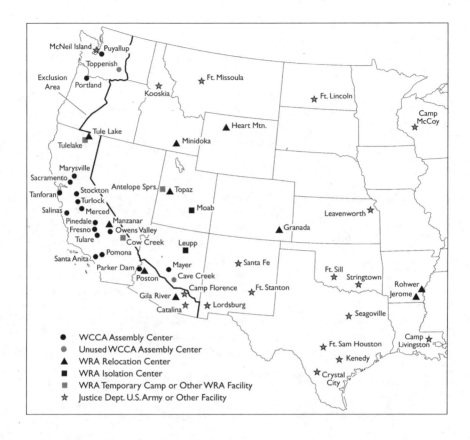

MAP 2.

"Labyrinth of (Un)freedom": The Japanese American internment
complex. Adapted from "Sites in the western U.S. associated with
the relocation of Japanese Americans during World War II." Courtesy
of the United States National Parks Service.

a whole but every member, so that he can ensure the salvation of each and all. The
shepherd is responsible for knowing the inner conscience of every individual, while
the individual must submit to the shepherd's guidance. However, in this relationship power is not supposed to be experienced as working through negative means.
The individual is not even supposed to realize that he or she is being led. As Foucault puts it, "The pastorage gave rise to an art of conducting, directing, leading,
guiding, taking in hand, and manipulating men, an art of monitoring them and urging them on step by step, an art with the function of taking charge of men collectively and individually throughout their life and at every moment of their existence."

Moreover, in the new pastoral power of modern governmentality, freedom is "an element that has become indispensable to governmentality itself. Henceforth, a condition of governing well is that freedom, or certain forms of freedom, are really respected. Failing to respect freedom is not only an abuse of rights with regard to the law, it is above all ignorance of how to govern properly. The integration of freedom, and the specific limits to this freedom within the field of governmental practice has now become an imperative."[1]

Common sense would have us believe that Japanese American internment ought to be understood strictly as a system of unfreedom, of exclusions, confinement, and restrictions—for example, the absence of freedom of movement and lack of civil liberties. Yet this chapter analyzes the campaign for army volunteers and the linked political ritual called "registration," together with the questionnaires that served as its key instruments, in order to demonstrate how they reflect rather than contradict the positive methods of liberal governmentality in managing rather than simply restricting freedom. I will argue that the fundamental and new premise of the questionnaires—with their key questions asking for willingness to soldier and unqualified allegiance to the nation—required the active participation of internees as free subjects making rational decisions, not as slaves or nonhuman objects displaying passive obedience. This premise fundamentally contradicted the original assumption behind the evacuation, which was that the Japanese were like animals without subjectivity.

At the same time, liberal governmentality required the exclusion of those considered incapable of citizenship and it threatened or used violence to purify the camps into spaces of freedom. In a nation where the governing elite were almost all Christian, the metaphor contrasting goats and sheep must have been related, whether consciously or not, to the passage in Matthew (quoted in the epigraph above) where it is said that the "Son of man will . . . separate them one from another as a shepherd separates the sheep from the goats," and that while the sheep would inherit the Kingdom of God, the goats would be condemned to eternal fire. Like the liberalism outside the camps that had put Japanese Americans behind barbed wire in the first place, liberalism inside would work through exclusions from the primary "relocation centers." We thus find a series of interlocked spaces of (un)freedom, each one constituted as unfree in relation to larger exterior spaces of freedom, but free in relation to contiguous spaces of unfreedom. In other words, the relocation centers constituted the space of America as a space of freedom; but the linked system of camps and prisons to which allegedly dangerous internees were expelled from the primary relocation centers and the periodic FBI and military police invasions into centers at moments of crisis in turn constituted the relocation centers (with the exception of the Tule Lake camp) during what were called "normal" times into spaces of freedom.

Yet the web of authorities could not leave the determination of trustworthiness completely up to the self-avowal of the "subject individual," as internees subjected to loyalty investigations were called. She or he could be dangerous and lying. In fact, the most dangerous would tend to lie. In principle, in terms of admissibility into the nation, the freely made individual choices to soldier and vow allegiance could trump racial ascription, but not without the subject passing background and other security checks. Again, this condition resonates with the pastoral metaphor, for the pastor must know the intimate details of each and every member of the flock, and the jurisdiction of the pastor or shepherd includes the power to "expel those sheep that by disease or scandal are liable to contaminate the whole flock."[2] Thus the questionnaires included far more questions that plumbed the individuals' social backgrounds and life experiences than those (just two) that required self-professions. On the basis of responses to these questions, which were checked against other intelligence reports, evaluators completed detailed profiles that measured the trustworthiness of the subject individual's own profession of willingness to join the military and pledge loyalty. An analysis of the guidelines for evaluating questionnaires will provide a glimpse into how culture (including religion) and political ideology, in addition to material connections to the enemy nation, came to stand in for biological race as a measure of admissibility into the national community.

THE QUESTIONNAIRES AND DEATH

Structurally, the demand imposed by total war for civilian and military labor as well as the plan to mobilize Japanese Americans in a global propaganda campaign led almost inevitably to the development of a joint program by the War Department and the War Relocation Authority to register and assess the loyalty of all adult Japanese Americans. With its already-noted commitment to a policy of leaves and resettlements by at least the fall of 1942, the WRA needed a streamlined system for determining the security risks of individual internees. For its part, the War Department required a means by which to assess the loyalty of army volunteers and of workers seeking employment in areas critical to the war effort. Thus the two agencies combined their efforts in a massive registration campaign that utilized not only background checks but also self-professions through questionnaires establishing loyalty and willingness to militarily defend the country.[3] These questionnaires became the key instruments in the political ritual of "registration" that gripped the entire relocation center complex from the second week of February to mid-March 1943.

At a meeting held in the office of the assistant secretary of war (ASW) on 2 January 1943, the deputy chief of staff instructed the assistant chief of staff (AC of S), G-2 (Intelligence), and the Office of the Provost Marshal General (OPMG) to jointly devise a plan to determine the loyalty of Japanese American citizens under the jurisdiction of the WRA. Its purpose would be to ascertain "(a) permit of their release by the War Relocation Authority from war relocation centers, and (b) whether those so released may be inducted into the military service or be employed in plants and facilities important to the war effort." A committee made up of officers from those two organizations did as instructed, after consulting with representatives of the ASW, the Office of Naval Intelligence (ONI), and the WRA. Dillon Myer, commenting on a preliminary sketch of the plan, advised that the program for determining loyalty "be extended to all those of the army age group on the outside of the centers as well as to those in the centers."[4]

The 20 January 1943 War Department directive that emerged out of these discussions stipulated teams "consisting of an army officer and three enlisted men, including one Japanese-American soldier of the Nisei class. The teams will assist the War Relocation Authority in supervising the execution of questionnaires" in the camps. It charged the Selective Service with administering these questionnaires to Nisei men of military age on the outside. The Bureau of Public Relations would tightly and exclusively control publicity concerning the entire program. Questionnaires completed by Nisei electing to volunteer for the army would be forwarded directly to military intelligence (AC of S, G-2) for approval or disapproval. The questionnaires of those volunteering for work outside of the camps but not for induction would be forwarded to the OPMG. The questionnaires of those not volunteering, as well as any other information pertinent to ascertaining the loyalty of these "subject individuals," were to be sent directly to the OPMG. The directive instructed the OPMG to also check FBI and ONI records and, if the action was deemed useful, to send a copy of the completed questionnaire to the Western Defense Command (WDC) and request the latter to conduct a further investigation.

Furthermore, the directive called for the establishment of a joint board that would make negative or positive recommendations concerning the release of individuals from the relocation centers for indefinite leave; it would also indicate if it had any "objection to the employment in plants and facilities important to the war effort" of any Nisei whom the WRA released on the basis of its recommendation. With regard to the board's composition, the directive explained that the Department of Justice, the Navy Department, and the WRA had agreed that it would consist of representatives from the FBI, ONI, WRA, AC of S (G-2), War Department General Staff, and OPMG. Thus the questionnaires for citizens were to be evaluated along two lines, one for army volunteers and the other for everyone else.[5] The directive made no mention of non-citizen Japanese. However, during the ten-day training program for soldiers who would administer the questionnaires in the camps, the WRA decided to extend registration to aliens.[6]

The directive reveals that despite differences in degrees of suspicion with which they regarded the Japanese in America, the more liberal-minded civilian agency (the WRA) and the more security-minded intelligence and military communities had found common ground. These civilian and military agencies had become braided into a massive security system that started with the premise that individual Japanese could be distinguished from one another in terms of their loyalty to the United States. This was of course completely at odds with what many believed had been the original premise for the mass evacuation of Japanese from the West Coast.

But the position of the War Department had shifted away from such vulgar racism, and the changed situation forced highly placed officials such as Assistant Secretary of War John J. McCloy to begin explaining why the loyal could now be differentiated from the disloyal if doing so had not been possible prior to the wholesale evacuation. For example, about a month after the questionnaire-based registration program in the camps had been completed, McCloy sent a letter to Albert B. Chandler, head of the Senate Subcommittee to Investigate the War Relocation Centers. Writing in response to Chandler's invitation to comment on wartime policies toward Japanese, McCloy explained that wartime conditions had changed. Earlier, when "faced with the prospect of imminent Japanese attack on our West Coast, the decision was made to evacuate all, rather than to chance fifth column activity, which other nations facing the Axis had found so fatal. It is important to appreciate, however, that it was a mass evacuation and did not constitute an indictment of the individual loyalty of any evacuee." In other words, McCloy emphasized that exigency and not a belief that it was impossible to ascertain the loyalty of individual Japanese was behind the mass evacuation program. Reflecting the new common sense, McCloy held that while it was imperative to identify and segregate the disloyal and the dangerous, it was just as important to utilize the remainder in the war effort. In short, he stressed, "The point I want to make is that internment other than of those both disloyal and dangerous may not only be, from the point of view of military security, unnecessary but from the manpower point of view unwise."[7]

To be sure, in their subsequent relations the WRA and the OPMG often clashed over what degree of caution should be exercised when evaluating individuals for release and work in areas critical to the war effort. The OPMG functioned as the "police arm of the military forces," which in addition to its other duties was specifically charged with supervising "the War Department's internal security programs for the protection of war production."[8] Therefore, its staff tended to deny release and permission to work far more often than the WRA thought necessary. Nonetheless, it is important to recognize that despite WRA officials' common disavowals of racism, including Dillon Myer's consistent criticism of racial discrimination, they made up a part of the web of agencies that believed that the Japanese in America deserved to be treated with special caution. Like the War Department, the OPMG, and officials such as McCloy, the WRA did not maintain that all Japanese Americans should be considered innocent until proven otherwise; indeed, it advocated imposing special security measures not applied to any other group, including German Americans and Italian Americans.

The questionnaires used in the registration program have become quite well-known, if only for their infamous questions 27 and 28. In answering them, individuals were asked to affirm or deny their willingness to enlist in the military as well as to pledge or disavow their loyalty to the United States. For instance, John Okada's brilliant and widely read novel about internment and military service, *No-No Boy* (1977), used the trope of two negative answers to this pair of questions to evoke the impossibility of making any reasonable choices given the conditions of life in camp. Nevertheless, despite their importance the questionnaires and the registration process have been subjected to surprisingly little analysis beyond the most straightforward and basic descriptions or uncomplicated condemnations of their racism.[9] Therefore, my purpose is not only to provide additional empirical details and to correct some common errors of fact but, more importantly, to highlight the political rationality that the questionnaires and the registration campaign reveal for managing this American subpopulation.

The War Department's official history of the military clearance program for Japanese Americans during World War II indicates that the "idea of the questionnaire originated with certain naval officers familiar with Japanese intelligence."[10] Indeed, at the 2 January 1943 conference on the "use of Japanese in Army" already mentioned in chapter 2, Acting Director of Naval Intelligence Captain Ellis M. Zacharias and his colleague at ONI, Lieutenant Commander Cecil H. Coggins, spoke on the need to involve the navy in formulating a strategy for determining Japanese American loyalty. Within military circles, both Zacharias and Coggins were widely considered experts on the Japanese and Japanese Americans. Zacharias suggested that the navy had much stronger records on the Japanese than the army and that it was important to quickly recognize the loyalty of those Japanese Americans who were in fact loyal, "lest their loyalty be broken."[11]

Coggins, the reader may recall, was a strong critic of biological racism directed against the Japanese and a major force in promoting the view that the overwhelming majority of Japanese Americans were loyal. At this conference Coggins explained that he had been "an undercover man in Hawaii" and that he had developed a "40-point check system" to gauge the loyalty of the Japanese there. According to a firsthand account of the conference by Colonel W. E. Crist of the Military Intelligence Service (MIS), Coggins "expressed the opinion that his 40-point system was adequate for determining loyalty; that probably 80% of all Nisei were loyal; and that the Navy would be willing to process them."[12] Within the next few days MIS came to the conclusion that it would devise a "questionnaire based chiefly upon the experience of the Office of Naval Intelligence," because it believed that "answers to this questionnaire should provide a reasonable index of loyalty, according to the Office of Naval Intelligence experts."[13] Shortly thereafter the AC of S, G-3 (Organization and Training Division), informed the assistant secretary of war that a questionnaire authored by Coggins would serve as the basis for the loyalty checks.[14]

Each of the ten recruitment teams, made up of the soldiers and WRA staff who had received training in Washington, D.C., in preparation for the project, arrived in one of the camps during the first week of February and commenced the actual registration on or about 10 February. All the teams completed their work by mid-March. During the initial phase of registration, internees received one of two versions of the questionnaire. All male citizens exceeding minimum draftable age— that is, those seventeen years of age and older—received Selective Service Form 304A, "Statement of United States Citizen of Japanese Ancestry." Although bearing the Selective Service System seal, it was in fact a War Department document. Questions 27 and 28 of this form read as follows.

(27) Are you willing to serve in the armed forces of the United States on combat duty, wherever ordered?

(28) Will you swear unqualified allegiance to the United States of America and faithfully defend the United States from any or all attack by foreign or domestic forces, and forswear any form of allegiance or obedience to the Japanese emperor, or any other foreign government, power, or organization?

Army team personnel gave each male citizen of draftable age a personal interview prior to his responding to these two questions; and if the registrant expressed a willingness to serve, he was further interviewed about volunteering. If the individual wished to volunteer, he executed the necessary Selective Service forms. All of this documentation was then transmitted to AC of S, G-2, for evaluation, as instructed in the 20 January directive. If approved by military intelligence, the applicant was supposed to be inducted following successful completion of a physical examination.[15]

All other adults ages seventeen or older—in other words, noncitizen male adults and all adult women regardless of citizenship—were instructed to complete WRA Form 126 Rev., "War Relocation Authority Application for Leave Clearance." This document followed Form 304A very closely; but with a total of thirty-three as compared to twenty-eight questions it was slightly longer and reflected special concerns having mainly to do with its targeted group's being noncitizens or women, as well as special considerations relevant to nonmilitary employment or leave. Most prominently, questions 27 and 28 differed considerably in their wording. Thus on Form 126 Rev. they read as follows:

(27) If the opportunity presents itself and you are found qualified, would you be willing to volunteer for the Army Nurse Corps or the WAAC [Women's Army Auxiliary Corps]?

(28) Will you swear unqualified allegiance to the United States of America and forswear any form of allegiance or obedience to the Japanese emperor, or any other foreign government, power, or organization?[16]

As is often noted, these various renderings of the two questions created enormous confusion and anxiety among the internees. Here question 27 in effect asked noncitizen males and elderly women if they would be willing to serve in the Army Nurse Corps or the WAAC. The WRA's version of question 28 was even more troubling, as it had simply dropped the clause "and faithfully defend the United States from any or all attack by foreign or domestic forces," but still included "and forswear any form of allegiance or obedience to the Japanese emperor, or any other foreign government, power, or organization?" The form's authors had not considered that aliens ineligible by U.S. law from naturalizing as citizens would become stateless if they forswore allegiance to all other foreign governments, including that of the Japanese emperor. The WRA recognized this problem fairly quickly and on 12 February ordered all centers to replace the question for aliens (but not for female citizens) to read:

Will you swear to abide by the laws of the United States and to take no action which would in any way interfere with the war effort of the United States?[17]

Before we proceed with a more detailed analysis of the questions and their broader implications, one obvious but preliminary observation should be made about both the War Department's and WRA's versions of the questionnaires—perhaps an obvious point that could be anticipated from the conclusions of the previous chapter: namely, at this moment the state fully recognized the right of an individual to live as a citizen only if that individual vowed that he or she would volunteer to die as a soldier. This did not technically require volunteering, although some thought that answering question 28 affirmatively was tantamount to doing so. Rather, the interrogators sought citizens willing in principle to enlist. So concerned were the interrogators to have respondents express their willingness to participate in war that they asked males to vow to take up arms twice, the second time in question 28 with the phrase "faithfully defend the United States from any or all attack." Furthermore, while the choice to volunteer for Japanese American soldiering in World War II is usually assumed to have been presented to men alone, it is important to observe that the WRA form asked Nisei women if they would be willing to serve as army nurses or in the Women's Army Auxiliary Corps. Only carelessness can explain why the WRA asked Issei men this latter question, but clearly some thought had been given to devising a question for women that would be comparable to the military question for males. In this ritual of inclusion, Japanese Americans who were legally citizens by birth but who had been excluded from the political and bio-political nation by race were invited to cross over to the inside of the national community, but only at the threshold of death. Conversely, in deleting the phrase "and faithfully defend the United States from any or all attack by foreign or domestic forces" from the form intended for noncitizens, the WRA reflected its understanding that those not fully allowed inside the political and bio-political community could not be compelled to take up arms in its defense.

One further mishandling of the situation took place at Manzanar, where the administrators, quickly realizing the problem of statelessness for aliens if they responded affirmatively to the original question 28, revised the question before registration began. The new version read:

Are you sympathetic to the United States and do you agree faithfully to defend the United States from any and all attack by foreign or domestic forces?[18]

Such a wording for aliens—"defend the United States from any and all attack"—would seem to contradict my argument above, since it would require noncitizens to be prepared to die for a nation that would not promise to include them regardless of their responses. However, the WRA community analyst who reported on the Manzanar registration specifically noted that the local administrators had not properly understood the relationship between citizenship and taking up arms. "To many Japanese aliens, a 'yes' answer seemed equivalent to an agreement to take up arms against the country in which they hold citizenship," he said. "Such an agreement or action, according to the laws of most nations, including those of the United States and Japan, is considered treason, and is punishable by the loss of citizenship and worse." In other words, the Manzanar administrators' unique wording reflected a complete lack of understanding about the limits to the state's right to demand the lives of noncitizens. The WRA's Washington administrators, who did understand those limits, revised 28 accordingly.[19] And ultimately, in April, Manzanar administrators replaced their rendering of 28 for aliens with the one produced by the Washington WRA.[20]

FROM "BLOCKS OF WOOD" TO FREE SUBJECTS

Beyond crystallizing the linkages between life, death, and citizenship, the political ritual of answering questions 27 and 28 reveals that a fundamental transformation had taken place in the governors' stance toward the subjectivities of the governed. Reflecting the old view, Lieutenant General John L. DeWitt continued to argue in the critical months of December 1942 and January 1943—just as the War Department and WRA were working out the mechanics of the army recruitment campaign and registration for Japanese Americans—that it was impossible to definitively assess their loyalty. It was not only possible but necessary to segregate the most obviously dangerous from the others. However, he had no faith in any test of loyalty, let alone in questionnaires that depended on the internees themselves for answers. Unlike those committed to the rationality of liberal governmentality, DeWitt had no interest in knowing the inner life of the internees or guiding them toward the aims of the total war effort. Thus in December he submitted a general plan for segregation in which those falling into four categories of especially suspect individuals and the family members who wished to accompany them would without notice be picked up and transferred on a specific day to a camp designated as a segregation center. These categories were those who had requested repatriation or expatriation to Japan, aliens who had been paroled from other detention or internment camps, those who had amassed "evaluated" police records in the assembly or relocation centers, and those whom the intelligence service had listed and judged to be potentially dangerous. On roundup day, the military would take complete control of the centers and business as usual would stop. Unlike the final plan for registration, his proposal did not call for the internees themselves to swear or forswear their allegiance.[21]

In a letter addressed to the army chief of staff and dated 27 January 1943, just days before the ten teams were to depart for the relocation centers from Washington, D.C., DeWitt harshly criticized the plan they were about to carry out. As Eric Muller, who has also analyzed this document, has already explained, DeWitt held that the shift to the view that the loyal could be separated from the disloyal would undermine the original justification for evacuating the Japanese from the West Coast en masse. If the authorities now claimed that such a distinction could be made, then it would follow that the mass evacuation had been a mistake or at least that individual determinations should have been made earlier, while the internees were being held in the temporary assembly centers. The new plan would also cast doubt on the continued necessity of excluding those deemed loyal from the evacuated zone. Moreover, as Muller has noted, DeWitt maintained that the dearth of information on individual Nisei made an accurate assessment of loyalty unimaginable.[22]

Beyond these points, DeWitt's criticisms highlight the contrast between his increasingly anachronistic views and WRA's and the War Department's new governing practices. In one of his numerous appendices to his letter to the chief of staff, DeWitt rejected the questionnaire method as a "suitable means even of beginning an investigation of this type. . . . A person who is actively loyal to an enemy nation will certainly not be truthful in any questionnaire he might submit, even though the questionnaire be made under oath. A check of his record, if any, plus investigation and questioning may lead to a fair index of active disloyalty—not the converse."[23] In other words, DeWitt explained with a reason that was both logical and increasingly out of touch with the new governmental practices that the disloyal, precisely because they were not loyal, would be unlikely to respond truthfully to questionnaires. Existing records and investigations could ferret out "active disloyalty"; but loyalty could never be confidently determined. In an "alternate plan" emerging out of his December scheme, he insisted that the public should continue to be told that the wholesale evacuation had been necessary because "we could not tell the sheep from the goats" and that there should be no change in this stance. But DeWitt did make some concessions in response to manpower needs, building on the views he had transmitted in July 1942 to the Board of Officers that had in September recommended against further inductions of Japanese Americans. After the segregation of those with "bad records," the remainder would be released for employment in the interior or for military service. Segregation should separate out the most dangerous, but "there should be no such thing as 'loyalty' determination or 'clearance.'"[24]

In one sense DeWitt's criticisms of the questionnaire-based plan can be explained by his continuing well-known distrust of all the Japanese as a race. Yet the WRA solicitor's characterization of DeWitt's segregation plan is even more suggestive about the dissonance between the lieutenant general's views of governing and the emerging new liberal governmentality. That plan, said the solicitor, would have treated "the evacuees as though they were so many blocks of wood, with complete disregard for the rights and liberties, not to mention the fears and sensibilities, they share with other human beings."[25] In other words, while the new governmentality would be concerned to treat the internees as human beings with "rights and liberties" as well as "fears and sensibilities," DeWitt did not care to preserve such rights and freedoms or even know the internees' sentiments or interiority. When he looked at the internees he saw only "blocks of wood" or what he himself characterized as "evasion" or a "blank wall of silence"[26]—an inscrutable and impenetrable mass of indistinguishable faces—and he wished to know nothing more about their individual subjectivities.

Under liberal governmentality, however, administrators felt compelled to penetrate into the conscience of each and every individual and to know them as individual human beings so that they could be guided toward free and rational choices. Their strategy for governing, in Foucault's words, "implies a knowledge of the conscience and an ability to direct it."[27] They sought to preserve the imaginary of the camps as democratic and free, or at least as democratic and free as possible under wartime conditions. These liberal (racist) administrators distinguished themselves from their Nazi enemies and insisted that they believed in the democratic rights of all citizens regardless of race and despite the evacuation. Moreover, DeWitt could not understand that one of the main purposes of registration lay in the very asking of questions. In this political ritual the answers of course mattered, but the submission of all adult internees to a system that would compel them to make choices was of even greater importance. Paraphrasing Foucault, we might say that DeWitt would have allowed the internees to remain silent, but that the WRA and War Department compelled them to speak as free agents. While DeWitt continued to privilege force alone, in the new governmentality the WRA and War Department would make them subject(ed) to freedom.[28]

Thus in the "Relocation Center Address," which they read verbatim at meetings in every center in order to explain their undertaking, team members stressed that the success of their efforts to recruit volunteers for the army and to complete the registration depended "finally upon the voluntary acts of free American citizens." "You may object that this—your life here—is not freedom," they conceded, but they explained (if clumsily) that in moments of national crisis the "interests of the few must sometimes be temporarily sacrificed or disregarded for what seems the good of the many. The proof of a nation's good faith is to be found in whether it moves to restore full privileges at the earliest opportunity." They acknowledged that the internees had gone through a "period of considerable hardship and great anxiety," but declared that American society always afforded its members freedom of choice.

> Not all Japanese Americans are loyal to their government. Not all members
> of any group of our population—even those whose ancestors came here
> hundreds of years ago—are fully loyal to their country. That is so because
> ours is a free society permitting the individual often to choose in what measure
> he will contribute to the common good. In all groups there are individuals who
> will not accept any obligation to the land which gives them their opportunity.
> Wherever you find them and whatever their blood may be they are the disloyal
> ones.[29]

On the one hand, this statement unwittingly captures a general characteristic of the structure of national belonging that theorists of nationalism such as Ernest Renan and Elie Kedourie long ago emphasized: namely, that nationalism rests ultimately on the voluntary choice of its members—not ascription. As we will see in later chapters on the perhaps unexpected structural fit between the self-determination of Korean individuals and their submission to Japanese nationalism and the emperor, this is why Kedourie emphasized the doctrinal importance of Kant and his notion of the categorical imperative, a concept that coupled transcendental freedom with submission or obedience to a moral inner command. As Kedourie notes, in a remark with obvious implications for individuals held in camps: "A man can be imprisoned in the worst of dungeons, or suffer the most odious of tyrannies, but he may still be free if his will is free; and his will is free when it is acting in accordance with the categorical imperative, as Kant denotes this inward law." Renan also captured this essential quality of nationalism in his plainly put observation that national existence is "a daily plebiscite," a matter of repetitive election.[30] Therefore in explaining that each member of the national community of whatever "blood" could "choose in what measure he will contribute to the common good," the team members made the not unusual claim that national belonging rests ultimately on the free will of its members.

On the other hand, prior to this moment, Japanese Americans had been excluded by race ascription from the ability to choose American nationality—they had no choice in the matter. By law Issei could not choose to apply for naturalization; and although Nisei were legally citizens, internment had unilaterally expelled them from the national community and even prior to that from a range of legal rights guaranteed to whites. Now, ironically, in a space and time that so obviously signified unfreedom, the civilian and military officers told the inmates that they were welcome to choose to fight for their nation and to pledge their loyalty. To make this point about the shift toward voluntarism even clearer, it may also be noted that on 1 July 1944, President Roosevelt signed Public Law 405 as an amendment to the Nationality Code. In keeping with the principle that nationality is ultimately a matter of choice and that therefore individuals ought to be able to freely denaturalize, this law allowed any citizen the right to renounce nationality in time of war. Interestingly, when after the war Wayne Collins defended renunciants who wished to reverse their decision to renounce, he argued that their actions had not been "the product of free will,"[31] again showing that whether affirming or renouncing nationality, the individual subject must be judged to have acted freely for the act to be genuine.

Of course, Issei would not be able to participate in this general principle of nationalism for some time, but following the trend toward racial inclusion and choice over ascription, it became possible on 11 September 1944 for noncitizen males of Japanese ancestry to volunteer for the army. Tellingly, as the adjutant general announcing this change in policy emphasized, in the case of such applicants an extra signed copy of the "Application for Voluntary Induction" (DSS 165) should be filed with local boards so that it could be forwarded to the appropriate armed forces induction station. The point was to provide "conclusive evidence that application for service was voluntary."[32] As explained in the War Department's official history of the military clearance program for Japanese Americans, the State Department had recommended this exaggerated demonstration of free choice "as a way to avoid any appearance of pressure on the alien volunteer," since international law "forbids the compulsory induction of enemy aliens." This care in processing the applications for voluntary induction of noncitizens not only testifies to government concerns that acts of inclusion be understood as voluntary by both the volunteer and other third parties; it also suggests a shared understanding even among enemy nations that national belonging should not be coerced but must be determined by freely acting subjects. Whether actual coercion existed in many cases is beside the point: the State Department as well as enemy nations had agreed in principle by law to act as if only voluntary acts would be recognized as legitimate. Such a logic also made it possible for the army to accept those in Japanese "occupied countries," such as Korea, even though they were legally Japanese nationals, presumably because they had become Japanese against their will.[33]

In any case, the team members explained that the time had come for the internees to willingly participate in the fight against the nation's enemies, either in battle or in war plants and facilities, and that they would be restored as soon as possible to their "normal and rightful share in the present life and work of the people of the United States." Moreover, anticipating charges that the restriction of Japanese Americans to a segregated unit was evidence of continuing discrimination, the speakers tried to explain that such an arrangement would give greater visibility to their accomplishments and thereby provide a "living reproach to those who have been prejudiced against you because of your Japanese blood." At the same time, "to the nations abroad, and especially to the peoples of the East, you would provide the measure of the solidarity of people who get together in the name of democracy." In short, the "Relocation Center Address" told the internees, the government needs you, the government trusts you, your lives will return to normalcy in the near future, and so you are encouraged to volunteer for the army and to affirm your loyalty. The choice, the team members meant to say, was up to the internees themselves.[34]

EXCEPTIONS THAT CONSTITUTED LIBERAL RULE

The believability of such a discourse on freedom and the strategy of guiding the internees toward the right choices, however, depended in large part on Myer's and his administrators' success in making the relocation centers appear as replicas of liberal democratic societies. That undertaking necessitated some commitment to open debates, self-government, community meetings, communication between camp administrators and elected or nonelected representatives of internees, and freedom of the press.

Yet when faced with the practical necessity of completing their assigned task, camp administrators and War Department teams used varying degrees of compulsion to goad the internees toward the correct choices. For instance, the "General Instructions to Team Captains" advised the teams that they could warn internees about the provisions of the Sedition Act, which made those engaged in "seditious or disloyal acts or words" during wartime subject to severe punishments. Offenses under the act included intentionally causing or attempting to cause "insubordination, disloyalty, mutiny, or refusal of duty, in the military or naval forces of the United States," and it specifically targeted those who "shall willfully obstruct the recruiting or enlistment services of the United States." The "Instructions" took care to say that the statute should not be posted, but should be "conveyed to the people in some other less pointed way, such as by talks or conferences with the Center leaders or block managers. It should not be used as a threat, but merely offered as a piece of pertinent information." No overt threats were to be made about refusal to complete the questionnaires. Instead, the individual should be "urged to comply for his own benefit." The distinction between informing in these terms and threatening was certainly not very clear, but the authorities appear to have crossed that line without much hesitation. At Topaz and Tule Lake, at the least, center officials overtly threatened internees with possible charges of sedition and most likely did so at Granada as well.[35]

The team captain at Granada reported that he gave the names of those who had answered question 28 negatively or with a qualified "yes" to the project director. The director or the camp's chief of police passed these names on to the block managers, who then attempted to compel these internees to change their answers to an unqualified "yes." The team captain concluded with some amazement that "after being told that the chances were that they would be placed in a prison camp or in a concentration camp, it is surprising to me that all those who answered 'NO' to twenty-eight did not change their answers."[36]

At the same time, such practices of guiding the internees toward compliance required far more ruthless and often violent practices of expelling and incarcerating those whose views and political activities could not be tolerated in the supposed space of liberty. In other words, the condition for liberalism inside the camps, replicating the condition for liberalism on the outside, was expulsion of those deemed unfit for freedom. The unfit would be considered exceptional and their freedom would be denied without apology. Thus, shortly after registration began, with reports of chaos, confusion, and resistance coming to him daily from the relocation centers, Myer instructed the project directors (the heads of the individual relocation centers) to deal with troublemakers firmly. But he also assured them that while the task at hand seemed daunting, the end result was likely to be a "purifying process."

I have told several of the project directors over the phone and I want to repeat: Nothing must be permitted to interfere with the complete success of the registration, and no interference with volunteering can be countenanced. Agitators seem to be at work in some of the centers. When you have reasonable evidence of interference, don't hesitate to make arrests. At Gila, Le Roy Bennett asked the FBI for help and on February 16 placed 13 aliens and 14 kibei under arrest. The FBI removed the aliens, and WRA removed the kibei who are on their way to the isolation center at Moab, Utah. Harvey Coverley at Tule Lake indicates that probably some arrests of trouble makers will be necessary there. Heart Mountain is experiencing a similar crisis that may require drastic action. The registration promises to be a purifying process.[37]

In short, Myer expected his project directors to work with the FBI to identify and without hesitation arrest suspected dissidents solely on the vague grounds of "reasonable evidence." On the bright side, such a process would lead to cleansing the relocation centers of unwanted elements. Myer was right about the impending crisis at Tule Lake, which turned out to be the most radically uncooperative of the centers. Only three days after the date of his letter, WRA internal security—supported by a caravan of military police carrying machine guns and bayonets—arrested and removed twenty-eight men. This represented most of the thirty-five from the center's Block 42 who had with a jointly signed petition requested repatriation in lieu of registration. As they had powerfully if not very elegantly put it: "We the undersigned do not wish to sign to selective service. But to repatriate we will sign any time so until then there won't be any business." On 10 March Project Director Coverley wrote to Myer informing him that as of the previous evening a total of 105 persons were being held in an isolation center and that 61 of these had been identified through a "screening process" targeting Kibei (U.S. citizens who had returned to the United States after being educated for a period of time in Japan).

There were other arrests as well. In his late March summary of "loose ends" relating to nonregistrants in Tule Lake, Myer noted that roughly 130 arrests had been made. Twelve of these individuals had pleaded guilty to participating in a riot and had been sentenced to terms in the Modoc county jail in Alturas. One individual had been taken to an internment camp for enemy aliens and five others were likely to receive the same fate. Seventeen Kibei were about to be transferred to Moab, the WRA's isolation camp in Utah. Myer also observed that another 400 to 450 nonregistrants had not been arrested. He provided ad hoc suggestions for a range of possible punishments for them, including jail sentences or suspension of welfare provisions that had been enabled by what I have described as the regime's "right to make live"—for example, disallowing "clothing allowances, any unemployment compensation to which they might otherwise become entitled, and any public assistance grants for which they might otherwise become eligible." Dorothy Swaine Thomas and Richard S. Nishimoto, the authors of *The Spoilage*, gave a figure of "approximately 100" for the total number of Kibei who had been removed to a nearby abandoned Civilian Conservation Corps camp. They noted that the WRA, with army assistance, operated the CCC camp for several weeks under extremely tight security, including censoring all incoming and outgoing mail.[38]

Tule Lake's team captain, First Lieutenant Evan W. Carroll, explained that while in the past discipline had been a problem, no arrests or removals had ever taken place in this project.[39] Thus these arrests might have seemed like the beginning of a "purifying process" for Tule Lake. Indeed, the cleansing even reached into the camp administration. By 6 March, two of a number of teachers who were "opposed to war as a means of settling international disputes and who would probably refuse to perform war service if they were required to do so" complied with requests for their resignation. In a letter of 31 March, Myer further informed Coverley that he was "receiving disturbing reports" on activities of WRA employees who were "pacifists and conscientious objectors." Naming some seventeen individuals, he instructed the Tule Lake director to take corrective measures and informed him that since the WRA had employed most of them for less than an year, they could be dismissed without the filing of formal charges.[40]

Rather than undertaking a purification for the purpose of maintaining freedom, however, administrators at Tule Lake continued to apply repressive measures to such an extraordinary degree that by stages they transformed the camp into the major exception to liberal rule. This dynamic was even more striking in the nearby CCC camp run by the WRA, where prisoners were subjected to forced labor.[41] The WRA's Community Analysis Section put it in a way that resonates with Foucault's distinction between the deployment of sheer force and a liberal governmentality that operates through freedom: Tule Lake after these arrests was "marked by persistent efforts of the administration to effect registration by force—a course of action to which they were irrevocably committed after the initial arrests and the open opposition which followed them." Administrators abandoned an earlier policy of "reasoning with the colonists," and through their use of force, they exacerbated the internees' combativeness. As a writer for the Community Analysis Section insightfully summed up: "The people were so outraged at the continuing application of force that their civil rights protest became identified with a refusal to register. To register was to become a dog—read administration stooge—in the eyes of thousands of Tule Lake residents, including many friends and neighbors."[42]

This collapse of liberal governmentality at Tule Lake reached a point of no return several months after the registration campaign when the WRA's Administrative Instruction No. 100, dated 15 July 1943, designated the center as the site for the segregation of "those persons of Japanese ancestry residing in relocation centers who by their acts have indicated that their loyalties lie with Japan during the present hostilities."[43] Among those designated for segregation were such obvious targets as individuals who had requested expatriation or repatriation and those who had refused to answer question 28, or had responded "no." The latter underwent a Board of Review hearing, during which they had the opportunity to change their responses and convince their hearing officers that they were not disloyal. A third category was more vague, encompassing all those denied leave clearance by the WRA for a variety of reasons, including, "No-noes who had asked to have their negative answers changed to affirmative after registration, repatriates who had asked to have their applications withdrawn, and a miscellaneous group of persons, technically 'loyal' by registration criteria but against whom various intelligence agencies or WRA project officials had filed 'adverse' reports."[44] This category allowed administrators to target persons under poorly specified criteria, including, as a WRA pamphlet delineating the procedure explained, those having interests "not in harmony with those of the United States" and "people who have indicated their desire to follow the Japanese way of life." Conversely, the pamphlet indicated that the loyal were those who "wish to be American" and "whose interests are bound with the welfare of the United States."[45]

The transformation of Tule Lake into the internment system's "segregation center" meant that unlike at other centers, its administrators no longer needed to prioritize the goal of making their impounded community appear to be a simulacrum of liberal democratic society. Instead, Tule Lake would become the compound to which those deemed unfit for freedom could be expelled and permanently incarcerated with little apology. Its existence as a space of unfreedom made it possible for individuals in the other relocation centers to be constituted as free. Thus, in its final quantitative report on internment, the WRA acknowledged that its concept of "free individual" was a relational category deriving its meaning from the individual's position within differentiated but interlocked spaces of confinement. It stated that in the fall of 1943, those marked for segregation streamed into Tule Lake, while "certain 'free' individuals" (note the scare quotes around "free" in the original) flowed out (see figure 2). Conversely, suggesting that Tule Lake also operated as a space of freedom in comparison with even more restrictive sites, it noted that from September 1943 to May 1944 the segregation center accepted some 134 "paroled" aliens who had been incarcerated in Justice Department Internment Camps. In the period of mass entrainments to and from Tule Lake between mid-September and mid-October 1943, 6,289 "free" individuals were pulled out of the segregation center and deposited in one of six relocation centers, while Tule Lake accepted 8,559 of the segregated and their immediate family members who had been newly "unfreed" from the nine other relocation centers.[46]

During the process of separating the loyals from the disloyals, the segregation center had been remade to embody physically, which is to say symbolically as well as practically, the logic of rule by force. Here is how Thomas and Nishimoto described the transformation:

FIGURE 2.
"Free individuals" arriving in the Granada Relocation Center
from Tule Lake. *War Relocation Authority Photographs of Japanese-
American Evacuation and Resettlement,* BANC PIC 1967.014—PIC.
John McClelland, photographer. 15 September 1943. Courtesy
of the Bancroft Library, University of California, Berkeley.

A double "manproof" fence, eight feet high, was constructed around the
whole area, and a new gate was built between Ward VII and the administrative
area. The external guard of military police was increased from a couple of
hundred soldiers to full battalion strength, and new barracks were built to
accommodate them. In the military area, half a dozen tanks, obsolete but
impressive, were lined up in full view of the residents. At this point there
followed numerous resignations among the Caucasian personnel in protest
against the transformation of Tule Lake into what had the aspect of a concentration camp. Notable among these were some socially minded persons
who had been in close and cooperative relations with the evacuees and had
promoted their efforts to develop a democratic organization within the center.[47]

While the WRA sought in general to release internees from the other relocation
centers into mainstream society, it prohibited direct resettlements out of the Tule Lake

segregation center. It also abandoned the pretense of internee self-government by eliminating the usual community government program. Elementary and high school education became optional rather than compulsory, a change that contrasts sharply with the establishment and accreditation of a junior college in the Manzanar relocation center just about a month before Tule Lake's new designation. To be sure, Tule Lake continued to operate with some semblances of liberal governmentality, such as hospital services, freedom of religion (except Shinto), a community newspaper, and voluntary rather than forced employment. But continued conflicts between administrators and internees over working conditions, the corruption of WRA employees, and the lack of self-government, as well as inadequate food and medical services— all culminating in a massive protest in the fall of 1943 to which the administration responded with extreme brutality—made it clear that in the balance between force and guidance that characterized all the camps, at Tule Lake force would rule.[48]

As Richard Drinnon uncovered in much detail some time ago, on 4 November internal security officers literally cracked down on protesting internees with beatings and baseball bats. Suspension of all pretensions to freedom followed immediately when the army entered the camp on the same day and placed it under martial law, a condition that did not end until January of the following year.[49] In this arrangement there would be no complex relationship of guiding and being guided between the white governors and the governed but rather a strict divide, as was symbolized by the high barbed wire, manproof fence that was built to separate what was called the Caucasian section of the camp (the administration building, living quarters, warehouses, and hospital) from the rest of the center. In addition, immediately after their takeover of the camp the army fenced off a high-security area within the center and operated it as a heavily militarized stockade for hundreds of alleged "troublemakers" who were held for indefinite periods of time. Labeled "Area B" or the "Surveillance Area," this was yet another zone of unfreedom carved into and thereby constituting the rest of the center as the relatively free space of Area A. The army, and then in its last months the WRA, continued to operate the stockade until August 1944.[50]

But Tule Lake and the general practice of exclusions were the exceptions that enabled liberal governmentality to further develop in the other relocation centers. For example, registration and army enlistment went relatively smoothly at Poston, resulting in 100 percent compliance with registration and 236 army volunteers, the second-highest number of any camp (Minidoka had 308). But as the center's team captain, First Lieutenant John H. Bolton, explained, the FBI's removal of two troublemakers had been partly responsible for the relatively few complications. Anticipating the conversion of Tule Lake into the segregation center, Bolton further recommended a general policy whereby the "small percentage of *disloyal* and trouble makers" would be removed and held in one of the existing centers. This should be done "quietly and without any publicity," he said, just as had been done in Poston.[51]

At Gila River the "purifying process" during February and March 1943 proceeded as follows. The teams commenced registration on 10 February, but responses to the loyalty questions in the first days proved extremely disappointing. When the Japanese American team member, a sergeant, addressed a meeting of internees on the 10th, he was subjected to "severe heckling interspersed with threats of bodily violence plus obscene and profane abuse. . . . Sergeant Aburamen was followed to his car by a jeering mob singing the Japanese National anthem. . . . Other members of the Military staff were subjected to taunts and insulted while traveling about the Center, in both Japanese and American [*sic*], during this period." As the team leader, Captain Norman R. Thompson, reported: "Another favorite antic was performed chiefly by truck drivers who swerved their trucks at us at the moment of passing, whether we were on foot or in a car, counting on the dust to obscure their license plate." On the 12th, Colonel W. F. Scobey, executive officer of the assistant secretary of war, and Lieutenant J. D. Hughes of OPMG arrived at the center. Scobey met with internee leaders and tried to persuade them not to interfere with registration and recruitment. The authorities reacted to these difficulties by suspending registration on the 13th and 14th while determining that groups composed primarily of Kibei were hurting responses. Registration and recruitment of volunteers resumed on the 15th.[52]

In the meantime, following a phone conversation with Myer on the 12th, Gila River Project Director L. H. Bennett initiated an investigation of "subversive activities." This investigation involved rechecking the list of ten names that he and his staff had already given to Myer and investigating "every evacuee and appointed personnel who we," said Bennett, "thought could contribute something to the identification of the subversive persons." Bennett, two members of his staff, and Thompson met with the U.S. Attorney in Phoenix, a Mr. Flint, and provided him with information about twenty suspect persons, of whom sixteen were aliens. Flint agreed to request a presidential warrant for the arrest of the noncitizens on the list as long as the FBI took responsibility for making the arrests. Bennett and other staff then consulted with the assistant FBI agent in charge, a Mr. Colter. The latter agreed to cooperate; and following the warrant's issuance on the morning of the 16th, Colter sent twelve agents to arrest the aliens. Thompson, Bennett, and his staff decided to add more Kibei names to the four that were on the list of twenty, after which Bennett instructed the camp internal security force to escort all the suspect Kibei to Moab.

The sweeping arrests of twenty-seven aliens and Kibei on the 16th required the close coordination not only of the WRA, FBI, and the Justice Department but also of the military police. Bennett, in consultation with the others involved, arranged to have military guards posted at the entrance to the center as well as "at the fence gates at each community [of which there were two, 3 miles apart] to stop traffic to and from the communities and disburse [*sic*] crowds gathering during the removal of these persons." At the appointed hour of 3 P.M. sharp, FBI cars driven by WRA staff moved into first the Butte, and then the Canal communities making up the project. The agents removed targeted individuals from the center, one at a time, and transferred each onto a truck waiting at the military police headquarters. This headquarters had been set up in advance, at the intersection of the roads leading away from the two camps and to Phoenix. WRA internal security followed this same procedure for the Kibei, transferring each suspect to a second truck waiting near the one for aliens. A platoon of military police armed with submachine guns stood in readiness near the trucks. It took a mere two hours and twenty-five minutes to complete the operation, enabling Bennett to report that by 6 P.M. the entire center had been "restored to normal." By that time the truck carrying aliens was on its way to a Justice Department internment camp at Lordsburg, New Mexico. At 7 P.M. the truck with Kibei U.S. citizens was en route to the Moab Isolation Center. Subsequent to the sweep, internees who had made negative entries on their loyalty questions were recalled and allowed to change their answers. Registration of males and females, citizens and noncitizens, continued until its completion on 15 March.[53]

In his 11 February 1943 testimony before the Chandler Subcommittee of the Senate Committee on Military Affairs, Dillon Myer succinctly outlined the system by which the Japanese were to be made free through a labyrinthine system of segregation. The date is significant in that Myer was presenting the WRA's position at the start of the campaign to recruit volunteer soldiers out of the camps and to subject all adults to loyalty questionnaires. "It is our policy at the present time to utilize categories of different kinds as a basis for special investigation," he began. However, he continued,

> it is not the policy of the War Relocation Authority to carry on a segregation
> program by categories without considering individual cases. In summary, then,
> I would like to state that the segregation policy of the War Relocation Authority
> is about as follows:

First, that the most positive form of segregation and most satisfactory is indefinite leave for work outside the centers, and for relocation of those eligible in the fighting forces.

Secondly, placement of aliens that may be considered subversive or trouble makers in Justice dentention [sic] camps or Army internment camps, and we now have an understanding with the Department of Justice that the War Relocation Authority may document any cases, and where we have reasonable grounds they will accept any aliens we may recommend from relocation centers. It is being handled on that basis.

Third, in the case of either aliens or citizens, if crime can be definitely proved, they are being processed through the Federal courts or local and State courts.

Fourth, in the cases of certain citizens of the United States for whom we do not feel we have enough evidence as yet to go through the regular court procedures, we are maintaining at least temporarily an isolation center where they may be isolated from the rest of the groups, and it will perhaps be necessary to continue such centers.

That, Mr. Chairman, I think summarizes the policy at the moment.[54]

In this summary Myer concisely explained that the WRA hoped to return most Japanese Americans—including young men eligible for military service—to the freedom of mainstream society. In order to achieve this goal, the agency conducted investigations based on categories. By "categories" Myer presumably meant classifications such as Issei (first-generation immigrant legally ineligible for citizenship), Nisei (second-generation Japanese American holding U.S. citizenship by birth), or Kibei Nisei (a Nisei who had returned to the United States after having received an education in Japan). But Myer also stressed that judgments by category were not enough. Instead, individual determinations of loyalty were being made.

Myer's testimony, however, revealed the contradiction between the principle of freedom and equality for Japanese Americans and the continuing discrimination against them on account of their "race." For even as Myer stressed the goal of mass release on a case-by-case basis, the term "indefinite leave" suggested that the proper place for Japanese in America during wartime remained the camps, and that as long as the war against Japan continued the released would remain members of a suspect racial group. In fact, under questioning from members of the Chandler subcommittee, Myer assured the senators that the WRA continued to monitor all Japanese Americans after resettlement. Myer told the panel that while only released aliens were legally obligated to keep the WRA informed of their addresses, the WRA required

Japanese American citizens to do so as well because "we think it is essential and practical."[55] When questioned at a later hearing, Myer claimed to know the whereabouts of all 1,760 individuals who had by then received permission for "indefinite leave."[56] This surveillance of all freed internees would last through the war years, thus continuing their contradictory situation of being both freed from the camps and targeted for special tracking. Moreover, until the rescission of the mass exclusion order on 17 December 1944 (effective 3 January 1945), they were not at liberty to move back to the West Coast. The WRA also continued to employ the term "indefinite leave" until 20 December 1944, when, in the wake of the Western Defense Command's announcement that the West Coast exclusion order would be revoked, it announced its plan to close the relocation centers. WRA considered anyone subsequently released to be a "terminal departure."[57]

As for those considered not qualified for "freedom" either outside or inside the WRA camps, Myer described two types of special camps, one intended for noncitizens and the other for citizens. With regard to the former, Myer explained that the Justice Department and the army were holding "aliens that may be considered subversive or troublemakers in Justice dentention [sic] camps or Army internment camps." What he had in mind were the camps administered by the Justice Department or the army, and not by the WRA, that held Japanese and other enemy alien nationals regarded as "dangerous." Civil and military intelligence communities had been monitoring individuals they regarded as especially suspect—usually on very flimsy evidence, such as their status as community leaders or as owners of radios (for example, fisherman)—well before December 1941. Within hours after the Pearl Harbor attack the FBI began arresting them under the authority of the 1918 Alien Enemies Act, which was based on the much older Alien Enemies Act of 1798. By November 1942 some 5,534 persons of Japanese ancestry, in addition to nearly 5,000 of German and more than 2,000 of Italian background, had been taken into custody.[58]

In his testimony Myer failed to mention that in addition to Issei, a considerable number of Nisei had been arrested in the early sweep of "dangerous" individuals, although the Alien Enemies Act clearly did not justify such detentions. Furthermore, a considerable number of Nisei could be found among those excluded from the WRA camps and held in Justice Department camps intended for aliens until the latter were closed down after the war. As Tetsuden Kashima points out, the FBI's early arrests may not have been legal, since its agents began taking suspect Japanese nationals into custody before the United States had officially declared war against Japan. Furthermore, by the end of the war the Justice Department had exceeded its jurisdiction on numerous occasions and had arrested and interned thirty-one Nisei—that is, American citizens—in addition to Japanese nationals.[59]

The Justice Department conducted hearings on those arrested, but on the mainland they did not allow the accused to obtain legal counsel and in both Hawaii and on the mainland appeals were practically impossible. Depending on the result of a hearing, the following actions were possible: repatriation to Japan, release or parole (in Hawaii, but not available on the mainland after the West Coast evacuation), return to Latin America for the few who had immigrated to the United States via that region, and, for most, long-term detention in Justice Department or army camps. After the West Coast roundup, of course, freedom from these camps led directly to reinternment in the temporary "assembly centers" or later the more permanent WRA relocation centers. As Myer explained, the WRA continued to have an arrangement in which those whom administrators regarded as "troublemakers" could be expelled from the "relocation centers" and placed in Justice Department camps. Near the end of the war 5,211 individuals out of the 7,364 internees in the Justice Department camps were of Japanese ancestry. In his impressively comprehensive account of the network of incarceration centers that housed persons of Japanese ancestry during the war years, Tetsuden Kashima estimates that the Justice Department interned a total of some 17,477 persons of Japanese ancestry—or about 54.8 percent of the total number of internees, which, in addition to the Japanese, included individuals of German, Italian, and other backgrounds.[60]

Even more striking in the testimony cited above, however, is Myer's unabashed description of an isolation center for select Japanese American U.S. citizens whom administrators lacked evidence to charge with any crime. Myer described a situation in which WRA administrators were not bound by law or even clear criteria for singling out "troublemakers" who could be expelled from the WRA camps and incarcerated in what amounted to a maximum security prison. The WRA established this camp, the Moab isolation center in Utah, shortly after the so-called Manzanar Riot—a disturbance in the Manzanar relocation center in December 1942 that had erupted within the context of dissatisfaction with camp conditions and a drive to recruit Japanese American linguists into the army. And as Myer predicted in his testimony, although the Moab isolation center was closed in April 1943, its role was taken up first by the Leupp isolation center in Arizona and later by the stockade that was established inside the Tule Lake relocation center.[61]

To sum up, the imaginary of the WRA relocation centers as replicas of the liberal nation-state could be sustained symbolically and practically only in relation to spaces and practices that signified increasing exclusion and unfreedom—namely, the Justice Department and army camps, the Moab and Leupp isolation centers, eventually the Tule Lake Segregation Center, and, within the latter, the stockade. In this connection it should also be remembered that Myer's testimony of 11 February was given at a hearing to consider Senate bill S. 444, which would have transferred WRA responsibilities to the War Department. Myer's success in addressing the concerns of his audience turned out to be of enormous consequence, since had the bill passed, the emerging labyrinthine arrangement for producing the appearance of healthily functioning liberal democratic societies in the relocation centers would have ceased to function and develop. The army would simply have taken over all the centers, as in a permanent state of martial law, and put a halt to the WRA's experiment of ruling the camps through practices of liberal governmentality. Conversely, the bill's failure signaled the establishment of this political rationality as the new common sense for ruling the Japanese American subpopulation.

Even the War Department opposed the bill, as explained by Colonel William P. Scobey of the General Staff, executive officer for Assistant Secretary of War McCloy, because the army was not "particularly qualified to handle" a responsibility that was "of a social nature rather than a military nature." He assured his interlocutor that the army's military police were well prepared to protect the communities outside the relocation centers from being "molested by the Japanese" and that they would respond without hesitation to crises. "Our troops are armed with machine guns, rifles, shotguns, tear gas, the normal complement of weapons that a military force of that size and type would have in its possession," he affirmed. "They are prepared to use them; they are trained in them and will not hesitate to use them in case of emergency." But his main point was that this was the army's role, which did not extend to social management.[62]

Rather than derail the scheme that Myer described to the Senate subcommittee on 11 February, the hearings actually assisted him in moving forward with plans already under way that would satisfy the demands of the War Department, the Senate, the media, the various intelligence communities, and the public at large. The bill's failure to pass signified that the vision of segregation, coupled with spaces of relative but never complete freedom, had come to reflect an emerging consensus on the part of America's civilian and military governors as well as the various intelligence communities about how to manage this still suspect minority. This is not to deny that the senators' interrogations were riddled with unabashedly racist expressions, including frequent use of the term "Japs." Senator Chan Gurney of South Dakota even believed that because released Japanese were "of a different race than most of us in this country," "they should report at least monthly, possibly weekly, as to where they are, so that you hear from them right along and can put your finger on them any day."[63] Yet even the persistence of such vulgar racist sentiments could not subvert the liberal plan that depended to some extent on trusting released Japanese to conduct themselves as loyal Americans.

The report of the House committee whose investigation of the WRA began 8 June 1943 also confirmed the growing if not complete unanimity of the governors. Dated 30 September, the report of the Dies Committee on Un-American activities basically reiterated the fundamental principles that the WRA had already begun putting into operation: namely, it called for further publicity concerning the separation of the loyal from the disloyal, for a board to investigate and consider internee requests for leave clearance, and for the WRA to begin a rigorous Americanization program in the centers.[64]

Much as he had done in his widely publicized letter to Stimson of 1 February 1943, in which he expressed his approval of the formation of the Japanese American combat team, the president himself announced the new consensus about how to manage Japanese Americans in a message of 14 September 1943. This time he not only affirmed the principle of racial equality; he also endorsed the WRA plan for separating the disloyal and possibly disloyal from the loyal, keeping the former group unfree while pressing forward in the release of the latter into mainstream society. Formally, this message had been crafted in response to Senate Resolution No. 166 (6 July 1943), which had called on the president to issue an executive order (1) to segregate the disloyal and those "whose loyalty is questionable" from the loyal; and (2) "to direct the appropriate agency of the Government to issue a full and complete authoritative statement on conditions in relocation centers and plans for future operations." In his message, Roosevelt explained that such an executive order would be doubly redundant. Not only had the WRA already formulated such a segregation plan, but the trains were already transporting internees into and out of the Tule Lake Segregation Center. Furthermore, the Office of War Mobilization had issued a short statement on conditions in the centers and a full report was being made public in conjunction with the president's message. Put differently, Roosevelt observed that Congress and the WRA were in agreement and so he, as president, would simply acclaim the current state of understanding about confinement, freedom, voluntary choice ("they can, and want to"), and race during wartime.

With the segregation of the disloyal evacuees in a separate center, the War Relocation Authority proposes now to redouble its efforts to accomplish the relocation into normal homes and jobs in communities throughout the United States, but outside the evacuated areas, of those Americans of Japanese ancestry whose loyalty to this country has remained unshaken through the hardships of the evacuation which military necessity made unavoidable. We shall restore to the loyal evacuees the right to return to the evacuated areas as soon as the military situation will make such restoration feasible. Americans of Japanese ancestry, like those of many other ancestries, have shown that they can, and want to accept our institutions and work loyally with the rest of us, making their own valuable contribution to the national wealth and well-being. In vindication of the very ideals for which we are fighting this war it is important to us to maintain a high standard of fair, considerate, and equal treatment for the people of this minority as of all other minorities.[65]

DISLOYAL BY REASON OF CULTURE, RELIGION, AND POLITICS

In order to complete the profile of this modality for governing Japanese Americans in time of total war, it is necessary to return to an examination of the questionnaires and trace their travels through the extensive network of authorities and security agencies that made final determinations about an individual's trustworthiness or "loyalty." It is usually forgotten that the questionnaires' two versions each contained far more items than numbers 27 and 28 and that the WRA and War Department based their security evaluations on an overall assessment of the questionnaires in combination with information available from other intelligence sources. Therefore in the case of an individual adult male completing Form 304A and desiring to volunteer, simply submitting an "Application for Voluntary Induction" (Form DSS 165) and answering questions 27 and 28 in the affirmative did not, from a security standpoint, suffice to make him eligible for induction. Instead, a special clearance section within the Counter Intelligence Group (CIG) of the War Department's Office of the Assistant Chief of Staff, G-2 (Intelligence), evaluated the loyalty of every volunteer according to a standardized point system for Form 304A. They also checked individuals against records held by the Military Intelligence Division (MID), ONI, WRA, and FBI. Local Selective Service boards could act on only the applications of those Japanese American volunteers deemed acceptable by the War Department through this screening procedure. Although AC of S, G-2, discarded the rigid point system when it began processing young men for the draft (which followed the phase of recruiting volunteers) because it felt that a more flexible and individualized approach to evaluating potential draftees was warranted, it nevertheless continued to utilize Form 304A and to follow the general assessment guidelines established under the volunteer program.[66]

The criteria and point system used by CIG's Japanese Section to evaluate Form 304A were clearly written down in a document titled "Analysis Chart of Special Questionnaires Relating to Citizens of Japanese Ancestry Who Make Application for Voluntary Induction Into the Army of the United States for Service with the Combat Team." This "analysis chart" is extremely suggestive about how the army and by extension the government understood admissibility into the nation in the wake of the official disavowal of biological racism. First, given CIG's desire to identify links to the enemy nation and people, a number of fairly obvious scoring criteria highlighted assessments of the individual's familial, social, and other material connections to Japan. These items were citizenship of marriage partner; citizenship of parents; existence of relatives already in the military; residence of family members; educational background; frequency of travel to and investments in Japan (for example, rejection of anyone who had purchased yen since 1935); contributions made to societies, clubs and organizations; magazines and newspapers of choice (English-language publications such as the Japanese American Citizens League's *Pacific Citizen* were favored), birth registration with Japanese consulate (better if not registered), and any previous applications for repatriation to Japan. Besides such unsurprising instructions, the chart advised evaluators to award positive points to individuals whose responses indicated cultural (including religious) distance from Japan, assimilation to (white) "anglicized" culture, and participation in mainstream rather than radical politics of any kind.

Thus the first response on Form 304A for which evaluators gave or subtracted points was question 1, name. The chart instructed: "If first name is anglicized and Japanese given name is no longer used—(1 point in favor). If Japanese given name is still used (1 point against)." Although much has been made about the oppressiveness of the "name-changing campaign" in colonial Korea, where the colonial authorities compelled Koreans to take up "Japanese" names in favor of Korean ones (see chapter 8), this item reveals a similar conflation of culture and nation. Reflecting the extreme assimilationist pressure especially on nonwhite communities outside as well as inside the camps to name properly, in Hawaii some 2,400 individuals in 1942 petitioned to anglicize their names.[67] Question 16 concerned religion: "Christian—(2 points in favor). Buddhist—(1 point against). Shintoist—(2 or 3 points against him). Worships regularly at Shintoist shrine—reject him." We have already seen in the previous chapter how military authorities and intelligence communities feared a global alliance of color led by the Japanese and united by the religion of Islam, but here we see another instance in which religion mattered in assessing admissibility to the nation. Not surprisingly, Japan's total war empire exhibited a similar collapsing of religion onto national belonging, but with "Shintoist" on top and "Christian" as most suspect, particularly in a colony such as Korea. With regard to language, in wartime Japan discourses on national admissibility increasingly emphasized ability to speak the "national language," an acquired cultural skill rather than the supposedly natural attribute of ethnicity. But item 18 took foreign-language ability to what appears to be an almost hysterical level of suspicion. It noted: "Facility in reading Japanese—(3 points against him); Speaking Japanese—none. No knowledge of Japanese—(2 points in favor). If subject speaks a foreign language other than Japanese—(1 point in favor)." The last concession to the value of knowledge of languages other than English in time of war stands in sharp contrast to the almost absurd contradiction between the negative points given to those who could read Japanese and the military's simultaneous effort to identify and train such individuals as interpreters and translators for national defense. Item 13, on education, also dismissed any form of education that might have promoted facility in Japanese, warning that if the individual attended Japanese language school in the United States a point should be deducted and worse yet, "if he continued language school while in high school, it shows less Americanization than if he told parents he didn't have enough time to go. Also in the higher grades he gets more Shinto-Yamato race instruction."

The chart advised evaluators to be attentive to a category that might appear to be innocuous but was judged to reveal much about an individual's trustworthiness from the point of view of culture: namely, "sports and hobbies." The guidelines for question 19 indicated that negative points should be assigned to those interested in what were regarded as quintessentially Japanese and nationalistic sports such as "Kudo [sic; archery], Judo, or Kendo. "If high Judo—Best to reject him. Judo instructor—reject." Conversely, "If sport is typically American—(1 point in favor). If sport is typically Japanese—(1 point against him)." Most likely reflecting fears of spying, the instructions noted: "If hobby is collecting anything—this is not too good—(1 point against him). If hobby is photography or radio—(1 point against him)."

This fear of "fifth column" activities most likely explains the deductions to be taken for some types of employment. Next to working directly for a Japanese government agency and as a "sea-going radio operator," both of which warranted immediate rejection, employment in a "semi-official firm such as Mitsubishi or Mitsui," work as a "newspaper man" in Japanese-language newspapers or periodicals in Japan or the United States, "Japanese-language instructor," and just holding a license as an "amateur radio operator" were most suspicious—all warranted two- or three-point deductions. But obsessive anxieties about the duplicitous Japanese made a number of other less obvious occupational categories grounds for assessing one negative point: "fisherman," "hotel owner or operator," "taxi driver," "importing or exporting business," "merchant marine," "steel foundry, automobile, heavy machinery," and "steamship line." For whatever reason, military intelligence determined that working in agriculture was a good sign ("1 point for him") while one occupation was neither positive nor negative: "miner—(zero)."

Finally, reflecting liberal governmentality's strategy of constituting self-conscious subject-citizens rather than passive objects of rule, the chart instructed evaluators to award points for positive forms of involvement in mainstream political and social activities and organizations. Thus item 7 indicated: "If a registered voter—(1 point in favor). If registered in first national election subsequent to his coming of age (here see date of birth)—(1 point in favor)." Conversely, they were to deduct points and even reject some individuals for political tendencies they thought threatened the liberal democratic form of government: "If registered in the Communist Party, rejection must be made." This principle had nothing to do with loyalty to Japan, since the Japanese empire's security policies were even more rabidly anticommunist than those of the U.S. government. Scoring for question 17 likewise reflected this logic. While membership in the Japanese American Citizens League (JACL), the hyper-American organization guided by wealthier Japanese Americans, warranted the addition of two points, belonging to the Congress of Industrial Organizations (CIO) counted "1 point against." Perhaps a bit alarmed at the constitutional issues involved in this assumption of disloyal tendencies on account of political views, one evaluator added a handwritten comment next to this stipulation: "Heavens!" Elsewhere he or she had written, "How important is the 'collecting'?"[68]

As briefly noted earlier, the files of volunteers who met these guidelines and passed supplementary background checks were forwarded to the Selective Service, after which the applicants became eligible for physical examinations and induction. AC of S, G-2, returned the files of those found unacceptable to the WRA, and the latter forwarded these files to the OPMG and the Japanese-American Joint Board (JAJB) for processing. AC of S, G-2, continued to screen Japanese Americans for military service until 25 July 1944. At that time the War Department transferred this clearance function to the OPMG, where the responsibility was taken up by what became its Military Clearance Section, Japanese-American Branch, Personnel Security Division.[69]

The OPMG and the JAJB also cooperated in screening the files of all adult female citizens and adult nonvolunteer (that is, most) male citizens as they were considered for indefinite leave and employment in "plants and facilities important to the war effort." Within the OPMG, the Japanese-American Section (later Branch and then Class IV Installation) in the Industrial Employee Security Branch, Personnel Security Division, evaluated each case on the basis of the subject's questionnaire, the WRA's Form 26 (Employment Data Form), and other intelligence checks. The Japanese-American Section carried the strong imprint of the army volunteer and registration campaign, since it was initially headed by Captain Norman R. Thompson, who had been the team captain charged with registration at the Gila Relocation Center. Moreover, seven former team captains assisted Thompson, and nine of the twenty-three sergeant investigators were also former team members. Twenty-one civilians filled out the original staff of fifty-two.[70]

As originally intended, the Joint Board was then supposed to make a recommendation regarding indefinite leave and eligibility for work in "plants and facilities important to the war effort." However, because of the volume of cases, in the first months of the arrangement the Joint Board often made assessments regarding leave without determining eligibility for war plant employment. This failure to make recommendations, combined with the Joint Board's advisory status, allowed the WRA to release some 10,000 internees from the relocation centers in May and June 1943 and the employment of hundreds of them in vital war plants without its approval. In part to deal with what it considered a security problem, the War Department issued another directive on 14 October 1943, which it made it possible for the OPMG to determine eligibility for war plant employment without involving the Joint Board. As a result the OPMG considered 3,381 applications for employment in facilities, approving 1,921, disapproving 810, and withholding a decision on 650 cases. In making these determinations the OPMG ordered agents out in the field to make local investigations, and those agents increasingly moved toward interviewing the subjects themselves. This was a practice that the OPMG had tried to avoid in the past, for "it had never been considered good form to interview American citizens because of the possibility of invasion of the sacred constitutional rights." The Joint Board continued to make recommendations concerning indefinite leave, and by 1 May 1944 it had done so for about 40,000 adult U.S. citizens; but it was finally disestablished on 25 May 1944, and its duties were transferred to the OPMG.[71]

In the above I have tried to demonstrate that the February–March 1943 army recruitment and registration campaigns constituted an important moment in the decisive shift toward managing the Japanese American population through the political rationality of liberal governmentality. This modality of governing coincided with the shift away from vulgar racism as analyzed in the previous chapter and operated through the recognition of internees as free and self-conscious subjects. The commitment to governing through the free will of the internees was most paradigmatically embodied in questions 27 and 28, which asked for voluntary professions of willingness to risk life in military service and uncompromised loyalty.

At the same time, exceptions enabled liberal rule. These included violent and repressive means such as the declaration of martial law (ironically, inside the Tule Lake Center, thereby constituting the center in normal times as a space of freedom); sweeping arrests of alleged "troublemakers" with the aid of the FBI and the army to "purify" the relocation centers; the elaboration of a labyrinthine system of spaces of incarceration that required the cooperation of the WRA with the FBI, the Department of Justice, and the War Department; and exceptional security instruments and practices, beginning with the questionnaires. In this system of (un)free spaces, America external to the camps signified the most freedom, but even on the outside Japanese through the war years continued to be objects of special security attention as a matter of race, even as markers of culture, class (JACL), and political ideology (Communists and Japanists) continued to be used to determine who among the (formerly) despised could be admitted into the army, war plants, other sensitive places, and the nation at large. Even after the Western Defense Command on 17 December 1944 publicly announced its decision to revoke the order barring Japanese from the West Coast, the OPMG continued to make recommendations concerning individual admissibility into the nation. In the interim between the announcement of the order's rescission and its effective date of 2 January 1945, OPMG recommended that some 11,000 individuals continue to be excluded from the area as exceptions to the reversal of the mass exclusion policy.[72]

The WRA and the OPMG often appear in the archival records as mutually antagonistic and in fundamental conflict, the one criticizing the other for excessive severity or laxity in managing the Japanese American population. OPMG personnel complained that since its and the Joint Board's recommendations concerning indefinite leave were technically only advisory, the WRA often released individuals it had unfavorably reviewed or whose cases it had not even considered. Also, since the Joint Board in principle assessed only citizens, the WRA acted alone in releasing noncitizens. The OPMG further accused WRA officials of sometimes failing to inform potential employers when recommendations had been made against clearing released internees to work in war plants. In short, OPMG's personnel charged the WRA with security recklessness.[73]

Conversely, WRA administrators tended to regard the OPMG as overly zealous about restricting employment in war plants and facilities. Indeed, despite the OPMG's official criticism of discrimination, its staff often made remarks of the "vulgar racist" kind. For example, even at the close of March 1945, when the war's end was well in sight, the director of OPMG's Personnel Security Division explained to the assistant secretary of war why he opposed the relaxation of security precautions for Japanese Americans seeking employment in vital war plants. After offering a litany of reasons for continuing to regard Japanese Americans as extremely suspect, he concluded that factors of an intangible quality but of significant importance such as the "racial distinction itself" set this segment of population apart for special consideration.[74]

Similarly, the eight-hour "Japanese-American Course" that many Japanese-American Branch investigators took to prepare them for conducting field investigations on individuals perpetuated the idea that assimilation to (white) "anglicized" American culture indicated admissibility into the nation, while also at times blurring the boundary between culture and race. Thus, like the guidelines for evaluating army volunteers, the "Outline of Japanese-American Course" told agents to regard proficiency in the Japanese language as suspect and emphasized that "one who is unable to speak English with reasonable clarity can hardly be said to be American." Similarly, reflecting the common though misguided and arrogant assumption that religion in the United States had little to do with nationalism, as a result of its healthy separation of church and state, whereas religion for the Japanese was "far more nationalistic than with other people," the outline advised investigators to be wary of Buddhists and Shintoists while Christianity "should be held in the Subject's favor." In its conclusion the course outline emphasized the pathology of the Japanese American population, which was "so completely disassociated from the way of life which is normally considered American that it can be profitably approached by an investigator only after considerable preparation and study of its peculiar culture and philosophy." And finally, "In conducting investigations of Japanese, you may rest assured that you are dealing with one member of a race which has on many occasions demonstrated its capacity for deceit."[75]

However, to view the OPMG and the WRA as fundamentally in conflict with each other, with the one understood as repressive and the other as liberal, would be to misrecognize their operations as two agencies that along with other intelligence communities—in particular the ONI, the FBI, the Justice Department, and the War Department's own military intelligence—meshed together to form the web of authorities making up the same wartime liberal state. Much as the unabashedly repressive and exclusionary character of the Tule Lake Segregation Center and the pastoral guidance practiced in the other nine camps were interlocked, so these two agencies supplemented one another while sharing information and interacting with the other intelligence communities. Together they constituted the regime of liberal governmentality that enveloped the labyrinthine internment complex but extended far beyond it to the nation's borders, and that after the war would become part of its strategy for achieving global hegemony. Moreover, even as WRA administrators such as Myer consistently assailed those he called "race-baiters" and advanced the liberal position of the time that Japanese Americans should be drafted into the military just like all other Americans, he simultaneously and unapologetically targeted these same people for special surveillance and subjected Japanese American citizens and noncitizens alike to tests of loyalty that the government required of no other U.S. minority. In other words, whatever these liberals might have said, they never relinquished the idea of the Japanese as a suspect race—a race presumed unfit for citizenship until proven loyal through background checks and self-professed oaths of allegiance.

Completion of questionnaires by some 74,703 of the 77,957 internees eligible to register meant that the civil and military authorities as well as the intelligence communities had produced an enormous database on the internees, both as an aggregated population and as individuals. This enabled the authorities to make distinctions between individual Japanese, separating those they considered trustworthy from the untrustworthy; to tabulate the data by social categories; and to facilitate the return of Japanese Americans into mainstream society, where they could help fill shortages in the civilian and military labor pool. At the same time, the ritual of filling in the questionnaires compelled every adult citizen internee, male or female, to make a clear choice between declaring loyalty to the United States or to Japan. Even the OPMG's official history of its involvement in the loyalty investigations of Japanese Americans during the Second World War recognized and celebrated its roles both in collecting data on a specific minority population and in obliging individual Japanese Americans to constitute themselves into self-conscious subjects through repeated rituals of choice.

OPMG has contributed to the future solution of the Japanese problem by compiling the most complete record that has ever been accumulated on any segment of our population and which will be of inestimable value to governmental agencies in the future social, economic, and political readjustments of those persons of Japanese descent. In this connection it may be fairly stated that while the original policy and program was so directed that the Japanese were in many instances permitted to evade commitments for or against his country, the subsequent modifications including particularly the re-institution of Selective Service, segregation, and renunciation of citizenship, tended to a crystallization of thought and action among Japanese. They were gradually brought into a position where they were obliged to make a positive choice between this country and the homeland of their fathers[76]

The OPMG correctly noted that repetitive trials within the internment experience, beginning with the ritual of registration, forced Japanese Americans to make choices about national belonging. Yet it is important to note that the supposed accomplishment of coercing Japanese Americans into choosing one national affiliation to the exclusion of the other inadvertently reveals that American citizens of Japanese ancestry had never previously been presented with such clear options. As the WRA's solicitor put it, earlier they had been like so many "blocks of wood." Ironically, the nation formally welcomed Japanese Americans into the nation more aggressively than at any previous time precisely at the moment when they seemed so obviously to be targets of special racist discrimination. The choice was theirs to make—and if they chose noncompliance with registration or to answer the key questions with "no," they had to be prepared to face what amounted to absolute exclusion from the national community, to be cursed and condemned to a kind of eternal fire prepared for the unwilling.

CHAPTER FOUR

Reasoning, Counterreasonings, and Counter-conduct

> [I]t seems a universal observation that one cannot have
> self-management in any kind of community without
> struggles and politics, sometimes more disturbing, some-
> times less, but always there. . . . The alternative is toward
> force, to which there is always resistance and this leads by
> action and reaction to extremes of suppression, resulting
> in tyranny, slave labor and undercover antagonism. Ineffi-
> cient self-rule, charged with good will, sloppy as it may
> be, seems to be better and more economical than anything
> else attainable.
>
> ALEXANDER H. LEIGHTON (on the Poston Relocation
> Center), *The Governing of Men* (1946)

In the previous chapter I charted the shift in modality of governing Japanese Americans toward a complex governmentality that mobilized exceptions and force precisely for the purpose of enabling liberal rule. As Dillon S. Myer put it in response
to aggressive questioning in the Senate about the need to more strictly police the internees, "it is a question whether we are going to make more fifth columnists by one
kind of treatment"—that is, by severity—"or whether by another type of treatment
we are going to make more good citizens."[1] Yet in the process I have only in passing observed the internees as they lived through this historical juncture, and how
they participated in or refused volunteering for the army and registration. In this
chapter I attend to this task, not through lenses that focus and simplify using the binary framework of resistance or collaboration, and even less with an intent to prove
that most Japanese Americans were basically loyal Americans. Such objectives would
unwittingly reproduce the framework of the authorities themselves, who had shifted
to the view that the overwhelming majority of Japanese Americans were loyal and
that registration was intended to separate out the unredeemable from those who
could be safely released into mainstream society or the "free" spaces of the nine cen-

ters other than Tule Lake. Instead, I explore the utterances and acts of the governed in relation to the demand that they speak as supposedly free subjects. As we will see, governing in this modality was a messy affair.

One of the most striking aspects of Japanese American responses to registration and the campaign for army volunteers is the intensity and frequency with which they produced counterquestions. For example, while the War Relocation Authority (WRA) and War Department questionnaires contained 33 and 28 questions, respectively, after a series of meetings the Community Council of Tule Lake presented their project director with some 150 queries about volunteering, registration, and the questionnaires. Tule Lake was a particular hotspot in the registration effort, but the ferocity and quantity of their questions were by no means atypical. Most internees responded to the numerous questions not with answers but with a barrage of counterquestions, some effectively if only momentarily sabotaging the reasoning of all those civilian, military, and intelligence agencies that had come together to collect information about them and to make them speak. Nevertheless, over the long run their dialogue with the governors resulted in the elaboration of a liberal model for governing a society that would include suspect minorities.

The internees' prerogatives to question, to submit petitions, and to expect answers emerged within the context of liberal governmentality. Since this was a modality of governance that was supposed to operate through reason and the mobilization of supposedly free subjects, the authorities had to give the internees opportunities to listen to official rationale and to ask questions. Of course, many authorities attributed to the American-educated, Christian, more assimilated, and wealthier among them a greater capacity for reason than laborers and those they considered uneducated. For instance, at Minidoka, where no one refused to register and the army recruited the most volunteers, the team captain Stanley D. Arnold attributed these circumstances to the belief shared by many that internees in the center from Washington State (who made up the overwhelming majority of the internees in Minidoka) were of a better and "different class, generally speaking, from others of their race on the Pacific Coast." On the one hand, the Japanese who had immigrated to California and Oregon

> were largely lower class peasants in Japan with little education, no money, and bound to old country religions through fear and ignorance. The Washington Japanese on the other hand came to this country of their own accord, with some education and either money or business connections. They came because it was the land of opportunity and not a land of necessity. They had done will [sic]

financially in the Puget Sound area. . . . [A] large majority of the younger generation have [*sic*] adopted Christianity. . . . There were few, if any, Buddhist volunteers.[2]

In his study of Poston, the social scientist Alexander H. Leighton similarly displayed this Orientalist understanding of raucous internees as somehow out of time and lacking reason when he invoked the historian Hugh Borton's study of peasant uprisings in Tokugawa Japan (1600–1867) to analyze the famous Poston Center strike of fall 1942.[3]

Notwithstanding such class-based, religious, and Orientalist prejudices, the War Department was so committed to dialogue that it provided the team captains not only with the "Relocation Center Address," in which they assured the internees that "words of explanation are owed to you," but also with answers to anticipated queries from the internees. Many of these questions concerned mundane details about the volunteer program, but others touched on the contradictions between the government's disavowal of racism and its actually existing policies. They pointed to soft spots in the reasoning of the authorities, and the teams administering the questionnaires had to be able to somehow answer them. "Is the formation of a Japanese American combat team a type of segregation?" "Will the combat team be officered by Americans of Japanese blood throughout?" "Have Japanese Americans already in the military service been discriminated against?" "Why were some Japanese Americans discharged?" "Will my family be permitted to return to the West Coast?"[4]

Of course, any attempt to recuperate and narratively represent Japanese American responses to the calls to volunteer for the military and to complete the questionnaires is bound to failure. Such a task can never completely succeed, because as difficult, or rather as impossible, as it is to fully recapture the subjectivity of even one individual, the impediments are multiplied by the tens of thousands if the task is such retrieval for all Japanese Americans based on fragments of evidence and the inevitably politicized postwar memories of internment. As Joan Scott in her classic essay on the "evidence of experience" argued some time ago, there are no pure unmediated texts through which we can access the experience of our subjects, since representations, even by the subjects themselves, are always already mediated. And as Gayatri Spivak offered in a much-cited and provocative essay on the dilemma of subaltern studies, any attempt to recuperate subaltern pasts must in the end face a wall of inaccessibility. Any summarizing of Japanese American experiences of volunteering, registration, and internment will always involve an erasure or forgetting of tens of thousands of singular experiences.[5]

My strategy in acknowledging this aporia will be to begin by transcribing and clustering together examples of the major types of questions that internees asked at their many meetings with the War Department teams and WRA administrators. This cacophony of counterquestions produced conversations among the internees themselves, responses from the authorities, and further counterresponses, resulting in rather coherent discursive formations. All of these discourses had precedents in the months before registration, as we will see, but they circulated widely and in logically consistent form through the registration process. The dominant discourses included two versions of Americanism that I will call "unconditional loyalty" and "conditional loyalty." These discourses shared many characteristics even as they produced and reflected conflicts among the internees. The common elements included, most importantly, valorization of the supposedly unique universal ideals of America: freedom, equality, security, and happiness. This overlapping made it possible and common for individuals to move from the logic of "conditional" to "unconditional" loyalty as a result of dialogues with or compulsion from other internees or the authorities. On the other hand, discourses that explicitly rejected the truthfulness of America's claims to embody these universal ideals existed as well and had the potential to radically sabotage the governors' reasoning

A FLOOD OF QUESTIONS

Several WRA staff and War Department teams transcribed or summarized internee questions, and they can be clustered together around several broad themes that reflect internee sentiments.[6] To simplify citation, I use the following codes:

GMH42   Gila, "Butte Community Open Meeting," 10 February 1943,
         Mess Hall #42

GMH52   Gila, "Butte Community Open Meeting," 9 February 1943,
         Mess Hall #52

TL304A   Tule Lake, "Questions Pertaining to Form 304-A"

TL126   Tule Lake, "Questions Pertaining to WRA Form 126-Revised"

RC   Rohwer Relocation Center, Summary of Questions at Block
         Meetings

PI   Poston, "Minutes of Meeting for Registration: Meeting for
         Registration of Roku I," 10 February 1943

PII   Poston, "Minutes of Meeting for Registration: Meeting for
         Registration of Roku II," 11 February 1943

In addition, to aid readability I have added question marks to those transcriptions that do not have them and I have omitted the use of *sic* to indicate typographical errors and ungrammatical sentences, since its repetition would have been tiresome. The word "note" prefaces an observation made by me in reference to an internee question.

1.   Some questions professed an inability to comprehend the reasoning of the questions.

>   "I would like to know your definition of a loyal American citizen. Japanese or not." (GMH52)

>   "I don't understand the loyal and unloyal citizen." (GMH52)

>   "What does the phrase 'unqualified allegiance to the United States of America' as stated in question 28 of WRA126-Rev. mean specifically?" (TL126)

>   "What is the definition of the word loyalty? (Issei standpoint)" (TL126)

>   "Clarification of question 27 in forms requested." (PII)

>   "Question 28 explanation requested." (PII)

>   "If the answer to question #27 is 'no' does that mean that said person is disloyal to the U.S.?" (Note: Answer was, "My interpretation is either that person is disloyal to the United States or he is a pantywaist.") (GMH52)

2.   Others more aggressively challenged the reasonableness of the questions, sometimes asking the governors to put themselves in the internees' place and view the questions from their perspective.

>   "What would you do under the same circumstances as us, Captain?" (GMH52)

>   "If you were evacuated from your home and brought out to a concentration camp like this, would you still feel loyal to U.S. after they push you around like an enemy alien (4-C)?" (GMH52)

>   "In case of a Nisei whose father was put in the internment camp forcefully and by the evacuation his mother being very poor economically, does the U.S. War Department think that that Nisei can contribute to the U.S. wholeheartedly? What is the U.S. Department opinion?" (TL304A)

3.   Others challenged the capacity of questions 27 and 28 to reflect internee sentiments, often suggesting the inadequacy of the simple binary option of affirmative or negative answers.

> "Could Question 28 be modified or struck out entirely? Also question
> 27, can it be modified or struck out?" (TL304A)
>
> "Must all questions be answered by only 'yes' or 'No'?" (GMH52)
>
> "Should make three (3) answers possible; namely, 'yes,' 'no' or 'neutral.' "
> (TL304A)
>
> "Regarding Question #27, can we describe the reason for putting
> down 'no'?" (TL304A)
>
> "Is it possible to answer question 27 with a conditional 'yes'?"
> (TL304A)
>
> "Would it be satisfactory to write 'undecided' at present?" (TL126)

4. One of the three most frequently asked types of questions in varying degrees
   contested the reasonableness of questions 27 and 28, given the history of
   discriminatory treatment and the failure of the government to protect life.
   Most internees felt that their lives had been ruined; and with ongoing agitation against them in Congress as well as in mainstream society, many had
   great reservations about their future lives in the United States. On this point
   the authors of *The Spoilage* long ago succinctly and accurately observed,
   "The questions, and their method of presentation, aroused a strong protest
   reaction among Nisei, who, having had almost all their rights as citizens
   abrogated through evacuation and forcible confinement, questioned the justice of the restoration of just the one 'right' of serving in the armed forces."
   Dorothy Swaine Thomas and Richard S. Nishimoto pointed to the extremely
   high percentage of Nisei males answering "no" to question 28, far higher
   than the comparable figure for alien males, and declared that negative responses signified not necessarily disloyalty but rather protest. The highest
   proportion of such protest "no's" came from Manzanar, where some 52 percent of citizen males answered 28 in the negative, as did only a little more
   than 1 percent of their noncitizen counterparts.[7]

   a. Some made it plain that the past history of discrimination made it unreas-
      onable to request volunteering or active participation in the war effort.

      > "How are you expecting us to volunteer after depriving of practically
      > everything what we have? Will you tell us where is liberty and justice
      > for us to fight for? What do you mean by saying 'fair treatment'?"
      > (GMH42)
      >
      > "What have we got to fight for—especially now that we are in a camp
      > like this?" (GMH52)

"Wouldn't the war department have gotten larger number of volunteers if we had been left in our homes?" (PI)

"When all Japanese (Nisei and Isseis) were officially ignored from some Oregon cities, when an attempt was made to take nisei's citizenship away, when citizens and aliens were put behind fences, and even Nisei Volunteers were refused before evacuation and Kibeis discharged, is it necessary to register or volunteer? Personally, the answer is *NO*." (emphasis in original) (TL304A)

"Can Japanese soldier or civilian nisei go back to California? If we . can't go back, why should we go into the Army?" (TL304A)

"Is the Army informed about the prejudices and discrimination toward the beet field workers last year? (Those men went out to relieve the labor shortage, thereby aiding the war effort, but were the American people willing to accept that as a symbol of loyalty and good faith toward the U.S. No. Prejudice and discrimination shows that they were not willing to recognize the contribution made by the beet workers.)" (parentheses in original) (TL304A)

b. Some contrasted the treatment of Japanese Americans with that of Americans of Italian and German background or worried about differential treatment in general.

"Do you think evacuating Japanese citizens out of California, leaving Germans and Italians, aliens, who don't have to fight for this country have more privilege than citizens of Japanese ancestry? Why?" (GMH52)

"Are other citizens of other nationals answering the same questionnaire? If not why are we required to do so?" (GMH52)

c. Others suggested that internees wanted assurances that the government would restore civil rights, reimburse material losses, and protect Japanese Americans against violence and racism before they could answer affirmatively.

"If we volunteer, would our citizenship rights be restored to us?" (Note: response is "You have lost sight of one essential point. The rights of citizenship have never been taken from you." To which the countercomment is, "But indirectly, privileges have been taken away.") (PI)

"What guarantee have we that our citizenship won't be removed when laws are being passed preventing us from owning land, et cetera, in some states even if we do serve in the Armed Forces?" (RC)

"A request for the guarantee of equal and undiscriminated rights accorded to Caucasians to be added to Question 27 and 28 in Form 304-A." (TL304A)

"Will Government compensate all Japanese for loss of time and money due to evacuation?" (TL304A)

"Has the Army of Government squelched foul propaganda talk made by leading statesmen, editors and writers of various papers and magazines who play on our weakness (Japanese) for their own personal gains by heavily published such undemocratic articles as: (1) deportation of all Japanese and Japanese-Americans after the war (2) not permitting Japanese blood to return to their homes after the war and (3) revoking the citizenship rights from all people of Japanese blood?" (TL304A)

"What will be our economic security and status, if relocated?" (TL126)

5. Another of the three most frequently asked categories of questions concerned more specifically the military and they implied, charged, or expressed fear that the military's policy toward Japanese Americans was racist.

a. Many questions took special aim at the segregated unit as emblematic of racism and pointed out that such a policy was incommensurate with democratic principles. Here and elsewhere, commentators often invoked the term "Jim Crow" and, reflecting their understanding of African Americans as the most abjected group within the military, worried about themselves falling into the category of "Negroes." There were also concerns of being used as cannon fodder.

"By forming a separate Japanese combat unit will it not tend to retard the understanding of Japanese and the Caucasians, rather than increase close understanding?" (GMH42)

"For sake of principle, would it not be of more value to be taken into the Army without segregation in order to prove that niseis can prove that they can fight shoulder to shoulder with other Americans, even sacrificing special opportunities for advancement in rank and also sacrificing an opportunity to prove their loyalty by group achievement of a separate battalion?" (GMH42)

"Is not the Nisei battalion a rank discrimination, to be compared with the negro volunteers in the last war?" (PI)

"Does not a 'special' combat team set a dangerous precedent in the treatment of minority groups?" (GMH42)

"In the last World War the Canadian Army sent the Japanese volunteers and Negroes in the front lines and white soldiers behind them and many Japanese and Negroes were slain. Can you guarantee that the U.S. would not do likewise?" (GMH52)

b. Some asked for an explanation of the War Department's inconsistent policy, which changed from excluding Japanese Americans from the military to now mounting an aggressive campaign to recruit them.

"Why does the U.S. Government change it's mind so quick, a year ago they didn't want us in the Army?" (GMH52)

"Today I received a card dated February 5, from my local board classifying me as 4C. Just what is this classification?" (Note: Ironically, this internee received notification of his ineligibility for selective service about a week after announcement of the voluntary program and just before the enlistment campaign began in the camps.) (GMH42)

"A few months after the war, I volunteered and was accepted. Three months after induction, I was suddenly informed that I was no longer wanted in the service and also informed to leave the premises within 24 hours, and not to don my uniform again. After such treatment, how do you expect me to volunteer again?" (GMH52)

"Why were soldiers with parents or relatives in Japan 'kicked out' of the Army and called a spy by some officers? There have been many complaints about this sarcastic discrimination." (GMH42)

c. Some pointed to several inconsistencies between policies for Japanese Americans and other groups while asking for assurances of equal treatment.

"Why aren't we drafted in the same manner as other Caucasians?" (RC)

"What guarantee have we that if drafted, we will have the same rights to deferments for dependents, et cetera, that the Caucasians have?" (RC)

"Will the families of those who enter Army Service be aided in resettlement, or will they have to remain and 'rot' in camp with all its abnormal conditions?" (GMH42)

"If it is the purpose of the U.S. to accept Nisei as loyal why not draft them as other Americans, including Negroes?" (GMH42)

"Japanese aliens in the last war had to fight for 14 years in order to get citizenship. Then they had to go to the Supreme Court. Clarification desire on this point. Also, the American legion posts in San Francisco and Los Angeles dismissed these veterans." (PI)

"Even when we are in uniforms why can't we travel all over the Union like the rest of the persons in Uniform?" (TL304A)

"Are the isseis and neiseis who served in the First World War in the Relocation Centers? Why?" (GMH42)

"Will the Japanese-American Girls be allowed the same privileges as Caucasian nurses and W.A.A.C.?" (TL126)

6. The final set of the three most frequently asked types of questions also concerned the military but were not necessarily accusatory. They simply sought more details about volunteering, the draft, and what volunteers might expect while in service. Many suggest less passion about the contradiction between racism and the demand to volunteer than a rather calm calculation of the benefits and costs that might come with particular choices. Here I give only a very small sampling.

"Will medical physicians, etc. be restrained from volunteering?" (Note: Respondent says they can volunteer but erroneously suggests that if there are too many they may serve in other units.) (PI)

"Is there an opportunity for us to join the Army Dental Corps Reserve and continue our dental education?" (GMH52)

"Will we be able to attend an officers' training school?" (GMH52)

"Will the Kibeis also be accepted?" (PI)

"Is the volunteering for 4 years or for the duration and 6 months after?" (PI)

"What does the Army have in mind when it is stated that we, 'the Japanese Americans, have superior qualifications for the purposes in which they intend to use you.'?" (GMH52)

"Will poor eye sight keep a person out of the armed forces?" (GMH52)

"If we don't volunteer, can we expect to be drafted through the selective service into other units for duty?" (PI)

"If a person has dependents or children, will he be drafted?" (GMH42)

"Do volunteers have preference in advancement?" (GMH42)

"Will those who want to finish his college education which was interrupted by the evacuation have a chance to finish it before induction?" (GMH52)

"What length of time must we be in the service before we are eligible
for a furlough?" (GMH52)`

"How about those interested women who wish to join the WAAC's?"
(GMH52)

"Is it the intention of the U.S. Army to send Japanese (Nisei) combat
team to the pacific area to fight against Japanese Army?" (GMH42)

"Will the Japanese Combat Team have a Tank Corps?" (GMH42)

"Is drafting of Niseis, a bill that has been passed by Congress or is it
just an Army order?" (TL304A)

"Can a person marry after he enlists?" (GMH52)

7. Many questions reflected a concern that the government provide for the
family members of soldiers. Clearly, internees and the authorities assumed
that the government was expected to promote life. Internees commonly
raised questions so that the authorities would reasonably consider the implications of soldiering and soldiers' deaths for the living. Some queries again
suggest a reasoned calculation of benefits at least as much as passion connected with refusing or accepting the call to volunteer.

"What will happen to the parents who will be left in camp?" (Note:
The captain replies that parents will receive the same benefits as other
soldiers' parents. However, they will in fact receive perhaps more
than "75% of the parents of other Americans because while you are
gone, they have a roof over their heads, enough to eat, and hospitalization." This exchange reveals both internees' expectations that the
government promote life and the authorities' attempt to show, if with
some twisted logic, that they were providing an excess of benefits to
life.) (GMH52)

"Are elderly parents and young children considered as dependents in
our case when we are here in relocation centers?" (GMH52)

"After the war who is going to look after the security of the old people?"
(GMH52)

"There are many families with many children and financially they are
in a critical situation and their future is uncertain because of their
property settlement back in California. What if I were the only son
in the family and I was drafted. Is the Government going to assure
us of the security of the family after the war?" (Note: Aside from the
general concern this question reflects, it should be noted that because

of the laws prohibiting Issei from owning land, titles to land were often in the names of children. If so, what would happen to the property if an only son in whose name that land was held was killed?) (GMH52)

"If a colonist is drafted for military duty in the U.S. Army, will the U.S. Government provide or make available provisions for the continuing welfare of the dependents of the draftee? By dependents is meant the unemployable parents, minor children or invalids. If so, how will it be done? And will they be kept in some camp such as Tule Lake or forced to live in their own way on the outside?" (TL304A)

"Will dependents of Nisei soldiers be given same care as other Americans in case of death, assuming parents remain in the WRA center?" (TL304A)

"After the war what will happen to the war risk insurance which was taken when in service?" (GMH42)

"If a nisei is killed in action, will he receive the insurance in lump sum? And if disabled, what provisions are there?" (PII)

"If a man joins, how much, in dollars, will he be allotted for his wife?" (PI)

"Will the wife be subject to income tax?" (PI)

"If a person goes out to defense war work and leaves his family in the center, will he be charged subsistence until he is settled?" (PI)

8. Scholars as well as administrators and WRA community analysts have often remarked on the confusion caused by the title of WRA Form 126 Rev., "Application for Leave Clearance." Many initially thought that filling out the form was tantamount to actually applying for leave clearance, a logical if erroneous conclusion. Even after clarification, many worried that in filling out the form they could later be compelled to leave before they were prepared to do so. Although this may seem odd, leaving camp was an unwelcome prospect for many who did not want to be separated from their families or to be forced back out into a country that appeared as hostile as ever. Furthermore, as has been explained earlier, internees found it unreasonable to ask Issei to forswear allegiance to their country of citizenship when U.S. law made it impossible for them to become U.S. citizens.

    "Mr. Coverley or the Army representative stated today [10 February 1943] that those issei who do not care to apply for leave clearance as such may change the title of this particular application form to

'Registration' when filling it out. However, the question which remains is: Since the questions to be answered remain unchanged, cannot this particular document still be considered an application for *leave clearance* in spite of the fact that the registrant intends it only to be a 'registration' and nothing more?" (TL126)

"What necessitated the WRA to use the same form for the two groups of people who are of two entirely different category—namely, female U.S. Citizens and the enemy aliens?" (TL126)

"Does the Geneva Conference Treaty carry provisions about asking such a question of the Issei as the questionnaire?" (TL126)

CONDITIONAL AND UNCONDITIONAL LOYALTY

These questions reflect an enormous variety of sentiments, from skepticism and anger about the unreasonableness of registration and the right of the government to ask internees to die, to immense anxiety about the fate of families and the protection of life, and to an apparently far more dispassionate desire for more information so that internees might simply make the best choices given their miserable circumstances. It would be possible to list many more questions that suggest these and other concerns, but I want to shift now to thinking about the effects of registration on the internees and especially of engaging in dialogue or attempting to reason with the authorities.

In the first place, the internees came to understand that they could not escape making choices about pledging allegiance to the nation. They could refuse to register, which some 3,254 men and women out of 77,957 eligible internees chose to do; they could refuse to answer both or either of questions 27 and 28; or they could give a qualified answer to the questions, as 1,041 did for question 28.[8] However, in no case could an adult individual escape subjection to the demand that he or she indicate a choice about loyalty. This may seem like an unremarkable fact, but it is important to remember that no racialized group in the United States had ever been subjected en masse to such an individualized ritual of pledging national allegiance, as if they were all being considered for naturalization, and none has been subjected to such a process since. The uniqueness of their situation was not lost on most of the internees themselves, who commented as much. Of course, we cannot assume that "no's" on the two key questions reflected disidentification with America, just as "yes" did not necessarily signify unqualified identification. A "no" to question 27 might reflect, for example, parental pressure or worry about leaving aging parents. A "yes" might have nothing to do with national identification, but reflect instead a desire to acquire professional skills in the army or simply to choose the least problematic option.

In reflecting on the successes and failures of the registration process, the WRA's community analysts recognized that it had been inconsistent and inept in many respects. They observed that administrators had approached the task with great optimism, but with little detailed and centralized preparation. Therefore, they conducted registration in ways and with success that varied greatly, leading the WRA's community analysts to warn against attributing single meanings to "yes" or "no" answers to questions 27 and 28, and therefore also against assuming that meaningful statistical comparisons across centers were possible. "There were so many differences in the manner in which registration was presented to center residents," the WRA reported, "in the manner in which registration was conducted, in the methods used by the administration to deal with crisis situations, indeed in the kinds of crises which arose at various projects, that each relocation center must be considered as unique in its registration returns. For this reason similar responses on the questionnaires from different projects simply do not have the same meaning and they should not be added together as though they did."[9]

Though we cannot reliably depend on "yes's" and "no's" as signs that point to specific and limited meanings about loyalty, the process itself solidified and circulated ways of understanding loyalty to the United States. While the War Department teams and the WRA administrators sought unconditional loyalty based on trust in America and the good faith efforts of the government—including the War Department's decision to open the army to Japanese American volunteers—only a small minority of internees followed this reasoning. The most common counter-reasoning among the internees might most appropriately be called "conditional loyalty," which respected the truth claims of the universal ideals of American nationalism in theory, but desired assurances and even guarantees that racist discrimination would end in practice. Many internees explicitly expressed such an attitude when they qualified their answers to question 28 by adding, "Yes, if my constitutional rights are guaranteed in writing."[10]

But such internees reasoned that they were not about to pledge their willingness to die for a nation whose governors seemed bent on destroying them. Some administrators and team members felt that such an attitude contradicted the very meaning of loyalty. Captain John A. Holbrook, the team captain at Rohwer, concluded that this quid pro quo stance was no different than disloyalty. "The Japanese-Americans of military age, that is, between the ages of seventeen and thirty-seven inclusive, as a group, are not interested in volunteering in the Armed Forces because they are not loyal citizens. At least to the extent that they care to express themselves without some material recompense for their loyalty. . . . They confuse the term with doing something for somebody for which they must receive advancement, socially and materially."[11] The team captain at Jerome, Eugene Siler, called the unconditional loyalists the "conviction group," while he criticized those whose loyalty was conditional by calling them the "expediency group" or "opportunists." At the same time, some internees exhibited a far more radical counterreasoning that challenged the very legitimacy of American nationalism and questioned its ability to ever treat nonwhites equally. They sought to sabotage the truth claims of the American nation in a more fundamental way, unveiling the unreasonableness of pledging loyalty to a nation in which the governors repeatedly proved themselves anything but committed to racial equality. Siler suggested using the term "poisonous group" to encompass many of this type of people.[12]

Registration at Topaz offers a useful case study for observing in a more dynamic way the process by which internees voiced their concerns about the Issei and how the community split between the proponents of conditional and unconditional loyalty, while also providing a glimpse into the mechanisms by which power operated under liberal governmentality through both reason and coercion. Some in Topaz appear from early on to have believed that active and unconditional participation in the war effort, including volunteering for the army, would provide an avenue to fulfill the promises of American freedom, equality, and democracy and to prove themselves and their people worthy of full inclusion in this supposedly unique nation. However, most of the internees required a great deal of coaxing, both through reasoning and the administration's use of overt or veiled threats, before they volunteered for the army or even consented to filling out the forms.

At Topaz administrators and the teams faced tremendous initial opposition to enlistment and registration. Issei had concerns about question 28, particularly in its initial wording. They also worried about their general security and the possibility of being forced to move out, just when they had begun to adjust to life in the camp. Nisei and Kibei hesitated because they felt that they had been deprived of their civil rights and that the proposed segregated combat team was emblematic of ongoing racist discrimination. Many were "loath to enlist now after all the bitter experiences of evacuation," while some parents pressured their children against it. On the afternoon of 14 February, Topaz's thirty-three block representatives held a meeting in which much of the discussion hinged on the question of whether to register or to first struggle for civil rights. As John Embree, who was the community analyst on the scene, observed, "if a vote had been taken it might well have gone negative."

However, the project director averted such a vote by threatening to invoke the Espionage Act.[13] Even in doing so, however, the director continued to act as if free speech would be respected by telling the internees that "they were free *as individuals* to say anything they cared to on the subject and that the Act referred only to *organized* interference with registration" (emphasis in original).[14]

Following this large meeting, the internees formed a subcommittee (the Committee of Nine) to draft a set of resolutions concerning civil rights that could be sent to Secretary of War Henry L. Stimson. Aside from one "fiery" Kibei, Embree saw the subcommittee as offering a rather "good cross-section of opinion" that "was probably reasonably representative of the various groups at the afternoon meeting." Given Embree's better-known reputation as a pioneering structural-functionalist anthropologist of Japan—he had published *Suye Mura*, his classic ethnography of a Japanese village, only four years previously—some readers may be surprised to find him operating as a participant observer in the Topaz registration crisis. Nevertheless, in his report Embree went on to note that he joined a meeting with the project director, two staff members, and the Committee of Nine, which lasted late into the night. At this meeting both the administrators and the internees made concessions on the resolutions, resulting in a moderate document that could be sent to the secretary of war. The internees agreed to continue the registration process even as they waited for Stimson's response. The meeting, with Embree involved, had helped avert a more serious turn of events for the WRA.[15]

The Committee of Nine lodged their protest from their position as loyal American citizens. They emphasized that they were making their requests to the secretary of war "in order to perform our duties as loyal citizens of the United States and in order to uphold the principles of democracy as established in the Constitution of the United States." After explaining that they had cooperated to the fullest in the evacuation, surrendered many of their rights and privileges, and suffered financial and other personal losses and that they hoped to prevent the future evacuation or confinement of citizens without trial and believed in equal treatment of all races as well as "the principle of freedom of speech, freedom of worship, freedom of the press, and freedom of assemblage as embodied in the Constitution and its amendments"—after prefacing their petition with such explanations of who they were and their outrage, they requested the following. They did not demand immediate release of all internees: they sought "absolute freedom of movement and a choice of returning to their homes," but only after a "thorough investigation of the Military Intelligence and the Federal Bureau of Investigation and other Federal authorities." Their reasoning did not differ greatly from that of the authorities, except, very importantly, they made allegiance of loyalty conditional. They asked the president to first confirm their rights as American citizens. They wanted security for the Issei and the recategorization of those not disloyal as "friendly aliens." Although they had been told that a segregated unit would make their military accomplishments more visible to the public, they argued that dispersal throughout the army would provide better publicity and that "education of [the] Caucasian soldier" could be accomplished by the "deep comradeship" that would follow. They wanted the democratic principles of the Four Freedoms that "we are fighting for" to be applied to them. Finally, they pledged: "If satisfactory answers can be given by a government spokesman, preferably the President of the United States, to these questions, we can go and fight for this our country without fear or qualms concerning the security of our future rights."[16]

On the afternoon of the 15th, the Issei had a meeting with the project director during which they expressed their many concerns. They lamented the financial losses caused by evacuation and the inadequate compensation for their labor in sugar beet work the previous summer. They made a special effort to chastise the government for treating their children as if they were aliens despite the sacrifices they as parents had made to provide them with education and to raise them as law-abiding citizens. The Issei also worried about the meaning of their form titled "Leave Clearance Form." Did this imply that they might be made to move yet again? Embree, again the good administrator (as opposed to a neutral social scientist), described this meeting as "a sort of catharsis for them."[17]

On that evening the team captain, Lieutenant William L. Tracy, explained to the Committee of Nine that a "friendly group in the Army" had been behind the registration plan. Reminding them of a situation about which they surely did not need to be alerted, Tracy cautioned them that a number of members of Congress and many in the public at large were "unfriendly to the Japanese Americans." Furthermore, he tried to dispel rumors that the army needed Japanese Americans because of an acute manpower shortage, even though, as we have seen, this "rumor" had some basis in fact. He wanted the internees to trust that the friendly group in the army had Japanese American interests in mind and that these friends would be sorely disappointed if the registration drive failed. More importantly, Tracy thought that plans for admitting Japanese Americans into the army might be dropped if registration did not go well, spoiling what should be viewed as an opportunity for Japanese Americans.[18]

The committee members made a very conciliatory gesture at this point, assuring Tracy that they would "get the whole camp fully behind registration by Wednesday [the 17th]." In addition, an even more cooperative group of young men and women, mostly "young Americans of a literary and intellectual bent," visited the director and protested against his forwarding of the Committee of Nine's petition. They also criticized the tactics of the "obstructionists," while charging that they had not been consulted. On the afternoon of the 16th Embree met for four hours with this second group. At that time he learned that they wanted the education department and the camp newspaper, the *Topaz Times*, to take a more positive role in properly informing the internees about WRA policy. They incidentally informed him that some of the teachers were racist ("anti-Japanese") and that many Kibei were "misrepresenting the whole registration." One of the many rumors circulating through the camp, they reported, was that the combat team would be sent to "a front where casualties will be high. Another is that the combat group will shortly be put on a ship and sunk in the middle of the Atlantic. Another rumor is, and this one appears to stem from the anxiety of the older people, that the combat group will all be trained as pilots and sent to bomb Tokyo." Given the 442nd's extraordinarily dangerous missions and inordinately high casualty rates, the first rumor appears to have been a rather accurate prediction; but that aside, these internees suggested that they wanted the administration to take a firmer guiding hand in registration through support of the "pro-democratic element," by which they meant the unconditional loyalists.[19]

A group calling itself the "Other Residents of Topaz," whose membership appears to have included those with whom Embree met on the afternoon of the 16th, drafted a statement that day in which they explicitly took "exception to the resolution presented to the Honorable Secretary of War Stimson as the expression of the majority." Like those represented by the Committee of Nine, they presented themselves as loyal American citizens. But unlike the protestors they stressed that their loyalty was unconditional—that "loyalty to our country is something to be expressed without reference to past grievances or wounds." They went on:

> We feel that the issue of expressing our loyalty has been confused. We
> believe in fighting for our rights, but we believe that fighting for our country
> and our ideals is the most important thing when our country is at war trying
> to uphold those ideals for which we stand.
> We shall register, we are loyal, we shall fight for the United States.

Edwin Iino topped the list of signatories, which included Miné Okubo, undoubtedly the "noted young woman artist" whom Embree identified as one of the Young

Democrats. As some readers may know, Okubo became the first internee to publish a book on the internment experience: her now well-known classic, *Citizen 13660* (1946).[20]

Thus the Committee of Nine and the Other Residents shared a great deal with each other and embraced many of the overall aims of the new (white) American consensus on how to manage Japanese Americans. They did not criticize the segregation plan in principle, and they both unequivocally affirmed the supposedly universal values for which America's citizens were being asked to fight. In the end, even the conditional loyalists of the Committee of Nine came around fully to the administration's position, promising to assist in the completion of the registration program. Furthermore, following responses from Myer and the War Department published in the camp newspaper, in which the director urged that it was no time to "quibble or bargain" while the latter reminded loyal internees that their civil rights could be restored only on the basis of mutual confidence and cooperation—after such responses the Committee of Nine issued a statement affirming "this registration as a indication of the government's good faith."[21]

Embree pointed out that even the "fiery Kibei" who had argued so wildly for the immediate restoration of civil rights had experienced a "redemption." This individual explained to Embree that he had become "embittered" through his experiences at the Tanforan Assembly Center and at Topaz. He had lost "faith in the sincerity of the American government." But through the process of making his views known and receiving "some recognition from the Administration," he had become "much more reasonable, and finally had come around to a state where he not only could review calmly the whole crisis, but through a better understanding of the motives of WRA he could even bring himself to cooperate with the very government he had attacked three days before."[22]

Although the authors of *The Spoilage* noted the continuing "strength and persistence of the underlying doubts and resentments" at Topaz, as was "indicated by the fact that 32 percent of the male citizens [at Topaz] answered question 28 in the negative"—despite this, the administration's and team members' handling of the registration crisis exemplified liberal governmentality. They met the Committee of Nine as well as the Other Residents not with direct force but through what they described as "reason" and recognition of their legitimate complaints. They worked with the American nationalist sentiments of the interned, guiding them toward cooperation. On the advice of the Other Residents, they also started to make better use of the camp newspaper while the project director worked with the community to plan a gathering for Washington's birthday that would heal the wounds of division and "bring them close together again."[23] Moreover, Embree's role reflects another distinctive characteristic of modern governmentality—namely, the important function that social scientists have played in governance even though they are often not made a formal part of the state until moments of crisis such as occur in total war. At such times, the nonstate/state distinction becomes even more blurred than in what are regarded as normal times. The explosion of quantitative and qualitative data and statistics produced by the WRA with its community analysts, as well as the contributions made to governance by social scientists making up the Japanese American Evacuation and Resettlement Study, also come to mind and caution us to use these materials against the grain of their authors' intentions.

HYPERIDENTIFICATION

Topaz produced a total of only 116 volunteers,[24] but many of those who professed their desire to enlist made strong efforts to show their eagerness. As Project Director Charles F. Ernst explained to Myer after he learned of the problems the relocation centers were having in enrolling volunteers, he called in twelve of the approximately fifty-five men who had signed up from Topaz up to that point. As a result of this meeting the twelve started a recruitment drive that resulted in the list growing to around one hundred. The volunteers also composed a "credo" in which they proclaimed their belief in democracy and their desire to "destroy every form of tyranny, oppression, and violation of human rights." Placing their "faith in America," they asserted that "volunteering in the armed forces of this country is a step towards the realization of these ends, and a positive manifestation of our loyalty to the United States." The Topaz volunteers asked the project director to pass the credo on to the other centers, which he did after conferring with Myer, in the hopes that volunteers from other camps would be inspired to express their mutual solidarity.[25] The circulation of the Credo of the Topaz Volunteers to the other camps had its desired effect. For example, the Heart Mountain Volunteers echoed exactly the words of their Topaz fellow volunteers in their own "Credo of the Nisei Volunteers" and further explained what they meant. They reiterated their commitment to fighting for their country based on their faith in the government and not the immediate restoration of civil rights. They hoped for "due recognition . . . for speedy reestablishment into all spheres of society in the post-war reconstruction." But they offered that "we reserve the expectation of results only after proving our mettle in the field."[26]

The Resident Council for Japanese American Civil Rights in Topaz published a newsletter titled "Volunteers for Victory," just before the enlistment campaign was to end. In it volunteers explained their motivations for choosing to serve. As if anticipating their own sacrifices while placing them within the long American history of the struggle for freedom and democracy, they printed Abraham Lincoln's iconic speech at the National Cemetery at Gettysburg as a preface to their own testimonies. They resolved, in words that can be found sprinkled throughout volunteer testimonies in the archives, to dedicate themselves to the great cause of ensuring that those who came before them "shall not have died in vain; that this nation, under God, shall have a new birth of freedom, and that government of the people, by the people, and for the people, shall not perish from the earth."

A strong theme running through the pamphlet is faith in the government's protection of life and happiness that echoed the practices of liberal governmentality. The pamphlet begins with an illustration of an armed soldier poised for battle against the backdrop of a family of four walking toward a big city bathed in sunlight. Obviously, the soldiers' battle is not only against the enemy but also against forces that might endanger the safe resettlement of their families into mainstream society. The opportunity to volunteer, the pamphlet explained, "told us that our government is definitely interested in our welfare." Taro Katayama testified that "whatever benefits I have received as an American citizen, Whatever I may make of my life in the future, I want to do so in this country." Henry H. Ebihara similarly explained that "I want to assure happiness and security in America for my parents, brother and sisters. This is their country. This is my country." Others emphasized their commitment to the fight against "fascism," "totalitarianism," or "military-fascist dictatorship." Above all, they stressed that this was a dramatic opportunity to prove their loyalty and that the voluntary character of their acts heightened the drama of this demonstration. The pamphlet also reported the extraordinary case of "the oldest person in Topaz to offer his services," who was not only sixty years old but an Issei. Although doubly ineligible by age and citizenship, he had wanted to "spend the remaining days of his life serving the cause of democracy in this present war," and his application had been accepted for consideration. Moreover, the pamphlet informed the internees about the availability of insurance for inductees and assured them that volunteers would be covered by the 1942 Servicemen's Dependents Allowance Act.[27]

The Japanese Americans who contributed most to the position of unconditional loyalty and helped administrators fashion the new modality of managing the internee population were individuals such as Mike "Moses" Masaoka, many of whom shared his affiliation with the Japanese American Citizens League (JACL). Asian American activists and other scholars have long criticized JACL members and especially

Masaoka for their hyperidentification with (white) America, but a further analysis of their activities may help deepen our understanding of the processes by which those located at the intersection of the governors and the governed occupied a pivotal position in developing the new governmentality and advancing the shift from vulgar to polite racism.[28] "Responding" to registration and the questionnaires as well as the call for army volunteers is too weak a word to describe the activism of some of these men and women, for they were not just being guided but in fact helped guide administrators toward concrete policies that would resolve the contradictions between the actually existing racism and its disavowal. Here the binary of governors and governed breaks down, because these Japanese Americans placed themselves at points at which the two categories intersected. In fact, Masaoka always acted as if *he* had been responsible for giving Japanese Americans the opportunity to volunteer; and he called himself "Moses" Masaoka, a telling moniker even if one does not accept Foucault's point that Christian pastoral power harks back to the Hebraic concept of the pastor-God.[29] Frank Miyamoto, a sociologist and researcher for the wartime Japanese American Evacuation and Resettlement Study, once wrote that when the army removed the Japanese from the West Coast, "the JACL was far more efficient in administering the process of evacuation than in organizing against it."[30] This statement may well apply to the JACL through the entire war, in that its leadership continued to be cogs in the machinery of administration as well as a segment of the administrated.

Ironically, one of the best critical studies we have available for analyzing the wartime activities of the JACL and Masaoka was commissioned by the organization itself. Following a 1988 resolution that the organization issue a formal apology for the wartime "injuries, pain, and injustice" that the JACL and individuals associated with it had inflicted on Japanese Americans, the organization contracted Dorothy Lim, an attorney and instructor at San Francisco State, to study the JACL's activities just before and during the war. Given access to JACL archival records, newspaper, and meeting minutes, and directed to use other available archives as well as secondary resources, Lim completed a ninety-five-page document in late 1989 that has come to be called the "Lim Report." While this report has circulated informally, some JACL leaders sought to repress its more damaging revelations about the organization and eventually produced a watered-down and in many places innocuously padded twenty-eight-page version of the original.[31]

The original Lim Report as well as a number of other studies provide undeniable proof that in the years immediately preceding Pearl Harbor and throughout the war, the leading members of the JACL actively cooperated with intelligence communities, the military, and other government agencies, starting with the WRA, rather than challenging their policies. They collected information about their fellow Japanese Americans and provided it to the FBI, the Office of Naval Intelligence, and military intelligence. They actively supported the removal of this population from the West Coast and its later management. For example, testifying for the JACL as its national secretary and field executive, Masaoka pledged before the Tolan Committee—which Congress had established early in the war to consider the removal of Japanese Americans and others from strategic areas—that the JACL would fully cooperate in their removal if the federal authorities and the military deemed it necessary. Most immediately relevant to the topic of registration, in February 1942, just before the forced removal, the JACL—in almost a trial run for the registration that would be conducted in the relocation centers about a year later—attempted to survey the Kibei population with background questionnaires oriented toward gauging loyalty. Moreover, although its effort does not appear to have been very successful, the JACL tried to create a comprehensive database of all Japanese American individuals it could locate through Japanese directories. Again, prefiguring the system of governing Japanese Americans through the exclusion of those regarded as unredeemable, Masaoka explained that such data would be useful in "ferret[ing] out the bad in order to protect the rest of the community."[32]

With regard to military service, the JACL did not wait for the government, the military, or the intelligence agencies to suggest that willingness to die could be a method by which Japanese Americans could demonstrate their loyalty and worthiness as citizens. At its mid-November 1942 convention in Salt Lake City the JACL went further than offering its assistance in recruiting internees for the Military Intelligence Language School at Camp Savage, Minnesota. Through a resolution it pledged to deliver Nisei volunteers if such an opportunity became available. Most astonishingly, Masaoka claimed in a report written in April 1944 that in a last-minute effort to avert evacuation, he had suggested the formation of a "volunteer 'suicide battalion' which would go anywhere to spearhead the most dangerous missions. To assure the skeptics that the members of the 'suicide battalion' would remain loyal . . . the families and friends of the volunteers would place themselves in the hands of the government as 'hostages.' "[33]

Thus, focusing narrowly on the February to March 1943 ritual of registration and army recruitment cannot adequately capture the long-term participation of men such as Masaoka in promoting and actualizing what had become by the winter of 1943 the dominant reasoning of the web of military, civilian, and intelligence authorities. Of course, we should be careful not to overestimate the JACL's and Masaoka's influence on policy making, despite Masaoka's own enormous claims. In a September 1942 report to the National Headquarters that was cited by the Dies Committee (the House's Special Committee on Un-American Activities) on 7 July 1943, Masaoka boasted that "Myer deals with us like he deals with his own staff. We have discussed every major policy with him before its adoption. . . . Congressmen would jump down their respected throats [of the WRA] if they knew the part we play in forming WRA policy." Despite such claims, the JACL and Masaoka could provide only ideas or concrete policies that coincided with the more general trends toward which the ruling authorities were already moving. As Myer, refuting Masaoka, put it in a way that was much more suggestive of the vector of power, "He [Masaoka] often took credit for policies formulated by others."[34] Nevertheless, the JACL and Masaoka may be credited with continuously pushing the authorities to eliminate contradictions between vulgar racism and the new polite racism—for example, untiringly encouraging the authorities to release the loyal back into mainstream society and to make male adult citizens eligible for the draft, and in the postwar years agitating for passage of the McCarran-Walter Act, which made it possible for Japanese aliens to naturalize as citizens.

Masaoka's and the JACL's position, it should be stressed, was not the dominant one among Japanese Americans. Rather, they offered a minority position while presenting it as the one that best represented all Japanese Americans. At a Dies Committee hearing on 3 July 1943, in which he offered that he had "worked on the evacuation and volunteered information to Naval Intelligence," Masaoka testified that the JACL had in fact become unpopular because of its involvement in evacuation and as a result of the activities of "certain militant minorities." He noted that membership had dwindled from 20,000 to 5,000, but even the latter figure appears to have been an overestimate: the committee investigator working with JACL records counted only 1,800 regular and 600 associate members. Masaoka admitted that the "JACL misrepresented and exaggerated its membership because it is the only group in a position to represent Japanese-Americans in the United States."[35] Nevertheless, Masaoka's and the JACL's position has become the most widely narrated and portrayed in mainstream representations of Japanese American history, in large part because it provided the partial truth from which the myth of Japanese American unconditional loyalty could expand out of all proportion to the number of its believers.

So who was Moses Masaoka, and how might we account for his eager self-inclusion on the side of the governors, even as he acted as self-acclaimed spokesperson for the governed? As the JACL's first executive secretary and probably the most well-known Japanese American lobbyist in Washington during and after the war, he was, as one publication has put it, "arguably the most famous and most influential Japanese American of his time."[36] And he has left an intriguing autobiography[37] that, although written many years after internment, is highly suggestive about what can be described as his hyperidentification with white America.

They Call Me Moses Masaoka reveals the splitting effects of nationalism on the racialized subject-citizen that results in an extreme identification with the Nation. Tracing his life back to his youth in Utah, Masaoka unwittingly reveals much about the intertwined structures of nationalism and racism that predated the period of total war, but that intensified with the looming prospect of military conflict with Japan. As in many modern nation-states, the message generated by the inclusionary and universalist discourses of U.S. nationalism and the exclusionary discourses of racism has been *duplex*, to use the language of electronics, where the term describes the ability to send two messages simultaneously in opposite directions. On the one hand, for even racialized subjects such as Masaoka it promises equality, freedom, and opportunity, while on the other hand it maintains a hierarchy of differences whereby all subjects are evaluated on a basis of standardized qualifications or distinctions and are compelled toward normalization. Some of these qualifications can be acquired—through educational achievement, through correction of social behavior (acquiring civility in a general way, speaking properly, keeping clean, eating "properly," and so on), or through exceptional military service. But others are presumed to be inherent and therefore cannot be easily overcome by individual effort, such as perceived race, ethnicity, or gender. The latter "deficiencies" can be compensated for only by extraordinary efforts to attain the former qualifications. This is the structure, reduced to its bare essentials, of modern nationalist and racist discourses that compel some members of minoritized groups toward extreme demonstrations of "love" for the national community. In other words, overcompensation or hyperidentification has been one reasonable response to the contradictory ways in which national subjects are interpellated as both equal and as less than the same.

Frantz Fanon noted long ago that "to speak is to exist absolutely for the Other."[38] Speaking appears as an obsession in Masaoka's life and autobiography. Throughout the autobiography Masaoka repeatedly refers to his extraordinary ability to speak as the (white) Other.[39] He writes proudly of his enormous successes as an award-winning member of debating teams, of his superb qualifications as a spokesman for Japanese American and American interests, and he seems to have had just as much pride in his *in*ability to speak Japanese. However, as much as he sought recognition from the Other, his anxiety intensified when that Other repeatedly reminded him that he was precisely other than white. Yet this rejection appears only to have generated an even greater desire for recognition as the same.

Masaoka tells a tragic and pathetic story of his own desire to speak as the (white) Other, coupled with the Other's unwillingness to recognize him as a white speaker. He prefaces the story of his own discovery of oratory with reflections on the racism that he experienced as a Japanese. He remembered that at the movies, for example, the Nisei were forced to sit in the "topmost seats in the balcony—then known as nigger heaven—along with the blacks" (p. 30). Yet despite the discrimination that he and other Japanese faced, he participated in typical schoolboy activities and through them became infatuated with public speaking. "I had always been articulate. Sometimes I was contentious. The thought of standing before an audience and speaking was both exciting and frightening. Oratory at that time in Salt Lake City, when radio was just beginning to come in, was a major youth activity. . . . A good speaker was looked up to, like a football or basketball star" (p. 31).

After a self-professed illustrious high school career as a debater, Masaoka entered the University of Utah and joined the university forensics team. Despite the Depression and the burdens of working his way through college, he writes of happy days on the debating team, of his successes and what he took to be full acceptance by other squad members. He liked rubbing shoulders with these young men of the university social elite and describes them as later becoming enormously successful in business or politics: "Traveling to various parts of the Intermountain West to debate, we shared dreams and hopes of the future. All my teammates had excellent minds and were stimulating company. Despite the differences in backgrounds, I was fully accepted. In fact, I might have been considered their leader. I was welcome in their homes and became acquainted with their girls" (p. 41). Speaking seemed to offer an avenue to become the Other, as well as to share the company of what he describes as the possessions ("their girls") of these young white elite men.

But as the narrative proceeds, we soon learn that the moment of Masaoka's greatest speaking triumph in youth also presented him with a devastating reminder that white America would usually choose to recognize him as anything but white. The incident occurred in 1936 at the National Invitational Tournament in Denver, "the biggest challenge we [the university debate team] had faced." Masaoka came away from the challenge with the highest honor, yet the leading newspaper in the intermountain West carried an editorial that showed Masaoka the extraordinary lengths to which he would need to prove his whiteness in the face of America's racial exclusionism:

This Republic is a land of liberty, democracy, and equal opportunity. . . .
In an oratorical contest held recently in Denver, a young Japanese student
of the University of Utah carried off the honors as the most effective speaker
at the conference. . . . When an alien of Asiatic parentage is able to master the
intricacies and absurdities of our orthography and to overcome lingual handi-
caps in pronunciation and articulation, to acquire an ability to think, to arrange
his ideas in logical sequence, and to express them clearly and forcefully, there
is no excuse for failure among American students. (pp. 42–43)

In other words, the *Salt Lake Tribune* had simply assumed that Masaoka was an
"alien," and when the editorial concluded by saying that his performance "should
also remind the world that neither race, nor creed, nor color constitute a bar to advancement here when merit asserts itself," it inadvertently revealed that being of
the other race, creed, or color was automatic grounds for being regarded as outside
the Nation. Masaoka observed, "No matter what we do to demonstrate our Americanism, no matter how many generations we have been in the United States, many
see our nonwhite faces as evidence of alien status" (p. 42). Tellingly, as a similar experience in John F. Aiso's life reveals, speaking superbly as the white Other was no
guarantee of recognition as an American.[40]

Yet this episode led not to Masaoka's abandonment of the desire for acceptance
but to an even greater vigilance over the (nonwhite) Other within, including the
Other within that would speak as other than white. Although he does not mention
it in his autobiography, it is known that in April 1942 he advised Milton Eisenhower,
then director of the WRA, that a central part of its policy of turning Japanese in
the camps into Americans should be to correct their habits and speech. "Special stress
should be laid on the enunciation and pronunciation of words," he implored, "so
that awkward and 'Oriental' sounds will be eliminated."[41]

The American dream of steady progress toward the elimination of racism had
an even hallucinatory effect on Masaoka. In his 1940 statement for the JACL National Convention, "The Japanese-American Creed"—written down, as he put it,
"in one furious writing session" and then publicly circulated (it even found its way
into the *Congressional Record*)—Masaoka simply pretended to be living the American dream. Stating his pride in being an "American citizen of Japanese ancestry,"
he began a litany of praises for all that America had given him, including "liberties
and opportunities such as no individual enjoys in this world today." Moreover, he
wrote that "She," the woman America, had "permitted me to build a home, to earn
a livelihood, to worship, think, speak, and act as I please—as a free man equal to

every other man." Yet as Masaoka later reflected, some of what he had written had been completely falsified. In fact, "I was barely earning a livelihood, and certainly I was in no position to build a home. But I had hopes, I was looking into the far future, I wrote in all sincerity; and never have I had occasion to change my mind about the meaning of America" (p. 50). The American dream would be deferred, but he would act as if he lived it.

Throughout the autobiography, Masaoka displays what can best be described as an obsessional neurosis in which he must always locate the national/racial/cultural source of every attribute of his personality, as well as of other Japanese Americans around him. Fanon described a comparable if not exactly similar situation under colonialism. "Because it is a systematic negation of the other person and a furious determination to deny the other person all the attributes of humanity," he said, "colonialism forces the person it dominates to ask themselves the question constantly: 'In reality, who am I?' "[42] For Masaoka, the Japanese side of the binary is not necessarily entirely negative, and therefore the split between the (white) Other and the (nonwhite) Other within does not have quite the rigid Manichaean quality of the colonial subjectivity described by Fanon. Rather, it dovetails with what I will in a later chapter describe as the logic of modernization theory and the "model minority" ideal, according to which the unique quality of the nonwhite nation/race/culture is allowed to exist insofar as it does not upset the dominant position of the white nation/race/culture and in fact assists the subject in becoming the (white) Other. Moreover, because of the shift from vulgar to polite racism across the transwar years, Masaoka did not recall such a harsh denial of his humanity. Nevertheless, the constant self-questioning and obsessive need to order the self that Fanon described for racialized, colonized peoples are still relevant.

Thus Masaoka writes that he learned the virtue of patient fortitude from the Japanese side of his upbringing: "The Japanese have a word for that: *gaman*. It means to hang tough, endure, stick it out. That is what my parents did, and by example that is what they taught their family. . . . [B]ut I learned more than the virtue of enduring. I learned to fight for my rights. That was the American part of my heritage" (p. 22). In his estimation, his wife Etsu, sister of Congressman and later Transportation Secretary Norman Mineta, also had this split and hierarchized identity. "Although she is American through and through, she combines her American strength, initiative, and independence with the finest qualities of Japanese womanhood, which are loyalty, dependability, compassion, and thoughtfulness" (p. 368). And so on. Above all, Masaoka needs constant reassurance that despite his numerous setbacks from (white) American racism, his vigilant subordination of the (non-white) Other within will lead eventually to acceptance.

Thus Masaoka's almost fanatical desire to prove his (white) Americanness through the call for a "suicide battalion" and hostages should be understood as a means by which to compensate for the (white) Other's recognition of him as anything but white. As Masaoka states explicitly in the autobiography, he welcomed the opportunity to redeem his race with Japanese American blood. "Unfair as this discriminatory action [of internment] was, our national leaders laid down another condition: since we were untested as Americans, only in blood could we demonstrate loyalty to our country in its hour of peril." Masaoka and his four brothers all took up the challenge; one brother was killed in action and another returned home severely disabled. But Masaoka was far from bitter about America, for he emphasized that through this sacrifice in blood, he, his brothers, and his fellow Japanese American soldiers overcame racial prejudice and proved their "right to share the American dream" (pp. 22–23).

OTHER REASONINGS AND COUNTER-CONDUCT, OR SABOTAGING YOUR REASONING

Very few of Masaoka's fellow Japanese Americans in camp followed his reasoning. Long ago, in her classic history of the internment camps, Michi Weglyn accurately concluded that those "patriots who roundly cheered the development [of allowing Nisei enlistment in the military] were vastly outnumbered, and in centers where feelings ran high, those who volunteered did so secretly, fleeing the camps in the dead of the night."[43] In the end, although the recruitment effort was a spectacular success in Hawaii, where there had been no wholesale internment, it was a dismal failure on the mainland. According to the internal official history of the Office of the Provost Marshal General (OPMG), the War Department had anticipated 4,286 volunteers from the mainland United States to fill a quota of 3,000 soldiers, and 1,500 from Hawaii. However, almost two months after the announcement of Japanese American eligibility, only 1,253 had enlisted out of an estimated 23,606 eligible male citizens (19,606 inside the camps and 4,000 outside), so that "it became clear by the end of March [1943] that the recruiting drive had failed because the evacuees resented what they considered to be unjust treatment at the hands of the War Department and other government agencies." By the end of June, only 1,208 men had volunteered from the ten relocation centers. These figures contrasted sharply with those for Hawaii, where by early March some 9,509 out of roughly 25,000 eligible men had applied for voluntary induction.[44]

The effort to recruit Japanese American women into the military was also a "complete failure." In early April 1943, Assistant Secretary of War John J. McCloy suggested to Oveta Culp Hobby, director of the Women's Army Auxiliary Corps, that Japanese American women should be allowed to volunteer for the WAAC. After exchanges involving McCloy; Hobby; the assistant chief of staff, G-1 (Personnel); the AC of S, G-2 (Intelligence); and the OPMG, the War Department on 28 July 1943 authorized the enlistment of Japanese American women. The WAAC had just been fully incorporated into the United States Army and renamed the Women's Army Corps. Unlike its policy for Japanese American men, the War Department determined that the women would not be segregated but would be assigned without discrimination. However, following precautionary procedures similar to those for males, the War Department decided to subject female volunteers to special screening to determine loyalty. While the Military Intelligence Division conducted investigations on male volunteers, the War Department assigned clearance for women to the OPMG, the rationale being that as a result of the program for screening all Japanese Americans, its Japanese-American Joint Board had already accumulated extensive files on women as well as men.[45]

The military authorities optimistically set the upper limit for Japanese American WAC volunteers at 500. Their sanguine attitude was perhaps in part the result of reports from registration at the relocation centers that noted the high rate of women's affirmative responses to the loyalty questions, especially compared to the men's, and the astonishing belief (given the context of internment) that Japanese American women appreciated the liberties in America that they were not accustomed to experiencing as Japanese. Displaying the type of arrogance about America's supposed liberation of women of color that Lisa Yoneyama has shown is so often deployed to justify U.S. military invasions and occupations, Captain Norman R. Thompson, a team leader, had reported the following responses to questions 27 and 28 from Gila River: "The splendid record established by the female citizens whereby 87% of them volunteered their services for the WAAC or the Army Nurse corps [in principle by answering yes to question 27], and showed an 88% loyalty factor, can be attributed in part to the fact that Japanese women have in the past, enjoyed few of the privileges and little of the liberty, that women in the United States take for granted."[46]

Certainly, there are records of enthusiastically patriotic women volunteers, such as a Kathleen Iseri who had applied from outside the relocation centers, in New York.

In a letter to the WAC Recruiting Headquarters she asked why it was taking so long for her application to be processed and ended her inquiry by quoting Masaoka's "Japanese-American Creed" in its entirety. Overall, however, the recruitment efforts produced very few volunteers, especially from the centers. In mid-July 1943, just before the War Department's directive authorizing the enlistment of Japanese American women was distributed, Calvert Dedrick, who was then chief economist for the Japanese American Branch within the OPMG, produced data broken down by center on the pool of women eligible to volunteer. According to his calculations, there were 19,031 "Native-born Japanese females 17 years of age and older." However, fewer than 50 of them volunteered from all of the ten relocation centers combined, and by October 1945 only 142 Japanese American women from inside and outside the camps had volunteered.[47]

Of the few men and women who volunteered, many exhibited far less enthusiasm for proving their loyalty than we are usually led to believe. At Poston, for example, Elizabeth Colson, then a young anthropologist and researcher for the camp's Bureau of Sociological Research, observed a general lack of overt excitement, either negative or positive, about registration and volunteering. While she admitted the difficulty of gauging the "attitude in camp toward volunteering and volunteers" and that it "seems to vary from place to place," she reported a general quietude despite block parties for applicants in two of the Poston units and some limited organized resistance. One block even seemed completely uninterested in the matter. "Two men volunteered and were given the block party, but now the whole matter seems to have been forgotten and the people are only interested in when the volunteers are to leave." Another block had apparently criticized two of its three volunteers, while another had a "faction against volunteering." As for the few reasons she had heard for volunteering:

One [volunteered] because he thought he was pretty sure to be rejected anyway, another because he knew that he'd probably be drafted and might just as well go now. I understand this is a fairly common feeling. One man who is married and has a small son said he did it because none of the younger men seemed to be going and he thought it was an opportunity for the Japanese to show their loyalty. Some of the doctors and dentists are volunteering if they can get a commission. I understand they aren't interested in going if they can't. One is said to have been influenced by the fact that the doctors in the last war had a good chance to improve their skill by being in the army.[48]

Other researchers at Poston, some of whom were internees themselves, sometimes reported that Nisei volunteers told them that they had made the commitment because they wanted to "show loyalty to America";[49] but much more often internees frankly revealed that they had not been motivated primarily by loyalty. The wife of a physician who volunteered out of Poston explained that although "the problem of loyalty" had been a factor for a number of doctors who volunteered, they had primarily hoped to acquire "very good training." She noted that during the "Spanish Am war, some of the Drs. who went to war became some of the best surgeons."[50] Another volunteer from Poston similarly explained that he wanted to get out of camp and that army service might help him in his future profession. "I want to leave camp so this is an opportunity. I think there's a future for me in the field of art. I plan to continue my art in the army, sketching and drawing. I want to go into the camouflage painting department while in the Army. Yes, I think there is a good future for me in that field."[51] When asked to confirm that one of his sons had volunteered, one father casually offered, "Yes, but he volunteered with rejection possibility in mind. You see, his eyes aren't specially good." To which the interviewer asked: "Then why did he volunteer?" "Well he figures he might be drafted. If he is drafted later then there isn't much chance for good positions. If he is accepted now, he has a chance of becoming a quartermaster."[52]

To be sure, as we have already seen, the WRA's mishandling of various practical aspects of registration, including its poor phrasings of questions 27 and 28, contributed to the internees' lack of enthusiasm. However, the foremost reason why so few volunteered was that the overwhelming majority of internees were left with too many unanswered or unsatisfactorily answered questions, even after repeated meetings and opportunities to engage in dialogue. On the eve of registration and the enlistment campaign, internees had already been ill-disposed toward the government and the army. As the Community Analysis Section reflected in its general report titled "Army and Leave Clearance and Registration at War Relocation Centers": "In January, 1943, the residents of relocation centers felt that they had been discriminated against in the evacuation, that they had blundered in failing to protest it, that their future in the United States was being threatened from many quarters, that WRA and the government generally could not be trusted, and that the Army, in particular, was responsible for their present situation."[53]

In February and March the internees had pushed the authorities to explain, most importantly, why they should volunteer to perhaps die for a nation that had discriminated so blatantly against them. As a team member at Rohwer put it, "[S]ome believe the race prejudice in the United States has become so great that they will never again enjoy the rights and privileges of loyal citizens, therefore, why volunteer to risk life for something that looks so dark and uncertain."[54] Internees who made volunteering conditional upon the enactment of concrete policies to end racism, as opposed to what appeared to them to be empty disavowals of discrimination, pressured the authorities to explain how so many obviously unequal policies could exist alongside claims that neither the government nor the military practiced racial discrimination. But even the War Department in its official history of the military clearance program for Japanese Americans admitted that de facto discrimination had been a difficult contradiction to explain.

> Although the War Department was against a policy of segregation as such, the practical application of the rule permitting Japanese-Americans to serve only in the 442nd Infantry Regiment amounted to segregation as no person of Japanese ancestry could enter the armed services except by volunteering for the special all-Japanese combat team. The provisions of Selective Service were still suspended as far as these men were concerned. Although certain prominent naval officers played an active part in persuading the army to utilize Japanese-Americans, the Navy refused to accept any of them for service in the naval forces. This policy of exclusion applied similarly in the Marine Corps and the United States Coast Guard. Within the Army, the Air Forces would not accept any person of Japanese ancestry. Therefore, the Japanese-American citizen felt, with some justification, that he was being discriminated against because of his racial background.[55]

But besides the unwillingness of Japanese Americans to volunteer unconditionally on the basis of the logic of conditional loyalty, many refused either because they had never believed claims about America as the nation that uniquely guaranteed freedom, equality, security, and happiness to all regardless of race or because the internment experience had convinced them that such claims were groundless. Rather than respond affirmatively to the key questions, let alone volunteer, they denied the reasonableness of the questions posed to them and the false justice of their governors. As one internee at Tule Lake explained his refusal to answer question 28: "I have not been given citizenship rights so I don't have to answer questions like that."[56] Although the contexts are a world and time apart, his attitude of defiance brings to my mind the one expressed by the Brazilian contemporary rappers, Racionais MC's (Rational MC's). In one of their best-known raps from the late 1990s, "Capítulo 4, Versiculo 3," which interestingly enough is a reference to Psalm 23 ("The Lord is my shepherd"), the Racionais MC's shout: "I came to sabotage your reasoning! / I came to shake your nervous system and your blood system!" After all, they were the Racionais. In her marvelous reading of this rap, Teresa P. R. Caldeira suggests that the sabotage has multiple meanings. Many of these are, of course, particular to the world of these rappers as they speak of the daily imminence of death and violence in the peripheries of a "democratized" and neo-liberalized São Paulo. Nevertheless, the undermining of an entire regime of truth, knowledge, and reason; the sabotaging of "the system, the statistics, the reasoning of the elites"; the conceptualization of justice "in more moral than in legal and institutional terms"—these all resonate with the responses of many Japanese American internees to the rationality of liberal (racist) governmentality in the camps. And as the lyrics to another Racionais MC's rap titled "Juri Racional" ("Rational Jury") express, such a subversion of governmental rationality often inspired harsh and sometimes violent attacks on the "white sheep of the race, betrayer," of those who in the case of the Japanese Americans were called *inu* (a term that literally means "dogs" and suggests informers).[57]

Foucault would call this type of response "counter-conduct in the sense of struggle against the processes implemented for conducting others." In other words, if we can accept that the administrators attempted to govern the internees through a type of pastoral power that sought to conduct (or direct) conduct—or, put differently, to govern self-governing—then counter-conduct would describe not so much "misconduct," a term that Foucault thought too passive because it implied only improper compliance, but an aggressive struggle against an entire regime of practices. Counter-conduct would mean a type of refusal that says, "We do not wish to obey these people. . . . We do not want this pastoral system of obedience. We do not want this truth. We do not want to be held in this system of truth. We do not want to be held in this system of observation and endless examination that continually judges us, tells us what we are in the core of ourselves, healthy or sick, mad or not mad, and so on."[58]

Many internees simply became convinced that America was a white man's world and that because Japanese Americans had no hope of ever being treated equally, some sort of identification with what they understood to be the ideals of the Japanese empire was their most viable alternative. Because they had experienced so much racism in the prewar and wartime years, American disavowals of racial discrimination seemed far less believable than the declarations of the Japanese empire's leaders, who claimed that they stood on the side of liberating Asians and other peoples of color throughout the world from white racism. Team Captain Thompson estimated that about 5 percent of those internees who had been willing to talk to him at Gila about their reasons for refusing service in the armed forces had said that "they did not believe that public opinion in the United States would ever permit the assimilation of orientals, at least not in their lifetime, and in consequence felt their future lay in Japan."[59] Whether the 5 percent figure is accurate is less important than the general observation that the truth claims of the Japanese empire rang truer to a considerable number of Nisei internees than those of the government that had placed Japanese Americans in camps, and of the army that now offered enlistment under conditions that smacked of Jim Crow and suggested the utilization of "Japs" as cannon fodder.

At Tule Lake, Thomas and Nishimoto also observed that even before the war the "Orient" had been idealized "as a place of unlimited possibilities. . . . Within the confines of the barbed-wire fence, the feeling that there was no longer a chance for success in America was intensified. The hope of a future without discrimination in Japan-controlled Java or Manchuria became, in many cases, the basis of plans for the future. One Kibei explained that there would be a good future in Manchuria for Nisei who spoke both English and Japanese. He himself planned a career there where he could 'enjoy his Japanese face.' "[60] More recent research has begun to recover the experiences of perhaps thousands of Japanese in Hawaii and the mainland United States who not only failed to serve in the U.S. military but chose to emigrate to Manchuria before Pearl Harbor as part of the Japanese imperial project. In the face of racism, Japanese Americans sometimes rejected the claims of U.S. nationalism by actively participating in Japanese expansionism on the Asian continent.[61] That even second-generation Japanese Americans such as Joseph Kurihara, who had never lived in Japan and had fought in the U.S. Army during the First World War, adopted a pro-Japan stance as a result of racism and the internment experience has long been known (though the memory has usually been suppressed). As Kurihara put it, if he was going to be repeatedly subjected to racist discrimination as a "Jap," he would "become a Jap 100 percent."[62] In post-segregation Tule Lake, a "Japanese" cultural and political renaissance took place. Moreover, whatever their individual reasons might have been, it has been estimated that some 8,000 people of Japanese descent— a number that includes Issei, Nisei, and Kibei—left the United States for Japan during or immediately after the war years.[63]

To observe such a radical version of counter-conduct before, during, and after registration and the call for volunteers is not to celebrate it as "resistance." Instead, it should be recognized that in the world of the Asia-Pacific, where the propaganda machineries of the powerful empires based on the U.S. and Japanese nation-states competed against each other, each claiming that its respective empire stood for racial equality while the other's practiced only duplicity, it was not illogical for Japanese

Americans to disown one totalizing and exclusionary regime in favor of the other. Months before registration, U.S. racism thus helped produce underground associations in the camps whose names often reveal imagined filiations with right-wing groups in Japan. At Manzanar, for example, groups such as the Manzanar Black Dragon Society, Southern California Blood Brothers Corps, Southern California Justice Group, and Patriotic Suicide Corps alarmed the civil and military authorities as well as the intelligence communities.[64] Following their multimonth investigation of the relocation centers, the Dies Committee expressed special concern about such "gangs" and named in addition the likes of the Dunbar Gang and the Yogores, whose names are less closely connected with the Japanese right wing and may signal that "gangs" were not necessarily pro-Japanese in any simple sense.[65] Thus "Yogores" means literally, "the defiled ones," suggesting a self-identity as the abjected rather than a strong identity with Japanese right-wing ideology.

In any case, the Dies Committee asserted that in early November 1942 the Manzanar commission on self-government—which had been established to develop a system of self-government in Manzanar that would privilege the position of Nisei who would cooperate closely with the WRA administration—received letters from the Blood Brothers Corp. One letter expresses a hatred of the army and a critique of the U.S. government and its proposed system of self-government, even pointing out that since internees had been put in camps against their will, self-government was an absurdity.

> **Think of the shame the American Government has put us into.** Think of the disruption of properties and the imprisonment of the Nisei.
>
> To start a self-government system now is nothing but a dirty selfish scheme. As the Army put us in here without regard to our will, **we should leave everything up to the Army, whether they want to kill us or eat us.**[66]

Mothers too—a usually forgotten presence in scholarly and popular narratives of internment and military service—often quietly and outside the public spaces of meetings or beyond the earshot of the administrators attempted to sabotage the reasoning of the governors. While it has often been noted that Nisei found it difficult to volunteer, given resistance from the Issei generation, we might draw special attention to the influential position of mothers. In John Okada's novel *No-No Boy*, Ichiro's mother exists in a state of apparent unreason, unable to fathom why any young Japanese American man should wish to join the army and even less why other mothers would allow their sons to do so. She considers herself better than other mothers who let their sons die in war, and who have as a result continued to live as the living dead ("it is she who is to blame, and it is she who is dead"). After the war Ichiro's mother even refuses to believe that Japan has lost the war and warns her son that "the boat is coming and we must be ready." And the draft resister Ichiro cannot deny that his mother's madness exists in himself as he thinks, "See in the mirror the madness of the mother, which is the madness of the son." While Ichiro's mother can be understood in various ways, I read her madness as the specular reason of American nationalism: it is only when American nationalism is seen as an inverted reflection of Japanese nationalism that it is recognizable as a kind of unreason. Her "crazy" commitment to Japanese nationalism is only as "mad" as unquestioning commitment to American nationalism.[67]

Complementing the imaginative and literary power of this novel, the archival record reveals the figure of the mother as capable of sabotaging the reasoning of the authorities and her formidability in the eyes of the administrators and the military. Like the mothers of Korean youth whom we will encounter in a later chapter, these first-generation women were politically and culturally located so far outside the boundaries of the national community, with no possibility of choosing inclusion, that they had little to lose from complete disidentification with America. In her personal journal, a researcher at Poston remarked on the activism of some women in criticizing the mothers of volunteers. In one case a volunteer's mother professed, "I have had no moment of happiness since my son volunteered, until last night when a church service was held in Parish II in honor of the volunteers. I have been so unhappy because many of the women have been making unfavorable comments to me directly and indirectly." Another mother purportedly said, "I think it would be absolutely dumb for my [son] to volunteer for the army when my husband is interned. I can never allow my son to volunteer as long as my husband is interned."[68] A community analyst at Granada recorded that in one case a mother reportedly accompanied her son on a visit to the project director to discuss the matter of enlisting. Each time the young man expressed his desire to enlist, the "mother addressed him in Japanese, and turning to the Project Director bowed and smiled . . . . It turned out that she had been saying to the boy, 'You are a disgrace to your father and your country.' " In another instance, one young man contemplating volunteering "reported that no less than seven mothers had called upon his mother to try to persuade her that he should be prevented from enlisting."[69] An army officer who toured the relocation centers during the army's enlistment campaign reported that not only were Issei and Kibei pressuring eligible men not to volunteer but "in some cases mothers threatened to commit suicide and parents disowned their sons."[70]

This is not to say that Issei mothers could respond only by "madness" to the gap they saw between the racism their sons faced and the government's pretense of equal treatment. For example, roughly two months after the War Department determined that Japanese American male citizens would again be eligible for the draft, hundreds of Issei mothers at Topaz signed a petition addressed to the secretary of war. In it they explained, with the painfully good reasoning of what I have been calling "conditional loyalty," that they opposed reimposition of the military obligation on their sons. Suggesting that they were not protesting their own bondage in the camps, but only that of their sons, they asked why the latter remained "in the Centers, in the similar classification, as we ourselves," even though they had sworn allegiance to America during registration. They criticized not only the conflation of their own and their sons' relationships to the national community but also the discriminatory conditions in the segregated army. Acknowledging their own abjection from the national community, they asked nothing for themselves, but only restitution of their sons' civil rights. "Most of us being aliens," they noted, "we understood why our rights and privileges were curtailed. But we cannot understand why our children who are American citizens were placed in the similar category as ourselves . . . . As we think of our brave sons dead, and surmise the thought of Sergeant Ben Kuroki who met with discrimination despite his distinguished service, we mothers feel anguish in our hearts . . . we humbly request that Civil Rights be restored to our children now."[71]

In either case, the civilian administrators and military officials understood that mothers could be a disruptive force, sometimes radically and sometimes subtly obstructing their plans. Therefore, it is not surprising to see special efforts to appease them during the remainder of the war, especially after the restitution of selective service. Dillon Myer, for instance, made sure to send personal letters of condolence to mothers and wives of deceased soldiers. In these letters he emphasized not only pride in the son, for his willingness to "give his blood as his last great measure of devotion [to his country]," but also in the parent, "who instilled these manly qualities in your son and prepared him to meet the greatest test of our times."[72] The War Department also made presentations of gold stars and special medals to mothers of the war dead. But as the photograph of Colonel Polk Atkinson presenting the Distinguished Service Cross to the mother of Pfc. Kiyoshi Muranaga suggests, the mother remained a potentially subversive figure (see figure 3). While probably not the intent of the photographer, the stern face of the mother looks more pensive and defiant than honored. It appears as though she sees the medal as a pathetically inadequate substitute for her son. And it is not she, the nonwhite woman, who quiv-

FIGURE 3.
Mother as potential subversive. *War Relocation Authority
Photographs of Japanese-American Evacuation and Resettlement,*
BANC PIC 1967.014—PIC. Iwasaki Hikaru, photographer.
Amache, Colorado. 21 April 1945. Courtesy of the Bancroft
Library, University of California, Berkeley.

ers and seeks recognition of the white male military officer, but rather the reverse. The colonel offering the medal looks uneasily toward the mother, as if needing her recognition, but the mother does not return his timid gaze.

Others who engaged in counter-conduct did so in a variety of ways that cannot be reduced to either Japanese or American nationalism. For instance, Team Captain Thompson noted that a rather large group (15 percent) of those who had revealed to him their reasons for refusing to serve in the army were "either pacifists or slackers." As Thompson explained, these were mostly Kibei who had returned to the United States once war with China had been declared because they had wanted to "escape military service in the Japanese Army against the Chinese." "This group," he felt, "is truly radical and apparently holds no loyalty for any country or government," because of the desire of individuals in this category to avoid military service in both Japan and the United States. Some, like agitators in Tule Lake, evinced a distrust, as the rap lyrics above indicate, of "the system, the statistics, the reasoning of the elites," by agitating against the collection of information. They posted a mimeographed statement titled "Why You Should Not Register" on all latrines, and in it they warned that any written responses might be turned against individuals. Congress and the army, it said, could use the information collected to "define all of us disloyal, they could cancel our citizenships, making us enemy aliens . . . [and thus] confiscate legally our properties."[73]

.   .   .

In this chapter I have tried to recuperate, if only imperfectly, some of the myriad ways in which Japanese American men and women in the relocation centers experienced, questioned, rejected, and participated in registration and the army recruitment campaign. While the strategies of liberal governmentality, which included expulsion and confinement of the most unruly and "unreasonable," continued to "purify" the spaces of the nine relocation centers other than Tule Lake, some forms of defiance continued, usually by those swayed by the discourse on "conditional loyalty." Although limitations of space preclude full investigation of draft resistance, in recent years activists and scholars have begun to excavate this long-forgotten history. Hundreds of men from the relocation camps refused to ignore the logical incommensurability of the nationalist discourse that disavowed racism and the racist practices that continued to confine Japanese Americans. Some 315 Japanese American men were convicted of draft evasion, and most spent around two years in prison. The reasoning of most of them, as Frank Emi, one of the draft resistance leaders has succinctly put it, was that "if we were citizens what the hell were we and our families doing in these concentration camps without semblance of due process. If we were not citizens, the draft does not apply to us." Likewise, Tamotsu Shibutani has given us an account of how one group of Japanese American men, far from exhibiting exemplary heroism in military service, became so thoroughly demoralized by discrimination and their inability to live up to the high expectations placed on them that they came to form "one of the more disorderly units in United States history." According to Shibutani, Company K became an object of scorn to many, in-

cluding many Nisei veterans, and it was commonly identified as a "fuck-up outfit."
And most recently, Shirley Castelnuovo has excavated the history of roughly 200
Japanese American soldiers who in return for their defiance against discrimination
were either imprisoned or placed in a hard labor army company that was eventually organized as Company B of the 1800th Engineer General Service Battalion.[74]

Unfortunately for the military resisters, however, the Japanese American minor
discourse on "unconditional loyalty" came to be most vigorously appropriated and
mobilized by the civil and military authorities to resolve the contradiction between
actually existing racism and its disavowal. The authorities never recognized the logic
of conditional loyalty as initially proposed but later given up by the Committee of
Nine at Topaz. Conversely, the willingness of some internees and JACL leaders such
as Mike Masaoka to join the army and profess loyalty unconditionally came back to
haunt draft resisters in the following years. The governors could not submit to the
idea that internees were obliged to fulfill their duties as citizens only if their civil
rights were fully restored.

Eric Muller provides some hints for understanding this rationale in his fine analysis of the legal, as opposed to the more commonsensical and perhaps more ethical,
reasoning about Japanese American draft resisters.[75] Although it might seem plausible and justifiable to argue that a citizen held in bondage by the government should
not be asked to risk his or her life to protect the freedom he or she does not have,
the law does not see the situation in this way. Legally, the government's alleged vi-
olations of civil rights is a matter separate from the duty to give one's life for the
nation. An individual must continue to fulfill the obligations of citizenship regardless of the possibility that the government has violated his or her rights as a citizen.
As I have argued, registration centered on a ritual of choosing to vow allegiance to
the United States. In this situation, crossing the boundary between noncitizen and
citizen was demonstrated in large part by freely indicating willingness to volunteer
for military service. However, once recognized as a citizen, even if an individual
believes his or her civil rights have been violated, he or she has no choice in the matter of serving. Thus, while Muller's analysis is suggestive, the title of his book, *Free
to Die for Their Country*, is in one sense not quite accurate.

As citizens recognized from January 1944 as eligible for the draft, even men held
behind barbed wire were not free to die for their country. They were obliged to do
so. This strange moral conundrum can best be explained by returning to the question of bio-power and population. As Foucault would say, since the state makes citizens live for its own interests, it (and not the citizens) is free to take those lives when
necessary. The state claims to provide life ("life, liberty, and the pursuit of happi-

ness"), and can therefore take it unilaterally. Unfortunately, the unconditional surrender to the state that the "Other Residents" at Topaz and the JACL offered prefigured precisely this logic as it eventually came to be applied to the Nisei draft resisters. For the Other Residents had categorically vowed to risk laying down their lives, despite their recognition that the government had only taken the "first step to restore us all rights as citizens of the United States." Conversely, when many draft resisters later claimed that they were loyal to the nation but would not follow the call to military service until their civil rights were restored, they replicated the Committee of Nine's original and failed position of conditional loyalty.

As a community analyst observed of antidraft sentiment in Heart Mountain, those who believed that application of the draft to internees was unfair became so convinced of the righteousness of their views that they lost touch with the logic of the state and the selective service apparatus.

> Their faces were toward each other; their backs toward the rest of the country and the government. They tended to lose touch with larger reality, to half-forget that the machinery of selective service was grinding on inexorably. Their opinions, reiterated and reinforced constantly, seemed so utterly reasonable and correct that they ought to make some difference. It was almost as if they believed that, if they felt hard enough and talked hard enough, the operations of selective service would somehow stop or be modified in the direction of their wishes.[76]

But what was reasonable based on a commonsensical notion of justice failed in the courts and in the logic of the bio-political state, resulting in the sentencing of draft resisters to jail terms and not only their expulsion from the national community but even their marginalization for many years in their own Japanese American communities.

Despite the numerous crises that the civil and military authorities produced and encountered during the February–March 1943 campaign, the WRA judged it to have been an overall success. As the WRA explained, even though the army had managed to secure only roughly 1,200 volunteers out of the camps, this was a number sufficient to activate the unit when combined with the large number of volunteers who had been recruited from Hawaii. Moreover, despite the War Department's complaints about the small number of volunteers and the high proportion of the apparently "disloyal" according to their answers on the questionnaires, by enabling the formation of the 442nd the campaign could contribute to the realization of the War Department's main objectives.

As we have seen, these aims included both filling a military manpower need and launching a propaganda campaign that would show domestic and global audiences a minority population fighting for America's supposedly universal values. The WRA likewise recognized this importance: "The volunteering of these young men in relocation centers is outstandingly important as a symbol of Nisei loyalty. Enlisting in the Army from behind wire fences, these volunteers have demonstrated their supreme devotion to the United States."[77] Even the extremely limited success of the volunteer program provided the tiny partial truth from which to invent the myths of Japanese American unconditional loyalty and produce an image of Japanese Americans as the "model minority." Through the remainder of the war and beyond, the many counterreasonings or counter-conduct of all those who refused to volunteer, of all those who found the promises of the Japanese empire more believable than those of the American empire, of all those who challenged the righteousness and justice of military service under discriminatory conditions, of all those who did not want to serve in any military force whether Japanese or American, of all those who questioned their objectification through statistics—all such counterreasonings and other inconvenient responses from the perspective of the authorities have been silenced or marginalized, often with the passionate complicity of some who have deemed themselves spokespersons for Japanese America. Conversely, the small minority's pledge of unconditional allegiance to America has come to achieve a disproportionate dominance in mainstream representations of Japanese American military service and loyalty, precisely because such representations have been so convenient for America's wartime and postwar multiracial nationalism.

CHAPTER FIVE · *Go for Broke,* the Movie

The Transwar Making of American Heroes

> In any stories concerning the use of Japanese-Americans
> by the American Army, we should go into considerable
> detail on the fact that these Japanese-Americans will
> be equipped with and trained in the use of all modern
> weapons, which shows our confidence in the patriotism
> of our Japanese fellow-citizens. This is a useful contrast
> to Japan's inability to use non-Japanese troops except as
> the lowest grade of cannon-fodder sandwiched in with
> Japanese units and watched over by machine-guns and
> with artillery in back of them. This story properly told
> will be effecting to the Axis satellites. Emphasize the
> voluntary basis of Japanese-American enlistment. The
> Japanese-Americans have conducted a long campaign
> in order to be allowed to volunteer.
>
> Overseas Operations Branch, Office of War Informa-
> tion, "Bulletin," for Week Feb. 5–12 (1943)

> Mr. and Mrs. K. Sakamoto, parents of four United States
> army veterans, one killed in action and two decorated
> for bravery, returned today to find their modest ranch
> home near Rocklin had been burned to the ground[.] . . .
> [T]hreats had been made recently in Placer County that
> Japanese ranch houses occupied by white families during
> the occupation would be found in ashes when the Japa-
> nese owners returned to take possession.
>
> "Parents of Japan G.I.s Homeless," *Seattle Port
> Intelligence,* 20 September 1945

Despite the failure of the Japanese American volunteer program to produce a large
number of volunteers from the mainland United States, by commonsense standards
those eventually inducted into the army from Hawaii and the mainland United States

(mainly through the draft) cumulatively performed astonishing feats of military heroism while sacrificing their lives and bodies in numbers out of all proportion to their presence in the military. Perhaps most famously they served as combatants in Europe, first with the 100th Infantry Battalion, an outfit originally made up of Hawaiian Japanese, and then with the 442nd Regimental Combat Team.[1] When war broke out with the Pearl Harbor attack, some 1,500 Hawaiian Japanese, most of whom had been conscripted, were already serving in the Hawaii National Guard. In the next few months great uncertainty arose about the fate of the Hawaiian Japanese in the Guard's 298th and 299th Regiments. However, in May 1942 Hawaii's provisional military governor, General Delos Emmons, recommended that these troops be formed into a special battalion and sent to the mainland for training. The following month, 1,432 men belonging to what was to become the 100th Battalion set sail for the mainland, where they commenced training at Camp McCoy in Wisconsin and then Camp Shelby in Mississippi. Although sixteen out of the 100th's twenty-four original officers were Nisei, the top two in command as well as all the company commanders were white. The 100th began fighting in Italy in September 1943. From their initial frontline action in Salerno, they moved northward through Italy, gaining much media recognition for their efforts while incurring enormous casualties. By June 1944, when the 100th became attached to the newly arrived 442nd Regimental Combat Team, it had suffered 900 casualties, a huge figure given that it had numbered around 1,300 when originally deployed.

As we have already seen, President Roosevelt announced the formation of the Japanese American 442nd Regimental Combat Team on 1 February 1943 after much deliberation concerning the approximately 5,000 Japanese Americans already in the military and the possibility of future enlistments. The 442nd accepted volunteers from the mainland, where most joined directly out of the camps, as well as from Hawaii. Training began in Camp Shelby in May 1943, but the RCT did not ship out to Europe until May 1944. The combat team deployed to Italy was nearly as self-sufficient as a full army division and consisted of the following: Regimental Headquarters Company, Antitank Company, Cannon Company, medical detachment, Service Company, Second and Third Battalions, 522nd Field Artillery Battalion, 232nd Combat Engineer Company, and the 206th Army Ground Force Band. The 442nd's original First Battalion remained behind to serve as a source of future replacements, so that when the 442nd joined the 100th in June 1944, the latter served as the RCT's first battalion. The 100th/442nd saw heavy fighting in seven major campaigns in Italy and France, and like the 100th sustained a huge number of casualties: 9,486, or triple its original strength. This figure included about 600 killed. In

one particularly costly mission that undoubtedly reveals as much about the low regard in which some high-ranking white officers held the lives of Japanese Americans as it does about the latter's heroism, the 442nd took 800 casualties in order to
save 211 men of a Texas battalion that had been trapped behind enemy lines in the
Vosges Mountains. In March 1945 the 522nd Field Artillery Battalion became a rov-
ing battalion, serving with different commands as needed, and participated in the
liberation of prisoners from the Dachau death camp. It is often said that for their
size and length of service the 100th Battalion and the 442nd Regimental Combat
Team were the most decorated units in U.S. military history. To name some of the
most significant, these decorations include 21 Medals of Honor, 52 Distinguished
Service Crosses, 559 Silver Stars, 8 Presidential Unit Citations, 1 Distinguished Service Medal, and 9,486 Purple Hearts.[2]

Thousands of Japanese Americans who graduated from the army's Military Intelligence Service Language School served during the war in combat areas throughout the Asia-Pacific as interpreters, translators, and P.O.W. interrogators. Although
called linguists, they were often involved in extremely dangerous missions, including occasions on which they placed themselves at great risk by trying to persuade
Japanese civilians and military personnel to surrender. After the war they continued their work under the Allied Occupation of Japan. In addition, Japanese Americans served in the 1399 Engineer Construction Battalion, a unit that was activated
in April 1944 in order to work on construction projects in Hawaii. A very small number evaded the army's segregation policy and the War Department's exclusion of
Japanese Americans from the other armed services. For example, Ben Kuroki fought
as a gunner in the Army Air Force, subsequently becoming a much-publicized war
hero for his exploits in North Africa and Europe.

Yet the unique nonwhite prominence in public discourse and representation of
Japanese American soldiers today cannot be explained by their heroism and sacrifices
alone. We ought not to imagine that the sheer weight of their achievements and their
enormous sacrifices were such irrepressible forces in themselves that they could not
but compel their fellow (white) Americans to overcome racism and to treat Japanese Americans as their equals. Certainly, we know that African Americans as well
as other minorities within the continental United States and its colonies have similarly demonstrated many times in modern history, including during the Pacific War,
what would be regarded as military heroism and sacrifice and in many cases served
in far greater numbers.

During World War I, the U.S. Selective Service made no exemptions by race, resulting in the conscription of almost 370,000 African Americans into the army. In

World War II, roughly 1.25 million black Americans were drafted into the four major services: the U.S. Army, U.S. Navy, U.S. Army Air Forces, and U.S. Marines.[3] A large number of Mexican Americans have likewise served, and by official estimate the armed forces enrolled anywhere between 250,000 and 500,000 "Hispanics" during World War II.[4] Roughly half the "American Indian" population did not have U.S. citizenship in 1917, and the government decided to exempt all of them from the draft during World War I. However, about 10,000 volunteered for service, resulting in Congress's granting citizenship to all American Indians in 1924. In World War II American Indians became subject to the draft, even though Arizona, New Mexico, and Maine did not allow them to vote. About 25,000 male and several hundred female American Indians joined the armed forces from July 1940 to December 1945. While the numbers may not seem large, this meant that over one-third of all physically qualified American Indian men between the ages of eighteen and fifty served.[5]

Besides the Japanese from Hawaii, other U.S. colonial soldiers likewise contributed in large numbers to the total war effort. Between 1940 and 1946, the armed forces enrolled some 53,000 Puerto Ricans into its ranks.[6] Although statistics on Filipinos' participation in World War II can only be very rough because of the complicated character of America's recognition of them, and the postwar denial of them as full-fledged U.S. military personnel, it has been estimated that in addition to members of the Filipino First and Second Infantry Regiments, which were Filipino American units, some 200,000 Filipinos served under the U.S. military and survived the war. While mainstream media reports almost always marginalize Filipino contributions and sacrifices to the Allied effort in the Philippines, some 90 percent of the Allied forces that took their last stand against the Japanese on the Bataan peninsula were Filipinos, as were all but 600 of the 7,000 to 10,000 men who died on the Bataan death march. Shortly after the Bataan surrender, the valor of Filipinos became widely known in the United States metropole, and in February 1942 the First and Second Filipino Infantry Regiments were formed so that Filipinos residing in the United States could join the war effort. In March 1942 the Second War Powers Act granted noncitizens in the armed forces the right to become U.S. citizens, with many formal procedures waived.

Yet after U.S. victory, the war record of Filipino veterans fell quickly out of public view and memory. Through the February 1946 Rescission Act, Congress rescinded FDR's promise to the Filipino soldiers who had fought with U.S. troops that they would be allowed U.S. citizenship and veterans' benefits. This law specifically stipulated that duty in the Philippine Commonwealth Army and U.S.-authorized guerrilla units "were not to be considered as active military service for the purposes of veterans benefits." Tens of thousands of Filipino veterans were thus forced to wait for almost forty-five years until passage of the U.S. Immigration and Naturalization Act in 1990 to once again become eligible for citizenship. But as of this writing, the now elderly and in many cases destitute Filipinos who fought for the United States still do not qualify for full benefits distributed by the Department of Veterans Affairs. Paralleling the case of Korean veterans of the Japanese military, their home country's national "liberation" facilitated the former colonial power's renunciation of political and bio-political responsibility for Filipino military service.[7]

But if the sheer irrepressibility of Japanese American military heroism cannot explain the relative abundance of public memorializing about them, especially in comparison with other soldiers of color, what factors have produced such a rich narrative about their triumphs; and how, specifically, have these Japanese American soldiers been represented in radio, film, and popular writings? What do these representations tell us about the management of race in the transwar years? To answer these questions it will be necessary to revisit the issue of U.S. propaganda aimed at both domestic and global audiences; but it will now be possible to demonstrate the obsessiveness and reach with which military and civilian authorities as well as agencies of American propaganda utilized Japanese American soldiers during wartime to construct an image of them as a loyal minority fighting for a nation that denounced racist discrimination.

The production of Japanese American soldiers as war heroes continued into the postwar years, with Hollywood as well as academics joining in the effort. Throughout the transwar period the politics of representing and producing memories of Japanese Americans and Japanese American soldiers have consistently been tied both to the domestic politics of racial management and to U.S. relations with peoples of color throughout the world, especially in Asia. As I have already suggested and will elaborate further in this chapter, during the war years the need to gain allies of color to win first the war, and then the projected peace, facilitated the rehabilitation of Japanese Americans into model soldiers and Americans. In the postwar and particularly Cold War period the production of these images continued, but with the very important difference that Cold War memory making shifted away from an assimilationist to a multiculturalist model. Such a turn away from the idea that cultural difference necessarily signified cultural pathology or lagging development to the idea that some aspects of cultural difference might be celebrated was directly related to the Cold War and the postcolonial scheme for U.S. hegemony in East Asia that gave the nation of Japan a unique location in the global community as the United States' capitalist and "almost, but not quite white" younger sibling. Japanese Americans within the re-racialized postwar U.S. society came to be positioned in a way that was in some important respects homological to the new location of Japan within the American imperium. Just as Japanese Americans continued their transwar transition into American's model minority, so Japan became American's model minority nation.

STAGING FREEDOM AND EQUALITY

As the epigraph above from the Office of War Information (OWI) indicates, the propaganda machinery of the U.S. government was already preparing to spin the story of Japanese American war heroes even before the campaign to recruit them had begun. Even earlier, in order to ensure complete control and management of information released to the public about the camp loyalty investigations, the War Department directed its Bureau of Public Relations to coordinate and take charge of all public relations regarding the program. It was to work closely with the assistant chief of staff (AC of S), G-2 (intelligence), War Department General Staff, Office of the Provost Marshal General (OPMG), Office of Naval Intelligence (ONI), War Relocation Authority (WRA), and OWI, and all information releases required "approval of the Deputy Chief of Staff."[8]

The point of propaganda would be to show that the United States equipped its soldiers with modern weapons and that unlike the non-Japanese soldiers in Japan, who were used only as "cannon-fodder sandwiched in with Japanese units and watched over by machine-guns and with artillery in back of them," the Japanese Americans willingly joined as volunteers. Interestingly, as we will see, on the other side of the Pacific not only did the Japanese military already boast a number of very high ranking Korean officers but Japan's special army volunteer program for Koreans was in its fifth year and the Japanese military and civil authorities had much earlier launched a comparable propaganda campaign in which they tried to show that the Korean people had shown an intense desire to join the Imperial Army out of their rising sense of patriotism to Japan. Japanese propaganda represented the integration of Koreans into the military ranks alongside metropolitan Japanese not as sign of distrust but as an indication that the Japanese empire did not practice racist segregation of military units. As the reader will recall, this was also the logic that Japanese Americans and other U.S. minorities used to argue for ending segregation in the military—a segregated army contradicted the principle of equality. Although John Hall of the Assistant Secretary of War's Office informed the OWI that as of

8 February 1943 it might be premature to "exploit the foreign propaganda aspect of the Japanese American soldiers . . . because of the possibility that things would not work out as planned," he also indicated that the War Department did not object to such a plan in the future.[9] Indeed, once some factual basis for celebrating Japanese American military exploits started to accumulate, the propaganda agencies accelerated efforts directed at both domestic and global audiences.

Following the very well orchestrated propaganda timetable, on 28 January 1943, roughly one week before the army teams arrived in the internment camps to administer the loyalty questionnaires, the War Department's Bureau of Public Relations issued a press release in which it announced formation of the all–Japanese American special army unit. Paralleling Japanese propaganda concerning Korean soldiering, the War Department attributed the new program to the desire of Japanese Americans to serve and to the nation's commitment to freedom and equality. Thus it noted that the action had been taken "following study of the War Department of many earnest requests by loyal American citizens of Japanese extraction for the organization of a special unit of the Army in which they could have their share in the fight against the Nation's enemies." And anticipating President Roosevelt's February 1 announcement, the press release quoted Secretary of War Henry L. Stimson's affirmation of "the inherent right of every faithful citizen, regardless of ancestry, to bear arms in the Nation's battle." The release also introduced the term "Nisei," explaining that it meant "American-born citizens of Japanese parentage," and emphasized that formation of the unit was part of a "larger program which will enable all loyal American citizens of Japanese ancestry to make their proper contribution toward winning the war—through employment in war production as well as military service."[10]

The media blitz accelerated on 1 February, the same day as the president's announcement, with press releases concerning the Japanese American soldiers from Hawaii who were already in training. The bureau explained that these soldiers of the 100th Infantry Battalion resented being called "Japs" and preferred "J.A.'s" or "nisei." Ignoring their exclusion from the Pacific except as language experts, it explained that these loyal and patriotic Americans had "a rendezvous with Tojo and his cohorts to avenge the sneak attack upon their relatives and friends at Pearl Harbor." The news media throughout the country picked up these releases very quickly, so that even in places such as Memphis, Tennessee, readers could see photographs of Japanese Americans in training with the caption "Don't Call 'Em Japs."[11]

In mid-February, WRA personnel surveyed nationwide newspaper coverage of the proposed Japanese American unit and noted that "with few exceptions the comments have been favorable." The *Springfield Republican* (Mass.) stated that its formation "would surely create a good impression among the mass of Americans." Explicitly interpreting the War Department's and the president's decision as evidence of America's condemnation of racism, especially in contrast to the stance of Axis powers, the *Baltimore Sun* proclaimed that the unit was "a visible, tangible denial of the German theory that this is a racial war." Even on the West Coast, where the call for Japanese American exclusion had been so strong and decisive, newspapers such as the *Portland Oregonian* and the *San Francisco Chronicle* praised the action, with the former calling it "Bad News for Hirohito" and the latter saying that the decision "will gratify all who have felt that the only proper test in their (Japanese-Americans') case is loyalty, not racial origin" (parentheses in original).[12]

Other mainstream media also quickly followed suit. The February issue of the *Reader's Digest* carried an article on the Japanese American soldiers from Hawaii that had been condensed from the *Baltimore Sunday Sun*. Titled "U.S. Soldiers with Japanese Faces," it used this trite expression to present Japanese American soldiering as an anomaly that showed America's ability to transcend race. It described the "American doughboys of Japanese ancestry" as "lads with Japanese faces and American hearts" who were "intensely loyal to the United States." They showed their loyalty by buying war bonds and wanted revenge for the Pearl Harbor attack. The article also invoked their shared Christian religion and ignorance of the Japanese language to testify to their Americanness. The chaplain for the 100th reported that his chapel was "filled to overflowing" with these soldiers and that "not one of the men was a Shintoist." "Most of the boys at Camp McCoy do not even speak Japanese," the article assured its readers, and they went by good American nicknames like "Pee Wee," "Pool Shark," "Alibi Joe," and "Peesight."[13]

In the spring and summer of 1943, however, mainstream reportage on Japanese Americans had little to say about Japanese American soldiering. In the first place, there was not much to report, since the 100th did not land in Europe until late September and the 442nd did not ship out until May 1944. Yet even in this period, Cecil H. Coggins, the naval intelligence officer who had been so instrumental in crafting the loyalty questionnaires, used *Harper's Magazine* as a forum to depict Japanese in Hawaii and their soldiers as model soldier-citizens in all respects, except for their "Oriental" appearance. He described the sad fate of the citizens of Japanese ancestry in the army and Hawaii Territorial Guard who had been relieved of their duties after the Pearl Harbor attack, but who through their perseverance eventually began serving in labor units in Hawaii, and then in the 100th Battalion. Like other liberals, Coggins did not condemn the West Coast evacuation and internment, but voicing what became the dominant official position around the time the Costello sub-committee released its final report on 30 September 1943, he asked only that Japanese Americans from Hawaii and the mainland be given an opportunity to prove themselves individually as good Americans. Using the increasingly common expression that was meant to suggest Japanese American loyalty, but that in fact also implied that the category of "American" was equated with whiteness, he wrote: "Their faces were Oriental; their ideas and language were pure American."[14]

Following the Costello subcommittee's essentially positive final assessment of the WRA's work at the end of September 1943, other well-known figures chimed in to praise the Japanese for being good Americans and the government for devising a system to separate the "goats from the sheep." Continuing its series of liberal articles on the Japanese American problem that went back to September 1942, *Harper's* carried a piece in October 1943 by the Pulitzer Prize–winning journalist S. Burton Heath. He did not condemn the evacuation and internment but stressed that continuing the categorical lockup of all Japanese Americans without giving individuals an opportunity to prove their loyalty might well be compared to Hitler's actions against the Jews. He thus defended the conclusion already reached by the WRA, the Costello subcommittee, and so many others—namely, that the goats should be separated from the sheep and that the process for releasing those deemed loyal should be accelerated.

Heath embodied the paternalism and self-congratulatory stance of the liberal and polite racists. For while he strongly condemned the vulgar racism of the Nazi type and warned against continuing a "pogrom against the Japanese Americans," at the same time he praised the judge who had commented on Gordon Hirabayashi's famous challenge to the exclusion order. This judge had purportedly advised white Americans to understand that some Asians (if not all) were as good as "Caucasians." As he put it, "their Mongoloid features and yellow skins have among them persons of the same high spirit, intellectual integrity and consciousness of social obligation as have the surrounding Caucasians." Heath also urged Americans to uphold the American principle of nondiscrimination and to treat Japanese Americans as well as one white family had treated the main subjects of his article, Hugh and Ruth Kiino. For upon their release from Camp Jerome, "[t]hey were exceedingly fortunate. Ruth found a housekeeping job with a family that is willing to let Hugh and their child live with her while Hugh finds work."[15]

Similarly, around the same time Eleanor Roosevelt, wife of the president who had presided over the evacuation and internment of Japanese Americans, wrote an article for *Collier's* on Japanese American loyalty. Essentially she defended the program of dividing the loyal from the disloyal, even if families might be split by the process, because "American Sportsmanship" and the principles of freedom and equality demanded that loyal Japanese Americans be granted the right to freedom. To help make her point, the article prominently featured a picture of the Toyama family, which showed two parents who had since returned to Japan and a son in the uniform of a U.S. Army sergeant.[16]

Although instances of ongoing racist discrimination against Japanese Americans and the resistance of some internees to the draft in 1944 complicated the production of Japanese American war heroes, as the military exploits of the soldiers mounted in the fall of 1943, the War Department increasingly worked to facilitate favorable media reports on the new soldiers. The Japanese American soldiers were not unaware of the War Department's exploitation of them for propaganda purposes. As censors who in mid-January 1944 intercepted and read letters sent by members of the 100th Infantry Battalion to relatives and friends in Hawaii explained: "Much publicity has followed the movements of this colorful battalion. Their eagerness to meet the enemy, heroism in battle, pride in the United States Army and in themselves as soldiers—these have been often reported by the press." However, they pointed out that while some of the soldiers enjoyed this coverage, "some feel that they have been made a publicity instrument." And it cited one letter that read: "You have probably been reading about the glorious 100th—well, don't believe all you read in the papers—we are a very much overpublicized bunch of guinea pigs."[17]

Whatever the soldiers themselves felt, the War Department continued to stage and report on the superb battlefield performances of the Japanese American soldiers. When Abe Fortes, undersecretary of the interior, inquired at the Office of the Assistant Secretary of War about publicity for the 442nd around the time it first began to participate in combat in Italy, the executive officer of the assistant secretary of war responded that "action has been initiated in the theater to obtain full press, still, and newsreel coverage of both Japanese American units [the 442nd and 100th] now overseas. Several top writers have been assigned to features and stories on these units, and in addition the Army Pictorial Service now has crews at the front with these units. Films will be completed and shipped within the near future. The press release line on these units has been lifted so that newspaper and radio coverage may be obtained of current operations."[18] Despite the last arrangement, the War Department continued to issue releases to the press lauding the Japanese American soldiers. For example, on 10 August 1944 the War Department explained to the press that Japanese American soldiers had participated in "virtually every front established in the drive through Italy" and had garnered a special citation for having completely "destroyed the enemy flank position in a critical conflict in the vicinity of Belvedere and Sassetta, Italy," on 26 and 27 June. "In ten months of almost continuous fighting," it declared, "only two soldiers of the 100th Infantry have been captured by the Germans, while the battalion has taken hundreds of prisoners, killed hundreds more, and destroyed vast quantities of enemy materiel." Members of the unit had been awarded "1,000 Purple Hearts, 44 Silver Stars, 31 Bronze Stars, nine Distinguished Services Crosses and three Legion of Merit medals." Although no desertions or absences without leave had occurred, the press were informed that two cases of "reverse AWOL" had taken place: "Before their battle wounds were completely healed in a field hospital behind the lines," the War Department said, "two soldiers left the hospital and hitch-hiked back to their companies on the battlefield."[19]

The media increasingly lauded the heroics of the Nisei soldiers and represented them above all as "normal" Americans. A Hearst newsreel segment titled "Japanese-Yank Troops Join U.S. Army in France," for example, showed the individual faces of Nisei soldiers and remarked that they were "Americans of Japanese parentage fresh from the U.S." The footage tried to give the impression that these soldiers faced wartime difficulties that were no different from those that confronted other Americans. Thus, while the narrator failed to mention the internment camps and racism, he reported that for these soldiers, "How to speak French is their first problem." And we see a handful of mostly Japanese faces poring over what appears to be a textbook with the title *French*. These are, the newsreel informs us, "loyal Japanese Americans." What we are seeing are "signal corps films of U.S.-born Japanese fighting in the cause of freedom."[20]

In the fall of 1944, the WRA in collaboration with the War Department issued a pamphlet called *Nisei in Uniform*.[21] It cited Roosevelt as it proclaimed, once again, that Americanism rested not on race but spirit. "Every race and nation from which our population has been drawn is represented among the young Americans who are fighting side by side to overthrow the Axis powers." This was true of Germans fighting the Nazis, of Italians waging war on the Italian Axis forces, and of course of "men whose parents came from Japan [who] are showing that devotion to America and gallantry in action are not determined by the slant of the eyes or the color of the skin." The text told of the Japanese American evacuation from the West Coast, but the emphasis lay elsewhere. Photographs showed Nisei soldiers involved in activities that one might expect of any soldier: engaging in military exercises, fighting in combat, searching for mines, standing guard, and so on. Above all, the Japanese American soldier appeared as a recognizable likeness of the white soldier. "American soldiers with Japanese faces," read one caption, inadvertently revealing that

Americanness was indeed associated with whiteness, "Edwin Iino, Saburo Ikuta, and Robert Yonemitsu were all born and raised in California where they were educated in American schools. They have never visited Japan." The individuals pictured were in most respects unremarkable in their resemblance to their typical white counterparts: a former bantamweight boxing champion, a star on a wrestling team, graduates of the University of Washington or the University of Utah, a minister of a Congregational Church, and the brother of a stage dancer. They liked mail call, they went sightseeing, their pastimes were no different from those of other Americans, their brides wore wedding gowns and they cut wedding cakes at their marriages, and they enjoyed Christmas packages from home. Nisei WACs mimicked their white counterparts, while male Nisei soldiers showed heroism and sometimes suffered severe injuries and dismemberment. Yoshinao Omiya of Honolulu, for example, "fought bravely until both eyes were blown out by a land mine." Race did not conflict with Americanness, so it seemed, as long as signs of cultural difference disappeared.

In the last year of the war, the nation's newspapers reported widely on the military exploits of the Japanese American soldiers, sometimes contrasting their heroics with the poor treatment they received when returning to their hometowns. For example, the Associated Press circulated a photo and report on a bespectacled and rather average-looking Mrs. William Insigne of Walnut Grove, California. She had been sent to county jail for thirty days for "threatening to burn house of Pvt. Yoshio Matsuoka unless his family moved" and had received only a reduced sentence with the proviso that "SHE leave town" (emphasis in original).[22] Although soldiers were not specifically mentioned, the *Los Angeles Daily News* (23 June 1945) reported that the well-known comedian Joe E. Brown, who had just returned from entertaining U.S. troops in the Pacific, had spoken for the Nisei. The "boys overseas," he said, "think attacks against Japanese Americans in California are 'terrible.' " "We don't terrorize persons of German descent, just because we were fighting the Germans in Europe," he said. "It certainly would be ridiculous to hate Eisenhower because he is of German ancestry." The *Fresno Bee* (30 June 1945) reported that Corporal George T. Morishita had served in the 442nd and received the "Silver Star for gallantry in action" as well as a Purple Heart. The *Great Falls Tribune* (2 July 1945) reported that although the Spokane Veterans of Foreign Wars had rejected the membership application of Pfc. Richard H. Naito, a "wounded Japanese-American veteran of the Italian campaign," 580 combat veterans had signed a petition in protest against this action. The petition of the veterans stated that "the prejudice of a few members which resulted in his (Naito's) rejection has no place in American life and particularly not in an organization with such a history, public importance and high, democratic ideals. This is not what we fought for in this war and it will not help our buddies in the Pacific who still have a job to do." The *Minidoka Irrigator* (Idaho, 21 July 1945) carried an article listing the accomplishments of Japanese American soldiers. According to the WRA, it reported that "at least 20,529 persons of Japanese ancestry are now in the armed forces of the United States, and Japanese Americans had suffered more than 9,000 casualties in the European and Pacific theaters of war." It also quoted a letter from General Jacob L. Devers, commanding general of the Sixth Army in Europe, who said: "It is my fervent wish that Americans will never forget the struggles and sacrifices of the fighting men, including these Nisei who, like the rest, have fought so courageously for our democratic ways of life. The Japanese American soldiers . . . are, now in my opinion, among the first soldiers in the United States Army." Excerpting an article from the *Reader's Digest*, the *Minidoka Irrigator* (31 July 1945) praised the 100th as "probably the most decorated unit in the history of the U.S. Army." The Japanese American soldiers, it said, had fought against not only the Axis powers but also discrimination at home and had shown that "democracy is stronger than race." It celebrated individual acts of heroism, including that of "little Kenny Yasui, dubbed 'Baby York' for his capture of 16 Japs." Conveniently ignoring that just a little more than two years previously Yasui's competence in Japanese would have made him particularly suspect as an American, the article explained how he had accomplished this feat. "Calling out in Japanese learned at Waseda University in Tokyo, Kenny convinced the 16 who were hiding in foxholes, that he was a Jap colonel." The *San Francisco Chronicle* (28 July 1945) reported on a speech by Captain George H. Grandstaff, who had fought with Nisei soldiers. He urged "fair play and fair treatment" and noted how the Japanese American soldiers had suffered 40 percent losses in their attempt to rescue the "Lost Battalion," a unit of the Thirty-fifth Texas Division. He condemned racism against these soldiers, saying, "Many mothers and fathers of these Texas boys thank God for these little half-pints whom some of you still call 'yellow-bellies.'" The *Oregonian* (25 July 1945) described the angry reaction of a white soldier who read about several Japanese American veterans, one of whom had lost an arm and another a leg, who had been refused service and thrown out of a Seattle soda fountain. He said: "Everyone here who read the article is plenty sore. I wish we had more soldiers like the Japanese-Americans. I guess some people didn't realize that some of the Japanese are better Americans than some white people."

Frank Capra's infamous propaganda film *Know Your Enemy—Japan* is perhaps one of the most blatant examples of wartime racism against the enemy.[23] Surprisingly, however, it begins not with a general statement about the "Japs" over there but with praise for Japanese Americans and particularly the Nisei soldier. The film informed its audience that the children of Japanese immigrants to America were citizens and that not only had they been educated in American schools and speak "our" language, but "a great many of them share our love of freedom and our willingness to die for it," including and most especially the Nisei soldiers in Europe. This film, the statement concluded, was not about Japanese Americans. Instead, it told "the story of Japs in Japan to whom the words 'liberty' and 'freedom' are still without meaning." Thus Capra seemed to say that race did not matter, only national belonging. Yet at the same time, the film repeatedly blurred the distinction between the "Jap" over there and the "Jap" over here. It showed fishermen off the coast of California and warned that they were part of the same family of treacherous Japanese people. And it cautioned Americans to beware of "Jap" spies in their midst: shopkeepers, barbers, and flower shop owners, all working for Tokyo. Thus, while in the Rooseveltian fashion disavowing race as a standard of Americanism, it nevertheless warned of the particular dangers that inhered in those perceived as racially different.

Among the most celebrated moments in (white) America's recognition of the Nisei soldier were victory celebrations following the war's conclusion. At Leghorn, Italy, some 3,000 Nisei troops were selected to take the lead position of honor for the V-J Day Parade. The *New York Times* (19 August 1945) reported that they would head up 15,000 troops and that they had garnered such respect from their fellow white soldiers that D Company of the 168th Infantry Regiment had promised to give "full aid to the Nisei boys during the readjustment problems back in the States." Among their heroics, only six Japanese Americans had ever gone AWOL. "These six," the *Times* noted, "were men who escaped from hospitals without leave to return to combat."[24]

The culminating event in the Nisei soldiers' immediate postwar heroization was President Truman's awarding of a presidential citation to the 442nd on the White House lawn in July 1946. After marching down Constitution Avenue, the men of the 442nd listened to Truman's speech explaining the significance of their accomplishments. Like others, he began by placing himself in the Rooseveltian mode of disavowal: "I believe it was my predecessor who said that Americanism is not a matter of race or creed, it is matter of the heart." He congratulated the Nisei soldiers for their contributions to the nation and to the world and then noted, "You fought not only the enemy, but you fought prejudice, and you have won." Yet the speech also made it clear that the accomplishments of the Nisei soldiers would always be overwritten by the teleological narrative of American progress. "Keep up that fight," he exhorted, "and we continue to win—to make this great Republic stand for just what the Constitution says it stands for: the welfare of all the people all the time."[25]

The emphasis on the grand American narrative is even more powerfully in evidence in Hearst newsreel footage of the ceremony.[26] In it we see the Japanese American troops marching in formation, but these men are not clearly individualized, and in fact appear not so different from the "Jap" soldiers in the Capra film who were described as just like so many "photographic prints off the same negative." The newsreel ceremonial is about the Nisei in only a secondary way, for it is Truman, standing in for America, whose gaze, face, and speech dominate the proceedings. He is the only person marked as an individual and his are the only words that we hear. The president is there to validate the Nisei, but in his recognition of them he affirms that their victories should be read only as victories for America. When he declares that the Nisei have made the Republic "stand for just what the Constitution says it stands for," he is insisting that all heroisms are always already foreordained by the Constitution. He guards against any slippage of meaning that might throw the grand narrative of progress under suspicion.

Thus, by the end of the war and its immediate postwar celebrations, the heroization of the Japanese American soldier had been framed to accentuate their "normality," which meant assimilation to white America, and in such a way that their exploits would always be overshadowed by the American nationalist claim that the nation's exceptional greatness stemmed from its denunciation of racism. Ronald Reagan—incidentally, a man who sometimes seemed to confuse movies with reality—expressed this idea while participating in a 1945 award ceremony for a Japanese American hero: "America stands unique in the world, the only country not founded on race, but on a way—an ideal. Not in spite of, but because of our polyglot background, we have had all the strength in the world. That is the American way."[27]

Yet we must also recall that the Japanese American soldiers were supposed to perform America's denunciation of racist discrimination for a global as well as domestic audience. If the decision to recruit Japanese Americans as soldiers was in large part triggered by the desire to employ them in a propaganda campaign directed at allies or potential allies of color, then we should expect to see them used in direct campaigns that specifically targeted those whom Edwin O. Reischauer and others described as the "yellow and brown" peoples of the world, including the Japanese people.

Indeed, in its 15 September 1944 plan for propaganda publications to be used in the Philippines, the Overseas Branch of OWI proposed the distribution of a special booklet titled "Orientals in the U.S. Forces," which presumably would have covered the contributions of Japanese Americans. It was to be prepared and published in four languages: 200,000 copies in English, 50,000 in Tagalog, 50,000 in Bisayan, and 25,000 in Iloko. Other booklets were to treat Chinese Americans in the Burma campaign as well as "Filipinos in the War." Such pamphlets were supposed to further the general objective of projecting the United States

> as a peace-loving democratic nation, dedicated with the other United Nations to the winning of the war and the securing of the peace; as a country whose resources have been developed by free men for the common good, and whose achievements bear witness to the soundness of the democratic process; as a country where freedom of speech and freedom of the press are cherished in war and peace; as a people who, through their racial origins and thanks to their educational opportunities, are becoming more and more interested in other peoples everywhere; as a country which is especially concerned with the progress of the Philippines.

In other words, propaganda aimed at the Philippines was supposed to emphasize that the future postwar American presence in this region would be part of a democratic project founded on the principles of freedom and racial equality.[28] Similarly, in its directive concerning "Radio Informational Activities to China," the same Overseas Branch of the OWI did not specifically mention Japanese American soldiers but laid down the principle that propaganda toward Asia should show the *"diversity of the American scene"* (emphasis in original) and should avoid the use of racial epithets even in referring to the Japanese, because these "might conceivably be equally applicable to the Chinese or Asiatics in general. 'Almond-eyed people' or 'Asiatic barbarians' are cases in point."[29]

However, the most striking and concerted efforts to mobilize Japanese American soldiers in direct propaganda to Asia were ironically against the Japanese themselves. Even while the Japanese Hawaiians were still in training in the mainland United States, the OWI was already circulating laudatory information about them across the Pacific in the Japanese language. For instance, on 13 May 1943 they broadcast a special radio program called "Splendid Record of the U.S. Soldiers of Japanese Ancestry." The program emphasized the superior qualities of the Japanese American soldiers, that in fact their "average record proves to be better than that of other American soldiers." It remarked on their sincere loyalty, enthusiasm, and self-determination. All had volunteered and many had made great monetary sacrifices in order to take part in the war effort. The program quoted an officer charged with training them who carefully avoided explicitly racializing the enemy, while at the same time clearly distinguishing between the Japanese people and their government. He testified that the Japanese American soldiers "have a deeper hatred toward the military government of Japan than the average American soldier." Why? Not only because of their fervent desire to "crac[k] down on the Axis," but also because many of them had lost family members and friends in the Pearl Harbor attack. The program concluded on a note about the fair and equal treatment they were receiving. "Like other American soldiers," it said, "these Japanese-Americans are receiving the same treatment in promotion of rank and other priveledges [sic]."[30]

The OWI's outline history of radio broadcasts to Japan indicates that as part of its psychological warfare campaign against the enemy, beginning on 1 July 1944 it featured a daily ten-minute program called "Nisei, USA," which "related the activities of Japanese-Americans, particularly in military activity." While the show appears to have ceased on 18 May 1945, the OWI continued to include reports on Nisei soldiers in its subsequent radio broadcasts to Japan.[31] Thus, a plan for radio broadcasts to Japan in June 1945 explained that Nisei soldiers should be used to counter the "Misrepresentation of Western People" as racist "barbarians": "American justice and fair play toward Oriental people is reflected in the honor, loyalty and courage of American soldiers of Japanese extraction, and in the friendly attitude of Japanese civilians once they realize we are not the barbarians their militarists claim we are. The accomplishments of the Nisei and American reaction to their achievements prove that Occidentals and Orientals do cooperate to the mutual advantage of both."[32]

In the last months of the war, the U.S. military as well as various civilian agencies joined to vigorously project the wartime contributions of Nisei soldiers, and Japanese Americans in general, as proof to the Japanese people and their allies that the United States did not countenance racial discrimination and that it would therefore treat the vanquished well upon their surrender. As Reischauer had urged, these authorities mobilized representations of Japanese Americans, including their soldiers, to win not only the war but also the peace that would follow. Thus a late war - time document, "Preliminary Plan for Leaflet Campaign Against Japan," whose main purpose was to outline a strategy to reduce the Japanese peoples' "mental obstacles to surrender," included skillful manipulation of Nisei soldiers for propaganda. "With pictures and text tell the story of the Nisei soldiers in this war," it said, "to show that Americans do not hate the Japanese as a race." This was to be part of a larger plan to show that "Occidentals" were "humane" and treated such people as the Filipinos and Japanese POWs well.[33] Finally, once the Japanese had surrendered, the United States sent hundreds of Japanese American soldiers to Japan, in no small part because of the long-standing plan to employ them as living proof to the former enemy that America would treat its former enemy fairly and without racial prejudice.

TRANSWAR MATTERS: *GO FOR BROKE*

According to the film historian Richard Slotkin, the 1943 feature *Bataan* established the prototype for the Hollywood combat film genre that has as one of its primary themes the multiethnic and multiracial unity of the diverse men making up the U.S. armed forces. Such films, he argues, have exceeded the immediate context of the military and express "a myth of American nationality that remains vital in our political and cultural life: the idealized self-image of a multiethnic, multiracial democracy, hospitable to difference but united by a common sense of national belonging." *Bataan* proved to be a great success, and other films such as *Sahara* (1943), *Guadalcanal Diary* (1943), *Gung Ho!* (1944), and *Objective Burma* (1945) followed in quick order. Each was unique and some had more internationalist angles, but all manifested the greater theme of multiracial unity—a theme that required viewers to exercise a considerable leap of faith, since in World War II the U.S. military still continued to segregate its personnel by race, even isolating blood plasma drawn from African Americans from that of whites. This genre did not end with the war but continued in such films as *Home of the Brave* (1949), *Red-Ball Express* (1952), *All the Young Men* (1959), and *Pork Chop Hill* (1959). In popular culture the theme of multiethnic/multiracial unity in war has stayed with us into the recent past and the present, although it is sometimes projected through stories that could hardly have been imagined in 1943, including *Alien* (1979), *Star Trek* (various television series from 1966, movies from 1979), and *Independence Day* (1996).[34]

I will have more to say in chapter 7 about *Bataan* and its surprisingly direct relevance for thinking about comparabilities between Hollywood and Japanese colonial film making on multiethnic or multiracial soldiering; but for the moment I would like to consider how one film that Slotkin places in this genre, *Go for Broke*, both carried on the theme of multiethnic/multiracial unity for the national cause and also projected the specific image of Japanese Americans into a major feature film for the first time.[35] As we have seen, pamphlets, newspaper and magazine articles, and celebratory newsreel footage had already created a public image of the Japanese American fighting men, but the 1951 movie was a Hollywood feature film starring one of the industry's leading actors, Van Johnson, and it circulated images of the Nisei as citizen and soldier with unprecedented reach and effect. Its premiere took place in Washington, D.C., and millions eventually saw it. The film's director and screen-writer was Robert Pirosh, an army combat veteran who had earlier won an Acad-emy Award for the movie *Battleground* (1949), and its producer was Dore Schary. Schary, it seems, had originally contemplated making a film about the identity of a soldier in the Tomb of the Unknowns, whose lack of identity suggests that he might have been from any ethnic background.[36] One scholar has also identified Schary as the source for the idea of putting an African American in *Bataan*.[37] Another eerie conflation of life inside and outside the movies as well as the continuity of rather than break between the wartime and postwar periods should be mentioned: all the men performing in the roles of soldiers in the 442nd were actually veterans of that unit, except for the actor who played the important role of Tommy (see figure 4). Thus these men performed America's disavowal of racism two times: once for the news media on actual battlefields, the second time for the movies after the war.

There are at least two central narratives that run through *Go for Broke*. The first and most obvious is the story of the Nisei soldiers' achievements—from training in Camp Shelby, Mississippi, to combat in Europe—as they battle both racism within American society and the national enemy. The film does not hide that many Nisei soldiers from the mainland have families in camps. A soldier sends a package of gifts to his loved ones who are suffering under miserable camp conditions, and Nisei main-landers on the war front await letters from loved ones back home, in camp. The high-lights of Nisei glory include victories in Italy and France, the capture of enemy officers who cannot comprehend the appearance of their captors—"What kind of troops are these, Chinese?"—and the 442nd's famous rescue of the all-Texan "Lost Battalion" in France.

However, it is the other story that dominates the film and subsumes the 442nd's heroism. This is the odyssey of Lieutenant Grayson (played by Van Johnson), who begins his spiritual journey as a man who despises the "Jap" soldiers that he must lead, but who in the course of the film comes to disavow that racism. When Gray-son initially reports to Camp Shelby he immediately requests a transfer out. He denies that his reason for doing so is that the men under his command will be "Japs," but the movie makes it clear that this is indeed the problem. Two officers in succession lecture Grayson, explaining that the Japanese Americans are loyal citizens. A colonel castigates Grayson: "They're not Japs; they're Japanese Amer-icans, Nisei; or as they call themselves, Buddhaheads; all kinds of Buddhaheads, lieu-tenant.... They're all American citizens and they're all volunteers, remember that."

FIGURE 4.
The cast of *Go for Broke*. Aside from Van Johnson in the lead role
(center) and Henry Nakamura as "Tommy" (to Johnson's right),
the other actors pictured had actually served in the 442nd. Film
still courtesy of Library of Congress, Motion Picture Division.

But Grayson is not convinced. He is repulsed by the culture of the Hawaiian
"Japs"—by their ukulele playing, singing, and hula dancing. Finally, he experiences
a moment of relief when he learns that his platoon sergeant will be Sergeant O'Hara.
But as it turns out, the sergeant's full name is Takashi Ohara—a Japanese name,
not an Irish one.

On his way to the battlefront in Europe, Grayson reads his orders. They tell him
that the Italian leaders are trying to convince their people that Americans are racist,
but that in truth "racial prejudice is abhorrent to our American concept of democracy." He pauses to reflect on his own negative feelings toward his men, but he is
as yet unrepentant and still looks forward to transferring out. "A guy gets in to fight
the Japs and winds up fightin' with them," he says. As he observes the Nisei soldiers' exploits in battle, however, Grayson is gradually won over. When he meets
an old friend named Culley from the Texas Division, he is offended and angered by

this man's racist attitude toward the Nisei. They're not "Japs," he tells his old friend, and he gets into a fistfight to defend those whom he had not long ago himself despised. Soon Culley too becomes an admirer of the Nisei, especially after he is rescued by them; and like them he begins to shout the 442nd slogan, "Go for Broke." The struggle against racism has apparently prevailed.

Grayson's and Culley's denunciations of racism are clearly allegories of America's overcoming of it. America's disavowal is foretold at the movie's beginning with the famous quote from Roosevelt—that Americanism is a "matter of mind and heart" and not of "race or ancestry"—and the possibility of interpreting both Nisei heroics and the white men's rejection of racism as anything but the realization of America's promise is foreclosed by the film's ending. The film concludes with the Nisei soldiers' triumphal return to the United States, followed by newsreel footage of the previously described ceremony in which Truman confers the presidential citation on them. Certainly, the men of the 442nd are much more individualized in the movie than in earlier newsreels and Truman is less of a presence, for instead of Truman's face we see a succession of blurred faces of the individual heroes of the 442nd. Yet, as the film comes to its close, the Nisei soldiers drop from sight. The camera pulls away to reveal anonymous soldiers marching down the Pennsylvania Avenue processional route. The White House looms sublimely over the capital. The End.

Despite similarities with earlier representations of the Nisei soldiers—most significantly, the teleological narrative's overwriting of the Nisei valor story—some major noteworthy departures link the film more directly to the "model minority" discourse of the 1960s and beyond. Most important, unlike earlier representations of the soldiers, the film shows greater tolerance for both individual and cultural difference; as a result, there is much in the film that prefigures today's moderate liberal multiculturalism. However shallowly developed, these are real, not stereotyped, Japanese American people, and the film asks its viewers to recognize that these men have a culture that is different from, but quite as respectable as, that of (white) Americans. They have their own pastimes, such as playing the ukulele, singing, and hula dancing, that even Lieutenant Grayson comes in time to appreciate. They use their own "pidgin English," and sometimes even speak in Japanese. They call themselves "Buddhaheads" and the officers "haoles," but this does not interfere with their work as American soldiers. A Nisei soldier lies wounded in the attempt to rescue the Lost Battalion. A white Catholic chaplain sees him holding a rosary and wonders why he has not seen him in Catholic services. The reason, the soldier responds, is that this is "a different kind of rosary." He is a Buddhist. Ignoring the army's actual prohibition of Buddhist chaplains from serving in its ranks, the film represents religious difference as unproblematic.[38] The chaplain leaves with a gesture of tolerance: "I'll be here if you want me."

Indeed, the film sometimes represents cultural differences as assets in the war effort. At one point, Grayson and Culley are separated from the U.S. troops, and when they hear the 442nd's soldiers at a distance they must identify themselves with a password. But Grayson does not know the new password, so in one of the film's more humorous scenes he shouts out the only Japanese that he has learned, *bakatare* (damned idiot). The Nisei soldiers conclude that he must be one of them and stop firing their rifles. In effect, Grayson and Culley are saved by a white American's multicultural literacy. In another episode, the Germans have captured a field telephone and are calling into headquarters in English. They pretend to be a part of the 442nd so as to sabotage the efforts of the U.S. troops. But a quick-witted Nisei minding the headquarter's phone suspects that something is amiss, so he begins to speak to the German in Japanese. He assumes that if the man on the other end is really a part of the 442nd he should be able to understand and respond. The German has no idea what is being said to him and can only keep repeating that his name is Sergeant Sugimoto. A white officer at headquarters commends the Nisei soldier for his resourcefulness and the soldier responds, "Thank you sir, it's just that good old Yankee know-how."

The cultural or ethnic differences evoked in the film are not critical ones that could upset the unspoken but assumed racial hierarchy. In the film as in life, the officers are almost all white, with one low-ranking exception. One of the Nisei men is seemingly always grumbling about racism, but none is unruly. There is, moreover, an overall emasculinization of the Nisei soldiers that serves to domesticate them in such a way as to safely position them in the existing racial hierarchy. U.S. propaganda such as *Know Your Enemy* had only a few years earlier created an almost superhuman image of the "Jap" soldier. It was said that although physically small, averaging "five foot three inches and one hundred and seventeen pounds," "Jap" soldiers were tough and hardened, fantastic soldiers who would "just as soon go over a mountain as around it." And fear of "yellow men" living in the United States was often expressed as a fear of their sexual insatiability.[39]

Go for Broke helped harness these menacing images of Japanese American male physicality and sexuality. Most pertinent is an odd subplot of the film involving Tommy, the smallest of the small soldiers. When Grayson first sees him he is wearing a uniform that is grossly oversized. Tommy is nearly childlike in his personality as well as his physical size. He confesses in tears one day that he wants to fight against the Japanese because both his parents were killed at Pearl Harbor. He has

FIGURE 5.
In *Go for Broke*, Tommy's pet pig is sacrificed to feed a poor
French family. Film still courtesy of the Library of Congress,
Motion Picture Division.

no parents, no girlfriend, and he longs to receive letters. One day while in combat
he finds a baby pig, which he decides to adopt and which he physically embraces
throughout the film. Only a little earlier, Grayson is shown listening to records, kiss-
ing, and drinking wine with a beautiful local Italian woman, but the closest Tommy
gets to the erotic is in his adventures with the pig.

As the film proceeds the piglet gets bigger. A local Italian peasant says he would
like to buy Tommy's pig so that he can mate it with his female pig. This is the first
intimation we have that Tommy's pig has a sex, and as the pig turns his hindquar-
ters toward us, we can see that he is indeed a male. *"Bambinos, amore,"* the Italian
implores, but Tommy misunderstands and thinks the Italian and his family want to
buy his pig to eat. The Italian peasant's children assure him, "No eat, no eat." Tommy
finally gets the point, smiles, but protests that the pig is too young. He will grow
bigger, the peasant responds. Yet Tommy refuses the offer and appears disturbed by
even the thought of such a union.

Soon the men of the 442nd ship out from Italy on their way to France, and Tommy smuggles his pet on aboard. But we can see that the pig is growing quite large and is rambunctious as well. Tommy can barely hide the squirming animal in his duffle bag. In France, Tommy must ask a poor peasant family to care for the pig while he himself goes off to combat. Later, Tommy returns for his pet and rewards the peasant with two packs of cigarettes. The peasant is grateful but disappointed, for his large family, which includes several children, has very little to eat. Tommy looks down at the pig, but decides not to offer it as food. But as he walks away he sees the Frenchman's wife cradling a small infant while looking nearly lifeless herself. Tommy returns to the Frenchman's barn and comes out alone. The fat pig is presumably eaten and Tommy's flirtation with the sexual ends (see figure 5). Tommy's desexualization and infantilization is one condition for postwar acceptance of Japanese Americans into (white) America. There is some irony in this, as the masculinist discourse of military heroism has been one element mobilized by Japanese American men to recuperate their self-esteem. Moreover, one consequence of the discourse of the male Japanese American soldier as citizen has been the figuring of Japanese American women as citizens of secondary rank.

"MODEL MINORITY" AND THE COLD WAR

Go for Broke was the product of the postwar transition to a discourse on the nation and on the racialized peoples within it that countenanced cultural difference insofar as it did not upset the racial hierarchy. As we have seen, while earlier representations of Japanese Americans as soldiers and citizens had celebrated their heroism and participation in the war effort, they tended to erase difference as the condition for acceptance in (white) America. *Go for Broke* and the discourse on the "model minority" that followed it are to be contrasted with this radically assimilationist view—a view that had been held by leading figures in the internment administration such as Dillon S. Myer, as well as by other liberal officials and citizens—according to which cultural differences, described as dangerously "nationalistic," would eventually be erased altogether as racial minorities blended into communities throughout the nation. *Go for Broke* included new patterns of representations and discourses that celebrated values considered to be traditional in Asian societies insofar as they seemed conducive to Americanism.

As others have already pointed out, the heyday of the "model minority" discourse took place in the mid-1960s, when Chinese Americans, and Japanese Americans to an even greater degree, came to be represented as the exemplars toward which all

Americans, including whites, should aspire. At that time, articles such as the sociologist William Petersen's "Success Story, Japanese-American Style" and "Success Story of One Minority Group in U.S." began to appear in the mainstream media.[40] These articles made a connection between what were perceived to be traditional Asian values and high achievement in education and employment. Respect for authority, love of learning, a work ethic, and so on were supposed to hold the secrets of Asian American success. In addition, to focus more specifically on Japanese Americans and military heroism, Petersen argued that unlike what he called the "problem minorities," Japanese Americans had practically overcome racial discrimination and succeeded as citizens in American society "by their own almost totally unaided effort." And he cited their military record against the backdrop of internment as evidence of Japanese American efforts and abilities to transcend prejudice on the way to becoming model citizens. While he noted that some Japanese Americans had understandably refused to serve, "most accepted as their lot the overwhelming odds against them and bet their lives, determined to win even in a crooked game."[41]

Many activists and scholars have already pointed out the utility of this logic in the 1960s for conservative denials of the debilitating effects of racism. Following the rise of the civil rights movement, black militancy, urban uprisings, and a move toward greater state intervention in race relations, the model minority success story could be mobilized to delegitimize the demands of other minorities for more aggressive measures to achieve social justice. In other words, it could be argued that Asian Americans and especially Japanese Americans had succeeded through their own efforts despite racial prejudice and that other minorities should do the same. Ultimately, minorities who failed had only themselves to blame for their miserable circumstances.

Yet explanations for the minor explosion into the public arena of a discourse on Japanese Americans as the model minority must also look beyond the domestic scene. The prominence of Japanese Americans as the "almost, but not quite white" minority coincides in both logic and historical timing with the construction of a discourse on Japan as the honorary white nation. As we have seen, as early as the summer or fall of 1942, some civil and military officials as well as advisers such as Edwin O. Reischauer were beginning to envision Japan as a potential ally in the struggle to establish U.S. hegemony in East Asia. Over the transwar years, this notion triggered a fundamental transformation of popular images about Japan and the Japanese people that clearly accelerated in the postwar and Cold War years. Dominant images of Japan underwent a miraculous metamorphosis, from those of a backward nation peopled by an insectlike or herdlike population to those of the United States' most reliable, friendly, and democratic ally (although racism and stereotypes obviously continued to exist in latent and sometimes blatant form). As the democratic, capitalist, and almost, but not quite white nation, "Japan" came to be deployed as the new model for aspiring peoples of color throughout the world.

Though critical scholarship on Cold War modernization theory has already unveiled its ties to U.S. imperialism, much less has been made of the transwar linkages between this theory and U.S. plans for hegemony in Asia that were already being hatched during the hot war.[42] The reader may recall that in the September 1942 memo analyzed at some length in chapter 2, Reischauer had already presented a scheme by which the United States would win the peace in the region by establishing a "puppet regime" in Tokyo and also by presenting itself as a nation that condemned racism. As Reischauer himself noted, he proposed this plan as a way to "win our ideological battles," a coded phrase that meant that the "yellow and brown" peoples needed to be swayed to follow the path of American-style liberal democracy and capitalism. In January 1945 some of the most forward-looking East Asian specialists in the United States advanced this line of thinking to another level of theorization around the concept of "modernization."

In their "guidance" to the OWI on what we might call "hot war modernization theory," a group identified as "Far Eastern Regional Specialists in N.Y. and Washington" strongly urged the OWI to desist from using the term "Westernization," which would associate the project of liberal democracy and industrial capitalism with American propaganda, and to advance what they believed was the more neutral and world-historical term "modernization." The experts argued that the theme of modernization was meant "to demonstrate that Far Eastern peoples like peoples everywhere can and must modernize their way of life. To modernize means to establish modern technological and scientific methods, and modern social and political institutions—in brief, science and democracy." This was not just a postwar plan, but a postcolonial plan for establishing U.S. hegemony in Asia. Therefore, modernization was to be accomplished not by forcing the peoples in the region to adopt such essentials as urban industrialization, communications, scientific agriculture ("i.e., an agrarian revolution"), and "democratic processes," but by persuading them to adopt these elements of the project on their own. "The present theme [of modernization]," they said, "is to show Asiatics what they can do for themselves, building partly on our experience but mainly on principles and methods which are a common inheritance of mankind, adaptable the world over." "Democratic processes" would include a commitment to harness industrialization to benefit individuals as well as the state and to prevent misuse for "selfish class aims or chauvinist political aims." "[Education] in the practices of democracy; universal literacy, free speech, a free press, free elections of a representative civilian government"—all these had to be established in order to propel the larger modernization project.[43]

The experts stressed that while the people of Asia would benefit from modernization, ultimately it was in the U.S. national interest to promote these processes. They foretold that the entire world was moving toward harnessing the physical forces of the globe to such an extent that all peoples had the potential to achieve "living standards never known before." But successful modernization for everyone was not a foregone conclusion, and if Asia was left behind, disaster and havoc for the United States might follow. "Asia should not be allowed to lag behind in this world process," they said, "for if Asia remains backward, or becomes relatively more backward, there will be grave dangers of imperialism, revolution, and world war. For example, the new nationalism which Japan has aroused in Asia must be given constructive outlets. Modernization in Asia is of vital interest to us because backwardness in Asiatic life will produce a constant menace to our way of life" (p. 2).

The logical inconsistency in the experts' proposal, however, was that while they urged Asians as self-determining subjects to make the choice of adopting liberal democracy and industrial capitalism, they sought to ensure that these backward people chose no alternative path into the future. To some extent, the United States would have to stand on the "sidelines" and allow the Asians themselves to "transform the life of Asia's millions." But since "we" occupied the position of "one of the major sources of modernization," we had a "heavy responsibility to see that the potentialities of modern life become fully known to peoples who are in some respects more backward than ourselves" (p. 2).

So, how did these experts plan to push the "backward" Asians forward in the modernization project while at the same time convincing them that doing so was not part of a plan to extend American power in the region? The last and "most important [point] in this whole paper" took on this question. The best method would be "to show that modernization is not an American monopoly but a world-wide growth in which all peoples can and should take part. The more international we can make it appear, the less likely is this theme of modernization to seem like American propaganda which is attempting to 'sell' to Asia a mechanical or materialistic or disruptive, peculiarly American change of life. Bring in developments in Sweden, or Canada, or especially in *Asiatic* countries" (p. 5; emphasis in original). Nowhere did the experts explicitly mention communism, and in one section they highlighted the benefits of "union organization and collective bargaining . . . as well as the rights and duties of the laboring man" (p. 3). However, they clearly advanced a noncommunist New Deal model of liberal capitalism in which workers would benefit from "mass production as the key to plenty" (p. 3) and propaganda should downplay Americanization while celebrating "Asiatic" models of and for modernization.

Thus, these experts' paper exhibited all the basic elements of what would later develop into the full-blown ideological project of modernization theory as it concerned East Asia. These included the ideas that (1) it is in the interests of the United States to promote liberal democracy and industrial capitalism throughout the world, since the failure to do so could lead to regional political instabilities; (2) modernization is not a mode of development unique to a particular part of the world, the West, but is a universal process in world history; and (3) although modernization is not Westernization, the United States is at the forefront of world history and is therefore duty bound to guide the rest of the lagging world toward modernization's telos. Furthermore, even as this paper and later Cold War modernization theory made the liberal gesture toward a common humanity by indicating that models for this process should be sought especially within the "Asiatic countries," it betrayed the extreme attentiveness of strategies for U.S. hegemony in the region to the management of race. Shift the terms of questioning about modernization, they said, so that Asians asked not " 'How has America modernized?,' but rather: 'How can Asia modernize?' Examples from many lands will get the point across better than examples from USA alone. Examples from modern Asia will be the most effective of all" (p. 5).

This hot war version of modernization theorizing did not specifically recommend Japan as the ideal nation to promote as the sign of successful "Asiatic" modernization, but the Cold War version did precisely that. Cold War modernization theory as applied to Japan emerged toward the end of the 1950s and reached the height of its popularity in the 1960s and early 1970s—in other words, precisely at the moment when the model minority discourse achieved its first explicit articulation.[44] In effect, Cold War modernization theory developed the less well articulated plans of the hot war, and completed the process of remaking Japan into the "global model minority." Japan, it came to be argued, had waited a long time to modernize. The roots of its ability to modernize, which primarily meant to industrialize and to become an economic superpower, had already existed in Japan centuries ago in the Tokugawa period. Among the most influential of such works was that of the sociologist Robert N. Bellah, who found in the religious beliefs and practices of seemingly all Japanese people in the Tokugawa period Japanese analogues to Max Weber's famous Protestant ethic.[45] In other words, it was as if the Japanese people, possessed of an ethic of hard work and frugality, had already desired to be the same as (white) Americans and Western Europeans even before the West's arrival. The related message to the rest of the non-Western (nonwhite) world, however, was that they had only themselves and their culture or lack of culture to blame for their backwardness or absence of development. They were deficient in the necessary cultural attributes, particularly the positive traditional values of the Japanese global model minority, and should aspire to be like them. In addition, it was often argued that the other nations of the non-Western world should be patient. It had taken a long time for Japan to modernize, and it would take a long time for other nations to develop as well.[46]

The locations of Japan in the world and of Japanese Americans in U.S. society were both homological and mutually reinforcing, with the direct influence of modernization theory on the production of the domestic model minority discourse especially salient. Petersen, for example, set up the terms of his problematic by asking why Japanese Americans, in contrast to "Negroes, Indians, Mexicans, Chinese and Filipinos," had been able to overcome "color prejudice." The Japanese immigrant group had been like every white ethnic immigrant group, each of which had within a generation or two taken "advantage of the public schools, the free labor market and America's political democracy; it climbed out of the slums, took on better-paying occupations and acquired social respect and dignity."[47] Why, he asked rhetorically, had the Japanese been the sole nonwhite minority group to successfully emulate the white minorities? For the answer, Petersen turned to the work of social scientists of Japan such as Bellah. The secret to Japanese American success, it seemed, was to be found in the quality of the culture that the Japanese immigrants had brought with them from Japan. As Petersen put it: "The issei who came to America were catapulted out of a homeland undergoing rapid change—Meiji Japan, which remains the one country of Asia to have achieved modernization. We can learn from such a work as Robert Bellah's 'Tokugawa Religion' that diligence in work, combined with simple frugality, had an almost religious imperative, similar to what has been called 'the Protestant ethic' in Western culture" (p. 41).

Moreover, like Bellah with his functionalist interpretation of the Japanese version of the Protestant ethic, Petersen praised Japanese American values not for their explicit surface details—it mattered little, for example, whether Japanese Americans were Christian or Buddhist (an echo of *Go for Broke*)—but for their utility in providing the motive force for Japanese American success. Again, to make this point,

Petersen used the negative example of "Negroes." The inability of the "Negroes" to overcome racism, he said, could be explained not by their distance from "American culture" but rather by their alienation from African culture. "Negroes," he maintained, are the "minority most thoroughly imbedded in American culture, with the least meaningful ties to an overseas fatherland." Therefore, the "Negro" has "no refuge when the United States rejects him. Placed at the bottom of this country's scale, he finds it difficult to salvage his ego by measuring his worth in another currency." In contrast, the Japanese "could climb over the highest barriers our racists were able to fashion in part because of their meaningful links with an alien culture" (p. 43). In other words, according to Petersen, the inability of African Americans to succeed in American society resulted directly from the inadequacy of their culture, whereas Japanese American success was due precisely to the fact that they were not alienated from their cultural legacy. This is a far cry from the earlier radical assimilationist model for Japanese American disappearance into white America. It marks the postwar and Cold War racialization of U.S. society, whereby Japanese Americans and some other Asian Americans became the almost, but not quite white model minority, whereas "Negroes" and other racial minorities were represented as incompetent citizens because of their allegedly dysfunctional culture.

Looking through an even longer historical lens stretching back to the mid-nineteenth century, we see that this shift represents a dramatic reversal in the way in which dominant discourses assessed the admissibility of Asians, in contrast to African Americans, on the basis of their respective cultures. In 1869 the economic reformer Henry George had argued that Chinese were hopelessly unassimilable because they had too much cultural baggage, whereas blacks could be assimilated because they had no culture to unlearn.[48] But nearly a century later it was being asserted that Japanese Americans and some other Asians could be assimilated to America precisely because they had rich, non-Western cultures that helped them flourish in modern capitalist, liberal democracies. "Negroes," on the other hand, were doomed to exclusion and failure because they were so alienated from what should be their own African culture. We may gain further insight into the polite racism of liberals when we recall the influential work of the Swedish scholar Gunnar Myrdal and his assistants, whose 1944 book, *American Dilemma: The Negro Problem and Modern Democracy,* had such an enormous impact on postwar liberal views of race. While criticizing biological theories of race and calling for the extension of democracy, equality and justice to African Americans, Myrdal also maintained that only assimilation to an unmarked white America could cure what he called the "pathological" culture of blacks.[49]

．　　　．　　　．

It has surely been of great comfort for many Americans—from FDR and Truman to Ronald Reagan and George H. W. Bush as well as his son, George W. Bush, to mention just a few named in this chapter and this book's introduction—to imagine and then remember that Nisei wartime heroism stemmed from this minority's irrepressible love of country. The Japanese Americans loved their country so much, so the story goes, that they were able to look beyond the discrimination they experienced and in time to overcome racism and realize the promised land that had already been foretold in the nation's origins. Nisei heroism in this warmed-over, often sentimentalized, and sometimes even hallucinatory explanation was a way to demonstrate a natural and unproblematic love of country.

Yet I have tried to show with some historical specificity that heroism was as much made as found by U.S. civil and military propaganda organs, as well as by the mainstream media during and after the war. While this process began prior to formation of the 442nd and even before the 100th had seen any combat in Europe, the production of these heroes accelerated during the last phase of the war and was completed during the Cold War, with both "hot war" and Cold War versions of modernization theory helping to ensure the production of public representations of Japanese Americans as war heroes. In short, it is clear that the making of Japanese American soldiers into national heroes owes as much and perhaps more to the politics of repositioning Japan and Japanese Americans as global and domestic model minorities as to their empirically verifiable military accomplishments.

In offering this perspective on Japanese American military heroism, I need to reiterate that I do not by any means intend to slight the accomplishments of the Japanese American soldiers. Instead, I have wanted to suggest that heroism in the public eye is always figured by power and interests. Ignoring the politics of representing Japanese American military heroism and its attendant narrative of national progress carries with it the risk not only of occluding ongoing racism but also of forgetting other histories, both domestic and global, that do not fit so neatly into American national myths. To critically examine the politics of representing Japanese American war heroism is thus not a debunking of the enormous sacrifices and accomplishments of the Japanese American soldiers, but rather a cautionary move against the drive to make the story of Japanese American war heroism appear as a success story for all of America and as the model for other historically marginalized groups to follow.

PART THREE · KOREANS AS JAPANESE

CHAPTER SIX · National Mobilization

> In fact the discourses of race and nation are never far
> apart, if only in the form of disavowal.
>
> ETIENNE BALIBAR, *"Racism and Nationalism"* (1988)

U.S. psychological warfare during the Second World War had as one of its key strategies the exploitation of class, racial, and regional divisions within the Japanese nation and larger colonial empire. While most Americans in the postwar United States have tended to believe that the Japanese are a homogeneous people, and wartime propaganda represented the Japanese as just like so many "photographic prints off the same negative,"[1] to use the filmmaker Frank Capra's famous phrase, U.S. intelligence agencies understood that the enemy's façade of unity veiled a nation and colonial empire fractured by deep cleavages. Even as U.S. propaganda tried to demonstrate to the world that America treated its minorities with fairness and equality, its intelligence agencies simultaneously studied and monitored the condition of racial discrimination in the enemy camp—not in hopes of improving the situation of Japan's colonial subjects and minorities, but with the unabashed aim of finding ways to worsen their circumstances. In its April 1942 propaganda plan for Japan, the Foreign Intelligence Service advised that minorities such as the "Christian minority and the eta" should be targeted for the purpose of furthering "national disunity." Even more explicitly, the May 1942 draft for general propaganda toward Japan (discussed more fully in chapter 2) specifically listed among its nine primary "propaganda objectives "to exploit the fear of minorities entertained by the leaders of Japan, inciting the leaders to persecute minorities in every case where the result will be impaired morale, reduced efficiency, or both." It further recommended persuading the "common Japanese people" that "Korea is still a potential menace to Japan."[2]

The concern to manage race and colonial divisions in the interests of promoting the enemy's disunity prompted U.S. and other Allied forces to interrogate captured Korean soldiers about their attitudes toward Japan and the war. Not surprisingly—given the harsh and discriminatory conditions prevailing in Korea as well as the obvious advantage for prisoners of war held by the Allies to distance themselves from the Japanese empire—most of these POWs expressed dislike of Japan. Some complained of discrimination, and those who had volunteered sometimes asserted that they had been in one way or another coerced or enticed to enlist for reasons other than loyalty.

Take the instance of Private First Class Yamamoto Takenaga (K. Che Nam Char). According to his interrogator's report, Yamamoto was relatively highly educated, as he had received fourteen years of education, including three years in a commercial college before enlistment. He volunteered for the Japanese army in late 1943 and was inducted into the Seventy-third Infantry Regiment in Nanam, Korea, in January of the following year. He was obviously one of the Korean "student soldiers" whose enlistment had been enabled by the Army Special Volunteers Extraordinary Induction Regulations of October 1943. Yamamoto completed basic training in a very short period of time and then underwent "special gas training." After serving in the region around Nanam, he shipped out to the Philippines in December 1944, where he "participated in operations against Filipino guerrillas." But in early February 1945 he deserted his unit and surrendered to a Filipino civilian, who escorted him to the headquarters of guerrilla forces just west of Acops.

According to the report, Private Yamamoto resented Japan and the Japanese. Affirming the finding of the historian Kang Duk-sang (Tŏk-sang) that the authorities applied tremendous pressure on Korean students to volunteer, Yamamoto claimed that he had tried to evade recruitment into the military and complied only when the authorities retaliated by imprisoning his parents. He and the report thus explained his desertion as the logical consequence of his having been "forced to volunteer." In addition, Yamamoto testified that "Koreans in the Army were not accepted as equals. They were often forced to do the hardest work." He also held the Japanese officers responsible for "non-promotion of Koreans and the ill-treatment they received."[3]

Similarly, another student soldier who had surrendered on 26 March 1945 in Burma informed his interrogator that many Koreans were then serving in his division, the Forty-ninth, and that "all Koreans shared his feelings toward the Japanese, and that they would attempt to escape and surrender." In fact, he reported that Koreans had held at least three meetings at which they discussed the "prospects of escape." The report noted that while the "more intelligent" Koreans were aware of the Geneva Convention and believed that they would be treated fairly upon surrendering, the "less intelligent" were more skeptical. The interrogator obviously regarded this thirty-year-old POW as among the "more intelligent" and noted that he had received eleven years of education in Korea and had subsequently studied law for four years at Nippon University in Tokyo. Interestingly, the Office of War Information (OWI) intended to use this "Outpost Report" from New Delhi to help formulate propaganda strategy directed specifically at Koreans in the Japanese military.[4]

However, other Korean POWs revealed far more ambiguous sentiments, sometimes uncertainty, and even in some cases strong support for Japan among Koreans inside and outside of the military. Superior Privates Kanekawa Tokimoto (K. Kim, Shiwani) and Kanaoka Juntaku (K. Kungan, Suntek) who most likely had been conscripted and whose duty was listed as horse transport, gave their interrogator a dismal picture of their division, the Twentieth, which at the time of their surrender in July 1945 was believed to have been reduced from its original strength of 25,000 to 800 men. Kanekawa and Kanaoka, who had been captured in Maprik West, New Guinea, offered that Allied surrender leaflets had a considerable impact on Koreans and that they increased Korean "objections to fighting the war for the Japanese." Furthermore, when asked if Allied airmen shot down over Korea could expect assistance from Koreans, they both replied affirmatively. However, they also indicated that "there were many pro-Japanese Koreans," and thus downed airmen would be at some risk. Finally, while they had heard about the Korean Independence Movement, they knew little "about this beyond the fact that it existed and that it occasionally organized attacks on the Japanese."[5]

Superior Private Kaneshiro Masao, who had volunteered in December 1939, surrendered in the Ulufu area of New Guinea on 13 July 1945. He had had the minimum six years of education necessary to qualify as an army special volunteer. Like Kanekawa and Kanaoka, Kaneshiro gave a picture of an almost completely exhausted and demoralized Twentieth Division. Not only had Kaneshiro deserted while recovering from beriberi and malaria, he also claimed that he had volunteered only to land "a secure job." Overall, he testified that all the soldiers in his regiment, not just Koreans, had such low morale that "more than half the men are talking of surrendering." In June a platoon leader and three of his men had in fact deserted. Kaneshiro claimed to be a Christian who wished to see Korea become independent, and he praised Kim Il-sŏng as a kind of Robin Hood who rode on horseback while stealing from rich Japanese, first in northern Korea and then in Manchuria, in order to support his movement and to give to the poor. Yet Kaneshiro also stated that not all Koreans in the military harbored antipathy toward the Japanese. In particular, he mentioned a Korean who had gone to the Japanese Officer Training School in Tokyo and risen to the rank of at least colonel.[6]

An unnamed private first class, who had volunteered in June 1941 and served in the Seventy-eighth Infantry Regiment before Australian troops captured him in New Guinea on 5 October 1943, gave a considerably different view of his experience within the Japanese military. This former farmer who had attended elementary school in Korea for six years explained that the forty Koreans in his battalion had been paid and treated in the same manner as Japanese. While new recruits may have been "slapped and kicked by senior soldiers and NCO's for slightest misdemeanor," this had not been a result of discrimination, for "both Jap and Korean troops were accorded similar treatment." This POW offered that Koreans actually "made better soldiers, as they were quicker witted." Moreover, rather than suggest any kind of discrimination, he testified that many Koreans made the rank of superior private after only one year of service. Though he thought that conscription would not be popular in Korea and that Koreans in general "had no real interest in the war and hoped it would soon be over," he also claimed that "people were fairly happy and contented as the younger generation had gradually assimilated Jap ideas through teaching and propaganda. Taxes were light and the people were not interfered with to any great extent."[7]

Finally, Sergeant Morogata Yoshio (K. Ri Daiko), section leader in the Seventy-seventh Infantry Regiment heavy machine gun company, responded to his American interrogator as an extraordinarily loyal Japanese soldier who believed in the Japanese military's official proclamations of equality. Sergeant Morogata was a man of considerable education, with six years of elementary school and five years of middle school, which meant that he had just one year less schooling than a high school graduate would have today. As a civilian he had worked as a clerk in the Chosen (Chosŏn) Life Insurance Company. Thus, when he volunteered in February 1940 in Keijō (Seoul), he was undoubtedly one of the more educated Koreans to volunteer before the start of the "student soldier" system in late 1943. After undergoing military training and assignment to the Seventy-sixth Infantry Regiment in Nanam, he left for Tokyo where he underwent training to become a noncommissioned officer. He completed NCO training in late November 1942 and then returned to Nanam; and after several transfers and almost perishing after an Allied submarine sank his transport ship, he began working on road construction on Mindanao. About six weeks after relocating to Ipil, Leyte, he left his unit in the mountains and surrendered.

Despite good reasons as a POW to disclaim enthusiasm for the Japanese army,

Sergeant Morogata told his interrogator that he had been "keenly interested in becoming a soldier," and that "knowing that conscription of Koreans was inevitable, he volunteered for service when 20 years of age." He claimed that far from observing "any discrimination against Koreans by officers or enlisted men . . . officers treated him with exceptional care and this often embarrassed him in front of his men. His duties were much easier than those of other noncommissioned officers." As further evidence that he had been enthusiastic about the Japanese military, Sergeant Morogata explained that while at Korean Army Headquarters in Keijō he had been engaged in morale improvement (*seishin kōyō kakari*). Along with as many as 150 Japanese officers and Japanese and Korean noncommissioned officers, he had indoctrinated "Korean youth with Japanese military ideals" in order to persuade them to volunteer for the army. For this task, "officers and noncommissioned officers were instructed to promote discussions and give short lectures on the brighter side of Army life and the intimate relationship existing between JAPAN and KOREA."[8]

I begin with this summary of several POW interrogation records to make the point that as was true of the responses of Japanese Americans to the call to bear arms, Korean attitudes toward Japanese military service cannot be reduced to any simple categorization, such as the conventional nationalist one that seeks to place every individual into the neat rubrics of collaborator or resister, with all but a few Koreans emerging as essentially resistant to Japanese rule. This would correspond to the typical attempt to force the incredible heterogeneity of Japanese American positions toward soldiering into the binary of loyal or disloyal and then to argue that almost all Japanese Americans were essentially loyal. In addition, we again bump up against the aporia resulting from the desire to represent experience, even as we acknowledge that our subjects can speak only through the web of multiple mediations that leave us just fragments with which to produce a coherent and ethically responsible narrative about their pasts.

The POW records suggest the difficulties of this task, for prisoners gave these testimonies while under extraordinary duress, and we cannot know all the conditions under which they were spoken. Did some Koreans emphasize their hatred and that of the Korean people for the Japanese military and Japanese rule because they had always held such feelings, or did factors such as the demoralization and imminent defeat of the Japanese forces or POWs' desires to present themselves to their captors as enemies of the Japanese influence their self-presentations? If so, why did other Korean POWs refuse such a logic of survival? Because they were truly loyal to Japan? Or had they received harsh treatment from the Australians or Americans that compelled them to defy their captors' expectations? Furthermore, who were the interrogators who wrote down the POWs' stories? Most likely, most of them were Japanese Americans. Did this make a difference? Did the structural similarity in the circumstances of Korean Japanese soldiers and their Japanese American interrogators make the latter more receptive to narratives of loyalty? Did a sense of shared race as Asians make the POWs more forthcoming, or was this tempered by the assumption that the Japanese American interrogators were actually Japanese? The problems become even more complex when one listens to former Korean soldiers speak today about their experiences as Japanese soldiers or reads their memoirs. How have the postliberation politics of memory helped shape these narratives? Is it ethically defensible to listen to individuals speak with apparent honesty and sincerity about their pasts while constantly doubting, or conversely naively accepting, everything they say?

These are all difficult questions for which no simple answers exist. Nevertheless, my strategy is not to abandon the recuperative dimension of this book but to accept that I can only reflect the partial truths that I see glimmer through the questions that I ask of the record and the already-mediated archive. This chapter analyzes a diverse record of Korean responses to the opportunity and then demand for young men to become Japanese soldiers, while continuing the work of chapter 1—namely, by situating this record within the context of the expansion of the late colonial state and closely associated nongovernmental organizations and individuals as they increasingly incorporated the Korean people into the regime of governmentality. Such a regime operated not by physical and brutal force alone, but also through an explosion of bureaucrats, statistics, background checks, and technologies that sought to constitute individuals into self-reflexive subjects who would ideally regulate themselves and make normative choices.

In this historical moment individuals within the aggregated colonial population made choices, but under conditions that were not of their own choosing. In this chapter I chart the variety of choices that they made under such conditions, including those framed by communist and Korean ethnic nationalist ideologies whose rationality paralleled that of the colonial state. Throughout, I stress the imperfect interpellation of the Korean populace as Japanese imperial subjects. They made a myriad of choices, including those based on logics that skirted around or deflected the rationality of the state, and that the state therefore dismissed as not within reason.

This is not to say that the colonial state and its authorities created all the conditions of colonial society as they wished and that the Korean populace could only respond. As I have already suggested in chapter 1, the colonial authorities themselves were forced to negotiate in some ways with actual and expected responses from the colonial subjects. Moreover, no absolute divide separated the colonizers and colonized, although there was clarity about the vector of power and certainty about who possessed the legitimate right to imprison, punish, and kill. In particular, many within the Korean elite participated in the production and fashioning of colonial policy. They contributed to the decision to mobilize Koreans into the military, and as we will see here and there throughout this chapter, they also helped fashion technologies to implement this mobilization.

MOTIVATIONS

Historians have made the plausible argument that the large number of Koreans who volunteered for the Japanese army did so not as a show of patriotism to Japan, but either because authorities pressured them to do so or because the army offered a means of livelihood. Private Kaneshiro's testimony, above, that he had joined in order to acquire "a secure job" certainly corroborates this latter motivation. To arrive at these conclusions, historians have utilized official data from the colonial period such as that captured in table 1.

Table 1 shows that the Army Special Volunteer System began in 1938 on a very modest scale, in terms both of numbers of Koreans who volunteered and of selectees who entered the Government-General of Korea's (GGK's) Training Center for Army Volunteers (Chōsen Sōtokufu Rikugunhei Shigansha Kunrensho). However, in subsequent years Koreans enlisted in extraordinarily large numbers, which peaked in 1943 when 303,294 volunteered for a quota of only 6,300 slots. This represented a more than 10,000 percent increase compared to 1938. Rather than explain these figures as indications of the Korean people's rising patriotism and enthusiasm for the opportunity to serve in the military—as the military and civil authorities and the empire's media emphasized—serious historians have pointed to contradictory evidence such as seen in table 2.[9]

The historian Ch'oe Yu-ri notes that only 35 percent of volunteers are listed as having volunteered "of their own volition" (J. *jihatsuteki ni*, K. *chabalchŏk ŭro*) and that the overwhelming majority of the remainder had been induced in some way by government offices. She stresses the "coercive character" (*kangjesŏng*) of volunteer mobilization, especially the use of local Patriotic Associations (*aegukpan*) in recruitment efforts. Furthermore, Ch'oe uses the psychological survey of volunteers summarized in table 3 to buttress her argument.

Referring to the figures in table 3, Ch'oe points out that only 27.9 percent of volunteers from throughout Korea's provinces indicated that they had volunteered out

TABLE 1   Korean Special Army Volunteers and Entrants into Training Centers

	Category			
Year	Number of Volunteers	Increase (%) (base year, 1938)	Number of Entrants into Training Center	Increase (%) (base year, 1938)
1938	2,946	100	406	100
1939	12,348	419	613	150
1940	84,443	2,866	3,060	753
1941	144,743	4,913	3,208	790
1942	·254,273	8,631	4,077	1,004
1943	303,294	10,295	6,300	1,551

SOURCE: Ch'oe Yu-ri, *Ilche malgi singminji chibae chŏngch'aek yŏn'gu* (Seoul: Kukhak Charyŏwŏn, 1997), 188. Ch'oe's original source is Naimushō (Ministry of the Interior), Chōsen oyobi Taiwan no genkyō, July 1944, as collected in Taiheiyō senka no Chōsen oyobi Taiwan, ed. Kondō Ken'ichi (Chigasaki-shi: Chōsen Shiryō Kenkyūkai, 1961), 33.

NOTE: In chapter 1 I used slightly different figures for the total number of volunteers who were accepted and then served, from Yoshida Toshiguma, "Chōsenjin, shiganhei/chōhei no kōgai," 21, ca. 1945, box 30, Manshū Chōsen 2, Chōsengun Kankei Shiryō, Military Archival Library, the National Institute for Defense Studies, Japan Ministry of Defense, Tokyo. However, the difference is very small and insignificant.

of "earnest patriotism" and that even the concrete content of this "patriotism" is unclear. She reaches the conclusion that whether for honor, for a utilitarian purpose, or for any other reason, the overwhelming majority in this survey volunteered as a means of securing a livelihood. She indicates that the data in this table corroborate Miyata Setsuko's observation that the poorer the province the greater the tendency to volunteer, and she then reproduces table 4 to show the actual economic circumstances of the individual volunteers.

As Ch'oe and Miyata have argued, the data collected by the Korean Government-General in preparation for the seventy-ninth Diet certainly show that young Korean men volunteered with far less patriotism than official propaganda claimed. It is undeniable that they were motivated by a variety of reasons that in most cases had little to do with loyalty to Japan. Moreover, both historians make the valuable observation that economic incentives probably played a strong part in the decision of some Korean men to volunteer.[10] Yet the data also raise a number of questions that considerably muddle the strong tone of certainty in their conclusions. First, despite the lack of detail concerning the content of "sincere patriotism" in table 3, the

TABLE 2 Survey by Age of Motives of Army Special
Volunteer Soldiers for Volunteering (1941)

Motive	Age									TOTAL
	17	18	19	20	21	22	23	24	25	
Persons volunteering of their own volition	5,673	6,943	7,771	7,591	6,486	5,357	3,965	2,694	3,704	50,184 (35%)
Persons volunteering in response to inducement by government offices	9,355	11,089	12,117	11,844	10,704	8,722	6,682	4,347	4,812	79,672 (55%)
Other	1,915	2,012	2,318	2,125	1,742	1,610	1,132	1,146	1,190	15,190 (10%)
TOTAL	16,943	20,044	22,206	21,560	18,932	15,689	11,779	8,187	9,706	145,046

SOURCE: Ch'oe Yu-ri, *Ilche malgi singminji chibae chŏngch'aek yŏn'gu* (Seoul: Kukhak Charyŏwŏn, 1997), 189. Ch'oe's original source is Chōsen Sōtokufu, "Dai 79 kai teikoku gikai setsumei shiryō," December 1941, ORKB #1236.

NOTE: The table in Ch'oe shows 1,694 24-year-olds "volunteering of their own volition," but this is clearly an error, which leads to the total for 24-year-olds and total of "persons volunteering of their own volition" being short by 1,000.

TABLE 3　Survey of Mental State of the Volunteers for the Army Special Volunteers (1941)

Region	Persons [Volunteering] from Earnest Patriotism	Mental State		Persons Selecting [the Army] as a Profession	Other	TOTAL
		Persons led to Volunteer Merely for Honor	Persons Volunteering from Individual Personal Utilitarian Motives			
Kyŏnggi	2,657	1,957	2,102	1,482	3,032	11,230
N. Ch'ungch'ŏng	2,720	1,594	997	960	1,816	8,087
S. Ch'ungch'ŏng	4,747	3,542	1,709	1,172	1,853	13,023
N. Chŏlla	921	1,504	1,284	583	477	4,769
S. Chŏlla	5,675	5,468	4,360	2,655	4,161	22,319
N. Kyŏngsang	3,465	5,225	3,275	2,263	9,299	23,527
S. Kyŏngsang	2,930	1,896	967	619	2,193	8,605
Hwanghae	1,422	1,466	634	542	647	4,711
S. P'yŏngan	2,603	1,887	1,324	1,152	2,664	9,630
N. P'yŏngan	2,256	1,351	903	587	1,457	6,554
Kangwŏn	4,017	2,877	1,551	1,065	2,221	11,731
S. Hamgyŏng	4,342	2,853	1,817	1,358	3,115	13,485
N. Hamgyŏng	2,698	1,834	872	643	1,328	7,375
TOTAL	40,453	33,454	21,795	15,081	34,263	145,046
	(27.9%)	(23.0%)	(15.0%)	(11.4%)	(23.6%)	

SOURCE: Ch'oe, *Ilche malgi singminji*, 190. Ch'oe's original source is Chōsen Sōtokufu, "Dai 79 kai teikoku gikai setsumei shiryō," December 1941.

NOTE: Ch'oe or the original source appears to have made some errors of addition or transcription and I have corrected them as follows. Ch'oe gives the total number of "Other" as 24,263 (16.7%), but the numbers given for the individual provinces in this category add up to 34,263 (23.6%). Only with the latter correction can we arrive at the survey total of 145,046 (100%). Also, the S. Hamgyŏng total is given as 13,483, but it should be 13,485.

TABLE 4   Survey of Assets of Volunteers for the Army Special Volunteers (1941)

Assets

Region	Less Than 100 Yen	More Than 100 Yen	More Than 1,000 Yen	More Than 5,000 Yen	More Than 10,000 Yen	More Than 100,000 Yen	More Than 500,000 Yen	TOTAL
Kyŏnggi	262	2,170	1,574	375	148	7	–	4,536
N. Ch'ungch'ŏng	1,622	2,852	1,626	390	107	1	–	6,598
S. Ch'ungch'ŏng	465	4,726	3,001	768	197	12	–	9,169
N. Chŏlla	161	1,414	752	182	52	–	–	2,561
S. Chŏlla	815	3,760	5,357	1508	326	16	–	11,782
N. Kyŏngsang	659	4,693	4,975	3798	884	197	7	15,213
S. Kyŏngsang	594	1,571	5,228	947	261	4	–	8,605
Hwanghae	89	892	1,675	452	178	5	–	3,291
S. P'yŏngan	1,277	2,459	1,719	522	111	6	1	6,095
N. P'yŏngan	184	1,412	1,460	681	385	5	–	4,127
Kangwŏn	968	4,088	4,801	1,414	440	19	1	11,731
S. Hamgyŏng	292	2,650	2,419	913	361	5	–	6,640
N. Hamgyŏng	257	1343	2,031	873	180	2	–	4,686
TOTAL	7,645	34,030	36,618	12,823	3,630	279	9	95,034
	(8%)	(35.8%)	(38.5%)	(13.5%)	(4%)			

SOURCE: *Ch'oe, Ilche malgi singminji*, 192. Ch'oe's original source is Chōsen Sōtokufu, "Dai 79 kai teikoku gikai setsumei shiryō," December 1941.
NOTE: Ch'oe's table has small but insignificant errors; I have corrected her 198 for S. Ch'ungch'ŏng, "more than 10,000 yen," and 7,654 for the total of "less than 100 yen."

figure of 27.9 percent signifies more than a small minority; indeed, it represents the largest single category of motivation. Second, despite the strong evidence that local authorities pressured young men to volunteer, the 35 percent figure in the category of volunteering "of their own volition" is likewise not insignificant.

Third, despite the plausibility of the argument that many volunteered as a means of escaping poverty, according to table 4 more than half of the volunteers (56 percent) had assets of more than 1,000 yen and nearly 18 percent had assets in excess of 5,000 yen, suggesting a standard of living far above that of the very poor. The table even notes more than a few with assets greater than 100,000 and 500,000 yen. To put these large sums in their historical context, we can note that according to Government-General data, in 1941 a skilled Korean worker such as a house builder (*kasaku*) might average a daily wage of only 3.44 yen. The daily pay for an unskilled manual laborer (*hira ninsoku*) was far less, averaging 1.61 yen, and in poorer regions the wage could be half that amount.[11] Thus those with assets exceeding 1,000 yen did not come from the poorest strata and probably did not need to join in order to secure a military salary, which—as late as 1944—ranged from 6 to 9 yen per month for privates second class. Trainees in the Army Special Volunteer Training Center, an institution that will be discussed below, received only room and board in 1938 and were required to pay for many incidental expenses associated with their education and daily living (for pencils, soap, stamps, etc.); beginning in 1939, they received an educational allowance of 3 yen per month.[12]

Thus, although Ch'oe's and Miyata's data and conclusions offer important insights about some volunteers, in their rush to debunk the colonial authorities' inflated claims of Korean patriotic fervor, they oversimplify the subjectivities of the colonized. At the least, we need to first recognize that however difficult it may be to fathom Koreans' volunteering out of patriotism to Japan, the tables confirm that a significant number of them at least acted as if this was the reason they chose to serve. We might say that if the colonial authorities during wartime had to act as if the Japanese colonial empire denounced discrimination and practiced equality—in some cases even convincing themselves that they were not racist—some of the colonized learned that they should act as if they truly believed these claims and in some cases convinced themselves of the truthfulness of this official stance.

In retrospect, it is fairly easy and for many preferable to express disbelief at the possibility of Korean patriotism toward Japan, but the fragmentary evidence out of which we must construct an understanding of the past suggests that from the perspective of the late 1930s and early 1940s, with Korean independence by no means assured, for some Koreans believing in or at least acting as if they believed in the promises offered by the colonial authorities presented the most reasonable way to live. The idea that they might respond with patriotism to a regime that continued to discriminate against them despite official disavowals of racism is only as absurd or reasonable as the notion that patriotic Japanese Americans volunteered out of internment camps to defend the freedom they did not have. But to acknowledge that a sector of the Korean population volunteered out of a sense of patriotism to Japan, however vague, is not tantamount to affirming Japanese colonialism as a positive force for the Korean people. Instead, it is to confirm that despite ongoing discrimination and the reality of continuing colonial violence, for some the new moment of inclusionary and polite racism presented unprecedented opportunities and the possibility of happiness. One of the tasks of those who wish to understand the power of nationalism should be to further our understanding of why individuals and groups in positions of enormous disprivilege often appear to choose loyalty rather than resistance to the nation.

Moreover, we must recognize that the tables themselves do not just reflect the interiority of colonized men, their "state of mind," but were part of the arsenal of technologies employed by the colonial authorities to manage the population. They simplified infinitely varied subjectivities into categories useful for administration and mobilization; thus, we would be guilty of reproducing the very logic of the colonial state if we were simply to accept the tables as direct reflections of social reality and volunteers' consciousness. Nevertheless, it is possible to read the data against the grain of the authorities' intentions. In particular, the open-ended categories of "individual, personal utilitarian motives" and "other" motives, together making up more than 38 percent of volunteers' responses, offer intriguing room for conjecturing on the attitude of Korean males toward Japan and the Japanese military. And that the authorities failed to fit almost one-quarter (23.6 percent) of the volunteers' "mental states" into any useful category suggests a range of responses that lay outside the parameters of state utility.

The data provided in anticipation of the seventy-ninth session of the Imperial Diet thus urge us to exercise caution rather than claim certainty about the subjectivities of colonial men. We should recognize that more than a few, whatever their class background (and exemplified by the POW Sergeant Morogata Yoshio), may have been inspired to join out of some kind of patriotism to Japan. In fact, it is quite easy to imagine that relative prosperity (but not exorbitant wealth) as much as poverty might have motivated some, since those who benefited materially from colonialism and the possibility of incorporation into the expanded concept of "Japan" had the most to gain from acting as if they were loyal to the Japanese nation. Yet it is even more likely that individuals responded to the call for volunteers out of a mix of circumstances and contingencies that do not fit neatly into any one category. A hesitant patriotism, enormous pressure from Japanese and Korean authorities, accidents, uncertainties, and so on—these make up some of the messy factors that propelled many young men toward the normative choice of enlisting. Take the case of Kim Sŏng-su (not to be confused with the well-known wealthy businessman and educator of the same name), the veteran of the Japanese Imperial Army who has on numerous occasions sued the Japanese government for compensation for his service and injuries suffered during the war.

When I met Kim Sŏng-su in September 2000, he did not have much interest in discussing the details of his wartime experience. Instead, he took me on a tour of Pusan and talked most of all about the present and events dating back to his trip to Japan in 1978, when he had walked alone into the Ministry of Welfare and asked to see official records of Korean soldiers and civilian workers for the Japanese military. After no more than thirty or forty minutes, he and a staff person located pertinent records for the 144th Infantry, the unit to which he had been transferred after his injuries. Despite the casual way in which he told his story, this finding was a miraculous feat, given the Japanese government's grossly incomplete records of Koreans who served as Japanese servicemen and civilian military employees, as well as its usual unwillingness to cooperate with individual and group efforts to investigate the mobilization of Koreans into the war effort. On the basis of his discovery, Kim Sŏng-su secured documentation verifying that he had served and then been injured as a Japanese soldier under the name of Ōdate Toshio. It subsequently became the necessary piece of evidence that enabled him to make legal claims against the Japanese government for compensation.[13]

Kim Sŏng-su launched this campaign with the help of supporters in Japan and Korea—first together with some others in a class action suit in 1990 and then as an individual in 1992—because he and other Korean veterans and civilian workers had received no compensation from the Japanese government after liberation, except for the shamelessly small amount of 300,000 wŏn awarded to a very limited number of families of the war dead under the provisions of the 1965 Treaty on Basic Relations between Japan and the Republic of Korea.[14] Kim Sŏng-su's commonsensical argument, like those of some other Koreans with similar wartime experiences, is that he fought and received injuries as a Japanese soldier. Therefore, he should receive the same benefits as the other Japanese soldiers. Korea's liberation should not absolve the Japanese government of its responsibilities to its former national subjects. During our time together he emphasized that he harbored no animosity toward the Japanese people; and like several other Korean veterans I interviewed, he downplayed the discrimination within the Japanese military. He wanted attention directed toward the postwar treatment of former Japanese nationals from the colonies such as himself, who had been treated and mobilized as Japanese under such slogans as "the equality of all under the emperor's benevolent gaze" (*isshi dōjin*) and the "unity of metropolitan Japan and Korea" (*Naisen ittai*), but whom the Japanese government unilaterally excluded from benefits after the war's conclusion because they were no longer Japanese.

When I asked Kim Sŏng-su several times about his experiences in the Japanese military, he repeatedly directed me to his book, a volume that I had already read. Like any other document the book is not politically unbiased. Written with Kim Sŏng-su as the first-person narrator, it is based on a manuscript of roughly one hundred pages originally penned by Kim Sŏng-su's friend Kim Kyu-ch'ŏl, primarily for use in Sŏng-su's lawsuit against the Japanese government. Fujita Hiroo then added to and edited the manuscript following numerous interviews with Kim Sŏng-su.[15] Yet the book is not fashioned out of any established ideological narrative on colonialism, the war, or the postwar years. It is a remarkable text that, through the lens of one man's life, presents a frank look at life under Japanese colonialism and in postliberation Korea. Rather than construct a simple narrative of national victimhood or heroism, the author and his collaborators present a candid account that even sometimes includes unflattering information about Kim Sŏng-su's life and family, while at other times offering modest praise for several individual Japanese.

According to the book, Kim Sŏng-su was born on 12 December 1924 into a relatively well-to-do family in a village of about a thousand households within the township of Chwabyŏngyŏng in eastern Ulsan county, S. Kyŏngsang Province. While his father had done quite well financially by operating a rice mill, other investments failed around the time of Sŏng-su's birth. This setback, coupled with the difficulties he faced when his new son's mother died of complications related to childbirth, forced the father to give up his business. Nevertheless, the family as a whole, with children of different ages already employed, was not impoverished. Thus Sŏng-su was able attend elementary school, partly in his natal village and partly in Pusan, where he lived at times with his elder brother, a teacher at an elementary school in the central part of the city. Moreover, while Korean boys rarely advanced to middle school, Kim Sŏng-su did well enough on his entrance exam to be admitted to Tongnae Upper Ordinary School (J. Tōrai Kōtō Futsū Gakkō, K. Tongnae Kongnip Pot'ong Hakkyo) in Pusan. He attributes a large part of his success on the exam to the efforts of a committed Japanese teacher who tutored Korean students in his own home (pp. 14–26). Under the educational system then in place in colonial Korea, upper ordinary school (renamed middle school in 1938) consisted of five years of education beyond six years of elementary school.

Kim Sŏng-su's memoir suggests something of the complex character of identity formation for the relatively educated under Japanese colonialism that was in part responsible for his volunteering for the army. He recalls the absolute reality of discrimination and the existence of a few anti-Japanese leftists and ethnic nationalists at his school. For example, he recounts a major protest against discriminatory judging at one intermural competition between Koreans and Japanese, as well as the brazen act of a Korean student who defecated in front of the small school shrine housing the emperor's portrait. However, he himself does not appear to have resisted or supported the colonial regime in any remarkable way. Instead, he recalls his resignation to life under Japanese rule, observing that despite some vague sense of opposition to the imperial regime (*tennōsei*), he also felt that the emperor was "an absolute being, something like a god" (*zettaiteki na sonzai de, kami ni chikai yō na ki ga shita,* p. 31).

The beginning of all-out war with China in July 1937, coming only a few months after Kim Sŏng-su's entry into middle school, unleashed the well-known wave of policies intended to incorporate Koreans into the war effort. Therefore, the years of Kim Sŏng-su's middle school education coincided exactly with implementation of the most extreme measures to incorporate Korea into a larger concept of Japan, including the obliteration of local customs and traditions. In 1939 his family adopted the Japanized surname of Ōdate, and he became Ōdate Toshio. He remembers feeling as though he was forced to wear "someone else's ill-fitting clothes." In an example of what Althusser has famously described as interpellation, he confesses that "each time I heard the name, it felt like I was becoming the disembodied, mysterious person, the Japanese 'Ōdate Toshio,' and not Kim Sŏng-su. That fictional name of a Japanese person began to menace the actually existing me" (p. 34).

Education included drills by a military officer attached to the school and daily repetition of the infamous "Oath of Subjects of the Imperial Nation" (*shinmin kōkoku no seishi*), with which reciters vowed their loyalty, mutual love and cooperation, and perseverance and self-cultivation for the imperial cause. From 1938 on, the state limited the language of education to Japanese, although Kim Sŏng-su notes with some irony that even as Korean-language instruction ceased, students continued to learn English, the language of the enemy. Thus by the time he volunteered to enlist in the army in his fifth and final year of middle school, he had been subjected to intense schooling and indoctrination as a Japanese national. While Kim Sŏng-su was aware of resistance to colonial rule—both organized and spontaneous, as in the case of the student who left some half-digested bean sprouts in front of the emperor's portrait—he admits to having had only a vague desire to live "an unremarkable life of an ordinary person" (p. 42).

Contradicting the apparent clarity of tables such as those reproduced earlier, in his book Kim Sŏng-su considers with self-doubt, even incredulity, and most of all anguish the decision he made just before his eighteenth birthday—a decision that would lead him to suffer catastrophic battlefield injuries, including a severed right arm and debilitating damage to his left leg and spine. These would continue to profoundly affect him for the rest of his life. He recalls that one day in the fall of 1941, his homeroom teacher called him and about thirty or forty other students together and lectured them about volunteering for the army. The students who had been subjected to this call for volunteers represented the superior among his classmates in terms of academic grades, physique, and family background, and he wondered why he had been included in this group since he was physically small and not a strong student. When he asked his teacher why he had been called in, he was told that with his cheerful personality and sufficient physique he would make an ideal soldier. In fact, he could become an officer. Then, as he recalls, he first hesitated but then blurted out, "Yes, I will go."

Kim Sŏng-su confesses that he is not sure exactly what motivated him to volunteer in such an unplanned and thoughtless way and that he did not realize the weightiness of those few words. He knows that he did not have any strong desire to cooperate in the "holy war" or to impress his teacher, but he sensed that the draft would soon be coming and that he would be taken anyway. But most importantly, he felt that his decision might contribute to the release of one of his brothers, Yang-su, who had been arrested as an anti-Japanese activist and who was being held by the police in Seoul. For this reason he names the training center that he entered before enrolling the "Forced Volunteers Training Center" (pp. 28–47, 54). However difficult it is to sort through the different elements in his "state of mind," as the authorities would have it, Sŏng-su—a product of wartime education, personal circumstances, and happenstance—thus became one of the 254,273 men, each undoubtedly with a unique story, who volunteered for the army in 1942. After his decision to enlist, Sŏng-su had regrets and even considered absconding, but eventually he became one of the 4,077 Korean men selected that year from among the volunteers to begin training. He would be unfortunate enough to be the only one from his class to enter the army that year.

VOLUNTEERING AND TRAINING AS IMPERIAL SUBJECTS

Like the Japanese Americans who were guided toward the ostensibly free choice of volunteering, but who were then subjected to rigorous background checks to assess their loyalty, once Korean men made their desire to enlist known, the colonial authorities and the army deployed an extensive network of offices and agents to gauge individual qualifications, reliability, and especially loyalty to Japan. These civil and military authorities in general did not wish to coerce the unwilling or unfit to join the army. In the first few years they had very low quotas to fill, and in the later years of the program they had an extraordinarily large number of volunteers. They also feared the presence of anti-Japanese activists within the military ranks. Thus they carefully excluded dangerous persons while selecting those who were, or who could be trained to be, effective and trustworthy. They therefore set out procedures both for making these determinations and then for training those selected in such a way as to have them actively discipline themselves in service to the nation.

In its November 1937 outline of procedures for carrying out the Korean volunteer soldier system, the Government-General indicated the qualifications for volunteers. They should be "sound in thought, of upstanding moral character, of excellent temperament; and they must have complete consciousness of themselves as subjects of the imperial nation." They should not be guilty of past errors, and those who have been involved in "ethnic nationalism or communist movements should not be selected." It added a warning against those with a record of any family members who had participated in "isms and movements." Confirming Kim Sŏng-su's sense that the authorities wanted not the poor and uneducated but the physically sound, educated, and financially stable, the outline of procedures further added such qualifications as "physically strong and healthy"; a minimum of six years of elementary school education, preferably with experience in a "disciplinary organization such as a Youth Training Center or a Youth School"; and "competence in the national [Japanese] language." Moreover, it instructed that volunteers be from "families with an above average livelihood and of good character" and warned against recruiting men whose absence would bring undue hardship to their families.[16]

Reader for Army Special Volunteers, a 1939 publication intended to inform official personnel and potential volunteers about the procedures for processing and training Korean army volunteers, provides considerable detail on the ways in which local authorities, the Government-General, the Korean Army, and the police cooperated to select and train Korean volunteer soldiers. Its author, Oka Hisao, who meticulously incorporated descriptions of the numerous legal measures taken to implement the volunteer system while offering clear and practical guidelines for carrying it out, had been an official employed in the Government-General's Bureau of Education at the time when the volunteer system was established.[17] As Oka explained, individuals wishing to volunteer were to submit a completed volunteer application form (*fukueki negai*), along with an abbreviated transcript of their household registries, to the police chief of the area in which their families were registered. The application form asked for such information as birth date, place of household registry, current place of residence, occupation, special abilities (*tokugyō*) or skills, and the units into which they preferred to be enrolled.[18]

The police chief appended three documents to the application before sending it forward to the provincial governor: the applicant's personal history and qualifications, a registration form for men of conscript age, and a table appended to the latter. The form covering the applicant's personal history and qualifications asked for some of the same information already in the application, but also for further details concerning the individual's background and life circumstances, such as "character and conduct" of the individual, reputation of the applicant's native place, education in preparation for enlistment, summary of courses in youth schools or their equivalent, family financial circumstances, description of family, and impact of enlistment on the family. Oka emphasized that significant details should be provided concerning the applicant's family's financial circumstances and its composition. The registration form and table sought further detail, including information that would normally have been asked of Japanese men of conscript age in the metropole (hence use of the term "youth of conscript age" [*sōtei*] even though Koreans were not yet subject to the draft), such as the applicant's family circumstances, education, occupation, and physical characteristics. Specifics concerning the applicant's physical condition were to be filled in after he had taken the provincial physical examination required of applicants (pp. 34–37).

The provincial governor examined the documents received from the local police chiefs and compiled a comprehensive registry of applicants, which was given to the commander of the Korean Army; the commander would make the final determinations of which applicants would be successful. To do so, he convened a selection committee of officers stationed in Korea. They assessed the documents forwarded to them and, after other necessary examinations, selected candidates qualified for enrollment. Oka emphasized that in judging the applicants' personal background and qualifications (*minoue chōsa*), taking into account a written examination on academic subjects and an oral examination, nothing was more important than "consciousness as a national subject." He also advised potential volunteers that for the oral portion of the examination, which entailed assessing the entire person, they should be prepared to discuss their motivation for volunteering and the "national essence" (*kokutai*, pp. 38–39). And as knowledgeable "imperial subjects" they should know the dates of national holidays such as National Foundation Day and Meiji Day (Emperor Meiji's Birthday) (p. 104).

However, War Department Ordinance No. 11, which set forth in detail the regulations for the Army Special Volunteer System, stipulated that individuals enlisting through this program must have completed or be expected to complete training in an Army Volunteer Training Center administered by the Government-General. Therefore, the potential volunteer soldier had to submit two applications almost simultaneously. In addition to applying for induction into the army through the Army Special Volunteer System, he had to apply for admission into the Army Volunteer Training Center. Both applications were processed at the same time, through two separate but overlapping channels, and the Korean Army could not make its final decisions until applicants to the Training Center had already been screened and were well into their training. For example, those in the first class of the Army Volunteer Training Center began their course on 13 June 1938, but did not take their final examination for entry into the army until 18 October of that year (p. 102).

The documents required to apply for admission to the center were the application itself (*nyūsho negai*), a résumé, a statement of financial assets and income, a letter of assurance from the head of the local government authority (that is, municipalities, townships, or village districts for Korea; their equivalents for Koreans living in Japan; and Japanese consulates for those living outside of Japan in places such as Manchukuo), a physical exam chart prepared by a licensed physician, and an abbreviated transcript of the applicant's household register. Most of the information included in these documents overlapped with that provided for the War Department application. However, the letter of assurance from the local government authority added another filter to the process of selecting reliable loyal subjects, for it asked the authorities to verify the "constancy of the [individual's] principles" (*shisō kengo*) and "good moral conduct" (*gyōjō hōsei*). After the applicant submitted all these materials to the police chief of the area of his household register, the police examined his records and made a determination as to his basic qualifications (for example, age, height, minimum of six years of elementary school education or the equivalent) and the presence of any disqualifying factors, such as a record of imprisonment or evidence that his absence would cause undue hardship to his family (pp. 78–82; for the quotes, 80).

Assuming that data from 1938 and 1939 provide a rough picture of the selection process for the program until it concluded in 1943, we see that an enormous proportion of applicants did not meet the minimum requirements for admission into the Army Volunteer Training Center as stipulated by GGK Ordinance No. 71. In 1938 only 1,663 out of 2,946 applicants were found to be minimally qualified; and in 1939 only about half, or 6,247 out of 12,348, could meet the basic standards.[19] It is highly likely that at this point many of those who might have considered volunteering for the army, and hence the training center, to at least be housed and fed were dropped from consideration. The police chief compiled a comprehensive register of those who met the minimum standards, to which he attached personal histories and qualifications reports based on the materials they had submitted. The police chief then forwarded all of these documents to the provincial governor. The police chiefs did not make selections from among the qualified applicants but offered their opinions about the applicants' suitability as trainees. The provincial governors made final recommendations to the training center director regarding admission (pp. 74–83).

Each provincial governor based his recommendations on the deliberations of a selection committee that he appointed; from that pool, the successful candidates were chosen by lottery. In assessing the qualified applicants, the committee relied on the materials submitted to the provincial governor and the results of three examinations: physical, oral, and subject-specific. The oral examination gauged the applicant's overall character and personality. It included questions on his thought (*shisō*), attitudes (*taido*), fluency in the Japanese language, and common sense (*jōshiki*). Examiners assigned a numerical grade, which took into account the exam's results and information culled from the personal history and qualifications report that had been prepared by the police. The subject-specific exam consisted of three parts: the Japanese national language, history, and arithmetic. Applicants who had gone to middle school or beyond, or had comparable academic ability, could be exempted from the subject-specific exam. In ranking the examinees, the selection committee did not simply rely on numerical calculations but also gauged the overall "human value" of each individual from a "spiritual perspective." The selection committee's purpose was to select "true subjects of the imperial nation" (p. 88). But Oka suggested that in order to introduce an "impartial" (*kōhei*) element into the process that did not strictly reflect ability, the final rankings were produced by a lottery. This added step introduced a mass democratic element and was consistent with the slogan of equality. Each governor, having been given a quota for the number admitted to the training center (say, twenty admissions), selected the equivalent of roughly 150 percent of the quota (thus thirty applicants) from the top of the selection committee's rankings, and then placed them in a lottery to determine their final ordering. Thus it was quite possible that the applicant ranked at the top by the selection committee would by luck of the draw be placed at the bottom of the final list and therefore be rejected, while the applicant who placed lowest among the larger group of thirty might be ranked first for admission. This rather complex selection process ensured both the admission of highly qualified trainees and the appearance of imperial impartiality (pp. 84–91).

The first class of 202 individuals selected by the procedures described above entered the temporary training center that the Government-General set up on the campus of Keijō Imperial University and began their six-month course on 15 June 1938. Construction of the permanent Army Volunteer Training Center, located in Nohae on the outskirts of Keijō (Seoul), was not completed until March 1939. To accommodate the increasing number of trainees, in 1940 the Government-General reduced the training period from six to four months while admitting three rather than two classes per year, and in December 1942 it opened a second training center in P'yŏngyang.[20]

Instruction in the Army Special Volunteer Training Center did not focus directly on combat training; rather, it sought to cultivate the spiritual and physical qualities of the Koreans so that they could later be trained alongside metropolitan Japanese men to become soldiers. This meant assimilating them to an idealized Japanese way of life that included self-discipline. It also entailed practice in group living. These lessons were to be experienced as "intense joy," as Colonel Kaida Kaname, the first head of the Keijō Training Center explained. In short, "while the facilities and the educational methods of the Training Center resemble those of the army, it is very different in that while the army gears everything toward combat, the Training Center emphasizes cultivation of character, hardening of will, guidance in everyday living, and physical development."[21]

The training center's curriculum was made up of three parts: cultivation of character (kun'iku), a course of study that included instruction in the "uniqueness of the Japanese national essence, reflection on duties of subjects of the imperial nation, national morals," and so on; an "ordinary curriculum" (futsū gakka), made up of "national [Japanese] language, mathematics, national history, geography, and science"; and a "technical course" (jukka), which entailed "physical exercise, military drills, martial arts." While these three components constituted the overall curriculum, they all were supposed to advance the first element—namely, cultivation of character.[22]

Indeed, in his memoir Kim Sŏng-su, the volunteer soldier introduced above, remembered that education in becoming a loyal subject of the emperor and the imperial system took place alongside marching and other types of military exercises. Thus he recalls the daily "worship of the emperor from afar" (in which trainees bowed toward Tokyo and the Imperial Palace), morning recitation of the "Oath of Subjects of the Imperial Nation," and memorization of the "Imperial Rescript for Soldiers and Sailors." Although he could not quite accept the imperial system in the same way as the Japanese, he admits that somehow the emperor "had become an absolute presence, a presence close to the gods." He very suggestively conjectures that the difference between him and his older brothers who were involved in anti-Japanese activities is that he was from a new generation that did not have firsthand experience of the March 1 independence movement.[23]

A schedule of daily activities at the First Training Center in Nohae as of late 1942 shows that the day began with wake-up at 6 A.M., followed by toilette and roll call, and then, from 6:30 to 7, a morning assembly that included worshipping the Imperial Palace in Tokyo and Ise Shrine (the shrine to the progenitor of the imperial line, Amaterasu), recitation of the "Oath of Subjects of the Imperial Nation," group singing of the military song "When Going to the Sea" ("Umi yukaba"), and basic physical exercises. This was followed by breakfast, cleaning and inspection, and then preparation for classes. Three fifty-minute classes and two ten-minute rest periods filled the time from 9 A.M. to noon. After a sixty-minute lunch break, trainees attended four more fifty-minute classes, with breaks between each of them and after the last. From 4:50 to 6 P.M., trainees cleaned and attended to grooming and laundry, received mail, and (on four assigned days each week) took baths. Trainees took no more than forty minutes for dinner, after which they had a seventy-minute study period, and then prepared for the evening roll call. The time from 8 to 8:30 was reserved for the evening roll call as well as for silence and self-reflection. The trainees were to retire at 9 P.M. with "gratitude for that day's life of training."[24]

The moment of evening contemplation was supposed to include "self-reflection on the day's instructions, and prayers for the safety and repose of their parents." This was part of a regimen that sought to constitute trainees into subjects of self-reflection and self-discipline who would have a sense of responsibility to their families, their superiors, their nation, their military units, and themselves. They were not to be mindless cogs in the Japanese military machinery. This strategy of disciplinary and pastoral power is also reflected in the pocketbook-sized "training journal" (*kunren techō*) that the center required each trainee to keep on his person at all times. This journal carried all the most important rescripts and oaths necessary for recitation and for self-reflection as an imperial subject and imperial soldier. It also contained a record of the trainee's life before and after entering the center, including awards, good conduct, infractions, academic course grades, technical course grades, and a list of absences. With this objectified record of accomplishments and faults, the trainee was supposed to be ever-vigilant in his own self-discipline, training, and consciousness.[25] As we will see in the following chapters, self-discipline or self-regulation and the inner turmoil that these generated in the souls of those in schools, trainee centers, and the army became a prominent theme in literary and cinematic representations of military life.

A remarkable set of surveys from the First Army Special Volunteer Training Center provides a general picture of the social backgrounds of trainees for the period 1938–42—that is, for all but the last year of the program. These data reflect both the characteristics of the applicants and the multiple screening mechanisms of the civil and military authorities. Very few successful applicants came from the big cities. Over the entire five-year period, only 555 trainees came from the twenty largest cities. Keijō produced just 119 trainees, P'yŏngyang 18, Pusan 74, Ch'ongjin 14, Taegu 42, and so on. The ages of trainees ranged from eighteen to twenty-seven, with most between nineteen and twenty-three.[26] As tables 5 and 6 show, the educational levels and occupations of trainees suggest a great deal about the Government-General's and the army's successes in mobilizing a volunteer force that met their basic goals, but also reveal some problems, including a failure to secure many trainees from the upper strata of Korean society.

The overwhelming majority of trainees in any year were six-year elementary school graduates and therefore just met the basic educational requirement. But in 1940 the training center began to accept a few graduates of four-year elementary schools, perhaps a sign of some difficulty in meeting increasing quotas unless the stipulation that those with the "equivalent" of a six-year elementary school education could qualify was brought into play. Still, between 1938 and 1942 only 8 percent of those admitted had less than six years of formal elementary school instruction. Course completion rates suggest that the quality of entrants stayed consistent at least until 1942. From 1938 to 1941, graduation rates were 99%, 97.2%, 98.5%, and 96.9%, respectively, but in 1942 the rate dropped suddenly to 56.9 percent.[27] Furthermore, while it is difficult to make broad generalizations about the income and assets of those in the categories employed in table 6, we can see that the great majority of trainees were from farming families. Trainees' occupations varied—they included lower white-collar, skilled, and manual workers—but overall it appears that the trainees generally came from the middle to lower middle range of the Korean population, with a few exceptions at the top and bottom. While some occupations whose salaries are very low are in evidence, such as "station manual laborer," "waiter

TABLE 5   Survey of Educational Background (of Trainees)

Education

Year	4-Year Elementary School Graduates or Less	6-Year Elementary School Graduates	Upper Elementary School Graduates	Continuation School Graduates	Some Middle Schooling	Middle School Graduates	Professional College (senmon gakkō) Graduates	TOTAL
1938		313	25	53	8	7		406
1939		499	31	62	13	8		613
1940	218	2,454	61	232	76	19		3,060
1941	336	2,622	46	101	72	31		3,208
1942	342	3,208	98	270	115	42	2	4,077
TOTAL	896	9,096	261	718	284	107	2	11,364

SOURCE: Chōsen Sōtokufu Daiichi Rikugunhei Shigansha Kunrensho, "Gakureki chōsa," in "Seito shochōsa hyō," ca. January 1943, Kajimura Bunkō, Ariran Bunka Sentā Kawaguchi, Saitama Prefecture, Japan.

TABLE 6   Survey of Occupations (of Trainees)

Occupation	1938	1939	1940	1941	1942	TOTAL
			Year			
Farming	234	385	1,798	1,823	2,081	6,321
Commercial	19	22	153	144	284	622
Fishing			16	15	28	59
Government Official (kanri)			7	4	43	54
Local Official (kōri)			47	80	178	305
Teacher (including for Korean sŏdang)	5	12	45	39	69	170
Company or Office Worker	15	12	124	165	300	616
Menial Worker (kōin)	21	23	158	142	156	500
Supervisors (kanshu kanchō)			17	14	5	36
Station Manual Laborer (ekishu)			34	36	39	109
Driver	1	1	23	37	57	119
Factory Worker		7	113	181	330	631
Store Clerk	23	41	85	130	128	407
Apprentice	8	10	46	65	97	226
Waiter or Page (kyūshi kozukai)	36	43	149	110	97	435
Manual Laborer	21	21	107	87	46	282
Student		4	51	39	57	151
Unemployed	13	18	49	55	49	184
Other	10	14	38	42	33	137
TOTAL	406	613	3,060	3,208	4,077	11,364

SOURCE: Chōsen Sōtokufu Daiichi Rikugunhei Shigansha Kunrensho, "Shokugyō chōsa," in "Seito shochōsa hyō."

or page" and "manual laborer," they do not skew the overall data toward the extremely economically disadvantaged. In short, while the Government-General and Korean Army appear to have been forced to make a few minor compromises—accepting a few poor trainees who may have wished to join the army to have a livelihood—they generally used the extensive screening process to eliminate most of the poor, the uneducated, and those who did not meet physical norms, as well as individuals who might cause disciplinary and ideological problems. There is no indication that the authorities hoped to compel the poor and unwilling to volunteer.

This rigorous screening process, coupled with the intense spiritual training received by these young men, goes far to explain why Korean volunteer soldiers appear to have performed very well after induction and on the battlefield. In November 1939 the chief of staff of the Korean Army circulated a top-secret report on the combat performance records and casualties of some of the first Korean volunteers enrolled in the Twentieth Division. While the report did not offer a comprehensive assessment of the Korean soldiers, it contains detailed reports from each of the four infantry regiments constituting the division—namely the Seventy-seventh through Eightieth Infantry Regiments (IRs).[28]

The reports are revealing in a number of ways, but I will call attention to two. Most importantly, with a few minor exceptions they record the extremely high performance of the Korean volunteers in nearly every category of service and testify to the internalization by some of Japanese national subjectivity. There is no reason to believe that the writers of these reports sought to inflate the performance of these soldiers or to concoct almost unbelievable stories of their battlefield valor, a point that is highlighted by the fact that a few writers noted exceptions and warned about the necessity of continuing to educate the Korean soldiers and the Korean people in general. Moreover, the reports were supposed to offer a candid assessment of the soldiers for internal circulation within the army and evaluation of the special voluntary system. They were not for media propaganda.

In general the assessors lauded the Koreans not only as good soldiers but as at least above the average Japanese conscript in almost all cases, and superior in a good number of others. A significant portion even cited the Koreans as models that the metropolitan soldiers should follow. Thus the report of the First Company (c.), Seventy-seventh IR, testified that these soldiers "manifested no faults." Their thoughts were "moderate and proper," and their combat performance was "superior" overall, with "an extremely high degree of heroism and vigor on a scale of bravery and cowardice." They were "models for other soldiers in their enthusiasm and steadfastness to their daily duties," and their "sturdy physiques" combined with "spiritual strength" resulted in superior battlefield performance, even when "bullets rained down on them." This reporter believed that the soldiers' "superlative performance record, exceeding that of general soldiers enrolled in the same year[,] . . . was related to their sense that as the first class of Korean Special Volunteers, they were representatives of the Korean Peninsula." In other words, much as Japanese American veterans have often said that they fought to prove their collective worthiness as a minority group, so this report and those on the Ninth and Tenth Companies, Seventy-seventh IR, commented on the Korean soldiers' belief that their military heroism would contribute to the reputation of the Korean people.

The reporter for the Fifth c., Seventy-seventh IR, emphasized many of the same qualities in the Koreans of good conduct and spirit, but also noted a minor weakness that in stereotypical fashion he related to "a traditional attribute"—namely, that while they followed orders well and had a sense of responsibility, their "conduct and behavior generally lacked the subtle elements needed for resourcefulness." Though he likewise also felt that Koreans lacked "quickness and dexterity in various matters," a point that other reports actually contradicted, the Fifth c.'s reporter was forced to conclude that "it is currently difficult to find common faults in them since most of them come from good families" and that "the performance records of the superior among them are competitive with the best [Japanese] conscripts of the 1938 year; even the lowest of them rank with those at the midlevel." The reports on Koreans in the Ninth and Tenth Companies, Seventy-seventh IR, worried a bit about their lack of complete facility in the Japanese language, but the Ninth c.'s commentary concluded that Koreans displayed an "abundance of physical and spiritual strength" and that their record placed them with the top rank of first-year Japanese conscript soldiers in the company. The Tenth c.'s report testified that the Korean soldiers in most respects provided a model that other soldiers could follow and that all of them had been advanced to the rank of superior private at the first opportunity.

The assessment of the Twelfth c., Seventy-seventh IR, and the comprehensive reports from the Seventy-eighth and Seventy-ninth IRs were positive but less effusive in their praise for the Koreans. The first stated that Korean soldiers were neither superior nor inferior in their duties within the barracks, but gave them high marks in other areas including marching and combat. It noted their bravery in battle and that they always took the lead in the attacks. Moreover, unlike so many "physically weak first-year [Japanese] recruits," the Koreans "always kept up with the company commander"; they therefore tended to be "relied upon more than the other soldiers." The Seventy-eighth IR report praised many qualities of the special volunteers, including their "physical prowess," "stamina," "ability to withstand hardship and deprivation," "military spirit," and high-spirited willingness to "take the lead while charging into the face of death." On all counts, the reporter concluded, of the twenty-four Koreans in the regiment, nineteen equaled the Japanese soldiers while five were only slightly inferior in the limited area of "actual combat." The report from the Seventy-ninth IR gave a mixed impression, although weighing in on the side of average performance.

The most positive assessment of Korean volunteers came from the Eightieth IR. According to this report, these soldiers were "self-aware of the honor that they had received in being able to join the ranks of the Imperial Forces" and in order to preserve this honor they compiled "various good records of performance." Not only were there "no differences between them and the [Japanese] soldiers in general, from the perspective of soldiers entering in the same year, the special volunteer soldiers were actually looked to for models." Attributing their superiority in academic subjects to the process of their selection as soldiers, the report also verified that out of the twenty-two special volunteer soldiers in the regiment, nine had been promoted to superior private at the first opportunity and nine had been recommended for noncommissioned officer training.

The reports made special note of the physical strength and mental toughness of the Korean soldiers, enabling them to withstand hardship, wounds, pain, and deprivation. In all the reports from the Twentieth Division, only one criticized the battlefield cowardice of a Korean soldier (Fifth c., Seventy-eighth IR), who retreated from combat out of "panic and fear" after allegedly suffering only a bruise from a hand grenade. But other writers provided accounts of Korean heroism, even when wounded, that rivaled the propagandistic depictions that would eventually be found in films and officially sanctioned reports meant for wide circulation. Private First Class Chŏng Chong-t'ae (Fifth c., Seventy-seventh IR) was said to have suffered a neck wound from shell fragments, but then "appeared unaffected, and by his vigor it seemed as though he had suffered only a slight injury." Private First Class Cho Pong-hwan (First c., Seventy-eighth IR) was so filled with the "attack spirit" that even after he was shot through the thigh by a machine gun, he continued to move forward until he could no longer stand. Private First Class Mun Chae-hyŏk (Sixth c., Seventy-eighth IR) suffered wounds from hand grenade shrapnel to the chest and left lower thigh during a twilight attack by the enemy, but unfazed and fully composed he pulled out a roll of bandages and stopped his own bleeding. The most remarkable and almost unbelievable account of the Korean display of proper subjectivity as an imperial soldier came from the Seventy-ninth IR; because this report was otherwise relatively lukewarm, it seems highly likely that the episode was not excessively embellished. Apparently, the unnamed volunteer soldier suffered a devastating wound to his left thigh from a hand grenade. Shouting, "Oh! Oh!" (*aigo, aigo*), he seemed to have lost the "desire to fight and a concern for victory or defeat." Nevertheless, "on the verge of death," he told his comrades "please do your best," and mumbled three times *"banzai* to the Emperor."

The reports are of interest not only because they give us a candid, if sometimes sentimentalized, indication of the performance of the first Koreans to serve in the Japanese army, but also because they suggest the extent to which officers, noncommissioned officers, and enlisted men seemed obligated to follow the army's official stance of nondiscrimination. They tell us little about the interior life of these Japanese personnel. We cannot know how sincere they were in apparently rejecting ethnic discrimination. But as I have maintained throughout this study, I am less concerned to determine the sincerity of the Japanese than to analyze the effects of the campaign to mobilize Koreans for war. Moreover, the voices of the Korean soldiers are always mediated through the Japanese officers and noncommissioned officers who presumably wrote the reports, which therefore offer only limited glimpses into their interiority. For example, one of the reports (Fifth c., Seventy-seventh IR) praised the Koreans for speaking only in Japanese, even in their private affairs. But we cannot be sure that they were not using Korean among themselves, as Kim Sŏng-su remembers doing in the training center, when no one was around to observe them.[29]

Nonetheless, the reports clearly indicate that while they may not have completely hidden their personal prejudices, all Japanese personnel were supposed to act as if the army impartially welcomed the Korean special volunteers, their accomplishments were to be celebrated, and advancement in rank should be determined by merit. We find no evidence of efforts consistent with later appeals from the Ministry of Welfare in *Yamato minzoku* (see chapter 1) to denigrate Koreans and urge the state not to allow them to intermingle with metropolitan Japanese soldiers. Instead, the writers showed that at least in principle they were supposed to further the "unity of metropolitan Japan and Korea." They celebrated the smooth and mutually supportive integration of the army as when the commentary on First c., Seventy-seventh IR, noted with great satisfaction that the relations of "general [Japanese] soldiers and special [Korean] volunteer soldiers transcends the spirit of the 'unity of metropolitan Japan and Korea' so that they truly possess the harmonious intimacy of comrades in arms on the battlefield."

Koreans and soldiers from metropolitan Japan in the Tenth c., Seventy-seventh IR, were also said to have excellent relations. The special volunteers had a sense of responsibility as the first class of Koreans in the army, while the other soldiers had empathy and respect. These attitudes led to "a camaraderie without friction, the 'unity of metropolitan Japan and Korea,' in which the soldiers lived every day while cooperating as if they were brothers." And so on. In short, the reports reflect the army's official stance that it rejected ethnic discrimination and that it desired to create a well-integrated and harmonious army and nation in which Koreans and metropolitan Japanese bonded together in strength. This obviously did not prevent some of the writers from occasionally revealing their personal prejudices or stereotypes about Korean ethnic tendencies, but such remarks were couched in a language of a paternalism that disavowed racism—in other words, in the language of polite racism.

But what can we further conclude about this glowing report on the Special Army Volunteers and the apparent Japanese commitment to nurturing and rewarding the new soldiers? First, some Koreans within the Japanese army acted as if they were loyal subjects of the Japanese imperial nation and sometimes died expressing this belief. Second, the behavior of the Koreans and the Japanese within the integrated units provided slivers of truth for the propaganda machinery that represented the Japanese empire as the champion of the equality of metropolitan Japanese and Koreans and that celebrated their partnership in an expanded concept of Japan.

Finally, we must remember that although for propaganda purposes the Government-General and the Korean Army wished to recruit Korean volunteers who reflected Korean society at large, other considerations and realities militated against this goal. As we have seen, between 1938 and 1943 the civil and military authorities selected only 17,664 men out of 802,047 for admission into the Training Centers, or about 2.2 percent of applicants (calculated from table 1). Because they utilized the program not only to fill a manpower need but also to create an image of Koreans from "good families" freely choosing to live and die for the Japanese nation, the civil and military authorities, assisted by the police, produced an extremely unrepresentative sampling of individuals to represent the characteristics and will of the Korean people. Since these authorities controlled this subject population so closely—selecting only those who best approximated ideal national subjects and then training them in the special centers—they were remarkably successful in realizing the objective of enlisting Korean soldiers who could be trusted to serve the military and the nation properly, but not the goal of having the soldiers mirror Korean society at large.

In this connection, two enormous problems concerning the mobilization of Koreans as soldiers loomed before the Government-General and the military as the war intensified. First, the authorities never successfully recruited a significant number of young men from the very upper social strata through the volunteer system. As table 5 shows, from 1938 to 1942 only two trainees were graduates of professional colleges. Moreover, just 1,372 out of the total of 11,364 trainees, or about 12 percent, had gone beyond the basic six-year elementary school. Another table, not reproduced here, shows that of the trainees who entered the center between 1938 and 1942, 70.4 percent had assets below 3,000 yen. This was fairly consistent in every year.[30]

Early in the program, Kaida Kaname warned that class disparity in the ranks would have very negative consequences for the military. After reviewing data from 1938 and 1939, he remarked that the number of volunteers who were "the children of those with considerable status, educational background, financial assets, etc. is extremely minuscule." This suggested to him that Koreans still disparaged military service. But more importantly, he worried about a glaring contradiction—namely, that "at the critical moment of volunteering, the educated class and the leadership class who had raised up both arms to welcome the system's promulgation first encouraged others to join but did not urge their own children to answer the call." Moreover, the paucity of volunteers with a middle school education or above would lead to great practical problems in the future, for Korea needed to produce highly qualified young men who could serve on the level of metropolitan Japanese men, many of whom were very "cultured and educated" (shūyō). In a related way, Kaida emphasized that service in the contemporary army, even in the infantry, required soldiers with a high degree of scientific knowledge. If Koreans were to excel in the military, it would be necessary to produce many of "superior merit in both spiritual and academic strength."[31]

Although Kaida used the neutral-sounding word "contradiction" (mujun) to describe the sideline cheerleading of the "educated class and the leadership class," this was sharp criticism of the Korean social and political elite's tendency to financially and vocally support a system that required young men of moderate if stable means to risk their lives, while shielding themselves and their families from sacrifices. The archival record is filled with examples of prominent Korean men who supported the voluntary system and implementation of the conscription system but at no major cost to themselves. For example, Pak Hŭng-sik, the well-known entrepreneur under Japanese colonialism whose portfolio included ownership of the Hwasin department store in Seoul and a chain of stores throughout Korea, joined with other members of the Korean elite in January 1939 to form the Association in Support of the Korean Special Volunteer Soldiers (Chōsen Tokubetsu Shiganhei Kōenkai). They reportedly had wished to provide assistance to volunteers, since with almost no infrastructure in place in Korea for them, young men aspiring to enlist had to bear the burden of travel and lodging expenses they incurred to take the volunteer selection exams. Yun Ch'i-ho—who had emerged in political life as a prominent participant in the Korean independence movement, only to become an avid supporter of Japanese total war policies—served as president of the association.[32] Revealing in a particularly direct way the intimate ties between capitalist profiteering and support for Japanese militarism and nationalism, toward the end of the war Pak Hŭng-sik teamed up with Kim Yŏn-su in a joint venture with the Mitsui conglomerate to build kamikaze planes. Although it has been said that the venture started too late to produce any planes before the war's end,[33] Korean youths were among those who died as Japanese kamikaze pilots.

The Japanese military institutionalized a significant program to deal with the problem of insufficient representation from the Korean social and political elite only in October 1943 with inauguration of the "student soldier" system, which made it possible for Korean and Taiwanese students in higher education to enlist directly into the army without first undergoing mandatory training in the GGK's Army Volunteer Training Center. As Carter J. Eckert has already shown, during this campaign a good number of the Korean capitalist class who profited from the development of industrial capitalism under Japanese colonialism actively participated in efforts to recruit Korean youths into the military. They included the brothers Kim Sŏng-su (not the volunteer soldier) and Kim Yŏn-su of the Kyŏngsŏng Spinning and Weaving Company.[34]

CONSCRIPTION

The other more challenging matter concerning recruitment of Koreans as soldiers arose in conjunction with the realization that Japan's military manpower needs in the post–Pearl Harbor moment could be filled only if the draft were extended to Koreans and Taiwanese. The Government-General and the Japanese military thus had to rapidly transform the relatively small-scale voluntary system that allowed rigorous selection from among youths who were at least in principle willing to join, and that included an extended phase of pre-induction training, to mass conscription of Korean youths. While the vast majority of these potential conscripts were poorly educated, unable to speak or understand Japanese in any practical way, and did not accept that they had any obligation to fight for Japan, they also had to be transformed into active soldiers very quickly.

As suggested in chapter 1, however, in order to mobilize the population as civilian and military labor, the Government-General and the army first had to map the population to identify potential conscripts. Although household registers remained the most detailed and effective means for tracking Korean households and their individual members, officials such as Oka Hisao, the author of the *Reader for Army Special Volunteers*, had been presented with plenty of evidence of their unreliability. He made special note to those processing volunteer soldier applications that they should take great care to ensure the fit between the registers and the individuals, because in processing the first group of applicants in 1938, officials had discovered in some cases that "the abbreviated transcripts of the household registers did not include a column for the applicant himself, or recorded his sex as female, or had birthdates recorded in two different ways."[35] Thus, while the household registers were supposed to verify the person, the volunteer system served as an opportunity for the person and the authorities to verify the household registers. In addition, the initial inattention of applicants to the accuracy of their registers, as they sometimes even submitted transcripts that did not include themselves, suggests that most commoners did not understand the relationship between themselves and the state's representation of them in household registers.

The major inducement for perfecting this political technology so that it could effectively grasp the Korean people as an aggregate, as families, and as individuals—in other words, across the three main targets of the modern modality of governmentality—was the draft. To determine if it would be possible to even enforce conscription in the colony, the Government-General and military assembled 270 examination teams to conduct a massive peninsula-wide survey of eighteen- and nineteen-year-old males. During the first ten days of March 1942, the teams of military physicians and other staff, in large part modeling their efforts on conscription exams, recorded their subjects' physical characteristics, their fluency in the Japanese language, and the condition of their household registers. Pak Hŭng-sik, Kim Yŏn-su, and other members of the business elite helped finance this endeavor. After completing their work they arrived at the conclusion that military conscription could be implemented in the colony, but the scale of further efforts to map the population through the household registers, as has already been described in chapter 1, signifies both a recognition of the poor quality of the system then in place for knowing and regulating the Korean people and a new commitment to perfecting a technology that would make all the Korean people visible to power.[36]

Mapping the population, making it visible in its details, was but the first step in surveillance that enabled the authorities to better foster the health, education, and welfare of all the people. Thus, in its budget for the 1943 fiscal year the Government-General appropriated the following amounts for expenses related to laying the groundwork for the extension of military conscription to Korea: 1,776,228 yen to expand administrative mechanisms and personnel at the Government-General and in local government offices; 3,469,367 yen to hire more personnel whose duties would include "composing rosters of men of conscript age and to as necessary register into household registers the unregistered, to correct errors in household registers, and to clarify the situation of those temporarily domiciled in places other than those noted in their household registers"; and 6,034,783 yen to use the facilities of national people's schools (*kokumin gakkō*) to "provide language instruction and basic drills" for about 80,000 men of conscript age who had not finished primary school (that is, at this time the first six years of the newly named national people's schools) or undergone any kind of drilling. The government would use these funds to pay teachers in the national people's schools and others who would instruct these young men, as well as to expand the capacity of Army Special Volunteers Centers from 4,500 to 6,000 men.[37]

In his explanation of conscription-related items in the Government-General's budget for the following year, Mizuta Naomasa, head of the Treasury Bureau, noted that for 1944 another 650,000 yen would be appropriated to continue the work of the previous year in perfecting the system of household registers and temporary domicile notifications. But with most of this work accomplished, Mizuta stressed the importance of giving men of conscript age at least "an ability to understand the [Japanese] language and on top of that some degree of training in manners and morals (*shitsuke*)." At first the Government-General had estimated that youths of conscript age for the year 1944 numbered about 220,000 and that about half of them had received no elementary school (*shōgakkō*) education. In fact, owing to discoveries made during the campaign to put the household registers in order, the total number was revised upward to just over 250,000.[38] Later that year, the Government-General calculated an even larger number of 260,000, with 200,000 of them residing in Korea and the remainder living elsewhere. Of the latter only about 75,000 had graduated from primary school (*kōtō shōgakkō*, or the first six years of national people's schools), meaning that most of the remaining 125,000 "cannot understand the [Japanese] national language and they are mentally in a state of enormous anxiety, and more, regarding entering the army."[39] As Mizuta explained, the governor-general promulgated the Youth Special Training Ordinance (Seinen Tokubetsu Rensei Rei) in October 1942 in order to provide the needed language education and "training in manners and morals." It enabled 110,000 youths to begin training. The Government-General also appropriated funds for similarly training Korean youths residing in Manchukuo.[40]

The ordinance mandated the establishment of Youth Special Training Centers in every municipality, village district, and township, although exceptions could be made (article 9). The ordinance's "purpose was to provide Korean male youth with the spiritual and physical training, as well as other types of instruction necessary to ensure that those who would in the future join the military service would be prepared with the requisite qualities. At the same time, [it] was expected to provide for training in the ability to adapt to labor" (art. 1). It primarily targeted Korean male youths between seventeen and twenty years of age residing in Korea (art. 2), but it exempted primary school (*kokumin gakkō shotōka*) graduates (art. 4.1). The ordinance specified that the period of training would in principle be a year, but could be reduced to six months if necessary (art. 5).[41] According to data compiled by the Government-General, by late 1944, 2,534 Youth Special Training Centers had been established in Korea (2,400 public and 134 private), a number that it expected to grow to 2,738 by 1945.[42]

Because the young men generally worked at their jobs during the day, they took classes in the evening. Over the course of a year, students completed roughly 400 hours of Japanese-language instruction and 200 hours of other instruction and drilling. The course of instruction was weighted toward language education because this was obviously the basic skill needed to function in the military. Most of the instructors were schoolteachers in the national people's schools, and each training center sought to secure the part-time services of an active soldier. After taking their conscription exams, those in the Youth Special Training Centers who received the "A" (*kō*) classification took an additional intensive course lasting roughly one month at one of three Military Service Preparatory Training Centers (Gunmu Yobi Kunrensho) that covered the general areas of spiritual training, language instruction, and manners and morals.[43] Two of these new training centers were converted out of the Special Army Volunteer Training Centers located in Nohae and P'yŏng-yang, which ceased taking trainees in 1943 because the Special Army Volunteer System was phased out as conscription was extended to Korea. The Government-General founded a third Military Service Preparatory Training Center in Shihŭng, just outside of Suwŏn in Kyŏnggi Province, in May 1944.[44]

At the same time, in consideration of the length of time that had elapsed since their graduation, even youths of conscript age who had completed primary school were required to attend a Youth Special Training Center, but in a separate yearlong special course (*bekka*) consisting of 300 hours of instruction. This course also focused on spiritual training, language instruction, and manners and morals. After successfully completing this special course, those classified as "A" following their conscription exams undertook training for a month under the direct command of active military officers (ideally, one commissioned and five noncommissioned) at one of 120 Combined Youth Training Centers established in key places throughout Korea. Finally, the limited number of middle school graduates who were exempted from any of the courses described above, as well as some others with a relatively high level of education, were supposed to receive additional training from organizations such as the Military Reservists Association.[45]

In short, with cooperation from the army the Government-General sought to give almost all potential conscripts, and especially those most likely to be inducted, at least the equivalent of a primary school education followed by a finishing course more explicitly preparing them for military service. Figure 6, based on a chart produced by the Government-General, summarizes what has been described above for the year 1944.

The monitoring and education of the people for war were not limited to institutions aimed specifically at males of conscript age, however. In fact, promulgation of the imperial ordinances establishing in rapid order first the Army Special Volunteer System (22 February 1938) and then reform of the new Korean educational system (4 March 1938) indicated the inextricable relationship between educating Koreans as a whole, under the banner of their betterment and equality, and creating more civilian and military laborers. For example, the Government-General also established training centers for young women of marriageable age in an effort to turn them into good imperial subjects, workers, and household managers. The Government-General calculated that as of late 1944, about 100,000 young women were receiving instruction at these Young Women's Training Centers (Joshi Seinen Kunrensho).[46] In another major effort to advance fluency in the Japanese language among Koreans, especially those between the ages of fifteen and thirty, in 1938 the Government-General also began to provide funds, textbooks, and encouragement to establish language-learning courses (kōshūkai) in local communities. The Government-General calculated that in its first year, the campaign produced 3,660 courses with 210,373 participants, and an additional 99,302 individuals bought textbooks in order to study on their own.[47]

These campaigns resulted from the colonial administrators' acute awareness that while the Japanese colonial empire needed the Korean people to participate in the war effort, a huge language barrier made total war mobilization extremely cumbersome and ineffective. In its 1940 comprehensive history of colonial administration, the Government-General noted that only a very small improvement in knowledge of Japanese could be measured in the decade leading up to 1936. At that time,

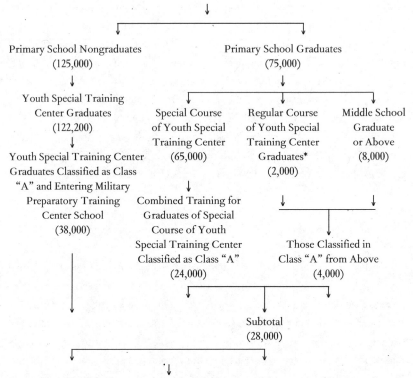

Korean Youths of Conscript Age Residing within and outside Korea in 1944 (260,000)

Korean Youths of Conscript Age in 1944 Residing in Korea (200,000)

Primary School Nongraduates (125,000) — Primary School Graduates (75,000)

Youth Special Training Center Graduates (122,200)

Youth Special Training Center Graduates Classified as Class "A" and Entering Military Preparatory Training Center School (38,000)

Special Course of Youth Special Training Center (65,000)

Combined Training for Graduates of Special Course of Youth Special Training Center Classified as Class "A" (24,000)

Regular Course of Youth Special Training Center Graduates* (2,000)

Middle School Graduate or Above (8,000)

Those Classified in Class "A" from Above (4,000)

Subtotal (28,000)

Total Korean Youths of Conscript Age Residing in Korea in 1944 Classified as Class "A" and Completing Finishing Courses Prior to Induction (66,000)

* "Regular Course of Youth Special Training Center Graduates" probably refers to those who completed training in Youth Special Training Centers that existed prior to the October 1942 ordinance mandating the establishment of Youth Special Training Centers throughout Korea. Such centers, following the model of metropolitan Japan, had existed in much smaller numbers since at least 1929.

FIGURE 6.
Pre-induction training for Korean youth of conscript age residing in Korea. Source: Chōsen Sōtokufu, "Shōwa 19 nen 12 gatsu dai 86 kai teikoku gikai setsumei shiryō," December 1944, as reproduced in Chōsen Sōtokufu, *Chōsen sōtokufu teikoku gikai setsumei shiryō*, vol. 10 (Tokyo: Fuji Shuppan, 1994); 56.

according to its first comprehensive national language survey in Korea, only about 8 percent of the total population had some competence in the Japanese language.[48] But in late 1944 the Government-General claimed that combined with the general expansion of primary school education, which would become compulsory by 1946, the expansion of language-learning courses, the Youth Special Training Centers, the Young Women's Special Training Centers, and efforts by other organizations had all contributed to a rapid rise in the proportion of the Korean population able to understand Japanese. While only 13.89 percent of the Korean people could understand Japanese in 1939, this percentage increased annually to 15.57, 16.61, and 19.9 percent, respectively, and finally reached 22.15 percent in 1943.[49]

The above campaigns, as well as the support of local units of new mass organizations such as the Neighborhood Patriotic Associations, contributed to the great success of the Government-General in registering and examining potential conscripts. In late November 1942, the Government-General established the Korea Central Committee to Maintain Household Registers (Chōsen Chūō Koseki Seibi Taisaku Iinkai) and charged it with developing policies for putting the registers in order. As a result, on 1 March 1943 each municipality, township, and village district in Korea simultaneously conducted investigations of household registers and temporary domicile notices involving males less than twenty years of age. It was discovered that out of 6,254,984 such cases, some 2,271,712 contained errors; by 1 September 1943, just under two million of these had been corrected. All of these preparations enabled the Government General to register 254,753 out of an estimated 266,643, or better than 95.5 percent, of all young men of conscript age during the registration that lasted from 1 October 1943 to 30 November 1943.[50]

The first Korea-wide mass examination of young men of conscription age began on 1 April 1944 and concluded on 20 August. Some forty examination teams gave mental and physical exams to 206,517 youths throughout the country. According to the Government-General this figure represented roughly 94.5 percent of those eligible who either were living in Korea or had returned to Korea even though they were domiciled elsewhere.[51] Of the examinees, 33.5 percent were classified as "A" (*kō*) and 30 percent as "B-1" (1 *otsu*), both classifications designating eligibility for active service. Examiners rated another 16 percent as "B-2" and 11.1 percent as "B-3," or qualified for reserve status. In September, the first Korean conscripts began enrolling in units of the Japanese army stationed in Korea in order to gradually accustom them to military life. They would then be distributed throughout the Japanese Imperial Forces. In the following year the colonial and military authorities conducted the second annual conscription exams in February and May, adhering to the previous year's model, and also trained them through the various centers that had been utilized in the first conscription year.[52]

"REASON"

As we have seen, in order to realize the material objectives of the total war regime, the colonial/national state reached its tentacles ever further down into the most remote of communities and stretched out even beyond Japan's expanded territorial borders on the Korea Peninsula. In collaboration with the army, the police, and many other local authorities, it made communities, households, and individuals visible to power in their numerous details, so that they could all be coordinated and mobilized for war. In official discourse, this totalizing as well as individuating project (that is, the aspect of the project that sought to constitute self-reflexive individuals who made normative choices) was always articulated as one that represented the unfolding of Reason, History, and Morality under Japanese rule. It was supposed to be part of a larger movement in the progress and increasing maturity of the Korean people, through which they could finally rise out of their low state of daily life, knowledge, and culture (*mindo*) and receive treatment as the full equals of the metropolitan Japanese. The advancing reason, progress, and maturity of the Korean people meant that they were at the cusp of realizing their telos as members of the leading people of East Asia. Service in the Japanese Imperial Forces was thus an honor and a duty that the Korean people should accept as part of their destiny as Japanese, as imperial subjects, and as a people at the forefront of world history.

Thus the Government-General celebrated the conduct of "informed Koreans in general" (*ippan yūshiki Chōsenjin*)—in other words, those literally "having knowledge and discernment" (*yūshikisha*)—for their support of the state's programs, including the recruitment of Koreans into the military. It claimed that they responded with tremendous "gratitude and enthusiasm" to the extension of military conscription to Korea because since the beginning of the special volunteer system in 1938, Koreans as well as metropolitan Japanese had assumed that their low educational level would make the conscription of Koreans impossible before compulsory education was established. Thus the "informed Koreans" interpreted the May 1942 announcement that conscription would begin in 1944 as recognition of their status as imperial subjects and regarded it as an indication that "discrimination between metropolitan Japanese and Koreans would soon be eliminated through the implementation of compulsory education, the granting of rights to vote and hold office, and so on." Reflecting such an attitude, many within this educated elite enthusiastically participated in preparations for implementing the draft.[53] To be sure, the Government-General's assessment may have reflected some wishful thinking among its officials, but given that the latter also honestly noted the lack of enthusiasm of some other sectors of the population and that the media found many such patriotic individuals to report about on its pages, the Government-General's official views cannot easily be dismissed as simply exaggerated.

Yet as the civil, police, and military authorities expanded this web of technologies for managing the entire population, they encountered others who did not accept the precise reasoning of the Japanese state and its authorities. Reason could also lead to conclusions that were at odds with state policy. For example, many in the older generation of the former *yangban* elite did not have a taste for war and disparaged the military. Others, self-aware of their position in world history, believed that the Japanese regime was likely to treat Korean conscripts much like other colonial powers had treated their colonial soldiers. As one "educated and informed" individual supposedly said, "There are many parents who are not eager to send their children into the army out of fear that they would be discriminated against like America's Filipino soldiers or Britain's Indian soldiers, or that they might be used as cannon fodder [literally, 'bullet shields,' *tamayoke*]."[54]

However, from the state's point of view, educating or encouraging Koreans to become useful and rational subjects who would willingly participate in national projects, including becoming soldiers, carried with it two very different kinds of dangers. First, while the Government-General consistently resisted the idea that benefits such as political rights should be granted in exchange for military service, many elite men of "knowledge and discernment" as well as commoners with plain common sense made precisely this argument—an argument that followed the logic of what I have in the case of Japanese Americans called "conditional loyalty." Why should conscription come even before the benefit of compulsory education? Or why should Koreans be compelled to serve in the military just like Japanese youths, when so many disparities in rights and benefits remained? Japanese intelligence agencies reported with great concern about this—about Koreans expecting much more from military service than superficial honors and praise.

Thus, in its special report on the reaction of various groups to the May 1942 announcement that military conscription would be extended to Korea, the Criminal Affairs Bureau of the Ministry of Justice noted in its internal intelligence report for June 1943 that although the Korean people in general approved this new development as a logical outgrowth of the volunteer system, "their excitement was not quite as great as that of Koreans living in Japan." As for the "upper class of intellectuals" (*jōsō chishiki kaikyū*) in Korea, the report warned that "among them are heard demands that all discriminatory treatment must be eliminated from compulsory education, travel to and from the metropole, salaries and housing subsidies, and rights to vote and hold office." It further indicated that such calls "even went so far as to insist on abolition of the Government-General system" and that this "demand also exists among Korean residents in metropolitan Japan." As evidenced by the views of an unnamed person from Sinŭiju who was listed on the report as an individual requiring special surveillance (*yōchū*), the latter demand was for Korea to be fully incorporated into Japan as a part of the nation and an end to all discriminatory policies (pp. 22–23).

To illustrate the view that Koreans ought to receive benefits in exchange for fulfilling the duty of military service, the report cited the stance of a Korean member of the aristocracy in Keijō (Seoul) who disparaged the army's special volunteer system as nothing but child's play, a bad "practical joke" (*kodomo no akugi*) that the upper strata had not welcomed. In contrast, he believed that the extension of military conscription truly offered Koreans "a status equal to that of metropolitan Japanese." Looking to the example of Europe and its colonies, he dismissed as unrealistic the dreams of some Korean youths for independence. Instead, he felt that with the extension of conscription to Koreans, they should be grateful for receiving "treatment equal to that of metropolitan Japanese," and that they should strive to produce Japanese military heroes of their own—"a second 'Three Human Bomb Patriots' (*bakudan sanyūshi*) [heroes of the Shanghai Incident] and a second the 'Nine Military Gods' (*kyūgunshin*) [heroes in the midget submarine attack at Pearl Harbor]." "In the near future," he predicted, Koreans would "probably also be granted political rights equal to metropolitan Japan's" (pp. 22–23).

The same report included considerable detail on the responses of Koreans residing in Japan. Overall, it gave the impression that the majority of these Koreans welcomed the new policy and considered it a hopeful sign that the principle of the unity of metropolitan Japan and Korea would finally be realized. As an example, it mentioned that immediately after the announcement a group of eleven led by Pak Ch'un-gŭm, the only Korean to serve in the lower house of the Imperial Diet (as he did twice), sent congratulatory telegrams to Governor-General Minami Jirō and Commander of the Korean Army Itagaki Seishirō. Then, following the ritual of bowing in the direction of the Imperial Palace, they visited the offices of the cabinet and the ministers of war, the navy, colonial affairs, and so on, bearing letters of gratitude. Noting that they also planned to worship at Meiji and Yasukuni Shrines, the report surmised that Pak Ch'un-gŭm's followers considered the new conscription policy the result of Pak's many years of effort (pp. 14–15).

However, like the U.S. civil and army intelligence branches that tended to be more suspicious of Japanese Americans and other minorities than other agencies, the Japanese police contributing to this report cast grave doubts on the true motives and sentiments of these colonial/minority subjects. While their descriptions of Korean responses may help us gauge the sentiments of Koreans in Japan, they also reveal that despite the official position of the Government-General, the central government, and the army that Koreans should be treated as equals, the intelligence communities contributed to continuing distrust of them. The report concluded:

> Today, as the fruits of the imperial subjectivization of the Peninsulars steadily appear, it could certainly have been anticipated that there would be more than a few who, grateful for the imperial benevolence, sincerely vow to serve. However, . . . delving a little more deeply and observing in more detail, it is evident that there are a considerable number among them who, while expressing the sentiment of gratitude for implementation of the conscription system, at the same time also immediately bring up not only the realization of compulsory education, but also acquisition of the rights to vote and hold office, the elimination of limits to traveling between the metropole and Korea, and the transfer of family registers [to the metropole]. And then they say that as long as the conscription system will be implemented, these matters should be re - solved all at once, or that these matters are likely to be resolved in the near future. Isn't it true that if their gratitude and enthusiasm were truly genuine, they would not raise the issue as a so-called consideration [that is, something given in exchange for a service]? From this it is evident that rather than pure elation out of gratitude and enthusiasm for this honor as subjects of the Imperial Nation, they are overjoyed by the elimination of one discriminatory treatment. This indicates that most Peninsulars do not yet truly have a thorough-going consciousness as Japanese (*Nihonjin*). (p. 15)

The report provided specific evidence about several representative Korean individuals who, in its writers' estimation, held the inappropriate idea that inclusion in the conscription system should be compensated with various rights and the elimination of unequal treatment. An individual in Kobe claimed to have supported implementation of conscription for more than a decade and was ecstatic and grateful to Governor-General Minami and Prime Minister Tōjō Hideki for finally bringing this about. Yet he insisted on the need to go one step further, because "the problem of the Government-General" itself remained. "Rather than use the phrase the 'perfect unity of metropolitan Japan and Korea' (*kanzen naru Naisen ittai*)," he maintained, the colonial relationship should be put to an end by "dismantling the Government-General system, giving [Korea] a prefectural name as is the case for metropolitan Japan, and placing it directly under the administration of the Home Ministry" (p. 17). In fact, this reasoning—which pushed the official discourse on unity and nondiscrimination to its limits—was so strong, widespread, and securely founded on the material necessity of employing Koreans in the war effort that, as the reader will recall (from chapter 1), although the government never went so far as to abolish the Government-General, in November 1942 it dismantled the Colonial Ministry and placed the Government-General directly under the Home Ministry's new Bureau of Administration.

An anonymous but well-informed individual in Kyoto similarly expressed gratitude and joy for the new policy; but using the phrase "conditional exchange" (*kōkan jōken*), which even he thought might be a bit "irregular" (*hen desu ga*), he pressed the government to go even further toward the complete elimination of discrimination. As explained in my introduction, Korean residents in Japan already possessed the rights to vote and hold office in Japanese national elections, but this individual argued that with the inclusion of all Koreans in the national conscription system, those resident in Korea should also be entitled to this privilege. He insisted that barriers to free travel between metropolitan Japan and Korea constituted a "type of discriminatory action" and should also be eliminated. Such views, he argued, were not his alone. "Probably all from the Korean peninsula" shared them.

From a practical standpoint as well, he reasoned that perhaps it would be better to first implement policies that would eliminate differences between the metropolitan Japanese and Koreans, and then commence the draft. He suggested that news reports about Koreans having a highly developed sense of "[Japanese] national consciousness" (*kokumin ishiki*) were products of a campaign promoted by only one segment of Korean intellectuals and that in reality almost none of the Koreans in Japan had such a consciousness. He did not reject the historical movement toward the unity of Koreans and metropolitan Japanese, but instead thought that compulsory education should come first. With it would come an "understanding of the national essence (*kokutai kannen*)" and "national consciousness as children of the Emperor" (pp. 16–17). In short, this individual was not a radical calling for Korean independence but rather a strong assimilationist who wanted the Japanese regime to first realize its claims of equality and to prepare the Korean people adequately as

Japanese nationals before exposing them to conditions under which they would be judged as Japanese. He worried, in other words, that inclusion in some aspects of national life without equality might in fact worsen discrimination.

While the logic of conditional loyalty and the material conditions of total war pushed the regime to make substantive changes in the structure and modality of governing Koreans, its commitment to provide the Korean people with more education presented another, more immediate danger to the successful wartime mobilization of Koreans. I am referring to the old problem of communists, ethnic nationalists, and students prone to these alternative modern ideologies—all of which predated the Asia-Pacific War. As the colonial government implemented new policies of exploitation such as military conscription, it and the police paid heightened attention to these groups and individuals. Thus the Government-General and intelligence agencies such as the Special Higher Police (that is, "thought police") continued and intensified covert surveillance of such persons and suppression of their activities. For example, in a survey of incidents and arrests of Koreans in Japan who broke the Peace Preservation Law, the Security Section of the Police Bureau recorded a case in August 1940 in which four Koreans, described as a "Korean ethnic nationalist group," were taken into custody. They had apparently planned to utilize the army's Korean volunteer system as well as the conscription system to launch an armed revolt. They had hoped to form a movement around the "bond of Korean nationalism" to bring about Korean national independence.[55]

In its assessment of these groups, the Government-General concluded that they remained a danger. In particular, while they had for a time been quieted by Japan's war victories, the recent stalemate had emboldened them. The ethnic nationalists, it claimed, spread unsubstantiated rumors about the empire's defeat and worked with the Allied Powers to throw off the imperial yoke. Their strategies also shifted away from quiet preparatory efforts to the praxis of "simultaneous uprisings, destruction and riots, and fomenting the people." As for the communists, they had retreated from the organizational efforts of the Communist Party and had adopted the strategy of the Popular Front. They therefore sought to direct the frustrations and enmity of the nation's people, who were overburdened by the demands of the wartime state, toward the destruction of the capitalist state. These communists, the Government-General warned, looked forward to the Soviet Union's entry into the war and planned a mass uprising and rioting of the people in conjunction with this opportunity. The communists also had a tendency to form a united front with the ethnic nationalists.[56]

While the governor-general's officials only vaguely mentioned the activities and dangers of students in higher education who were Korean ethnic nationalists, the historian Kang Duk-sang has identified in considerable detail a large number of student soldiers who had been pressured to join the army who refused to enlist, absconded after their enlistment, or in quite a few cases went so far as to plan mutinies and rebellions, or deserted while on the war front in China. Many of the deserters joined forces with the Chinese military or the military arm of the Korean Provisional Government, then located in Chongqing—namely, the Korean Restoration Army. Most famously, Kim Jun-yop (Chun-yŏp), the historian and former president of Korea University, has written a memoir—a best seller in Korea—that covers his deeds as the "first escapee" among student soldiers. After deserting, one of his first tasks in psychological warfare against the Japanese consisted of writing leaflets intended to persuade other Koreans to desert.[57]

Under the legal framework of the National Mobilization Law (1938) and National Conscription Ordinance (1939), which gave the state the authority to conscript civilian laborers, the Government-General forced those students in Korea who refused to volunteer for the army or who volunteered but failed to appear for their conscription exams either to join the army late or to become conscript laborers. In either case, the Government-General forced the unwilling in December 1943 to undergo a period of spiritual training lasting about two weeks at the former training center for Korean volunteer soldiers in Nohae. While they were undergoing training, the instructors made them write essays of self-criticism and reflection. The few who showed the proper contrition and expressed a desire to join the army were given another opportunity to enlist. As for the others, Kang shows that at least in the cases he was able to uncover, after their short training program they were sent to labor under tight surveillance, grueling conditions, and continued efforts to reform their souls. That the authorities gave these refusers another opportunity to prove themselves worthy of inclusion within the Japanese national community, even if it was to be as civilian laborers rather than soldiers, is evidence of the Japanese colonial empire's severe and worsening labor shortage. Yet the Government-General's Education Bureau explained to them that if they failed to prove themselves again, they would become "people shut out from the Nation and from their hometowns."[58] In short, while the authorities invariably presented the various avenues for Koreans to join the military as opportunities for them to become truly Japanese, the price of unwillingness to make the normative choice was expulsion from the national community.

The Ministry of Education ordered the administrators of universities, higher schools, and professional schools in metropolitan Japan to encourage the Korean students who had not volunteered for the army to either take temporary leave from school or withdraw altogether. If the students did not comply, the administrators were supposed to order them to take leave. At the same time, the police swept the country to determine the actual whereabouts of these Korean students. According to police records, they located some 283 of these individuals, persuaded 52 of them to enlist, and arrested the remaining 231. The police sent 98 of them back to Korea while compelling the remaining 133 to labor in Japan after a period of spiritual training. Police continued to search for the remaining 1,100 nonvolunteers, imprisoning some and driving at least one to suicide.[59]

Although a number of small-scale disruptions involving student soldiers took place not long after their recruitment in Yongsan, Taegu, Nanan, Taiwan, and other locations within Japan, the most formidable attempt to carry out a full-scale mutiny and rebellion took place in P'yŏngyang and involved the regiments of the 30th Division (Akiotsu Shidan). Kang reminds us that if the mutiny had succeeded, it would have launched the largest rebellion to emerge out of the military since the famous February 26 Incident of 1936, in which disgruntled young officers attempted to overthrow the government in Tokyo.

According to Kang's well-documented account, the leader of the plan was Pak Sŏng-hwa (J. name, "Uhara Akihiro"),[60] a young man predisposed to his later actions because he had tenaciously resisted efforts to enlist him in the army. After joining, like many other Korean student soldiers he reacted strongly against discriminatory treatment by metropolitan Japanese soldiers. Ethnic tension between the Korean and Japanese soldiers increased and reached a boiling point in June 1944 when Koreans learned that only 11 percent of Korean applicants for officer and noncommissioned officer training had been accepted while the corresponding rate for their Japanese counterparts was 86 percent. Although Pak Sŏng-hwa was among the successful Koreans, he so resented the fate of his fellow Koreans that, in the understated words of military court records, "he came to possess ethnic prejudice" against Japanese. Pak and others launched a plot to abscond with arms and ammunition while blowing up what they could not take with them. At the same time, they sought to encourage the liberation movement in the local area and then escape to Manchuria. From there they planned to join the Korean Independence Army to fight for national independence.

Initially, the conspirators split on ideological grounds between those who took the straightforward line of ethnic self-determination and those who advocated Korean independence from a socialist position. But after reaching a unified stance that they agreed would transcend ideology, they patched together an expansive and deep network of co-conspirators that encompassed not only all six P'yŏngyang units but also supporters from around the local area. The latter included men active in independence activities as well as female students and at least one woman employed as a nurse in the army hospital. A co-conspirator described one of the female students as originally from the Soviet Union. The organization in some ways replicated the Japanese military in that it was supposed to be highly disciplined and hierarchically ordered with all subordinating themselves to its orders. Unfortunately for these men and women, the military police uncovered their plan and arrested more than seventy Korean soldiers in mid-October 1944. About half of them faced military trials. The military court handed the leader Pak a sentence of thirteen years in prison, and gave many others sentences as long as nine years.[61]

IGNORANCE

In the previous section we have seen how various classes educated under Japanese colonialism responded sometimes with affirmation but at other times with hesitation or even resistance to the demand that they submit themselves or other male youths of appropriate age to the national conscription system. In each case, whether the proponents were enthusiastic about the draft, conditionally supportive, or literally violently opposed—regardless of such significant differences in their specific political views, they were all products of the Japanese colonial commitment, already evident before the 1930s, to produce at least a limited number of Koreans as self-reflexive, rational subjects who could be coaxed toward normative choices that would further Japanese colonial and national projects. Yet this long-term inclusionary movement into what other scholars have been calling "colonial modernity" had a limited reach prior to the period of total war. Its limitations were exposed in many ways, but perhaps most glaringly in the fact that when faced with the need to mobilize tens of thousands of Koreans through the draft, the authorities encountered a huge mass of the population that they could not accurately identify and certainly did not know. Thus the conscription system could not simply mobilize Korean males ready to serve as soldiers; instead, as we have seen, they first had to be educated in training centers to become properly "Japanese" in thought, physical abilities, and manners *after* conscription.

Thus another problem, in some ways even greater than that of addressing the contradictions produced by the commitment to educate and inform the relatively elite, was how to incorporate the great masses of the Korean people into the wartime regime of governmentality and reason. These people did not propose alternative plans to realize the modern ideology of nationalism (that is, Korean nationalism versus Japanese nationalism) or other modern ideologies such as communism. Instead, they appeared to the authorities as those who had not yet been made subject to the colonial regime's civilizing project—all those whom the empire of reason regarded as stupid, ignorant, lazy, and backward or out of time. These people—the poor, those without formal education or with alternative educations, "uninformed" youths, the elderly, and especially women of all ages—represented an as yet undomesticated chaotic world of interiorities that seemed incommensurable with the rationality of the modern colonial and national state.

It is for this reason that official discourse advanced the incorporation of the Korean masses into the war effort and the extension of the national conscription system as a project of edification. When Yoshida Toshiguma explained that the Government-General and the Korean League for Total National Manpower (Chōsen Kokumin Sōryoku Renmei) had worked closely with "powerful nongovernmental cultural organizations such as those involving newspapers, magazines, film, theater, etc.," he like many others called this campaign an "enlightenment movement" (*keimō undō*). As an example of the extent to which some organizations and individuals went to enlighten the Korean people about conscription, he cited the efforts of Lieutenant Colonel P'o Hun, a Korean graduate of the Japanese Military Academy, who had inspired the president of the *Maeil sinbo* newspaper company, the only Korean-language paper then in existence, to privately fund a propaganda troupe. This troupe traveled to the most remote regions by automobile and then used picture card shows, open-air talks, and comic performances to explain conscription in easily understood terms.[62]

The teams that began administering the conscription examinations in April 1944 also observed many instances of what they regarded as the people's ignorance. Though official observers such as Yoshida Toshiguma tried to put the potential conscripts in the best light—to show that many presented themselves enthusiastically for examination and rejoiced upon passing—given their civilizing project they could not ignore the many cases of what seemed to them backwardness, absurdity, or even madness. In the first place, with so many young men completely incapable of speaking Japanese, the exams often had to be conducted with the assistance of interpreters and while "gesturing with hands and feet, thus presenting a curious sight." But the encounter between examiners who often did not have sufficient knowledge of Koreans and Koreans who often had no knowledge about conscription presented many more "comical stories and freakish scenes" (*chindan kikei*).

For example, one conscript grabbed a knife off the desk of an examiner and was detained by the military police. It turned out that the youth had no intention of harming the examiner but had wanted to cut off his own finger to make a blood oath as a show of his patriotism. He said that as a man, he had felt ashamed that having contracted syphilis he would not pass the physical. As Yoshida put it, "Everyone was left speechless" (*ichidō aẓen tari*). In another case a young man who had been conscripted as a laborer and who was then working in the metropole sent his younger brother to take his exam in his stead. Yoshida was appalled not only by the person's "ignorance" (*muchi*) but also by the abysmal state of knowledge of the local official, who accepted the substitute in order to arrive at the proper head count. Yoshida also recounted the exploits of an extraordinary young man who seemed to live in an almost completely different temporality. When the examiners showed him the simple *hiragana* and *katakana* letters of the Japanese phonetic alphabet, all he could do was ignorantly shake his head. But when directed to write his place of residence and name, he did so in beautiful Chinese characters. As it turned out, this young man had been educated in one of the traditional *sŏdang* schools and had some exposure to Confucian learning. Although calligraphy in kanji was one of his strengths, he knew nothing of Japanese letters. Another small minority—perhaps 1 percent, in Yoshida's estimation—attempted to abscond, injure themselves, or feign illness in order to evade the draft. These, Yoshida concluded, were individuals who manifested the Korean ethnic tendency to place family above all else and who worried about the fate of their family members if they were forced to leave for the military, or who simply had anxieties and fears about military life (for example, believing that enrollment meant certain death).[63]

Those appointed to train and observe conscripts also saw "ignorance" and belated development in these young men. When two professors from Keijō Imperial University (Yano and Wada) came to observe those regarded as the most poorly qualified for military service in the Military Service Preparatory Training Centers (Gunmu Yobi Kunrensho), they determined that the Japanese-language competence of these individuals was that of metropolitan Japanese three-year-olds, while their intelligence equaled that of seven- or eight-year-olds. This finding was particularly striking since, the reader will recall, those in training at the Military Service Preparatory Training Centers had already received prior training in the Youth Special Training Centers and had been designated "class A," or fit for immediate active service. The purpose of the professors' study was to help them put together the training manual for conscripts analyzed in chapter 1.[64]

From the authorities' point of view, when Koreans did not understand why they should participate in the conscription system or when they absconded in large numbers (as in the first months after they began to join the ranks of Japanese soldiers in

September 1944), they did so out of ignorance or stupidity. Overall, like Yoshida, the Government-General found in its summaries of popular Korean reactions to the conscription system that most youths greeted it positively. It claimed that most of their fears disappeared after entering the barracks and that they blended in well with the metropolitan Japanese and performed their duties at a high level. In fact, because of their generally superior physiques, some even outperformed their metropolitan Japanese counterparts in drills. However, "among the elderly class, women and the lower class, and the ignorant or uninformed classes," a number believed that conscription meant certain death. They therefore tried to hide the whereabouts of youths subject to the draft or change the ages recorded for them in their family registers. Some youths even abandoned the idea of marrying, since they believed that they would surely die.[65]

When the Government-General admitted that a segment of the conscripts "remained bound by individualistic thinking and exhibited prejudiced grumbling" and that a small minority even absconded, it attributed these failings to the still unenlightened characteristics of a significant segment of the Korean people and the need to improve pre-induction education and training. The Government-General generally identified the deserters as being "mostly from the lower, uneducated class," who fell into three broad types: (1) "those with little sense of obligation who perform their duties as if they were working as day laborers," (2) "those who had become accustomed to a dissolute lifestyle and felt tormented by strict military discipline," and (3) "those who are ignorant and who with insufficient knowledge of the [Japanese] national language are unable to communicate what is on their minds and who have difficulties with following their course lessons." Nowhere did the Government-General identify Korean ethnic nationalism among the people or a commitment to a clearly formed communist, socialist, or anarchist ideology as motivation for their resistance. Instead, it stressed the absence of qualities necessary to perform as Japanese national subjects and even pointed out that many of the deserters had actually taken flight in "desultory fashion" (manzen dassō), without a clear purpose other than to relieve their longing for their hometowns.[66]

The authorities identified no greater obstacle to their project of enlightening and civilizing the people than what they regarded as the uninformed, stubborn, and even crazed actions of women, especially of mothers and wives of potential volunteers and conscripts. As the Government-General observed: "[I]n particular, there are some within the uneducated class, especially among women and children, who still believe that conscription leads inevitably to death, and they cannot bear to part. Embracing at the train stations, they lament, wail, or make an enormous racket, as if mad. These unseemly sights have the opposite effect of bursting the bubble of enthusiasm of these young men entering the military."[67] Although they often conflated categories of class, gender, and age by lumping women together with the elderly, who they claimed were mired in old ways of thinking, or men of the "lower" and "uneducated" classes, who were simply ignorant and unenlightened, they made women a special target of observation, condemnation, and reform. Here the authorities encountered not just another way of reasoning but a formidable mode of counter-conduct that we have already explored in the Japanese American internment camps.

Today, having some knowledge about the Japanese colonial regime's brutality against Korean women, we might imagine that it was always the colonized, and particularly colonized women, who feared their colonial masters. Accounts of Japanese men involved in the wartime mobilization of Korean women to serve as sexual slaves for Japan's military give the impression of the regime's unshaken confidence in its ability to control women and sex in the colony. For example, in his 1983 book Yoshida Seiji, a self-professed "war criminal," graphically described his involvement in what he called "slave hunting" (*dorei gari*) between 1942 and 1945. Operating under military orders and in an official capacity, he recalled that he had been so proficient in the task of forcibly recruiting "comfort women" that he had taken pride in being called the "conscription demon." Confessing that he had been driven by what he called an "inhuman patriotism," he testified to having personally participated in the capture of nearly 1,000 "comfort women" and that this often involved looking down into Korean homes from hilltops, rushing unannounced into homes with young women, and then literally stealing them away.[68]

To be sure, the colonial regime's near monopoly over the use of violence as well as the effects of its incessant threats of violence—resulting in what Tomiyama Ichirō calls "presentiments of violence" by the colonized[69]—should not be minimized. Yet the colonial records also reveal a regime not fully sure of itself, always mindful of the precariousness of its control over the people and indeed fearful that the macro-political system of domination might unravel from the bottom up, in terms of both class and gender, as well as from the intimate spaces of families.

The military authorities and the colonial government were extremely attentive to the gender gap in support of their efforts to mobilize Koreans as soldiers, even within families that produced volunteer soldiers. Thus a survey of the social backgrounds of the 1,709 Korean volunteers who entered the military training center in Nohae in the second half of 1942 used gendered tabulations to determine who—among the volunteers' friends and relatives whose views could be ascertained—

opposed or supported their enlistment. In almost every kinship category women overwhelmingly opposed their relatives' enlistment, while men even more strongly backed them. Thus, while 585 fathers sided with their sons and only 52 disapproved, the figures for mothers were 261 and 354, respectively. Wives disapproved 78 to 37, while only 4 brothers dissented compared to 533 who approved. The only male exceptions were grandfathers, the majority of whom joined grandmothers in opposition, and sisters, the majority of whom approved of their brothers' actions, although not as predictably as did male siblings.[70] A young volunteer soldier participating in a forum for the journal published by the Ryokki Renmei (Green Flag League)—a nongovernmental organization established to promote the Government-General's policies—described the problem in extremely blunt terms: "I feel that women are at fault. Whether it's the grandmother, mother, sister or wife—they are the ones who most strongly oppose [volunteering for the army]."[71]

Authorities reporting on Korean reactions to the volunteer program for Korean army recruits and then the announcement of the draft were often struck by what they considered the bizarre or ignorant behavior and attitudes of women. Reports of mothers wailing in front of army camps or setting themselves down outside of barracks for days on end in order to lovingly observe their newly recruited sons—such acts exacerbated general fears of the regime's inability to control the population. Yoshida Toshiguma saw firsthand that huge throngs of relatives accompanied recent conscripts to the barracks and that they continued to visit the conscripts even after induction. "In particular," he observed, "there was a considerable number of the likes of mothers who every day sat themselves down where they could command a view over the open spaces between the barracks and where they worried all day long over the circumstances of their beloved children. And the military units had an unimaginably difficult time dealing in any kind of orderly way with these visitors." Furthermore, he blamed the unsupportive behavior of women on their general ignorance. As he explained: "At that time [when Koreans were being conscripted], only a little more than roughly 1 percent of the stratum of Korean women, especially the mothers and sisters of young men of conscript age, had attended school. Under these conditions the majority were still insensitive to the trends of the times. Many remained shut up in the shell of past conventions, completely infatuated with blind love for their children; while very few were passionate about motherly love in service to the Nation (*kokkateki boseiai*)."[72]

The Ministry of Justice's Criminal Affairs Bureau likewise castigated Korean women for what it described as their stupidity concerning military service.[73] It found that "the superstitious fear of soldiering, in which it is believed that becoming a soldier inevitably leads to death, is an idea that is widely circulated in farming and fishing villages; and it is said that women in particular are absolutely persuaded of this" (p. 18). A Korean informant, then a student in Kyoto, offered that "in the thought of Korean women (*hantō fujin*) evasion of military service is a deeply rooted concept. They obstinately adhere to the idea that becoming a soldier means death" (pp. 19–20). Elsewhere, these agents charged that a considerable number of those in the "lower classes, the elderly, and legitimate mothers"[74] were prone to encourage evasion because they either "despised or feared soldiering" (*senpei kyōheiteki*; p. 22). Although she may have exaggerated, an informant described as a woman of the educated class (*yūshikisha fujin*) in Keijō (Seoul) claimed that "all the mothers of volunteer soldiers had been opposed [to their sons' decisions]"; and that since every Korean youth would from then on be subject to conscription, "the sizable resistance of ignorant women (*muchi na fujin*) would be something to be reckoned with (*sōtō ōkii*)." She warned of the danger of "motherly love"—that when the details of the new system became public it would most likely lead mothers to utilize whatever means they could to help their sons evade the draft. She concluded, "In any case, it is a fact that right now the state of mind of these women is one of apprehension and irritation toward the [conscription] system" (p. 22).

In short, the authorities concluded that ignorance or superstition, as well as protective and misguided "motherly love," presented enormous threats to the ability of the colonial empire to mobilize its subjects for the war effort. Therefore, from the inception of the voluntary system in 1938 through the end of the war, propaganda efforts to mobilize soldiers were directed almost as much toward women as they were toward men. The special committee within the Korean Army Headquarters charged with deliberating on implementation of the draft in Korea in fact advised that while efforts should be made to inform the Korean population about conscription, they "must place special weight on the edification of women, especially mothers."[75] In a December 1943 forum to discuss extension of the conscription system to Koreans, a representative of the Welfare Ministry stressed that it intended to make special efforts among Koreans residing in Japan to "deepen the understanding of parents, especially women, concerning the military conscription system." Similarly Sekiya Teizaburō, then director of the Kyōwakai (a governmental organization that had been established to regulate the activities of Korean residents in Japan) and a man with long experience in colonial administration, insisted on the importance of deepening the understanding of the draft held by the mothers and in fact the entire families of young men.[76]

Newspaper reports offered models of Japanese womanhood for Koreans. To give just one of many possible examples, Yi In-sŏk was the first Korean Japanese volunteer soldier to die in battle, and as such he became one of the most celebrated of Korea's Japanese war heroes. Interestingly enough, however, at the time that he volunteered the *Keijō nippō* utilized his story of loyalty and bravery to praise his mother. Reproducing the young man's written statement on his resolve to volunteer, the article quoted Yi's mother as having said, "There is a multitude of women who as mothers want to keep their children near them, but I do not want to obstruct your future." Emphasizing that Yi In-sŏk would not be the man he was without such a model of motherhood, the article lauded her for telling him to serve the nation and not worry about his family.[77]

. . .

In this chapter I have resumed the work of chapter 1 to show that the drive to incorporate the Korean people into Japan's imperialist war unleashed a massive machinery of institutions and agents that sought to make all the people visible to power, and then worked to turn them into usable Japanese subjects. This was a regime that proclaimed itself a force of reason, history, morality, and even freedom; thus, although it did not forsake sheer force and brutality—for example, confining and punishing the unwilling (or, as would have been said in the U.S. context, "separating the sheep from the goats")—it favored the use of positive means (albeit supplemented by force) to produce what it regarded as rational, informed, and self-disciplining national subjects. Disavowing racist discrimination, providing increased opportunities for education and training, allowing some Koreans to advance socially and economically within and outside the military, "enlightening" the masses—these were part of the regime of polite racism that, propelled by a "civilizing mission," sought to include all but the most recalcitrant and unwilling in the regime of governmentality. In fact, it gave hesitant subjects such as the student soldiers who refused to volunteer multiple opportunities to prove themselves.

The late colonial conditions that enveloped the Korean people, and that some of the colonized participated in producing, created a complex and contradictory situation in which individuals made choices based on their understandings of how best to advance their lives from their respective social positions. For many of the uppermost elite who prospered under Japanese colonialism, cooperation and conditional Japanese patriotism, even at the expense of the suffering of the great masses of the Korean people, were logical choices for living and thriving through total war. They regarded the colonial and national authorities' proclamations of equality as openings from which to push the authorities to actualize their claims of equality rather than as lies whose deceitfulness inspired support for national independence. In contrast, those who had been economically, socially, and politically marginalized for most of the colonial period, including women of various classes, were not predisposed to sacrifice themselves or their male family members. Certainly, it could be argued that reluctant volunteers, conscripts, and their supporters displayed good common sense rather than ignorance when they spread rumors that conscription meant death and when they refused to die for a regime that until then had provided them with few tangible benefits to their material well-being.

But for Koreans in between these extremes, the choices were not so clear and can seem so only in hindsight. Those youths educated after the 1 March 1919 independence movement, including those pressured to become student soldiers, might see the only practical avenue into the future either as the one that appeared to lead toward full inclusion into an expanded concept of Japan or as the one that turned toward the alternative modern ideologies of Korean ethnic nationalism or communism. Others, however—certainly the majority of the Korean people—reflected the incompleteness of colonial governmentality prior to the period of total war and were products of the Japanese regime's and of alternative modern ideologies' imperfect interpellations of them as political subjects. The "desultory desertion" that the Government-General noted as a minor phenomenon is surely indicative of a far more widespread uncertainty about the future among the great masses of the Korean people.

Although the Korean people situated themselves in relation to Japanese rule in these various ways, I have been able to suggest only a few patterns related to economic and social positions that in themselves still cannot adequately represent the myriad experiences of the people. Yet in concluding this chapter I am again compelled to insist that the Japanese military, despite its use of force both to mobilize the willing and to exclude the dangerous, was at least as consistent and in some ways perhaps even more consistent than the U.S. military in rejecting racial discrimination in principle. This is not to deny that most Japanese soldiers probably harbored prejudices against Koreans and that there were many instances of discrimination against the Korean soldiers, just as most white Americans surely continued to discriminate against "Negroes," "Mexicans," and "Japanese Americans" inside and outside of the military. But it is to recognize that like the U.S. regime, the Japanese system of rule was shifting decisively toward the condemnation of ethnic discrimination and that its leaders made this the official policy.

The case of discrimination that set off the P'yŏngyang student soldier uprising does not contradict this argument. Even in this instance the Japanese military did not peremptorily exclude Koreans from consideration for officer and noncommissioned officer training. Instead, it followed the merit-based principle that Korean soldiers should have the same opportunity as metropolitan Japanese soldiers to take the identical exam. The command then informed the soldiers that some had passed but others had failed. As it turned out, of course, it appears that prejudiced evaluation of the tests resulted in the recommendation of a disproportionate number of metropolitan Japanese as compared to Korean soldiers. Yet this was a problem of laxity or abuse in following the system of meritocracy, and is typical in regimes that claim not to practice racism; under exclusionary racism, in contrast, racial or ethnic difference is reason alone for precluding minorities or colonial subjects from even sitting for the exams. In short, equal opportunity to take the merit-based exam coupled with a low recommendation rate is the product of an inclusionary, polite racism, not of an exclusionary racism.

Moreover, despite the valuable information Kang provides in his book, he does not mention that while a large number of Koreans were put on trial and sentenced to years of imprisonment, the commander of the Thirtieth Division was also made responsible for the disorder and dismissed.[78] Furthermore, Kang reveals that more than a few Korean soldiers in the Thirtieth Division continued to act as if they believed in service to the Japanese military despite charges of discrimination. Most tragically, it was none other than a Korean officer in the auxiliary military police who uncovered and reported on the plot of the P'yŏngyang conspirators. Similarly, a Korean took the lead in an undercover operation of the military police in Himeji which disrupted a scheme by a group of student soldiers from Posŏng College that apparently would have included the assassination of the governor-general. And as the accused in the P'yŏngyang incident stood trial, Colonel Kim Sŏk-wŏn sat in the courtroom and observed them. He was a Korean graduate of the Japanese Military Academy who early in his career had served with Major General Yamashita Tomoyuki, the infamous "Tiger of Malaya." He had also occupied many positions of high military responsibility, including heading a special Korean detachment of the Japanese Imperial Army that was charged with suppressing Kim Il-sŏng, the guerrilla fighter and future head of North Korea. The colonel had a direct stake in the fate of the P'yongyang rebels, for he had taken an active role in recruiting soldiers from Korea.[79]

The complex and sometimes even subtle character of discrimination in the Japanese military was brought home to me in a particularly poignant way during an interview that I conducted with a former conscript soldier and his wife, whom I will call Mr. Chang and Mrs. Yun.[80] When I met this couple in April 2003, I was humbled by their hospitality and willingness to talk to me about a past that could not have been pleasant to recall and that appeared not to have provided them with many material comforts. The war and its aftermath, I learned, had led to a turbulent life for them. Mr. Chang had been drafted into the Japanese army and served in Japan. After his postliberation return to the northern part of Korea, unsettled conditions there forced him to migrate to Seoul for work. And then in the late 1970s the couple moved to the Pacific Northwest of the United States. There Mr. Chang worked in housekeeping in a hospital and Mrs. Yun took in sewing while they raised their children, who are a great source of pride and joy to them. Mr. Chang and Mrs. Yun repeatedly told me that they harbored no animosity toward the Japanese people or the Japanese emperor.

Mr. Chang recounted that he had been drafted in 1944 and was among the first Korean conscript soldiers. After preparatory training, he enrolled in a unit in P'yŏngyang, and then transferred out to Japan via Pusan, traveling through Shimonoseki, Hokkaido, Tokyo, Osaka, and finally Sakurajima in Kyūshū. As he explained, he was able to survive the war because by the time he arrived in Sakurajima the soldiers stationed there were no longer being shipped out.

I was particularly concerned to know about the circumstances of his conscription and treatment within the military. Had he resisted? How did his parents react? What about discrimination against Koreans? Mr. Chang responded that resisting was an impossibility. Even though it might seem natural for parents to shield their children from the draft, they resigned themselves to it because, after all, the police backed up the system. When I mentioned the planned uprising of the student soldiers in P'yŏngyang where he himself had been first enrolled, he remarked that he had never heard of the incident and that conscript soldiers who did not want to serve deserted rather than planned rebellions. With regard to discrimination, to my surprise he stated and then repeated on several occasions during the interview that discrimination did not exist within the military. Why, I asked? "They couldn't because we were soldiers, right? We all had guns, right?" And then he said, laughing, "So you know what would happen if they crossed us?" My question of discrimination caught Mrs. Yun's attention and she joined in, remarking that in her experience most Japanese discriminated against Koreans and said that they smelled of garlic and were dirty. She felt many good people among the Japanese did not discriminate, but that the ones who did, did so in an extreme way.

Near the end of my interview Mr. Chang pulled us back to the topic of discrimination. When I had pressed him a second time about any discriminatory incidents or attitudes, he could recall only one. Although he had ordered a very popular book from the commissary, when it arrived the clerk passed him over and sold it to a Japanese soldier. But Mr. Chang wanted to clarify. "In the military everyone was considered equal, so there was no reason to discriminate." He confessed that he did not know about politics, but within the military "Japan did well" (*umaku yatta*). He dismissed the case of the prejudiced commissary clerk as merely an "individual's actions" (*honnin no*) and not a military "policy" (*seisaku*).

I was also curious to know if either Mr. Chang or Mrs. Yun had seen or read any of the numerous films and literary pieces that had been produced during the war about Koreans serving heroically in the Japanese military. While they did not recognize the titles of the literary works that I named, their faces lit up when I mentioned several films. Yes, yes, they remembered the film *Wakaki sugata* (*Figure of Youth*), by the Japanese director Toyoda Shirō. When I asked if they had seen *Bōrō no kesshitai* (*Suicide Squad at the Watchtower*) by the Japanese film director Imai Tadashi and his Korean assistant director Ch'oe In-kyu, they became quite excited and seemed even nostalgic. He exclaimed, "That was a fine movie, wasn't it!" (*yoku dekita deshō*); and she repeated, "Yes, that was a fine movie." "Wasn't the actress Tanaka Kinuyo?" Mrs. Yun asked. Actually, it was Hara Setsuko, I replied. "Oh right, Hara Setsuko." Mrs. Yun explained that in those days no one thought liberation was possible, "So that's why we probably thought they [the films] were good." Lots of people saw those films, she offered.

When I told them that I had recently seen *Suicide Squad at the Watchtower*, they seemed amazed. I could imagine that they wondered how I, a Japanese American at least one generation removed from them and not yet born at the time of the war, might have come to see a film that they had viewed some sixty years earlier, and that they recalled with some nostalgia. Mrs. Yun exclaimed, "Oh my, *Suicide Squad at the Watchtower*, I'd really like to see it." Although I did not have the entire film with me, I happened to have some clips from it in my briefcase, so I naively asked them if they'd like to view them. Of course, they said, and so I placed the tape into the player and we watched three minutes of clips together. When it started Mr. Chang recognized one of the Korean stars, Ch'ŏn T'aek-i. Mrs. Yun again said that she felt great nostalgia. But as we watched we all seemed to feel odd and uncomfortable about watching clips from an old wartime film about Koreans fighting heroically for the Japanese empire, while sitting in the living room of a modest house in the Pacific Northwest—especially when one of our number was a Korean veteran of the Japanese Imperial Army. Even as the clips were still running Mrs. Yun asked me if I believed in God, to which I replied that I was raised Buddhist. She went on to talk about the evils of war, including America's war in Iraq. I did not feel entitled to ask them any more about the film, but the experience confirmed for me the powerful impact that cultural productions such as film must have had in the period of late colonialism. In the next two chapters, I turn to an analysis of films and literature that had as their primary theme Korean soldiering in the Japanese military.

CHAPTER SEVEN

Nation, Blood, and
Self-Determination

> Therefore, within the Japanese nation there should be
> no ethnic discrimination. Revering the Imperial House-
> hold as the main family, Japanese subjects who devote
> themselves to the great principle with the Emperor at
> its center—they all gradually become integrated so as
> to form a totally blended Japanese ethnos. . . .
>
> Moreover, the cultural policy of unifying metropoli-
> tan Japan and Korea is not limited to simply transform-
> ing Peninsular cultural life along the lines of metropoli-
> tan Japan. If in old Korean culture there is something
> clearly elegant and refined, this should be nurtured and
> aided within the Japanese cultural sphere. To supple-
> ment the delicate and subtle insular culture with the
> composed atmosphere of the continent—such is to
> retain elements that can add to the vigorous breadth
> and robust resilience of the new Japanese culture. . . .
> Because Japanese culture is moving gradually west-
> ward, penetrating into Manchuria, spreading through-
> out China, becoming the keynote of cultural life for all
> Orientals—because of this it must be said that what is
> especially called for today is a universalism and a persist-
> ence that will take root and flower in every corner of the
> continent.
>
> Defense Guidance Division, Korean Federation of
> National Total War, *The Doctrine of the Unity of
> Metropolitan Japan and Korea, and Outline of Policies
> for Its Realization* (June 1941)

The concerted disavowal of racism in the Japanese colonial empire during the late
war years operated through media other than the documents and directives produced
by the civil and military branches of the state. Newspapers, magazines, cinema, ra-

dio, literature, music, and other media also circulated stories about Japan's empire of equality throughout not only Korea but also the metropole and other places within the Japanese imperium. Already in the late 1930s, the Japanese media in the metropole—paralleling liberal efforts among the Allies to discontinue use of blatantly racist terms such as "nigger" and "Jap"[1]—conspicuously began to avoid the virulently discriminatory label *Senjin*, as well as *Futei Senjin* (or "unruly Senjin") to refer to Koreans. In place of these terms, which had been widely and unabashedly employed previously, the media substituted conciliatory labels such as "Peninsular compatriots" (*Hantō dōhō*), and "Peninsulars" (*Hantōjin* or *Hantō shusshin*).[2] The derogatory labels did not disappear, but it is telling that in Kansai, and probably elsewhere as well, by the late 1930s major newspapers including the *Ōsaka mainichi* and *Ōsaka asahi* went on record to advocate the "complete elimination of discriminatory treatment of metropolitan Japanese and Koreans in newspapers and magazines."[3]

Furthermore, many of these media representations focused on the figure of the Korean soldier, since it was said that he truly embodied the reality of the unity of the peninsula and the metropole. Little girls and boys, adult men and women, young and old, rich and poor—from the late 1930s to the end of the war, Koreans of every class, region, gender, and age were bombarded with textual, aural, and visual propaganda celebrating Korean soldiers and encouraging family members and communities to support them. For example, a 1944 publication intended for Korean schoolchildren, *Shōkokumin no tame no heitaisan monogatari* (*A Soldier's Story for the Nation's Little Subjects*), even introduced military life to its "little" male readers. It encouraged them to become Japanese by complete assimilation to a Japanese way of life, to support their older brothers who had already become soldiers, and to grow up to be Japanese soldiers themselves. Yi In-sŏk, the first Korean to die under the special volunteer soldier system, became a Japanese national hero from the colony, supposedly demonstrating that Koreans were in fact Japanese and that it was an honor to die for the emperor, nation, and empire.[4]

The Korean-language media obviously targeted such propaganda at the Korean people themselves, relentlessly publishing articles and columns in the vernacular, describing why Koreans ought to be thankful for the opportunity to serve in the military, insisting that many Koreans were anxious to serve, and showing the many ways in which Korean individuals and groups celebrated this concrete manifestation of the nation's principle of equality. For example, the Government-General's news organ the *Maeil sinbo* (which would become the only Korean-language newspaper in Korea after 1940) reported on individuals who were "inspired and moved (*kamgyŏk*)" as Koreans by the elimination of discrimination between metropolitan Japanese and

Koreans" (16 January 1938), and linked the demonstration of equality in the military to promulgation of the revised Educational Ordinance, which would come into force later in the year and expand educational opportunities for Koreans (18 January 1943).[5] It described the "great gratitude and emotion" throughout the country that had been inspired by this demonstration of "the unity of metropolitan Japan and Korea" (18 January 1943), as well as the "joy" (*hwanhŭi*) of Koreans in Manchuria who began volunteering and planning a "celebratory commemorative event" in anticipation of the official promulgation of the ordinance that would enable Koreans to serve in the army (19 January 1938). Similarly, it reported on commencement of the army volunteer system as a long-awaited opportunity and emphasized that more than 500 Korean men resident in Korea, metropolitan Japan, and even Manchuria had tried to sign up even before the ordinance's official promulgation (25 January 1938).

Following the 8 May 1942 cabinet decision to begin conscripting Koreans, the newspaper noted the immense gratitude of the Korean people, describing military service as "the highest honor" (10 May 1942) or the "highest privilege of imperial subjects" (12 May 1942). It reported that the number of army volunteers in that year had exceeded 250,000 (10 May 1942), a figure that as we have already seen was not an exaggeration, while the extension of the draft had elicited a "stream of letters of thanks to Governor-General Minami and Commander Itagaki . . . from Koreans on the Continent and in the Home Islands" (19 May 1942) as well as "blood oaths of Korean youths who were grateful for the honor of conscription" (16 May 1942). It described religious groups—including Buddhists (15 May 1942), Christians (12 May 1942), and even the Ch'ŏndogyo (Heavenly Way Religion; 21 May 1942), which had been so active in the 1 March 1919 anticolonial movement—sponsoring special activities of gratitude.

In the days before and after the effective date of changes to the Military Service Law made it possible to draft Koreans, the newspaper described Korean inclusion in the national conscription system as the "most inspirational moment of the century" (*segi ŭi kamgyŏk kojo*) (1 August 1943). Similarly, it noted that people throughout the peninsula were sponsoring events to commemorate the "stirring moment that occurs but once in a century" (*segijŏk kamgyŏk*) (2 August 1944), and it printed testimonials from Koreans declaring their "gratitude" and "resolve" (3 August 1944). The newspaper also printed the music and lyrics for two songs celebrating the inclusion of Koreans in the conscription system: "We Are Soldiers of the Empire" ("Uri nŭn cheguk kunin") and "Mother's Prayers" ("Ŏmŏni ŭi kiwŏn") (4 August 1943). And it glorified the masculinity and physicality of young recruits, a point that will be developed more fully in the following chapter, by showing the flesh of physically fit young men lining up to have their bodies inspected as "human bullets for victory" (*sŭngni ŭi yukt'an chŏnyŏl*) (16 April 1944). In short, Korean-language media increasingly portrayed the Korean soldier as less a colonial soldier than an ethnic national soldier who embodied the Japanese nation's transcendence of difference.

Yet such representations of Koreans, Korean soldiering, and the Japanese empire's rejection of ethnic discrimination were not directed only at the Korean people. Instead, they pervaded the entire Japanese-language media and targeted all the people of the colonial empire, including the metropolitan Japanese. For example, following the May 1942 Japanese cabinet resolution that announced extension of military conscription to Koreans, an article in the *Tokyo asahi* emphasized their great desire to participate in the draft and to become, in a commonly invoked phrase, "now indeed, truly Japanese" (*ima koso shin ni Nipponjin*).[6] They were being given the opportunity, it said, to realize their intense patriotism and to participate in the lofty goal of establishing the Greater East Asia Co-Prosperity Sphere. In this article and elsewhere, the media reprinted letters from Koreans thanking the government for allowing them to participate as equals in the Japanese war effort. The *Tokyo asahi*'s lead article announcing the decision offered that conscription "was a response to the exuberant popular will [of the Korean people]."[7] Another article in the same edition described the growing "unity of Korea and the homeland" as like a "fireball" (*naisen ichinyo, hi no tama ni*) burning with patriotism. The sincere feelings of what it called "love for the ancestral country" (*sokokuai*) were said to be "bubbling forth from every place throughout the length and breadth of the Peninsula" (*hantō tsutsu uraura ni wakiagari*). The writer then pointed to the enormous number of Koreans who had volunteered for service since the special voluntary system had been initiated in 1938 as further evidence of just how "ardent is the loyalty of our Peninsular compatriots and how enthusiastic is their participation in the war to build the Greater East Asia Co-Prosperity Sphere."

Public ceremonies featuring Koreans as model Japanese soldiers also took place, not only in Korea but also in major Japanese cities, most importantly Tokyo and Osaka. On 1 August 1943, the day that the new conscription law went into effect, mass rallies were held in Seoul (Keijō), Tokyo, and Osaka. In Tokyo more than 10,000 young men, both Koreans and metropolitan Japanese, gathered at Yasukuni Shrine and then paraded through the city before ending their celebration on the plaza fronting the Imperial Palace.[8] This integrated parade was said to be a living representation of the reality of Korean and Japanese unity. Similarly, in August 1944 the government sponsored a mass rally at Tokyo's Hibiya Park in order to celebrate the commencement of Korean conscripts' induction into the Japanese military. Minami Jirō, a former governor-general of Korea, gave a speech, and the Korean inductees received Rising Sun Flags and amulets from Meiji Shrine and then paraded around the capital.[9]

This chapter and the one that follows focus mainly on two media forms that most dramatically and compellingly articulated the dominant discourse on Korean soldiers or Korean male youth volunteering to become soldiers—namely, literature and film. My primary purpose is to analyze the ways in which they utilized soldiering both to diagram ideal forms of Japanese national subjectivity for Koreans and to narrativize normative personal, social, and other relationships. In this chapter I pay special attention to the recurring themes of blood, adoption, and self-determination to make the argument that these cultural productions helped blur the boundaries between Koreans and metropolitan Japanese, as well as between colony and nation, sometimes emphasizing common ethnic origins but in other cases transcending the symbolism of blood altogether. Moreover, as in the case of Japanese Americans choosing to become American or as is seen within the doctrine of modern nationalism more generally, they consistently represented the formation of the national subject as ultimately an act of choice or self-determination. The next chapter builds on this one while focusing on the mutually constitutive character of discourses on gender, romance, and family, on the one hand, and nation and colony on the other.

TOTAL WAR AT THE MOVIES

According to a July 1943 special issue of the popular motion picture magazine *Eiga junpō* focusing on Korean film, in 1941 Korean movie theaters had sold over 25 million tickets for admission, an impressive figure considering that the entire population of the colony at that time was about 24 million. While still relatively small in comparison to the number of individual movie viewings in the metropole, where there had been more than 440 million paid admissions in 1940, this represented a huge leap from the approximately 3.6 million tickets that had been sold in 1927. By 1943 Korea's moviegoers—about 20–30 percent of whom were Japanese and the re - mainder Korean—could view films at some 165 movie theaters spread across the thirteen provinces; and for those in places too remote to have nearby theaters, the movies came to them by way of the thirteen provincial mobile movie projection units that the Chōsen Eiga Haikyūsha (Korea Motion Picture Distribution Company) had established beginning in December 1942.[10]

Officials in the colonial government as well as their Japanese and Korean advisers often argued that film offered a powerful medium to further the "national mission" (*kokkateki shimei*) in Korea. It could provide "information, enlightenment, and edification" (*hōdō ni, keihatsu ni, kyōka ni*) and advance the constitution of the Korean people as imperial subjects. An official who headed the section within the Government-General that was most responsible for the administration of colonial film policy maintained that precisely because there were few institutions in Korea dedicated to entertainment, the importance of the movies there far surpassed their significance in the metropole. The scene of women in remote areas walking across great distances with children on their backs just to see the movies, and in winter enduring cold viewing rooms before walking back to their distant home villages— such thoughts made him reflect that nothing could compare to the movies as a medium of national importance. Cinema seemed to have a magic that could appeal to everyone and even transcend barriers of language and cultural understanding.[11] Commentators remarked that film appealed to a broad social spectrum, especially in contrast to other art forms, and for that reason alone was having a tremendous impact.[12]

In recognition of the need to effectively manage this powerful medium, the colonial government took strong measures in the 1940s to centralize its control over Korean film production and the circulation of films in the colony. The Korean Motion Picture Ordinance (Chōsen Eiga Rei)—which the governor-general promulgated in January 1940 and which went into effect in August of that year—was closely modeled after the metropole's 1939 Motion Picture Law and vastly increased the regulatory powers of the colonial government over film. This led in 1942 to the amalgamation of all ten independent movie companies in Korea into the Chōsen Eiga Kabushiki Kaisha (Korea Motion Picture Production Corporation), a process that was completed by September, as well as the establishment in April of the Korea Film Distribution Company. The latter assumed responsibility for all film distribution in Korea. Needless to say, this newly streamlined system for film production (including censorship) and distribution heightened the colonial government's ability to directly control practically all film-related activities in Korea.[13]

The important film critic Yi Yŏng-il once noted that the year 1942 marked the end of authentic *Korean* filmmaking under Japanese rule. As he put it: "I say this because it is a fact that at this moment the breath of life of Korean cinema in its proper sense was extinguished."[14] At the same time, in postwar Japan these films have for the most part been forgotten, hidden, destroyed, or simply dismissed as products of an era of misguided "war collaboration" (*sensō kyōryoku eiga*). Yet a serious postnationalist analysis of them can tell us a great deal about the complex and changing character of late colonial discourses and practices that may confound some commonly held assumptions about this era and the colonial situation. Late colonial motion pictures were certainly not as simple and predictable as might be expected. In the first place, while these dramatic films (*geki eiga*) were surely propagandistic, the filmmakers also sought to make their works entertaining, and they drew liberally from Hollywood for inspiration even after the colonial government prohibited all distribution of American and British films on the day of the Japanese attack on Pearl Harbor.

But even more importantly, although the Japanese and Korean filmmakers produced their films under tremendous state scrutiny, they negotiated between their various concerns and the changing needs of the expansive and multiethnic Japanese empire. In particular, though one of the intentions of these films was to provide dramatic models for turning "Koreans" into "Japanese," some of them, including the two that I will analyze at some length below, pointed in a direction that equated becoming Japanese not with a narrow ethnic particularism but with a kind of humanist and universalist nationalism that disavowed the symbolism of racial or ethnic blood. As was noted in the 1942 *Eiga nenkan* (the semiofficial yearbook for Japanese cinema), Korean film was moving beyond Korea itself. While these movies obviously had the purpose of edifying all Koreans, even those in the most remote areas, on such matters as the national (Japanese) language, lifestyle, and the obligations of being Japanese (most importantly, military duty), it emphasized that Korean cinema's future lay in transcending narrow depictions of Korean "local color." Noting that "it would be an enormous error to make Korean films too Korean (*Chōsenteki sugiru*)," the yearbook stressed that "if it is true that the future of Japanese film must be shared within the Greater East Asia Co-Prosperity Sphere, then of course Korean movies must also be a wing of Japanese movies that has the responsibility of carrying out the great mission of the Co-Prosperity Sphere." Therefore, the writers for *Eiga nenkan* insisted that the marketplace for Korean films should not be restricted to Korea itself. And they encouraged the active circulation of actors and cooperation among the cinemas of the empire, including those of the metropole, Korea, and Manchuria.[15]

Between 1940 and 1945 at least seven feature films were made on the theme of Koreans in the Japanese military, and another on Koreans in the border police. The seven were *Volunteer Soldier* (K. *Chiwŏnbyŏng*, J. *Shiganhei*, 1940), *You and I* (K. *Nŏ wa na*, J. *Kimi to boku*, 1941), *Figure of Youth* (K. *Chŏlmŭn mosŭp*, J. *Wakaki sugata*, 1943), *Korea Strait* (K. *Chosŏn haehyŏp*, J. *Chōsen kaikyō*, 1943), *Here We Go!* (K. *Nanŭn kanda*, J. *Warera imazo yuku*, 1942), *Mister Soldier* (K. *Pyŏngjŏngnim*, J. *Heitai-san*, 1944), and *Love and the Vow* (K. *Sarang kwa maengsŏ*, J. *Ai to chikai*,

1945).[16] Although administratively not part of the navy or army, the border police functioned much like a branch of the army in that its purpose was to protect Korea's borders. The well-known Japanese director Imai Tadashi took up the theme of Koreans in the border police in his *Suicide Squad at the Watchtower* (K. *Mangnu ŭi kyŏlsadae,* J. *Bōrō no kesshitai,* 1943), the film mentioned at the end of the previous chapter.

In addition, Korean and Japanese directors produced a number of documentaries on Korean military service. In fact, the well-known Korean director Pang Han-jun's *Victory Garden* (K. *Sŭngni ŭi ttŭl,* J. *Shōri no niwa,* 1940), which depicted the daily lives of Korean volunteers in training, was the first documentary in Korea to be officially recognized as a "cultural film" under the provisions of the Korean Film Ordinance (1940).[17] The state thereby certified that it was a nonfeature film that contributed to "cultivation of the national spirit and development of the national intellect." According to Nishiki Motosada of the Korean Government-General's Book Section, Korea's Army Volunteer Training Center served as the setting for Pang's film and everyone who appeared in it spoke only in Japanese.[18] Morinaga Kenjirō directed *Shōwa jūkyūnen* (*The Nineteenth Year of Shōwa*), a film released in 1943 to celebrate the inclusion of Koreans in the conscription system. *Eikō no hi* (*Day of Glory,* 1943) likewise commemorated the opening of the Japanese navy to Korean volunteers.[19]

I turn now to two films that fall into the category of the transregional or imperial film productions envisioned for the future by *Eiga nenkan* in 1942. In fact, *Eiga nenkan* specifically named one of them, *Bōrō no kesshitai* (*Suicide Squad at the Watchtower*), as an exemplar of this type of movie. *Suicide Squad at the Watchtower* and the other film, *Ai to chikai* (*Love and the Vow*), were co-productions of Korean and metropolitan film companies that employed directors, actors, and actresses from both Korea and the metropole.

SUICIDE SQUAD AT THE WATCHTOWER

Imai Tadashi, assisted by Ch'oe In-kyu, directed the 1943 action drama *Suicide Squad at the Watchtower.* The Japanese company Tōhō and Korea's Kōrai Eigasha—which was absorbed into the Chōsen Eiga Seisaku Kaisha while it was in production—co-produced the film.[20] One of postwar Japan's most distinguished filmmakers, Imai was to have a fifty-two-year directorial career that began in 1939 with *Numazu heigakkō* (*Numazu Naval Academy*), a historical drama set in the period just after the Meiji Restoration, and ended in 1991 with *Sensō to seishun* (*War and Youth*). By his own admission Imai became involved in leftist activism as a Tokyo University student, but later recanted and made mostly "collaboration films" during the war.[21] Imai is best known for the postwar films in which he criticized militarism and social inequality while celebrating what he regarded as democratic and antifeudal values and social relations. The famous kiss separated by a glass window in *Mata au hi made* (*Until We Meet Again*, 1950) that mildly transgressed wartime taboos of public intimacy, the tragic suicide scenes of young women during the Battle of Okinawa in *Himeyuri no tō* (*Monument to the Star Lilies*, 1953 and 1982)—such are the images from Imai's works that have come to dominate popular memory of him. Yet the film that first won Imai significant recognition was none other than *Suicide Squad at the Watchtower*.[22]

Imai's assistant, Ch'oe In-kyu, was a highly regarded Korean director who had been widely praised for his 1941 film *Homeless Angels* (K. *Chip ŏmnŭn ch'ŏnsa* , J. *Ie naki tenshi*), as well as the 1940 work that he directed with Pang Han-jun, *School Tuition* (K. *Suŏmnyo*, J. *Jugyōryō*).[23] When it was released, critics lauded *Homeless Angels* as Korea's most accomplished film and the Japanese Ministry of Education initially selected it as one of its "recommended films" for 1941, although the designation was later withdrawn for reasons that are not entirely clear.[24] Imai has said that Ch'oe's complete cooperation in the project ensured his ability to recruit an all-star Korean cast,[25] including Chŏn T'aek-i in the key role of Police Officer Rin (or Hayashi or Im) and Kim Sin-chae playing the important character Kin Eishuku (Kim Yŏng-suk) (see figure 7).

Suicide Squad at the Watchtower is a film about national community formation that mobilizes the space and metaphor of the border between Korea and Manchuria to visually and narratively produce a multiethnic nation made up not only of metropolitan Japanese but of loyal Chinese and Koreans as well. Shot largely on location along the Yalu River, its central drama involves the defense by the National Border Police (*kokkyō keisatsu*) of this national and not simply colonial border against the attacks of anti-Japanese guerrillas, or "bandits" (*hizoku*) as they are called. National security here is imperiled by two factors: one external to the nation, the other internal.

The external threat is that of "bandits" crossing over the river. While the borderland in the summer and fall is presented as an idyllic place of bountiful harvests and simple people living in harmony under Japanese rule, as winter approaches and then deepens nature turns harsh and, more importantly, creates conditions that enable the breakdown of the border. For in winter, when the river freezes over, it is transformed from a natural barrier protecting the community to a path over which

FIGURE 7.
Watchtower at the border, with cast from *Suicide Squad at the Watchtower*. Film still courtesy of Korean Film Archive.

guerrillas can attack at will. Suspense builds as we hear booming sounds from the direction of the river—not rifle shots, we learn, but the sound of ice forming.

The equally great danger is an internal one that is presented by the characteristics of the borderland community just inside the national border. It is a multiethnic community made up of individuals who are physically similar to one another. There is no visible physical means by which to determine whether anyone is ethnically Japanese or non-Japanese, except for their clothing, which of course can be changed. Early in the film, Imai plays on clothing and ethnic fluidity by cross-dressing the police chief as Chinese. We learn that the chief has been passing as such in order to collect intelligence information, but the suggestion is that enemy spies can just as easily go unnoticed within the community on the Japanese side of the border. In fact, during the course of the film we learn of the dangers of betrayal from within—particularly by Chinese such as the figure Wang Ko. Though the son of a loyal Chinese villager in the "Japanese" community, he has gone over to the side of the anti-Japanese "bandits."

Once the river has frozen over, the "bandits" begin their attack. They are represented as ruthless and unprincipled savages who set fire to the village and loot, driving the Chinese and Korean villagers into the safety of the walled border police outpost. Here community formation has nothing to do with a perceived common-

FIGURE 8.
Kin Eishuku (played by Kim Sin-chae) at her brother's grave site.
He is the first "Japanese" victim. Film still courtesy of Korean
Film Archive.

ality of race or ethnicity, such as could be found in the then-prominent discourse on the "common ancestral origins of Japanese and Koreans (*Nissen dōsōron*)." Instead, it is achieved through the constitution of Japanese, Chinese and Koreans as common victims of the enemy. The first "Japanese" victim is in fact a Korean policeman, Officer Kin Shunshoku (Kim Ch'un-sik), who is killed by the "bandits" (see figure 8); the second is Wang Ryū, father of the disloyal Wang Ko. In short, the Japanese multiethnic nation is formed through the constitution of the Other, the common "bandit" enemy, not by Japanese domination or even by an assumed ethnic or racial sameness. This is a story of Japanese innocence and vulnerability, and of the reciprocal relations of sympathy that Japanese have with the locals. In the process of their common victimization, all members without exception, including the one originally traitorous Chinese and one initially less-than-eager Korean, make the choice to be loyal Japanese.

Choice or self-determination—the ability to freely will oneself as a national subject—is crucial here. As was generally the case in late colonial discourse at this time, the colonized are represented as deciding to become Japanese. They are neither coerced nor born into this condition but become Japanese through acts of self-determination. Early in the film villagers have been allowed to choose whether to help build the fortresslike police outpost, and most do. When one of the policemen must leave the outpost to get reinforcements, it is none other than a Korean, Officer Rin, who volunteers. And most importantly, when it appears that all is lost, when no reinforcements have yet arrived, Japanese and Koreans alike, both men and women, choose death as Japanese over capture.

In scenes that eerily anticipate Imai's postwar films on the tragedy of wartime Okinawa—where soldiers and civilians, men, women, and children, seek refuge in dark, damp, and uncomfortable underground caves before committing suicide—individuals making up this diverse borderland community retreat into the shelter underneath the outpost, and then resolve to take their own lives. First Yoshiko, the police chief's wife, takes a pistol from her husband and prepares to kill herself. Next, Gyokuzen, the wife of the Korean policeman (Rin) who has gone off to bring reinforcements, is told by the police chief that although it is really her husband's responsibility, if necessary he will assist her in her suicide. But Gyokuzen politely refuses the chief's assistance and lets him know that she is prepared to kill not only herself but her new baby as well. Finally, the Korean woman (Eishuku) who is the sister of the Korean police officer (Kin) who had been the first victim of the "bandits" asks her betrothed to shoot her before taking his own life. Here it is important to recall that the Japanese word for such suicides was *jiketsu,* which literally means "self-determination."[26] The transformation of Koreans and especially Korean women into Japanese national subjects thus depends on their agency as self-determining subjects. In choosing death, they achieve subjecthood as Japanese nationals.[27]

This story ends differently from the Okinawan tragedy, however. Office Rin finally arrives on the scene with the awaited reinforcements. The "bandits" are killed or driven away, and the border police and the community they defend are rescued. The movie closes on the theme of triumph through sacrifice. A poignant funeral for those who have given their lives in defense of the community takes place. But subtle touches, such as a frontal shot of Officer Rin's wife in a Japanese kimono rather than in Korean clothing, suggest that the almost womblike experience in the darkness under the watchtower has resulted in the rebirth of the multiethnic community as a unified embodiment of the nation.

The rescue scenes are oddly reminiscent of "cowboys and Indians" movies from Hollywood in which the heroes on horseback return with the cavalry to save the whites under siege. However, also reminding us of the global context of imperialism and colonialism in which he made this film, Imai has noted that his model for the movie was *Beau Geste,*[28] the 1939 Hollywood classic produced by Paramount Pictures and starring Gary Cooper, which had been set in an outpost of the French

Foreign Legion in the Sahara Desert. While the unlikely storyline in *Beau Geste* revolves around the theft of a precious jewel, its central premise is that the French
Foreign Legion and the "friendly Arabs" who assist them are defending "twenty
millions of natives" and above all civilization from the attacks of the barbarians in
the desert.

Coming at a time when the screening of American and British films was prohibited in both Korea and the metropole, Imai's plundering of *Beau Geste* in particular
but also Hollywood motion pictures more generally for conventions, techniques,
and even the main storyline for *Suicide Squad at the Watchtower* is so transparent
that it is at times startling and would be almost laughable were the subject matter
not so serious (see figure 9). For example, as in Hollywood movies Imai tried to cap-
italize on the attraction of star power—in his case by using Hara Setsuko (see figure
10) and Takada Minoru in the lead roles as well as Chŏn T'aek-i and Kim Sin-chae
in the supporting cast.

Imai also deployed the classic Hollywood narrative form in which personal stories of heterosexual love and romance (in this case, between Eishuku and her betrothed) parallel larger themes of historical or public importance and some kind of
deadline, including a rescue just before time has run out, structures the temporal organization.[29] Even the props and siting of Imai's film were direct adaptations from
Beau Geste. In both films the action takes place in a military outpost with a watchtower, and these fortresses are located in natural environments that are physically
challenging—at least from the perspectives of Westerners and the Japanese—and
that allegorize the border zone between Civilization and Savagery. Yet perhaps the
most striking aspect of this connection between late colonial Korea and Hollywood
that confounds the simple binary of democratic Allies versus fascist Axis Powers is
that Imai's film is not simply a copy of a particular Hollywood motion picture. Instead, with only the most minimal "translation," it fits very neatly into an entire genre
of Hollywood motion pictures about the frontier and civilization that the film historian Richard Slotkin has called the "Victorian Empire film."[30]

According to Slotkin's formidable body of research, the Victorian Empire genre
emerged in the mid-1930s beginning with Paramount's *Lives of a Bengal Lancer*
(1935) and Warner Brothers' *The Charge of the Light Brigade* (1936). These were followed by such movies as *Wee Willie Winkie* (1937), *Drums* (1938), *Gunga Din* (1939),
and *Beau Geste* (1939). Slotkin argues that movies in this genre continued to be produced even into the fifties and sixties, but the point here is that almost all the key
elements of the genre that he has identified are important components of *Suicide
Squad at the Watchtower*.

FIGURE 9.

In *Suicide Squad at the Watchtower* (upper image) and *Beau Geste* (lower image), men in the fortress watchtowers are shot as they protect civilization from the attacking "savages."

FIGURE 10.
Hara Setsuko in the leading female role with the actor playing
Wang Ryū, father of the "bandit" leader. Film still courtesy
of Korea Film Archive.

Slotkin notes, for example, that

thematically, these movies deal with a crisis in which civilization—symbolized
by the Victorian Empire or its equivalent—is faced by a threat from an alliance
between the opposite extremes of savage license and totalitarian authority.
The Victorian or civilized order is embodied in a regiment or a military outpost whose values are nominally those of a liberal and progressive imperium
but whose heroes are warriors and whose politics are those of a justified and
virile patriarchy happily exercised over consenting White women and childlike
brown faces.[31]

In *Suicide Squad at the Watchtower* the "equivalent" of the "Victorian Empire" is
of course the Japanese empire, and "bandits" pose the crisis to civilization—a civilization that is embodied by an outpost of warriors. These "bandits" do in fact represent both extreme "savage license and totalitarian authority" in that they kill and
burn ruthlessly even as they hold each of their members in check by means of mutual surveillance and indeed assassination in the name of the authoritarian Kō Ryū
Band (*Kō Ryū Ichimi*). The "regiment" or "military outpost" is a "liberal or pro-

gressive imperium" that under its patriarchal police chief both civilizes and protects the local people. As for the "consenting White women and childlike brown faces" over whom the patriarch presides, we need merely substitute "consenting Japanese women and childlike faces of Chinese and Koreans."

Slotkin continues:

> A fanatical and perhaps even pseudo-messianic chieftain (usually a "Khan" of some sort) is uniting the hill tribes against our regimental utopia, and the blood politicians in Whitehall or Washington are too corrupt, inept, or locked into bureaucratic red tape to do what needs to be done about it. There is often a foreign power, an evil empire (Russia, Germany, Imperial China) working behind the scenes. As a result the British army and civil service (wives and children included) and all the little brown people who depend upon "us" are in peril of massacre by the chieftain and his deluded barbarians.

From the film itself it is difficult to know much about the "fanatical" or "pseudo-messianic chieftain" of the Kō Ryū Band, but knowledgeable viewers might have guessed that Imai's version of the "Khan" would have been modeled on the Chinese and Korean anti-Japanese Communist, nationalist partisans active in the border region, or both. Most famously, in June 1937 the future North Korean leader Kim Il-sŏng is known to have led a small force of armed men in an attack on the town of Poch'ŏnbo, just inside the Korean border, in which they killed police officers, set fire to police stations, and destroyed the homes of pro-Japanese Koreans.[32] Slotkin's reference to political ineptitude in London and Washington is one aspect of the 1930s' Victorian Empire film that does not find a parallel in *Suicide Squad at the Watchtower*. But certainly the wartime restriction on cinema's ability to criticize the government would have characterized both the United States and the Japanese empire in the period after Pearl Harbor. Moreover, there is scarcely a hint of any sinister empire working behind the scenes. If anything, the film explicitly states that Manchukuo is a powerful ally that has assisted in putting down the "bandits." Nevertheless, as in *Beau Geste*, the metaphorical "little brown people who depend upon us" are in danger of "massacre by the chieftain and his deluded barbarians."

And Slotkin concludes:

> The only one who can save us is the hero, a soldier who knows the natives well enough almost (or actually) to pass for one—a man who straddles the border

between savagery and civilization, fanaticism and religion, brown and white, them and us. And we *are* saved—though typically at the cost of the hero's sacrificial death, in company with his picked band of men, in some heroic last stand or suicidal charge.

Here again the tropes translate very easily, though with some variation. It is clearly the police chief, the hero after all, who freely traverses the borderline between "savagery and civilization, fanaticism and religion, brown and white, them and us." Toward the beginning of the film, as mentioned earlier, he passes as Han Chinese, dressing and speaking as the Other. And it is he who saves "us," even as others under the police chief's command have been sacrificed.

Yet there is one point of great contrast between *Beau Geste* and *Suicide Squad at the Watchtower* concerning their respective representations of the "little brown people." To be sure, paralleling Police Officer Rin's role in bringing additional officers to rescue the outpost under siege, in *Beau Geste* it is the "good Arab native" who goes back for reinforcements to rescue the French Foreign Legionnaires who are under attack by the "bad Arabs." But unlike *Beau Geste*—where the Arabs are never fully admitted into the ethnically diverse but strictly white multinational community of soldiers—Imai's film ostensibly promises the full inclusion of Koreans and Chinese within the Japanese national community. The two Korean policemen are for the most part treated as Japanese policemen, and all loyal Koreans and Chinese are in the end admitted into the watchtower's fortress, a metaphor for the Japanese nation. In telling contrast, the commanding sergeant in *Beau Geste* opens a small peephole in the fortress gate to tell an Arab scout to go for reinforcements, but then rapidly closes it (see figure 11).

The only condition seeming to limit the potentially universal inclusiveness of the Japanese empire is loyalty. And here it is important to reiterate that the film appears to transcend the symbolism of blood, whether of ethnic communities or of the blood ties that bind parents and children. Thus when the police chief is forced to decide between returning to Japan to care for his dying mother or to stay in Korea and defend the border and the multiethnic community living there, he of course stays. Nationalism, we can see, requires transcendence of the narrow particularism of the family, even though it must also build upon it. The police chief's wife, Yoshiko, has no biological children of her own but instead acts as if she were a mother to everyone, Japanese and Korean alike, caring for them when they are injured and serving them delicious meals. The Japanese nation and empire appear to aspire to a universalism that exceeds that of Hollywood's Victorian Empire films.

FIGURE II.
The "good Arab" is told to go after reinforcements but is not allowed inside the fortress. From *Beau Geste*.

To be sure, the disavowal of blood in the constitution of the national community does not necessarily mean that the film's only message is that of equality, for even as Koreans are admitted into the national community insofar as they accept cultural assimilation and dress in Japanese clothes, the film does not let its viewers forget that differences separate the newly admitted and the Japanese from the metropole. We do not forget that the Koreans have sung their ethnic songs, that their children need special instruction in pronouncing Japanese, and that they have eaten their meals differently from the Japanese. The hierarchy of gendered and ethnically marked individuals is left undisturbed despite representations of equality and admissibility. But while hierarchy in an earlier time might have been between two distinct communities—the Japanese colonial rulers on the one hand and the colonial subjects on the other—in this time of total war the hierarchy must be between Koreans and Japanese, as well as women and men, *within* the same national community, with an ambiguous and crossable line separating the civilized from the uncivilized.

With respect to the theme of the admissibility of Koreans into the national community, *Suicide Squad at the Watchtower* clearly went beyond the "Victorian Empire" film genre. Under conditions of total war, the "little brown people" of Japan could not be kept outside the boundaries of the nation, as allegorized by the outpost. They had to be included in both the community and the military forces fighting to protect the nation. In this sense, Imai's film shares even more with a new type of Hollywood film that was just starting to be produced in exactly the same year as *Suicide Squad at the Watchtower*—namely, the World War II combat film.

According to Richard Slotkin, the prototype for such films was MGM's *Bataan*.[33] Directed by Tay Garnett and starring Robert Taylor and Lloyd Nolan, this 1943 film inaugurated a cinematic genre that had as one of its primary themes the multiethnic and multiracial unity of American men, sometimes even fighting side by side with colonials against a savage enemy. *Bataan* featured a ragtag platoon made up of six white Anglo-Saxon Protestants and seven racialized or ethnic men, a highly unlikely mix given the segregated character of the U.S. military. The non-WASPs were a Jew, an Irishman, a Pole, a Latino, an African American, and two loyal Filipinos (one a Moro from Mindanao and the other named Yankee Salazar).

Like Imai's *Suicide Squad at the Watchtower*, *Bataan* portrays the mixed unit as a heroic group of men acting in mutually supportive harmony as they make a last stand against the enemy. Interestingly, it is once again the colonial subject who volunteers to seek reinforcements. The loyal Moro from Mindanao strips off his military uniform, covers his body with black ash for camouflage, and then runs through the jungle in the night for help. But before his ultimately unsuccessful attempt, this colonial soldier has apparently told his buddy that "it don't matter where a man dies, as long as he dies for freedom." Suicide is likewise a theme that connects the two films, for in *Bataan* there is no rescue but only a desperate stand against an enemy. The heroes fight to the last man and one of them even carries out a kamikaze-style attack: a lieutenant intentionally pilots a plane loaded with dynamite directly into a bridge to prevent the Japanese from utilizing it.

Bataan is also similar to Imai's film in making the gesture of liberal inclusion, while it continues to mark the non-WASPs with stereotypes such as the Jew with bad feet, the Latino obsessed with dance music, and the black man singing the blues in a beautiful deep voice. Moreover, the film represents the Moro "native" as always on the edge of reverting to a state of nature. Almost fully undressed in preparation for his flight through the jungle, he recalls his "onetime very murdering family," and the sergeant casually tells him to "put your clothes on and get civilized again" (see figure 12). Finally, even as this film is meant to be a celebration of equality and the transcendence of racial and ethnic discrimination, the WASPs occupy the high-

FIGURE 12.
The self-professed "Moro from Mindanao" has stripped off his
uniform and is ready to run through the jungle. From *Bataan.*

ranking positions and are portrayed as the most adept soldiers. In short, while Imai
may have modeled his work on a prewar film within the Victorian Empire genre,
the structural convergence of the American and Japanese total war systems stamped
Suicide Squad at the Watchtower with characteristics of the combat film—an emerging type of motion picture with which Imai would most likely not have been familiar as he was making *Suicide Squad at the Watchtower.*

LOVE AND THE VOW

Love and the Vow is a deeply disturbing film that is rarely mentioned by film critics
and is often not listed among Imai Tadashi's works. Interestingly, in his survey and
commentary on Imai's career, Satō Tadao writes that the 1944 film *Ikari no umi (Sea
of Anger)* was Imai's last wartime movie, even though an accompanying comprehensive list of his films includes *Love and the Vow* as a 1945 production. And in his
massive study of wartime films, Peter High notes that because *Love and the Vow* was

released so close to the war's ending (26 July 1945) and then discarded immediately after defeat, it was possible for Imai to attempt to conceal that he had made it.[34]

Like *Suicide Squad at the Watchtower, Love and the Vow* was a transregional and imperial film co-produced by the Japanese film company Tōhō and the Korea Motion Picture Production Corporation. Ch'oe In-kyu, Imai's assistant director for *Suicide Squad at the Watchtower*, co-directed. Once again the Japanese star Takada Minoru played one of the male lead roles; the young Korean actor Kim U-ho took the other. Suggesting the importance of the trope of the orphan in colonial and national discourse at this time, Kim U-ho played an orphan, a role he had already taken in Ch'oe In-kyu's *Homeless Angels*. Postwar Japanese cinema fans would most likely be surprised to see Shimura Takashi—perhaps best known for his important roles in such Kurosawa Akira films as *Stray Dog* (1949), *Rashōmon* (1950), *Ikiru* (1952), and *Seven Samurai* (1954), to name just a few—playing a Korean named Murai, who is the principal of an elementary school in the Korean countryside.

The main storyline shares the conventional narrative of the bildungsroman, the novel of formation, in that the protagonist overcomes the uncertainties of youth and develops into mature and civilized adulthood, while in the process reconciling with the national social order. Furthermore, as in the novel of formation and in modern bourgeois culture more broadly, in the end the main character overcomes the contradictions that emerge out of the tension between, on the one hand, the valorization of interiority and individual self-determination and, on the other, the demands of socialization, normality, or conformity to the normative order. As Franco Moretti puts it, in this modern bourgeois culture simple obedience is not enough (recall also Japanese American internment and the questionnaires). Instead, "it is also necessary that, as a 'free individual,' not as a fearful subject but as a convinced citizen, one perceives the social norms as *one's own*. One must *internalize* them and fuse external compulsion and internal impulses into a new unity until the former is no longer distinguishable from the latter" (emphasis in original).[35]

Love and the Vow advances this structure of the bildungsroman by telling the story of a wayward Korean youth's coming into adult, male, and Japanese subjecthood through his decision—his choice—to become a kamikaze pilot. To cite Moretti again, "Time must be used to find a homeland [in this case, 'Japan']. If this is not done the result is a wasted life: aimless, meaningless."[36] Following other historical, social scientific, and literary texts that were written during the colonial period, which likened Korea and Taiwan to orphaned children adopted by Japan (*yōshi* or *moraigo*),[37] *Love and the Vow* allegorizes the psychological torment of the colonized and by then increasingly nationalized subject through the trope of the adopted Korean child. The film examines the youth's neurosis, a neurosis that originates in his having been orphaned, and then asks its viewers to believe that he can achieve full subjecthood and self-determination only through willful submission to the adoptive relationship.

In analyzing this film, we can in some ways follow Frantz Fanon, who in his *Black Skin, White Masks* employed the psychoanalytical concept of the "abandonment neurosis" to diagnose Jean Veneuse, the black Antillean protagonist in a novel by René Maran.[38] In Fanon's reading, Jean Veneuse obsessively desires to receive the love of a white woman. But he is tormented: while he cannot live without love, he cannot accept it because he fears abandonment. In fact, perpetually fearing desertion, he "unconsciously does everything needed to bring about exactly this catastrophe" (p. 76, quoting Germaine Guex). Having been forsaken by his love-object as a child, when he was one of the "intermittent orphans" in a boarding school, Veneuse is a man who needs the white woman's repeated affirmations of love, as well as the white man's recognition that he is really one of them—that he has nothing "in common with real Negroes" (p. 69). Veneuse obsesses about past frustrations, feels anguish with every rejection, becomes aggressive, lacks self-esteem and affective security because he feels unworthy of love. As a result he feels "an overwhelming feeling of impotence in relation to life and to people, as well as a complete rejection of the feeling of responsibility" (p. 73, quoting Guex). I do not mean to suggest that the "abandonment neurosis" necessarily typified Korean colonial consciousness itself, but it does help us analyze *Love and the Vow*'s representations of the colonial subject's condition.

Kin Eiryū (Kim Yŏng-yong) was literally an orphan. How he came to lose his parents and family is one of the great mysteries of the story, but he has been adopted—or, as Mrs. Shiraishi puts it, "picked up" (*hirotte kita*)—by a Mr. Shiraishi, bureau chief of the Keijō Shinpōsha newspaper company. Eiryū wishes to be loved by his foster parents and needs their constant affirmation of his worth, yet all his actions seem to be driven by the desire to prove his unworthiness. He is so afraid of abandonment that he behaves as if intent on doing whatever he can to bring about the dreaded but expected result. Eiryū is unable to stay focused on any activity. He has the habit of wandering about, much as he must have as a waif on the streets. Eiryū consistently devalues himself and purposely disappoints his parents even when given the opportunity to please them. Fanon, quoting Germaine Guex to explain Jean Veneuse's abandonment neurosis, could just as easily have been describing Eiryū's condition: "This lack of esteem of self as an object worthy of love has grave consequences. For one thing, it keeps the individual in a state of profound inner insecurity, as a result of which it inhibits or falsifies every relation with others. It is as something that has the right to arouse sympathy or love that the individual is uncertain of himself. The lack of affective self-valuation is to be found only in persons who in their early childhood suffered from a lack of love and understanding" (pp. 75–76).

The solution to Eiryū's abandonment neurosis is complete acceptance of the love of father and nation, and reciprocation in kind. Following Murai's path, Eiryū comes to the realization that he must volunteer to become a kamikaze pilot. As in *Suicide Squad at the Watchtower*, full subjecthood results from the self-determining act of volunteering to die. While he had previously always cowered in front of every adult, mumbled when speaking, behaved like a child, and shunned all responsibilities, once he has decided to become a kamikaze pilot he is transformed into an articulate and respectable young man who holds his head high and his body straight. In the movie's last scenes we see Eiryū in the seat of a kamikaze plane looking proud, brave, and resolute as he goes off on his suicide mission.

The trope of the adopted child that features so prominently in *Love and the Vow* is at the same time a familiar element in Japanese colonial discourse and a radical version of it that is particular to the end of the total war period in which it was made. As far back as 1918, the theorist Ōshima Masanori explained: "Of course, the Koreans are not of the same ethnos as us. However, to take them into our Nation (originally a Nation-Family) like adopted children, foster children, or foundlings, and to view them spiritually as family and then to treat them as family—such is the way to expand our National Polity."[39]

This leads us to the question of why colonial discourse employed the metaphors of the orphan and adopted child so widely and how they functioned. They are in many ways ideal tropes for colonial regimes (as well as modern nation-states) that are simultaneously assimilationist and racist, because they have the effect of incorporating new subjects while infantilizing them and marking them as different. The tropes appear to transcend the logic of consanguinity because they disavow its centrality in the constitution of the family, the nation, and the colonial relation. In fact, the logic of adoption would appear to have a universalizing ability to incorporate all difference. Hence the linkage to empire. Yet at the same time, terms such as "adopted" and "foster" reinscribe the symbolism of blood in the very act of disavowing its importance.[40]

Judith S. Modell, building on David Schneider's pathbreaking critiques of the biologism in anthropological kinship studies, has very astutely observed that the modern discourse on adoption in the United States, which appears to transcend the symbolism of biological ties, in fact reinstates the primacy of blood because it operates under what she calls an "as-if" axiom. In her terms, adopted children are "as-if-begotten" and parents are "as-if-genealogical." In other words, in the dominant American discourse the adoptive relationship can at best imperfectly mimic what is believed to be the "natural" family: "The adoptive family is 'just like' a biological family."[41] As Schneider put it long ago, "adoption is not ruled outside the 'kinship' system but is understandable as a kind of 'kinship' relationship precisely in terms of the fact that it is modeled after the biological relationship. Without the biological relationship, in this view, adoption makes absolutely no sense."[42] Put conversely, adoption defines the biologically bound parent-child relationship as the one that is natural.

If we can accept this argument about the supplementary rather than contradictory relationship between the adopted and the biologically begotten child, it can be seen that while the adoption trope as used to represent the colonial relationship seemed to promise the recognition of colonial subjects as equals, it also had the effect of indicating that the relationship was always naturally suspect. This is undoubtedly how the adoption trope usually operated in Japanese colonial discourse. But *Love and the Vow* represents an extreme version of the disavowal of the ideology of blood.

Love and the Vow confounds any certitude its viewers might have about the fixity and importance of blood sameness or difference, whether within families or across the divide between colony and metropole. Most importantly, although the adoptive father and mother dress, speak, and act as if they are Japanese, well into the film it is hinted that they are actually Korean themselves. First, while at the rural school where the father of the deceased war hero Murai is the principal, Shiraishi explains to the pupils that he had attended the very same school. He had received instruction from the wise principal who is, incidentally, both Korean and a model Japanese. Second, early in the film we learn that Eiryū's adoptive father had actually been a "forlorn orphan" (*tengai no koji*) himself. Thus adoption is at least partially naturalized by the commonness of orphans and their upbringing by foster parents. Third, while the adoptive parents have a child who is apparently their biological son, Eiryū receives far more attention than his younger brother.

Finally, there is a rather complicated subplot in which Eiryū—who is persistently troubled by his original abandonment and seeks to know who he is and the circumstances by which he was forsaken—eventually comes to the realization that his biological genealogy and the past mean nothing. Eiko, the kamikaze hero's widowed wife, recollects that she and her brother had been separated in Shanghai at the time of the Shanghai Incident (1932). She tells a sad story of how her brother had tried to revive their mother, who had been killed by the Chinese, by calling out, *"kaachan, kaachan," "ŏmŏni, ŏmŏni."* Though Eiko was later adopted by her uncle, her brother had never been found. This is again a case of common victimization by an enemy helping to constitute Koreans as Japanese; but more importantly, Eiko posits the possibility of her own biological tie to Eiryū. Might Eiryū really be Eichū, her brother? Eiryū looks a great deal like her brother, but she cannot be sure. Did Eiryū remember riding on a big ship? No, he responds, but he seems to faintly recall the blue color of the ocean. Eiryū continues to wonder if Eiko might be his sister. He is distressed and finds relief only when upon volunteering to become a pilot he decides that biological genealogy means nothing. Instead he will think of himself as the younger brother of Murai, the deceased Korean kamikaze hero, a man with whom he has no consanguineous relation. Eiryū achieves his Japanese subjecthood not only by volunteering to die but also by denaturalizing the symbolism of blood.

In thus naturalizing adoptive relationships over those of blood, I suspect that *Love and the Vow* went as far as was possible under colonialism to renounce differences between the colonizer and the colonized. There are at least two reasons for the film's radicalism in this respect. First, the movie was most likely intended primarily for a Korean audience. As a propaganda film that sought to mobilize young Korean men and their families for the war effort, it presumably was not as necessary to stress the hierarchy of differences between colonizers and colonized. But we should also consider the lateness of the period in which the film was produced. In general the material and manpower needs of fighting a total war necessitated the production of a discourse of sameness between Koreans and Japanese. As war conditions worsened for the Japanese state, and as a mood of desperation increased, the disavowal of blood and the discourse on sameness between colonizers and colonized reached its most extreme form.

"VOLUNTEER SOLDIER IWAMOTO"

While the films analyzed above downplayed the symbolism of blood in imagining the unity of Japan and Korea, many works of fiction emphasized that blood mattered. Its importance, however, was not in separating metropolitan Japanese from Koreans but in providing a primordial foundation upon which cultural and biological ethnic unity had been forged.

In what follows I will analyze a very imaginatively crafted story by the Korean Japanese writer Chō Kakuchū (K. Chang Hyŏk-chu) titled "Iwamoto shiganhei," or "Volunteer Soldier Iwamoto," that drew heavily from the widespread discourse on Korean and Japanese sameness. Like many of Chō's other writings, the work was undoubtedly read by a wide audience not only in Korea but in other places in the empire as well, including the metropole. Originally serialized in the major Japanese national daily newspaper *Mainichi shinbun* between 24 August and 9 September 1943, it was later collected in book form along with three other major short stories about Korean soldiers.[43]

As for the identity of the writer, one of the few scholars to have written comprehensively about Korean writers in Japan has argued that he was the first Korean composing works in Japanese to be recognized as a legitimate writer in mainstream Japanese literary circles (*bundan*).[44] Born in 1905 in Korea, Chō started his literary career while a teacher in rural Northern Kyŏngsang Province, but immigrated to Japan in 1936.[45] He came to the attention of a wide Japanese readership with a short story published in 1932 titled "Gakidō" ("Hell of Hungry Ghosts").[46] This was a passionate indictment of Japanese colonialism and landlordism and their oppressive effects on the Korean peasantry; but the works that I will examine here and in the following chapter are primarily those that followed the author's remarkable conversion to Japanese nationalism in the late 1930s. It may also be noted that Chō was one of the most prolific Korean authors writing in Japanese from the mid-1930s to the end of the war. Indeed, with a total of twenty-nine books published in Japanese between 1934 and 1945 (three of them coauthored), together with an extraordinary number of short stories, essays, and even translations, Chō was surely one of the most productive and cosmopolitan authors of his era writing in Japanese.[47]

While different from the films previously analyzed in that it borrowed heavily from the discourse on the common ancestry of the Japanese and Koreans, Chō's stories of Korean soldiers, including "Volunteer Soldier Iwamoto," nevertheless complemented the more universalist message that disavowed blood in that its main purpose was to dramatize that Koreans and Japanese shared the same identity. Furthermore, like *Love and the Vow,* "Volunteer Soldier Iwamoto" played on the neurosis of a forlorn child. Though Private Iwamoto's biological parents are not dead, he is an orphanlike character who cannot tolerate his drunken and abusive father and who was raised in a home for juvenile delinquents. Like Eiryū in *Love and the Vow,* Chō's Iwamoto is an internally troubled and misguided youth who can succeed in becoming a complete and affectively secure subject only through submission to the love of the patriarch, as symbolized both by the principal of the home for juvenile delinquents and by the Japanese emperor. But as in *Suicide Squad at the Watchtower* and *Love and the Vow,* the story achieves its drama precisely because submission is not guaranteed. Instead, it is premised on the possibility that the protagonist will not make the normative choice of acquiescing to the demands of the emperor and nation. More than any other story analyzed here and in the next chapter, Chō's "Volunteer Soldier Iwamoto" reveals how nationalism worked through the constitution of subjects who have the freedom to choose their own subjection to the national community. The inner conflict stemming from this subjection to choice is fully comparable with the inner turmoil described in chapter 3 of Japanese Americans faced with the choice of complying with the call to arms.

As in several of his other works, in "Volunteer Soldier Iwamoto" Chō is attentive to the ways in which space, place, and memory interpellate Koreans as Japanese national subjects.[48] The narrative begins at Koma Station in the Musashino region, a rustic town just northwest of Tokyo. While the history of this area is not yet evident to readers, an intimation of the place's associations with Korea is given by the figures of the deities that stand near the station exit. They are the paired images of Tenka Daishōgun and Chika Joshōgun, guardian spirits called *changsŭng* in Korean (see figure 13). Seeing these figures jolts the first-person narrator—who, the book's preface has already informed us, is modeled on the author—into a flashback that takes him on a memory journey through time, space, and history. It begins with a recollection of his childhood in Korea, when he had once been startled by the frightening figure of a Daishōgun, and ends in Koma. The core of the story revolves around the narrator's relationship with a volunteer Korean soldier named Iwamoto. What had Iwamoto felt when he had visited Koma and seen these figures? Iwamoto's feelings were probably different from his own, the narrator conjectures, for while he himself had been raised in Korea, Iwamoto had been brought up in the metropole. Yet by the time his memory journey circles back to Koma at the story's end, we see that the doubled travels of the narrator and Iwamoto, which take them in opposite directions between Korea and the metropole, end in the erasure of the imaginary borders between the two geographical spaces.

Near the beginning of the memory journey, the narrator recalls his boyhood and his great sadness and envy at watching Japanese soldiers march through the streets of his native place in Korea. He had been a child with no hope of ever achieving the soldierly manhood that he had witnessed. And yet, the voluntary system and recent changes in the conscription law had made it possible for Koreans to participate in the military, thus presumably allowing him to finally fulfill his childhood dream. When he receives an invitation to enter the Training Center for Army Volunteers in Keijō (Seoul), he accepts with the full intention of becoming a regular trainee. The narrator's and hence Chō's travel back to Korea can thus be read as a journey to recuperate the manhood and national subjecthood that he had earlier been denied.

FIGURE 13.

Today's Koma Station, still fronted by its *changsŭng*.
Photo by author.

However, upon his arrival at the training center the narrator is informed that he is too old to be a regular trainee, and he accepts a position within the school as an instructor's apprentice. The narrator's and Iwamoto's lives first intersect when one day the narrator notices Iwamoto sobbing during the moment of silence that trainees daily observe to remember their gratitude to their parents. This sparks the narrator's intense curiosity about the young man's past. He soon learns that the youth has had a troubled life. Iwamoto had attended an academy for delinquent boys, and his father had until recently been a drunkard. But Iwamoto had somehow managed to become a model youth in service to the nation, and by volunteering for military service had caused his father to change his ways and inspired other young men in the academy to also volunteer.

The little that the narrator initially learns only whets his appetite to know more. Iwamoto responds to all of his questions, describing the life processes through which a desultory Korean boy had come to be constituted as a well-disciplined, Japanese national subject. As a child he had gotten into trouble, mainly out of frustration that as a Korean he was ineligible for military service. But perhaps, he reflects, he would not have given up on himself had it not been for his father. The narrator understands how discrimination against Koreans with regard to their military eligibility, Iwamoto's family situation with an irresponsible father and a stepmother, and the poverty of Korean immigrants might all have contributed to Iwamoto's despair.

Iwamoto recalls that unlike most of the other boys in the academy, he had not been forced to resign himself to its care. Instead, following the advice of someone from the local Kyōwakai branch (a governmental organization that had been established to regulate the activities of Korean residents in Japan), he had entered of his own volition so that, as he put it, "I could rigorously reform my past self" (p. 43). Although the academy's Principal Maruoka had taught the boys that they were the "Emperor's children" and that they should be reborn as "true Japanese" (*shin no Nipponjin*) (p. 48), he was sometimes troubled with doubts about his ability to achieve that end. At those times he regretted having entered the academy.

As a youth one further question had weighed heavily on Iwamoto's mind. While he had heard that Korea and metropolitan Japan had been one since ancient times, such an idea seemed disconnected from his daily life. Only on making a pilgrimage to Koma Shrine did the reality of "the unity of metropolitan Japan and Korea" become real to him in "a flash of illumination" (pp. 50–51). The materiality of the landscape showed Iwamoto that Koreans had come to metropolitan Japan more than 1,200 years earlier and that they had become completely Japanese.

At this point in the story the narrator begins his own travel back to Japan, first visiting northern and middle Korea and witnessing throughout the provinces the training of imperial subjects and young men of draftable age. Somehow, Iwamoto is constantly on his mind, and we find him retracing the youth's spiritual journey. Thus he visits the Maruoka Academy and sees the disciplined lifestyle of its students. Principal Maruoka explains to the narrator his philosophy of teaching: the main purpose of the academy is to impress upon the boys "that they are Japanese" and "that they are subjects of the imperial nation." As for Iwamoto, the principal reaffirms, only upon making the pilgrimage to Koma Shrine did he learn that "his own ancestors were the same as those of the Yamato Race (*Yamato minzoku*)" (p. 55).

After calling on Maruoka the narrator makes his own pilgrimage to Koma, returning us to the time and place at which the story began. The narrator leaves behind Tenka Daishōgun, making his way to the shrine itself. Along the way, as he retraces the route that Iwamoto had taken, he recalls the history of the oneness of Korea and metropolitan Japan in that region. And following the historical scholarship of the time, he notes that 1,797 immigrants led by a Korean prince from Koguryŏ (J. Kōkuri) had settled in Koma more than 1,200 years earlier. Just then, he passes by the Koma elementary school, where some children have begun to leave the school grounds. He observes the faces of the children and it seems to him that "two out of five look so much like recent [Korean] immigrants that they could be misrecognized as such." He thinks of Iwamoto again and conjectures that he too must have been shocked and moved by these faces, but then reflects that "in the same way that the faces of 1,200 years ago have become metropolitan Japanese faces (Naichika), Iwamoto's face is also changing." The metropole and Korea are, after all, one and the same (p. 57).

The story comes to its dramatic conclusion when the narrator finally reaches his destination. Like Iwamoto, it is here that he is most impressed by the reality of the unity of Korea and the metropole. He thinks back again to Iwamoto and toward the future, when many other pilgrims will also be moved by this site. But most importantly, he reflects that "in ancient times Koreans had come not only to this place, Musashino, but to every corner of the country and are also prospering in this fashion." Furthermore, he calculates that more than a hundred other shrines in metropolitan Japan could be traced back to Korea. The narrator's final vision of the landscape, then, is of the metropole covered with sacred sites such as Koma Shrine that bear visual witness to the complete melding of Korea and the metropole in ancient times. The story ends with the narrator praying that Iwamoto will become an even better soldier and that "all Korean comrades will even a day earlier complete the task of becoming imperial subjects" (p. 58).

Chō's attentiveness to Koma Shrine as a mnemonic site that could awaken forgotten memories of an original national unity between Korea and the metropole was part of an official discourse on Korean and Japanese sameness that interjected the history of Korean immigration into the history of Japan. "Volunteer Soldier Iwamoto" and Chō's other stories of Korean men becoming Japanese soldiers and citizens call our attention to the ways in which spaces and places work to constitute them as national subjects. Famous sites on the national symbolic topography—places such Ise, Meiji, and Yasukuni Shrines as well as the Imperial Palace—interpellate Chō's characters as Japanese. But Chō and others also attempted to emplot other far less well-known shrines with some relationship to Korea onto the national memoryscape. Such shrines as Koma and religious sites in the metropole that were regarded as having been founded by immigrants from the Korea Peninsula, as well as various shrines throughout the "Peninsula" with connections to the metropole—writers, ideologues, and the media reconstituted these so as to offer them as material evidence for the claim that metropolitan Japan and Korea had been and should be one.

In order to advance his thesis on Korean and Japanese sameness, Chō also takes the apparently odd position that cultural assimilation might have the capacity to trump biological inheritances of physical appearance—"the faces of 1,200 years ago have become metropolitan Japanese faces (*Naichika*), Iwamoto's face is also changing." Such an idea may seem absurd and particular to Japanese colonial discourse. However, even the most cosmopolitan of intellectuals among Chō's contemporaries in the modern world freely espoused the idea that corporeal transformations tended to accompany cultural assimilation.

For instance, at exactly the moment that the *Mainichi shinbun* was serializing "Volunteer Soldier Iwamoto," the renowned writer Yi Kwang-su published a short essay with the title "Kao ga kawaru" ("Faces Change").[49] Yi's novel *Mujŏng* (*Heartless*, 1917) is often regarded as the "first major modern novel in Chosŏn (Korea),"[50] and he was a major participant in the Korean independence movement. However, by the time he wrote "Faces Change" he had taken on the Japanized name of Kayama Mitsurō in addition to his Korean name and was publishing on behalf of the Japanese empire. Elsewhere, as we will see, Yi would also argue that a kind of post-racial Japanese universalism ensured the equality of Koreans and metropolitan Japanese; but here he argued strongly for common blood and the propensity of Korean faces to change as they literally incorporated Japanese culture. Remarking on the power of culture to transform Korean physiognomy over the course of some thirty years of Japanese colonialism, Yi explained: "It is not only the faces that have changed. The style of dress, the manner of walking and decorum, and the way of thinking have probably changed. It is likely that all of these things have come together to have the effect of changing faces" (p. 27).

Koreans were dressing in Japanese clothes, intermarrying, receiving the same education as Japanese, worshipping at the same religious institutions, speaking the same language, thinking the same thoughts—all of these factors fused the peoples in such a thoroughgoing way, he reasoned, that eventually the phrase "the unity of Korea and the Metropole" would become obsolete, an anachronistic expression for a time before complete union.

Again, like Chō, Yi held that an original unity of blood enabled Koreans and metropolitan Japanese to become one people in both appearance and culture. In contrast, "in all likelihood the English would not in several tens of thousands of years come to have the faces of Indians" (p. 27). Furthermore, while Koreans and metropolitan Japanese had the closest consanguineous ties, an undercurrent of common blood also bound together all the peoples of East Asia in the Co-Prosperity Sphere. In this sense the unity of Korea and the metropole was but the harbinger of the eventual unity of "Japanese, Manchus, and Chinese," and under Japanese leadership they would come to form one "Great Ethnos" (*ichi daiminzoku*). "Moreover," he said, "I have the feeling that the day is not far when the faces of Annamese, Malays, and South Pacific Islanders will also become alike" (p. 28).

The idea that culture might transmute bodies, despite the importance of blood, also was not uncommon in the United States in the first half of the twentieth century. Following David Palumbo-Liu's richly documented and incisive research,[51] we know that the Immigration Commission (otherwise known as the Dillingham Commission), which was established by Congress in 1907 to assess the effects of immigration on the United States, was very attentive to the corporeal transmutability of immigrants—at least those of eastern and southern European stock. As one of the commission's publications put it: "For instance, the east European Hebrew, who has a very round head, becomes more long-headed; the south Italian, who in Italy has an exceedingly long head, becomes more short headed; so that in this country both approach a uniform type, as far as the roundness of the head is concerned."[52] By the 1930s, some Americans even observed that Asian bodies and visages were changing as a result of their environment. In his *The Oriental in American Life* (1934), the clergyman Albert Palmer held that "American-Japanese" were taller, heavier and had longer legs than those born in Japan. "Changes in eyelids and eyelashes are also evident, but the most noteworthy adjustment is in the shape of the mouth and the general openness and responsiveness of the countenance." Palmer hoped that American public opinion would recognize that these young Asians were "a new type" and that they were not "just replicas of the old type foreign-born Chinese or Japanese."[53] That culture had the power to transform physicality even appears to have been a common belief among War Relocation Authority personnel charged with overseeing Japanese Americans in the camps. As its self-authored history explained: "Superficially too, WRA staff members were quick to note, these [Nisei] youngsters gave every appearance of being more American than their elders. They looked generally taller and straighter, and in some cases even seemed to have a less pronounced oriental cast of features."[54]

NATIONALISM AND SELF-DETERMINATION

National belonging for Koreans and Japanese, however, was not founded solely on the premise of shared blood, culture, or even a humanity that transcended the symbolism of blood. While these factors certainly mattered, nationalism rested on the doctrine that individuals could become genuine national subjects only through their self-determination, not by ascription. In all three "texts" that I have considered at some length—"Volunteer Soldier Iwamoto," *Suicide Squad at the Watchtower*, and

Love and the Vow—the authors represent even those in disprivileged positions under Japanese colonialism as making the choice to become Japanese. It was apparently not enough for Koreans to be shown contributing to and indeed dying in the war effort. They had to be seen as agents of their own decisions who struggle internally with the alternatives of disloyalty and loyalty to Japan, because only through such an inner conflict could the normative choice appear as a matter of freedom or self-determination. Rather than reading this contradiction between submission and freedom as exceptional to a duplicitous Japanese national and colonial regime, these texts expose the mechanisms of nationalism more generally.

In his classic treatise on nationalist thought, Elie Kedourie argued that the idea of self-determination is one of the most fundamental philosophical foundations of nationalist doctrine.[55] Those who formed the French nation in the late eighteenth century, for example, assumed that they came together in a "free union with one another," and such people as the Alsatians were said to be acting of their own will in uniting themselves with the French people (p. 17). In Kedourie's interpretation, Kant's achievement was to articulate a notion of freedom that could serve as the philosophical basis for the nationalist idea of self-determination. This "freedom in the strictest, i.e., transcendental sense," as Kant put it, was opposed to the simple idea that freedom meant doing whatever one pleased. Instead, for Kant freedom meant submission or obedience to the categorical imperative, to the laws of morality, which were to be found not in the external world but within the souls of individuals. Submission to this inward law is freedom in that it is not obedience to an external or even divine command. Freely recognized and freely accepted, it enables a critique of the world as it is. Thus in Kant's formula, "the good will, which is the free will, is also the autonomous will" (p. 24). But since this moral rigor must be based on inner freedom, the result is constant internal struggle. In Kedourie's words, "The autonomous man is a stern activist, a perpetually tormented soul" (p. 30).

Kedourie located this familiar description of the modern self-constituting, autonomous subject as explicated by Kant at the very heart of nationalism by showing that Kant's celebration of the dynamic notion of self-determination was taken up by later nationalist thinkers such as Fichte. The latter also valorized freedom as the highest good and a self-imposed internal state, but shifted its grounding so that true individual freedom was said to be possible only through complete identification with the whole. Thus, "[I]t is only when he and the state are one that the individual realizes his freedom" (p. 38). The nationalist appropriation of Kantian ethics thus managed to celebrate simultaneously individual self-determination and submission to the whole. For Kedourie, however, this was a resolution that opened the way for the massive abuse of state power. The articulation of political issues in such terms as "development, fulfillment, self-determination, [and] self-realization" (pp. 47–48) occluded relations of power and state violence while nationalist leaders spoke in the language of aesthetics, religion, and love. Yet even though nationalists often referred to ties of language, race, or religion, in the end it was the "will of the individual [that] must ultimately indicate whether a nation exists or not" (p. 80). "National self-determination is, in the final analysis, a determination of the will; and nationalism is, in the first place, a method of teaching the right determination of the will" (p. 81).

Kedourie may be faulted for his inattention to the ways in which his criticisms of nationalism might have been applied to the United States and Great Britain, especially in contrast to his hyperattention to the political abuses of third world nationalists (pp. 74, 108–12). Nevertheless, his tracing of nationalist doctrine through the idea of self-determination helps us see that the Japanese brand of nationalism—both in its formative moment in the late nineteenth and early twentieth centuries and in the late colonial or late wartime period when Korea was being included in the larger idea of Japan—is fully comprehensible within the larger parameters of nationalist doctrine's emphasis on freedom with submission.

In my running commentaries on *Suicide Squad at the Watchtower* and *Love and the Vow*, I have already alluded to representations of the inward agitation of Koreans and Chinese as they freely strove to arrive at the choice of becoming Japanese, but we may find in Chō Kakuchū's writings an extremely well diagrammed exposition of the relationship between freedom and submission that I have described through Kedourie and my earlier work on Japanese nationalism.[56] Many of the spaces that Chō constructs are "spaces of confinement"—namely, military training schools (*kunrenjo*), military barracks (*heiei*), an academy for delinquent youth, and so on: bordered spaces of visibility where individuals are both objectified and constituted as self-disciplining subjects. It is in these places that Koreans not only learn to become national subjects but contend with the internal turmoil that exists precisely because they are supposed to be free.

Like Korea as a whole in the dominant Japanese discourse on the colony, Iwamoto is represented as a lost and confused adolescent until he finds his own subjectivity as a Japanese imperial subject. Iwamoto seeks of his own volition to have his soul reformed in the disciplinary space of an academy for troubled youth. There are some successes, but Iwamoto's subjectivity is incompletely formed and his soul wanders. Iwamoto confesses that on one occasion he lied to the principal so that he could temporarily escape from the academy. If the academy as a micro-space of confinement guards against such an unreflexive soul, escape from it at first seems to foster laxity.

But as he and a friend wait at a bus stop at Hibiya, Iwamoto happens to catch a glimpse of the Imperial Palace's moat. Until then he had "completely returned to [his] past [degenerate] self," but the instant he sees the moat (obviously associated with the emperor) he "suddenly froze in fear." His "heart was violently smashed to bits" (*ganto kokoro ga tatakikudakareta*). Then, after sending his confused friend off alone, Iwamoto walks to the Nijū Bridge in front of the Imperial Palace, "as if [he] were being unwittingly sucked toward it" (*suitsukarete yukuyō ni*). There he remembers his monthly patriotic trips to worship the palace and he feels as if he is seeing the "face of Principal Maruoka standing there." After worshipping the palace in tears, Iwamoto returns to the academy and confesses to the principal (p. 49).

In the end the space outside the academy, the Nation, is yet another and far more expansive "space of confinement" where the individual soul remains subject to a disciplinary gaze. The imperial moat and the palace function like the tower in Foucault's description of Bentham's Panopticon (as does the face of the patriarch Maruoka), and by their presence on the physical landscape they help constitute the self-disciplining self that is the subject of the modern Nation. Iwamoto returns to the academy, but the implication is that he no longer really needs to be confined there; for he can be both free and obedient, and eventually he "volunteers" to become a soldier. In other words, Iwamoto's self-determination, as well as by extension Korea's, results in self-subjectification to the nation of Japan.

.   .   .

While the explicit articulation of the primacy of blood continued to appear in late wartime discourses on the colonial/national relationship—more often to stress the blood sameness of Japanese and Koreans than the superiority of a pure Yamato race—such a discourse was supplemented by a humanism and universalism that disavowed blood symbolism altogether. Rather than interpreting the humanistic and universalist messages found in these examples of late colonial/national literature and film as merely insincere lies or false ideologies, I read them as indications of the turn toward polite racism and the disavowal of racism that became the very means through which a recalibrated system of racial exploitation was sustained. The promise of the essential admissibility of all into the Japanese nation set the conditions for Koreans to choose to become Japanese, but it also legitimated the discrimination and exploitation of those regarded as culturally inadequate or immature. And yet, this promise of admissibility and the imperative to act as if such an admissibility existed enabled the constitution of some colonial subjects into exemplary Japanese citizens, whether in film and literary representation or in life outside fiction and the movies.

Such a reading of late wartime colonial films and literature once again compels us to reconsider the easy binaries that are usually constructed to separate so-called fascist Japan from liberal democratic nation-states—including those of the Allied Powers in the 1930s and '40s, their postwar incarnations, and postcolonial Japan. The translatability of the Hollywood Victorian Empire film and the World War II combat film into the Japanese colonial context is suggestive in this regard, as is the coexistence of racism and its disavowal in wartime and postwar America. The case of Japanese American soldiers during World War II who fought for freedom and democracy while their families were imprisoned in internment camps is but one of the glaring examples of the compatibility of racism and its denunciation in an avowedly liberal regime. Likewise the scheme of the model Japanese American leader Mike Masaoka to form a "suicide battalion" during the war to prove the loyalty of Japanese Americans—this demonstrates less an exotic borrowing from "Japanese culture" than Masaoka's insight that such a plan might work within the context of the American nation. In fact, as Slotkin points out, one of the conventional tropes of the Hollywood combat film genre is the mission that will "require total sacrifice for the cause," including the heroic deaths of soldiers and sometimes even "suicidal martyrdom."[57]

CHAPTER EIGHT

The Colonial and National
Politics of Gender, Sex,
and Family

> Gender power was not the superficial patina of empire,
> an ephemeral gloss over the more decisive mechanics
> of class or race. Rather, gender dynamics were, from
> the outset, fundamental to the securing and maintenance
> of the imperial enterprise.
>
> ANNE MCCLINTOCK, *Imperial Leather: Race, Gender and
> Sexuality in the Colonial Contest* (1995)

> His thoughts leaped back to all the fuss they had made
> over Japanese-Korean marriages during the occupa-
> tion of [Korea by Japan]. Then such things weren't the
> makings of slander and humiliation. Rather, they were
> thought quite natural by many, if not possibly even a
> mark of distinction.
>
> CHŎN KWANGYONG, *"Kapitan Ri"* (1962)

In recent years some of the most incisive scholarship on the cultural politics of empire has emphasized that the management of families, gender, and sex was not of
secondary concern for colonial and imperial powers, but was central to and impli-
cated in the constitution and maintenance of larger structures of exploitation and
domination. Thus, as Ann Stoler has put it, she has been concerned to interrogate
"how and why microsites of familial and intimate space figure so prominently in
the macropolitics of imperial rule," a problematic that echoes with other feminist
calls for attentiveness to why "gender dynamics were, from the outset, fundamental to the securing and maintenance of the imperial enterprise."[1] With regard to colonialism in East Asia, while in their pioneering work on gender and Korean nationalism Chungmoo Choi and Elaine H. Kim focus primarily on the postcolonial effects

and conditions of Korean nationalism, they also operate from an understanding that Japanese colonialism and its successor, U.S. neocolonialism, were and are gendered and sexualized formations. Such works and a few earlier studies such as those by Frantz Fanon have helped us see that the construction of masculinity, the cult of domesticity, the regulation of sexual relations, and the production and maintenance of particular types of heterosexual families and the like—all these exceeded the supposed realm of the private, as well as the limited level of metaphor, and worked in a mutually constitutive relationship to race, class, and imperial domination.[2] To be sure, they were tropes that helped authorize asymmetrical colonial and imperial power relations, as in the Saidian formulation of the masculine imperial power and the feminized Orient.[3] But beyond that, colonial and imperial powers have worked to actually fashion gender, sex, and families in ways that have been enabling for colonial and imperial rule.

In one respect, such a perspective should sound familiar to historians of Japanese colonialism in Korea, for it is fairly well-known that one of the Japanese colonial government's core policies for managing the Korean people in the interests of the war effort involved transforming the structure of Korean families. For example, while the so-called *sōshi kaimei* campaign is often translated as the "name-changing campaign"[4]—the point being that this was a movement to force Koreans to adopt Japanese-style names—it was also something more. Through *sōshi kaimei* the colonial government sought above all to regulate Korean families along the model of the Japanese-style household, which had one surname (*shi*) for all household members. In conventional Korean naming practices, women marrying into households had retained their patrilineal descent names (J. *sei*, K. *sŏng*) and had not adopted their husband's surnames after marriage. As a result, multiple descent names existed within the same domicile, while women's patrilineal kinship ties complicated kinship bonds within and beyond the household. In order to execute the strategy of turning unified households into the basic unit of population management above the individual, the colonial government made it legally obligatory to establish one surname for an entire household. This was literally *sōshi*, "establishing household surnames." As Kim Yŏng-dal has stressed, voluntarism in "establishing household surnames" did not exist, because even if the head of a household neglected to register a new household surname (*shi*) during the six-month campaign period that began on 11 February 1940, his patrilineal descent name (*sei*) automatically became his household surname (*shi*) after 10 August 1940. At the same time, while Koreans experienced enormous pressure to adopt Japanized household surnames and given names, the law did not require them to do so.[5] Thus *sōshi kaimei* entailed the legally obligatory adoption of unified household surnames and the formally voluntary, albeit usually coerced, changing of names. Hence, to capture the intent of the policy it would be better to translate *sōshi kaimei* as "establishing household surnames and changing names," rather than simply "changing names."

Some historians have also understood that while there was no shortage of those in Japan who advocated racial eugenics, strict sexual separation, and endogamy, colonial policy in Korea had from the 1920s encouraged intermarriage and significantly advanced the campaign for the conjugal coupling of Japanese and Koreans during the war. At one level this colonial politics of marriage and sex operated through the highly visible liaisons of several scions of the former Korean monarchy to the Japanese extended imperial family (*kōzoku*) and aristocratic elite. The first and most spectacular case was the marriage of Princess Nashimoto Masako to Prince Yi Ŭn in April 1920. Prince Yi Ŭn was none other than the son of Kojong, the Korean monarch who had reigned until 1907, when Japanese military and political pressure forced his abdication. He was also the brother (by a different mother) of Sunjong, Kojong's successor, who was on the throne in 1910—that is, when the Japanese state formally annexed Korea, abolished the Korean monarchy, and established the former Korean royal family as a new Japanese royal house (Ri'ōke) under the Japanese emperor. Prince Yi Ŭn's bride, Princess Masako, was the daughter of Morimasa, head of the Nashimoto house, a collateral house within the extended imperial family (*kōzoku*). In 1931 the male to female marriage exchange went first in the opposite direction, with the wedding of Kojong's youngest daughter, Princess Tŏk-hye, to Count Sō Takeshi, who was descended from the lords of the Tsushima domain. Then, in the same year, one of Kojong's grandsons wedded Matsudaira Keiko, who was related to Princess Masako on her mother's side.[6]

Such marriage arrangements among those broadly categorized as "blue bloods" could be read as throwbacks to premodern aristocratic practices, in which strategic couplings advanced kinship alliances of the elite across territories but had little to do with constituting heterogeneous populations as unified peoples. The deployment of marriage alliances by premodern European monarchies is perhaps the most familiar example of this strategy. In the Japanese case, we might recall the marriage of the next-to-last shogun, Tokugawa Iemochi, to Emperor Kōmei's sister Kazu-nomiya on the eve of the Meiji Restoration. That had been an effort to form a political alliance between the faltering Shogunate and the newly rising Imperial Court. But this earlier instance of marriage and sexual politics preceded the formation of the modern nation-state, occurring at a time when the common people were yet but irrelevant bystanders.

However, the colonial regime began to expand its strategy of conquest through miscegenation far beyond the couplings of a few representatives of the "blue-blooded" class, particularly in the period of total war. The Korean Government-General's Law Concerning Intermarriage of Metropolitan Japanese and Koreans (Naisenjin tsūkon hō), which passed in June 1921, expressed in legal terms the government's official position that marriage unions between the colonizers and the colonized were conducive to the larger colonial aim of "amalgamating" (*yūgō dōka*) the Koreans with the metropolitan Japanese. Yet only in the period after the outbreak of full-scale war against China (1937–45)—in other words, precisely when the wartime demands for civilian and military labor pushed the discourse of equality and inclusion to its limits—can we observe a much more vigorous official campaign for intermarriages.

This was the moment when cross-ethnic marriages shifted from existing strictly as a metaphor for the unity of Korea and metropolitan Japan to becoming also an instrument of rule. For example, the Commission on Policies for the Current Situation (Jikyoku Taisaku Chōsakai)—an advisory body established within the Government-General in August 1938—produced a report proposing specific measures to achieve the complete "fusion of Koreans with the metropolitan Japanese." Most tellingly, one of its twelve recommendations for realizing this end suggested the thoroughgoing implementation of the new system allowing Korean men to volunteer for the Japanese army, while another offered that it was necessary to "devise appropriate steps to encourage intermarriage between Metropolitan Japanese and Koreans."[7] When the Government-General's official history of thirty years of colonial rule over Korea noted the manifold increase in mixed couples between 1925 and 1937, it did so in celebratory fashion, observing that many more common-law mixed couples that had not been registered undoubtedly existed, and that these intermarriages signified the excellent progress made in the unification of Korea with metropolitan Japan.[8]

Minami Jirō, governor-general of Korea from August 1936 to May 1942 and well-known for his promotion of policies designed to assimilate Koreans to what was said to be Japanese imperial culture, also strongly advocated intermarriage. In his May 1939 instructions to the Korean Federation for Mobilization of the National Spirit (Kokumin Seishin Sōdōin Chōsen Renmei)—the organization that had been established in July 1938 to lead the movement to foster and unify the (Japanese) national spirit of the Korean people and thereby to realize the national mission in a time of crisis—Minami implored his readers to understand that *Naisen ittai*, the melding of Koreans and metropolitan Japanese into one body, should be understood as more than just a metaphor. It did not mean just "tepidly holding one another's hands, melding into one form, and so on." Instead, it signaled that "it is necessary in form, in spirit, in blood, and in the flesh—in each and everyone of these ways to become one body." Under Minami's administration, the Government-General continued to make changes enabling the legal formation of mixed households, including making it possible for Korean households to adopt Japanese individuals, and vice versa. The Korean Federation for the Mobilization of the National Spirit even presented formal commendations and gifts to mixed conjugal couples in recognition of them as models of and for the unity of Korea and the metropole.[9]

The data reported by the colonial government give the impression that the actual number of intermarriages was never very high. For example, according to records incorporated into Suzuki Yūko's analysis, 404 such couples could be identified in 1925, and their number apparently rose to 1,206 by 1937.[10] Another set of data prepared by Government-General officials in anticipation of the eighty-sixth Imperial Diet (December 1944) indicates 907 mixed couples in Korea in 1938, and 1,528 in 1942. Yet the colonial bureaucrats who tabulated these data from household registries recognized that their figures represented gross undercounts. As they explained, only as recently as 1921 had the colonial state institutionalized the system for recording marriages through the household registration system (*koseki*). And Koreans customarily had not even possessed household surnames (*shi*), a factor central to the ability of the household registration system to accurately track the population.

Moreover, Koreans had only recently become subject to military conscription. While the document's authors did not explain the connection between instituting the draft and having a precise record of marriages, they undoubtedly shared the common understanding that Korea's household registration system had been extremely unreliable until plans for military conscription made it imperative for the colonial state to accurately know the composition of Korean households. The authors of the document therefore concluded that "the actual figures [for intermarriages] are several tens of times or several hundreds of times those in the table." In fact, although circumstances in the metropole differed in some very important respects from those that obtained in Korea, the colonial authorities found that when it attempted to count common-law marriages between Koreans and metropolitan Japanese in the home islands in addition to those officially registered, they found 10,700 intermarriages in the metropole alone.[11]

In short, although the official count of intermarriages may have been relatively small, given Korea's estimated population of around 16.9 million in 1920 and 23.55 million in 1940,[12] the colonial authorities nevertheless celebrated the conjugal couplings of Koreans with Japanese as the figurative and literal embodiment of the slogan "the unification of Korea with metropolitan Japan." Even when they reported small figures for officially registered marriages, they claimed that many more Koreans and Japanese had coupled and that this was a positive development. Popular memory of this official encouragement of intermarriage was captured by the writer Chŏn Kwangyong in his 1962 short story "Kapitan Ri" when he has the protagonist reflect back on the approbation given to cross-ethnic marriages in the late colonial period (quoted in an epigraph to this chapter).[13]

Expanding on arguments introduced in chapter 1, I want to highlight the fit between this intensified attention to gender, sex, and the family and the inclusion of Koreans within the Japanese regime of bio-power and governmentality. Conventional scholarship has understood *sōshi kaimei* as strictly a negative policy designed to obliterate Korean cultural practices, but it was also an integral part of the turn toward actualization of a productive modality of power that sought to transform Korean families into positive sites of political intervention. While marriages between Japanese and Korean royalty and the nobility may have been symbols of the unity of Korea and metropolitan Japan beginning in 1920, from especially the late 1930s on we witness in the Japanese colonial context what Foucault describes as the transformation of the family from a model or metaphor of government into "an element internal to population, and into an instrument of its government." Throughout this chapter we will see that while Foucault may too easily discount the enduring power of family and familial relations as metaphors when he says that the "theme of population" made "elimination of the family as model" possible,[14] his observations on reconstituting the family into an apparatus to regulate populations are fully applicable to the changing character of power in late colonial, wartime Korea. In short, not only did the family continue as a metaphor for the Korea/metropolitan Japan relationship; the multiplicity of families making up "segments" of the population became instruments through which to manage the people.

In this chapter I seek to more explicitly discuss the imbrications of familial, gendered, and sexual microspaces with the macropolitical, for although scholars have paid some attention to mobilization of the discourse on ethnic sameness between Japanese and Koreans (*Nissen dōsoron*) to legitimate Japanese colonial rule in Korea, there has been virtually no analysis of the ways in which discourses and practices regarding gender, sex, and the family supplemented and helped constitute those on ethnic unity. Such a problematic will require me to untangle the knots of colonial discourses and practices and demonstrate how the simple binary of colonizers and colonized can show us only one dimension, however important, of Japanese colonial rule—especially during the late colonial period, when official discourses and practices increasingly included Koreans in an expanding conception of the Japanese nation.

The reader attentive to such questions may already have noticed the ways in which the films and literature examined in the previous chapter show that the colonial and increasingly nationalized discourse concerning the relationship between Korea and Japan was articulated and constituted at the sites of gender, sex, and the family. Within these texts, individuals are represented not just as ethnically Korean, Japanese, or Chinese but also as men and women who aspire to "Japanese" norms of masculinity or femininity within the context of "Japanized" nuclear families, as well as in class and other relations that transcend families and ethnicity.

Not surprisingly, soldiering offers a particularly illuminating window on this relationship between gender, sex, and the family, on the one hand, and nationalism and colonialism on the other. When Korean soldiers became models for and of the idealized Japanese male, they were constituted not only as Japanese national and war heroes but also as lovers, husbands, and sometimes fathers. As might be expected, images of Korean soldiering in literature, film, and the media more generally consistently invoked images of their militarized yet civilized hypermasculinity. But at the same time, the soldiers in these cultural productions were unfailingly constituted in their relations with women, even as women were constituted in their relationships with men. Moreover, the terrain of families—either already or about to be formed from heterosexual couples—was never far from the apparently grander site of soldiering and the telos of becoming Japanese.

And in a way that is tied to the themes of self-determination and freedom that have already been discussed in the previous chapter, the ideal coupling of young men and women is almost always represented as a freely chosen pact. Here the apparently personal world of romantic love is interbraided with the larger world of social and national life. The lovers desire to choose their partners, but such a choice is intermingled with choosing to become Japanese. The challenges that lovers face in consummating their personal passion are the same as the obstacles thrown in the way of Korea's destiny as a part of Japan. If the national hero is at the same time the male lover, husband, and sometimes father, then the national heroine is at the same time the female lover, wife, or mother. As part of the drive by the colonial government (as well as by Japanese and Korean artists and other collaborators) to turn the "private" sphere of families into an instrument of rule, literary and filmic representations of heterosexual intimacy not only depicted parents sacrificing their sons for the nation; they also encouraged readers and viewers to identify the consummation of romantic love with the achievement of unity between Korea and metropolitan Japan, even when the consummation of love coincided with self-sacrifice for the nation. As Doris Sommer has so elegantly and convincingly demonstrated in the case of the Latin American novel, "[R]omance doesn't distinguish between ethical politics and erotic passion, between epic nationalism and intimate sensibility. It collapses the distinctions."[15]

THE MASCULINIST BONDS OF NATION AND EMPIRE

As in colonialisms throughout much of the rest of the world, Japanese colonial discourse generally worked to infantilize and feminize the colonized in such manner as to make masculinist imperial domination appear warranted and natural.[16] It was commonly said, for example, that Korea had become effeminate because of its long history of valorizing the literary over the military arts. One of the Korean subjects of Carter J. Eckert's fine study of colonial industrialization echoed this view; as Eckert explains, he blamed the reluctance of Korean students to volunteer for the Japanese military on "Korea's historical degeneration into 'effeminacy,' the result of the country's traditional pursuit of the literary arts to the neglect of the military."[17]

Yet the practical necessity of incorporating Koreans into the Japanese war effort and into the Japanese nation, particularly as soldiers, made it impossible to sustain a rigid binary logic of masculinized colonizers and infantilized and feminized colonial subjects. Instead, even as it feminized Korean males, colonial discourse and practice presented them with the opportunity to attain their (Japanese) adult manhood through service for the nation. Colonialism and nationalism thus sought, albeit with mixed results, to mobilize their subjects not simply through repressive means but also by producing gendered desires and presenting opportunities to fulfill them. For instance, the *Keijō Nippō* reported that in his speech to the 202 first graduates of the military training program for Korean volunteers, Governor-General Minami Jirō observed and praised them for the improvement of their manly physiques and deportment. "If naked [your bodies] would reveal muscles that have become hardened. . . . [Y]our speech and bodily manners are expeditious and you have become filled with strength in a manly kind of way."[18] When Lower House Member Pak Ch'un-gŭm stood up in a formal session of the Diet to thank his "seventy million metropolitan Japanese compatriots" on behalf of his "twenty-three million Peninsular compatriots" for making it possible for Koreans to volunteer for the Japanese army, he described the joy of Koreans as that of "babes who have become adults" (*akambō ga otona ni natta yō ni*)—to which, it was reported, all the Diet members in attendance responded with applause.[19]

Suicide Squad at the Watchtower, which I have analyzed at some length in the previous chapter, also shows very clearly that in late wartime discourse, for Korean males Korean ethnic difference was associated with femininity while becoming Japanese was tied to masculinity, and that a movement from one ethnicity to the other entailed a transition from one pole of gender to the other, and vice versa. In an early scene, two Korean policemen, Officers Kin (Kim) and Hayashi (Im), are made to sing in Korean and dance in Korean style to entertain their Japanese comrades. As in Hollywood films (including *Bataan*), singing and dancing are used to mark racial or ethnic difference in a way that is not clearly either cultural or racial, because those activities are so closely associated with the physical body. A Japanese officer tells Kin that were it not for his dancing he would be "just like a Japanese from the metropole in every way" (*maru de Naichijin*). Most relevant here on the issue of feminization, or at least the emasculinization, of Koreans is that in this scene of singing and dancing, the part of the film that most strikingly marks the Koreans as ethnically different, the Koreans are most emasculated. For as they sing and dance the Korean officers wear only their undershirts and their trousers with cuffs rolled up. They lack the full uniform that is the masculinized sign of their complete transformation into Japanese male subjecthood (see figure 14). It is only through their heroic deeds and their commitment to being loyal Japanese that they acquire the uniform— a multivalent sign of both masculinity and Japaneseness. Coming into full subjecthood is thus presented as a masculinist and Japanese nationalist opportunity.

Like his short story "Volunteer Soldier Iwamoto," Chō Kakuchū's "Shuppatsu" ("A Beginning") and "Atarashii shuppatsu" ("A New Beginning") are stories of Korean youth living in the Japanese metropole who overcome the frustrations of their colonial and emasculated status by enlisting in the military. And like "Volunteer Soldier Iwamoto," a very large multiethnic public within the metropole and Korea undoubtedly read or heard these literary pieces. *Kokumin sōryoku,* the wartime journal that had been launched in Korea as part of the national wartime mobilization effort, began serializing "A New Beginning" on 15 July 1943. Japan's national radio station, Dai Nippon Hōsō Kyōkai, commissioned "A Beginning" and aired it in August 1943 as part of a weeklong assortment of special programs commemorating the extension of military conscription to Koreans.[20] Although much could also be gleaned from "A Beginning," let us look in more detail at "A New Beginning."

Like the other short stories, "A New Beginning" is a parable of progress in the national disavowal of differences and the inclusion of Korean men into the fraternity of the nation. But even more than "A Beginning" and "Volunteer Soldier Iwamoto," the narrative demands the self-disciplinization of Korean individuals and

FIGURE 14.
In *Suicide Squad at the Watchtower*, Officers Kin (Kim) and
Hayashi (Im), third and second from the right, have just sung
and danced while wearing undershirts rather than full uniforms.
Film still courtesy of Korean Film Archive.

the normalization of the entire Korean community to what are imagined to be Japanese culture and values. In other words, becoming truly Japanese is seen as requiring not just the opportunity bestowed by the nation and emperor but also constant self-reflection on the practices of everyday life. Excessive talkativeness, excitability, loss of reason, extreme valuation of filial piety at the expense of loyalty to nation and emperor, and so on—these are understood to be the character traits not simply of individuals but of Koreans generally. And it is this Koreanness that must be shed in order for those from "the Peninsula" to become completely Japanese. The taut contradiction between the possibility of Koreans' inclusion into the nation and their abjection as Koreans generates their self-disciplining subjectivity as national and imperial subjects. Thus the story is filled with such expressions as "self-subjectification as an imperial subject" (*jiko kōminka*), "training of Peninsulars in becoming imperial subjects" (*Hantō no kōminka rensei*), "the self-consciousness of Peninsulars" (*Hantōjin no jikaku*), and the "training of the soul" (*tamashii no rensei*) (pp. 75, 142). When a group of Korean youths send off one of the story's heroes at a train station, they agree to do so solemnly, in a "model way" (*mohanteki*), not noisily as they say Koreans are prone to do. Moreover, Chō represents the military training center as a place where young men are Japanized, where they first learn the proper relation between filial piety and loyalty and then "reform their everyday lives to the metropolitan Japanese style (*Naichishiki ni*)" (pp. 115, 135). Furthermore, "A New Beginning" is remarkable for the ways in which it demonstrates the logic by which ethnic difference for men is to be transcended through the renaturalization of gender difference and the abjection of women.

The initial drama of "A New Beginning" is provided by its two main characters, Sawada and Shimamura, who have been driven apart for personal and political reasons but who are eventually reunited through the new possibility of Koreans serving in the military. The story's narrator explains in retrospect that years before the China Incident (1937)—during a time when they had used their Korean descent names Pak and Yi—the two families had quarreled and the two young men had become estranged. Only through rumors did Sawada hear that Shimamura had married a metropolitan Japanese woman.

Over the years Sawada gave little thought to Shimamura, but one day he unexpectedly receives two letters, the first apologizing for the quarrel that had taken place so many years earlier and a second announcing that Shimamura would be volunteering for the military. Shimamura asks Sawada to meet him at the train station, but Sawada is conflicted: while he is happy that Shimamura has decided to volunteer, he still cannot forget the past wrongs that he and his family have endured. Yet Sawada decides that he will go to the station, and upon noticing other men in military uniform, he is glad about his decision. Seeing these men while looking for Shimamura, Sawada muses on his new sense of inclusion in the nation.

In the past he had always tended to think of himself as a Japanese patriot. And yet, whenever he had sent off soldiers he had felt that "somehow, in a way it seemed like someone else's affair." But now, he had come to see his fellow Korean, Shimamura, and "this feeling of dissatisfaction melted away in an instantaneous flash of illumination." At that moment, the faces of the Japanese soldiers looked like Shimamura's. Self and Other, Peninsula and Metropole, Korean and Japanese, had all become one and the same (p. 78).

In the course of their reconciliation Shimamura explains to Sawada that the true reason he had forsaken Tokyo and Sawada so many years earlier was his sense of frustration at being unable to take the military conscription exam with his close Japanese friend Sugimoto. As a Korean Shimamura had not been eligible for the draft, and in those days he could not even volunteer. Just at that moment, Sawada and Shimamura had quarreled because Sawada thought Shimamura was spending too much time with Sugimoto rather than with him. Frustrated in his relations with both Sawada and Sugimoto, Shimamura had decided to flee from Tokyo. Thus, we learn that the estrangement of the two Korean youths had had nothing to do with the past relationship between their families. Instead, the exclusion of Korean men from the national fraternity of potential soldiers had ultimately resulted in the interpersonal problems separating all three young men. Shimamura's apparent character flaw had stemmed from the Nation's incomplete rejection of discrimination. But now Korean men could join the military and become part of the Nation. Chō makes the Nation stand for progress in the denunciation of ethnic discrimination that enables Sawada, Shimamura, and all other Koreans to be completely delivered from their internal distress.

It could be argued that there is a great deal of homoeroticism in this story. Sugimoto and Shimamura are like lovers, "studying together, taking walks together, sharing interests, reading the same books, thinking the same things[.]" Shimamura remarks, "In the Korean fashion you could say we were so close that we would even have shared what was in our mouths" (p. 91). Similarly, Sawada had acted like a spurned lover, jealously interrogating Shimamura about his relations with Sugimoto. And Shimamura insists that had his relationship with Sugimoto been more secure, he and Sawada might have been able to "tenderly make up" (p. 93). In fact, throughout his short stories Chō notes the attractiveness of the young soldier's uniforms and the fitness of their bodies. Later, as recounted in "A New Beginning," when Shimamura has already gone off to a training center, Sawada imagines him in uniform "losing himself in the regularity of the manly daily routine" (p. 117).

Yet the allure of the military is not strictly its underlying homoeroticism: rather, inclusion in the Nation through acceptance into the military is understood by Chō as the confirmation of masculinity. Moreover, this confirmation is constituted through a misogynous process of homosocial bonding. For Shimamura, rejection by Sugimoto results in marriage to a woman in whom he cannot confide. She cannot be an intimate partner in the manner of either Sugimoto, a metropolitan Japanese, or the Korean Sawada. At one point in the story Shimamura confides to Sawada that only Sawada, not his wife, can understand him (p. 73). And when Shimamura is finally on the train bound for the training center, even after his wife has dutifully seen him off, he resists any signs of affection, only noting, "In my heart I no longer have a shop or a wife. There is only the Emperor and the Nation" (p. 112). We might recall that in the film *Love and the Vow*, the Korean youth who eventually becomes a kamikaze pilot rejects the possibility of being the sibling of a woman and instead chooses to consider himself the younger brother of the Japanese war hero Murai, a Korean with whom he has no blood relationship.

In her important book on American masculinity and the Vietnam War, Susan Jeffords argues that one of the most prominent motifs in U.S. representations of the war involved the masculine bond's ability to overcome racial and class differences. Camaraderie among soldierly men enabled the military unit to become "the location for the eradication of social, class, ethnic, and racial boundaries."[21] Yet she also incisively argues that the constitution of this masculinist bond depended on the rejection of women and their exclusion from the national community of heterogeneous men. Only by marking women as absolutely different from men could Vietnam narratives constitute diverse men as the same: "Although Vietnam narratives show the bonding of soldiers from diverse and often antagonistic backgrounds, those bonds are always and already masculine. At no point are women to be included as a part of this collectivity. . . . It is through this elision—'America's collective consciousness' as a masculine consciousness—that the claim of collectivity is most safely made, as the firmly established structure of gender difference maintains a frame within which other change can (apparently) occur, change circumscribed by the masculine bond."[22]

As the above descriptions of Chō's short stories make clear, a similar argument could be made about his gendered representations of metropolitan Japanese and Koreans during the total war years of colonial rule. Like representations of the Vietnam War, Chō's narratives construct the military as the site at which metropolitan Japanese and Koreans reject their ethnic and colonial differences through their male bond. Moreover, this bonding is enabled by the absolute and hierarchized boundary that is formed between men and women. All men, metropolitan Japanese or Korean, must first reject all women, metropolitan Japanese or Korean, in order for the heterogeneous men to realize their sameness. Therefore, in the passage cited above the Korean Shimamura rejects his metropolitan Japanese wife in order to join the fraternity of Japanese men, even though in another context he might have continued to possess her as a token of his having become Japanese.

FEARING WOMEN, LOVING WOMEN

In such stories of the inclusion of ethnic and colonial men in the nation in exchange for the exclusion (or at least second-order inclusion) of all women, including metropolitan Japanese women, women are figured as threats to warfare, to the masculine bond, and hence to the nation. Mothers and wives are potentially menacing presences who may endanger the nation through their propensity to love their men excessively or to be objects of inordinate male affection. As Peter High points out in his masterful study of Japanese film during the Asia-Pacific War, Japanese films in general during this period warned against the "selfish, possessive feeling of parents toward their children." And films as well as other media commonly celebrated the self-sacrificing mother of militarized Japan, the *gunkoku no haha*, who encouraged her son to sacrifice himself for the nation and emperor.[23] In a related way, Jeffords makes the point that "when women appear in Vietnam narratives, it is never as part of the 'brotherhood' that is created in battle. They are instead usually trying to stop their husbands, sons, or lovers from going to Vietnam."[24]

And to continue our observations on points of comparability across the wartime Pacific, it is instructive to note that John Wylie's *Generation of Vipers* became a best seller in 1942. In her recent study, Rebecca Plant has observed that Wylie's attack on "momism" was part of a broader reassessment and critique of "maternal glorification" during the 1940s and 1950s and that his book was particularly popular among military servicemen. Plant further notes that during this period a widespread psychiatric discourse charged mothers with unhealthily dominating family life, thereby creating overly dependent sons through excessive affection, and upbraided them for producing weak men prone to "combat exhaustion." As George Lipsitz puts it, *Generation of Vipers* "blamed overprotective mothers for undermining the nation's strength by raising insufficiently masculine sons lacking in patriotic resolve."[25]

If it is the homosocial bond that unifies the fraternal nation through its work of transcending differences among men and expelling women, then the heterosocial bond between mothers and sons, or husbands and wives, constantly threatens to unleash a process of degeneration into the narrow particularism of family interests. Therefore, women no less than men must be reformed, and for Korean women the model of womanhood was the metropolitan Japanese woman.

As in many other Japanese colonial texts, Korean women in Chō's writings are always suspect. Even when they are lauded for their behavior, this praise is premised on their acting contrary to the expectation that they are probably not "good women." When Shimamura in "A New Beginning" is in a training center, he encounters a simple but pure-hearted trainee named Yoshimura. The noncommissioned officers "loved (*aishite iru*) Yoshimura for his ingenuous personality" (p. 137). But one day Yoshimura bursts out crying during the evening moment of silent self-reflection. Shimamura repeatedly asks him why he is so sad, each time suspecting that Yoshimura longs inappropriately for his wife or children and is not attentive enough to his soldierly duties. When Yoshimura mentions that he has left his wife and children behind, Shimamura is angered and responds that many trainees have wives and children. When Yoshimura says his wife has taken ill, Shimamura finds the situation laughable. But Shimamura is taken by surprise. Yoshimura's tears are not the result of selfish longing to be with his wife and family; instead, they come from thoughts of the incredible sacrifices that his wife and mother have made in order to help him become a good soldier—in fact, to become a man who can do without them. As it turns out, Yoshimura's wife's illness had been caused by the daily cold-water rigors she had undergone at a local shrine to pray that he might become a good soldier. Furthermore, when Yoshimura expressed concerns about who would care for his aging and frail widowed mother, she had scolded him for worrying about his family even though he was an "imperial soldier" (p. 140).

While Yoshimura's mother and wife are good women because they do not threaten to dismantle the boundary that separates them from the world of soldiers, they also defy expectations about the characteristics of Korean women. When Shimamura tells Yoshimura's story to his instructor, the latter is surprised: "What a splendid mother. We've got to have a better opinion about the Peninsular mother (*hantō no hahaoya*)." The instructor is astonished because, as Shimamura explains, it had been said that "the Korean mother is obsessed with loving only her own children, and does not give a thought to training her children or offering them to the nation" (p. 143). Yoshimura's mother is splendid because in tempering her son's soul she is not behaving like "the Korea mother." Indeed, the instructor concludes that she is nothing other than "a splendid Japanese mother" (*rippa na Nippon no haha oya da*) (p. 142).

Paralleling the demands placed on Korean men to rid themselves of what were deemed Korean tendencies and to become "Japanese," the narrative thus calls on Korean women to eradicate what are described as their Korean ways and to become Japanese mothers. In fact, by the end of the story we learn that the parable of Yoshimura's splendid "Japanese" mother has had a deep impact on many people. Shimamura's friend Sawada is greatly moved by the thought that "even in Korea there is such a splendid mother." And as a result of hearing the story, not only has Sawada's mother begun to reform her old ways, but she and Shimamura's sister have decided to start a "mother's association" (*haha no kai*). "In other words," Sawada concludes, "they have decided to start training as mothers" (p. 148).

Toyoda Shirō's 1943 film, *Figure of Youth (Wakaki sugata)*, interbraids the theme of soldiering as a means of achieving both manhood and Japaneseness with a minor romantic subplot that requires the reform of Korean women into Japanese women. Like Imai Tadashi, Toyoda Shirō is commonly regarded as one of Japan's most distinguished filmmakers. Born in 1906 and therefore six years older than Imai, he released his first film in 1929 and his last in 1973. His film career thus spanned the Asia-Pacific War (1931–45) and continued through the entire postwar period of high economic growth (1955–73). He is perhaps best known as the director who most often and with great success (as well as some failures) sought to translate major works of literature into the cinematic medium. At the same time, he has been praised for his skillful and realistic depictions of the everyday lives of common people, most notably in *Meoto zenzai* (*Bravo to the Man and Wife*), his 1955 classic set in one of the well-known amusement quarters of Osaka.

While not much discussed, it is no secret that Toyoda made films that supported Japanese imperialism. His 1940 work, *Ōhinata Mura* (*Ōhinata Village*), based on Wada Tsutō's widely read documentary novel of the same title, depicted the grinding poverty of life in a mountain village in Nagano Prefecture while presenting emigration to the expansive and bountiful spaces of Manchuria as the solution to the poor farmers' seemingly hopeless situation. *Figure of Youth*, his major film contribution to Japanese rule over Korea, is likewise known, but very little has been written about it.[26] So well did *Figure of Youth* capture the dominant discourses of the late colonial period on the Korea/Japan relationship and on gender, family, and sex that the Japanese Ministry of Education designated it one of its "recommended movies" (*monbushō suisen eiga*) of 1943. It was thus one of only two films produced about Korea during the colonial period to be recognized with this national honor. The other was *You and I,* a film made in 1941 by the Korean director Hŏ Yŏng (or Hinatsu Eitarō), which I will discuss at some length later in this chapter.[27]

Chōsen Eiga Kabushiki Kaisha (Korea Motion Picture Production Corporation) produced *Figure of Youth* with the support of the major studios Tōhō, Daiei, and Shōchiku, as well as the Government-General of Korea and the Korean Army. Toyoda lined up a first-rate staff for the film, including the cameraman Miura Mitsuo and scriptwriter Yata Naoyuki. The cast included major Japanese and Korean stars such as Maruyama Sadao in the lead role of Major Kitamura, an army officer assigned to a Korean middle school to administer the military training of the young male students, and Hwang Ch'ŏl, playing a Korean schoolteacher named Matsuda Masao.[28]

The central drama in *Figure of Youth* concerns the education, character building, and militarized training of young male students in middle school as they look forward to becoming Japanese military men. It thus is another example of a film that manifests the structure of the bildungsroman, for here the trials that the young men face are less strictly obstacles that must be overcome than opportunities to incorporate experiences into their character.[29] In fact, all of the trials, including the cul-

minating cross-country ski excursion, are elements of training—in other words, or-
deals purposely concocted to strengthen the youths' mettle.

The film likewise presents soldiering as a masculinist and nationalist opportunity.
The students who collectively form the main subjects of the film are all young men,
but like Eiryū in *Love and the Vow* and the youthful Iwamoto of "Volunteer Soldier
Iwamoto" before his transformation into a soldier, they are incompletely developed,
either as men or as Japanese national subjects. These seventeen- or eighteen-year-
olds are at a major turning point in their lives: they are confronted with many tests
of their character, intelligence, responsibility, and ability to endure pain and deprivation, and if they fail in their preparation to assume the duties of the Japanese
soldier, they cannot achieve their maturity. The film begins with a scene of the students marching in formation while Major Kitamura inspects them. But one of the
youths, Yanagi Yoshio, marches clumsily, faltering at every other step in almost comical fashion. Later we learn that Yanagi's shoe had become so worn that a nail had
become exposed, leaving his foot bloody. Why has he endured such pain? Because,
as Yanagi explains, he has been taught that the meaning of "the Japanese Spirit is
to stick [to a task] until one collapses, no matter what kind of adversities one might
encounter."

The most challenging test of the students' transition into manhood occurs during a cross-country ski excursion. The snow-covered mountainous landscape is as
challenging for the youths as it is stunning in its beauty. In fact, they are caught in
a snowstorm and lose their way, but the army determines that it will do everything
possible to rescue them, and they are saved. While this incident might be read as an
indication of the students' immaturity and incompetence, the film shows it as yet
another adversity that has helped them develop their character. As one of the students exclaims joyfully on his return: "What a wonderful ordeal that was" (*ii shiren
datta*). "I'm envious," Yanagi responds. "I wish I could have gone."

Yanagi's most difficult trial concerns his body. The film makes much of the
strength and beauty of the young men's bodies. One student stripped to the waist
is told "You've got a pretty good physique," and each of the young men's bodies is
examined. But Yanagi is deeply disturbed to learn that a doctor has discovered something seriously wrong with his health. While the illness is not mentioned, grave concerns over his breathing suggest tuberculosis. Yanagi is depressed but the doctor
tells him that with the proper care he can recover. For Yanagi, his illness is simply
another hurdle to be overcome on the way to becoming a Japanese soldier and a
mature man. Yet the story of Yanagi and the other students is an allegory for all of

Korea. Their figures as youths represent the passage of the Korea people from an immature and emasculated stage to a new phase of masculinized subjecthood.

A second theme that we have already encountered is the essential equality of Koreans and metropolitan Japanese. For example, the film emphasizes the fundamental sameness as Japanese of the Korean schoolteacher Matsuda and the metropolitan Japanese schoolteacher Ōki, despite their differences. In fact, the conventional assumption that it is natural for metropolitan Japanese to speak Japanese and unnatural or difficult for Koreans to do so is completely deconstructed by Ōki's unwillingness or inability to break his habit of speaking in a strong Kyushu or "Satsuma" dialect. In contrast, the Korean teacher Matsuda skillfully and seemingly with ease uses perfect standard Japanese. We are led to believe that it is just as natural for the Korean to speak Japanese as it is difficult for a Japanese from the provinces to speak standard Japanese. Moreover, Matsuda is a refined Japanese in every way—for example, in his reserved mannerisms, etiquette, and knowledge of Japanese literary culture—while Ōki has an abrupt, country bumpkin personality that, although endearing to some, marks him as different from the other metropolitan Japanese.

For the purposes of this chapter, one of *Figure of Youth*'s most striking themes is a subplot of romance and the transformation of Korean women into Japanese women within the domestic sphere, which takes place alongside the great public drama of Korean male youths developing into Japanese men. Not only does Major Kitamura endeavor to turn his male students into soldierly men, but throughout the movie he acts as a go-between in a plot to marry the Korean schoolteacher Matsuda to Yoshimura Eiko, a beautiful young woman within a Korean family that in almost every respect, except clothing, is a model Japanese family. In fact the Yoshimura family is an almost but not quite perfect replica of Major Kitamura's family, led by a father who rejoices with the sinking of every American ship. Each of the patriarchs has a lovely and refined wife and daughter, and both men appear to have the same calligraphy on the folding screens in their homes. The only major difference in family composition is that the Korean patriarch has a son who is a volunteer soldier, while Major Kitamura does not have a son—or so it only seems. For Yoshimura says that his own son "surely thinks of you [Major Kitamura] as his father."

While Yoshimura Eiko is graceful and lovely, she has one fault. At the Kitamura home Matsuda asks Eiko if she raises the family's pigs. She answers in very feminine language that she does not, because "Well, they're just so smelly." Echoing the common complaint of colonial administrators that upper-class Korean women refused to do such dirty work, Matsuda reprimands her by saying, "That's the worst thing about the Korean woman."[30] And yet the Korean woman can become the Japanese woman, and Kitamura tells his wife to "train her a bit." Kitamura's wife is agreeable and gives her own opinion about upper-class Korean women: "Yes, aren't they just like decorative pieces." As the camera shifts away from this domestic scene—where Kitamura's wife pours her husband's tea as he reads his newspaper—we sense that this metropolitan Japanese wife will indeed guide Eiko toward becoming the model wife of the Japanese home.

Yet alongside the discourse on colonized women as objects of fear, in need of either abjection or reform, colonial films and literary works also worked young women into more thrilling stories of romance and even subtle eroticism. In all cases—whether women are presented as objects of fear, abjection, or reform, or as partners in heterosexual romantic love, or even in a combination of the two opposing views—late colonial/national discourse, like classic Hollywood narratives as well as so many representative novels in national literary canons, mobilized representations of men and women in intimate relationships to help weave together large themes of historical and public importance. In the remainder of this section and in the next, I argue through a reading of several films and literary pieces on Korean soldiering that romantic love did more than serve to create excitement and interest; it also helped constitute Korea, now becoming nationalized as a part of an expanded concept of Japan, into a space of freedom from the boundaries of ethnicity, class, and what are represented as the retrograde customs of Korean patriarchy. Consummating, or at least the possibility of consummating, heterosexual love was inextricably bound up with a type of national consolidation that transcended barriers of ethnicity, class, and local customs.

Consistent with one of the central arguments of the previous chapter, these works conflate the freedom to choose partners in heterosexual love with the freedom to choose submission to the nation. For example, although the theme of romantic love is not as strong in *Suicide Squad at the Watchtower* as in some of the other films that I analyze below, it is nonetheless an important subplot. The romantic subnarrative focuses on Kin Eishuku and her betrothed, who partway through the film begin an innocent courtship. Yet the pair narrowly escape a fate that might be described as being the ultimate star-crossed lovers, in that they must experience and pass safely through the harrowing ordeal of almost committing suicide. Their personal fate as lovers on the precipice of death is inextricably linked to national destiny. They serve as both a metaphor and a metonym of the Japanese nation in that their survival as romantic lovers is at once a metaphorical analogy to the flourishing of the national totality and a part standing for the collectivity.

In this connection, many years after the war, the director Hirosawa Ei, perhaps most well-known for his 1974 film *Sandakan Brothel No. 8*, reflected back on watching the Victorian Empire films that, as we have seen, influenced Imai Tadashi in his making of *Suicide Squad at the Watchtower*. Not only did he notice parallels on the theme of self-sacrificial death that linked the Hollywood film *Lives of a Bengal Lancer* to the Japanese films celebrating the heroic suicides of the "Three Human Bomb Patriots," he also became a fan of Gary Cooper movies such as *Beau Geste*, *Dawn Patrol*, and *Morocco*, and recalled that these films produced in him similar sentiments about romantic love and national sacrifice. "Still, the hero who dies for the nation and the hero who dies for love," he remembered, "both became images of heroism to me. I was thrilled by each of them."[31]

Volunteer Soldier (K. *Chiwŏnbyŏng*, J. *Shiganhei*, 1940), directed by An Sŏk-yŏng, is a story about a young Korean man, Ch'un-ho, who achieves his completeness as a man, a Japanese, and a lover by volunteering to become a soldier. The most important women in his life are his sister, who is still a young girl; his widowed mother; and his future bride, Pun-ok. Pun-ok is played by Mun Yae-bong, who has often been described as the most beautiful Korean actress of her day. Initially the main character is frustrated by his life as a student and as the manager of tenanted land for an absentee landlord in Keijō (Seoul). This distress only grows when he learns that the landlord will no longer have him as manager. He is to be replaced by Kim Tŏk-sam, who is none other than the man who stands in the way of his desire to wed Pun-ho. Pun-ho's father had long ago promised Kim Tŏk-sam that he would give his daughter in marriage to the man's son.

At the same time, as in so many other stories of Korean soldiering, Ch'un-ho is tortured by his inability to volunteer for the Japanese army. He sympathetically watches Korean boys who pretend to be soldiers as they play. His younger sister also admires soldiering, but Ch'un-ho is unable to become a soldier because implementation of the Special Volunteer System is still in the future. But one day he learns that the army will begin to accept Korean volunteers. Now he can join, and he becomes self-assured and manly in appearance and in his resoluteness about life.

In the meantime, the obstacles to Ch'un-ho's progress in his livelihood and romance evaporate. When the wealthy landlord learns that the young man has successfully passed the examination for volunteer soldiers, he reconsiders his earlier decision to replace Ch'un-ho as manager of his tenanted land and wants only to help Ch'un-ho's family. Pun-ok's father also refuses to keep his earlier promise to give the evil Kim Tŏk-sam's son his daughter in marriage. He realizes that Pun-ok loves Ch'un-ho and comes to believe that parents cannot force their wishes upon their children, who must be free to choose their own partners. Moreover, in keeping with other

FIGURE 15.

The "modern girl" in *Volunteer Soldier* helps persuade her brother,
the landlord, to assist the volunteer and his family.

representations of the new Korea under Japanese rule as a space of freedom, the
landlord's sister is the strongest influence on her brother in his decision to care for
Ch'un-ho's family. She is figured not as a bulwark of either Korean or Japanese tradition but as a "modern girl" who dresses in Western clothing, has her hair permed,
and carries around a handbag (*handobaku;* see figure 15).

The story ends with the most precious women in Ch'un-ho's life—his mother,
sister, and future bride—at the train station, sending him off to the battlefield (see
figure 16). Ch'un-ho has now taken the position of the Japanese soldier, a multivalent position of both masculinity and Japaneseness, and at the same time has secured
his future marriage with Pun-ok. Becoming a man, becoming Japanese, overcoming class (vis-à-vis the landlord), and gaining success in romantic heterosexual love
are thus achieved all at once in a way that makes it difficult to separate the personal
from the larger social and public themes.

Pak Ki-ch'ae's 1943 film *The Korea Strait* (K. *Chosŏn haehyŏp,* J. *Chōsen kaikyō*)
is perhaps the most dramatically successful film I will analyze whose theme is the

FIGURE 16.
The protagonist's lover and sister in *Volunteer Soldier* send him
off at the train station. Adult women wear the Patriotic Women's
Association sash.

desire for both romantic love and national belonging. Before making this film Pak Ki-ch'ae had worked at Tōa Kinema and Takarazuka Eiga, had founded the Korea Film Corporation, and had directed such works as *Heartless* (K. *Mujŏng*, J. *Mujō*, 1937) and *Here We Go!* (K. *Nanŭn kanda*, J. *Warera imaʒo yuku*, 1942).[32]

The story's pathos derives from the sacrifice made by the protagonist, Yi Sŏng-ki (Seiki, in the film), and his partner, Kŭm-suk (Kinshuku, in the film), of their pure love so that they can fulfill their respective duties for the nation. Seiki chooses to forsake his partner in order to undergo training as a volunteer soldier. He must do so, he says, "as a man" (*otoko toshite*), and he enters the Training Center for Army Volunteers. Although apparently abandoned by Seiki, Kinshuku dutifully serves the nation as an "industrial woman warrior" (*sangyō josenshi*) in a clothing factory, and also gives birth to their child.

One day Seiki's sister Kiyoko leaves a message for Kinshuku, informing her that Seiki and his fellow Korean soldiers will be parading through the city. Kiyoko has

FIGURE 17.
In *Korea Strait*, Kinshuku (played by Mun Yae-bong) moves through
the crowd with her baby in her arms to view Seiki marching in the
military parade.

learned of this happy event from her father, who brims with pride in his son the volunteer soldier. Seiki's father, mother, and Kiyoko mix in with the throngs of people
who have lined up along the streets to observe the parade. At least one Japanese contemporary writer noted at the time that these were the first scenes of large crowds
in Korean cinematic history—an observation which if true would be unsurprising,
since one of national cinema's roles is to represent the nation's people on-screen so
that they might imagine themselves as a unified mass. In any case, Kinshuku receives
the message and rushes with baby in arms to view Seiki in the parade—but she takes
care not to be seen by him or his parents. For Seiki's parents, especially his father,
have disapproved of the relationship: Kinshuku is poor and of humble status, while
they are from the Korean social elite. Kinshuku desperately makes her way past the
well-wishers until she catches glimpses of Seiki marching in formation. Close-ups
of her face show her marveling at his newly uniformed appearance, perhaps suggesting an even erotic fascination (see figures 17–19).[33]

Kinshuku must endure great hardships because social differences make it seem-

FIGURE 18.
In *Korea Strait*, Seiki (in the foreground, played by Nam Sŭng-min) as seen by Kinshuku.

ingly impossible for her to marry Seiki. Kinshuku must raise the baby with the help only of her friends and neighbors, while working long, grueling hours in the factory. The tragic story of missed opportunities and obstacles to reunification continues on the day that Seiki is scheduled to depart from the train station. Kiyoko informs Seiki that Kinshuku has given birth to his son, and he hurries to Kinshuku's living quarters to see her and his child. However, she is not there; and although she rushes from her workplace to try to meet up with him, the two lovers just miss each other. Kiyoko once again attempts to intervene, as she takes a cab with Kinshuku to the train station in the hopes of allowing Seiki and Kinshuku to meet before his departure; but again, she is a little late. Thus Seiki departs for the battlefront without having seen his lover and their child, and Kinshuku misses the opportunity to present him with the "thousand-stitch belt" (*sennin bari*) that she had lovingly prepared for his protection on the battlefield.

As a result of her exhaustion Kinshuku becomes gravely ill, but while in a Korean hospital she has an intimate telephone conversation with Seiki. He has been wounded and is recovering in a hospital in the metropole. They do not speak about

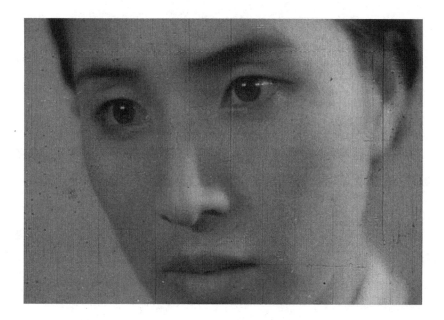

FIGURE 19.

In *Korea Strait* Kinshuku marvels at Seiki's new militarized appearance.

their respective bodily ailments, but communicate their unselfish and undying love for each other through the brief call across the sea. Though Seiki has left his wife and child in the interests of the nation, the telephone conversation—a metaphor for the unity of Korea and the metropole across the beautiful Korea Strait—is their redemption. Seiki tells Kinshuku that the future is theirs.

Redemption operates at the personal, social, and national levels, for Seiki's upper-class parents finally accept Kinshuku as their son's legitimate wife. Seiki's father apologizes to Kinshuku and accepts her as both his son's wife and the mother of his grandson. Like *Volunteer Soldier*, *Korea Strait* critiques the customs of what are figured as the outmoded practices of Korean patriarchal authority, through which parents and especially the father determine marriage partners for their children while valuing "family pedigree" (*iegara*) and "social appearances" (*sekentei*). In contrast, the Japanese nation is made to appear as a progressive force that not only transcends class differences but also values children's wishes, human feelings, freedom to choose, and even romantic love.

Moreover, the promise of romantic love's realization again intermingles with

FIGURE 20.
In the last scene of *Korea Strait,* Seiki looks longingly from Japan
across the Korea Strait.

the larger public theme of the unification of the Japanese metropole and Korea.
In the last scene, as Seiki and his nurse look across the sparkling water of the Korea Strait toward Korea (see figure 20), his nurse remarks, "She must be a wonderful wife (*ii okusama deshō ne*) [long pause] oh, so lovely (*maa kirei*) [long pause],
so beautiful (*suteki dawa*). On the other side of the ocean, that's the Korea Peninsula isn't it? (*ano umi no mukō wa hantō desu ne*)." With these halting if poignant
words, Seiki's and the nurse's thoughts move almost imperceptibly from Kinshuku
to Korea. The subject of the nurse's sighs of "so lovely" and "so beautiful" is suspended in uncertainty between the lover and Korea until the final phrase—"that's
the Korea Peninsula isn't it?"—making it difficult for the viewer to separate the
desire to see the lovers united from hopes for the unification of Korea and metropolitan Japan.

Nevertheless, as in all the films discussed and in conventional wartime Hollywood
films as well, audiences are not supposed to confuse the relative value of heterosexual love and love for the nation. As if to emphasize this point, despite the film's
ambiguity on the matter of Kinshuku's survival, leaving open the possibility that

the couple may be rejoined, the detailed synopsis of the movie provided by an article in the film magazine *Eiga junpō* curiously notes that she dies. The suggestion there, as in the more straightforwardly misogynist stories analyzed earlier, is that ultimately women as well as heterosexual love must be sacrificed if necessary for the nation.[34] And even if in watching the film we believe that the couple will reunite, this redemption must be deferred until victory in war. Seiki and Kinshuku must first fulfill their respective roles for the war effort and nation as soldier, worker, and now the mother of a future soldier before they can fully consummate their relationship. This is a recurring theme in stories of cross-ethnic romance as well.

CROSS-ETHNIC ROMANCE

I have attempted to show how sites of personal intimacy in literature and film were inextricably bound up with the larger themes of politics and administration, but none of the stories I have discussed so far crossed the romantic and sexual boundary between Koreans and metropolitan Japanese, except in a very muted way in Chŏ's "A New Beginning." And there the Korean Shimamura forsakes his metropolitan Japanese wife as a condition of cross-ethnic male bonding. However, consistent with the late colonial government's official celebration of interethnic marriages, in some cases film and literature crossed over, or at least implied the transgression of, the sexual border that might have enforced the ethnic separation of the colonizers from the colonized. Two stories that I will take up below, the script for the film *You and I* as well as the novel by Yi Kwang-su titled *Kokoro aifurete koso* (*Truly, When Hearts Meet*),[35] have as one of their most important themes the coupling of Korean men with metropolitan Japanese women and Korean women with metropolitan Japanese men. These relationships are not condemned, but rather glorified.

The life story of Hinatsu Eitarō, the director and scriptwriter of *You and I,* is an amazing one, told in great detail by Utsumi Aiko and Murai Yoshinori in their very well researched book.[36] Soon after illegally entering the Japanese mainland, Hŏ Yŏng, using the Japanized name "Hinatsu Eitarō" and passing as metropolitan Japanese, launched his career with Makino Motion Pictures in the midst of the Japanese film industry's transition from silent movies to talkies. The first film to use a Hinatsu script came out in 1931, when he was only twenty-three years old. After the collapse of Makino, Hinatsu moved to Shōchiku, where he had the unfortunate experience of accidentally blowing up a "national treasure" during the filming—namely, a section of the Himeji Castle's stone wall. The explosion also killed one person and injured seven others. Undaunted even after this mishap and aided by a pardon, Hinatsu continued to work, first returning to Shōchiku and then moving to Shinkō Kinema. Shinkō Kinema gave him the opportunity to direct his first film, *You and I.*

Only months after *You and I*'s December 1941 release, Hinatsu participated in the Japanese assault on Java as a member of a propaganda corps attached to the Sixteenth Army. As his fortunes would have it, his ship was sunk by the Allied Fleet, but he survived and was soon writing and then directing another propaganda film, *Gōshū e no yobigoe (Calling Australia)*. Unlike *You and I,* this was not a major feature film. Instead, it was a short film completed in 1943 about Allied POWs and interned women and children in Java that was intended to demonstrate how wonderful life could be under Japanese rule. It showed the POWs swimming, fishing, eating steak and freshly baked bread, drinking beer, receiving excellent medical care, and so on—everything to make camp life seem safe, comfortable, and even relaxing. Hinatsu also cleverly made it appear as though the POWs had produced the film themselves in order to send their message of the good life in camp to Australia. Sometime toward the end of the war Hinatsu became acquainted with Sukarno, the future president of Indonesia. Then, following the Japanese defeat, he took up the Indonesian name "Dr. Huyung" and played an important role in the development of post-independence Indonesian filmmaking.

Like the literary and cinematic works previously analyzed, *You and I* depicts Korean youths successfully becoming soldiers and, through that rite of passage, acquiring their manhood and national subjecthood.[37] Furthermore, not only do Korean men expel women from the core national community of metropolitan Japanese and Korean men; they also exchange women as a sign of masculine camaraderie. In the end, Korean men are represented as potentially interchangeable with metropolitan Japanese men, and Korean women with metropolitan Japanese women, but this transcendence of ethnicity occurs through and not across gender, thereby reinforcing and naturalizing the sharp boundaries distinguishing men from women.

Much as in "Volunteer Soldier Iwamoto," physical sites of memory that give a materiality to the historical roots of "Korean and metropolitan Japanese unity" (*Naisen ittai*) constitute an important mise-en-scène for *You and I.* The story's leading character, the Korean youth Kaneko Eisuke, as well as his fellow volunteer soldier Kinoshita Tarō are both from the town of Puyŏ in South Ch'ungch'ŏng Province. Two metropolitan Japanese enthusiasts of the *Naisen ittai* idea who are central to the plot's unfolding, Kubo Ryōhei and his wife Fusako, also live there, and Puyŏ is the setting for more than half the story. The Paekche kingdom's capital of Sabi had been located on the Puyŏ plain, and when Eisuke takes his Japanese love interest Mitsue and her friend Yi Paek-hŭi on a tour of the area, he shows them the remains of the ancient court. Puyŏ was important in the discourse of *Naisen ittai*, as Mitsue and Fusako's brother Asano Kenzō partly explains, because it had been said that ancestral connections between metropolitan Japanese and Koreans could be traced to this area (p. 142). While the details of this connection are not explicitly described, we know that proponents of the *Naisen ittai* thesis commonly argued that when the Paekche kingdom on the Korea Peninsula fell to the Tang and Silla forces in the seventh century, many exiles from Paekche migrated to the Japanese archipelago, where they established communities and subsequently blended into the population.[38] Therefore, as in "Volunteer Soldier Iwamoto," the realization of unity between metropolitan Japanese and Koreans in the narrative present is understood to be the natural result of an original communal identity.

The transcendence of ethnic difference through gendered relations, together with the exchange of women between men that is allowed by the gendered hierarchy in such a discourse, forms the core theme of *You and I*. The rite of passage in Kaneko Eisuke's development into manhood and national subjecthood begins with the enactment of a masculine if still unequal bond between this pure-hearted Korean youth and the metropolitan Japanese soldier, Asano Kenzō. In an early scene, before he has entered the training center for Korean volunteers, Eisuke welcomes Japanese soldiers at the Keijō (Seoul) train station, wishing them well as they depart for the war front. Eisuke is distributing good luck amulets and he gives one to Kenzō, one of the metropolitan Japanese soldiers. Kenzō stretches out his huge hands to take a charm and recognizes Eisuke with the words, "Thank you, brother." Eisuke takes Kenzō's hand and says, "I'm depending on you. Do your best." As Kenzō takes the amulet, he promises to "always keep it next to my body." Kenzō is so moved by the sendoff that he gives Eisuke a note expressing his gratitude for the reception the Koreans have given him. But folded inside the note is also a ten-yen bill that Kenzō says will be of no use to him in the battlefield. Eisuke refuses what might appear to be purely monetary compensation for his loyalty and patriotism by in turn donating the money to a patriotic organization for national defense. In the end, as we will see, the payoff for Eisuke's loyalty, patriotism, and eventual growth into manhood is not money but coupling with a metropolitan Japanese woman, since he is eventually presented with Kenzō's sister, Mitsue. Yet this final exchange between men cannot take place until Eisuke becomes a truly Japanese man, and to do so he must become a soldier. For as we have already been told, to become a soldier is the "natural duty of a virile son of Japan." At the station, Eisuke is still placed in the submissive, feminized position of asking Kenzō, who has the demeanor of a "warrior" (*bujinrashiku*), to fight for him and the nation (pp. 133, 135).

Eisuke first meets Mitsue and her Korean classmate, Yi Paek-hŭi, at the station. As they walk away from the scene Eisuke announces that he also intends to become a soldier. Mitsue looks toward him, as if she feels that she can depend on him. They part, and because they are strangers who have been brought together only by the Japanese soldiers passing through, we cannot know that they will cross paths in the future. But Eisuke and Mitsue are brought together again by the beauty of the military. One day Mitsue and Paek-hŭi notice the Korean volunteers marching in town, and when they run to have a glimpse of the "splendid" sight, they see Eisuke. They then decide to take a tour of the volunteer training center. This is perfectly believable, for as part of the campaign to win over mothers, wives, and women in general as supporters of Korean volunteers, women were offered opportunities to visit the volunteers' training center in Yongsan.[39] In the story, Eisuke serves as guide for the two young women. Hinatsu presents Mitsue there and elsewhere as an object of Korean male desire. She is described as "an extremely beautiful metropolitan Japanese young lady" (p. 137), and her respectability is signified by her playing the violin and her status as a student in music school. Moreover, she and her fellow classmates, including Paek-hŭi, are called "maidens" (*otome*), marking their sexual purity.

Eisuke and Mitsue part company yet another time, and Eisuke continues on his soldierly journey to equality. He graduates from the training center and finally enters the Imperial Army. In the first scene to show him as a true soldier, Eisuke and his fellow Korean volunteers are seen wearing the brand-new uniforms of privates second class. No longer are all the soldiers around Eisuke and his friends Koreans. Instead, Koreans and metropolitan Japanese are intermingled. Eisuke has come a long way from the scene at the train station, when he had been dressed in Korean clothes and had infantilized himself by imploring the Japanese soldiers for protection and sending them off with good luck charms. Now at last Other and Self—or, as the directions for the scene stress, "Kimi to boku," "you and I"—blend together as one (p. 138).

Now that Eisuke has overcome his ethnic difference, he can finally take Mitsue as his bride. The immediate conduit is another homosocial, transethnic bond that forms between Eisuke and Kubo Ryōhei, who is the husband of Mitsue's sister. When Eisuke and his Korean fellow volunteer Kinoshita return to their native town to visit their families before leaving for the war front, they are befriended by Ryōhei. The latter takes an immediate and "enormous liking" to Eisuke because he is a soldier and a "splendid young man" (p. 141). Although neither he nor his wife, Fusako, has any inkling that Eisuke and Mitsue already know each other, Ryōhei decides that he would like to arrange the marriage of this Korean youth to his sister-in-law. Of course, Ryōhei is successful because Eisuke and the beautiful Mitsue have already chosen one another; and by the story's end we know that they will become husband and wife if he returns safely from battle. Thus the masculinist bonds between the volunteer soldier Eisuke, on the one hand, and Mitsue's brother Kenzō and brother-in-law Ryōhei, on the other, enable Eisuke not only to become Japanese but also to acquire a metropolitan Japanese wife. With regard to Eisuke's relationship to Kenzō, Eisuke had been feminized in the early train station scene, since sending men off to war with good luck charms was behavior typical of women, children, and civilian men. But just as Ryōhei is plotting to arrange the marriage, Kenzō writes to Mitsue from the battlefield praising Koreans, amplifying on the theme of *Naisen ittai*, and also revealing how much he still holds dear the "noble figure of one [Korean] youth," who we know is Eisuke. Through this scene Hinatsu allows Kenzō to finally repay the colonial subject Eisuke for his loyalty and patriotism by recognizing his manhood and offering him his own sister. The unpaid debt signified by Eisuke's earlier rejection of the monetary transaction is repaid in the currency of a "maiden."

A highly unexpected twist in the story further shows how the discourse on *Naisen ittai* operated through the promise of the interchangeability of metropolitan Japanese and Koreans along, but not across, gendered boundaries. Mitsue and her Korean classmate Paek-hŭi are extremely close friends. Throughout the film they are almost always together. Paek-hŭi accompanies Mitsue to her sister Fusako's home in Puyŏ, where she is treated as a house guest. One evening the two of them bathe together. When they have finished, Mitsue decides to clothe Paek-hŭi in her own Japanese kimono. Mitsue remarks that Paek-hŭi looks nice in the kimono, that it "suits her very well," and suddenly she asks if Paek-hŭi would like to be her brother Kenzō's bride. She also says that more Koreans ought to wear Japanese clothes. Paek-hŭi protests that it is difficult to know how to put on Japanese clothes properly, but Mitsue remarks that she herself wears Korean clothes and does not give the matter a second thought. With that she proceeds to put on Paek-hŭi's Korean clothes, and Paek-hŭi this time assists Mitsue in dressing. After having ethnically cross-dressed each other, the two show themselves off to Eisuke and Ryōhei. It has already been decided that Eisuke and Mitsue will eventually marry, and when Mitsue sits next to Eisuke wearing Paek-hŭi's Korean outfit, Ryōhei comments that she looks like his bride. Thus paralleling Eisuke's transformation into a Japanese man, Mitsue's and Paek-hŭi's cross-dressing represents the ability of women to transcend ethnic difference. At the same time, it is again clear that whether they are metropolitan Japanese or Korean, women achieve inclusion in the nation through their relations with men. Finally, through the intimation that the Korean "maiden" Paek-hŭi and the metropolitan Japanese soldier Kenzō may marry, a completely equal exchange of women has been accomplished (pp. 144–45).

The structure of Yi Kwang-su's unfinished novel *Truly, When Hearts Meet*,[40] originally published in five parts in 1940 in the colonial journal *Ryokki*, in many ways replicates that found in *You and I*. Like Hinatsu's film script as well as the other texts I have already examined, the novel has a central plot that revolves around the themes of military service for emperor and nation, the unity of metropolitan Japan and Korea, and the transcendence of ethnic difference through gendered bonds. Moreover, as in *You and I*, cross-ethnic romance and friendship serve as both the means for and the symbols of the fusion of colony and metropole.

The novel opens with a young Korean man named Kim Ch'ung-sik (Kin Chū-shoku) and his sister Sŏk-ran (Sekiran), who rescue an injured metropolitan Japanese youth, Higashi Takeo, and his sister Fumie in the mountains. In the course of the rescue and the friendships and romances that subsequently develop, each set of siblings gradually discards its misconceptions and discriminatory attitudes toward the other brother-and-sister pair. The Japanese sister Fumie is initially wary of Ch'ung-sik's Korean accent, but "within less than an hour that anxiety had completely disappeared and it seemed that her heart was completely filled with the type of trust and gratitude one might feel toward someone like a real brother" (p. 316). Fumie's brother Takeo likewise becomes completely infatuated with the young Korean woman Sŏk-ran. As he is convalescing in the Kim home he wonders at his inability to detect any differences between her and a Japanese woman. "Whether her Japanese speaking, her manners, or the shape of her face—wasn't there anything at all that differed?" he asks (p. 319). Only her Korean garb distinguished her; but since Takeo discovers that he himself had been changed into Korean clothing while unconscious, and since he sees Fumie also wearing Korean clothes, he realizes that dress is only superficial and does not signal any essential differences. As in *You and I* and *Suicide Squad at the Watchtower*, ethnic cross-dressing illuminates the fluidity of identity. The warm feelings that Takeo and Fumie develop toward Ch'ung-sik and Sŏk-ran are reciprocated, and the Korean siblings, who had never before had intimate relations with any Japanese, come to see them as good people. They are forced to change their negative views of the metropolitan Japanese. In short, Takeo falls in love with Sŏk-ran and Fumie with Ch'ung-sik, while Takeo and Ch'ung-sik develop a deep and open friendship as do Sŏk-ran and Fumie. It is through their personal love and friendship that progress in the larger project of the unity of metropolitan Japan and Korea is possible.

In contrast to these two sets of siblings who represent the new Korea, the new metropolitan Japan, and the nation's heightened disavowal of ethnic discrimination, their respective parents are depicted by Yi Kwang-su as decent and principled people who are moved by their children's views, but who cannot completely shake their old prejudices. Ch'ung-sik and Sŏk-ran's father Kim Yŏng-chun (Kin Eijun) had been a leader among the disloyal "Korean malcontents" (*futei senjin*). He had been arrested and even spent time in jail, but he had refused to repent. Despite his intelligence, his learning in Japanese history and classics, and his belief that Japan deserved to be the leader of Asia, he continued to insist on the self-determination of the Korean people and remained indignant about the apparently permanently degraded treatment of the colonized. To Yŏng-chun, Governor-General Minami's pronouncements about the "unity of metropolitan Japan and Korea" "must have seemed like no more than the smooth words of a politician" (p. 342). Even as Yŏng-chun grew fond of the Higashi siblings and respectful of their political views, unlike his children he could not change his own political positions. Similarly, even as Takeo and Fumie's parents begin to develop some affection for and understanding of the Kim family, they are not free of prejudices. Worrying about the shame that Takeo might bring upon them if he were to develop a romantic relationship with Sŏk-ran, the mother Kikuko remarks that "it would be no different than wiping mud on the Higashi family" (p. 348). Takeo and Fumie's father is a colonel in the Japanese army who had been opposed to admitting Koreans into the Japanese military as volunteers or as draftees. He had always said that "to include inferior Koreans in the national military is no way to strengthen the services" (p. 328). Colonel Higashi comes to respect Kim Yŏng-chun as a man of deep principles, but he cannot make a clean break with the past.

Thus Yi Kwang-su represents the older generation—both the Korean "malcontent" and the upright but still prejudiced Japanese army colonel and his wife—with sympathy and understanding. He seeks reconciliation through the "meeting of hearts," a reconciliation that in the end depends on the leadership of the younger generation. The destinies of metropolitan Japan, Korea, all of Asia, and indeed the world depend primarily not on the older generation but on the youth. And it is in the remainder of the story, once Takeo has become a soldier and gone off to war, that the deepening cross-ethnic romances come to stand for the promise of the eventual complete unity of metropolitan Japan and Korea.

The story reaches a critical moment when Takeo confesses to Ch'ung-sik in a letter from the front that he would have married Sŏk-ran were it not for his anticipation of resistance from the older generation (p. 361). Moreover, Takeo indicates that despite their feelings for one another, Ch'ung-sik and Fumie could not have married because of familial obligations. But for Yi Kwang-su the story cannot end there, because he must carry on the theme of the progressive movement of history toward the realization of *Naisen ittai*. Thus the story continues.

Not long after Takeo goes off to the front, Ch'ung-sik, who had completed medical school at Keijō Imperial University, volunteers to become a doctor in the Japanese army. Despite his political views, Kim Yŏng-chun had given his son his blessings, in large part because of his belief that, as he put it, "There is nothing more deeply moving for a man than to fight for one's ancestral country" (p. 365). Yŏng-chun himself had desired such an opportunity but had never been blessed with one, and he would not now stand in the way of Ch'ung-sik's chance to fight for Japan as his "ancestral country." Soon thereafter, the good friends Fumie and Sŏk-ran decide to become special volunteer nurses. They bond as women in the same way that Takeo and Ch'ung-sik have bonded as soldiers and men. They vow to "truly become just like sisters"; and in what we can now recognize as a repetitive theme in the literature on soldiering, the two young women both transcend ethnic difference and reinforce the naturalness of the gendered divide as they join the war effort in a supportive, secondary role. As Fumie explains: "In the same way that our brothers are doing what they can as men, let us do what we can as women. In so doing, let us build up a splendid Japan" (p. 373).

The paths of all four of the brothers and sisters cross again on the battlefield when, in a highly unlikely scenario, the two young women arrive at the very field hospital in China where Ch'ung-sik is treating the wounded. But even more miraculously, one day as Ch'ung-sik cares for a soldier whose face has been so severely wounded that it is difficult to even make out its contours, Sŏk-ran notices that the patient is Takeo. At this point the weight of the novel shifts to the relationship between the now blind Takeo and Sŏk-ran. We can presume that Fumie will continue to assist Ch'ung-sik and that their love will grow, but it is the story of Takeo and Sŏk-ran that Yi Kwang-su tells in detail. Even though Takeo has lost his eyesight, he still desires to serve the nation. He therefore plans to infiltrate the Chinese with the intention of winning the enemy over to Japan's side. He believes that if he can but "explain Japan's true intentions and the great currents of the times in Asia" to enemy commanders, it might be possible to gain their allegiance (p. 385). He vows to go behind enemy lines on this mission and to never return. Predictably, Sŏk-ran pledges that she will join Takeo on this mission to certain death. She will serve not only as his eyes but also his translator, the latter a role that she is able to fulfill superbly because she had spent time in China with her father after elementary school.

The cross-ethnic love story between Takeo and Sŏk-ran becomes further conflated with the chronicle of their devotion to the nation and emperor when they are married in a "provisional wedding ceremony" (*kari kekkon no shiki*) in which the field unit's commanding officer plays the role of ceremonial marriage go-between (p. 390). Takeo and Sŏk-ran then dress up as Chinese refugees, intending to go behind enemy lines and prepared never to return. In the meantime, Ch'ung-sik continues his devoted work as a doctor with Fumie by his side. The Japanese nurses who had looked on him disparagingly for being Korean completely rid themselves of such views, while they come to regard Sŏk-ran as a heroine.

In the last scenes of the unfinished novel, Takeo, using Sŏk-ran as his interpreter, tries to convince a Chinese division commander and his officers that Japan is winning the war and that Japan and China must join together as brothers. Chiang Kai-shek, he says, is nothing but a puppet of the communists, the British, and the French. The commander listens intently while other officers show mixed reactions to Takeo's arguments. We cannot know if Takeo and Sŏk-ran will be successful in winning this division over to the Japanese side—most likely not—but Yi Kwang-su is concerned to show that the success or failure of their efforts narrowly construed is less important than the fruition of their love and the unification of metropolitan Japan and Korea in the great cause of establishing Asia for Asians. While Takeo and Sŏk-ran are kept under guard in a dark and filthy room, they bow in the direction they think faces the east, toward Tokyo's Imperial Palace. Despite their apparently miserable condition and the uncertainty of their fate, the two lovers declare their happiness. When Takeo asks Sŏk-ran if she is happy because she is thinking that this is a "joyful honeymoon trip," she replies that no, "it is something more" (p. 405). Yi Kwang-su's message is clear enough. The happiness of this cross-ethnic couple comes from both the joy of marriage and the greater elation that comes from total sacrifice for the nation and emperor.

In closing this discussion of soldiering and cross-ethnic marriage, it might be worthwhile considering the incompleteness of the novel *Truly, When Hearts Meet,* as well as the final deferral of marriages between Koreans and metropolitan Japanese in this novel and in the film script for *You and I.* Yi Kwang-su ended his serialized novel with the notations "to be continued" and "incomplete." This lack of finality is replicated in the marriage between Takeo and Sŏk-ran, for their wedding ceremony is described as a "formalistic provisional wedding ceremony," presumably because it is a makeshift wedding and they have not received their parents' blessings. Similarly, in *You and I* we are led to believe that the Korean youth Eisuke may eventually marry Mitsue and the Japanese youth Kenzō might couple with Paek-hŭi, but the marriages are ultimately deferred. Like the novel with its incomplete ending, Yi Kwang-su and Hinatsu Eitarō seem to suggest that these stories of love and the unity of metropolitan Japan and Korea can be completed only with victory in war. Only then will the soldiers return home to marry and only then will the stories reach their telos.

REFORM, RAPE, AND NATIONALISM

In the literary and cinematic works considered here, Korean men and women were compelled to overcome their ethnic difference with metropolitan Japanese through parallel and supplemental bonds of gender. Proper manliness and respectable womanliness provided the avenues through which colonial subjects might imagine their sameness with metropolitan Japanese; but the boundaries of gender were not to be transcended. The imaginary equalities existed within and not across gender categories. But when viewed against the horrors of the ethnically differentiated sexual slavery that is euphemistically called the "comfort women system," representations of Korean women becoming proper Japanese women might appear as nothing but cruel fantasies calculated to obscure the real violence that Korean women faced in their everyday lives under colonialism. How could such a contradiction be sustained?

Here we might recall Fanon's observations in his powerful essay "Algeria Unveiled," where he noted the duplicity of the colonial enterprise, which apparently made the supposed liberation of Algerian women a political doctrine even as it authorized sexual violence against them. He unveiled the hypocrisy of European men asking Algerian husbands, for instance, "Does your wife wear the veil? Why don't you take your wife to the movies, to the fights, to the café?"—even as the French conquest validated the rape of Algerian women as part of the erotic "sadism of the conquerer."[41]

To be sure, there seems to be more than a hint of masculinist sexual possessiveness in Fanon's fear that the colonizer would seek to "destroy the structure of Algerian society, its capacity for resistance," by having as its guide the thought that "we must first of all conquer the women; we must go and find them behind the veil where they hide themselves and in the houses where the men keep them out of sight."[42] The entire essay signals the hypermasculinist alarm of the manly nationalist who is wary not only of the colonizer but of betrayal by *his* local women.[43] Nevertheless, Fanon incisively alerts us to the way in which the macropolitical structures of colonialism operated at the site of sex and gender—that they sought to unravel the bonds of anticolonial women with anticolonial men through the apparently nonviolent and "civilizing" call to reform gendered and sexualized customs.

In the Japanese colonial situation as well, reform and rape came as two sides of an avowedly civilizing enterprise that was at once gynophobic and misogynist. We have seen that Korean women might have respectable positions within the nation, but in the dominant discourse these were almost always mediated through social relations with men. In such figurations ethnicity could be overcome, but only through gender-differentiated and hierarchical avenues of inclusion. As Ueda Tatsuo—an ardent Korean proponent of the theory of *Naisen ittai* and Korean assimilation to Japan—put it shortly after the official announcement that military conscription would be extended to Korea: "[T]he time has come for [Korean] women to work toward the creation of their majestic qualifications as mothers, wives, older sisters, and younger sisters of heroic imperial soldiers."[44] Thus, although the discourse on the "unity of metropolitan Japan and Korea" suggests an undifferentiated and nongendered inclusion, it promised full incorporation for men alone and rested on the exclusion of all women, whether metropolitan Japanese or Korean, from complete membership in the nation. In modern Japanese history one of the most obvious examples of the supplementary relationship between the inclusion of ethnically marked men, on the one hand, and the exclusion of women, on the other, is the "universal" manhood suffrage law of 1925. At that time Japanese suffrage law extended the vote and the right to hold public office to adult Korean male residents in Japan; but including Korean men under the general provisions of the new law (as "male imperial subjects over the age of twenty-five") also meant writing out all women, whether Korean or metropolitan Japanese.[45]

This understanding of women as Japanese national subjects of a second order opened up possibilities for blatant forms of misogyny and brutality. While the colonial authorities sought to reform Korea's women in order to restructure families and society, they also staffed a regime that by the best estimates sexually enslaved tens of thousands of mostly non-Japanese women, the majority of whom were Korean. This ethnically or racially differentiated system of sexual slavery reflected the racist relationship of the metropolitan Japanese to Koreans and other peoples, and yet the misogynist and class-inflected character of sexual slavery ensured that Japanese women from disprivileged backgrounds were not exempted from mobilization, and Korean women from poorer families were much more likely to be taken than those from wealthier families.[46]

While recognizing the importance of Fanon's perspective on the compatibility of reform and rape, we should also note that within the context of Korea's forced incorporation within an expanded concept of the Japanese nation, the Japanese colonial regime's official stance toward sex and marriage between the colonizers and colonized moved, in some key respects, in a direction exactly opposite to that of Euro-

American colonial policies. Most importantly, scholars have shown that in the nineteenth and twentieth centuries European colonial regimes generally shifted away from their earlier tolerance for, and even encouragement of, the formation of households between white colonial men and indigenous women. These regimes moved from openly condoning the existence of a white/native mestizo population (despite countervailing anxieties about it) to absolute disapprobation of racial mixing and the solidification of racial separation.

In late colonialism European wives were supposed to police the boundaries of white rule, not only by marrying and bedding their men in the colonies but also by serving as custodians of white bourgeois culture and protecting their men from cultural contamination by the colonized. In this new sexual, gendered, cultural, and class-based clarification of racial boundaries, lower-class whites as well as those considered of "mixed-race" were either excluded from the ranks of the colonizers or disciplined to live up to the standards of bourgeois whiteness. In short, as Ann Stoler has written, "The impulse was clear: away from miscegenation toward white endogamy; away from concubinage toward family formation and legal marriage; away from, as in the case of the Indies, mestizo customs and toward metropolitan norms." As for the Philippines under U.S. rule, Vicente Rafael has demonstrated that despite the absence of antimiscegenation laws, white bourgeois women worked to mark the bodily and cultural separation of the colonized and colonizers, most conspicuously in domestic spaces.[47]

Thus the Japanese colonial state's official promotion of mixed marriages ran counter to global trends, where miscegenation came to be unambiguously condemned and colonial endogamy promoted. However, the Japanese strategy of rule through miscegenation should not be understood either as more progressive than that of the West—as the official Japanese position had it—or as simply the sinister obliteration of the Korean people through blood mixing. Instead, consistent with the regime's offer to Korean men of a masculinist opportunity to become Japanese, it constituted one of the formal gestures of inclusion and liberation necessary in a time of total war. While this policy celebrated the essential sameness of Koreans and Japanese and made it possible to praise mixed couples as conjugal models for the empire, such gestures of inclusion preserved the possibility of extreme violence against those judged incapable of living up to expectations of cultural Japaneseness. In other words, it was precisely the assumption that Koreans and Japanese had the opportunity to be equals that legitimated abuse against those deemed (in)different. Men as well as women were susceptible to such mistreatment. But since Korean men's sense of ethnic sameness with Japanese men so often rested on the abjection and relegation of all women to subjects of a second order, Korean women would suffer more than their double oppression under colonialism as women and as colonials: this legacy of the colonial order would continue to haunt them even after national liberation.

POSTCOLONIAL CODA

The interdependency of discourses on gender, on the one hand, and nationalism and colonialism, on the other, is further suggested by a revealing text titled "Japanese Women" ("Nihon no josei") authored by Chō Kakuchū. Chō published this short essay several months before the full-scale invasion of China (July 1937) and therefore before his transformation from critic of Japanese colonialism to Japanese patriot. Instead of praising Japanese women as models to be emulated by colonized women as he would do in his later writings, here he criticized them for their soft-spoken and reserved demeanor, their dependence on men, their general "weakness" (*yowayowashisa*) and inability to express their own selves, their "fragility" (*moroi*), and their "passivity" (*judōteki, shōkyokusei*). In short, he complained that "Japanese women are too womanly" (*amari ni joseiteki de arisugiru*).[48]

Most strikingly, Chō suggested that Japanese women should emulate the women of Korea and China. Korean and Chinese women, he noted, spoke with vigor and authority, as independent individuals who could talk face-to-face with men. Japanese women, in contrast, merely flattered men and sought dependence. Furthermore, Chō urged Japanese feminists toward more political activism while asserting that massive and welcome changes would result from women's gaining suffrage. Though the significant limits to Chō's feminism foreshadow his later misogynist turn, he at least recognized the possibility of including women in the national political community independent of their social relations with men. Moreover, in suggesting that Korean and Chinese women might be models for Japanese women, he confounded the colonial mimetic relationship and held open the possibility of an anticolonial heterosocial bond of collaboration between non-Japanese men and women. However limited and problematic his representations of non-Japanese women might have been, Chō's early praise of Korean and Chinese women clearly contradicted his later Japanese patriarchal nationalist view that Korean men ought to emulate Japanese men while Korean women should seek to become Japanese women. Chō's conversion from critic to enthusiast of Japanese colonialism and nationalism, then, was paralleled by his transformation from critic to admirer of the "Japanese woman," as well as by the narrowing of his vision of the possibilities for women as independent political subjects. Put even more strongly, for Chō the enlargement of opportunities for Korean men within Japanese nationalism seems to have been inextricably linked to his increasingly derogatory view of Korean women.

The importance of unveiling the necessary entanglement of gender, race, ethnicity, and class with nationalism and colonialism during the prewar and wartime period is not limited to that bygone era. Instead, such an exercise may help further our interrogations of the continuing effects of colonial and national modernity on the postcolonial world. As feminist scholars have already insisted, anticolonial nationalisms have tended to be masculinist formations and have resulted in the doubly layered oppression of colonized women. For instance, Chungmoo Choi points out that even in their resistance, colonized Korean men mimicked the colonizers in oppressing Korean women, so that "in the sacred mission of anti-colonial nationalism, the object of which is often to restore national masculinity, women of the colonized nation are doubly oppressed."[49] In the same volume, Seungsook Moon shows how Korean nationalist views of history have followed an androcentric and masculinist logic. The official discourse on national history, she demonstrates, has been one of national defense; and in this logic, the "continuous necessity to defend the Korean nation masculinizes it by linking citizenship to soldiering." Other work has maintained that the masculinist and patriarchal shame of postcolonial Korean nationalists colluded with other factors to silence discussion of the issue of "comfort women" over so many postwar decades.[50]

My final point builds on such feminist critiques of postcolonial nationalism. As can be seen in the writings of Chō, Hinatsu, and others, the masculinist logic of nationalism typified the thinking not only of anticolonial Korean nationalists but also of many Korean proponents of Japanese nationalism. In either case, the masculinist bond opened up an avenue for inclusion in the nation, whether Korean or Japanese. Such a perspective makes it easier to understand the relatively noncontradictory movement of someone like Park Chung Hee (Pak Chŏng-hŭi) from graduate of the Japanese Military Academy and first lieutenant in the Manchukuo army to president of the Republic of Korea and, according to Moon, "the main architect of official nationalism" in the postcolonial regime, who sought to establish a national history that represented the Korean nation as primarily a community of men.[51] My purpose is not to locate the ultimate origins of such a masculinist logic in Japanese colonial and nationalist discourse, but to say that such a logic was integral to maintaining the Japanese nation and empire, that it was nurtured within the modern nationalist and colonial context, and that its effects remain with us today.

> Because so many things pile up, one after the other,
> things we remember and things we wish to remember
> are steadily forgotten. It is regrettable, but in a way
> unavoidable. The episode I am going to relate here is
> one such thing. While I'd like to include it in a novel,
> considering that I don't know when I can write that
> novel and such, I thought it best to at least write it
> down. In that way, perhaps it might be possible to
> avoid forgetting.
>
> NAKANO SHIGEHARU, "Yonin no shiganhei" (Four
> Volunteer Soldiers), *Minshu Chōsen*, March–April 1947

In April 1947 Nakano Shigeharu, the Marxist writer, poet, and critic, published a short essay titled "Four Volunteer Soldiers." More a column than an extended essay, Nakano tells the story of his encounter on a train with four young men in Japanese army uniform in September 1945—four men who had belonged to the first cohort of Koreans who had volunteered for the Japanese army in 1938. Like the youths, Nakano had just been demobilized, so when they met they shared a common history as soldiers in the Imperial Army. However, while Nakano was middle-aged, they were in their twenties; and while he was traveling to rejoin his children in Fukui Prefecture, they were bound for Shimonoseki. From there they intended to board a ship to Pusan, and then make their way back to their hometowns or villages in Korea, three of which were located north of the thirty-eighth parallel.[1]

The Korean youths had come of age during the last phase of Japanese rule in Korea, when Korea was increasingly becoming a part of an expanded concept of Japan, and Nakano's attentiveness to their mannerisms, language use, and general sensibilities allows us to see that they embodied some of the strange symptoms of the inclusionary racism of that period. As Nakano watched them on the train, he observed their almost disembodied Japaneseness. He "sensed" (*kankaku*) from their speaking that they were Korean. But he admonished his readers not to assume that that they spoke Japanese poorly. Rather, their spoken Japanese sounded "far purer" (*kissui no Nihongo*) to Nakano than the "very strange Japanese" (*zuibun okashii . . . Nihongo*) used by a rustic middle-aged woman who asked one of the young men something about the train. Nakano explained that it was precisely because their spoken language was so perfect, so pure or unadulterated in that it gave no hint of an upbringing in any particular region of metropolitan Japan, that he recognized them as Koreans. They spoke perfect Japanese, but they spoke it as a national language, not as a vernacular with an organic relationship to a place.

As for the interregnum between the death of the former sovereign power and the birth of the new,[2] Nakano observed that even though the war had ended, most Japanese in the train around him did not yet seem able to "understand the enormous significance of Japan's defeat." And though the defeated Japanese soldiers wore their uniforms, they did so almost as ghostly apparitions, with their shoulder insignia removed. Colonialism seemed not yet to have died. As Nakano observed, even though "the young men knew of Korea's independence, they were still far from completely freed from the sort of feeling (*kankaku*) that the power of the Japanese government still ruled over Korea. It seemed that as an embodied sensibility (*nikutaiteki na kankaku*) they were still not fully living the idea that they were but outsiders passing through the foreign country of Japan, on their way back to their home country" (p. 53).

In fact, it could hardly be denied that the dying colonial power continued to exercise some control over their destiny, for they depended on the travel documents issued by their Japanese commanding officer to guarantee their passage home. Yet even here the former power was but a skeleton of its former self. The Korean youths worried that their travel documents indicated that they were bound only as far as Shimonoseki in southern Japan. They wondered how it would be possible to cross the strait to Pusan. And even if they made it to Pusan, how would they return to their hometowns or villages? Nakano reminded them that the Japanese were no longer the authorities in charge. Still optimistic about the U.S. occupation of Korea and the presence of People's Committees, particularly in the north, Nakano told the young men that they should simply write in their destinations in Korea and boldly board the ship to Pusan. If any Japanese military men should raise questions once they had arrived in South Korea, Nakano advised, the youths should call on the American troops to come to their aid.

Although Nakano described this interregnum as one of ruin, ghostliness, and possibilities, he wrote about the Koreans with happiness and optimism, albeit in a subdued way. To him, their general bearing and their expressions appeared very different from those of the Japanese around him. The other demobilized soldiers appeared wasted, in despair, and ready to turn against their siblings and even their own people, if not the government and the emperor, but the Korean youths had a quiet and calm air about them. Moreover, while they knew little about contemporary political affairs in Korea, or of revolutionary writers such as Im Hwa and Kim Sa-ryang, he felt heartened by their fresh responsiveness to his discussions about such matters. With such youth as its foundation, he thought, Korea's future looked bright.

At the same time, the essay cast an ominous cloud over the fate of the history and memories of colonialism and the war. Nakano begins by remarking on signs of the memory crisis that he could already sense, even in the context of demobilization. "Because so many things pile up, one after the other," he says in the passage quoted in the epigraph, "things we remember and things we wish to remember are steadily forgotten." He had wanted to include the encounter with the four Korean youths in a novel, but he did not know when he would be able to write such a story, and therefore he had resolved to "at least write it down. In that way, perhaps it might be possible to avoid forgetting" (p. 67).

Nakano worried that his pragmatic recounting of the episode, intended simply to prevent him from forgetting, might be beneficial from the point of view of memory, but harmful from the perspective of producing a "work of art." And yet, "Four Volunteer Soldiers" is by no means an artless production of the period. Using the imagery of trains moving in several directions, of railroad tracks destroyed by floods, of detours, and of choices made about when and where to go, Nakano evocatively captured a moment of many possibilities and multiple routes into the future, while at the same time suggesting that memories of those such as the "four volunteer soldiers" were already fading and in danger of being lost to history. For Nakano observes that while all the other deactivated Japanese soldiers were traveling toward Tokyo, he and the Koreans moved in the opposite direction—against the tide of returnees and seemingly against the flow of Japanese national history and memory.

Nakano recalls that in Miyamoto Yuriko's 1947 novel *Banshū heiya*, the protagonist hurries up the Sanyō Line, even walking the stretch where flooding has washed out a section of the tracks in order to make a connection with the train heading to Tokyo. He realizes that at almost the same moment, the Korean former volunteer soldiers had been taking that same trip but in reverse, heading away from the capital and beyond Japan. The essay ends with his reflection that through all the hours that he had spent talking with the former volunteer soldiers, "no one had the faintest idea that I had been talking with Koreans. No one had the faintest idea that four Korean youths were talking with a solitary Japanese man" (p. 70). And then he notices that while it is still warm in Japan, the Koreans have lined their coats for warmth in anticipation of the cold autumn in northern Korea. The piece leaves its readers with the feeling that that though the Koreans might face a positive future, the Japanese homecoming was already producing a forgetting about the complex history of late colonialism, when the Japanese regime had sought to incorporate the Korean people into a new concept of Japan.

Indeed, there would be no celebrations of Korean soldiers comparable to the big parades, newspaper headlines, and even Hollywood movies for Japanese American troops, and those who returned home to Korea would find a country whose immediate future would be further violence, warfare, and division rather than the happiness hoped for by many, including Nakano. Korean officers who had been trained in the Manchurian and Japanese military academies quickly changed uniforms: from 1945 to 1980 they predominated as the leading officers in the South Korean military. Their number included Kim Sŏk-wŏn, a former colonel in the Japanese army and the courtroom observer of the P'yŏngyang student soldier mutineers discussed in chapter 6, who on the eve of the Korean War was a division commander in the southern Korean forces.[3] Like Kim Sŏk-wŏn, Chŏn Sang-yŏp also served in both the Japanese and later South Korean military forces. However, very unlike the celebrated courtroom observer Colonel Kim, Chŏn enlisted in the imperial army under the Japanized name of Takayama Jun'ichi, had been only a private first class, and had been a co-conspirator in the P'yongyang mutiny. For his alleged crime a secret Japanese military court sentenced him to eight years in prison, a judgment that only the war's end cut short.

When I interviewed Chŏn in 1999, he told me of his harrowing experiences—of overcoming his prison guard and escaping from solitary confinement, where he had been kept unclothed and unshaven, only to be recaptured as he fled to the north. Imagine, he urged me, how he must have appeared to local people who saw a naked, barefoot, and heavily bearded man in flight. Even as an elderly man in his late seventies, Chŏn related to me in tears how his mother, hearing only rumors of his imminent return after the war, waited every day at one of the two stations where he might get off the train, while his brother waited at the other. After his return home there would be no peace or physical safety for Chŏn, for while fighting for the southern Korean forces he suffered a severe gunshot wound to the chest. Although Chŏn gave some indications of family celebrations for his multiple homecomings from war, the politics of history and memory making on the Korea Peninsula, Japan, and the United States have pushed the Second World War experiences of men such as Chŏn and his fellow Korean veterans of the Japanese military into the scrapheap of the past.[4]

Japanese filmmakers destroyed their wartime films about Koreans as Japanese national war heroes, and only within the past few years have Korean film archivists begun to "repatriate" the "lost" wartime films made by Korean directors on this theme. The Korean film director Ch'oe In-kyu, who in 1943 and 1945 had collaborated with Imai Tadashi to make two films on Korean war heroes fighting for Japan, quickly reversed course and in 1946 released *Hurrah for Freedom* (*Chayu manse*), a celebration of the wartime anti-Japanese resistance. Actors who had only a few years earlier played central roles in movies celebrating the Japanese empire began taking parts completely at odds with those films. Perhaps most strikingly, and indicative of the speed with which historical forces produced a forgetting of Koreans as Japanese, a mere three years after taking the female lead in *Suicide at the Watchtower*, Hara Setsuko starred in the 1946 Akira Kurosawa film ironically titled *No Regrets for Our Youth* (*Waga seishun ni kui nashi*). There she played a young woman who refused to cooperate with the Japanese wartime authoritarian regime. By 1950 Shimura Takashi, who had played the Korean school principal in *Love and the Vow*, appeared in Akira Kurosawa's *Rashōmon*, voicing his condemnation of war and his faith in humanity. The forces of the Cold War—with the United States and the leaders of its client states of Japan and South Korea all eager to forget or at least only selectively remember the war and colonialism and get on with the task of economic rebuilding—further pushed memories of Koreans and Taiwanese who had fought as Japanese soldiers into the margins of history, even as those same forces accelerated memory making about America's model minority citizen-soldiers.

Japan's defeat and the Cold War impacted the Korean population very differently from the way in which the Allied victory and the Cold War affected Japanese Americans. Japan's surrender disrupted the trajectory of the Korean people's inclusion into the political and bio-political nation; and shortly after the war the Japanese state, backed by the United States, unilaterally stripped all of them, including those residing in Japan, of their legal status as Japanese nationals. In doing so it deprived them not only of their political rights but also of their rights to life through welfare. Power in that relation then recoiled back into an uncomplicated mode of the "right to kill," a power that had never ceased to operate alongside the "right to make live." This is why postwar political activism of Korean residents in Japan has largely focused as much on rights to education and welfare as on political rights in the conventional sense. And, as Tessa Morris-Suzuki shows in her revealing book, this is also why many Koreans who had resided in Japan during the war felt it necessary to migrate to North Korea just to secure a basic livelihood.[5]

Japanese Americans, in contrast, continued their passage across the 1945 divide into the mainstream American population, as the landmark McCarren-Walter Act of 1952 finally permitted Japanese to become naturalized citizens. In national politics, much as the Japanese empire had sought to decolonize Korea through its wartime nationalization policy, so the United States accelerated its nationalization of Hawaii, as well as Japanese Americans in Hawaii and on the mainland. This made it possible for the 442nd's decorated war hero from Hawaii, Daniel Inouye, to become the first Japanese American to serve in Congress when he was elected to the House of Representatives in 1959, and then the first Japanese American to take a seat in the Senate in 1963. Likewise, this enabled the people of Hawaii to send a twice-wounded veteran of the 100th Battalion, Masayuki "Spark" Matsunaga, to the House of Representatives in 1962, and then to the Senate in 1976.

In that same year, the voters of California, the state that had seen some of the worst examples of vulgar racist sentiment and violence against Japanese Americans during the war, sent S. I. Hayakawa, a Canadian-born Japanese American, to Washington as one of their senators. Like Inouye and Matsunaga, Hayakawa had been an enthusiast of Japanese American soldiering, if only from a distance. In February 1943, in the midst of the failing campaign to mobilize Japanese American army volunteers out of the camps, Hayakawa had enthusiastically offered to assist Dillon Myer in the effort to enlist the Nisei even as he said he regretted that his Canadian citizenship (retained until 1954) made him ineligible to serve himself.[6] Despite ongoing periodic explosions of racial violence against Asian Americans and other people of color in the United States, many other prominent Japanese Americans have likewise secured highly visible and prestigious positions in local, state, and national government, including U.S. Representatives Mike Honda, Robert Matsui, Doris Matsui, Norman Mineta, and Patricia Mink.

On the cultural front, *Hell to Eternity* was the next major Hollywood film after *Go for Broke* to condemn racism against Japanese Americans and to celebrate their wartime contributions as well as their inclusion in America. Directed by Phil Karlson, the production starred one of the movie industry's top leading men, Jeffrey Hunter, with co-stars David Janssen and Vic Damone in important sidekick roles. It also cast Sessue Hayakawa and Tsuru Aoki Hayakawa—the two great Japanese actors who had become well-known in the United States and Europe through their work in Hollywood silent films—in the prominent roles of the Japanese commander on Saipan and the Japanese American mother (or "Mama-san"). Made in 1960, the film was part of the Cold War cultural machinery that worked to rehabilitate Japanese Americans and Japan into the domestic American and global communities, respectively, with the one process inextricably bound to and even at times conflated with the other. A few scenes remind the audience that the Japanese American "boys," George and Kaz, belong to the valiant 442nd, but the most important sites of rehabilitation are the Une family's Japanese American home and the Saipan battlefield.[7]

Guy Gabaldon, an Italian American boy who grows up to be the hero of the story on Saipan, is taken in and raised by the Une family. In an early scene we see Guy as an adolescent fighting and constantly getting himself into trouble. The cause of his delinquency: lack of a proper family. When the older son Kaz, who works as a schoolteacher, visits Guy's home to meet the boy's parents, he discovers not only a house without adult supervision but a home in shambles. The camera pans to show rubbish scattered throughout the place, dirty dishes, and unkempt furniture. "Where is your mother?" Kaz asks. As it turns out, she has been hospitalized, and Guy's father had died some time ago. Kaz decides that his family must adopt Guy.

As the two enter the Une house, Guy is overwhelmed by its almost aseptic cleanliness and fastidious good order. If the point is not made clearly enough by the camera shots, we find Mama-san hard at work with the laundry, and in a later scene Guy and Mama-san clean house while teaching each other the Japanese and English words for "broom," "carpet sweeper," and "vacuum cleaner" (see figure 21). These scenes are typical of the ways in which the Cold War popular media often made it seem that the racial divide between Japan and the United States could be transcended, or at least made tolerable, by their shared appreciation of cleanliness—in other words, that hygiene in the sense of cleanliness might compensate for loosening the boundaries of racial hygiene. For example, in the well-known 1957 film *Sayonara*, when the Japanese entertainer Hana-ogi (played by Miiko Taka, who also had an important role in *Hell to Eternity*) wonders how she can marry her white American lover (played by Marlon Brando) when they are bound by conflicting duties and obligations in a world troubled by racial discrimination, he responds in his affected southern accent that their first obligation is to get married and "raise some clean, sweet children." Those babies, he adds, would be "half Japanese, half American; they'd be half yella and half white; they'd be half you and half me; that's all they gonna be."[8]

The good and clean, heteronormative Une family is completed by the quiet and hardworking Father Une. Thus, far from posing a threat to the national community, the Une family is a part of it as an instrument of liberal governmentality, and

FIGURE 21.
"Mama-san" and Guy tidy up the perpetually clean Une house
as the camera zooms in on the broom. From *Hell to Eternity.*

is even able to provide a model toward which ethnic whites can aspire. In short, Japanese American cultural differences from mainstream society are figured as merely superficial and quaint variations on white bourgeois decency.

If it is the domestic space along with intimations of military service that serves to incorporate Japanese Americans into the national community, then Saipan presents the site for Japan's postwar rehabilitation and its conflation with the domesticated Japanese Americans. While the film does not minimize the mutual killing, General Matsui dramatizes Japan's complete, dignified, and finally easy surrender to American benevolence. Utilizing the Japanese he has learned growing up in the Une household, Guy singlehandedly captures hundreds of Japanese civilians and military men by coaxing them out of the caves in which they are hiding with promises of aid and comfort. Guy also convinces General Matsui that he must give up his plan to fight till the end, so that eventually the general and Guy work together to make the completely weakened and demoralized Japanese fighters surrender to American mercy. In the calculus of war and reconciliation, however, someone must be sacrificed for the deaths of so many. Thus the general commits suicide in front of the hundreds of Japanese whom he, with Guy behind him, has persuaded to surrender.

Through his courage Guy is represented as repaying many times over the love

FIGURE 22.
The figures of the Japanese Americans "Mama-san" and George
are superimposed upon a Japanese mother and child who jump to
their deaths in Saipan. From *Hell to Eternity*.

and material comfort he has received from the Une family. For not only does he signal his intention to adopt a little Japanese boy named Kiyoshi with the casual promise "I'm gonna take him home with me," he does so in a scene that shows him with
the hundreds of Japanese prisoners who he has saved from certain death. And lest
the film's message be too oblique, when he sees the horrific suicide of an anonymous Japanese mother and her resistant son who throw themselves off a Saipan cliff
(see figure 22), the projector superimposes on them the figures of his adoptive Mama-
san and brother George. The families of the devastated Japanese soldiers and civilians, he reasons, are no different from the Japanese American family that had provided him with the "only love I ever knew." They are all potentially good people,
not animal-like threats to America and the global community.

Amazingly, the true-life story of a man named Guy Gabaldon who had grown
up in East Los Angeles among Japanese Americans served as the basis for *Hell to
Eternity*'s miraculous plot. The real Gabaldon had been able to pick up the rudi-
ments of Japanese from a Japanese American family, the Nakanos, who had taken
him in when he was a youth. Moreover, as in the film's Japanese American family,
the Nakano boys, Lane and Lyle, had actually served in the 442nd, and Lane played
a major role as a member of the unit in the film *Go for Broke*. The real Gabaldon is

also known to have captured more than 1,000 prisoners, largely on his own, and on a single day supposedly took in 800 Japanese military personnel and civilians.

The one major falsehood in the film, however, is very revealing about the ways in which the making of Cold War memories of the Second World War depended on forgetfulness[9] and, in particular, the segregation of war memories concerning each racialized American minority. Guy Gabaldon was not an Italian American at all. Instead, he self-identified as a Chicano from East Los Angeles with a lineage he traced back to New Mexico. The film completely erased the deep and rich history of intimacies among people of color in mixed communities such as Boyle Heights, Los Angeles, while making it appear that one racialized minority's history could be told only in relation to the history of white Americans. In other words, while the liberal racist road from wartime propaganda about Japanese American military heroism to *Go for Broke* and then *Hell to Eternity* helped produce an image of Japanese Americans as a model minority, this narrative was also guilty of and dependent on marginalizing other stories such as that of Chicano military service and admissibility into the nation, as well as of intimacies across racialized U.S. minorities.

The postwar and Cold War incorporation of Japanese Americans into the U.S. nation, however problematic as a patronizing form of inclusionary racism, thus stands in stark contrast to the immediate postwar expulsion of Koreans from the Japanese national community, including of Korean residents in Japan. Nevertheless, it is also important to recognize that in the postwar order—in the wake of Nazi defeat and the widespread disavowal of racist discrimination by all those nations and empires that had sought to mobilize multiethnic or multiracial political communities for the war effort, including as soldiers—few nation-states could for long sustain racism in its "vulgar" form alone.

As for Japan's political leaders, even as they expelled their former colonial subjects from the national community, reversed the trajectory of inclusionary racism, and promoted what Oguma Eiji has called the "myth of [Japanese] ethnic homogeneity,"[10] they also guaranteed through the postwar constitution that "all of the people are equal under the law and there should be no discrimination . . . because of race, creed, sex, social status or family origin" (Article 14). In the United States, even as "polite racism" continued to evolve beyond simple assimilationism and to take hold as liberal multiculturalism, the more vulgar right to take life without explanation continued in everyday brutality against targeted subpopulations. With regard to the latter it is necessary to at least mention the infamous Tuskegee Syphilis Study that began in 1939 and did not end until 1972. In this experiment, hundreds of mostly poor black sharecroppers were denied medical care for syphilis in order to study the effects of the untreated disease.[11] Tellingly, during the war years the United States Public Health Service, the agency that headed this study, was also responsible for the health and physical well-being of Japanese Americans in the camps.

Regardless of concrete differences from nation to nation, then, one of the most profound legacies of the Second World War is that racism and its disavowal so often still continue to haunt us in their uneasy compatibility. "Vulgar racism," as Fanon warned us long ago, may have been forced to go underground during the transwar years but has never disappeared. To borrow a musical metaphor, it continues to stay with us as a kind of ground or literally "obstinate bass" (*ostinato basso*), working sometimes to thwart but also to supplement and enable "polite racism."[12]

NOTES

PREFACE

1. T. Fujitani, "*Go for Broke*, the Movie: Japanese American Soldiers in U.S. National, Military, and Racial Discourses," in *Perilous Memories: The Asia Pacific War(s)*, ed. T. Fujitani, Geoffrey M. White, and Lisa Yoneyama (Durham, N.C.: Duke University Press, 2001), 239–66.

2. Lisa Lowe, *Immigrant Acts: On Asian American Cultural Politics* (Durham, N.C.: Duke University Press, 1996).

3. George Lipsitz, *The Possessive Investment of Whiteness: How White People Profit from Identity Politics* (Philadelphia: Temple University Press, 1998), esp. chap. 10.

4. Revised versions of the conference paper were published as "The Masculinist Bonds of Nation and Empire: The Discourse on Korean 'Japanese' Soldiers in the Asia Pacific War," in *Japanese Civilization in the Modern World: Nation-state and Empire*, ed. Takashi Fujitani, Umesao Tadao, and Kurimoto Eisei, a special issue of *Senri Ethnological Studies* (Suita, Japan: National Museum of Ethnology, 2000), 133–61; and in Japanese as "Kokumin kokka to teikoku no danseishugiteki na chūtai: Ajia-taiheiyō sensō ni okeru Chōsenjin 'kōgun heishi' ni kansuru gensetsu," in *Shokuminchishugi to jinruigaku*, ed. Yamaji Katsuhiko and Tanaka Masakazu (Nishinomiya, Japan: Kansai Gakuin Daigaku Shuppankai, 2002), 313–42.

5. "Raishawā no kairai tennōsei kōsō," *Sekai*, no. 672 (March 2000): 137–46; "Raisyawŏ ŭi koeroe ch'ŏnhwangje kusang," *Silch'ŏn munhak*, no. 61 (15 February 2001): 359–81; "The Reischauer Memo: Mr. Moto, Hirohito, and Japanese American Soldiers," *Critical Asian Studies* 33, no. 3 (September 2001): 379–402.

6. My paper was published as "Singminji sidae malgi 'Chosŏn' yŏnghwa ŭi hyu -

mŏnijŭm pop'yŏnjuŭi kŭrigo injong ch'abyŏlchuŭi: Imai T'adasi ŭi kyŏngu rŭl chungsim ŭro," in *Han'guk yŏnghwa ŭi mihak kwa yŏksajŏk sangsangnyŏk,* ed. Yŏnsedae midiŏ at'ŭ sent'ŏ (Seoul: Sodo, 2006), 189–214; Japanese version: "Shokuminchi shihai kōki no 'Chōsen' eiga ni okeru kokumin, chi, jiketsu/minzoku jiketsu," in *Kioku ga katarihajimeru,* ed. Tomiyama Ichirō (Tokyo: Tokyo University Press, 2006), 33–57.

7. T. Fujitani, "Senka no jinshushugi: dainiji taisenki no 'Chōsen shusshin Nihon kokumin' to 'Nikkei Amerikajin,' " in *Kanjō, kioku, sensō, Iwanami kōza: kindai Nihon no bunkashi,* ed. Narita Ryūichi et al., vol. 8 (Tokyo: Iwanami Shoten, 2002), 235–80; and "Korosu kenri, ikasu kenri: Ajia-Taiheiyō sensō-ka no Nihonjin toshite no Chōsenjin to Amerikajin toshite no Nihonjin," in *Dōin, teikō, yokusan, Iwanami kōza: Ajia-taiheiyō sensō,* ed. Kurasawa Aiko et al., vol. 3 (Tokyo: Iwanami Shoten, 2006), 181–216; English version: "Right to Kill, Right to Make Live: Koreans as Japanese and Japanese as Americans during WWII," *Representations,* no. 90 (Summer 2007): 13–39; revised Korean version: "Chugil kwŏlli wa sallil kwŏlli: 2 ch'a taejŏn tongan Migugin ŭro sarattŏn Ilbonin kwa Ilbonin ŭro sarattŏn Chosŏnindŭl," *Asea yŏn'gu* 51, no. 2 (2008): 13–47.

INTRODUCTION: ETHNIC AND COLONIAL SOLDIERS AND THE POLITICS OF DISAVOWAL

1. Utsumi Aiko, *Chōsenjin "kōgun" heishi tachi no sensō* (Tokyo: Iwanami Shoten, 1991), 39; for a slightly different translation, see "Korean 'Imperial Soldiers': Remembering Colonialism and Crimes against Allied POWs," trans. Mie Kennedy, in *Perilous Memories: The Asia Pacific War(s),* ed. T. Fujitani, Geoffrey M. White, and Lisa Yoneyama (Durham, N.C.: Duke University Press, 2001), 200.

2. Ōshima Nagisa, "People of the Forgotten Army," in *Cinema, Censorship, and the State: The Writings of Nagisa Oshima, 1956–1978,* ed. with an introduction by Annette Michelson, trans. Dawn Lawson (Cambridge, Mass.: MIT Press, 1992), 71.

3. Kang Duk-sang, "Mō hitotsu no kyōsei renkō," *Ningen bunka,* preparatory volume (March 1996): 25–38.

4. For the official count as of 2001, see Takahashi Tetsuya, *Yasukuni mondai* (Tokyo: Chikuma Shobō, 2005), 93.

5. This is fairly common local knowledge among those involved in building the monument and was reported to me on a visit in 1998.

6. *Pacific Citizen,* 2–15 April 2004.

7. Takashi Fujitani, "National Narratives and Minority Politics: The Japanese American National Museum's War Stories," *Museum Anthropology* 21, no. 1 (Spring 1997): 99–112.

8. Cathleen K. Kozen shows the ubiquity of the discourse on Japanese American soldiering in congressional debates on the Civil Liberties Act in "Achieving the (Im)possible Dream: Japanese American Redress and the Construction of American Justice" (master's thesis, University of California, San Diego, 2007).

9. Robert Reinhold, "Pearl Harbor Remembered," *New York Times*, 8 December 1991; President George H. W. Bush's speech as heard on *From Hawaii to the Holocaust: A Shared Moment in History*, executive producer, Judy Weightman (Hawaii Holocaust Project, 1993).

10. "Asia/Pacific American Heritage Month, 2006: A Proclamation by the President of the United States of America," Proclamation 8008 of 28 April 2006, http://edocket.access.gpo.gov/cfr_2007/janqtr/pdf/3CFR8008.pdf (accessed January 2011). For more examples, see T. Fujitani, "*Go for Broke*, the Movie: Japanese American Soldiers in U.S. National, Military, and Racial Discourses," in Fujitani, White, and Yoneyama, eds., *Perilous Memories*, 239–66.

11. The national media reported on the memorial in the days before and after the 9 November 2000 dedication ceremony. For example, see Melissa Lambert, "California and the West; The Washington Connection; A Place of Honor for Japanese Americans," *Los Angeles Times*, 7 November 2000. The National Japanese American Foundation's website, www.njamf.com, gives a fairly detailed description of the memorial, its history, and its significance.

12. For silences or absences in memories that trouble mainstream narratives of internment, see Marita Sturken, "Absent Images of Memory: Remembering and Re-enacting the Japanese Internment," in Fujitani, White, and Yoneyama, eds., *Perilous Memories*, 33–49; and Carolyn Chung Simpson, *An Absent Presence: Japanese Americans in Postwar American Culture, 1945–60* (Durham, N.C.: Duke University Press, 2001).

13. Mark Mazower, *Dark Continent: Europe's Twentieth Century* (New York: Vintage, 1998), esp. 138–81.

14. Prasenjit Duara has very convincingly demonstrated the seriousness of the scheme to present Manchukuo to the world as a self-determining and authentic nation-state rather than a Japanese colony in *Sovereignty and Authenticity: Manchukuo and the East Asian Modern* (Lanham, Md.: Rowan & Littlefield, 2003).

15. In questioning the dominant contrastive logic, I align this book with the important volume edited by Yamanouchi Yasushi, Victor Koschmann, and Narita Ryūichi, *Sōryokusen to gendaika* (Tokyo: Kashiwa Shobō, 1995).

16. Frantz Fanon, "Racism and Culture," in *Toward the African Revolution*, trans. Haakon Chevalier (New York: Grove Press, 1967), 35–37; for Balibar, see, for example, "Is There a 'Neo-Racism'?" in Etienne Balibar and Immanuel Wallerstein, *Race, Nation, Class: Ambiguous Identities*, trans. Chris Turner (London: Verso, 1991), 17–28.

17. Ito Abito et al., eds., *Chōsen o shiru jiten* (Tokyo: Heibonsha, 1986), 217.

18. John J. McCloy, quoted in Bernard C. Nalty, *Strength for the Fight: A History of Black Americans in the Military* (New York: Free Press, 1986), 169.

19. Chōsen Sōtokufu, "Chōsenjin shiganhei seido jisshi ni kansuru sūmitsuin ni okeru sōtei shitsumon oyobi tōben shiryō," ca. 1938, Ōno Rokuichirō Kankei Bunsho (ORKB) #1276–2, unpaginated, Kensei Shiryōshitsu, National Diet Library, Tokyo, as repro-

duced in *Sengo hoshō mondai shiryōshū*, ed. Sengo Hoshō Mondai Kenkyūkai (Tokyo: Sengo Hoshō Mondai Kenkyūkai, 1991), 3:92 (hereafter *SHMS*). *SHMS* contains many photocopied archival documents. However, it is not commonly available. Therefore, whenever possible, when I first cite a document from this collection I have included information for the archive where the original is located.

20. Monbushō Kyōgaku-kyoku, ed., *Shinmin no michi*, reprinted in *Kokutai no hongi/Shinmin no michi*, ed. Kaizuka Shigeki (Tokyo: Nihon Tosho Sentā, 2003), 24–26; for the long quote, 26.

21. Oguma Eiji, *Tan'itsu minzoku shinwa no kigen: "Nihonjin" no jigazō no keifu* (Tokyo: Shinyōsha, 1994), published in English as *A Genealogy of 'Japanese' Self-images*, trans. David Askew (Melbourne: Trans Pacific Press, 2002); Tessa Morris-Suzuki, *Reinventing Japan: Time, Space, Nation* (Armonk, N.Y.: M. E. Sharpe, 1998), 79–109; Naoki Sakai, "Ethnicity and Species: On the Philosophy of the Multi-ethnic State in Japanese Imperialism," *Radical Philosophy*, no. 95 (May/June 1999): 33–45; Naoki Sakai, "Subject and Substratum: On Japanese Imperial Nationalism," *Cultural Studies* 14, nos. 3/4 (2000): 462–530; and Komagome Takeshi, *Shokuminchi teikoku Nihon no bunka tōgō* (Tokyo: Iwanami Shoten, 1996).

22. For Sakai, in addition to the two works cited in the previous note, see *Translation and Subjectivity: On Japan and Cultural Nationalism* (Minneapolis: University of Minnesota Press, 1997) and *Shisan sareru Nihongo/Nihonjin* (Tokyo: Shinyōsha, 1996); Balibar and Wallerstein, *Race, Nation, Class*.

23. Akira Iriye, *Power and Culture: The Japanese-American War, 1941–1945* (Cambridge, Mass.: Harvard University Press, 1981); Gerald Horne, *Race War! White Supremacy and the Japanese Attack on the British Empire* (New York: New York University Press, 2004).

24. For example, see Reed Ueda, "The Changing Path to Citizenship: Ethnicity and Naturalization during World War II," in *The War in American Culture: Society and Consciousness during World War II*, ed. Lewis A. Erenberg and Susan E. Hirsch (Chicago: University of Chicago Press, 1996), 202–16, esp. 210–11.

25. John Dower, *War without Mercy: Race and Power in the Pacific War* (New York: Pantheon, 1986).

26. Ibid., 203, 234.

27. Balibar, "Is There a 'Neo-Racism'?"

28. The concept of "as if" is an integral part of modern thought, paradigmatically in Kant's philosophy of the categorical imperative wherein one must act *as if* one's maxims are universal law (see, for example, the entry for "As-if," in Howard Caygill, *A Kant Dictionary* [Oxford: Blackwell, 1995], 86–87). In civil society or the public sphere we are supposed to act as if we are all social and economic peers, although critics of this Habermasian model have argued that such a world is more fanciful than practical. In a

later chapter on the adoption metaphor in relationship to colonialism, I use the concept of *as if* somewhat differently than I use it here.

29. Dower, *War without Mercy*, 263. The work is Kōseishō Kenkyūbu Jinkō Minzokubu, *Yamato minʐoku o chūkaku to suru sekai seisaku no kentō* (1943), reprinted in *Minʐoku jinkō seisaku kenkyū shiryō*, vols. 3–8 (Tokyo: Bunsei Shoin, 1982–83).

30. For the estimate of *gunʐoku*, see Higuchi Yūichi, *Kōgun heishi ni sareta Chōsenjin: jūgonen sensōka no sōdōin taisei no kenkyū* (Tokyo: Shakai Hyōronsha, 1991), 12–17.

31. William L. O'Neill, *A Democracy at War: America's Fight at Home and Abroad in World War II* (1993; reprint, Cambridge, Mass.: Harvard University Press, 1995), 9.

32. For "approximately 33,000," see, for example, United States Commission on Wartime Relocation and Internment of Civilians, *Personal Justice Denied* (Seattle: University of Washington Press, 1997), 253. The commission's figure is drawn from the United States Selective Service System's publication *Special Groups*, special monograph no. 10, vol. 1 (Washington, D.C.: Selective Service System, 1953), 142. However, Colonel Norman A. Donges, chief of the Strength Accounting Branch, Adjutant General Office, reported on 14 April 1947 to Colonel E. J. Fielder of the Information Division, War Department, that "from 1 July 1940 to 30 November 1946, 33,330 enlisted or inducted personnel gave their race as Japanese upon entrance into the Army" (G-1 [Personnel], Decimal File, June 1946–48, Entry 43, Box 799, 291.2 Japanese to 292, War Department General Staff, Record Group [RG] 165, National Archives at College Park, College Park, Md. [NACP]). In other words, the "approximately 33,000" count includes all those who entered the army in the more than fifteen months that elapsed between the war's end in mid-August 1945 and November 1946.

A War Relocation Authority (WRA) document authored by Director Dillon Myer about two months after the war's end states that he had been informed by the War Department that a total of 22,532 Nisei and "Alien volunteers" had served in the U.S. Army between 1 July 1940 and 30 June 1945. Of the total, 10,707 (109 officers and 10,598 enlisted personnel) were from Hawaii, while 11,825 (142 officers and 11,683 enlisted personnel) came from the mainland (D. W. Myer, War Relocation Authority, "Administrative Notice No. 322," 29 October 1945, Personnel Security Division, Japanese-American Branch [JAB], General File, 1942–46, Entry 480, Box 1740, Records of the Office of the Provost Marshal General, 1941–, RG 389). Myer also received a detailed list of all Japanese American officers and enlisted men who had served in the army during this period that includes not only the names but also serial numbers and places of residence for each individual ("Listing of all Japanese with Service in the U.S. Army 1 July 1940 through 30 June 1945" [XTN-89], no date, Administrative Services Division, Strength Accounting Branch Strength Returns, 1941–1954, Entry 389, Box 2166, Records of the Adjutant General's Office, 1917–, RG 407). The WRA's statistical analysis of its history indicates that according to releases of the War Department, from November 1940 to December

1945 "25,778 Japanese Americans were inducted into the Armed Forces—438 officers and 25,340 enlisted men—with an estimated 13,528 from the mainland and 12,250 from Hawaii" (United States War Relocation Authority, *The Evacuated People: A Quantitative Description* [Washington, D.C.: U.S. Government Printing Office, 1946], table 49, p. 128).

A memo from R. W. Berry (deputy assistant chief of staff, G-1) to the Under Secretary of War, 1 August 1945, states that 21,102 Americans of Japanese descent were inducted into the army from 1 November 1940 to 31 May 1945, including 162 officers and 79 members of the Women's Army Corps (WACs) (Personnel Security Division, JAB, General File, 1942–46, Entry 480, Box 1717, RG 389). Berry's figures corroborate those given in "Army Personnel of Japanese Ancestry by Month of Enlistment or Induction" (XTM-23), ca. March 1946, Administrative Services Division, Strength Accounting Branch Strength Returns, 1941–1954, Entry 389, Box 2166, RG 407. This latter document has the most detailed breakdown I have been able to find of Japanese Americans who were inducted into the army between November 1940 and February 1946. From its summary table it is possible to calculate that between November 1940 and August 1945, the month of the war's ending, 23,168 Japanese were inducted into the army, including 186 officers and 81 WACs. From these documents we can calculate that the total for those who served during the war years was roughly the sum of all those inducted between November 1940 and August 1945 (23,168) plus a few hundred men who may have enlisted prior to November 1940, minus a small number who may have been discharged prior to the Pearl Harbor attack, minus those who were inducted in the latter half of August 1945. A different method of calculation yields practically the same results: if we add the number of men inducted into the army in July and August of 1945 (17 officers and 1,029 enlisted men) to Dillon Myer's figure of 22,532 for the number of men who served in the army between July 1940 and June 1945, we come up with a total of 23,578 for men who served between July 1940 and August 1945. Thus the number of Japanese Americans who served during the war proper was undoubtedly around 23,500. This would mean that as many as 9,000 to 10,000 Japanese Americans were inducted between September 1945 and November 1946.

33. See United States Bureau of the Census, *Sixteenth Census of the United States: 1940. Population: Characteristics of the Nonwhite Population by Race*, 5; and *Sixteenth Census of the United States: 1940. Population: Second Series Characteristics of the Population, Hawaii*, 5; and *Sixteenth Census of the United States: 1940. Population: Characteristics of the Population*, vol. 2, part 1, 19 (all published in Washington, D.C.: U.S. Government Printing Office, 1943).

34. Memorandum of Dillon Myer to Secretary of the Interior, 5 April 1944. Ickes agreed with Myer and wrote a letter to the Secretary of the Navy urging the latter to rescind the exclusion of Japanese Americans from branches under the Navy Department's jurisdiction (7 April 1944). The memorandum and letter can be found in File 13.607,

Headquarters Subject-Classified General Files, 1942–46, entry 16, box 92, Records of the War Relocation Authority, RG 210, National Archives Building, Washington, D.C. (NAB). The navy remained closed to Japanese Americans throughout the war, but as we will see, Myer's reasoning had great sway throughout the War Department and the government.

35. See, for example, United States Bureau of the Census, *Sixteenth Census of the United States: 1940. Population: Characteristics of the Nonwhite Population by Race.*

36. United States Selective Service System, *Special Groups;* for the extended quotes, 4, 13.

37. Giorgio Agamben, *Homo Sacer: Sovereign Power and Bare Life*, trans. Daniel Heller-Roazan (Stanford: Stanford University Press, 1998); Giorgio Agamben, *State of Exception*, trans. Kevin Attell (Chicago: Chicago University Press, 2003); Achille Mbembe, "Necropolitics," *Public Culture* 15, no. 1 (2003): 11–40.

38. Lisa Lowe, *Immigrant Acts: On Asian American Cultural Politics* (Durham, N.C.: Duke University Press, 1996), 5; David Palumbo-Liu, *Asian/American: Historical Crossings of a Racial Frontier* (Stanford: Stanford University Press, 1999), 1. I follow his interpretation of the solidus in later chapters.

39. Peter Duus, *The Abacus and the Sword: The Japanese Penetration of Korea, 1895–1910* (Berkeley: University of California Press, 1995), 397–413.

40. For example, see Carter J. Eckert et al., *Korea Old and New: A History* (Seoul: Ilchokak for the Korea Institute, Harvard University, 1990), 276–304.

41. See, for example, Duus, *Abacus*, 413–23; Kim Il-myŏn, *Tennō to Chōsenjin to sōtokufu* (Tokyo: Tabata Shoten, 1984), 168–84.

42. Oguma, *Tan'itsu minzoku*, 151–53, 246.

43. Kita Ikki, "Nihon kaizō hōan taikō," in *Kita Ikki chosakushū,* vol. 2 (Tokyo: Misuzu Shobō, 1959), 331. Oguma makes similar points using Kita's earlier "Kokka Kaizōan genri taikō," but I have thought it more appropriate to use the later version that was made widely available in 1923. See Oguma, *Tan'itsu minzoku*, 155.

44. See Matsuda Toshihiko, *Senzenki no zainichi Chōsenjin to sanseiken* (Tokyo: Akashi Shoten, 1995), on which I draw for my discussion.

45. Etienne Balibar, "Racism and Nationalism," in Balibar and Wallerstein, *Race, Nation, Class*, 37–67; for the quote, 37.

46. I have borrowed the term "vulgar racism" from Frantz Fanon, and "polite racism" from David Theo Goldberg, while elaborating on these concepts. See Fanon, "Racism and Culture"; and David Theo Goldberg, *The Racial State* (Malden, Mass.: Blackwell, 2002).

47. For the data, see Matsuda, *Senzenki*, 81 (table III-1).

48. Since it is no longer unusual to call for such a bridging of disciplinary and area bounded fields of study, I will not name all who have done so. I should note, however, the recent appearance of two laudable transnational studies of Japanese Americans: Brian

Masaru Hayashi, *Democratizing the Enemy: The Japanese American Internment* (Princeton: Princeton University Press, 2004), and Eiichiro Azuma, *Between Two Empires: Race, History, and Transnationalism in Japanese America* (Oxford: Oxford University Press, 2005). Overall, studies that act on the call for transnational projects that transcend older area and ethnic studies formations are still rare.

49. Such a perspective characterizes works by not only Japanese American veterans and veterans' organizations but also by journalists, historians, and filmmakers. Major publications by veterans or veterans' organizations include, in order of publication date, Chester Tanaka, *Go for Broke: A Pictorial History of the Japanese American 100th Infantry Battalion and the 442th Regimental Combat Team* (Richmond, Calif.: Go for Broke, 1981); John Tsukano, *Bridge of Love* (Honolulu: Honolulu Hosts, 1985); and Tad Ichinokuchi, ed., *John Aiso and the M.I.S.: Japanese-American Soldiers in the Military Intelligence Service, World War II* (Los Angeles: Military Intelligence Service Club of Southern California, 1988). The Internet site established and maintained by the Go for Broke Educational Foundation, www.goforbroke.org, is an impressive contribution to this discourse on Japanese American heroism and citizenship. Major works by others include Thomas D. Murphy, *Ambassadors in Arms: The Story of Hawaii's 100th Battalion* (Honolulu: University of Hawaii Press, 1954); Joseph D. Harrington, *Yankee Samurai: The Secret Role of Nisei in America's Pacific Victory* (Detroit: Pettigrew Enterprises, 1979); Masayo Duus, *Unlikely Liberators: The Men of the 100th and 442nd*, trans. Peter Duus (Honolulu: University of Hawaii Press, 1987); Lyn Crost, *Honor by Fire: Japanese Americans at War in Europe and the Pacific* (Novato, Calif.: Presidio Press, 1994); and U.S. Commission on Wartime Relocation and Internment of Civilians, *Personal Justice Denied*, 253–60. A large number of videos also exist.

50. Miyata Setsuko, *Chōsen minshū to "kōminka" seisaku* (Tokyo: Miraisha, 1985); Higuchi, *Kōgun heishi;* Utsumi, *Chōsenjin "kōgun" heishi tachi no sensō;* Kang Duk-sang (Tŏk-sang), *Chōsenjin gakuto shutsujin: mō hitotsu no wadatsumi no koe* (Tokyo: Iwanami Shoten, 1997), Higuchi Yūichi, *Senjika Chōsen no minshū to chōhei* (Tokyo: Sōwasha, 2001), Ch'oe Yu-ri, *Ilche malgi singminji chibae chŏngch'aek yŏn'gu* (Seoul: Kukhak Charyŏwŏn, 1997), 179–251.

CHAPTER 1. RIGHT TO KILL, RIGHT TO MAKE LIVE: KOREANS AS JAPANESE

1. Chōsen Sōtokufu, *Shisei sanjūnenshi* (Keijō: Chōsen Sōtokufu, 1940); reprinted as *Zōho Chōsen sōtokufu sanjūnenshi*, vol. 3 (Tokyo: Kuresu Shuppan, 1999), 448–49.

2. See esp. Michel Foucault, *The History of Sexuality*, vol. 1, trans. Robert Hurley (New York: Vintage, 1978), esp. 135–59; "Governmentality," in *The Foucault Effect: Studies in Governmentality*, ed. Graham Burchell, Colin Gordon, and Peter Miller (Chicago: University of Chicago Press, 1991), 87–104; *Society Must Be Defended*, trans. David Macey (New York: Picador, 2003), 239–64; and *Security, Territory, Population: Lectures*

at the Collège de France, 1977–78, ed. Michel Senellart, trans. Graham Burchell (Basingstoke: Palgrave Macmillan, 2007).

3. Foucault, *History of Sexuality,* 137.

4. Foucault, "Governmentality," 101.

5. Michel Foucault, "The Subject and Power," in *Michel Foucault: Beyond Structuralism and Hermeneutics,* ed. Herbert L. Dreyfus and Paul Rabinow, 2nd ed. (Chicago: University of Chicago Press, 1983), 221. As Foucault summarizes, in this complex system of governmentality population is the main target of power, political economy is its "principal form of knowledge," and "apparatuses of security" are its primary technical means ("Governmentality," 102–3).

6. For example, Todd Henry, "Sanitizing Empire: Japanese Articulations of Korean Otherness and the Construction of Early Colonial Seoul, 1905–1919," *Journal of Asian Studies* 64, no. 3 (August 2005): 639–75; Sonja Myung Kim, "Contesting Bodies: Managing Population, Birthing, and Medicine in Korea, 1876–1945," (Ph.D. diss., University of California, Los Angeles, 2008); Jun Yoo, *The Politics of Gender in Colonial Korea: Education, Labor, and Health, 1919–1945* (Berkeley: University of California Press, 2008).

7. This shift in view can also be seen in recent scholarly works on Manchukuo and Taiwan. For Korea, see, for example, the pioneering collections by Gi-Wook Shin and Michael Robinson, eds., *Colonial Modernity in Korea* (Cambridge, Mass.: Harvard University Asia Center, 1999), and Miyajima Hiroshi et al., eds., *Shokuminchi kindai no shiza: Chōsen to Nihon* (Tokyo: Iwanami Shoten, 2004); as well as Bruce Cumings, *Korea's Place in the Sun* (New York: W. W. Norton, 1997), 148–50. Matsumoto Takenori has provided a useful summary of some of the major works along these lines in "(Kenkyū dōkō) 'Shokuminchiteki kindai' o meguru kinnen no Chōsenshi kenkyū," in Miyajima et al., eds., *Shokuminchi kindai no shiza,* 247–72.

8. Itagaki Ryūta presents a very insightful overview of some current debates concerning the concept of "colonial modernity" among scholars writing in Japanese and Korean in " 'Shokuminchi kindai' o megutte," *Rekishi hyōron,* no. 654 (October 2004): 35–45. See also Itagaki's book on what he calls "the colonial experience." In it he seeks to go beyond simple application of the "colonial modernity" concept while emphasizing the multiple as well as contradictory spaces and temporalities in colonial Korea during the 1920s and '30s (*Chōsen kindai no rekishi minzokushi: Keihoku sanju no shokuminchi keiken* [Tokyo: Akashi Shoten, 2008]).

9. Yoo, *Politics of Gender,* 109, 181.

10. Kim, "Contesting Bodies," 140.

11. Hong Kŭm-cha, "Nittei jidai no shakai fukushi seisaku oyobi shakai fukushi sābisu," in *Shokuminchi shakai jigyō kankei shiryōshū: Chōsen hen,* ed. Kin-gendai Shiryō Kankōkai, supplement: *Kaisetsu* (Tokyo: Kin-gendai Shiryō Kankōkai, 1999), 33–93; Yun Chŏng-uk, *Shokuminchi Chōsen ni okeru shakai jigyō seisaku* (Osaka: Osaka Keizai Hōka Daigaku Shuppanbu, 1996); and Sin Yŏng-hong, *Kindai Chōsen shakai*

jigyōshi kenkyū: Keijō ni okeru hōmen iin seido no rekishiteki tenkai (Tokyo: Ryokuin Shobō, 1984).

12. Chōsen Sōtokufu, *Shisei sanjūnenshi*, 823–24.

13. These phrases are inspired by Giorgio Agamben insofar as they are meant to suggest a condition of uncertainty, indeterminacy, or the indefinite (not only in the temporal sense), with regard to worthiness for life within political arrangements (*Homo Sacer: Sovereign Power and Bare Life*, trans. Daniel Heller-Roazan [Stanford: Stanford University Press, 1998], and *State of Exception*, trans. Kevin Attell [Chicago: University of Chicago Press, 2003]). But I especially wish to stress the triple possibilities of unconcern, exclusion, and inclusion, and the wartime movement from the first two to the third.

14. Foucault, *Society Must Be Defended*, 256.

15. The 24 November 1937 Korean Army report under the signature of Kunō Seiichi is "Chōsenjin shiganhei seido ni kansuru ken kaitō," and is enclosed with Rikugun Chōbōka, "Chōsenjin shiganhei seido ni kansuru ken," Microfilm Reproductions of Selected Archives of the Japanese Army, Navy and Other Government Agencies, 1868– 1945 (hereafter MRSA), T678, Library of Congress, Washington, D.C.; reproduced in Sengo Hoshō Mondai Kenkyūkai, ed., *Sengo hoshō mondai shiryōshū* (Tokyo: Sengo Hoshō Mondai Kenkyūkai, 1991), 3:11–24 (hereafter *SHMS*). Yoshida Toshiguma, "Chō - senjin shiganhei/chōhei no kōgai," 4, ca. 1945, box 30, Manshū Chōsen 2, Chōsengun Kankei Shiryō, Military Archival Library, the National Institute for Defense Studies, Japan Ministry of Defense, Tokyo (hereafter MAL).

16. Yoshida, "Chōsenjin shiganhei/chōhei," 4.

17. While similar arguments can be found elsewhere, the generalizations made here are especially based on Rikugun Chōbōka, "Chōsenjin shiganhei seido ni kansuru ken," and Chōsen Sōtokufu, "Chōsenjin shiganhei seido shikō ni kansuru sūmitsuin ni okeru sōtei shitsumon oyobi tōben shiryō," ca. 1938, Ōno Rokuichirō Kankei Bunsho (hereafter ORKB), #1276–2, unpaginated, Kensei Shiryōshitsu, National Diet Library, Tokyo, in *SHMS*, 3:79–151.

18. Rikugun Chōbōka, "Chōsenjin shiganhei seido ni kansuru ken," in *SHMS*, 3:18.

19. Chōsen Sōtokufu, "Chōsenjin shiganhei seido shikō ni kansuru sūmitsuin," in *SHMS*, 3:132–42.

20. Ibid., esp. 3:83–86, 106–16; Chōsen Sōtokufu, "Shōwa 13 nen 12 gatsu dai 74 kai teikoku gikai setsumei shiryō," December 1938, as reproduced in Chōsen Sōtokufu, *Chōsen sōtokufu teikoku gikai setsumei shiryō*, vol. 3 (Tokyo: Fuji Shuppan, 1994), 53.

21. Rikugun Chōbōka, "Chōsenjin shiganhei seido ni kansuru ken," in *SHMS*, 3:21.

22. This report, "Sankō shiryō," unpaginated, ca. Nov. 1938, is a supplement to Rikugun Chōbōka, "Chōsenjin shiganhei seido ni kansuru ken," MRSA, unpaginated (not reproduced in *SHMS*).

23. Ibid.

24. Ibid.

25. *SHMS*, 4:14.

26. Naimushō, "Chōsen oyobi Taiwan no genkyō," July 1944, in *Taiheiyō senka no Chōsen oyobi Taiwan*, ed. Kondō Ken'ichi (Chigasaki-shi: Chōsen Shiryō Kenkyūkai, 1961), 33–34.

27. *SHMS*, 4:23–25.

28. Kondō Masami, *Sōryokusen to Taiwan: Nihon shokuminchi hōkai no kenkyū* (Tokyo: Tōsui Shobō, 1996), 50–51.

29. For the army data, see Yoshida, "Chōsenjin shiganhei/chōhei," 7. The army figures Yoshida provides for the years 1940–43 are 3,000; 3,000; 4,500; and 5,330. Slightly higher numbers are given in Naimushō, "Chōsen oyobi Taiwan no genkyō," 33, raising the total to 17,664. According to the latter source, the navy accepted 1,000 Koreans and an equal number of Taiwanese for the first class of navy special volunteers, which began training in specially established training centers on 1 October 1943. The second class, which began training on 1 April 1944, took 2,000 volunteers from each of the colonies. This makes a total of 3,000 volunteers from each colony. The Koreans trained at Chinhae (J. Chinkai), and the Taiwanese at Gaoxiong (Kaohsiung, or J. Takao). However, the total number of Korean and Taiwanese volunteers accepted into the navy was probably larger than 6,000, because the navy continued to take them even after implementation of the conscription systems. From the same source it is possible to calculate that the army enrolled a total of 4,525 Taiwanese volunteers (1,020 in 1942, 1,008 in 1943, and 2,497 in 1944). See ibid., 33–35.

30. Law No. 4 is reproduced in *SHMS*, 4:33. Although Koreans were considered Japanese nationals, they were not subject to the metropole's Household Registration Law (*kosekihō*), and their position outside that law generally served as the legal foundation for their formal exclusion from various rights and duties granted to metropolitan Japanese. Thus each time the Japanese military opened up limited avenues for Koreans and Taiwanese to enter the military, it needed to explicitly circumvent or amend language that established exclusions on the basis of the Household Registration Law. For example, the Special Volunteer Soldier Law of April 1938 stipulated that if other conditions were met, "male imperial subjects seventeen years of age and older to whom the Household Registration Law does not apply" could be enlisted into active service (*gen'eki*) or the first reserves (*dai'ichi hojū hei'eki*). Then, in order that Koreans might be conscripted into the military it became necessary to revise the Military Service Law so that it included not just those subject to the Household Registration Law but also those bound by "the Household Registration Law in Korean civil law."

31. For useful data on the volunteer and conscription systems in Taiwan, see Kondō, *Sōryokusen to Taiwan*, esp. 46–55, 371–97.

32. Higuchi Yūichi, *Senjika Chōsen no minshū to chōhei* (Tokyo: Sōwasha, 2001), 101–8. Aside from official documentation of the 110,000 drafted directly into active service, Higuchi has rather ingeniously relied on piecemeal evidence and conjecture to

arrive at the additional 80,000 conscripts. Because of the imprecision of this method, the actual total may be slightly more or less.

33. Yoshida, "Chōsenjin shiganhei/chōhei," table 9. According to this table, 29,388 out of 45,000 Korean army conscripts in 1944 were assigned to the infantry. A manuscript edited just after the war (ca. 1946) by a staff officer within the General Staff's Organization and Mobilization Department (Sanbō honbu hensei dōin-ka) gives these same figures. It also indicates that in the following year, 29,780 out of 45,000 Korean army conscripts were assigned to the infantry and that the army conscripted a total of 8,000 Taiwanese (*Shina jihen daitōa senso-kan dōin gaishi;* reprint, ed. Ōe Shinobu [Tokyo: Fuji Shuppan, 1988], table 2, 435).

34. Ōe, ed., *Shina jihen daitōa senso-kan dōin gaishi,* 436.

35. Katō Yōko, *Chōheisei to kindai Nihon* (Tokyo: Yoshikawa Kōbunkan, 1996), 248–53.

36. Kang Duk-sang (Tŏk-sang), *Chōsenjin gakuto shutsujin: mō hitotsu no wadatsumi no koe* (Tokyo: Iwanami Shoten, 1997), 1–38, 370. Alternatively, Yoshida ("Chōsenjin shiganhei/chōhei," 7) gives a total of 3,893 Korean student volunteers inducted.

37. Ch'oe Yu-ri, *Ilche malgi singminji chibae chŏngch'aek yŏn'gu* (Seoul: Kukhak Charyŏwŏn, 1997); Higuchi Yūichi, *Kōgun heishi ni sareta Chōsenjin: jūgonen sensōka no sōdōin taisei no kenkyū* (Tokyo: Shakai Hyōronsha, 1991); Higuchi, *Senjika Chōsen;* Miyata Setsuko, *Chōsen minshū to "kōminka" seisaku* (Tokyo: Miraisha, 1985); Utsumi Aiko, *Chōsenjin "kōgun" heishi tachi no sensō* (Tokyo: Iwanami Shoten, 1991); Wan-yao Chou, "The *Kōminka* Movement in Taiwan and Korea: Comparisons and Interpretations," in *The Japanese Wartime Empire, 1931–1945,* ed. Peter Duus, Ramon H. Myers, and Mark R. Peattie (Princeton: Princeton University Press, 1996), 40–68.

38. For an early attempt to articulate and emphasize the mutually constitutive character of the colonial relationship, see Frederick Cooper and Ann Laura Stoler, eds., *Tensions of Empire: Colonial Cultures in a Bourgeois World* (Berkeley: University of California Press, 1997).

39. Chōsen Sōtokufu, "Chōsen dōhō ni taisuru chōheisei sekō junbi kettei ni tomonau sochi jōkyō narabi sono hankyō," May 1942, unpaginated, ORKB #1262, in *SHMS,* 3:158.

40. Tessa Morris-Suzuki, *Re-inventing Japan: Time, Space, Nation* (Armonk, N.Y.: M. E. Sharpe, 1998), 94–95.

41. Chōsen Sōtokufu, "Chōsen dōhō ni taisuru chōheisei," in *SHMS,* 3:159–61.

42. Rikugun Heibika, "Daitōa sensō ni tomonau waga jinteki kokuryoku no kentō," 20 January 1942, collected in *Jūgonen sensō gokuhi shiryōshū,* 1st ser., ed. Takasaki Ryūji (Tokyo: Ryūkei Shosha, 1976), unpaginated.

43. Kōseishō Kenkyūbu Jinkō Minzokubu, *Yamato minzoku o chūkaku to suru sekai seisaku no kentō* (1943), reprinted in *Minzoku jinkō seisaku kenkyū shiryō,* vols. 3–8 (Tokyo: Bunsei Shoin, 1982–83). Although some of my emphases and readings are different, I

fundamentally agree with Oguma Eiji's richly contextualized analysis of this text in *Tan'itsu minzoku*, 235–70, 430 n. 28.

44. Kōseishō Kenkyūbu Jinkō Minzokubu, *Yamato minzoku*, 7:2360–63.

45. Ibid., 3:327–30; for the quotes, 329–30.

46. Chōsengun Shireibu, "Chōsenjin shiganhei seido ni kansuru iken," June 1937, MRSA, in *SHMS*, 3:25–60; for the quote, 30.

47. Chōsen Sōtokufu, "Chōsenjin shiganhei seido shikō ni kansuru sūmitsuin," in *SHMS*, 3:87–88.

48. Chōsengun Shireibu, "Daini-kō iinkai uchiawase kettei jikō," 24 April 1942 (revisions 1 May), ORKB #1204–2.

49. "Takumu daijin kakugi setsumei an," ORKB #1279–2, in *SHMS*, 3:219–24; for the quotes, 223.

50. "Rikugun daijin kakugi setsumei an," ORKB #1279–3, in *SHMS*, 3:225–29; for the quote, 227.

51. Chōsengun Shireibu, "Chōsenjin shiganhei seido ni kansuru iken," in *SHMS*, 3:31–32.

52. Rikugun Chōbōka, "Chōsenjin shiganhei seido ni kansuru ken," in *SHMS*, 3:23.

53. Chōsengun Shireibu, "Chōsenjin shiganhei seido ni kansuru iken," in *SHMS*, 3:40.

54. Chōsen Sōtokufu, "Chōsenjin shiganhei seido jisshi yōkō," MRSA, in *SHMS*, 3:69.

55. Chōsen Sōtokufu, "Chōsen dōhō ni taisuru chōheisei sekō junbi kettei ni tomonau," in *SHMS*, 3:161.

56. Dipesh Chakrabarty, *Provincializing Europe: Postcolonial Thought and Historical Difference* (Princeton: Princeton University Press, 2000), 8.

57. Kyōiku Sōkanbu, *Chōsen shusshinhei no kyōiku sankō shiryō*, 2 vols. (Kyōiku Sōkanbu, 1944), MAL. The discussion and page numbers in this passage refer to vol. 1 (published in February). The second volume (August) elaborated on the first volume's basic points. The pathbreaking work on Japan's version of Orientalism is Stefan Tanaka, *Japan's Orient: Rendering Pasts into History* (Berkeley: University of California Press, 1993).

58. Kyōiku Sōkanbu, *Chōsen shusshinhei*, 1–3.

59. Ibid., 9.

60. Ibid., 11–14. The remainder of my analysis of *Chōsen shusshinhei* is drawn from 17–45.

61. The classic text in this tradition pertinent to East Asia is, of course, Max Weber's *The Religion of China: Confucianism and Taoism*, trans. and ed. Hans H. Gerth (Glencoe, Ill.: Free Press, 1951), which presented the ethic spawned by Chinese religion as the antithesis of the spirit of capitalism that had grown out of Puritanism.

62. Ruth Benedict, *The Chrysanthemum and the Sword: Patterns of Japanese Culture*

(1946; reprint, Boston: Houghton Mifflin, 1989). Japanese colonial discourse commonly charged that Koreans lacked a sense of responsibility. For example, at a 19 February 1943 gathering of officials responsible for implementing the conscription system, Tanaka Tokutarō, a longtime bureaucrat in the Government-General of Korea, explained that Koreans did not possess "conscience" (ryōshin) and a sense of "responsibility" (sekinin). Overall, Tanaka's lecture "Korean Thought and Character" attributed basically the same negative qualities to the Korean people as the army manual, while similarly emphasizing their ability to overcome them. Furthermore, Tanaka proposed a post-racial understanding of Amaterasu (the Sun Goddess), not as the progenitress of the Yamato Race but as an object of veneration for all Japanese, including Koreans (Tanaka Tokutarō, "Chōsenjin no shisō to seikaku," transcript of lecture and discussion at Inchonkaku, ORKB #1299, esp. 4, 45–47).

63. Kyōiku Sōkanbu, Chōsen shusshinhei, 35.

64. Peter Duus provides vivid examples of turn-of-the-century Japanese discourses on Korean "filth, squalor, and indolence" in The Abacus and the Sword: The Japanese Penetration of Korea, 1895–1910 (Berkeley: University of California Press, 1995), 399–406; the quotes are from Okita Kinjō's Rimen no kankoku (Osaka: Kibunkan, 1905), as cited in ibid., 401–3.

65. United States War Department, Command of Negro Troops, pamphlet no. 20–6 (Washington, D.C.: U.S. Government Printing Office, February 1944); for the quotes, 1, 3, 12. For an even more extensive manual intended for use in training officers that similarly denounced racial discrimination while attributing differences to history and environment, see United States Army Service Forces, Leadership and the Negro Soldier, Army Service Forces Manual M5 (Washington, D.C.: U.S. Government Printing Office, October 1944).

66. U.S. War Department, Command of Negro Troops, 4, 6–7.

67. For example, in answer to a possible question from Diet members regarding the response of Koreans to military conscription, the GGK made the point that some Korean youths who passed their physicals possessed "ethnic prejudice" (minzokuteki henken; Chōsen Sōtokufu, "Shōwa 19 nen 12 gatsu dai 86 kai teikoku gikai setsumei shiryō," December 1944, as reproduced in Chōsen Sōtokufu, Chōsen sōtokufu teikoku gikai setsumei shiryō, 10:120).

68. Shisō Taisaku Kakari, "Hantōjin mondai" (August 1944), collected in Senjiki shokuminchi tōchi shiryō, vol. 7, ed. Mizuno Naoki (Tokyo: Kashiwa Shobō, 1998), 318–19. As Mizuno Naoki points out, while the affiliation of the study group is not specifically noted on the manuscript, the report was submitted under the name of Nishi Minoru, an adviser to the Kyōchōkai ("Kaisetsu," in ibid., 1:27). From this and the fact that the manuscript was found in the Kyōchōkai Collection of the Ōhara Institute for Social Research at Hōsei University, it seems fairly certain that the study group was organized under the Kyōchōkai.

69. Chōsen Sōtokufu, "Shōwa 19 nen 12 gatsu dai 86 kai teikoku gikai setsumei shiryō," 10:5–7.

70. The information in this paragraph is extracted from the excellent short summary of the history of the hardship allowance published as a note to Tanaka Takeo et al., "Sanseiken shikō no kei'i o kataru—Tanaka Takeo Koiso naikaku shokikanchō hoka" (tape-recorded 26 August 1958), in *Jūgonen sensōka no Chōsen tōchi, Mikōkai shiryō Chōsen sōtokufu kankeisha rokuon kiroku (1)*, Miyata Setsuko, supervising editor, *Tōyō bunka kenkyū* 2 (March 2000), 170 n. 2.

71. The draft of Mizuta's lecture (29 March 1944), which was a report on the GGK's 1944 budget, was published as "Shōwa jūkyūnendo Chōsen sōtokufu yosan ni tsuite," *Chōsen kindai shiryō kenkyū shusei*, no. 4 (15 December 1961): 1–50. On the hardship allowance problem and for the quotes, see 38–41.

72. Miyata, *Jūgonen sensōka no Chōsen tōchi*, 170 n. 2.

73. Chōsen Sōtokufu, "Shōwa 19 nen 12 gatsu dai 86 kai teikoku gikai setsumei shiryō," 10:14–16. In a postwar roundtable, several former colonial officials recalled the late colonial push to increase the number of Koreans in the colonial and central governments' bureaucracies (Tanaka et al., "Sanseiken shikō no kei'i o kataru," 152–53). Han has been described as a "classic collaborator" for his leading role in fostering cooperation between Japanese and Korean business interests (Carter J. Eckert, *Offspring of Empire: The Koch'ang Kims and the Colonial Origins of Korean Capitalism, 1876–1945* [Seattle: University of Washington Press, 1991], 242, 296 n. 24).

74. Wartime U.S. intelligence was extremely sensitive to Japan's treatment of its minorities and colonial subjects and reported on this question regularly. For example, the Office of Strategic Services collected information about Koiso's speech and subsequent efforts developing out of it to improve the condition of Koreans and Taiwanese; see Office of Strategic Services (Honolulu), "Programs of Japan in Korea: with Bibliographies," Assemblage #60, 10 February 1945, 12–14, Overseas Branch, Bureau of Overseas Intelligence Central Files, 1941–1945, Entry 370, Box 406 C, Records of the Office of War Information, Record Group (RG) 208.

75. Koiso Kuniaki, "Shisei enzetsu," *Dai 85 kai teikoku gikai kizokuin giji sokkiroku dai ichi gō*, published as *Kanpō gōgai*, 7 September 1944.

76. Okamoto Makiko, "Ajia/Taiheiyō sensō makki ni okeru Chōsenjin/Taiwanjin sanseiken mondai," *Nihonshi kenkyū*, no. 40 (January 1996): 53–67; Okamoto Makiko, "Ajia/Taiheiyō sensō makki no zainichi Chōsenjin seisaku," *Zainichi Chōsenjin kenkyū*, no. 27 (September 1997): 21–47; Mizuno Naoki, "Kaisetsu," esp. 14–19.

77. Chōsen Sōtokufu "Chōsenjin chōshū ni kansuru gutaiteki kenkyū," ca. May 1942, ORKB #1279–5, unpaginated, in *SHMS*, 3:249.

78. Tanaka et al., "Sanseiken shikō no kei'i o kataru," 151.

79. Okamoto, "Ajia/Taiheiyō sensō makki ni okeru Chōsenjin/Taiwanjin."

80. Tanaka et al., "Sanseiken shikō no kei'i o kataru," 139–79, esp. 144–48.

81. Mizuno Naoki, "Senjiki no shokuminchi shihai to 'naigaichi gyōsei ichigenka,'" *Jinbun gakuhō*, no. 79 (1997): 77–102. Mizuno tends to downplay the actual impact of this apparent unification of domestic and colonial administration.

82. Tanaka et al., "Sanseiken shikō no kei'i o kataru"; Tanaka Takeo et al., "Koiso sōtoku jidai no gaikan—Tanaka Takeo seimu sōkan ni kiku" (tape-recorded 9 September 1959), as published in Miyata, *Jūgonen sensōka no Chōsen tōchi*, 95–138.

83. Tanaka et al., "Sanseiken shikō no kei'i o kataru," 145.

84. Tanaka et al., "Koiso sōtoku jidai no gaikan," 113–14.

85. Ibid., 114.

86. Okamoto, "Ajia/Taiheiyō sensō makki ni okeru Chōsenjin/Taiwanjin"; and Tanaka et al., "Sanseiken shikō no kei'i o kataru," 172 n. 7.

87. T. Fujitani, "Kindai Nihon ni okeru kenryoku no tekunorojī: guntai, chihō, shintai," trans. Umemori Naoyuki, *Shisō*, no. 845 (November 1994): 163–76.

88. Kyung Moon Hwang, "Citizenship, Social Equality and Government Reform: Changes in the Household Registration System in Korea, 1894–1910," *Modern Asian Studies* 38, no. 2 (May 2004): 355–87.

89. Although my argument concerning the relationship between bio-power and governmentality, on the one hand, and the household registration and temporary domicile notification systems, on the other, is original, this paragraph relies heavily on Higuchi, *Senjika Chōsen*, 35–51.

90. "Musekisha no shūseki narabi ni kiryū ni kansuru hōrei sekō ni tomonau jimu shori ni yōsuru keihi hojo," ca. 1942, ORKB #1200–3, unpaginated.

91. Higuchi, *Senjika Chōsen*, 45.

92. Sheldon Garon, *Molding Japanese Minds: The State and Everyday Life* (Princeton: Princeton University Press, 1997), 58. Historians of the United States have noted the relative shift away from New Deal–type social service agencies in wartime toward welfare for the military, especially as embodied in the 1944 G.I. Bill. For example, see Michael S. Sherry, *In the Shadow of War: The United States since the 1930s* (New Haven: Yale University Press, 1995), 111–12.

93. Chōsen Sōtokufu, "Shōwa 19 nen 12 gatsu dai 86 kai teikoku gikai setsumei shiryō," 10:63–65.

94. Ibid., 10:64–70.

95. This paragraph is based on Hong, "Nittei jidai no shakai fukushi seisaku," esp. 67–79, and Sin, *Kindai Chōsen shakai jigyōshi*, 450–90.

96. Sin, *Kindai Chōsen shakai jigyōshi*, 430–34; for the quote, 432.

97. Chōsen Sōtokufu, "Dai 85 kai teikoku gikai setsumei shiryō" (1944), reprinted as "Dai 85 kai teikoku gikai setsumei shiryō fukkoku—sōtoku tōchi makki no jittai (4)," in *Chōsen kindai shiryō kenkyūkai shūsei*, supervising ed. Kondō Kenichi, vol. 4 (Tokyo: Yūhō Kyōkai Chōsen Shiryō Kenkyūkai, 1961), 110–15.

98. Hong, "Nittei jidai no shakai fukushi seisaku," 78.

99. For example, see Shō Kashin, *Nihongata fukushi kokka no keisei to "jūgonen sensō"* (Tokyo: Mineruba Shobō, 1998); Gregory J. Kasza, "War and Welfare Policy in Japan," *Journal of Asian Studies* 61, no. 2 (May 2002): 417–35.

100. The proposal, which was passed by the cabinet on 22 December 1944, is collected in Mizuno, ed., *Senjiki shokuminchi tōchi shiryō*, 1:130–46.

101. Komagome Takeshi makes the important point that the segregation of the metropolitan and colonial household registration systems functioned to distinguish Japanese from Taiwanese "on the basis of consanguinity" ("Japanese Colonial Rule and Modernity: Successive Layers of Violence," in *"Race" Panic and the Memory of Migration*, ed. Meaghan Morris and Brett de Bary, special issue of *Traces* [Hong Kong: Hong Kong University Press, 2001], 236). References to Okamoto Makiko in this paragraph are from Okamoto, "Ajia/Taiheiyō sensō makki no zainichi Chōsenjin."

102. Okamoto, "Ajia/Taiheiyō sensō makki no zainichi Chōsenjin," 23.

103. For more on the Kyōwakai, see Higuchi Yūichi, *Kyōwakai: senjika Chōsenjin tōsei soshiki no kenkyū* (Tokyo: Shakai Hyōronsha, 1986).

104. Yoshida, "Chōsenjin shiganhei/chōhei" (above, note 15), 22.

105. Ibid., 20.

106. Beginning with Pak Kyŏng-sik's *Chōsenjin kyōsei renkō no kiroku* (Tokyo: Miraisha, 1965) and Senda Kakō's *Jūgun ianfu* (Tokyo: San'ichi Shobō, 1978), there are now quite a number of scholarly works and collections of testimonials on this topic. For a recent concise discussion in English of Korean forced laborers, see Naitou Hisako, "Korean Forced Labor in Japan's Wartime Empire," in *Asian Labor in the Wartime Japanese Empire*, ed. Paul H. Kratoska (Armonk, N.Y.: M. E. Sharpe, 2005), 90–98. The issue of comfort women will be discussed more fully in chapter 8.

107. Michel Foucault, "The Political Technology of Individuals," in *Technologies of the Self: A Seminar with Michel Foucault*, ed. Luther H. Martin, Huck Gutman, and Patrick H. Hutton (Amherst, Mass.: University of Massachusetts Press, 1988), 145–62; for the quotes, 147, 152, 160.

108. Agamben, *Homo Sacer* and *State of Exception;* Achille Mbembe, "Necropolitics," *Public Culture* 15, no. 1 (Winter 2003): 11–40.

CHAPTER 2. "VERY USEFUL AND VERY DANGEROUS": THE GLOBAL POLITICS OF LIFE, DEATH, AND RACE

1. Important works that have connected the evacuation and internment of Japanese Americans to the long history of U.S. racism, particularly against Asians, include Roger Daniels, *Concentration Camps, USA: Japanese Americans and World War II* (New York: Holt, Rinehart & Winston, 1972), and Richard Drinnon, *Keeper of the Concentration Camps: Dillon S. Myer and American Racism* (Berkeley: University of California Press, 1987).

2. William Seltzer and Margo Anderson, "After Pearl Harbor: The Proper Role

of Population Data Systems in Time of War," paper presented at the panel "Human Rights, Population Statistics, and Demography: Threats and Opportunities," Population Association of America, annual meeting, Los Angeles, March 23–25, 2000, esp. 5–23, 38–40.

3. Natalia Molina, *Fit to Be Citizens? Public Health and Race in Los Angeles, 1879–1939* (Berkeley: University of California Press, 2006), esp. chap. 3; Roger Daniels, "Japanese America, 1930–1941: An Ethnic Community in the Great Depression," *Journal of the West* 34, no. 4 (October 1985): 35. Nayan Shah's work shows a similar exclusionary logic in public health discourses and practices regarding San Francisco's Chinese population, at least until the 1940s and 1950s (*Contagious Divides: Epidemics and Race in San Francisco's Chinatown* [Berkeley: University of California Press, 2001]).

4. *Los Angeles Times*, quoted in Daniels, *Concentration Camps, USA*, 62.

5. Chase A. Clark, governor of Idaho, quoted from a newspaper report in United States War Relocation Authority, *The WRA: A Story of Human Conservation* ([Washington, D.C.]: Department of the Interior, War Relocation Authority, ca. 1946), 7. Dower's pioneering study of such nonhuman racist images of the Japanese is *War without Mercy: Race and Power in the Pacific War* (New York: Pantheon, 1986), esp. 77–93.

6. These facts are well-known. See for example, United States Commission on Wartime Relocation and Internment of Civilians, *Personal Justice Denied* (Seattle: University of Washington Press, 1997), 137–40.

7. Achille Mbembe, *On the Postcolony* (Berkeley: University of California Press, 2001), 190.

8. See introduction, note 33.

9. Philip L. Martin, *Promise Unfulfilled: Unions, Immigration, and the Farm Workers* (Ithaca: Cornell University Press, 2003).

10. U.S. Commission on Wartime Relocation and Internment of Civilians, *Personal Justice Denied*, 181–84; U.S. War Relocation Authority, *The WRA*, 27–41.

11. Several scholars have already suggested, albeit in different ways, a close relation between liberalism and internment. See esp. Gordon H. Chang, " 'Superman is about to visit the relocation centers' and the Limits of Wartime Liberalism," *Amerasia Journal* 19, no. 1 (Fall 1993): 37–59; Brian Masaru Hayashi, *Democratizing the Enemy: The Japanese American Internment* (Princeton: Princeton University Press, 2004), esp. chaps. 1, 4; Colleen Lye, *America's Asia: Racial Form and American Literature, 1893–1945* (Princeton: Princeton University Press, 2005), esp. chap. 4; Mae M. Ngai, *Impossible Subjects: Illegal Aliens and the Making of Modern America* (Princeton: Princeton University Press, 2004), esp. 167–201; Carolyn Chung Simpson, *An Absent Presence: Japanese Americans in Postwar American Culture, 1945–60* (Durham, N.C.: Duke University Press, 2001), esp. chap. 2.

12. Adjutant General J. A. Ulio reported the figure of "4,670 Japanese-Americans now in the United States Army" in his 5 November 1942 letter to John F. Embree, Senior

Archivist, War Relocation Authority, File 13.607, Headquarters Subject-Classified General Files, 1942–46, entry 16, box 92, Record Group (RG) 210.

13. Office of the Assistant Chief of Staff, G-2, and Office of the Provost Marshal General (OPMG), "Monograph on History of Military Clearance Program (Screening of Alien Japanese and Japanese American Citizens for Military Service)," 1–5, for the quotes, 1–2; Military Clearance Br. File (activities, functions, branch reports, etc.), Personnel Security Division, Japanese-American Branch (JAB), General File, 1942–46, entry 480, box 1726, RG 389. A slightly shorter but almost verbatim narrative of this situation is contained in OPMG, "World War II: A Brief History," no date (ca. November 1945), 247–49, Records of the Office of the Assistant Chief of Staff, G-2 (Intelligence), Historical Studies and Related Records of G-2 Components, 1918–1959, Box 31-Miscellaneous Files, Records of the Army Staff, RG 319.

14. Memorandum of Major Karl R. Bendetsen for the Adjutant General, 16 January 1942, 291.2 Jan–Mar 1942, Army-AG Classified Decimal File, 1940–42, entry 360, box 147, RG 407.

15. Memorandum of Brigadier General James E. Wharton for the Assistant Chief of Staff, G-1, 28 March 1942, 291.2 Jan–Mar 1942, Army-AG Classified Decimal File, 1940–42, entry 360, box 147, RG 407.

16. A memorandum compiled by the Office of the Commanding General, Headquarters Western Defense Command and Fourth Army, indicates that "an order dated March 30, 1942, stopped all induction of Japanese in this (the Western Defense Command) area" (Memorandum of J. L. DeWitt to Chief of Staff, U.S. Army, 20 November 1942, ASW 342.18, Formerly Security Classified Correspondence of John J. McCloy, 1941–45, entry 180, box 22, Records of the Office of the Secretary of War, RG 107). M. W. Pettigrew, chief of the Far Eastern Group in the War Department's Military Intelligence Service, noted that Nisei "induction and enlistment was stopped March 31, 1942" (Memorandum of M. W. Pettigrew to Mr. McCloy, 17 November 1942, 291.2 Army-AG Classified Decimal File 1940–42, Entry 360, Box 147, RG 407).

17. Memorandum of John W. Martyn, Administrative Assistant, to Chief of Staff, 7 February 1942, 28 March 1942, with attached anonymous handwritten note asking "Why Japans" [sic], in 291.2 Jan–Mar 1942, Army-AG Classified Decimal File, 1940–42, entry 360, box 147, RG 407.

18. Letter of Mrs. Sarah Usuda Lindsey to Colonel W. M. Dixon, 12 February 1942; memorandum of W. M. Dixon to the Chief of Finance, 14 February 1942 enclosed with memorandum of Ralph P. Cousins to the Chief of Staff, 1 January 1942: both in 291.2 Jan–Mar 1942, Army-AG Classified Decimal File, 1940–42, entry 360, box 147, RG 407.

19. U.S. Commission on Wartime Relocation and Internment of Civilians, *Personal Justice Denied*, 187, 253–56; Stimson quote, from letter to Major General Lewis B. Hershey, 17 June 1942, 291.2 (Alphabetically), G-1 (Personnel), Decimal File, 1942–June 1946, entry 43, box 445, RG 165.

20. Masayo Duus, *Unlikely Liberators: The Men of the 100th and 442nd*, trans. Peter Duus (Honolulu: University of Hawaii Press, 1987), 18–21; U.S. Commission on Wartime Relocation and Internment of Civilians, *Personal Justice Denied*, 256, 268–77.

21. Letter of D. S. Myer to John J. McCloy, 18 February 1943; letter of William P Scobey to Mr. Myer, 23 February 1943; copy of the Adjutant General's letter to Commanding General, All Service Commands, 26 September 1942: all filed together in ASW 342.18, Formerly Security Classified Correspondence of John J. McCloy, 1941–45, entry 180, box 22, RG 107.

22. Roosevelt's declaration can be found in many places, including the now official history of Japanese Americans during the war years: U.S. Commission on Wartime Relocation and Internment of Civilians, *Personal Justice Denied*, 191.

23. Office of the Assistant Chief of Staff, G-2, and OPMG, "Monograph on History of Military Clearance Program," 29–43, 59–63.

24. To be sure, such employees were required to pass an elaborate security check. In October the War Department amended the policy so that even aliens became employable. JAB, OPMG, "History of the Japanese Program," no date (ca. 1 September 1945), p. 17, Personnel Security Division, JAB, General File, 1942–46, entry 480, box 1723, RG 389.

25. I borrow the expression "naturalistic racism" from David Theo Goldberg, *The Racial State* (Malden, Mass.: Blackwell, 2002).

26. Letter of Adjutant-General to Assistant Chief of Staff, G-2, appointing board of officers to consider military utilization of United States Citizens of Japanese Ancestry, 1 July 1942, 291.2 (Alphabetically), G-1 (Personnel), Decimal File, 1942–June 1946, entry 43, box 445, RG165. The Board of Officers' report quoted in the following passage is "The Military Utilization of United States Citizens of Japanese Ancestry," approved by order of Secretary of War 14 September 1942, 291.2 (Alphabetically), G-1 (Personnel), Decimal File, 1942–June 1946, entry 43, box 445, RG 165.

27. Memo of Major L. Duenweg to Colonel T. J. Koenig, 12 August 1942, enclosed with "The Military Utilization of United States Citizens of Japanese Ancestry." Colonel Theodore J. Koenig served as president of the Board of Officers.

28. Memo of Lieutenant General L. J. McNair to Chief of Staff, U.S. Army (Attention: G-1 Division), enclosed with "The Military Utilization of United States Citizens of Japanese Ancestry."

29. Memorandum of LeR. Lutes, Assistant Chief of State for Operations, Services of Supply, to Colonel T. J. Koenig, enclosed with "The Military Utilization of United States Citizens of Japanese Ancestry."

30. "Memorandum for the Record," recorded by Major J. L. Lowell (Recorder of Board), 9 July 1942, enclosed with "The Military Utilization of United States Citizens of Japanese Ancestry."

31. Letter of Lieutenant General John L. DeWitt to Colonel Theodore J. Koenig,

25 July 1942, enclosed with "The Military Utilization of United States Citizens of Japanese Ancestry."

32. "Memorandum for the Record," recorded by Major Lowell, 9 July 1942.

33. Letter of Congressman D. D. Terry to Lieutenant General Lesley J. McNair, 19 March 1943, enclosed with "The Military Utilization of United States Citizens of Japanese Ancestry."

34. Letter of Brigadier General F. B. Mallon to Commanding General, Seventh Corps Area, 20 March 1942, 291.2, Jan.–Mar. 1942, Army-AG Classified Decimal File, 1940–42, entry 360, box 147, RG 407.

35. Letter of D. Hodson Lewis to Congressman D. D. Terry, 18 March 1942, enclosed with "The Military Utilization of United States Citizens of Japanese Ancestry."

36. Evaluation Branch, Counter-Intelligence Group (CIG), Military Intelligence Division (MID), Assistant Chief of Staff, G-2, "Development of Our Own," 5 December 1942, Subversive Organizations, Personnel Security Division, JAB, General File, 1942–46, entry 480, box 1737, RG 389. For more on Takahashi, see Ernest Allen, Jr., "When Japan Was 'Champion of the Darker Races': Satokata Takahashi and the Flowering of Black Messianic Nationalism," *Black Scholar* 24, no. 1 (Winter 1994): 23–46. Takahashi's first name is sometimes rendered as Satokata rather than Satakata.

37. As quoted in Gerald Horne, *Race War! White Supremacy and the Japanese Attack on the British Empire* (New York: New York University Press, 2004), 57. According to Horne, one of these Japanese men was Hikida Yasuichi. Hikida was reportedly extremely knowledgeable about black history, wrote a biography of the Haitian revolutionary hero Toussaint L'Ouverture, and kept a mailing address at the YMCA in Harlem.

38. Evaluation Section, CIG, MID, "Japanese Racial Agitation Among American Negroes," 15 April 1942, Personnel Security Division, JAB, General File, 1942–46, entry 480, box 1730, RG 389 (hereafter cited parenthetically in the text). Marc Gallicchio has also discussed this report in *The African American Encounter with Japan and China: Black Internationalism in Asia, 1895–1945* (Chapel Hill: University of North Carolina Press, 2000), 128–32.

39. Memo of Major General J. A. Ulio to Commanding General, Army Ground Forces (McNair), 29 May 1942, 291.2, April–September 1942, Army-AG Classified Decimal File, 1940–42, entry 360, box 147, RG 407.

40. See especially Gallicchio, *The African American Encounter*, 122–58. Other valuable works that shed light on the positive images that many African Americans held of the Japanese, especially of Japanese struggles against white imperialism, include Allen, "When Japan Was 'Champion of the Darker Races' "; Horne, *Race War!*, 43–59, 105–27, 220–50; Reginald Kearney, *African American Views of the Japanese: Solidarity or Sedition?* (Albany: State University of New York Press, 1998), 92–127; and George Lipsitz, " 'Frantic to Join . . . the Japanese Army': Black Soldiers and Civilians Confront

the Asia-Pacific War," in *Perilous Memories: The Asia Pacific War(s)*, ed. T. Fujitani, Geoffrey M. White, and Lisa Yoneyama (Durham, N.C.: Duke University Press, 2001), 347–77.

41. Bob Kumamoto, "The Search for Spies: American Counterintelligence and the Japanese American Community, 1931–1942," *Amerasia Journal* 6, no. 2 (Fall 1979): 50–51.

42. Gallicchio, *The African American Encounter*, 144.

43. Evaluation Branch, CIG, MID, Assistant Chief of Staff, G-2, "Ethiopian Pacific Movement," 17 December 1942, Subversive Organizations, Personnel Security Division, JAB, General File, 1942–46, entry 480, box 1737, RG 389.

44. Letter of Brigadier General Mallon to Commanding General, Seventh Corps Area, 20 March 1942.

45. L. Duenweg to Assistant Chief of Staff, G-2, 6 July 1942, 5th endorsement (of the 29 May 1942 memo of Major General J. A. Ulio to the Commanding General, Army Ground Forces and the Commanding General, Southern Defense Command); memorandum of Thomas T. Handy, Major General, Assistant Chief of Staff to Chief of Staff, 18 July 1942, and memorandum of Joseph T. McNarney, Acting Chief of Staff to Commander in Chief, U.S. Fleet, 21 July 1942, Harny and McNarney memos in G-1 (Personnel), Decimal File, 1942–June 1946, entry 43, box 445, RG 165; Richard Donovan (Commanding General of the Eighth Service Command, Services of Supply) to Adjutant General, 9 September 1942, 12th endorsement (of the 29 May 1942 memo); the 5th and 12th endorsements are clustered together with the 29 May 1942 memo in 291.2, April–September 1942, Army-AG Classified Decimal File, 1940–42, entry 360, box 147, RG 407.

46. "The Military Utilization of United States Citizens of Japanese Ancestry," 3.

47. All the documents cited in this paragraph, except the last mentioned, can be found in the cluster of documents labeled "Enlistment of loyal American citizens of Japanese descent into the Army and Navy," 17 December 1942; 291.2 Army-AG Classified Decimal File 1940–42, Entry 360, Box 14 7, RG 407. For McCloy's 15 October 1942 letter to M. S. Eisenhower: Records of the Office of the Director and Predecessor Agencies, Records of the Director, 1942–45, entry 1, box 1, RG 208.

In her pathbreaking work on Japanese American soldiers, Masayo Duus briefly refers to some of these documents and to the propaganda factor (*Unlikely Liberators*, 57). Duus's wording is a bit ambiguous, but she could be read as arguing that propaganda utility was the decisive factor in the decision to allow Japanese Americans to volunteer for the military. The excellent encyclopedia edited by Brian Niiya, *Japanese American History: An A-to-Z Reference from 1868 to the Present* (New York: Facts on File, 1993), apparently reads Duus in this way and clearly states that the "primary factor leading to this decision [to form a Nisei unit] had to do with issues of image and propaganda" (137). However, it cites no primary documents on this matter and emphasizes the need to appeal to "allies." In contrast, as we will see, the propaganda campaign was directed not at domestic audiences and allies alone but at people of color throughout the world, especially in Asia, as a means of achieving American global hegemony. Brian Hayashi briefly discusses propaganda in *Democratizing the Enemy*, 139–40.

The U.S. Commission on Wartime Relocation and Internment of Civilians' *Personal Justice Denied* mentions the propaganda dimension (188–91), only to downplay it and highlight the "humanitarian overtones" in the decision to allow Japanese Americans into the military. My emphasis is the reverse—namely, that whatever "humanitarian overtones" can be found in the documents, they were secondary to the argument that Japanese Americans could be useful as propaganda material.

48. Third draft of memorandum, author unknown, to Secretary of War, 28 October 1942, 291.2 Army-AG Classified Decimal File 1940–42, Entry 360, Box 147, RG 407.

49. Memorandum of M. W. Pettigrew to Mr. McCloy, 17 November 1942, 291.2 Army-AG Classified Decimal File 1940–42, Entry 360, Box 147, RG 407. To be sure, Pettigrew's concrete recommendations went further than the War Department would eventually dare to go, including suspension of "all existing restriction against the conscription and voluntary enlistment of Nisei."

50. Memorandum of Colonel W. E. Crist, General Staff, to General Strong, 4 January 1943, Personnel Security Division, JAB, General File, 1942–46, entry 480, box 1717, RG 389.

51. John F. Embree, "Note on Treatment of American Citizens of Japanese Ancestry as an Aspect of Morale in Hawaii," copy attached to letter of J. R. Hayden to Dr. J. P. Baxter, 3rd, 19 January 1942, Records of the Office of Facts and Figures, Decimal File of the Director, 1941–42, Entry 5, Box 4, RG 208.

52. U.S. Commission on Wartime Relocation and Internment of Civilians, *Personal Justice Denied*, 187; Daniels, *Concentration Camps USA*, 145. Daniels also found that even earlier, on 25 February 1942, the "Joint Evacuation Board, composed of middle echelon military personnel and their opposite numbers from several executive departments and agencies" had proposed drafting or enlisting Japanese Americans into the armed forces.

53. All subsequent quotes from the Psychological Warfare Branch's plans, except for the final ones where I have specifically indicated "first draft," can be found in the 23 May 1942 draft titled "Japan Plan." It appears that the first draft, dated 13 May 1942 and called "Basis for a detailed plan for propaganda into the Japanese Empire," was authored solely or almost so by Solbert, and was then revised and expanded by him in response to "comments by a number of the experts of the government agencies involved" (cover letter to 23 May draft). The recommendations in the two drafts are very similar, although the second draft at 34 pages is much expanded from the earlier 18-page version. For both drafts: Records of the Historian, Historian's Records of the Psychological Warfare Branch, 1942–45, Entry 6G, Box 5; RG 208. I first discussed these two drafts as well as a number of other related documents in "The Reischauer Memo: Mr. Moto, Hirohito,

and Japanese American Soldiers," *Critical Asian Studies* 33, no. 3 (September 2001): 379–402. Since the publication of this article, Kato Tetsurō has discovered and written on a third draft of the plan, dated 3 June 1942, which he has put into the context of the origins of the "symbolic emperor system" (*Shōchō tennōsei no kigen: Amerika no shin-risen "Nihon keikaku"* [Tokyo: Heibonsha, 2005]).

54. On the OWI, see Allan M Winkler, *The Politics of Propaganda: The Office of War Information, 1942–1945* (New Haven: Yale University Press, 1978); for the quote, which is from the Executive Order (13 June 1942) establishing the OWI, 34.

55. Milton S. Eisenhower, letter to John J. McCloy, 22 August 1942. In his response to Eisenhower's letter, McCloy acknowledged that "I feel as you do about the Japanese and have already expressed my view to the General Staff." For both letters: Records of the Office of the Director and Predecessor Agencies, Records of the Director, 1942–45, entry 1, box 1, RG 208.

56. Edwin O. Reischauer, "Memorandum on Policy Towards Japan," 14 September 1942, with materials collected by War Department General Staff, Organization and Training Division, G-3, concerning "Enlistment of loyal American citizens of Japanese descent into the Army and Navy," 17 December 1942, 291.2 Army-AG Classified Decimal File 1940–42, Entry 360, Box 147, RG 407. I have reproduced the entire Reischauer memorandum as an addendum to my article "The Reischauer Memo."

57. Important works that have considered Reischauer's role in the politics of knowledge production in postwar area studies include John W. Dower, "E. H. Norman, Japan and the Uses of History," in *Origins of the Modern Japanese State* (New York: Random House, 1975), 3–101; four articles by Richard H. Minear: "Orientalism and the Study of Japan," *Journal of Asian Studies* 39, no. 3 (May 1980): 507–17; "Cross-Cultural Perception and World War II," *International Studies Quarterly* 24, no. 4 (December 1980): 555–80; "Helen Mears, Asia, and American Asianists," Asian Studies Committee, Occasional Papers Series No. 7, International Area Studies Program, University of Massachusetts at Amherst (1981); and "Wartime Studies of Japanese National Character," *The Japan Interpreter* 13, no. 1 (Summer 1980): 36–5; and H. D. Harootunian, "America's Japan/Japan's Japan," in *Japan and the World*, ed. Masao Miyoshi and H. D. Harootunian (Durham, N.C.: Duke University Press, 1993), 196–221.

58. Edwin O. Reischauer, *My Life between Japan and America* (New York: Harper & Row, 1986), 79–94.

59. This analysis owes much to Prasenjit Duara's *Sovereignty and Authenticity: Manchukuo and the East Asian Modern* (Lanham, Md.: (Rowan & Littlefield, 2003), as well as conversations that I have been having with Naoki Sakai over the years.

60. As early as July 1942, Stanley Hornbeck, adviser to the secretary of state, had also already stated in a private conversation that the emperor should be distinguished from the military and that after the war was over he could emerge once again as the leader of the Japanese people (Akira Iriye, *Power and Culture: Power and Culture:*

The Japanese-American War, 1941–1945 [Cambridge, Mass.: Harvard University Press, 1981], 59).

61. "OWI Board of War Inf. Minutes," 3 November 1942, Records of the Historian, Area File, 1943–45, Entry 6C, Box 3, RG 208.

62. Letter of Elmer Davis to Ralph Barton Perry, 7 November 1942, and memo of Col. Solbert to Davis, 6 November 1942, both in Records of the Historian, Area File, 1943–45, Entry 6C, Box 3, RG 208.

63. Nakamura Masanori, *The Japanese Monarchy: Ambassador Joseph Grew and the Making of the "Symbol Emperor System," 1931–1991*, trans. Herbert Bix et al. (Armonk, N.Y.: M. E. Sharpe, 1992), 18.

64. Robert E. Ward has noted that the imperial problem was "first mentioned in a paper of the Subcommittee on Political Problems of the Advisory Committee on Postwar Foreign policy, dated 10 March 1943, where it is simply identified as one among a series of major problems relating to the 'Treatment of Japan'" ("Presurrender Planning: Treatment of the Emperor and Constitutional Changes," in *Democratizing Japan: The Allied Occupation*, ed. Robert E. Ward and Sakamoto Yoshikazu [Honolulu: University of Hawaii Press, 1987], 3).

65. Grew gave his "queen bee" speech on 12 December 1944, during the Senate Foreign Relations Committee's hearings on his appointment as under secretary of state (see Joseph C. Grew, *Turbulent Era*, ed. Walter Johnson [Boston: Houghton Mifflin, 1952], 2:1415–19).

66. War Department General Staff, Organization and Training Division, G-3, concerning "Enlistment of loyal American citizens of Japanese descent into the Army and Navy."

67. There has been a great deal of scholarly work in Japanese and English that has charted the course by which MacArthur and Hirohito, along with their advisers and conservative Japanese politicians, endeavored not only to retain the imperial institution but also to exempt Hirohito from prosecution for war crimes and to keep him on the throne. In recent years Herbert P. Bix's *Hirohito and the Making of Modern Japan* (New York: HarperCollins, 2000), esp. 533–646, and John W. Dower's *Embracing Defeat* (New York: W. W. Norton / New Press, 1999), esp. 277–345, have brought a new level of detail to our understanding of this process.

68. JAB, OPMG, "History of the Japanese Program," 5.

69. "Talk by Colonel Miller," p. 6, in "Training Program for Teams Sent to War Relocation Centers," ca. January 1943, Personnel Security Division, JAB, General File, 1942–46, Entry 480, Box 1738, RG 389. Here and in the following notes, when I refer to individual talks, I will indicate the name of the speaker, the date of the lecture, and the relevant page(s) for the particular date. In some cases pagination in the documents restarts during the course of a talk. These second pagination sets will be indicated by the suffix "b," even though that suffix does not appear in the original document.

70. "Talk by Colonel Scobey," 25 January 1943, p. 2, in "Training Program."

71. "Talk by Commander Coggins," 26 January 1943, pp. 1b, 6b, in "Training Program."

72. "Talk by Mr. Fryer," 26 January 1943, pp. 9–10, in "Training Program."

73. "Talk by Mr. Dedrick," 30 January 1943, p. 10, in "Training Program." For some background on Dedrick, see Seltzer and Anderson, "After Pearl Harbor," esp. 10–12; William Seltzer and Margo Anderson, "The Dark Side of Numbers: The Role of Population Data Systems in Human Rights Abuses," *Social Research* 68, no. 2 (Summer 2001): 492.

74. "Talk by Mr. Dedrick," p. 12.

75. United States War Relocation Authority, Community Analysis Section (John F. Embree), "Project Analysis Series," no. 1 (February 1943): 9.

76. Daniels, *Concentration Camps, USA,* 89.

77. Gwenn M. Jensen, "System Failure: Health-Care Deficiencies in the World War II Japanese American Detention Centers," *Bulletin of the History of Medicine* 73, no. 4 (Winter 1999): 602–28.

78. Ruth E. Hudson, R.N., "Health for Japanese Evacuees," *Public Health Nursing* 35 (1943): 619.

79. Louis Fiset, "Public Health in World War II Assembly Centers for Japanese Americans," *Bulletin of the History of Medicine* 73, no. 4 (winter 1999): 580–82; U.S. Commission on Wartime Relocation and Internment of Civilians, *Personal Justice Denied,* 163–65.

80. U.S. War Relocation Authority, *The WRA,* 142.

81. "Comprehensive Statement in Response to Senate Resolution No. 166," p. 21, prepared for Director of War Mobilization James F. Byrnes by War Relocation Authority, 14 September 1943; as collected in *American Concentration Camps: A Documentary History of the Relocation and Incarceration of Japanese Americans, 1942–1945,* ed. Roger Daniels, vol. 7, *1943* (New York: Garland, 1989), "Archival Documents," unpaginated.

82. Jensen, "System Failure," 602.

83. In "Professional Health Care and the Japanese American Incarceration" a special issue of the *Bulletin of the History of Medicine,* Gwenn M. Jensen offers the more critical view ("System Failure"), while the more positive assessment is given by Louis Fiset ("Public Health in World War II Assembly Centers").

84. U.S. Congress, Senate, Committee on Military Affairs, *War Relocation Centers: Hearings. Before a Subcommittee of the Committee on Military Affairs,* 78th Cong., 1st sess., on S. 444, 20 January 1943, 41, and part 2, 11 February 1943, 146; as collected in Daniels, ed., *American Concentration Camps,* vol. 7, *1943,* "Hearings on War Relocation Centers, Chandler Subcommittee, January—February, 1943," unpaginated.

85. U.S. War Relocation Authority, *The WRA,* 62, 111–14. On "fancy food items," see letter of Congressman Elmer Thomas to Major General Allen W. Gullion (Provost Marshal General), 2 June 1943; as collected in Daniels, ed., *American Concentration Camps,* vol. 7, *1943,* "Archival Documents," unpaginated.

86. Corporal Fred J. Grant Post #1481 Veterans of Foreign Wars of the United States at Ogden, Utah, "Resolution," 1 September 1943; as collected in Daniels, ed., *American Concentration Camps*, vol. 7, *1943*, "Archival Documents," unpaginated.

87. Drinnon, *Keeper of the Concentration Camps*.

88. Dillon S. Myer, *Uprooted Americans: The Japanese Americans and the War Relocation Authority during World War II* (Tucson: University of Arizona Press, 1971), 91–107.

89. U.S. Congress, Senate, Committee on Military Affairs, *War Relocation Centers: Hearings Before a Subcommittee of the Committee on Military Affairs*, on S. 444, 53–54.

90. Myer's statement is reproduced in his *Uprooted Americans*, 99–100.

91. U.S. War Relocation Authority, *The WRA*, 16–19.

92. U.S. Congress, Senate, Committee on Military Affairs, *War Relocation Centers: Hearings Before a Subcommittee of the Committee on Military Affairs*, on S. 444, 127–28.

93. Ibid., 158.

94. U.S. War Relocation Authority, *The WRA*, 112.

95. "Telephone conversation—Mr. McCloy and Colonel Bendetsen—10 July 1943"; as collected in Daniels, ed., *American Concentration Camps*, vol. 7, *1943*, "Archival Documents," unpaginated.

96. U.S. War Relocation Authority, *The WRA*, 115; U.S. Commission on Wartime Relocation and Internment of Civilians, *Personal Justice Denied*, 226.

97. Dower, *War without Mercy*.

98. Edwin O. Reischauer, foreword to *The Korean Minority in Japan, 1904–1950*, by Edward W. Wagner (New York: Institute of Pacific Relations, 1951), i.

99. Dower, *War without Mercy*, esp. 77–93.

100. U.S. Congress, Senate, Committee on Military Affairs, *War Relocation Centers: Hearings Before a Subcommittee of the Committee on Military Affairs*, on S. 444, 117.

101. I borrow this term from Achille Mbembe because I find it evocative of the close and useful relationship between the white majority and its flock, most of which is supposed to be peaceful and obedient. However, he uses it in quite a different sense to refer to a much more overtly brutal relationship between the colonized and colonizer in Africa (Mbembe, *On the Postcolony*, esp. 102–41, 173–211, 235–43).

102. "Talk by Commander Coggins," 26 January 1943, pp. 1b, 6b, in "Training Program."

CHAPTER 3. SUBJECT TO CHOICE, LABYRINTH OF (UN)FREEDOM

1. Michel Foucault, *Security, Territory, Population: Lectures at the Collège de France, 1977–78*, ed. Michel Senellart, trans. Graham Burchell (Basingstoke: Palgrave Macmillan, 2007); for the quotes, 165, 353.

2. Ibid., 153.

3. United States War Relocation Authority, "Semi-Annual Report: January 1 to

June 30, 1943," collected in *War Relocation Authority Quarterly and Semiannual Reports*, vol. 2 (Tokyo: Nihon Tosho Sentā, 1991), 8–9.

4. Dillon Myer, handwritten note on memorandum of Allen W. Gullion, the Provost Marshal General, to the Deputy Chief of Staff, 13 January 1943, 291.2, Jan–April 1943, Army-AG Classified Decimal File, 1943–45, entry 360, box 1512, Record Group (RG) 407.

5. J. A. Ulio, the Adjutant General, "Loyalty Investigations of American Citizens of Japanese Ancestry in War Relocation Centers," 20 January 1943, 291.2, Jan–April 1943, Army-AG Classified Decimal File, 1943–45, entry 360, box 1512, RG 407.

6. Japanese-American Branch (JAB), Office of the Provost Marshal General (OPMG), "History of the Japanese Program," no date (ca. 1 September 1945), p. 11, Personnel Security Division, JAB, General File, 1942–46, entry 480, box 1723, RG 389.

7. Copy of letter of John J. McCloy to Albert B. Chandler, 24 April 1943, entry 480, box 1735, RG 389.

8. OPMG, "World War II: A Brief History," no date (ca. November 1945), p. 1, Records of the Office of the Assistant Chief of Staff, G-2 (Intelligence), Historical Studies and Related Records of G-2 Components, 1918–1959, Box 31–Miscellaneous Files, Records of the Army Staff, RG 319.

9. In *American Inquisition: The Hunt for Japanese American Disloyalty in World War II* (Chapel Hill: University of North Carolina Press, 2007), Eric L. Muller analyzes some of the same issues and provides much new and important detail on certain topics— especially on the Western Defense Command's continuing and virulent distrust of Japanese Americans throughout the war years. However, our approaches and analyses are very different. Most importantly, Muller emphasizes the conflicts between the military and the WRA, with the latter *reluctantly* following the military's desire to investigate the loyalty of all Japanese Americans. In contrast, I regard the military and civilian agencies as complementary and mutually supportive wings of the emerging regime of polite racism.

10. Office of the Assistant Chief of Staff, G-2, and OPMG, "Monograph on History of Military Clearance Program (Screening of Alien Japanese and Japanese American Citizens for Military Service)," p. 14; Military Clearance Br. File (activities, functions branch, reports, etc.), Personnel Security Division, JAB, General File, 1942–46, entry 480, box 1726, RG 389.

11. Memorandum of W. E. Crist for General Strong, 4 January 1943, entry 480, box 1717, RG 389.

12. Ibid.

13. Memorandum of John T. Bissell for General Strong, 8 January 1943, entry 480, box 1717, RG 389.

14. Memorandum of I. H. Edwards to Assistant Secretary of War, 14 January 1943,

ASW 342.18, Formerly Security Classified Correspondence of John J. McCloy, 1941–45, entry 180, box 22, RG 107.

15. Office of the Assistant Chief of Staff, G-2, and OPMG, "Monograph on History of Military Clearance Program," 11.

16. All four versions of question 28 discussed in this passage—the one used for male citizens, the original for female citizens and all aliens, the revised question given to aliens, and the Manzanar version—as well as versions of question 27 can be found in War Relocation Authority, Community Analysis Section, "Army and Leave Clearance Registration at War Relocation Centers," June 1943, Appendix A, p. 52, Nonserial Informational Issuances (1942–46), entry 6, box 1, RG 210.

17. U.S. War Relocation Authority, "Semi-Annual Report: January 1 to June 30, 1943," 10–11.

18. Most books on internment cover only sketchily the content of the two questions, the War Department and WRA alternatives, and the revised versions of WRA's question 28. They often also contain errors. For instance, in his classic work *Concentration Camps, USA: Japanese Americans and World War II* (New York: Holt, Rinehart & Winston, 1972), Roger Daniels surprisingly does not distinguish between the two versions of question 27 (113). Likewise, in her pioneering study *Years of Infamy: The Untold Story of America's Concentration Camps*, updated ed. (Seattle: University of Washington Press, 1996), Michi Weglyn erroneously writes that question 28 was "worded exactly alike for all registrants," whether citizens or Issei (136). U.S. Commission on Wartime Relocation and Internment of Civilians, *Personal Justice Denied* (Seattle: University of Washington Press, 1997), is accurate insofar as it goes but is sketchy about the differences between the two forms and does not give the final revised wording for question 28 on the WRA form (191–95). The very careful book by key researchers in the Japanese American Evacuation and Resettlement Study, Dorothy Swaine Thomas and Richard S. Nishimoto—namely, *The Spoilage* (Berkeley: University of California Press, 1946)—provides a relatively detailed account and is accurate in almost all respects. However, it implies that the WRA substituted its final revised wording for question 28 on all WRA forms (57–61). Instead, as the WRA's own publication that appeared only a few months after the registration process stressed by literally underlining the point, it substituted the new version only for aliens and not for female citizens (U.S. War Relocation Authority, "Semi-Annual Report: January 1 to June 30, 1943," 11). Brian Masaru Hayashi, in *Democratizing the Enemy: The Japanese American Internment* ([Princeton: Princeton University Press, 2004], 143), and Richard Drinnon, in *Keeper of the Concentration Camps: Dillon S. Myer and American Racism* ([Berkeley: University of California Press, 1987], 78), both succinctly and accurately summarize the two versions of each of the questions. However, of the above works only Thomas and Nishimoto mention the anomalous Manzanar rendering (70). This survey may strike the reader as excessively nitpicky. Indeed, I do not mean to contest the point that has often been made about the

mass confusion and anxiety that resulted from the characteristics of the questionnaires. But to give the forms the close critical reading they deserve and to understand the very close critical reading that internees must have given to the questionnaires—for them, even the smallest difference in wording had literally life-altering consequences (including death)—I have felt it necessary to be as precise as possible.

19. United States War Relocation Authority, Community Analysis Section, "Registration at Manzanar," *Project Analysis Series,* no. 3 (3 April 1943): 3.

20. Thomas and Nishimoto, *The Spoilage,* 71.

21. United States War Relocation Authority, *The WRA: A Story of Human Conservation* (Department of the Interior, War Relocation Authority, ca. 1946), 59–60.

22. Eric L. Muller, *Free to Die for Their Country: The Story of the Japanese American Draft Resisters in World War II* (Chicago: University of Chicago Press, 2001), 47–48; letter of J. L. DeWitt to Chief of Staff, United States Army, "Comments on Proposed Program for Army Recruitment of and Determination of Loyalty of Japanese Evacuees," 27 January 1943, entry 180, box 22, RG 107.

23. DeWitt, "Comments on Proposed Program for Army Recruitment," Tab D; for the quotes, pp. 1, 3.

24. Ibid., Tab G; for the quotes, p. 1.

25. WRA solicitor, as quoted in U.S. War Relocation Authority, *The WRA,* 60.

26. DeWitt, "Comments on Proposed Program for Army Recruitment," Tab D, p. 2.

27. Michel Foucault, "The Subject and Power," in *Michel Foucault: Beyond Structuralism and Hermeneutics,* ed. Herbert L. Dreyfus and Paul Rabinow, 2nd ed. (Chicago: University of Chicago Press, 1983), 214.

28. See Michel Foucault, "Politics and Reason," in *Politics, Philosophy, Culture: Interviews and Other Writings, 1977–1984,* trans. Alan Sheridan et al., ed. with introduction by Lawrence D. Kritzman (New York: Routledge, 1988), 83–84.

29. "Relocation Center Address," no date, collected in OPMG, "Field Reports: Loyalty Investigations of American Citizens of Japanese Ancestry in War Relocation Centers," March 1943, entry 480, box 1769, RG 389; for the quotes, pp. 1, 2, 3.

30. Elie Kedourie, *Nationalism,* 3rd ed. (1966; reprint, London: Hutchinson, 1985), 23; Ernst Renan, "What Is a Nation?" in *Nation and Narration,* ed. Homi K. Bhabha (London: Routledge, 1990), 19.

31. Wayne Collins, quoted in Weglyn, *Years of Infamy,* 256.

32. Letter of C. W. Ardery to the Provost Marshal General, "Induction of Alien Japanese," 11 September 1944, entry 480, box 1717, RG 389.

33. For more details on the history of the switch from alien Japanese unacceptability to acceptability for voluntary induction into the army, see Office of the Assistant Chief of Staff, G-2, and OPMG, "Monograph on History of Military Clearance Program," 59–63; for the quotes, 61.

34. "Relocation Center Address"; for the quotes, pp. 4, 6.

35. "General Instructions to Team Captains," collected in OPMG, "Field Reports: Loyalty Investigations of American Citizens of Japanese Ancestry in War Relocation Centers"; for the quotes, pp. 3, 4; for Topaz, see Hayashi, *Democratizing the Enemy*, 146; for Tule Lake, see Thomas and Nishimoto, *The Spoilage*, 75.

36. Captain William S. Fairchild, "Granada Relocation Center," p. 4, in OPMG, "Field Reports: Loyalty Investigations of American Citizens of Japanese Ancestry in War Relocation Centers."

37. Letter of Dillon Myer to All Project Directors (file copy), 18 February 1943, File 13.607, Headquarters Subject-Classified General Files, 1942–46, entry 16, box 92, RG 210.

38. First Lt. Evan W. Carroll, C.M.P., "Tule Lake Relocation Center," pp. 2–3, and petition copy, in OPMG, "Field Reports: Loyalty Investigations of American Citizens of Japanese Ancestry in War Relocation Centers"; letter of Harvey Coverley to Dillon S. Myer, 10 March 1943, entry 16, box 92, RG 210; War Relocation Authority, Community Analysis Section, "Army and Leave Clearance Registration at War Relocation Centers," June 1943, pp. 15–18, entry 6, box 1, RG 210; letter of D. S. Myer to Harvey W. Coverley, 29 March 1943 (file copy), entry 16, box 92, RG 210; Thomas and Nishimoto, *The Spoilage*, 77, 82.

39. Carroll, "Tule Lake Relocation Center," 2.

40. Letter of Harvey M. Coverley to Dillon S. Myer, 6 March 1943, and letter of Dillon Myer to Harvey M. Coverley, 31 March 1943: both in entry 16, box 92, RG 210.

41. Drinnon, *Keeper of the Concentration Camps*, 89–91. Drawing from the Japanese American Evacuation and Resettlement Study archives, Drinnon offers a number of compelling firsthand testimonies from individuals arrested at Tule Lake (83–97). While I much admire his work in uncovering a wealth of materials that testify to the ongoing force of racism throughout the war, he is not attentive to the ways in which racism and its disavowal, or spaces of freedom and unfreedom, worked together to sustain the new kind of racism that I am calling polite racism. He chooses to resolve the contradictions in policies toward Japanese Americans—for example, the gestures of benevolence and the acts of violence, or the avowals of freedom and the existence of slave labor—by criticizing all pretensions of liberal democratic governance as lies. In a related way, there is a problematic ahistorical bent to his interpretations in that he calls our historical attention only to lines of continuity with the "deep roots in our traditional racism" (xxii) going back for centuries and not with the transformation of racism over time. Furthermore, he includes Japanese American camps in the category of "concentration camps" that are "hardly modern inventions" (6). However, my point is that the political modality in the camps is precisely that of modern governmentality and that it is consonant with liberalism. With regard to the last point, while Drinnon points out that the men who ran the "concentration camps were liberals of the genus New Deal" (4),

he never explains the political rationality allowing a fit between liberalism and concentration camps.

42. War Relocation Authority, Community Analysis Section, "Army and Leave Clearance Registration at War Relocation Centers," 18.

43. WRA's Administrative Instruction No. 100, quoted in Thomas and Nishimoto, *The Spoilage*, 85.

44. Ibid., 85–86.

45. Pamphlet quoted in ibid., 87; for more detail on the categories, see 85–87.

46. United States War Relocation Authority, *The Evacuated People: A Quantitative Description* (Washington, D.C.: U.S. Government Printing Office, 1946), 166–67, 169.

47. Thomas and Nishimoto, *The Spoilage*, 106.

48. Ibid., 113–46; for Manzanar's junior college, see Brian Niiya, ed., *Japanese American History: An A-to-Z Reference from 1868 to the Present* (New York: Facts on File, 1993), 61.

49. Drinnon, *Keeper of the Concentration Camps*, 131–59 passim.

50. Thomas and Nishimoto, *The Spoilage*, 140; Drinnon, *Keeper of the Concentration Camps*, 110–11.

51. For the volunteer figures broken down by center, see U.S. War Relocation Authority, "Semi-Annual Report: January 1 to June 30, 1943," 10; for the quotes and other information, First Lt. John H. Bolton, C.M.P., "Colorado River Relocation Center," in OPMG, "Field Reports: Loyalty Investigations of American Citizens of Japanese Ancestry in War Relocation Centers."

52. Captain Norman R. Thompson, "Gila River Relocation Center," in OPMG, "Field Reports: Loyalty Investigations of American Citizens of Japanese Ancestry in War Relocation Centers"; for the quotes, see "Condensed Summary," p. 1, and main report, p. 5.

53. Ibid., and letter of L. H. Bennett to Dillon S. Myer (copy), 17 February 1943; latter enclosed with "Gila River Relocation Center"; for the quotes, see letter, p. 2. The FBI subsequently arrested an additional alien. Captain Norman R. Thompson's "field report" on registration and recruitment says a total of twenty-eight were arrested, half of whom were aliens and the other half Kibei. Since Bennett's letter says that twenty-seven were arrested during the main sweep of the 16th with an additional alien arrested subsequently, this total seems accurate. However, the math does not work for the division between aliens and Kibei. Bennett's letter notes a total of sixteen aliens in the original list of twenty, which would already be more than half the final total of twenty-eight. Perhaps some of the aliens did not make it onto the final arrest list. In any case, the most important point here is that both citizens and aliens in roughly the same numbers were arrested and hauled away as part of the process of camp purification.

54. U.S. Congress, Senate, Committee on Military Affairs, *War Relocation Centers: Hearings before a Subcommittee of the Committee on Military Affairs*, 78th Cong, 1st sess.,

on S. 444, part 2, 11 February 1943, 156–57; as collected in *American Concentration Camps: A Documentary History of the Relocation and Incarceration of Japanese Americans, 1942–1945*, ed. Roger Daniels, vol. 7, *1943* (New York: Garland, 1989), unpaginated.

55. U.S. Congress, Senate, Committee on Military Affairs, *War Relocation Centers: Hearings before a Subcommittee of the Committee on Military Affairs*, on S. 444, 20, 27, and 28 January 1943, 41, as collected in ibid., unpaginated.

56. U.S. Congress, Senate, Committee on Military Affairs, *War Relocation Centers: Hearings before a Subcommittee of the Committee on Military Affairs*, on S. 444, part 2, 11 February 1943, 133–34.

57. U.S. War Relocation Authority, *The Evacuated People*, 25.

58. Tetsuden Kashima, *Judgment without Trial: Japanese American Imprisonment during World War II* (Seattle: University of Washington Press, 2003), 25; for the numbers, 51.

59. Ibid., 52–53, 48, 64.

60. Ibid., 123–25.

61. For more on Moab and Leupp, see ibid., 139–59.

62. U.S. Congress, Senate, Committee on Military Affairs, *War Relocation Centers: Hearings before a Subcommittee of the Committee on Military Affairs*, on S. 444, January 20, 27, and 28, 1943, 83–84.

63. U.S. Congress, Senate, Committee on Military Affairs, *War Relocation Centers: Hearings before a Subcommittee of the Committee on Military Affairs*, on S. 444, part 2, 11 February 1943, 146.

64. U.S. Commission on Wartime Relocation and Internment of Civilians, *Personal Justice Denied*, 225–26; U.S. War Relocation Authority, *The WRA*, 111–16.

65. Franklin D. Roosevelt, "Segregation of Loyal and Disloyal Japanese in Relocation Centers: Message from the President of the United States," 78th Cong., Senate, 1st sess., Document No. 96, 14 September 1943, 2; as collected in Daniels, ed., *American Concentration Camps*, vol. 7, *1943*, unpaginated.

66. Office of the Assistant Chief of Staff, G-2, and OPMG, "Monograph on History of Military Clearance Program," 13–16, 43; "Analysis Chart of Special Questionnaire Relating to Citizens of Japanese Ancestry Who Make Application for Voluntary Induction into the Army of the United States for Service with the Combat Team" (with handwritten evaluator revisions, additions, and commentary); and "Revised Instructions for Use in Processing Citizens of Japanese American Ancestry for Induction into the Army of the United States," entry 480, boxes 1720 and 1723, RG389. The "Analysis Chart" in box 1720 is an early version that includes handwritten revisions or additions to the typed text and some commentary written by a sometimes skeptical evaluator. "Revised Instructions" includes the original "Analysis Chart" with its handwritten revisions and additions typed out. Except in the one case noted in the text, the quotes in this passage are from the full typed-out version, which copies the original version except for a very few insignificant changes in wording.

67. U.S. Commission on Wartime Relocation and Internment of Civilians, *Personal Justice Denied*, 280.

68. "Analysis Chart of Special Questionnaire Relating to Citizens of Japanese Ancestry."

69. Office of the Assistant Chief of Staff, G-2, and OPMG, "Monograph on History of Military Clearance Program," 55–56.

70. JAB, OPMG, "History of the Japanese Program" (see note 6, above), 38.

71. Ibid., 19–26; for the quote, 22–23.

72. Ibid., 36.

73. Ibid., 59–62.

74. Memorandum of Alton C. Miller to the Assistant Secretary of War, 31 March 1945, copy as Appendix E-8, JAB, OPMG, "History of the Japanese Program."

75. "Outline of Japanese American Course," no date (ca. 1 January 1944), Sixth Hour (unpaginated), Seventh Hour, pp. 1–2, and Eighth Hour, pp. 5–6, entry 480, box 1756, RG389. Though no author is given, this is clearly a JAB, OPMG document.

76. JAB, OPMG, "History of the Japanese Program," 55–56.

CHAPTER 4. REASONING, COUNTERREASONINGS, AND COUNTER-CONDUCT

1. U.S. Congress, Senate, Committee on Military Affairs, *War Relocation Centers: Hearings before a Subcommittee of the Committee on Military Affairs*, 78th Cong, 1st sess., on S. 444, 20, 27, and 28 January 1943, 54; as collected in *American Concentration Camps: A Documentary History of the Relocation and Incarceration of Japanese Americans, 1942–1945*, ed. Roger Daniels, vol. 7, *1943* (New York: Garland, 1989), unpaginated.

2. Second Lt. Stanley D. Arnold, "Minidoka Relocation Center," pp. 2–3, as collected in Office of the Provost Marshal General (OPMG), "Field Reports: Loyalty Investigations of American Citizens of Japanese Ancestry in War Relocation Centers," March 1943, entry 480, box 1769, Record Group (RG) 389.

3. Alexander H. Leighton, *The Governing of Men: General Principles and Recommendations Based on Experience at a Japanese Relocation Camp* (Princeton: Princeton University Press, 1946), 195.

4. "Relocation Center Address" (p. 4) and "Questions and Answers," collected in OPMG, "Field Reports: Loyalty Investigations of American Citizens of Japanese Ancestry in War Relocation Centers."

5. Joan W. Scott, "The Evidence of Experience," *Critical Inquiry* 17, no. 4 (Summer 1991): 773–97; Gayatri Chakravorty Spivak, "Can the Subaltern Speak?" in *Marxism and the Interpretation of Culture*, ed. Cary Nelson and Lawrence Grossberg (Urbana: University of Illinois Press, 1988), 271–313.

6. The Poston question lists are archived in #3830, box 11, Japanese-American Relocation Records, Division of Rare and Manuscript Collections, Cornell University Li-

brary (JARRC). The others are included in the respective center reports collected in OPMG, "Field Reports: Loyalty Investigations of American Citizens of Japanese Ancestry in War Relocation Centers."

7. Dorothy Swaine Thomas and Richard S. Nishimoto, *The Spoilage* (Berkeley: University of California Press, 1946), 62–63.

8. United States War Relocation Authority, *The Evacuated People: A Quantitative Description* (Washington, D.C.: U.S. Government Printing Office, 1946), gives two tables of data concerning the army enlistment and WRA leave clearance registration programs. Table 73 (p. 164) is compiled from the original responses of internees in the ten relocation centers that were given during the February–March 1943 campaign, plus all those who reached seventeen years of age and filled out the forms between March and September of the same year. According to this table 2,083 gave qualified "yes" answers to question 28. The figure 1,041 comes from table 74 (p. 165), which reflects changes made by internees subsequent to the initial campaign.

9. War Relocation Authority, Community Analysis Section, "Army and Leave Clearance Registration at War Relocation Centers," June 1943, p. 28, Nonserial Informational Issuances (1942–46), entry 6, box 1, RG 210.

10. As observed by David G. Erskine, Chief of the Countersubversive Unit, Counter Intelligence Group (CIG), in his memorandum to General Strong, 8 March 1943, entry 480, box 1717, RG 389.

11. Captain John A. Holbrook, "Rohwer Relocation Center," p. 5, as collected in OPMG, "Field Reports: Loyalty Investigations of American Citizens of Japanese Ancestry in War Relocation Centers."

12. Memorandum of Eugene Siler to Office of the Assistant Secretary of War, 22 March 1943, as collected in OPMG, "Field Reports: Loyalty Investigations of American Citizens of Japanese Ancestry in War Relocation Centers."

13. United States War Relocation Authority, Community Analysis Section (John F. Embree), "Registration at Central Utah: 14–17, February, 1943," *Project Analysis Series*, no. 1 (Washington, D.C., February 1943); for the quote, 2.

14. U.S. War Relocation Authority, Community Analysis Section, "Army and Leave Clearance Registration at War Relocation Centers," p. 19.

15. Ibid. There have been a number of very good works on the problematic involvement of social scientists and especially anthropologists in administering the relocation centers. For example, Peter T. Suzuki, "A Retrospective Analysis of a Wartime 'National Character' Study," *Dialectical Anthropology* 5, no. 1 (May 1980): 33–46; Peter T. Suzuki, "Anthropologists in the Wartime Camps for Japanese Americans: A Documentary Study," *Dialectical Anthropology* 6, no. 1 (August 1981): 23–60; and Orin Starn, "Engineering Internment: Anthropologists and the War Relocation Authority," *American Ethnologist* 13, no. 4 (November 1986): 700–720.

16. The "Resolution of the Committee of Nine" is available as Appendix I of U.S.

War Relocation Authority, Community Analysis Section, "Registration at Central Utah," 9–11.

17. Ibid., 4.

18. Ibid.

19. Ibid., 4–5.

20. "Statement of Other Residents of Topaz," is available as Appendix II of ibid., 11; for the signatures, see letter of The Other Residents of Topaz to Dillon Myer, 10 March 1943, File 13.607, Headquarters Subject-Classified General Files, 1942–46, entry 16, box 92, RG 210.

21. For the quotes, see Thomas and Nishimoto, *The Spoilage*, 65. For the full texts of Myer's and the War Department's responses: U.S. War Relocation Authority, Community Analysis Section, "Army and Leave Clearance Registration at War Relocation Centers," Appendix D.

22. U.S. War Relocation Authority, Community Analysis Section, "Registration at Central Utah," 7.

23. Thomas and Nishimoto, *The Spoilage*, 65; and U.S. War Relocation Authority, Community Analysis Section, "Registration at Central Utah," 7.

24. U.S. War Relocation Authority, "Semi-Annual Report: January 1 to June 30, 1943," 10.

25. Copies of the "Credo" and Ernst's letter of 12 March 1943 to Myer are enclosed with letter of Charles F. Ernst to Dillon S. Myer, 18 March 1943, RG 210.

26. The Heart Mountain volunteers' "Credo" and statement found their way to Eleanor Roosevelt, and are enclosed with memorandum of Grace G. Tully (Private Secretary to Mrs. Roosevelt) to Dillon S. Myer, 24 May 1943, entry 16, box 93, RG 210.

27. Resident Council for Japanese American Civil Rights, "Volunteers for Victory," entry 480, box 1716, RG 389.

28. For important works that challenged the JACL's historical perspective on internment in the critical period of the 1970s, see Gary Y. Okihiro, "Japanese Resistance in America's Concentration Camps: A Reevaluation," *Amerasia Journal* 2, no. 1 (Fall 1973): 20–34; Gary Y. Okihiro, "Tule Lake under Martial Law," *Journal of Ethnic Studies* 5, no. 3 (Fall 1977): 71–85; and Arthur A. Hansen and David A. Hacker, "The Manzanar Riot: An Ethnic Perspective," *Amerasia Journal* 2, no. 2 (Fall 1974): 112–57. For a nuanced recent treatment of the JACL during the internment period in relation to its Japanese American critics and sympathizers that especially highlights class conflicts within the Japanese American population, see Lon Kurashige, *Japanese American Celebration and Conflict* (Berkeley: University of California Press, 2002), 75–116.

29. Michel Foucault, *Security, Territory, Population: Lectures at the Collège de France, 1977–78*, ed. Michel Senellart, trans. Graham Burchell (Basingstoke: Palgrave Macmillan, 2007), 124–30, 151–53, 164–65.

30. Frank Miyamoto, quoted in Deborah K. Lim, "Research Report Prepared for

the Presidential Select Committee on JACL Resolution #7" (submitted 1990), 18. I thank William Hohri for giving me a copy of "The Lim Report" some years ago. It is now available online (unpaginated) at www.javoice.com, with an introduction written by Hohri.

31. This paragraph draws on Hohri's introduction to ibid.

32. Ibid., 21.

33. Ibid., 38, 13–14.

34. "Testimony Taken before the Dies Committee (7 July 1943)," as reported by I. V. Tiernman on 8 July and printed on 9 July, pp. 1–2, entry 480, box 1719, RG 389.

35. "Testimony Taken before the Dies Committee (3 July 1943)," as reported by I. V. Tiernman on 5 July and printed on 6 July, pp. 1–2, entry 480, box 1719, RG 389.

36. Brian Niiya, ed., *Japanese American History: An A-to-Z Reference from 1868 to the Present* (New York: Facts on File, 1993), 226.

37. Mike Masaoka with Bill Hosokawa, *They Call Me Moses Masaoka* (New York: William Morrow, 1987); hereafter cited parenthetically in the text.

38. Frantz Fanon, *Black Skin, White Masks*, trans. Charles Lam Markmann (New York: Grove Press, 1967), 17.

39. Conversely, Sansei in many communities, including in Berkeley, California, where I grew up, often mimicked the speech of the (black) Other as a tactic of disidentification with whites.

40. John F. Aiso, who headed the MIS Language School during the war, won a Hollywood High School oratorical contest sponsored by the American Legion, but a white classmate was sent to the finals in Washington, D.C., instead. Ironically, the subject of the contest was "The American Constitution" (Roger Daniels, "Japanese America, 1930–1941: An Ethnic Community in the Great Depression," *Journal of the West* 24, no. 4 [October 1985]: 45).

41. Letter from Masaoka to Eisenhower, 6 April 1942, quoted in Frank Chin, "Come All Ye Asian American Writers of the Real and the Fake," in *The Big Aiiieeeee!*, ed. Jeffrey Paul Chan et al. (New York: Meridian, 1991), 59.

42. Frantz Fanon, *Wretched of the Earth*, trans. Constance Farrington (New York: Grove Press, 1968), 250.

43. Michi Weglyn, *Years of Infamy: The Untold Story of America's Concentration Camps*, updated ed. (Seattle: University of Washington Press, 1996), 136.

44. For data on recruitment's failure, OPMG, "World War II: A Brief History," no date (ca. November 1945), 258–59 (quote, 259), Records of the Office of the Assistant Chief of Staff, G-2 (Intelligence), Historical Studies and Related Records of G-2 Components, 1918–1959, Box 31-Miscellaneous Files, Records of the Army Staff, RG 319; for the figure of 1,208 and volunteer numbers by relocation center, U.S. War Relocation Authority, "Semi-Annual Report: January 1 to June 30, 1943," 10.

45. OPMG, "World War II: A Brief History," 260–63.

46. Captain Norman R. Thompson, "Gila River Relocation Center," p. 8, as collected in OPMG, "Field Reports: Loyalty Investigations of American Citizens of Japanese Ancestry in War Relocation Centers." See Lisa Yoneyama, "Liberation under Siege: U.S. Military Occupation and Japanese Women's Enfranchisement," *American Quarterly* 57, no. 3 (September 2005): 885–910.

47. Letter of Kathleen Iseri to Major Kathleen McClure, 26 January 1944, entry 16, box 93, RG 210; Calvert L. Dedrick, Memorandum for the Record, "Tabulation of native-born Japanese females for the W.A.C. Headquarters," 16 July 1943, entry 480, box 1762, RG 389; OPMG, "World War II: A Brief History," 263. For a sympathetic and respectful account of Japanese American women in the military during the Second World War, see Brenda L. Moore, *Serving Our Country: Japanese American Women in the Military during World War II* (New Brunswick, N.J.: Rutgers University Press, 2003).

48. EC (undoubtedly Elizabeth Colson), no title, March 1943, p. 4, #3830, box 11, JARRC.

49. CTS, no title, 9 March 1943, #3830, box 11, JARRC.

50. CTS, "Volunteering," 8 March 1943, #3830, box 11, JARRC.

51. MF, "Selective Service, Informal Conversation—a Volunteer Speaks, Sentiments," 10 March 1943, #3830, box 11, JARRC.

52. CTS, no title, 8 March 1943, #3830, box 11, JARRC.

53. U.S. War Relocation Authority, Community Analysis Section, "Army and Leave Clearance Registration at War Relocation Centers," 7.

54. Memorandum of Sgt. George H. Buxton, Jr., to Office of Assistant Secretary of War, 9 March 1943, enclosed with Captain John A. Holbrook, "Rohwer Relocation Center," p. 5, as collected in OPMG, "Field Reports: Loyalty Investigations of American Citizens of Japanese Ancestry in War Relocation Centers."

55. Office of the Assistant Chief of Staff, G-2, and OPMG, "Monograph on History of Military Clearance Program (Screening of alien Japanese and Japanese American Citizens for Military Service)," p. 19, entry 480, box 1726, RG 389.

56. Internee, quoted in Thomas and Nishimoto, *The Spoilage*, 97.

57. Teresa P. R. Caldeira, " 'I Came to Sabotage Your Reasoning!': Violence and Resignifications of Justice in Brazil," in *Law and Disorder*, ed. Jean Comaroff and John L. Comaroff (Chicago: University of Chicago Press, 2006), esp. 126–31; for the full lyrics to "Capítulo 4, Versiculo 3," see 127–29; for the quotes from Caldeira, 129; for the full lyrics to "Juri Racional," 130–31.

58. Foucault, *Security, Territory, Population,* 201.

59. Thompson, "Gila River Relocation Center," p. 5.

60. Thomas and Nishimoto, *The Spoilage,* 100.

61. For an important attempt to reconsider the question of Japanese American "loyalty," see the articles in Yuji Ichioka, guest ed., *Beyond National Boundaries: The Complexity of Japanese-American History,* special issue of *Amerasia Journal* 23, no. 3 (Win-

ter 1997–98). In particular, John Stephan's "Hijacked by Utopia: American Nikkei in Manchuria" (1–42) discusses the allure of Manchuria for Japanese Americans who faced racism in Hawaii and the Americas; and Yuji Ichioka's "The Meaning of Loyalty: The Case of Kazumaro Buddy Uno" (45–71) presents a case study of a journalist in California, a onetime supporter of the assimilationist JACL, who ultimately responded to U.S. racism by writing propaganda for the Japanese expansionist regime. For a major transnational study of Japanese immigrants caught between the Japanese and U.S. empires, see Eiichiro Azuma, *Between Two Empires: Race, History, and Transnationalism in Japanese America* (Oxford: Oxford University Press, 2005). For the Tule Lake renaissance, see Weglyn, *Years of Infamy*, 229–48.

62. See the biographical notes on Joseph Yoshisuke Kurihara in Thomas and Nishimoto, *The Spoilage*, 363–70. He is well-known as one of the leaders of the famous Manzanar uprising of December 1942 and also as among the first to renounce his U.S. citizenship.

63. Donald E. Collins, *Native American Aliens: Disloyalty and the Renunciation of Citizenship by Japanese Americans during World War II* (Westport, Conn.: Greenwood, 1985), 120–21.

64. Hansen and Hacker, "The Manzanar Riot," 135–36.

65. United States Congress, House of Representatives, Special Committee on Un-American Activities, *Report and Minority Views of the Special Committee on Un-American Activities on Japanese War Relocation Centers*, Report No. 717, 78th Cong, 1st sess., 30 September 1943, 5.

66. Ibid., 6.

67. John Okada, *No-No Boy* (1976; reprint, Seattle: University of Washington Press, 1979); for the quotes, 41, 13, 43.

68. MF (probably Misao Furuta), "Personal Journal—MF, Sentiments—Volunteering for the Army," 5 March 1943, #3830, box 11, JARRC.

69. United States War Relocation Authority, Community Analysis Section, "Army Registration at Granada 1," *Project Analysis Series*, no. 2 (Washington, D.C., 19 March 1943), 6 n. 2.

70. "Extract from letter to D. S. Myer from Col. E. M. Wilson," 28 February 1943, enclosed with memorandum from Joseph D. Hughes to the Assistant Chief of Staff, G-1, 6 March 1943, ASW 342.18, Formerly Security Classified Correspondence of John J. McCloy, 1941–45, entry 180, box 22, RG 107.

71. "Statement from Mothers of Topaz, W.R.A. Center," enclosed with letter of Wakako Adachi et al. to Henry L. Stimson, 11 March 1944, 291.2, 1–1-44 to 7–11–44, Army-AG Decimal File, 1940–45, entry 363, box 1065, RG 407.

72. The quotes are from a form letter that was sent to mothers of deceased soldiers in Amache. See the sample letter attached to letter of D. S. Myer to J. G. Lindley, 31 August 1944, entry 16, box 92, RG 210.

73. Thompson, "Gila River Relocation Center," 5; Thomas and Nishimoto, *The Spoilage*, 80.

74. Frank Emi, "Resistance: The Heart Mountain Fair Play Committee's Fight for Justice," *Amerasia Journal* 17, no. 1 (1991): 49; Tamotsu Shibutani, *The Derelicts of Company K: A Sociological Study of Demoralization* (Berkeley: University of California Press, 1978), vii, 3; Shirley Castelnuovo, *Soldiers of Conscience: Japanese American Military Resisters in World War II* (Westport, Conn.: Praeger, 2008).

75. Eric L. Muller, *Free to Die for Their Country: The Story of the Japanese American Draft Resisters in World War II* (Chicago: University of Chicago Press, 2001).

76. U.S. War Relocation Authority, Community Analysis Section, "The Reaction of Heart Mountain to the Opening of Selective Service to Nisei," *Project Analysis Series*, no. 15 (Washington, D.C., 1 April 1944), 5.

77. U.S. War Relocation Authority, Community Analysis Section, "Army and Leave Clearance Registration at War Relocation Centers," 25.

CHAPTER 5. *GO FOR BROKE*, THE MOVIE: THE TRANSWAR MAKING OF AMERICAN HEROES

1. The outline of the history of Japanese Americans in the army and their accomplishments that follows is drawn from the following widely available sources: Thomas D. Murphy, *Ambassadors in Arms: The Story of Hawaii's 100th Battalion* (Honolulu: University of Hawaii Press, 1954); Joseph D. Harrington, *Yankee Samurai: The Secret Role of Nisei in America's Pacific Victory* (Detroit: Pettigrew Enterprises, 1979); Masayo Duus, *Unlikely Liberators: The Men of the 100th and 442nd*, trans. Peter Duus (Honolulu: University of Hawaii Press, 1987); "522nd Field Artillery Battalion," "442nd Regimental Combat Team," "Military Intelligence Service," "Military Intelligence Service Language School," "100th Infantry Battalion," in *Japanese American History: Japanese American History: An A-to-Z Reference from 1868 to the Present*, ed. Brian Niiya (New York: Facts on File, 1993), 137, 230–32, 276–77; Lyn Crost, *Honor by Fire: Japanese Americans at War in Europe and the Pacific* (Novato, Calif.: Presidio Press, 1994); United States Commission on Wartime Relocation and Internment of Civilians, *Personal Justice Denied* (Seattle: University of Washington Press, 1997), 253–60.

2. This tally is from a count of decorations maintained by the Go for Broke Educational Foundation at www.goforbroke.org (accessed 24 March 2011).

3. Bernard C. Nalty, *Strength for the Fight: A History of Black Americans in the Military* (New York: Free Press, 1986), 107–24, 143–203; United States Office of the Deputy Assistant Secretary of Defense for Equal Opportunity and Safety Policy, *Black Americans in Defense of Our Nation* (Washington, D.C.: [Department of Defense], 1985), 30, 34–38.

4. United States Office of the Assistant Secretary of Defense for Military Manpower

and Personnel Policy, *Hispanics in America's Defense* (Washington, D.C.: [Department of Defense], 1990), 24–33; for the estimate, 27.

5. Alison R. Bernstein, *American Indians and World War II* (Norman: University of Oklahoma Press, 1991), 22, 40, 138.

6. U.S. Office of the Assistant Secretary of Defense for Military Manpower and Personnel Policy, *Hispanics in America's Defense*, 27.

7. Ronald Takaki, *Strangers from a Different Shore: A History of Asian Americans* (Boston: Little, Brown, 1989), 357–63; Theo Gonzalves, " 'We hold a neatly folded hope': Filipino Veterans of World War II on Citizenship and Political Obligation," *Amerasia Journal* 21, no. 3 (Winter 1995–96): 155–74. Satoshi Nakano has neatly summarized the complex nature of U.S. recruitment/recognition of Filipinos as American military personnel in "Nation, Nationalism and Citizenship in the Filipino World War II Veterans Equity Movement, 1945–1999," *Hitotsubashi Journal of Social Studies* 32 (2000): 33–53, esp. 35–36. The marginalized history of these soldiers is symbolized by the very quiet granting of lump-sum payments to Filipino veterans through a minor provision of President Obama's economic stimulus initiative, the American Recovery and Reinvestment Act of 2009. See 10 U.S.C. § 1002.

8. J. A. Ulio, the Adjutant General, "Loyalty Investigations of American Citizens of Japanese Ancestry in War Relocation Centers," 20 January 1943, 291.2, Jan–April 1943, Army-AG Classified Decimal File, 1943–45, entry 360, box 1512, Record Group (RG) 407.

9. John Hall's note and the excerpted section of the OWI Bulletin can be found in "Reattached Memorandum for Files," 2 February 1943, ASW 342.18, Formerly Security Classified Correspondence of John J. McCloy, 1941–45, entry 180, box 22, RG 107.

10. War Department, Bureau of Public Relations, "Loyal Americans of Japanese Ancestry to Compose Special Unit in Army," 28 January 1943, Military Clearance Br. File (activities, functions, branch reports, etc.), Personnel Security Division, Japanese-American Branch (JAB), General File, 1942–46, entry 480, box 1726, RG 389.

11. War Department, Bureau of Public Relations, "Japanese Americans in Army Train to Avenge Pearl Harbor" and "Japanese-Americans in U.S. Battalions are Praised by Battalion Commander," both dated 1 February 1943, Military Clearance Br. File (activities, functions, branch reports, etc.), Personnel Security Division, JAB, General File, 1942–46, entry 480, box 1726, RG 389. The newspaper clipping from the *Memphis Press-Scimitar*, 1 February 1943, is filed together with the releases.

12. Office of Reports, War Relocation Authority, "Press Opinion Favorable to Combat Unit," 15 February 1943, enclosed with letter of John C. Baker, Chief of Office of Reports, to All Project Directors, 15 February 1943, File 13.607, Headquarters Subject-Classified General Files, 1942–46, entry 16, box 92, RG 210.

13. Blake Clark, "U.S. Soldiers with Japanese Faces," *Reader's Digest*, February 1943,

copy in Military Clearance Br. File (activities, functions, branch reports, etc.), Personnel Security Division, JAB, General File, 1942–46, entry 480, box 1726, RG 389. Here and in a number of other instances I take advantage of the War Department's obsessive collection of media reports on Japanese American soldiering and utilize the clippings in their files. However, when I do not indicate an archive location, I have accessed the original.

14. Cecil Hengy Coggins, "The Japanese-Americans in Hawaii," *Harper's Magazine*, June 1943, 75–83; for the quote, 78.

15. S. Burton Heath, "What about Hugh Kiino?" *Harper's Magazine*, October 1943, 450–58; for the longer quotes, 451, 458.

16. Mrs. Franklin D. Roosevelt, "A Challenge to American Sportsmanship," *Collier's*, 16 October 1943. Copies of the Heath and Eleanor Roosevelt articles as well as the Costello subcommittee's September report are included with a memorandum sent by Calvert L. Dedrick, Services of Supply, OPMG to Officers of the JAB, Military Clearance Br. File (activities, functions, branch reports, etc.), Personnel Security Division, JAB, General File, 1942–46, entry 480, box 1743, RG 389.

17. MID, Counter Intelligence Group, Censorship Branch, "Special Report—Morale of 100th Infantry Battalion in Italy," ca. January 1944, copy with ASW 342.18, Formerly Security Classified Correspondence of John J. McCloy, 1941–45, entry 180, box 22, RG 107.

18. Letter of Harrison A. Gerhardt to Abe Fortas, 11 July 1944, copy with ASW 342.18, Formerly Security Classified Correspondence of John J. McCloy, 1941–45, entry 180, box 22, RG 107.

19. War Department, Bureau of Public Relations, Press Branch, "100th Battalion has Fought on Virtually All Fronts in Italy," for release on 10 August 1944, Military Clearance Br. File (activities, functions, branch reports, etc.), Personnel Security Division, JAB, General File, 1942–46, entry 480, box 1726, RG 389.

20. "Japanese-American Troops," Hearst newsreel footage, UCLA Film and TV Archive (ca. 1944).

21. U.S. Department of the Interior, War Relocation Authority, in collaboration with the War Department, *Nisei in Uniform* (Washington, D.C.: U.S. Government Printing Office, 1945), unpaginated. A Department of the Interior press release indicates that the original illustrated pamphlet was issued on 31 October 1944: "Advance Release: For Tuesday Afternoon Papers, October 31, 1944," entry 82, box 251, RG 208.

22. This article from the *New York Daily Mirror* is one among a large number of newspaper clippings collected by the JAB. The news reports referenced in this paragraph can be found in Military Clearance Br. File (activities, functions, branch reports, etc.), Personnel Security Division, JAB, General File, 1942–46, entry 480, boxes 1743 and 1745, RG 389.

23. Frank Capra, dir., *Know Your Enemy—Japan*, U.S. Army Pictorial Service, Signal Corps, 1945.

24. Meyer Berger, "U.S. Nisei Troops Honored in Italy," *New York Times*, 19 August 1945.

25. President Truman, quoted in "Nisei Troops Get Truman Citation," *New York Times*, 16 July 1946. Truman's speech is almost always cited in commemorations of Nisei soldiers.

26. "Japanese-American troops," Hearst newsreel footage, UCLA Film and TV Archive (ca. 16 July 1946).

27. Ronald Reagan, quoted in Mike Masaoka, with Bill Hosokawa, *They Call Me Moses Masaoka* (New York: William Morrow, 1987), 178. On Reagan's experiencing of the movies as the hyperreal, see Michael Paul Rogin, *Ronald Reagan, the Movie and Other Episodes in Political Demonology* (Berkeley: University of California Press, 1987).

28. Office of War Information, Overseas Branch, "Publications Plan for Philippines," 15 September 1944 (Revised), Records of the Office of the Director and Predecessor Agencies, Records of the Historian Area File, 1943–1945, entry 6C, box 1, Records of the Office of War Information, RG 208; for the long quote, p. 1.

29. Office of War Information, Overseas Branch, "Directive on Radio Informational Activities to China," 27 October 1944, Records of the Office of the Director and Predecessor Agencies, Records of the Historian Area File, 1943–1945, entry 6C, box 1, RG 208; for the quotes, pp. 6, 10.

30. Office of War Information, Foreign Language Division, Washington, D.C., "Splendid Record of the U.S. Soldiers of Japanese Ancestry," 13 May 1943, English transcript of Japanese release, entry 535, box 3142, RG 208.

31. Office of War Information, Overseas Bureau, San Francisco, "Outline History of Japan Division," Records of the Historian, Draft Historical Reports, 1941–48, entry 6H, box 2, RG 208.

32. "Japan Radio Plan," 24–30 June 1945, Reports, Directives, Bulletins, and Other Papers Dealing with Psychological Warfare and Propaganda Activities in Overseas Theaters, 1939–45, entry 172, box 336, RG 165; for the quote, p. 1.

33. "Preliminary Plan for Leaflet Campaign Against Japan," Reports, Directives, Bulletins, and Other Papers Dealing with Psychological Warfare and Propaganda Activities in Overseas Theaters, 1939–45 (ca. June 1945), entry 172, box 329, RG 165; for the longer quote, p. 8.

34. Richard Slotkin, "Unit Pride: Ethnic Platoons and the Myths of American Nationality," *American Literary History* 13, no. 3 (Autumn 2001): 469–98; for the quote, 469. On blood plasma, see Nalty, *Strength for the Fight*, 148, 181.

35. Robert Pirosh, dir., *Go for Broke*, produced by Dore Schary, MGM, 1951.

36. See Masaoka, *They Call Me Moses Masaoka*, 216.

37. George H. Roeder, Jr., *The Censored War* (New Haven: Yale University Press, 1993), 46.

38. The first Buddhist chaplain to serve in the U.S. Armed Forces, Jeanette Shin, was

commissioned on 22 July 2004 ("U.S. Armed Forces Commissions First Buddhist Chaplain," *Pacific Citizen*, 6–19 August 2004).

39. Dennis Ogawa, *From Japs to Japanese: An Evolution of Japanese-American Stereotypes* (Berkeley: McCutchan, 1971), 14–16; the quotations are from the film.

40. William Petersen, "Success Story, Japanese-American Style," *New York Times Magazine*, 9 January 1966; William Petersen, "Success Story of One Minority Group in U.S.," *U.S. News and World Report*, 26 December 1966. For critiques of the "model minority" discourse, see, for example, Bob H. Suzuki, "Education and the Socialization of Asian Americans: A Revisionist Analysis of the 'Model Minority' Thesis," in *Asian Americans: Social and Psychological Perspectives*, ed. Russell Endo, Stanley Sue, and Nathaniel N. Wagner (Palo Alto, Calif.: Science and Behavior Books, 1980), 2:155–75; and Keith Osajima, "Asian Americans as the Model Minority: An Analysis of the Popular Press Image in the 1960s and 1980s," in *Reflections on Shattered Windows: Promises and Prospects for Asian American Studies*, ed. Gary Y. Okihiro et al. (Pullman: Washington State University Press, 1988).

41. Petersen, "Success Story, Japanese-American Style," 36.

42. Bruce Cumings is suggestive when he cites McGeorge Bundy, who once said that "the first great center of area studies . . . [was] in the Office of Strategic Services" ("Boundary Displacement: The State, the Foundations, and International and Area Studies during and after the Cold War," in *Parallax Visions: Making Sense of American-East Asian Relations at the End of the Century* [Durham, N.C.: Duke University Press, 1999], 173).

43. Office of War Information, Overseas Branch, "Guidance on Major Themes for Far Eastern Long Range Media Theme VIII—Modernization," 10 January 1945, Records of the Historian Area File, 1943–45, entry 6C, box 3, RG 208 (hereafter cited in the text); all quotes in this paragraph, p. 1. While the experts are not named, we can conjecture that they must have at least included the China scholar John K. Fairbank, who was at that time assistant deputy director of the Far Eastern Division of the State Department in Washington, and perhaps the Japanese American John Maki.

44. For example, the six volumes in the most ambitious publication project of the modernization theorists were published by Princeton University Press between 1965 and 1971, in the series Studies in the Modernization of Japan.

45. Robert N. Bellah, *Tokugawa Religion: The Values of Pre-Industrial Japan* (Glencoe, Ill.: Free Press, 1957).

46. I have written in more detail on modernization theory in "*Minshūshi* as Critique of Orientalist Knowledges," *Positions* 6, no. 2 (Fall 1998): 303–22.

47. Petersen, "Success Story, Japanese-American Style," 40; this work is hereafter cited in the text.

48. Reed Ueda, "The Changing Path to Citizenship: Ethnicity and Naturalization during World War II," in *The War in American Culture: Society and Consciousness Dur-*

ing World War II, ed. Lewis A. Erenberg and Susan E. Hirsch (Chicago: University of Chicago Press, 1996), 205.

49. Gunnar Myrdal, as quoted in Michael Omi and Howard Winant, *Racial Formation in the United States: From the 1960s to the 1990s,* 2nd ed. (New York: Routledge, 1994), 16–17.

CHAPTER 6. NATIONAL MOBILIZATION

1. Frank Capra, dir., *Know Your Enemy—Japan,* U.S. Army Pictorial Service, Signal Corps, 1945.

2. Foreign Intelligence Service, "F.I.S. Basic Propaganda Plan for Japan—I," 15 April 1942, pp. 9, 6; and O. N. Solbert, "Japan Plan," 23 May 1942, pp. 5, 13: both in Records of the Historian, Historian's Records of the Psychological Warfare Branch, 1942–45, Entry 6G, Box 5; Record Group (RG) 208. The FIS became a part of the new Office of War Information in June 1942.

3. Allied Translator and Interpreter Section, South West Pacific Area, "Interrogation Report No. 720," 11 May 1945, Microfiche 89/281, 10-IR-720, Wartime Translations of Seized Japanese Documents, ATIS reports, 1942–1946 (hereafter ATIS reports, 1942–1946), Library of Congress, Washington, D.C.; Kang Duk-sang, *Chōsenjin gakuto shutsujin: mō hitotsu no wadatsumi no koe* (Tokyo: Iwanami Shoten, 1997). The romanizations of Korean names in the ATIS reports are unusual but given as is.

4. U.S. Office of War Information (New Delhi), "Propaganda to Koreans serving in the Japanese Forces," Report no. JRA-366, 3 May 1945, Reports, Directives, Bulletins, and Other Papers Dealing with Psychological Warfare and Propaganda Activities in Overseas Theaters, 1939–45, entry 172, Box 330, RG 165.

5. Headquarters First Australian Army, First Australian Army ATIS Advanced Echelon, "Prisoner of War Joint Preliminary Interrogation Report," 335, Microfiche 89/281, 20-IR-335, ATIS reports, 1942–1946.

6. Headquarters First Australian Army, First Australian Army ATIS Advanced Echelon, "Prisoner of War Joint Preliminary Interrogation Report," 352, Microfiche 89/281, 20-IR-352, ATIS reports, 1942–1946.

7. Allied Translator and Interpreter Section, South West Pacific Area, "Interrogation Report No. 187," 9 November 1943, Microfiche 89/281, 10-IR-187, ATIS reports, 1942–1946.

8. Allied Translator and Interpreter Section, South West Pacific Area, "Interrogation Report No. 739," 3 June 1945, Microfiche 89/281, 10-IR-739, ATIS reports, 1942–1946.

9. I specify "serious historians," because in recent years neo-nationalists in Japan have used these figures to distort the level of enthusiasm shown by Koreans for military service.

10. For Miyata Setsuko, see *Chōsen minshū to "kōminka" seisaku* (Tokyo: Miraisha, 1985), 50–93.

11. Chōsen Sōtokufu, ed., *Shōwa 16 nen Chōsen sōtokufu tōkei nenpō* (Keijō [Seoul]: Chōsen Sōtokufu, 1943), 150–55.

12. United States War Department, *Handbook on Japanese Military Forces* ([1944]; reprint, Baton Rouge: Louisiana State University Press, 1991), 8; Oka Hisao, *Rikugun tokubetsu shiganhei tokuhon*, with a preface by Shiohara Tokisaburō (Keijō [Seoul]: Teikoku Chihō Gyōsei Gakkai Chōsen Honbu, 1939), 72.

13. Kim Sŏng-su, interview by author, 14 September 2000, Pusan, Republic of Korea.

14. In the past few years, negotiation documents that resulted in the Basic Treaty confirm that the South Korean government must bear some responsibility for the failure to compensate individuals such as Kim Sŏng-su: it took money, however limited, from the Japanese government that was targeted for reparations with the understanding that it would compensate victims of Japanese war mobilization. Unfortunately, those funds apparently were not used for this purpose. See, for example, "Compensation for Colonial Victims is Not Just a Legal Problem," *Chosŏn ilbo*, 17 January 2005.

15. Kim Sŏng-su, *Shōi gunjin Kin Seiju no sensō*, ed. Fujita Hiroo (Tokyo: Shakai Hihyōsha, 1995), 220–22 (hereafter cited parenthetically in the text).

16. Chōsen Sōtokufu, "Chōsenjin shiganhei seido jisshi yōkō," Microfilm Re-productions of Selected Archives of the Japanese Army, Navy and Other Government Agencies, 1868–1945 (MRSA), reproduced in Sengo Hoshō Mondai Kenkyūkai, ed., *Sengo hoshō mondai shiryōshū* (Tokyo: Sengo Hoshō Mondai Kenkyūkai, 1991), 3:63–64 (hereafter *SHMS*).

17. See the preface to Oka, *Rikugun tokubetsu;* this work is hereafter cited parenthetically in the text.

18. This form was included as an attachment to War Department Ordinance No. 11, effective 3 April 1938, which stipulated basic procedures for the Army Special Volunteer System. The ordinance and form are included in ibid, 110–15, as well as *SHMS*, 4:16–18.

19. Chōsen Sōtokufu, *Shisei sanjūnenshi* (1940), reprinted as *Zōho Chōsen sōtokufu sanjūnenshi* (Tokyo: Kuresu Shuppan, 1999), 3:806–7.

20. Yoshida Toshiguma, "Chōsenjin, shiganhei/chōhei no kōgai," ca. 1945, box 30, Manshū Chōsen 2, Chōsengun Kankei Shiryō, Military Archival Library, the National Institute for Defense Studies, Japan Ministry of Defense, Tokyo (MAL), 5, 7; Chōsen Sōtokufu, *Shisei sanjūnenshi*, 3:807.

21. Kaida Kaname, *Shiganhei seido no genjō to shōrai e no tenbō*, vol. 3 of *Konnichi no Chōsen mondai kōza* (Keijō [Seoul]: Ryokki Renmei, 1939), 9.

22. Oka, *Rikugun tokubetsu*, 64–66.

23. Kim, *Shōi gunjin Kin Seiju*, 51–52.

24. This schedule as well as several extremely valuable social surveys of trainees,

which I will analyze at more length later in this chapter, are included in a set of surveys compiled by the Government-General's First Training Center for Army Volunteers (Chōsen Sōtokufu Daiichi Rikugunhei Shigansha Kunrensho). The set carries the title "Seito shochōsa hyō" (Tables of Various Surveys of Trainees), ca. 1943, and can be found among the papers of the eminent historian Kajimura Hideki. His library is housed at the Ariran Center for Korean History and Culture (Bunka Sentā Ariran) in Kawaguchi (Saitama Prefecture, Japan).

25. For a copy of a "trainee journal," see Oka, *Rikugun tokubetsu*, 120–27.

26. "Shuyō toshi shusshinsha chōsa" and "Nenrei chōsa," both in Chōsen Sōtokufu Daiichi Rikugunhei Shigansha Kunrensho, "Seito shochōsa hyō."

27. "Nyūsho shūryō chōsa," in Chōsen sōtokufu daiichi rikugunhei shigansha kunrensho, "Seito shochōsa hyō." The figures for those who completed the course out of those admitted from 1938 to 1942 are 404 of 406, 596 of 613, 3,013 of 3,060, 3,110 of 3,208, and 2,318 of 4,077.

28. The larger report is titled "Rikugun tokubetsu shiganhei jōkyō chōsho," October 1939, and is archived in MAL. It is now available online (www.jacar.go.jp) under Chōsengun Sanbōchō, Katō Rinpei, "Rikugun tokubetsu shiganhei jūgun jōkyō ni kansuru ken," November 1939, reference code C04121631700.

29. Kim, *Shōi gunjin Kin Seiju*, 52.

30. "Shisan chōsa," in Chōsen Sōtokufu Daiichi Rikugunhei Shigansha Kunrensho, "Seito shochōsa hyō." The figures for each of the years 1938–42 are 74.9 percent, 76.5 percent , 66.4 percent , 71.7 percent, and 70.6 percent.

31. Kaida, *Shiganhei seido*, 27–28.

32. Yoshida, "Chōsenjin, shiganhei/chōhei," 6.

33. Carter J. Eckert, *Offspring of Empire: The Koch'ang Kims and the Colonial Origins of Korean Capitalism, 1876–1945* (Seattle: University of Washington Press, 1991), 120–21, 298 n. 52.

34. Ibid., esp. 224–52.

35. Oka, *Rikugun tokubetsu*, 33.

36. On the pre-conscription survey, see Yoshida, "Chōsenjin, shiganhei/chōhei," 7–8; Yūichi Higuchi, *Senjika Chōsen no minshū to chōhei* (Tokyo: Sōwasha, 2001), 18–24.

37. Chōsen Sōtokufu, "Shōwa 18 nen Chōsen sōtokufu tokubetsu kaikei yosan kōgai setsumei," December 1942, pp. 51–52, Ōno Rokuichirō Kankei Bunsho (hereafter ORKB) #1183.

38. Mizuta Naomasa, "Shōwa 19 nendo Chōsen sōtokufu yosan ni tsuite," 29 March 1944, as reprinted in *Chōsen kindai shiryō kenkyū shusei*, supervising ed. Kondō Ken'ichi, vol. 4 (Tokyo: Yūhō Kyōkai Chōsen Kenkyūkai, 1961), 23.

39. Chōsen Sōtokufu, "Shōwa 19 nen 12 gatsu dai 86 kai teikoku gikai setsumei shiryō," December 1944, as reproduced in Chōsen Sōtokufu, *Chōsen sōtokufu teikoku gikai setsumei shiryō* (Tokyo: Fuji Shuppan, 1994), 10:55.

40. Mizuta, "Shōwa 19 nendo," 23, 25.

41. The ordinance, Seirei No. 33, is reproduced in full in *SHMS*, 4:32.

42. Chōsen Sōtokufu, "Shōwa 19 nen 12 gatsu dai 86 kai teikoku gikai setsumei shiryō," 54.

43. Ibid., 56; here the training period is given as forty days (p. 56) or one or two months (p. 57), while Yoshida Toshiguma gives one month in "Chōsenjin, shiganhei/chōhei," 19.

44. Yoshida, "Chōsenjin, shiganhei/chōhei," 19.

45. Chōsen Sōtokufu, "Shōwa 19 nen 12 gatsu dai 86 kai teikoku gikai setsumei shiryō," 56.

46. Ibid., 58.

47. Chōsen Sōtokufu, *Shisei sanjūnenshi*, 823–24.

48. Ibid.

49. Chōsen Sōtokufu, "Shōwa 19 nen 12 gatsu dai 86 kai teikoku gikai setsumei shiryō," 58–59.

50. Ibid., 86, 88–89.

51. In other words, this figure did not include most of the 52,859 living outside of Korea (Chōsen Sōfokufu, "Dai 85 kai teikoku gikai setsumei shiryō—zaimu kyokuchō-yō," ca. 1944, reprinted as "Sōtokufu tōchi shūmatsuki no jittai," in *Chōsen kindai shiryō kenkyū shūsei*, supervising ed. Kondō Ken'ichi, vol. 2 (Tokyo: Yūhō Kyōkai Chōsen Kenkyūkai, 1959), 88.

52. Chōsen Sōtokufu, "Shōwa 19 nen 12 gatsu dai 86 kai teikoku gikai setsumei shiryō," 89. Individuals classified as "C" (*hei*, 5.6 percent) qualified only for limited service in the National Army (*kokuminhei*); those classed as D (*tei*, 3.2 percent) and F (*bo*, 0.02 percent) were ineligible for any type of service, although the former were subject to annual reexamination (Yoshida, "Chōsenjin, shiganhei/chōhei," 16, 18, 22). On the classifications, see U.S. War Department, *Handbook on Japanese Military Forces*, 2–3.

53. Chōsen Sōtokufu, "Shōwa 19 nen 12 gatsu dai 86 kai teikoku gikai setsumei shiryō," 119.

54. Shihōshō Keijikyoku, "Shisō geppō," no. 95 (June 1942): 18 (hereafter cited parenthetically in the text).

55. Keihokyoku Hōanka, "Kiō rokkanenkan ni okeru zaijū Chōsenjin chiihō ihan jiken kenkyo shirabe," 31 March 1942, p. 14; "Chōsenjin kankei shorui," no. T1473, R215, MRSA.

56. Chōsen Sōfokufu, "Dai 85 kai teikoku gikai setsumei shiryō—zaimu kyokuchō-yō," 89–90.

57. Kang, *Chōsenjin gakuto shutsujin*, 315–68; on Kim Chun-yŏp, 355–59. Kim's memoir has been translated into Japanese as *Chōsei: Chōsenjin gakutohei no kiroku*, trans. Huang Min-gi and Usuki Keiko (Tokyo: Kōbunsha, 1991).

58. Kang, *Chōsenjin gakuto shutsujin*, 315–26; for the quote, 317.

59. Ibid., 326–29.

60. The likely but impossible to confirm reading of the kanji ideographs that make up this Japanese name.

61. Kang, *Chōsenjin gakuto shutsujin*, 339–55.

62. Yoshida, "Chōsenjin, shiganhei/chōhei," 12.

63. Ibid., 15.

64. Ibid., 19.

65. Chōsen Sōtokufu, "Shōwa 19 nen 12 gatsu dai 86 kai teikoku gikai setsumei shiryō," 119–21.

66. Ibid., 121.

67. Ibid., 120–21.

68. Yoshida Seiji, *Watashi no sensō hanzai: Chōsenjin kyōsei renkō* (Tokyo: San'ichi Shobō, 1983), 1–4, 100–151. Although some scholars on both the left and right have discredited the veracity of Yoshida's account, my point here concerns the prevailing popular image of Korean women under Japanese colonialism—an image that I believe is warranted but not complete. On the controversy over Yoshida's account, see Sarah Soh, *The Comfort Women: Sexual Violence and Postcolonial Memory in Korea and Japan* (Chicago: University of Chicago Press, 2008), 152–55.

69. Tomiyama Ichirō, *Bōryoku no yokan* (Tokyo: Iwanami Shoten, 2002).

70. Chōsen Sōtokufu Daiichi Rikugunhei Shigansha Kunrensho, "Seito shochōsa hyō." The figures for grandfathers are 39 opposed and 19 supporting; for sisters, 13 and 83, respectively.

71. "Wakaki gakuto to shiganhei taidan," *Ryokki* 6.5 (May 1941): 119.

72. Yoshida, "Chōsenjin, shiganhei/chōhei," 21, 12.

73. Shihōshō Keijikyoku, "Shisō geppō" (hereafter cited parenthetically in the text).

74. I have taken some license in translating the Japanese word used in the text, *chakujo*, as "legitimate mothers." *Chakujo* literally means "oldest legitimate daughters," but such an expression does not make sense here and I suspect the author meant to say *chakumo*, "legitimate mothers" (as opposed to concubines). In any case, the author clearly means women in legitimate families.

75. Chōsengun Shireibu, "Daini-kō iinkai uchiawase kettei jikō," 24 April 1942 (revisions 1 May), ORKB #1204–2.

76. Pusan Nippōsha, *Chōsen mesaretari* (Pusan, Korea: Pusan Nippōsha, 1943), 10, 14–15.

77. *Keijō nippō*, 2 February 1938.

78. Yoshida, "Chōsenjin, shiganhei/chōhei," 14.

79. Kang, *Chōsenjin gakuto shutsujin*, 350–51, 353, 368 n. 2; Bruce Cumings, *The Origins of the Korean War*, vol. 1 (Princeton: Princeton University Press, 1981), 38.

80. Interview, 13 April 2003. I have given the couple pseudonyms to protect their privacy. They are not public figures.

CHAPTER 7. NATION, BLOOD, AND SELF-DETERMINATION

1. On "nigger," see Gerald Horne, *Race War! White Supremacy and the Japanese Attack on the British Empire* (New York: New York University Press, 2004), xiv. Dillon Myer frequently admonished others to desist from using the term "Jap."

2. Higuchi Yūichi, *Kyōwakai: senjika Chōsenjin tōsei soshiki no kenkyū* (Tokyo: Shakai Hyōronsha, 1986), 231–39.

3. Shinbun Yōgo Kenkyūkai, *Chōsen dōhō koshō narabini shinbun zasshi kiji toriatsukai zadankai* (1939), unpaginated. Similarly, by June 1935 the colonial government in Taiwan discontinued usage of the harsh word *seiban* (raw savages) to refer to the aborigines, and replaced it with less insulting name *Takasago-zoku*, or the Takasago people (Leo T. S. Ching, *Becoming Japanese: Colonial Taiwan and the Politics of Identity Formation* [Berkeley: University of California Press, 2001], 253).

4. Watanabe Katsumi, *Shōkokumin no tame no heitaisan monogatari* (Keijo [Seoul]: Kokumin Sōryoku Chōsen Renmei, 1944), for the quote, 152; Utsumi Aiko, *Chōsenjin "kōgun" heishi tachi no sensō* (Tokyo: Iwanami Shoten, 1991), 47–48.

5. In quoting from *Maeil sinbo*, I have used the 1989 reprint edition (Seoul: Kyŏngin Munhwasa).

6. *Tokyo asahi*, 15 May 1942.

7. *Tokyo asahi*, evening edition, 10 May 1942.

8. *Osaka asahi*, 2 August 1943.

9. Higuchi Yūichi, *Kōgun heishi ni sareta Chōsenjin: jūgonen sensōka no sōdōin taisei no kenkyū* (Tokyo: Shakai Hyōronsha, 1991), 64.

10. These figures are taken from various tables and narrative descriptions in *Eiga junpō* 87 (11 July 1943): esp. 35, 46, 51, 55. Similarly, according to its June 1942 survey of the metropole and its colonies, the Nihon Eiga Zasshi Kyōkai named 167 movie theaters in Korea (Nihon Eiga Zasshi Kyōkai, ed., *Shōwa jūshichinen eiga nenkan* [1942], reprinted as *Eiga nenkan*, vol. 9 [Tokyo: Nihon Tosho Sentā, 1994], section 10, 109–16).

11. The official was Mori Hiroshi, head of the Book Section in the Government-General's Police Administration Bureau. The quotes are from his article "Chōsen ni okeru eiga ni tsuite," *Eiga junpō* 87 (11 July 1943): 4; Tokizane Shōichi, "Chōsen no eigakan," in ibid., 52.

12. See, for example, a discussion on Korean cinema and its importance that involved representatives of the Korean media, the colonial government, and several members of the Korean film industry, including two important Korean film directors, Hinatsu Eitarō (Hŏ Yŏng) and Ch'oe In-kyu: "Chōsen eiga no zenbō o kataru," *Eiga hyōron* 1, no. 7 (July 1941): 54–60.

13. *Eiga junpō* 87 (11 July 1943): 22–26, 28–29. 32–38. The text of the Korea Motion Picture Ordinance can be found in Nihon Eiga Zasshi Kyōkai, ed., *Eiga nenkan*, vol. 9: section 7, 14–22.

14. Yi Yǒng-il, "Nittei Shokuminchi jidai no Chōsen eiga," trans. Takasaki Sōji, in *Kōza Nihon eiga*, vol. 3, ed. Imamura Shōhei et al. (Tokyo: Iwanami Shoten, 1986), 333.

15. Nihon Eiga Zasshi Kyōkai, ed., *Eiga nenkan*, vol. 9: section 7, 3–5.

16. The title of another feature film produced in this period strongly suggests that it also told a story of Korean military service: *Children of the Kamikaze* (K. *Sinp'ung ŭi adŭldŭl*, J. *Kamikaze no kodomotachi*, 1945).

17. Kim Chong-uk, ed., *Sillok Han'guk yŏnghwa ch'ongsŏ* (Seoul: Kukhak Charyowŏn, 2002), part 2, 607.

18. The quote is the official phrasing in both the Korean Motion Picture Ordinance and its model, the metropole's Motion Picture Law (Nishiki Motosada, "Chōsen eiga no daizai ni tsuite," *Eiga hyōron* 1.7 [July 1941]: 53). Chōsen Kōkoku Eiga (Korean Imperial Nation Motion Pictures) produced the film (*Eiga junpō* 87 [11 July 1943]: 21).

19. *Eiga junpō* 87 (11 July 1943): 34.

20. This information and the film's credits come from Nihon Eiga Zasshi Kyōkai, ed., *Eiga nenkan*, vol. 9: section 7, 4, and *Imai Tadashi*, a special issue of *Firumu sentā* 80 (2 December 1983): 63. The latter also includes a synopsis of the film.

21. Imai Tadashi, "Sensō senryō jidai no kaisō," in *Kōza Nihon eiga*, vol. 4, ed. Imamura Shōhei et al. (Tokyo: Iwanami Shoten, 1986), 204–5.

22. The observation that *Suicide Squad at the Watchtower* was the film that first garnered Imai fame as a director was made by the film historian and critic Satō Tadao. For this point and a general synopsis of Imai's career, see Satō's "Imai Tadashi," in *Nihon eiga no kyoshōtachi*, vol. 2 (Tokyo: Gakuyō Shobō, 1996), 215–32.

23. "Chōsen eigakai o seou hitobito no zadankai," in the special expanded Korean (*Chōsenban*) edition of *Modan Nippon* 11, no. 9 (1 August 1940): 242; and *Eiga junpō* 87 (11 July 1943): 19.

24. Sakuramoto Tomio notes that while the theme of vagrant children growing up to be Japanese imperial subjects would certainly have appealed to the selection committee, it was probably deemed less than an ideal film by the Ministry of Education because its characters spoke in Korean and wore Korean clothes, and because the institution that cared for them was Christian in spirit (Sakuramoto Tomio, *Daitōa sensō to Nihon eiga* [Tokyo: Aoki Shoten, 1993], 70–71). More recently, Lee (Yi) Yŏng-chae has made the sophisticated argument that the film did not pass the censors primarily because it gave too prominent a role to Korean elite males in the colonial enlightenment project ("Teikoku Nihon no Chōsen eiga: shokuminchimatsu no 'Hantō,' kyōryoku no shinjō, seido, ronri," master's thesis, Tokyo University, 2006, 70–96).

25. Imai, "Sensō senryō jidai no kaisō," 203.

26. Conversations with Naoki Sakai and Tomiyama Ichirō have helped me recognize the importance of the term *jiketsu*, and I thank them.

27. Following Hegel, we might say that the confrontation with death makes it possible for them to truly become subjects and that through this confrontation they are en-

abled to interject themselves into the movement of history—which in this case is of course the Japanese national history. See Achille Mbembe, "Necropolitics," *Public Culture* 15, no. 1 (Winter 2003): 11–40, esp. 12–16; and Georges Bataille, "Hegel, Death and Sacrifice," *Yale French Studies*, no. 78 (1990): 9–28.

28. Imai, "Sensō senryō jidai no kaisō," 203.

29. David Bordwell, "Classical Hollywood Cinema: Narrational Principles and Procedures," in *Narrative, Apparatus, Ideology: A Film Theory Reader*, ed. Philip Rosen (New York: Columbia University Press, 1986), 17–34.

30. Richard Slotkin, "The Continuity of Forms: Myth and Genre in Warner Brothers' *The Charge of the Light Brigade*," *Representations*, no. 29 (Winter 1990): 1–23; and Richard Slotkin, *Gunfighter Nation: The Myth of the Frontier in Twentieth-Century America* (1992; reprint, Norman: Oklahoma University Press, 1998), 265–71.

31. This and the quotes from Slotkin that follow are from Slotkin, *Gunfighter Nation*, 266.

32. Dae-Sook Suh, *The Korean Communist Movement, 1918–1948* (Princeton: Princeton University Press, 1967), 287.

33. Although I take his analysis of *Bataan* in some different directions (particularly regarding the role of the colonial soldier and the theme of suicide), much of the following is very much inspired by Richard Slotkin's "Unit Pride: Ethnic Platoons and the Myths of American Nationality," *American Literary History* 13, no. 3 (Autumn 2001): 469–98. See also Clayton R. Koppes and Gregory D. Black, *Hollywood Goes to War: How Politics, Profits and Propaganda Shaped World War II Movies* (Berkeley: University of California Press, 1987), 256–59.

34. Satō, "Imai Tadashi," 216–17; Peter B. High, *Teikoku no ginmaku: Nihon eiga to jūgonen sensō* (Nagoya: Nagoya Daigaku Shuppankai, 1995), 453.

35. In drawing this parallel between the Euro-American bildungsroman and the film *Love and the Vow* (as well as the colonial/national media culture of this era), I have been much inspired by Lisa Lowe's readings of several pieces of Asian American writing as alternatives to the conventional novel of formation (*Immigrant Acts: On Asian American Cultural Politics* [Durham, N.C.: Duke University Press, 1996], esp. chaps. 5, 6), and by Franco Moretti, *The Way of the World: The Bildungsroman in European Culture* (London: Verso, 1987); for the quote, 16.

36. Moretti, *The Way of the World*, 19.

37. For examples of the adoption trope and some thoughts on the implications of Japanese adoption practices and discourses for Japanese imperialism, see Oguma Eiji, *Tan'itsu minzoku shinwa no kigen: "Nihonjin" no jigazō no keifu* (Tokyo: Shinyōsha, 1994), 142–51, 377–94.

38. Frantz Fanon, *Black Skin, White Masks*, trans. Charles Lam Markmann (New York: Grove Press, 1967), 63–82 (this work is hereafter cited parenthetically in the text).

39. Ōshima Masanori, quoted in Oguma, *Tan'itsu minzoku*, 146. For a slightly different translation, see Oguma Eiji, *A Genealogy of 'Japanese' Self-images*, trans. David Askew (Melbourne: Trans Pacific Press, 2002), 119.

40. The analogy of colonial subjects to adopted children appeared frequently in modern colonial discourse and was not peculiar to Japanese colonialism. It was also sometimes mobilized in relation to the service and sacrifice of soldiers from the colonies. For instance, at the beginning of the French occupation of Syria and Lebanon following World War I, the new French high commissioner commented that "France has always found pleasure in this gift, to see marching by her side her adopted children like her own children. Who could believe that these Moroccans and Senegalese, after having spilled their blood for four years on the battlefield, would sacrifice themselves again yesterday, if France were not a true mother to them?" (quoted in Elizabeth Thompson, *Colonial Citizens: Republican Rights, Paternal Privilege, and Gender in French Syria and Lebanon* [New York: Columbia University Press, 2000], 40).

41. Judith S. Modell, *Kinship with Strangers: Adoption and Interpretations of Kinship in American Culture* (Berkeley: University of California Press, 1994), 225.

42. David Schneider, quoted in ibid., 3.

43. While the book's title page has the author's name as Chō Kakuchū, the copyright page gives Noguchi Minoru, Chō's adopted "Japanese" name: *Iwamoto shiganhei* (Keijō: [Seoul]: Kōa Bunka Shuppan Kabushiki Kaisha, 1944). The Korean translation of the short story was serialized in the Korean newspaper *Maeil sinbo* from 7 to 22 September 1943 under the title "Sullye" (Pilgrimage) (Shirakawa Yutaka, *Shokuminchi-ki Chōsen no sakka to Nihon* [Okayama, Japan: Daigaku Kyōiku Shuppan, 1995], 120).

44. Im Jon-hye, *Nihon ni okeru Chōsenjin no bungaku no rekishi* (Tokyo: Hōsei Daigaku Shuppankyoku, 1994), 202.

45. Shirakawa, *Shokuminchi-ki Chōsen*, 121–22.

46. Chō Kakuchū, "Gakidō," *Kaizō* 4 (1932): 1–39.

47. These numbers are based on Shirakawa Yutaka's very detailed research in *Shokuminchi-ki Chōsen*, 112–21. In addition, Chō wrote one novel in Korean during this period. It is not my intent to assess Chō in any comprehensive manner. Suffice it to note that while such literary historians and critics as Im Jon-hye (*Nihon ni okeru*, 202–12) and Im Chong-guk (*Shinnichi bungakuron*, trans. Ōmura Masuo [Tokyo: Kōrai Shorin, 1976], 331–42) have roundly condemned Chō for his collaboration with Japanese colonial domination, Kawamura Minato has offered a more sympathetic reading that, though still critical, attempts to go beyond the binary model of resistance versus submission ("Kin Shiryō (Kim Sa-ryang) to Chō Kakuchū (Chang Hyŏk-chu): shokuminchijin no seishin kōzō," in *Iwanami kōza, kindai Nihon to shokuminchi*, vol. 6, *Teikō to kutsujū*, ed. Ōe Shinobu et al. [Tokyo: Iwanami Shoten, 1993], 205–34).

48. Chō, *Iwamoto shiganhei*, 11–58; this edition is hereafter cited parenthetically in the text.

49. Yi Kwang-su, "Kao ga kawaru," *Chōsen gahō*, 1 September 1943, 26–28; this work is hereafter cited parenthetically in the text.

50. For example, Michael D. Shin, "Interior Landscapes: Yi Kwangsu's 'The Heartless' and the Origins of Modern Literature," in *Colonial Modernity in Korea*, ed. Gi-Wook Shin and Michael Robinson (Cambridge, Mass.: Harvard University Asia Center, 1999), 248–87.

51. David Palumbo-Liu, *Asian/American: Historical Crossings of a Racial Frontier* (Stanford: Stanford University Press, 1999), esp. 85–92.

52. Immigration Commission, quoted in ibid., 85.

53. Albert Palmer, *The Oriental in American Life;* quoted in ibid., 90.

54. United States War Relocation Authority, *The WRA: A Story of Human Conservation* (Department of the Interior, War Relocation Authority, ca. 1946), 3–4.

55. Elie Kedourie, *Nationalism*, 3rd ed. (1966; reprint, London: Hutchinson, 1985); this work is hereafter cited parenthetically in the text.

56. T. Fujitani, *Tennō no pējento: Kindai Nihon no rekishi minzokushi kara*, trans. Lisa Yoneyama (Tokyo: Nihon Hōsō Shuppan Kyōkai, 1994), esp. 139–69; "Kindai Nihon ni okeru kenryoku no tekunorojī: Guntai, 'chihō,' shintai," trans. Umemori Naoyuki, *Shisō*, no. 845 (November 1994): 163–76; *Splendid Monarchy: Power and Pageantry in Modern Japan* (Berkeley: University of California Press, 1996), esp. 24–28, 137–45.

57. Slotkin, "Unit Pride," 485–86.

CHAPTER 8. THE COLONIAL AND NATIONAL POLITICS OF GENDER, SEX, AND FAMILY

1. Ann Laura Stoler, *Carnal Knowledge and Imperial Power: Race and the Intimate in Colonial Rule* (Berkeley: University of California Press, 2002), 19; Anne McClintock, *Imperial Leather: Race, Gender and Sexuality in the Colonial Context* (New York: Routledge, 1995), 7.

2. Elaine Kim and Chungmoo Choi, eds., *Dangerous Women: Gender and Korean Nationalism* (New York: Routledge, 1998). For Fanon the key texts include "Algeria Unveiled," in *A Dying Colonialism*, trans. Haakon Chevalier (New York: Grove Press, 1965), and *Black Skin, White Masks*, trans. Charles Lam Markmann (New York: Grove Press, 1967).

3. Edward Said, *Orientalism* (New York: Vintage Books, 1979).

4. Wan-yao Chou, "The *Kōminka* Movement in Taiwan and Korea: Comparisons and Interpretations," in *The Japanese Wartime Empire, 1931–1945*, ed. Peter Duus, Ramon H. Myers, and Mark R. Peattie (Princeton: Princeton University Press, 1996), 40–68, esp. 55–61.

5. Kim Yŏng-dal, *Sōshi kaimei no kenkyū* (Tokyo: Miraisha, 1997). See also Miyata Setsuko, Kim Yŏng-dal, and Yang T'ae-ho, *Sōshi kaimei* (Tokyo: Akashi Shoten, 1992).

6. The information on "blue-blood" intermarriages is largely borrowed from Suzuki

Yūko, *Jūgun ianfu, Naisen kekkon* (Tokyo: Miraisha, 1992), esp. 73–75, 88–92. Watanabe Midori's *Nikkan kōshitsu hiwa: Ri Masako-hi* (Tokyo: Yomiuri Shinbunsha, 1998) does not pretend to be a scholarly work, but the author has for many years been a television journalist, researcher, and writer specializing on the Japanese Imperial Household and I have drawn what I consider to be some unproblematic facts from the book (esp. 20–46, 139–40). While it is often said that the Yi imperial house became but one of the branch families of the Japanese imperial family (*kōzoku*), this is not entirely true. Upon the Japanese takeover of Korea, *ōzoku* and *kōzoku* were invented as new categories to distinguish the Yi family from the other collateral families. *Ōzoku* has roughly the meaning of "royal family." While *kōzoku* as a term used for former Korean royalty is a homophone of the more common *kōzoku* designating the extended Imperial Family, its ideograph for *kō* differs; the character has a variety of meanings, including "public," "prince," and "lord." The originally Korean *ōzoku* and *kōzoku* were treated in many ways as one of the branch families, but they were in other matters sharply distinguished. Most obviously, they were not directly subject to the Imperial House Law (see Murakami Shigeyoshi, ed., *Kōshitsu jiten* [Tokyo: Tōkyōdō Shuppan, 1980], 22–23).

7. Suzuki, *Jūgun ianfu,* 75–87; for the report, 81–82.

8. Chōsen Sōtokufu, *Shisei sanjūnenshi* (Keijō: Chōsen Sōtokufu, 1940); reprinted as *Zōho Chōsen sōtokufu sanjūnenshi,* vol. 3 (Tokyo: Kuresu Shuppan, 1999), 474.

9. Suzuki, *Jūgun ianfu;* for the quote from Minami, 84.

10. Ibid., *Jūgun ianfu,* 76, 82–83.

11. Chōsen Sōtokufu, ed., "Shōwa 19 nen 12 gatsu dai 86 kai teikoku gikai setsumei shiryō," December 1944; reprinted in Chōsen Sōtokufu, *Chōsen sōtokufu teikoku gikai setsumei shiryō,* vol. 10 (Tokyo: Fuji Shuppan, 1994), 20.

12. Itō Abito et al., *Chōsen o shiru jiten* (Tokyo: Heibonsha, 1986), 217.

13. Chŏn Kwangyong, "Kapitan Ri," in *Land of Exile: Contemporary Korean Fiction,* trans. and ed. Marshall R. Pihl, Bruce Fulton, and Ju-Chan Fulton (Armonk, N.Y.: M. E. Sharpe, 1993), 62.

14. Michael Foucault, "Governmentality," in *The Foucault Effect: Studies in Governmentality,* ed. Graham Burchell, Colin Gordon, and Peter Miller (Chicago: University of Chicago Press, 1991), 99–100.

15. Doris Sommer, *Foundational Fictions: The National Romances of Latin America* (Berkeley: University of California Press, 1991), 24.

16. See, for example, Ashis Nandy, *The Intimate Enemy: Loss and Recovery of Self under Colonialism* (Delhi: Oxford University Press, 1983), esp. 1–63; and several essays in the volume edited by Julia Clancy-Smith and Frances Gouda, *Domesticating the Empire: Race, Gender, and Family Life in French and Dutch Colonialism* (Charlottesville: University Press of Virginia, 1998).

17. Carter J. Eckert, *Offspring of Empire: The Koch'ang Kims and the Colonial Origins of Korean Capitalism, 1876–1945* (Seattle: University of Washington Press, 1991), 246.

18. *Keijō nippō*, 1 December 1938, evening edition.

19. *Keijō nippō*, 28 January 1938.

20. Chō Kakuchū, *Iwamoto shiganhei* (Keijō: [Seoul]: Kōa Bunka Shuppan Kabushiki Kaisha, 1944), 1, 155; Ōmura Masuo and Hotei Toshihiro, eds., *Chōsen bungaku kankei Nihongo bunken mokuroku* (Tokyo: Ryokuin Shobō, 1997), 213. I have used the texts for "Shuppatsu" and "Atarashii shuppatsu" as collected in Chō's *Iwamoto shiganhei*, 209–48, 59–155; page references are hereafter given parenthetically in the text.

21. Susan Jeffords, *The Remasculinization of America: Gender and the Vietnam War* (Bloomington: Indiana University Press, 1989), 54.

22. Ibid., 59.

23. Peter B. High, *The Imperial Screen: Japanese Film Culture in the Fifteen Years' War, 1931–1945* (Madison: University of Wisconsin Press, 2003), for the quote, 391; on military mothers, 399–405.

24. Jeffords, *The Remasculinization of America*, 64.

25. Rebecca Jo Plant, "The Repeal of Mother Love: Momism and the Reconstruction of Motherhood in Philip Wylie's America" (Ph.D. diss., Johns Hopkins University, 2001), esp. 72–75, 193–214; George Lipsitz, *Rainbow at Midnight: Labor and Culture in the 1940s* (Urbana: University of Illinois Press, 1994), 286.

26. The above information on Toyoda is largely drawn from Satō Tadao's *Nihon eiga no kyoshōtachi* (Tokyo: Gakuyō Shobō, 1996), 2:101–24.

27. Sakuramoto Tomio, *Daitōa sensō to Nihon eiga* (Tokyo: Aoki Shoten, 1993), 70.

28. Iwamoto Kenji and Makino Mamoru, general eds., *Eiga nenkan*, Shōwa-hen I, bekkan (Tokyo: Nihon Tosho Sentā, 1994), 12. I viewed the copy of this film that is preserved in the Motion Picture, Broadcasting, and Recorded Sound Division, Library of Congress, Washington, D.C. Unfortunately, the copy is not in good condition and the reels appear to be in incorrect order. However, I have also been able to consult Yata Naoyuki's script for the film that was published in *Chōsen*, no. 337 (June 1943): 65–84. Having reviewed both the film and the script, I am confident in my understanding of most of the details and the story line of the film. All quotes are from the film itself. Another copy of the film is archived at the Korean Film Archive.

29. Franco Moretti writes: "Trial, in the *Bildungsroman*, is instead an opportunity: not an obstacle to be overcome while remaining 'intact,' but something that must be *incorporated*, for only by stringing together 'experiences' does one build a personality" (*The Way of the World: The Bildungsroman in European Culture* [London: Verso, 1987], 48; emphasis in original).

30. In general, colonial policy in this period not only encouraged women to labor within and outside the home, it also promoted the rationalization of domestic work so that women could devote more time to activities in service to the nation and emperor. The women's section of the Green Flag League (Ryokki Renmei), for example, encour-aged women to run their domestic affairs more efficiently and then to become more

involved in public campaigns such as those to recycle and to liquidate unwanted goods; see Kawa Kaoru, "Sōryokusenka no Chōsen josei," *Rekishi hyōron*, no. 612 (April 2001): 7–9.

31. Haruko Taya Cook and Theodore F. Cook, *Japan at War: An Oral History* (New York: New Press, 1992), 241–42.

32. *Eiga junpō* 87 (11 July 1943): 31.

33. In a personal communication, Baek Moon Im of Yonsei University has offered an alternative reading of Kinshuku's expression. She sees more despair and surprise than erotic attraction. Furthermore, Baek finds more resistance in Pak's film. Her comments serve as a good reminder that viewers during the colonial period and in the present might not necessarily see the film in the way that I am describing it. Nevertheless, I offer what I believe would have been the filmmaker's preferred reading.

34. *Eiga junpō* 87 (11 July 1943): 31.

35. I thank Su Yun Kim for first alerting me to this story. Her dissertation focuses on the theme of intermarriage in Korean literature ("Romancing Race and Gender: Intermarriage and the Making of a 'Modern Subjectivity' in Colonial Korea, 1910–1945" [Ph.D. diss., University of California, San Diego, 2009]).

36. Utsumi Aiko and Murai Yoshinori, *Shineasuto Kyo-ei no "Shōwa": Shokuminchika de eiga ʒukuri ni honsō shita ichi Chōsenjin* (Tokyo: Gaifūsha, 1985).

37. Unfortunately, like Utsumi and Murai, I have been unable to locate and view the actual film. The text that I will use is Hinatsu's film script: Hinatsu Eitarō and Iijima Tadashi, "Shinario kimi to boku," *Eiga hyōron* 1, no. 7 (July 1941): 132–45; it is hereafter cited parenthetically in the text. On the making of *You and I*, see Utsumi and Murai, *Shineasuto Kyo-ei no "Shōwa,"* esp. 57–121. Technically, Hinatsu was not the sole author of the script used here. Iijima Tadashi, the pioneering film scholar, is listed as coauthor, and an army press officer is known to have rewritten some parts of the text. But according to Utsumi and Murai, Iijima did not make a substantial contribution and Hinatsu was the primary author. It should also be noted that the film version differed from the script analyzed here.

38. Kim Il-myŏn, *Tennō to Chōsenjin to sōtokufu* (Tokyo: Tabata Shoten, 1984), 178–84.

39. See, for example, the advertisement for a tour of the training center in *Maeil sinbo*, 28 February 1943, aimed at women.

40. I have used Yi Kwang-su, "Kokoro aifurete koso," reprinted in *Kindai Chōsen bungaku Nihongo sakuhinshū*, sōsakuhen 1, ed. Ōmura Masao and Hotei Toshihiro (Tokyo: Ryokuin Shobō, 2001), 313–405; this edition is hereafter cited parenthetically in the text.

41. Fanon, "Algeria Unveiled," 35–67; for the quotes, 39, 45.

42. Ibid., 37–38.

43. The extent and significance of Fanon's misogynist tendencies is the subject of some debate. See, for example, McClintock, *Imperial Leather*, 360–68; and in *Frantʒ*

Fanon: Critical Perspectives, ed. Anthony C. Alessandrini (London: Routledge, 1999), see Rey Chow, "The Politics of Admittance: Female Sexual Agency, Miscegenation, and the Formation of Community in Frantz Fanon," 34–56; T. Denean Sharpley-Whiting, "Fanon and Capécia," 57–74; and a brief commentary on this issue in the editor's introduction, 9–10.

44. Ueda Tatsuo, *Chōsen no mondai to sono kaiketsu* (Keijō [Seoul]: Shōgaku Kenkyūjo, 1942), 70.

45. On the history of Korean residents' rights to vote and hold office in Japan, see Matsuda Toshihiko, *Senzenki no zainichi Chōsenjin to sanseiken* (Tokyo: Akashi Shoten, 1995).

46. As a result of the willful destruction of official records and the suppression of the "comfort women" issue for so many decades, quantitative data regarding the total number and ethnic composition of the women mobilized as "comfort women" remain extremely limited. Reasonable estimates of the total number range from 80,000 to 200,000. See Yoshimi Yoshiaki, *Comfort Women: Sexual Slavery in the Japanese Military During World War II*, trans. Suzanne O'Brien (New York: Columbia University Press, 2000), 91–96; Yuki Tanaka, *Japan's Comfort Women: Sexual Slavery and Prostitution during World War II and the US Occupation* (London: Routledge, 2002), esp. 31–60; and Sarah Soh, *Comfort Women: Sexual Violence and Postcolonial Memory in Korea and Japan* (Chicago: University of Chicago Press, 2008).

47. Stoler, *Carnal Knowledge*, 64; Vicente L. Rafael, *White Love and Other Events in Filipino History* (Durham, N.C.: Duke University Press, 2000), 52–75. See also Ann Laura Stoler, *Race and the Education of Desire: Foucault's History of Sexuality and the Colonial Order of Things* (Durham, N.C.: Duke University Press, 1995), esp. 42–54. For a discussion of this issue in interwar West Africa, see Alice L. Conklin, "Redefining 'Frenchness': Citizenship, Race Regeneration, and Imperial Motherhood in France and West Africa, 1914–40," in Clancy-Smith and Gouda, eds., *Domesticating the Empire*, 65–83.

48. Chō Kakuchū, "Nihon no josei," *Bungaku annai* 4 (1937): 86–88.

49. Chungmoo Choi, "Nationalism and Construction of Gender in Korea," in E. Kim and Choi, eds., *Dangerous Women*, 9–31; for the quote, 14.

50. Seungsook Moon, "Begetting the Nation: The Androcentric Discourse of National History and Tradition in South Korea," in E. Kim and Choi, eds., *Dangerous Women*, 43. The last point concerning Korean masculinist and patriarchal collaboration or shame is discussed to varying extents by several contributors to *Dangerous Women* and to Chungmoo Choi, ed., *The Comfort Women: Colonialism, War and Sex*, a special issue of *Positions* 5, no. 1 (Spring 1997). Sarah Soh's *Comfort Women* is a recent and thought-provoking study of militarized sexual slavery that interrogates Japanese colonialism while also tackling the question of Korean patriarchal nationalism head-on.

51. Carter J. Eckert, "Total War, Industrialization, and Social Change in Late Colonial Korea," in Duus, Myers, and Peattie, eds., *The Japanese Wartime Empire*, ed. 3–39; Moon, "Begetting the Nation," 34.

EPILOGUE

1. Nakano Shigeharu, "Yonin no shiganhei," *Minshu Chōsen*, no. 9 (March/April 1947), as reprinted in *Fukkoku minshu Chōsen*, vol. 2 (Tokyo: Akashi Shoten, 1993), 67–70; the latter edition is hereafter cited parenthetically in the text.

2. Chungmoo Choi, "The Discourse of Decolonization and Popular Memory: South Korea," *Positions* 1, no. 1 (Spring 1993): 77–102. Choi quotes Gramsci's famous line, "The crisis consists precisely in the fact that the old is dying and the new cannot be born; in this interregnum a great variety of morbid symptoms appear" (p. 77).

3. Bruce Cumings, "The Legacy of Japanese Colonialism in Korea," in *The Japanese Colonial Empire, 1895–1945*, ed. Ramon H. Myers and Mark Peattie (Princeton: Princeton University Press, 1984), 479; Bruce Cumings, *The Origins of the Korean War*, vol. 1 (Princeton: Princeton University Press, 1981), 38.

4. Chŏn Sang-yŏp, interview with author, 4 March 1999, Seoul. At the time of the interview Chŏn gave me a copy of the official certified judgment rendered in his case, which corroborates his personal background and sentence, and offers details on the mutiny and his role in it (Chōsengun kanku rinji gunpō kaigi, Heijō shikanku hōtei, "Hanketsubun").

5. Tessa Morris-Suzuki, *Exodus to North Korea: Shadows from Japan's Cold War* (Lanham, Md.: Rowman & Littlefield, 2007).

6. See the entries for Inoue, Matsunaga, and Hayakawa in Brian Niiya, ed., *Japanese American History: An A-to-Z Reference from 1868 to the Present* (New York: Facts on File, 1993), 158–59, 174–75, 228–29. For Hayakawa's offer of assistance, see letter to Dillon Myer, 25 February 1943, Headquarters Subject-Classified Files, Entry 16, box 92, Record Group 210.

7. Phil Karlson, dir., *Hell to Eternity* (Atlantic Pictures, 1960).

8. Joshua Logan, dir., *Sayonara* (Warner Bros., 1957). See also Carolyn Chung Simpson for some perceptive and related insights into the popular media's Americanization of Japanese in America, especially through representations of "war brides," in *An Absent Presence: Japanese Americans in Postwar American Culture, 1945–60* (Durham, N.C.: Duke University Press, 2001), 149–85.

9. For more on the processes by which Cold War power and interests shaped an understanding of the Second World War largely through a forgetting of issues that clashed with the representation of the United States as a force of liberation, see Lisa Yoneyama's forthcoming study, *Cold War Ruins* (tentative title). Guy Gabaldon is the subject of a fine documentary by Steven Jay Rubin, *East L.A. Marine* (Fast Carrier Pictures, 2006). Gabaldon's autobiography is *Saipan: Suicide Island* (n.p.: Guy Gabaldon, 1990).

10. Oguma Eiji, *A Genealogy of 'Japanese' Self-images*, trans. David Askew (Melbourne: Trans Pacific Press, 2002).

11. Tuskegee Syphilis Study Legacy Committee, "Report of the Tuskegee Syphilis Study Legacy Committee [1] Final Report—May 20, 1996," www.med.virginia.edu/hs-library/historical/apology/report.html (accessed 20 April 2004).

12. Maruyama Masao once used the metaphor of the *ostinato basso* to make a very different point about constancy in Japanese history; see "The Structure of *Matsurigoto: The Basso Ostinato of Japanese Political Life*," in *Sources of Japanese Tradition*, vol. 2, *1600 to 2000*, comp. Wm. Theodore De Bary, Carol Gluck, and Arthur E. Tiedemann, 2nd ed. (New York: Columbia University Press, 2006), 544–48.

SELECTED BIBLIOGRAPHY

ARCHIVES AND MANUSCRIPT COLLECTIONS (WITH ABBREVIATIONS)

Unpublished documents from these collections and archives are generally not listed in this bibliography.

ATIS   Allied Translation and Interrogation Section, Wartime Translations of Seized Japanese Documents: ATIS reports, 1942–1946, Library of Congress, Washington, D.C.

BSA   Bunka Sentā Ariran. Kawaguchi, Saitama Prefecture, Japan.

JARRC   Japanese-American Relocation Records, Division of Rare and Manuscript Collections, Cornell University Library

LC   Library of Congress, Washington, D.C.

MAL   Military Archival Library, The National Institute for Defense Studies, Japan Ministry of Defense, Tokyo.

MRSA   Microfilm Reproductions of Selected Archives of the Japanese Army, Navy and Other Government Agencies, 1868–1945, Library of Congress, Washington, D.C.

NAB	National Archives Building, Washington, D.C.
NACP	National Archives at College Park, College Park, Md.
NDLT	National Diet Library, Tokyo
ORKB	Ōno Rokuichirō Kankei Bunsho, Kensei Shiryōshitsu, National Diet Library, Tokyo.

RECORD GROUPS AT NAB

RG 210 Records of the War Relocation Authority

RECORD GROUPS AT NACP

RG 107 Records of the Office of the Secretary of War

RG 165 War Department General Staff

RG 208 Records of the Office of War Information

RG 319 Records of the Army Staff

RG 389 Records of the Office of the Provost Marshal General, 1941–

RG 407 Records of the Adjutant General's Office, 1917–

NEWSPAPERS IN JAPANESE AND KOREAN

Keijō nippō (Keijō [Seoul], 1938).

Maeil sinbo. Reprint. Seoul: Kyŏngin Munhwasa, 1989.

Mainichi shinbun (Tokyo, 1943).

Osaka asahi (Osaka, 1943).

Tokyo asahi (Tokyo, 1942.)

NEWSPAPERS IN ENGLISH

Los Angeles Times (Los Angeles, 2000).

New York Times (New York, 1946, 1991).

Pacific Citizen (Monterey Park, Calif., 2004).

SOURCES IN JAPANESE AND KOREAN

Chō Kakuchū [Chang Hyŏk-chu, Noguchi Minoru]. "Gakidō." *Kaizō* 4 (1932): 1–39.

———. *Iwamoto shiganhei.* Keijō [Seoul]: Kōa Bunka Shuppan Kabushiki Kaisha, 1944.

———. "Nihon no josei." *Bungaku annai* 4 (1937): 86–88.

Ch'oe Yu-ri. *Ilche malgi singminji chibae chŏngch'aek yŏn'gu.* Seoul: Kukhak Charyŏwŏn, 1997.

"Chōsen eigakai o seou hitobito no zadankai." Expanded Korean (*Chōsenban*) edition. *Modan Nippon* 11, no. 9 (1 August 1940): 240–45.

Chōsen Sōtokufu. *Chōsen sōtokufu teikoku gikai setsumei shiryō*. Vols. 3, 10. Tokyo: Fuji Shuppan, 1994.

———. "Dai 85 kai teikoku gikai setsumei shiryō." 1944. Reprinted as "Dai 85 kai teikoku gikai setsumei shiryō fukkoku—sōtoku tōchi makki no jittai (4)." In *Chōsen kindai shiryō kenkyū shūsei*, supervising ed. Kondō Ken'ichi. Vol. 4. Tokyo: Yūhō Kyōkai Chōsen Kenkyūkai, 1961.

———. "Dai 85 kai teikoku gikai setsumei shiryō—zaimu kyokuchō-yō." 1944. Reprinted as "Sōtokufu tōchi shūmatsuki no jittai." In *Chōsen kindai shiryō kenkyū shūsei*, supervising ed. Kondō Ken'ichi. Vol. 2. Tokyo: Yūhō Kyōkai Chōsen Ken - kyūkai, 1959.

———. *Shisei sanjūnenshi*. 1940. Reprinted as *Zōho Chōsen sōtokufu sanjūnenshi*. Vol. 3. Tokyo: Kuresu Shuppan, 1999.

———. "Shōwa 13 nen 12 gatsu dai 74 kai teikoku gikai setsumei shiryō." December 1938. Reprinted in Chōsen Sōtokufu, *Chōsen sōtokufu teikoku gikai setsumei shiryō*, vol. 3.

———, ed. *Shōwa 16 nen Chōsen sōtokufu tōkei nenpō*. Keijō [Seoul]: Chōsen Sōtokufu, 1943.

———. "Shōwa 19 nen 12 gatsu dai 86 kai teikoku gikai setsumei shiryō." December 1944. Reprinted in Chōsen Sōtokufu, *Chōsen sōtokufu teikoku gikai setsumei shiryō*, vol. 10.

Eiga junpō 87 (11 July 1943) [special issue on Korean film].

Fujitani, T. "Kindai Nihon ni okeru kenryoku no tekunorojī: guntai, chihō, shintai." Trans. Umemori Naoyuki. *Shisō*, no. 845 (November 1994): 163–76.

———. *Tennō no pējento: Kindai Nihon no rekishi minzokushi kara*. Trans. Lisa Yoneyama. Tokyo: Nihon Hōsō Shuppan Kyōkai, 1994.

High, Peter B. *Teikoku no ginmaku: Nihon eiga to jūgonen sensō*. Nagoya: Nagoya Daigaku Shuppankai, 1995.

Higuchi Yūichi. *Kōgun heishi ni sareta Chōsenjin: jūgonen sensōka no sōdōin taisei no kenkyū*. Tokyo: Shakai Hyōronsha, 1991.

———. *Kyōwakai: senjika Chōsenjin tōsei soshiki no kenkyū*. Tokyo: Shakai Hyōronsha, 1986.

———. *Senjika Chōsen no minshū to chōhei*. Tokyo: Sōwasha, 2001.

Hinatsu Eitarō and Iijima Tadashi. "Shinario kimi to boku." *Eiga hyōron* 1, no. 7 (July 1941): 132–45.

Hinatsu Eitarō et al. "Chōsen eiga no zenbō o kataru." *Eiga hyōron* 1, no. 7 (July 1941): 54–60.

Hong Kŭm-cha. "Nittei jidai no shakai fukushi seisaku oyobi shakai fukushi sābisu." In *Shokuminchi shakai jigyō kankei shiryōshū: Chōsen hen*, ed. Kin-gendai Shiryō Kankōkai. Supplement: *Kaisetsu*. Tokyo: Kin-gendai Shiryō Kankōkai, 1999.

Im Chong-guk. *Shinnichi bungakuron*. Trans. Ōmura Masuo. Tokyo: Kōrai Shorin, 1976.

Im Jon-hye. *Nihon ni okeru Chōsenjin no bungaku no rekishi*. Tokyo: Hōsei Daigaku Shuppankyoku, 1994.

Imai Tadashi. Special issue of *Firumu sentā* 80 (2 December 1983).

Imai Tadashi. "Sensō senryō jidai no kaisō." In *Kōza Nihon eiga*, vol. 4, ed. Imamura Shōhei et al. Tokyo: Iwanami Shoten, 1986.

Itagaki Ryūta. *Chōsen kindai no rekishi minzokushi: Keihoku sanju no shokuminchi keiken*. Tokyo: Akashi Shoten, 2008.

———. "'Shokuminchi kindai' o megutte." *Rekishi hyōron*, no. 654 (October 2004): 35–45.

Ito Abito et al., eds. *Chōsen o shiru jiten*. Tokyo: Heibonsha, 1986.

Iwamoto Kenji and Makino Mamoru, general eds. *Eiga nenkan*. Shōwa-hen I, bekkan. Tokyo: Nihon Tosho Sentā, 1994.

Kaida Kaname. *Shiganhei seido no genjō to shōrai e no tenbō*. Vol. 3 of *Konnichi no Chōsen mondai kōza*. Keijō [Seoul]: Ryokki Renmei, 1939.

Kang Duk-sang [Tŏk-sang]. *Chōsenjin gakuto shutsujin: mō hitotsu no wadatsumi no koe*. Tokyo: Iwanami Shoten, 1997.

———. "Mō hitotsu no kyōsei renkō." *Ningen bunka*, preparatory volume (March 1996): 25–38.

Katō Tetsurō. *Shōchō tennōsei no kigen: Amerika no shinrisen "Nihon keikaku."* Tokyo: Heibonsha, 2005.

Katō Yōko. *Chōheisei to kindai Nihon*. Tokyo: Yoshikawa Kōbunkan, 1996.

Kawa Kaoru. "Sōryokusenka no Chōsen josei." *Rekishi hyōron*, no. 612 (April 2001): 2–17.

Kawamura Minato. "Kin Shiryō (Kim Sa-ryang) to Chō Kakuchū (Chang Hyŏk-chu): shokuminchijin no seishin kōzō." In *Iwanami kōza, kindai Nihon to shokuminchi*. Vol. 6, *Teikō to kutsujū*, ed. Ōe Shinobu et al. Tokyo: Iwanami Shoten, 1993.

Kim Chong-uk, ed. *Sillok Han'guk yŏnghwa ch'ongsŏ*. Seoul: Kukhak Charyowŏn, 2002.

Kim Il-myŏn. *Tennō to Chōsenjin to sōtokufu*. Tokyo: Tabata Shoten, 1984.

Kim Jun-yop [Chun-yŏp]. *Chōsei: Chōsenjin gakutohei no kiroku*. Trans. Huang Min-gi and Usuki Keiko. Tokyo: Kōbunsha, 1991.

Kim Sŏng-su. *Shōi gunjin Kin Seiju no sensō*. Ed. Fujita Hiroo. Tokyo: Shakai Hihyōsha, 1995.

Kim Yŏng-dal. *Sōshi kaimei no kenkyū*. Tokyo: Miraisha, 1997.

Kita Ikki. "Nihon kaizō hōan taikō." In *Kita Ikki chosakushū*. Vol. 2. Tokyo: Misuzu Shobō, 1959.

Koiso Kuniaki. "Shisei enzetsu." *Dai 85 kai teikoku gikai kizokuin giji sokkiroku dai ichi gō*. Published as *Kanpō gōgai*. 7 September 1944.

Komagome Takeshi. *Shokuminchi teikoku Nihon no bunka tōgō*. Tokyo: Iwanami Shoten, 1996.

Kondō Masami. *Sōryokusen to Taiwan: Nihon shokuminchi hōkai no kenkyū*. Tokyo: Tōsui Shobō, 1996.

Kōseishō Kenkyūbu Jinkō Minzokubu. *Yamato minzoku o chūkaku to suru sekai seisaku no kentō*. 1943. Reprinted as *Minzoku jinkō seisaku kenkyū shiryō*. Vols. 3–8. Tokyo: Bunsei Shoin, 1982–83.

Lee (Yi) Yŏng-chae. "Teikoku Nihon no Chōsen eiga: shokuminchimatsu no 'Hantō' kyōryoku no shinjō, seido, ronri." Master's thesis, Tokyo University, 2006.

Matsuda Toshihiko. *Senzenki no zainichi Chōsenjin to sanseiken*. Tokyo: Akashi Shoten, 1995.

Matsumoto Takenori. "(Kenkyū dōkō) 'Shokuminchiteki kindai' o meguru kinnen no Chōsenshi kenkyū." In Miyajima Hiroshi et al., eds., *Shokuminchi kindai no shiza*.

Miyajima Hiroshi et al., eds. *Shokuminchi kindai no shiza: Chōsen to Nihon*. Tokyo: Iwanami Shoten, 2004.

Miyata Setsuko. *Chōsen minshū to "kōminka" seisaku*. Tokyo: Miraisha, 1985.

————, supervising ed. *Jūgonen sensōka no Chōsen tōchi, Mikōkai shiryō Chōsen sōtokufu kankeisha rokuon kiroku (1)*. A special issue of *Tōyō bunka kenkyū* 2 (March 2000).

Miyata Setsuko, Kim Yŏng-dal, and Yang T'ae-ho. *Sōshi kaimei*. Tokyo: Akashi Shoten, 1992.

Mizuno Naoki. "Kaisetsu." In Mizuno, ed., *Senjiki shokuminchi tōchi shiryō*, vol. 1.

————. "Senjiki no shokuminchi shihai to 'naigaichi gyōsei ichigenka.'" *Jinbun gakuhō*, no. 79 (1997): 77–102.

————, ed. *Senjiki shokuminchi tōchi shiryō*. Vols. 1, 7. Tokyo: Kashiwa Shobō, 1998.

Mizuta Naomasa. "Shōwa 19 nendo Chōsen sōtokufu yosan ni tsuite." 29 March 1944. Reprinted in *Chōsen kindai shiryō kenkyū shusei*, supervising ed. Kondō Ken'ichi, vol. 4. Tokyo: Yūhō Kyōkai Chōsen Kenkyūkai, 1961.

Monbushō Kyōgaku-kyoku, ed. *Shinmin no michi*. 1941. Reprinted in *Kokutai no hongi/ Shinmin no michi*, ed. Kaizuka Shigeki. Tokyo: Nihon Tosho Sentā, 2003.

Mori Hiroshi. "Chōsen ni okeru eiga ni tsuite." *Eiga junpō* 87 (11 July 1943): 4–5.

Murakami Shigeyoshi, ed. *Kōshitsu jiten*. Tokyo: Tōkyōdō Shuppan, 1980.

Naimushō. "Chōsen oyobi Taiwan no genkyō." July 1944. In *Taiheiyō senka no Chōsen oyobi Taiwan*, ed. Kondō Ken'ichi. Chigasaki-shi: Chōsen Shiryō Kenkyūkai, 1961.

Nakano Shigeharu. "Yonin no shiganhei." *Minshu Chōsen*, no. 9 (March-April 1947): 67–70. Reprinted in *Fukkoku minshu Chōsen*, vol. 2. Tokyo: Akashi Shoten, 1993.

Nihon Eiga Zasshi Kyōkai, ed. *Shōwa jūshichinen eiga nenkan*. 1942. Reprinted as *Eiga nenkan*. Vol. 9. Tokyo: Nihon Tosho Sentā, 1994.

Nishiki Motosada. "Chōsen eiga no daizai ni tsuite." *Eiga hyōron* 1, no. 7 (July 1941): 51–53.

Oguma Eiji. *Tan'itsu minzoku shinwa no kigen: "Nihonjin" no jigazō no keifu*. Tokyo: Shinyōsha, 1994.

Oka Hisao. *Rikugun tokubetsu shiganhei tokuhon*. With a preface by Shiohara Tokisaburō. Keijō [Seoul]: Teikoku Chihō Gyōsei Gakkai Chōsen Honbu, 1939.

Okamoto Makiko. "Ajia/Taiheiyō sensō makki ni okeru Chōsenjin/Taiwanjin sanseiken mondai." *Nihonshi kenkyū*, no. 40 (January 1996): 53–67.

———. "Ajia/Taiheiyō sensō makki no zainichi Chōsenjin seisaku." *Zainichi Chōsenjin kenkyū*, no. 27 (September 1997): 21–47.

Ōmura Masuo and Hotei Toshihiro, eds. *Chōsen bungaku kankei Nihongo bunken mokuroku*. Tokyo: Ryokuin Shobō, 1997.

Pak Kyŏng-sik. *Chōsenjin kyōsei renkō no kiroku*. Tokyo: Miraisha, 1965.

Pusan Nippōsha. *Chōsen mesaretari*. Pusan, Korea: Pusan Nippōsha, 1943.

Rikugun Heibika. "Daitōa sensō ni tomonau waga jinteki kokuryoku no kentō." 20 January 1942. Collected in *Jūgonen sensō gokuhi shiryōshū*, 1st ser., ed. Takasaki Ryūji. Tokyo: Ryūkei Shosha, 1976.

Sakai, Naoki. *Shisan sareru Nihongo/Nihonjin*. Tokyo: Shinyōsha, 1996.

Sakuramoto Tomio. *Daitōa sensō to Nihon eiga*. Tokyo: Aoki Shoten, 1993.

Sanbō honbu hensei dōin-ka. *Shina jihen daitōa sensō-kan dōin gaishi*. 1946. Reprint, ed. Ōe Shinobu. Tokyo: Fuji Shuppan, 1988.

Satō Tadao. "Imai Tadashi." In *Nihon eiga no kyoshōtachi*, vol. 2. Tokyo: Gakuyō Shobō, 1996.

Senda Kakō. *Jūgun ianfu*. Tokyo: San'ichi Shobō, 1978.

Sengo Hoshō Mondai Kenkyūkai, ed. *Sengo hoshō mondai shiryōshū*. Vols. 3, 4. Tokyo: Sengo Hoshō Mondai Kenkyūkai, 1991.

Shihōshō Keijikyoku. "Shisō geppō," no. 95 (June 1942).

Shinbun Yōgo Kenkyūkai. *Chōsen dōhō koshō narabini shinbun zasshi kiji toriatsukai zadankai*. 1939.

Shirakawa Yutaka. *Shokuminchi-ki Chōsen no sakka to Nihon*. Okayama: Daigaku Kyōiku Shuppan, 1995.

Shisō Taisaku Kakari. "Hantōjin mondai." August 1944. Collected in Mizuno, ed., *Senjiki shokuminchi tōchi shiryō*, vol. 7.

Shō Kashin. *Nihongata fukushi kokka no keisei to "jūgonen sensō."* Tokyo: Mineruba Shobō, 1998.

Sin Yŏng-hong. *Kindai Chōsen shakai jigyōshi kenkyū: Keijō ni okeru hōmen iin seido no rekishiteki tenkai.* Tokyo: Ryokuin Shobō, 1984.

Suzuki Yūko. *Jūgun ianfu, Naisen kekkon.* Tokyo: Miraisha, 1992.

Takahashi Tetsuya. *Yasukuni mondai.* Tokyo: Chikuma Shobō, 2005.

Tanaka Takeo et al. "Koiso sōtoku jidai no gaikan—Tanaka Takeo seimu sōkan ni kiku." Tape-recorded 9 September 1959. In Miyata, supervising ed., *Jūgonen sensōka no Chōsen tōchi.*

———. "Sanseiken sekō no kei'i o kataru—Tanaka Takeo Koiso naikaku shokikanchō hoka." Tape-recorded 26 August 1958. In Miyata, supervising ed., *Jūgonen sensōka no Chōsen tōchi.*

Tokizane Shōichi. "Chōsen no eigakan." *Eiga junpō* 87 (11 July 1943): 51–53.

Tomiyama Ichirō. *Bōryoku no yokan.* Tokyo: Iwanami Shoten, 2002.

Ueda Tatsuo. *Chōsen no mondai to sono kaiketsu.* Keijō [Seoul]: Shōgaku Kenkyūjo, 1942.

Utsumi Aiko. *Chōsenjin "kōgun" heishi tachi no sensō.* Tokyo: Iwanami Shoten, 1991.

Utsumi Aiko and Murai Yoshinori. *Shineasuto Kyo-ei no "Shōwa": Shokuminchika de eiga zukuri ni honsō shita ichi Chōsenjin.* Tokyo: Gaifūsha, 1985.

"Wakaki gakuto to shiganhei taidan." *Ryokki* 6, no. 5 (May 1941): 110–118.

Watanabe Katsumi. *Shōkokumin no tame no heitaisan monogatari.* Keijo [Seoul]: Kokumin Sōryoku Chōsen Renmei, 1944.

Watanabe Midori. *Nikkan kōshitsu hiwa: Ri Masako-hi.* Tokyo: Yomiuri Shinbunsha, 1998.

Yamanouchi Yasushi, Victor Koschmann, and Narita Ryūichi. *Sōryokusen to gendaika.* Tokyo: Kashiwa Shobō, 1995.

Yata Naoyuki. "Wakaki sugata." *Chōsen*, no. 337 (June 1943): 65–84.

Yi Kwang-su. "Kao ga kawaru." *Chōsen gahō*, 1 September 1943, 26–28.

———. "Kokoro aifurete koso." Reprinted in *Kindai Chōsen bungaku Nihongo sakuhinshū*, ed. Ōmura Masao and Hotei Toshihiro. Sōsakuhen 1. Tokyo: Ryokuin Shobō, 2001.

Yi Yŏng-il. "Nittei shokuminchi jidai no Chōsen eiga." Trans. Takasaki Sōji. In *Kōza Nihon eiga*, vol. 3, ed. Imamura Shōhei et al. Tokyo: Iwanami Shoten, 1986.

Yoshida Seiji. *Watashi no sensō hanzai: Chōsenjin kyōsei renkō.* Tokyo: San'ichi Shobō, 1983.

Yun Chŏng-uk. *Shokuminchi Chōsen ni okeru shakai jigyō seisaku.* Osaka: Osaka Keizai Hōka Daigaku Shuppanbu, 1996.

SOURCES IN ENGLISH

Agamben, Giorgio. *Homo Sacer: Sovereign Power and Bare Life*. Trans. Daniel Heller-Roazan. Stanford: Stanford University Press, 1998.

———. *State of Exception*. Trans. Kevin Attell. Chicago: University of Chicago Press, 2003.

Alessandrini, Anthony C., ed. *Frantz Fanon: Critical Perspectives*. London: Routledge, 1999.

Allen, Ernest, Jr. "When Japan Was 'Champion of the Darker Races': Satokata Takahashi and the Flowering of Black Messianic Nationalism." *The Black Scholar* 24, no. 1 (Winter 1994): 23–46.

"Asia/Pacific American Heritage Month, 2006: A Proclamation by the President of the United States of America." 26 April 2006. http://edocket.access.gpo.gov/cfr_2007/janqtr/pdf/3CFR8008.pdf (accessed 20 January 2011).

Azuma, Eiichiro. *Between Two Empires: Race, History, and Transnationalism in Japanese America*. Oxford: Oxford University Press, 2005.

Balibar, Etienne. "'Is There a 'Neo-Racism'?" In Balibar and Wallerstein, *Race, Nation, Class*.

———. "Racism and Nationalism." In Balibar and Wallerstein, *Race, Nation, Class*.

Balibar, Etienne, and Immanuel Wallerstein. *Race, Nation, Class: Ambiguous Identities*. Trans. Chris Turner. London: Verso, 1991.

Bataille, Georges. "Hegel, Death and Sacrifice." Trans. Jonathan Strauss. *Yale French Studies*, no. 78 (1990): 9–28.

Bellah, Robert N. *Tokugawa Religion: The Values of Pre-Industrial Japan*. Glencoe, Ill.: Free Press, 1957.

Benedict, Ruth. *The Chrysanthemum and the Sword: Patterns of Japanese Culture*. 1946. Reprint, Boston: Houghton Mifflin, 1989.

Bernstein, Alison R. *American Indians and World War II*. Norman: University of Oklahoma Press, 1991.

Bix, Herbert P. *Hirohito and the Making of Modern Japan*. New York: HarperCollins, 2000.

Bordwell, David. "Classical Hollywood Cinema: Narrational Principles and Procedures." In *Narrative, Apparatus, Ideology: A Film Theory Reader*, ed. Philip Rosen. New York: Columbia University Press, 1986.

Caldeira, Teresa P. R. "'I Came to Sabotage Your Reasoning!': Violence and Resignifications of Justice in Brazil." In *Law and Disorder*, ed. Jean Comaroff and John L. Comaroff. Chicago: University of Chicago Press, 2006.

Castelnuovo, Shirley. *Soldiers of Conscience: Japanese American Military Resisters in World War II*. Westport, Conn.: Praeger, 2008.

Caygill, Howard. *A Kant Dictionary*. Oxford: Blackwell, 1995.

Chakrabarty, Dipesh. *Provincializing Europe: Postcolonial Thought and Historical Difference*. Princeton: Princeton University Press, 2000.

Chang, Gordon H. " 'Superman is about to visit the relocation centers' and the Limits of Wartime Liberalism." *Amerasia Journal* 19, no. 1 (Fall 1993): 37–59.

Chin, Frank. "Come All Ye Asian American Writers of the Real and the Fake." In *The Big Aiiieeeee!*, ed. Jeffrey Paul Chan et al. New York: Meridian, 1991.

Ching, Leo T. S. *Becoming Japanese: Colonial Taiwan and the Politics of Identity Formation*. Berkeley: University of California Press, 2001.

Choi, Chungmoo, ed. *The Comfort Women: Colonialism, War and Sex*. A special issue of *Positions* 5, no. 1 (Spring 1997).

———. "The Discourse of Decolonization and Popular Memory: South Korea." *Positions* 1, no. 1 (Spring 1993): 77–102.

———. "Nationalism and Construction of Gender in Korea." In E. Kim and Choi, eds., *Dangerous Women*.

Chŏn Kwangyong. "Kapitan Ri." In *Land of Exile: Contemporary Korean Fiction*, trans. and ed. Marshall R. Pihl, Bruce Fulton, and Ju-Chan Fulton. Armonk, N.Y.: M. E. Sharpe, 1993.

Chou, Wan-yao. "The *Kōminka* Movement in Taiwan and Korea: Comparisons and Interpretations." In Duus, Myers, and Peattie, eds., *The Japanese Wartime Empire*.

Chow, Rey Chow. "The Politics of Admittance: Female Sexual Agency, Miscegenation, and the Formation of Community in Frantz Fanon." In Alessandrini, ed., *Frantz Fanon*.

Clancy-Smith, Julia, and Frances Gouda, eds. *Domesticating the Empire: Race, Gender, and Family Life in French and Dutch Colonialism*. Charlottesville: University Press of Virginia, 1998.

Coggins, Cecil Hengy. "The Japanese-Americans in Hawaii." *Harper's Magazine*, June 1943, 75–83.

Collins, Donald E. *Native American Aliens: Disloyalty and the Renunciation of Citizenship by Japanese Americans during World War II*. Westport, Conn.: Greenwood, 1985.

Conklin, Alice L. "Redefining 'Frenchness': Citizenship, Race Regeneration, and Imperial Motherhood in France and West Africa, 1914–40." In Clancy-Smith and Gouda, eds., *Domesticating the Empire*.

Cook, Haruko Taya, and Theodore F. Cook. *Japan at War: An Oral History*. New York: New Press, 1992.

Cooper, Frederick, and Ann Laura Stoler, eds. *Tensions of Empire: Colonial Cultures in a Bourgeois World*. Berkeley: University of California Press, 1997.

Crost, Lyn. *Honor by Fire: Japanese Americans at War in Europe and the Pacific*. Novato, Calif.: Presidio Press, 1994.

Cumings, Bruce. "Boundary Displacement: The State, the Foundations, and International and Area Studies during and after the Cold War." In *Parallax Visions: Making Sense of American-East Asian Relations at the End of the Century*. Durham: Duke University Press, 1999.

————. *Korea's Place in the Sun*. New York: W. W. Norton, 1997.

————. "The Legacy of Japanese Colonialism in Korea." In Myers and Peattie, eds., *The Japanese Colonial Empire*.

————. *The Origins of the Korean War*. Vol. 1. Princeton: Princeton University Press, 1981.

Daniels, Roger, ed. *American Concentration Camps: A Documentary History of the Relocation and Incarceration of Japanese Americans, 1942–1945*. Vol. 7, *1943*. New York: Garland, 1989.

————. *Concentration Camps, USA: Japanese Americans and World War II*. New York: Holt, Rinehart & Winston, 1972.

————. "Japanese America, 1930–1941: An Ethnic Community in the Great Depression." *Journal of the West* 24, no. 4 (October 1985): 35–50.

Dower, John. "E. H. Norman, Japan and the Uses of History." In *Origins of the Modern Japanese State*. New York: Random House, 1975.

————. *Embracing Defeat: Japan in the Wake of World War II*. New York: W. W. Norton / New Press, 1999.

————. *War without Mercy: Race and Power in the Pacific War*. New York: Pantheon, 1986.

Drinnon, Richard. *Keeper of the Concentration Camps: Dillon S. Myer and American Racism*. Berkeley: University of California Press, 1987.

Duara, Prasenjit. *Sovereignty and Authenticity: Manchukuo and the East Asian Modern*. Lanham, Md.: Rowan & Littlefield, 2003.

Duus, Masayo. *Unlikely Liberators: The Men of the 100th and 442nd*. Trans. Peter Duus. Honolulu: University of Hawaii Press, 1987.

Duus, Peter. *The Abacus and the Sword: The Japanese Penetration of Korea, 1895–1910*. Berkeley: University of California Press, 1995.

Duus, Peter, Ramon H. Myers, and Mark R. Peattie, eds. *The Japanese Wartime Empire, 1931–1945*. Princeton: Princeton University Press, 1996.

Eckert, Carter J. *Offspring of Empire: The Koch'ang Kims and the Colonial Origins of Korean Capitalism, 1876–1945*. Seattle: University of Washington Press, 1991.

———. "Total War, Industrialization, and Social Change in Late Colonial Korea." In Duus, Myers, and Peattie, eds., *The Japanese Wartime Empire*.

Eckert, Carter J., et al. *Korea Old and New: A History*. Seoul: Ilchokak for the Korea Institute, Harvard University, 1990.

Emi, Frank. "Resistance: The Heart Mountain Fair Play Committee's Fight for Justice." *Amerasia Journal* 17, no. 1 (1991): 47–51.

Fanon, Frantz. "Algeria Unveiled." In *A Dying Colonialism*, trans. Haakon Chevalier. New York: Grove Press, 1965.

———. *Black Skin, White Masks*. Trans. Charles Lam Markmann. New York: Grove Press, 1967.

———. "Racism and Culture." In *Toward the African Revolution*, trans. Haakon Chevalier. New York: Grove Press, 1967.

———. *Wretched of the Earth*. Trans. Constance Farrington. New York: Grove Press, 1968.

Fiset, Louis. "Public Health in World War II Assembly Centers for Japanese Americans." *Bulletin of the History of Medicine* 73, no. 4 (1999): 565–84.

Foucault, Michel. "Governmentality." In *The Foucault Effect: Studies in Governmentality*, ed. Graham Burchell, Colin Gordon, and Peter Miller. Chicago: University of Chicago Press, 1991.

———. *The History of Sexuality*. Vol. 1. Trans. Robert Hurley. New York: Vintage, 1978.

———. "The Political Technology of Individuals." In *Technologies of the Self*, ed. Luther H. Martin, Huck Gutman, and Patrick H. Hutton. Amherst, Mass.: University of Massachusetts Press, 1988.

———. "Politics and Reason." In *Politics, Philosophy, Culture: Interviews and Other Writings, 1977–1984*, trans. Alan Sheridan et al., ed. with introduction by Lawrence D. Kritzman. New York: Routledge, 1988.

———. *Security, Territory, Population: Lectures at the Collège de France, 1977–78*. Ed. Michel Senellart. Trans. Graham Burchell. Basingstoke: Palgrave Macmillan, 2007.

———. *Society Must Be Defended*. Trans. David Macey. New York: Picador, 2003.

———. "The Subject and Power." In *Michel Foucault: Beyond Structuralism and Hermeneutics*, ed. Herbert L. Dreyfus and Paul Rabinow. 2nd ed. Chicago: University of Chicago Press, 1983.

Fujitani, Takashi. "*Go for Broke*, the Movie: Japanese American Soldiers in U.S. National,

Military, and Racial Discourses." In Fujitani, White, and Yoneyama, eds., *Perilous Memories*.

———. "*Minshūshi* as Critique of Orientalist Knowledges." *Positions* 6, no. 2 (Fall 1998): 303–22.

———. "National Narratives and Minority Politics: The Japanese American National Museum's War Stories." *Museum Anthropology* 21, no. 1 (Spring 1997): 99–112.

———. "The Reischauer Memo: Mr. Moto, Hirohito, and Japanese American Soldiers." *Critical Asian Studies* 33, no. 3 (September 2001): 379–402.

———. *Splendid Monarchy: Power and Pageantry in Modern Japan*. Berkeley: University of California Press, 1996.

Fujitani, T., Geoffrey M. White, and Lisa Yoneyama, eds. *Perilous Memories: The Asia Pacific War(s)*. Durham, N.C.: Duke University Press, 2001.

Gabaldon, Guy. *Saipan: Suicide Island*. N.p.: Guy Gabaldon, 1990.

Gallicchio, Marc. *The African American Encounter with Japan and China: Black Internationalism in Asia, 1895–1945*. Chapel Hill: University of North Carolina Press, 2000.

Garon, Sheldon. *Molding Japanese Minds: The State and Everyday Life*. Princeton: Princeton University Press, 1997.

Goldberg, David Theo. *The Racial State*. Malden, Mass.: Blackwell, 2002.

Gonzalves, Theo. " 'We hold a neatly folded hope': Filipino Veterans of World War II on Citizenship and Political Obligation." *Amerasia Journal* 21, no. 3 (Winter 1995–96): 155–74.

Grew, Joseph C. *Turbulent Era: A Diplomatic Record of Forty Years, 1904–1945*. Ed. Walter Johnson. Vol. 2. Boston: Houghton Mifflin, 1952.

Hansen, Arthur A., and David A. Hacker. "The Manzanar Riot: An Ethnic Perspective." *Amerasia Journal* 2, no. 2 (Fall 1974): 112–57.

Harootunian, H. D. "America's Japan/ Japan's Japan" In *Japan and the World*, ed. Masao Miyoshi and H. D. Harootunian. Durham, N.C.: Duke University Press, 1993.

Harrington, Joseph D. *Yankee Samurai: The Secret Role of Nisei in America's Pacific Victory*. Detroit: Pettigrew Enterprises, 1979.

Hayashi, Brian Masaru. *Democratizing the Enemy: The Japanese American Internment*. Princeton: Princeton University Press, 2004.

Heath, S. Burton. "What about Hugh Kiino?" *Harper's Magazine*, October 1943, 450–58.

Henry, Todd. "Sanitizing Empire: Japanese Articulations of Korean Otherness and the Construction of Early Colonial Seoul, 1905–1919." *Journal of Asian Studies* 64, no. 3 (August 2005): 639–75.

High, Peter B. *The Imperial Screen: Japanese Film Culture in the Fifteen Years' War, 1931–1945*. Madison: University of Wisconsin Press, 2003.

Horne, Gerald. *Race War! White Supremacy and the Japanese Attack on the British Empire*. New York: New York University Press, 2004.

Hudson, Ruth E., R.N. "Health for Japanese Evacuees." *Public Health Nursing* 35 (1943): 615–20.

Hwang, Kyung Moon. "Citizenship, Social Equality and Government Reform: Changes in the Household Registration System in Korea, 1894–1910." *Modern Asian Studies* 38, no. 2 (May 2004): 355–87.

Ichinokuchi, Tad, ed. *John Aiso and the M.I.S.: Japanese-American Soldiers in the Military Intelligence Service, World War II*. Los Angeles: Military Intelligence Service Club of Southern California, 1988.

Ichioka, Yuji, guest ed. *Beyond National Boundaries: The Complexity of Japanese-American History*. Special issue of *Amerasia Journal* 23, no. 3 (Winter 1997–98).

———. "The Meaning of Loyalty: The Case of Kazumaro Buddy Uno." *Amerasia Journal* 23, no. 3 (Winter 1997–98): 45–71.

Iriye, Akira. *Power and Culture: The Japanese-American War, 1941–1945*. Cambridge, Mass.: Harvard University Press, 1981.

Jeffords, Susan. *The Remasculinization of America: Gender and the Vietnam War*. Bloomington: Indiana University Press, 1989.

Jensen, Gwenn M. "System Failure: Health-Care Deficiencies in the World War II Japanese American Detention Centers." *Bulletin of the History of Medicine* 73, no. 4 (Winter 1999): 602–28.

Kashima, Tetsuden. *Judgment without Trial: Japanese American Imprisonment during World War II*. Seattle: University of Washington Press, 2003.

Kasza, Gregory J. "War and Welfare Policy in Japan." *Journal of Asian Studies* 61, no. 2 (May 2002): 417–35.

Kearney, Reginald. *African American Views of the Japanese: Solidarity or Sedition?* Albany: State University of New York Press, 1998.

Kedourie, Elie. *Nationalism*. 3rd ed. 1966. Reprint, London: Hutchinson, 1985.

Kim, Elaine, and Chungmoo Choi, eds. *Dangerous Women: Gender and Korean Nationalism*. New York: Routledge, 1998.

Kim, Sonja Myung. "Contesting Bodies: Managing Population, Birthing, and Medicine in Korea, 1876–1945." Ph.D. diss., University of California, Los Angeles, 2008.

Kim, Su Yun. "Romancing Race and Gender: Intermarriage and the Making of a 'Modern Subjectivity' in Colonial Korea, 1910–1945." Ph.D. diss., University of California, San Diego, 2009.

Komagome Takeshi. "Japanese Colonial Rule and Modernity: Successive Layers of Violence." In Morris and de Bary, *"Race" Panic and the Memory of Migration*.

Koppes, Clayton R., and Gregory D. Black. *Hollywood Goes to War: How Politics, Profits and Propaganda Shaped World War II Movies*. Berkeley: University of California Press, 1987.

Kozen, Cathleen K. "Achieving the (Im)possible Dream: Japanese American Redress and the Construction of American Justice." Master's thesis, University of California, San Diego, 2007.

Kumamoto, Bob. "The Search for Spies: American Counterintelligence and the Japanese American Community, 1931–1942." *Amerasia Journal* 6, no. 2 (Fall 1979): 45–75.

Kurashige, Lon. *Japanese American Celebration and Conflict*. Berkeley: University of California Press, 2002.

Leighton, Alexander H. *The Governing of Men: General Principles and Recommendations Based on Experience at a Japanese Relocation Camp*. Princeton: Princeton University Press, 1946.

Lim, Deborah K. "Research Report Prepared for the Presidential Select Committee on JACL Resolution #7." Unpublished manuscript, 1990.

Lipsitz, George. "'Frantic to Join . . . the Japanese Army': Black Soldiers and Civilians Confront the Asia-Pacific War." In Fujitani, White, and Yoneyama, eds., *Perilous Memories*.

———. *The Possessive Investment of Whiteness: How White People Profit from Identity Politics*. Philadelphia: Temple University Press, 1998.

———. *Rainbow at Midnight: Labor and Culture in the 1940s*. Urbana: University of Illinois Press, 1994.

Lowe, Lisa. *Immigrant Acts: On Asian American Cultural Politics*. Durham, N.C.: Duke University Press, 1996.

Lye, Colleen. *America's Asia: Racial Form and American Literature, 1893–1945*. Princeton: Princeton University Press, 2005.

McClintock, Anne. *Imperial Leather: Race, Gender and Sexuality in the Colonial Context*. New York: Routledge, 1995.

Martin, Philip L. *Promise Unfulfilled: Unions, Immigration, and the Farm Workers*. Ithaca: Cornell University Press, 2003.

Maruyama Masao. "The Structure of *Matsurigoto:* The Basso Ostinato of Japanese Political Life." In *Sources of Japanese Tradition*, vol. 2, *1600 to 2000*, comp. Wm. Theo-dore De Bary, Carol Gluck, and Arthur E. Tiedemann. 2nd ed. New York: Columbia University Press, 2006.

Masaoka, Mike, with Bill Hosokawa. *They Call Me Moses Masaoka*. New York: William Morrow, 1987.

Mazower, Mark. *Dark Continent: Europe's Twentieth Century*. New York: Vintage, 1998.

Mbembe, Achille. "Necropolitics." *Public Culture* 15, no. 1 (Winter 2003): 11–40.

———. *On the Postcolony.* Berkeley: University of California Press, 2001.

Minear, Richard H. "Cross-Cultural Perception and World War II." *International Studies Quarterly* 24, no. 4 (December 1980): 555–80.

———. "Helen Mears, Asia, and American Asianists." Asian Studies Committee. Occasional Papers Series No. 7. International Area Studies Program, University of Massachusetts at Amherst, 1981.

———. "Orientalism and the Study of Japan." *Journal of Asian Studies* 39, no. 3 (May 1980): 507–17.

———. "Wartime Studies of Japanese National Character." *The Japan Interpreter* 13, no. 1 (Summer 1980): 36–59.

Modell, Judith S. *Kinship with Strangers: Adoption and Interpretations of Kinship in American Culture.* Berkeley: University of California Press, 1994.

Molina, Natalia. *Fit to Be Citizens? Public Health and Race in Los Angeles, 1879–1939.* Berkeley: University of California Press, 2006.

Moon, Seungsook. "Begetting the Nation: The Androcentric Discourse of National History and Tradition in South Korea." In E. Kim and Choi, eds., *Dangerous Women.*

Moore, Brenda L. *Serving Our Country: Japanese American Women in the Military during World War II.* New Brunswick, N.J.: Rutgers University Press, 2003.

Moretti, Franco. *The Way of the World: The Bildungsroman in European Culture.* London: Verso, 1987.

Morris, Meaghan, and Brett de Bary, eds. *"Race" Panic and the Memory of Migration.* Special issue of *Traces.* Hong Kong: Hong Kong University Press, 2001.

Morris-Suzuki, Tessa. *Exodus to North Korea: Shadows from Japan's Cold War.* Lanham, Md.: Rowman & Littlefield, 2007.

———. *Re-inventing Japan: Time, Space, Nation.* Armonk, N.Y.: M. E. Sharpe, 1998.

Muller, Eric L. *American Inquisition: The Hunt for Japanese American Disloyalty in World War II.* Chapel Hill: University of North Carolina Press, 2007.

———. *Free to Die for Their Country: The Story of the Japanese American Draft Resisters in World War II.* Chicago: University of Chicago Press, 2001.

Murphy, Thomas D. *Ambassadors in Arms: The Story of Hawaii's 100th Battalion.* Honolulu: University of Hawaii Press, 1954.

Myer, Dillon S. *Uprooted Americans: The Japanese Americans and the War Relocation Authority during World War II.* Tucson: University of Arizona Press, 1971.

Naitou Hisako. "Korean Forced Labor in Japan's Wartime Empire." In *Asian Labor in the Wartime Japanese Empire*, ed. Paul H. Kratoska. Armonk, N.Y.: M. E. Sharpe, 2005.

Nakamura Masanori. *The Japanese Monarchy: Ambassador Joseph Grew and the Making* of the *"Symbol Emperor System,"* *1931–1991*. Trans. Herbert Bix et al. Armonk, N.Y.: M. E. Sharpe, 1992.

Nakano, Satoshi. "Nation, Nationalism and Citizenship in the Filipino World War II Veterans Equity Movement, 1945–1999." *Hitotsubashi Journal of Social Studies* 32 (2000): 33–53.

Nalty, Bernard C. *Strength for the Fight: A History of Black Americans in the Military.* New York: Free Press, 1986.

Nandy, Ashis. *The Intimate Enemy: Loss and Recovery of Self under Colonialism.* Delhi: Oxford University Press, 1983.

Ngai, Mae M. *Impossible Subjects: Illegal Aliens and the Making of Modern America.* Princeton: Princeton University Press, 2004.

Niiya, Brian, ed. *Japanese American History: An A-to-Z Reference from 1868 to the Present.* New York: Facts on File, 1993.

Ogawa, Dennis. *From Japs to Japanese: An Evolution of Japanese-American Stereotypes.* Berkeley: McCutchan, 1971.

Oguma Eiji. *A Genealogy of 'Japanese' Self-images.* Trans. David Askew. Melbourne: Trans Pacific Press, 2002.

Okada, John. *No-No Boy.* 1976. Reprint, Seattle: University of Washington Press, 1979.

Okihiro, Gary Y. "Japanese Resistance in America's Concentration Camps: A Reevaluation." *Amerasia Journal* 2, no. 1 (Fall 1973): 20–34.

———. "Tule Lake under Martial Law." *Journal of Ethnic Studies* 5, no. 3 (Fall 1977): 71–85.

Omi, Michael, and Howard Winant. *Racial Formation in the United States: From the 1960s to the 1990s.* 2nd ed. New York: Routledge, 1994.

O'Neill, William L. *A Democracy at War: America's Fight at Home and Abroad in World War II.* 1993. Reprint, Cambridge, Mass.: Harvard University Press, 1995.

Osajima, Keith. "Asian Americans as the Model Minority: An Analysis of the Popular Press Image in the 1960s and 1980s." In *Reflections on Shattered Windows: Promises and Prospects for Asian American Studies,* ed. Gary Y. Okihiro et al. Pullman: Washington State University Press, 1988.

Ōshima Nagisa. "People of the Forgotten Army." In *Cinema, Censorship, and the State: The Writings of Nagisa Oshima, 1956–1978,* ed. with an introduction by Annette Michelson, trans. Dawn Lawson. Cambridge, Mass.: MIT Press, 1992.

Palumbo-Liu, David. *Asian/American: Historical Crossings of a Racial Frontier.* Stanford: Stanford University Press, 1999.

Petersen, William. "Success Story, Japanese-American Style." *New York Times Magazine,* 9 January 1966.

―――. "Success Story of One Minority Group in U.S." *U.S. News and World Report,* 26 December 1966.

Plant, Rebecca Jo. "The Repeal of Mother Love: Momism and the Reconstruction of Motherhood in Philip Wylie's America." Ph.D. diss., Johns Hopkins University, 2001.

Rafael, Vicente L. *White Love and Other Events in Filipino History.* Durham, N.C.: Duke University Press, 2000.

Reischauer, Edwin O. *My Life between Japan and America.* New York: Harper & Row, 1986.

Renan, Ernst. "What Is a Nation?" In *Nation and Narration,* ed. Homi K. Bhabha. London: Routledge, 1990.

Roeder, George H., Jr. *The Censored War: American Visual Experience during World War Two.* New Haven: Yale University Press, 1993.

Rogin, Michael Paul. *Ronald Reagan, the Movie and Other Episodes in Political Demonology.* Berkeley: University of California Press, 1987.

Said, Edward. *Orientalism.* New York: Vintage, 1979.

Sakai, Naoki. "Ethnicity and Species: On the Philosophy of the Multi-ethnic State in Japanese Imperialism." *Radical Philosophy,* no. 95 (May/June 1999): 33–45.

―――. "Subject and Substratum: On Japanese Imperial Nationalism." *Cultural Studies* 14, nos. 3/4 (2000): 462–530.

―――. *Translation and Subjectivity: On Japan and Cultural Nationalism.* Minneapolis: University of Minnesota Press, 1997.

Scott, Joan W. "The Evidence of Experience." *Critical Inquiry* 17, no. 4 (Summer 1991): 773–97.

Seltzer, William, and Margo Anderson. "After Pearl Harbor: The Proper Role of Population Data Systems in Time of War." Paper presented at the Population Association of America Annual Meeting, Los Angeles, 23–25 March 2000.

―――. "The Dark Side of Numbers: The Role of Population Data Systems in Human Rights Abuses." *Social Research* 68, no. 2 (Summer 2001): 481–513.

Shah, Nayan. *Contagious Divides: Epidemics and Race in San Francisco's Chinatown.* Berkeley: University of California Press, 2001.

Sharpley-Whiting, T. Denean. "Fanon and Capécia." In Alessandrini, ed., *Frantz Fanon.*

Sherry, Michael S. *In the Shadow of War: The United States since the 1930s.* New Haven: Yale University Press, 1995.

Shibutani, Tamotsu. *The Derelicts of Company K: A Sociological Study of Demoralization.* Berkeley: University of California Press, 1978.

Shin, Gi-Wook, and Michael Robinson, eds. *Colonial Modernity in Korea.* Cambridge, Mass.: Harvard University Asia Center, 1999.

Shin, Michael D. "Interior Landscapes: Yi Kwangsu's 'The Heartless' and the Origins of Modern Literature." In G. Shin and Robinson, eds., *Colonial Modernity in Korea*.

Simpson, Carolyn Chung. *An Absent Presence: Japanese Americans in Postwar American Culture, 1945–60*. Durham, N.C.: Duke University Press, 2001.

Slotkin, Richard. "The Continuity of Forms: Myth and Genre in Warner Brothers' *The Charge of the Light Brigade*." *Representations*, no. 29 (Winter 1990): 1–23.

————. *Gunfighter Nation: The Myth of the Frontier in Twentieth-Century America*. 1992. Reprint, Norman: Oklahoma University Press, 1998.

————. "Unit Pride: Ethnic Platoons and the Myths of American Nationality." *American Literary History* 13, no. 3 (Autumn 2001): 469–98.

Soh, Sarah. *The Comfort Women: Sexual Violence and Postcolonial Memory in Korea and Japan*. Chicago: University of Chicago Press, 2008.

Sommer, Doris. *Foundational Fictions: The National Romances of Latin America*. Berkeley: University of California Press, 1991.

Spivak, Gayatri Chakravorty. "Can the Subaltern Speak?" In *Marxism and the Interpretation of Culture*, ed. Cary Nelson and Lawrence Grossberg. Urbana: University of Illinois Press, 1988.

Starn, Orin. "Engineering Internment: Anthropologists and the War Relocation Authority." *American Ethnologist* 13, no. 4 (November 1986): 700–720.

Stephan, John. "Hijacked by Utopia: American Nikkei in Manchuria." *Amerasia Journal* 23, no. 3 (Winter 1997–98): 1–42.

Stoler, Ann Laura. *Carnal Knowledge and Imperial Power: Race and the Intimate in Colonial Rule*. Berkeley: University of California Press, 2002.

————. *Race and the Education of Desire: Foucault's History of Sexuality and the Colonial Order of Things*. Durham, N.C.: Duke University Press, 1995.

Suh, Dae-Sook. *The Korean Communist Movement, 1918–1948*. Princeton: Princeton University Press, 1967.

Suzuki, Bob H. "Education and the Socialization of Asian Americans: A Revisionist Analysis of the 'Model Minority' Thesis." In *Asian Americans: Social and Psychological perspectives*, ed. Russell Endo, Stanley Sue, and Nathaniel N. Wagner. Palo Alto, Calif.: Science and Behavior Books, 1980.

Suzuki, Peter T. "Anthropologists in the Wartime Camps for Japanese Americans: A Documentary Study." *Dialectical Anthropology* 6, no. 1 (August 1981): 23–60.

————. "A Retrospective Analysis of a Wartime 'National Character' Study." *Dialectical Anthropology* 5, no. 1 (May 1980): 33–46.

Takaki, Ronald. *Strangers from a Different Shore: A History of Asian Americans*. Boston: Little, Brown, 1989.

Tanaka, Chester. *Go for Broke: A Pictorial History of the Japanese American 100th Infantry Battalion and the 442nd Regimental Combat Team*. Richmond, Calif.: Go for Broke, 1981.

Tanaka, Stefan. *Japan's Orient: Rendering Pasts into History*. Berkeley: University of California Press, 1993.

Tanaka, Yuki. *Japan's Comfort Women: Sexual Slavery and Prostitution during World War II and the US Occupation*. London: Routledge, 2002.

Thomas, Dorothy Swaine, and Richard S. Nishimoto. *The Spoilage*. Berkeley: University of California Press, 1946.

Thompson, Elizabeth. *Colonial Citizens: Republican Rights, Paternal Privilege, and Gender in French Syria and Lebanon*. New York: Columbia University Press, 2000.

Tsukano, John. *Bridge of Love*. Honolulu: Honolulu Hosts, 1985.

Tuskegee Syphilis Study Legacy Committee. "Report of the Tuskegee Syphilis Study Legacy Committee [1] Final Report—May 20, 1996." www.med.virginia.edu/hs-library/historical/apology/report.html (accessed 20 April 2004).

Ueda, Reed. "The Changing Path to Citizenship: Ethnicity and Naturalization during World War II." In *The War in American Culture: Society and Consciousness During World War II*, ed. Lewis A. Erenberg and Susan E. Hirsch. Chicago: University of Chicago Press, 1996.

United States Army Service Forces. *Leadership and the Negro Soldier*. Army Service Forces Manual M5. Washington: U.S. Government Printing Office, October 1944.

United States Bureau of the Census. *Sixteenth Census of the United States: 1940. Population: Characteristics of the Nonwhite Population by Race*. Washington, D.C.: U.S. Government Printing Office, 1943.

———. *Sixteenth Census of the United States: 1940. Population: Characteristics of the Population*. Vol. 2, part 1, 19. Washington, D.C.: U.S. Government Printing Office, 1943.

———. *Sixteenth Census of the United States: 1940. Population: Second Series Characteristics of the Population, Hawaii*. Washington, D.C.: U.S. Government Printing Office, 1943.

United States Commission on Wartime Relocation and Internment of Civilians. *Personal Justice Denied*. Seattle: University of Washington Press, 1997.

United States Congress, House of Representatives, Special Committee on Un-American Activities. "Report and Minority Views of the Special Committee on Un-American Activities on Japanese War Relocation Centers." Report No. 717. 78th Cong., 1st sess. 30 September 1943.

United States Congress, Senate, Committee on Military Affairs. *War Relocation Centers:*

Hearings. Before a Subcommittee of the Committee on Military Affairs, 78th Cong., 1st sess., on S 444. In Daniels, ed., *American Concentration Camps,* vol. 7, *1943.*

United States Office of the Assistant Secretary of Defense for Military Manpower and Personnel Policy. *Hispanics in America's Defense.* Washington, D.C.: [Department of Defense], 1990.

United States Office of the Deputy Assistant Secretary of Defense for Equal Opportunity and Safety Policy. *Black Americans in Defense of Our Nation.* Washington, D.C.: [Department of Defense], 1985.

United States Selective Service System. *Special Groups.* Special monograph no. 10, vol. 1. Washington, D.C.: Selective Service System, 1953.

United States War Department. *Command of Negro Troops.* Pamphlet no. 20–6. Washington, D.C.: U.S. Government Printing Office, February 1944.

―――. *Handbook on Japanese Military Forces.* 1944. Reprint, Baton Rouge: Louisiana State University Press, 1991.

United States War Relocation Authority. "Comprehensive Statement in Response to Senate Resolution No. 166." Prepared for Director of War Mobilization James F. Byrnes. 14 September 1943. In Daniels, ed., *American Concentration Camps,* vol. 7, *1943.*

―――. *The Evacuated People: A Quantitative Description.* Washington, D.C.: U.S. Government Printing Office, 1946.

―――. "Semi-Annual Report: January 1 to June 30, 1943." In *War Relocation Authority Quarterly and Semiannual Reports,* vol. 2. Tokyo: Nihon Tosho Sentā, 1991.

―――. *The WRA: A Story of Human Conservation.* Department of the Interior, War Relocation Authority, ca. 1946.

United States War Relocation Authority, Community Analysis Section. "The Reaction of Heart Mountain to the Opening of Selective Service to Nisei." *Project Analysis Series,* no. 15. Washington, D.C., 1 April 1944.

―――. "Registration at Central Utah." *Project Analysis Series,* no. 1. Washington, D.C., February 1943.

―――. "Registration at Manzanar." *Project Analysis Series,* no. 3. Washington, D.C.: 3 April 1943.

United States War Relocation Authority, in collaboration with the War Department. *Nisei in Uniform.* Washington, D.C.: U.S. Government Printing Office, 1945.

Utsumi Aiko. "Korean 'Imperial Soldiers': Remembering Colonialism and Crimes against Allied POWs." Trans. Mie Kennedy. In Fujitani, White, and Yoneyama, eds., *Perilous Memories.*

Wagner, Edward W. *The Korean Minority in Japan, 1904–1950.* New York: Institute of Pacific Relations, 1951.

Ward, Robert E. "Presurrender Planning: Treatment of the Emperor and Constitutional Changes." In *Democratizing Japan: The Allied Occupation*, ed. Robert E. Ward and Sakamoto Yoshikazu. Honolulu: University of Hawaii Press, 1987.

Weglyn, Michi. *Years of Infamy: The Untold Story of America's Concentration Camps.* Updated ed. Seattle: University of Washington Press, 1996.

Winkler, Allan M. *The Politics of Propaganda: The Office of War Information, 1942–1945.* New Haven: Yale University Press, 1978.

Yoneyama, Lisa. "Cold War Ruins" (tentative title). Unpublished manuscript.

———. "Liberation under Siege: U.S. Military Occupation and Japanese Women's Enfranchisement." *American Quarterly* 57, no. 3 (September 2005): 885–910.

Yoo, Jun. *The Politics of Gender in Colonial Korea: Education, Labor, and Health, 1919–1945.* Berkeley: University of California Press, 2008.

Yoshimi Yoshiaki. *Comfort Women: Sexual Slavery in the Japanese Military during World War II.* Trans. Suzanne O'Brien. New York: Columbia University Press, 2000.

SELECTED FILMS AND VIDEOS

Film titles are given first in the film's primary language.

An Sŏk-yŏng, dir. *Chiwŏnbyŏng* (J. *Shiganhei*, E. *Volunteer Soldier*). Tonga Hŭngŏpsa, 1940.

Capra, Frank, dir. *Know Your Enemy—Japan*. U.S. Army Pictorial Service, Signal Corps, 1945.

Garnet, Tay, dir. *Bataan*. MGM, 1943.

Imai Tadashi, dir., and Ch'oe In-kyu, co-dir. *Ai to chikai* (K. *Sarang kwa maengsŏ*, E. *Love and the Vow*). Tōhō and Chōsen Eiga Seisaku Kabushiki Kaisha, 1945.

Imai Tadashi, dir., and Ch'oe In-kyu, asst. dir. *Bōrō no kesshitai* (K. *Mangnu ŭi kyŏlsadae*, E. *Suicide Squad at the Watchtower*). Tōhō and Chōsen Eiga Seisaku Kabushiki Kaisha, 1943.

"Japanese-American Troops." Hearst newsreel footage. UCLA Film and TV Archive, ca. 1944.

"Japanese-American Troops." Hearst newsreel footage. UCLA Film and TV Archive, ca. 16 July 1946.

Karlson, Phil, dir. *Hell to Eternity*. Atlantic Pictures, 1960.

Logan, Joshua, dir. *Sayonara*. Warner Bros., 1957.

Pak Ki-ch'ae, dir. *Chōsen kaikyō* (K. *Chosŏn haehyŏp*, E. *The Korea Strait*). Chōsen Eiga Seisaku Kabushiki Kaisha, 1943.

Pirosh, Robert, dir. *Go for Broke*. MGM, 1951.

Rubin, Steven Jay, dir. *East L.A. Marine: The Untold True Story of Guy Gabaldon*. Fast Carrier Pictures, 2008.

Toyoda Shirō, dir. *Wakaki sugata* (K. *Chŏlmŭn mosŭp*, E. *Figure of Youth*). Chōsen Eiga Seisaku Kabushiki Kaisha, 1943.

Weightman, Judy, exec. producer. *From Hawaii to the Holocaust: A Shared Moment in History*. Hawaii Holocaust Project, 1993.

Wellman, William A., dir. *Beau Geste*. Paramount Pictures, 1939.

INDEX

100th Infantry Battalion, 5, 85, 207, 215, 236, 380; casualties and decorations of, 207–8, 216, 218; desire to avenge Pearl Harbor and, 212–13; in Europe, 207–8, 215–16; resentment of "Jap," 212; "reverse AWOL" of, 216. *See also* Japanese American soldiers

442nd Regimental Combat Team, 5, 195, 207, 225*fig*, 227, 236, 380, 383; casualties and decorations of, 207–8, 217, 219, 226; in Europe, 207–8, 215–16; formation of, 86, 180, 212; Japanese American requests for, 212; as manpower, 205; presidential citation of, 219, 226; in propaganda, 204–5; publicity of, 215; units in, 207. *See also* Japanese American soldiers

1399 Engineer Construction Battalion, 208

Adams, Ansel, 113*fig*
Adjutant General's Office, 87
adoption, 303, 318–23, 439n40; and primacy of blood, 322

African Americans, 14; alliance with Japanese, 88, 90, 93, 407–8n40, 423n39; contrasted with Japanese, 20–21, 230, 234–35; Japanese agitation amongst, 90–96; likened to Japanese, 170–71, 188; marriages with whites, 50; naturalization and, 12, 79; as "pathological," 235; in propaganda, 99–100; and sexual intimacy with Japanese, 90–91. *See also* Tuskegee Syphilis Study

African American soldiers and sailors, 10, 400n65; as abjected, 170; in *Bataan*, 317; blood segregation of, 223; in World War I and II, 208–9, Japanese agitation amongst, 93. See also *Command of Negro Troops*

Afro-Asiatic League, 93
Agamben, Giorgio, 77, 396n13
Ainu, 24
Air Corps, 83, 88
Aiso, John F., 189
Akiyama Shōhei, 66–67
"Algeria Unveiled" (Fanon), 370

Cold War (continued)
445n9; U.S.-Japan relationship and,
101, 210, 231
collaborators, 9. See also under Korean
people; Korean soldiers and sailors
Collins, Wayne, 139
colonialism, 7; gender and, 335–36, 372;
racial and sexual boundaries in, 372.
See also Korea, colonial
colonialism, Japanese. See empire,
Japanese; Korea, colonial
colonialism, U.S. See empire, U.S.
Colonial Ministry, Japanese (Takumushō):
abolition of, 66, 282
colonial modernity, in Korea, 37–39, 286,
395n8. See also empire, Japanese;
Korea, colonial
Colson, Elizabeth, 193
Combined Youth Training Centers, 275
"comfort women," 76, 290, 370, 374,
435n68, 444n46,50
Command of Negro Troops (U.S. War
Department), 59–60
Commission on Policies for the Current
Situation, 338
Committee on Military Affairs (United
States Senate), 114
Community Analysis Section, 143, 194
Company B of the 1800th Engineer
General Service Battalion, 203
Company K, 202–3
comparabilities: defined, 30
conscription, Japanese American. See
Selective Service System
conscription, Korean, 1, 17–18, 48, 51,
271–81, 296; civilizing project and,
287–88; demand for political rights
and, 51, 65, 279, 281–82; gratitude
reported for, 301–2, 342; mass examinations of, 277–78; meritocracy and,
75; nondiscrimination and, 53, 61,
64, 280, 296–98, 301; national sub-

jectivity and, 286–87; numbers and
distribution of, 45, 397–98nn, 32, 33;
pre-induction survey and training and,
272–77; public opinion and, 48; views
of Koreans in Japan on, 279–80; welfare and, 70; women and, 371
Cooper, Gary, 310–11, 354
Correa, Matthias, 95
Counter Intelligence Group (CIG):
assessment of Japanese American
loyalty and, 154–55; fueling of race
panic and, 91–94
Coverley, Harvey, 141–43
Crist, W.E., 98, 132
cross-dressing, ethnic, 308, 310, 364–65,
366
cultural anthropology, 14
culture: power to transmute bodies and,
330; as stand in for biological race, 15,
121, 128
culture and customs, Japanese, 14–15; as
universal, 299. See also modernization
theory
culture and customs, Korean: as backward, 54–59, 299, 359, 399–400n62

Dachau death camp, 208
Damone, Vic, 380
Daniels, Roger, 80, 409n52, 415n71
Davis, Elmer, 97, 106
Dedrick, Calvert L., 110–12, 193, 412n71
Development of Our Own, 91
DeWitt, John L., 88–89, 135–37
Dies Committee, 114–15, 153, 186; Cos-
tello subcommittee of, 115, 117, 214
Diet, Japanese, 342: Korean and Tai-
wanese participation in, 23–24, 65–68
Dillingham Commission. See Immigra-
tion Commission
Donovan, Richard, 96
Dower, John W., 14–17, 119, 404n5,
410n57, 411n67

Drinnon, Richard, 146, 415n18, 417n41
Duara, Prasenjit, 103, 389n14
Duenweg, L., 87–88, 95
Dutch East Indies, 92
Duus, Masayo, 408–9n47

Earthquake, Great Kanto, 22
Ebihara, Henry, H., 183
Eckert, Carter J., 271, 342, 401n73
Educational Ordinance, 301
Education, Japanese Ministry of, 22, 284–85; *Principles of the National Entity* and, 48; "recommended movies" of, 350; "The Way of Subjects" and, 11
Eisenhower, Milton S., 97, 100–101, 189
Embree, John, 99, 111, 177–82; and plan for Hawaiian Nisei, 99; *Suye Mura*, 178
Emi, Frank, 202
Emmanual Gospel Mission, 93
Emmons, Delos C., 85, 207
emperor, Japanese, 39, 47; benevolent gaze of, 48, 54, 253; in Chō Kakuchū's stories, 324–325, 327, 333, 346; equality and, 48, 54, 253, 299; "imperial subjectification" and, 46–47; Japanese American allegiance to, 132–33; Korean feelings toward, 138, 254–55, 260–61, 268, 282, 300; loyalty to, 14, 48; MacArthur and, 411n67; national holidays and, 258; postwar U.S. treatment of, 119, 410–11n60, 411n64; as "puppet," 28, 102–108; related to Koreans, 22–23; as symbol, 106, 410n53
empire, Japanese: administration of, 66; appeal to Japanese Americans, 196–97; blood, significance in, 12, 22–23, 74, 303, 315–16, 321–33; brutality of, 8, 76, 290, 293, 372–73; decolonization of, 30, 375–78; as multiethnic, 4, 11–12, 74, 299, 305, 307–18; as post-racial,

329, 300–400n62; Yamato race and, 11, 15–17, 49–51, 268, 327, 333. *See also* Korea, colonial; Manchukuo
empire, U.S.: Civilization and, 311–17; colonial soldiers in, 209–10, 317; decolonization and, 30; Hawaii as colony of, 19, 81; postcolonial model, 7–8, 28; postwar plan for, 231–33; sexual and marriage policies in, 372. *See also* Filipinos as U.S. soldiers; modernization theory; Philippines
Enlisted Reserve Corps, 86
Espionage Act, 178
ethnicity, Japanese understandings of. *See* race: Japanese discourses on
ethnic nationalism, Korean, 244, 256, 283, 289, 294; in P'yŏngyang mutiny, 285–86; recanting of, 42; as reverse racism, 60; women's oppression and, 373–74
ethnic studies, 29
Ethiopian Pacific Movement, 93, 95

"Faces Change" ("Kao ga Kawaru") (Yi), 329
families, Japanese American: in camps, 82, 112, 173–75; during evacuation, 110; as hostages, 185; rehabilitation and, 381–82; in society, 183; of soldiers, 165, 171, 173, 222, 224, 229; split, 215
families, Korean, 290–94, 336–37, 339–40, 357–59; military benefits for, 70–71. *See also* household registers; interethnic marriage, Japanese and Korean; Korea, colonial: intimacy; *sōshi kaimei*
family, the, 7; as site of liberal governmentality, 381–82. *See also* families, Japanese American; families, Korean
Fanon, Frantz, 12, 13, 187, 190, 393n46, 443–44n43; on abandonment neurosis, 320–1; on sex and colonialism, 50, 336, 370–71; vulgar racism and, 9, 385
Far Eastern Group, 98

FBI, 91; Japanese American internees and, 127, 129–30, 141–142, 146–151, 154, 159, 161, 178–79, 418n53; Japanese American relations with African Americans and, 91; liberal state and, 161

Federal Bureau of Investigation. *See* FBI

Fichte, Johann Gottlieb, 331

Figure of Youth (*Wakaki sugata*), 297, 305, 349–54

Filipinos, 13, 20; as U.S. soldiers, 209–10, 223. *See also* Philippines

film, Japanese imperial: Allied POW representations in, 362; crowds in, 357; survey of, 436n10, under total war, 303–5, 436n10; transregional productions, 306, 319. *See also* "Victorian Empire film"; *specific film titles*

film, U.S. World War II: combat film, 223, 317–18, 334. *See also* Hollywood: conventions in Japanese imperial films; "Victorian Empire film"; *specific film titles*

First World War. *See* World War I

Fortes, Abe, 215

Foucault, Michel: on panopticon, 333; on the subject, 27, 128; on thanatopolitics, 76. *See also* bio-power; governmentality; pastoral, the; population; "right to kill"; "right to make live"; sovereign power

"Four Volunteer Soldiers" ("Yonin no shiganhei"), 375

Free Japanese Corps, 100

Fryer, E.R., 110

futei senjin (unruly Koreans) 300, 367

Gabaldon, Guy, 381–85

gaichi (outer territories): abolition of, 66

Garnett, Tay, 317

Garvey, Marcus, 93

Generation of Vipers (Wylie), 348

George, Henry, 235

German Americans, 79, 83–84, 101, 131, 150, 151, 169, 216, 217

Gila River, 141, 147, 192, 196–97

Go for Broke, 223–29, 234, 380, 383–84

Goldberg, David Theo, 393n46, 406n25

governmentality, 26–27, 395n5, 417–18n41; in colonial Korea, 37–40, 64–65, 68, 70, 74–75, 244, 272, 286, 293–94, 340; in colonial Taiwan, 64–65; counter-conduct and, 196; defined, 35–36; family and, 340, 381; force and, 135–37, 143–46, 151–52, 163–64, 181–82; Japanese Americans and, 78, 82, 89, 118, 125–28, 146, 151–52, 157, 159–161, 164, 196, 202; social science and, 182; in United States, 89. *See also* bio-power; Foucault, Michel; pastoral, the; population

Gramsci, Antonio, 22

Granada Relocation Center, 112, 141, 145*fig*, 199

Grandstaff, George H., 218

Greater East Asia Co-Prosperity Sphere, 31; Atlantic Charter, compared to, 7; film and, 305; "Great Ethnos" in, 329; Japan as leader of, 11, 17; Koreans and, 53–56, 302; movement to overthrow whites and, 92

Greater East Asia Ministry, 66

Greater Japan Broadcasting Organization, 343

Green Flag League, 291, 442–43n30

Grew, Joseph, 101, 106, 120–21; queen bee metaphor and, 107, 121

gunzoku. *See* civilian military employees

Gurney, Chan, 114, 152

Guzman, Memo de, 95

Hall, John, 211

Handy, Thomas T., 96

Hans, Martin J., 88

Hara Setsuko, 297, 311, 313*fig*, 379

Harper's Magazine, 213–14

Inspectorate General of Military Training, 54–60

interethnic marriage, Japanese and Korean: colonial policy and, 17, 337–40, 372; proscriptions against, 50–51; royalty and, 22–23, 337–38, 440–41n6. *See also* nationalism: romance and

International Military Tribunal for the Far East (IMTFE), 108

internment, Japanese American: conditional and unconditional loyalty in, 166, 175–81, 183, 186, 195, 202–5; counterconduct in, 196–202, 205; draft resistance in 202–4; education and, 112, 146; forced labor in, 143; freedom and unfreedom in, 117, 125–62 ; health and, 81–82, 110–114, 385, 412n83; as humane, 114–16; indefinite leave from, 81, 129, 149–50, 158–59; martial law in, 146, 152, 159; memory of, 5–6, 389n12; Sedition Act and, 140–1; social scientists in, 182, 421n15; social welfare and, 110–12, 117; underground associations in, 198. *See also* bio-power: in internment camps; governmentality: Japanese Americans; Japanese American Evacuation and Resettlement Study; registration and recruitment; *specific camp names*

Irish problem: compared to colonial Korea, 67

Iriye, Akira, 12

Isaka Kazuo (Yun Chong-hwa), 63

Ise Shrine, 261, 328

Iseri, Kathleen, 192–93

Islam. *See* Muslims

Islam Movement, 93

isolation centers (Leupp and Moab), 141–42, 148, 151–52

Issei (first generation Japanese Americans): arrests of, 150; as classification, 149; in modernization theory, 234; naturalization and, 138; property rights, 174; registration and, 134, 167, 172, 174, 175, 177, 415n18, 179, 200; volunteering for army and, 139, 141, 169, 183, 198–99. *See also* internment, Japanese American; Japanese Americans; Japanese American soldiers; registration and recruitment

Itagaki Ryūta, 395n8

Itagaki Seishirō, 280, 301

Italian Americans, 79, 83–84, 101, 131, 150, 169, 216; Gabaldon, Guy and, 382–85

Iwasaki, Hikaru, 201

Jamaica Progressive League, 93

Janssen, David, 380

Japan, expanded concept of, 7, 17, 341, 375

Japanese American Citizen's League (JACL): class and, 157, 159, 422n28; critical historiography of, 422n28; "The Japanese American Creed" and, 189; *Pacific Citizen* and, 155; unconditional loyalty and, 203–4; wartime activities of, 183–87, 424–25n61. *See also* Lim, Dorothy

Japanese American Evacuation and Resettlement Study, 182, 184, 415–16n18, 417–18n41

Japanese-American Joint Board (JAJB), 157; screening of females, 158

Japanese American National Museum, 5

Japanese Americans: animality and, 80, 111, 113, 114, 120–21, 127, 196; arrests of, 142, 147–48, 150–51, 159; assimilation of, 87, 97, 109, 115, 118, 155–56, 160, 197, 219, 220, 235; as civilian labor, 18–21, 79, 81, 85, 87, 108, 113, 119, 161, 169, 179; evacuation of, 79–80, 109, 111, 130, 136–37, 153–54, 403n1; exclusion from civilian military employment, 84; exclusions from military, 82–85, 87–96, 195; as goats and sheep, 125–28, 214; health of, 21, 79–81, 111–13; as homological to Japan, 119, 211, 234, 381–83; hyperfecundity of, 79–80; legal discrimination against, 78–79, 133, 138–39; as military manpower, 19–21, 81–82, 89, 96, 98, 100, 136, 205; multiculturalism and, 210–11, 229–35, 384; in occupation of Japan, 105, 108, 208, 223; postwar inclusion in United States, 381–85; in propaganda, 13, 20, 96–102, 104–5, 107–8, 113, 115–16, 118, 128, 214–15, 236, 408–9n47; readmission as army civilian employees, 86; readmission into army, 86, 96–102, 104–5, 107–8, 236, 408–9n47 98; repatriation to Japan and, 135, 142–143, 151, 155; resettlement of, 81, 128, 145, 149, 171, 183; sex and, 90–91, 227–29. *See also* bio-power: Japanese Americans; census: Japanese Americans; citizenship, Japanese American; governmentality: Japanese Americans; Hawaiian Japanese Americans; internment, Japanese American; Issei; Japanese American soldiers; Kibei; Nisei; model minority discourse; registration and recruitment; women, Japanese American

Japanese American soldiers: as cannon fodder, 170, 197; casualties of, 200, 207–8, 216, 218; as childlike, 227–29; cultural difference and, 226–29; decorations of, 200. 219, 226; desire to avenge Pearl Harbor and, 212–13, 222, 227–28; distrust of publicity, 215; doctors and dentists, 193–94; emasculinization of, 227–229; in Europe, 219, 228–29; and exclusion from the Pacific, 212; Go For Broke Monument and, 5; historiography of, 29, 394n49; in labor units, 203, 213; language and, 213, 226–27; "Lost Battalion" and, 218, 224; memory of, 5–6, 107–8, 210, 236,

389n11; as model Americans, 210, 213, 216, 218, 229–30; noncitizen volunteers, 86, 139, 391n32; as "normal" Americans, 213, 216, 220, 227; number of, 19, 83, 191–92, 391–92n32; number of volunteers, 146, 191–92, 418n51, 423n44; occupation of Japan and, 108, 208, 223; as officers, 207, 391–92n32; in propaganda, 96–102, 104–5, 107–8, 211–13, 215–223, 227, 236, 384, 408–9n47; public celebrations for, 219–20; quotas for, 191; religion and, 155–56, 160, 164–65, 213, 226–27, 234; segregation of, 20, 136, 165, 170–71, 177, 181, 195, 208, 211; sexuality and, 227–29; suicide battalion of, 27, 185, 191; training of, 90, 207, 212, 224; as translators and interpreters, 5, 85, 89, 208; voluntarism of stressed, 97–98, 139–41, 183, 206, 211; volunteer induction application for, 139, 154–58, 419n66; as war heroes, 4–6, 207, 394n49. *See also* 100th Infantry Battalion; 442nd Regimental Combat Team; *Go for Broke;* Hawaiian Japanese Americans: in army; *Hell to Eternity;* internment, Japanese American; model minority discourse; recruitment and registration; Selective Service System; Women's Army Auxiliary Corps

Japanese Buddhist Church, 93

Japanese Military Academy, 41, 287, 295, 374

Japanese soldiers and sailors: compared to Koreans, 265; despair of, 377; POWs, 223; prejudices of, 294; relationship with Koreans, 268–69; as superhuman, 227

Japanese studies, 30, 101

"Japanese Women" ("Nihon no josei") (Chō), 373

Jeffords, Susan, 347–48

Jerome, 177, 214

Meiji Shrine, 280, 303, 328
Mexican Americans: in armed forces, 209; public health and, 79. *See also* Gabaldon, Guy
Military Assistance Law, 70–71
Military Clearance Section, Japanese-American Branch, Personnel Security Division, 158
Military Intelligence Division, 89, 154, 192
Military Intelligence Language School, 185, 208
Military Intelligence Service, 98
Military Reservists Association, 275
Military Service Law, revision of, 45, 301
Military Service Preparatory Training Centers, 274, 288
Miller, A.C., 109
Minami, Jirō, 40, 280–81, 301, 303, 338–39, 342, 367
Mineta, Norman, 190, 380
Minidoka, 146
Ministry of Health and Welfare, Japanese, 16, 50, 70–74, 252, 268, 292
Mink, Patricia, 380
miscegenation: in Euro-American colonies, 371–72; U.S. laws against, 17. *See also* interethnic marriage, Korean and Japanese
Mister Soldier (K. *Pyŏngjŏngnim,* J. *Heitai-san*), 305
Miura Mitsuo, 350
Miyamoto, Frank, 184
Miyamoto Yuriko, 377
Miyata Setsuko, 246, 250–52
Mizuno Naoki, 400n68, 402n81
Mizuta Naomasa, 62–63, 273
Moab. *See* isolation centers
Modell, Judith S., 321–22
model minority discourse, 31, 205, 211, 226, 229–36, 379, 384
model minority nation: Japan as, 211, 230–36

modernization theory, 231–36; hot war version of, 231–33; Japanese Americans and, 190, 234–35
Molina, Natalia, 79
Monument to the Star Lilies (*Himeyuri no tō*), 307
Moon, Seungsook, 374
Moretti, Franco, 319
Morinaga Kenjirō, 306
Morishita, George T., 217
Morris-Suzuki, Tessa, 11–12, 48, 379–80
"Mother's Prayers" (Ŏmŏni ŭi kiwŏn), 301
Moto, Mr., 104
Muller, Eric, 136, 203, 414n9
Mun, Yae-bong, 354, 357*fig*
Murai Yoshinori, 361
Muranaga, Kiyoshi, 200
Murayama Chijun, 56
Muslims, 92, 156
Myer, Dillon, 85–86, 129, 182, 186, 229, 380; camp as model of liberal democracy and, 140–52; on discrimination of Japanese Americans in armed forces, 20, 392–93n34; on making good citizens, 163; mothers and, 200; as polite racist, 114–17; on surveillance of Japanese Americans, 131, 161
Myrdal, Gunnar, 235

Naito, Richard H., 217
Nakamura, Henry, 225*fig*
Nakamura Masanori, 106
Nakane Naka. *See* Takahashi Satakata
Nakano Shigeharu, 375–78
Nam Sŭng-min, 358*fig*
Nan'yō, 66
Nashimoto Masako, 23, 337
National Conscription Ordinance, 284
nationalism: anticolonialism and, 103; family and, 315; gender and, 342–47, 362–70; homosociality in, 347–49, 361; inclusionary character of, 28, 219,

nationalism *(continued)*
229; interpellation of subjects and,
254, 325, 328; masculinity and, 341,
346–47, 373–74; mnemonic sites and,
328; multiracial, 205; racism and, 24–
25, 176–77, 187, 220, 239, 251; romance
and, 341–42, 353, 355–56, 359–60;
universalism and, 24, 28, 305; as unreason, 199; voluntary choice and,
138–39, 324–34. *See also* self-
determination
National Japanese American Memorial
to Patriotism, 6
National Mobilization Law, 284
Native Americans, 14, 20, 21, 209
naturalization, 12–13, 79, 138, 175, 210
Navy Special Volunteer System, 44–45
Nazi regime, 9, 17, 384; contrasted with
U.S. and Japanese total war regimes,
7, 11; liberal views of, 137, 214
necropolitics, 21, 77
Neighborhood Patriotic Associations, 277
"A New Beginning" ("Atarashii
shuppatsu"), 343–49, 361
New Deal, 8, 80, 233, 402n92, 417–18n41
Nimitz, Chester W., 96
Nine Military Gods (*kyūgunshin*), 280
*The Nineteenth Year of Shōwa (Shōwa
jūkyūnen)*, 306
Nisei (second generation Japanese American): African-Americans and, 188;
arrests of 150–51; citizenship and, 138–
39; as classification, 149; in counterquestions, 167–70, 174; Japanese
empire's appeal to, 197; loyalty of,
109–10, 120, 132, 136, 171; mothers
of, 198–201; officers in army, 207;
in propaganda, 99, 205, 212, 216–18;
in questionnaire teams, 129; War Relocation Authority's privileging of, 198.
See also Hawaiian Japanese Americans;
internment, Japanese American; Japanese Americans; Japanese American

soldiers; registration and recruit-
ment; Women's Army Auxiliary
Corps
Nisei in Uniform (War Relocation Author-
ity), 216–17
Nishiki Motosada, 306
Nishimoto, Richard S., 142, 144–45, 168,
181, 197
Nissen dōsoron. See under Korea, colonial:
shared ancestry of Koreans and
Japanese
Nolan, Lloyd, 317
*No Regrets for Our Youth (Waga seishun ni
kui nashi)*, 379
*Numazu Naval Academy (Numazu
heigakkō)*, 306

"Oath of Subjects of the Imperial
Nation," 254, 261
Occupation: of East Asia, 31, 376;
of Japan, 28, 31, 57, 120. *See also*
Japanese Americans: in occupation
of Japan
Ōdate Toshio. *See* Kim, Sŏng-su
Office of Naval Intelligence (ONI), 91,
98, 109–10, 121, 129–31, 154, 161, 211
Office of the Provost Marshall General
(OPMG): enlistment of Japanese
American women and, 192; history
compiled by, 83, 191–92, 405n13;
loyalty investigations and, 109, 129–
31, 157–62; propaganda on Japanese
American soldiers and, 211
Office of War Information (OWI), 97,
100, 211, 231, 241; Japanese emperor
and, 106; "Nisei, USA," 222; "Orientals in the U.S. Air Forces," 220–21;
"Outpost Report," 241; Overseas
Operations Branch, 206; psychological warfare, 222; "Radio Informational Activities to China," 221; "Splendid Record of the U.S. Soldiers of
Japanese Ancestry," 221

public health (continued)
Japanese American internment and, 111–12, 385; Japanese Americans and, 79–80; mass death and, 76; Mexican Americans and, 79–80
Public Relations, Bureau of, 116, 129, 211–12
Puerto Ricans: in U.S. armed forces, 20, 209

questionnaires. See under registration and recruitment

race: Japanese discourses on, 11–12, 15–17, 384
Racionais MC's (Rational MC's), 195–96
racism, 7; biological critiqued, 11–12, 59–60, 120, 121, 132, 235; class and, 77; cultural, 9, 15, 63, 77, 104; as duplex, 187; historicism and, 25, 53–54; humanism and, 24–26, 333; liberal, 120–21, 137, 161, 196, 213–15, 235, 317–18, 384; modernity and, 15; nationalism and, 24, 187, 220, 239; naturalistic, 25, 87, 110; postwar anticommunism and, 120; racial purity and, 17; sex and, 76–77; universalism and, 12, 24, 26, 333. See also empire, Japanese: blood significance in; other entries beginning with racism
racism, disavowal of, 8, 239; internment and, 184, 195–96, 417–18n41; Japanese American soldiers and, 210–30; in Japanese empire, 48, 54, 75–76, 299–300; Japanese in Hawaii and, 99; Korean soldiers and sailors and, 300–03, 343, 367; in total war regimes, 8–25, 333–34, 384–85; in United States, 81–82, 99–100, 118–19
racism, exclusionary, 7, 21, 25, 38, 40, 80, 295
racism, inclusionary, 7, 21, 25, 28, 40, 54, 60, 75–77, 251, 295, 375
racism, polite: African Americans and,

235; animality and, 121; biologism and, 60; defined, 25; disavowal of racism and, 75–76; Goldberg, David Theo on, 393n46; governmentality and, 27, 125–27, 293; health and, 112–14; Korean patriotism to Japan and, 251; Masaoka, Mike and, 184–91; in meritocracy, 295; in military training manuals, 54–60; Myer, Dillon and, 114–16; paternalism of, 214, 269; transition to in camps, 30; transnational contingencies and, 82, 96–108; vulgar racism and, 7, 214, 333–34, 384–85.
racism, vulgar: Coggins, Cecil H. against, 110; defined, 25; Fanon, Frantz on, 9, 393n46; health and, 112–13; Japanese American evacuation and, 80, 113, 380; Japanese American exclusion from military and, 84, 87, 89, 94, 96; Masaoka, Mike and 186; as negativity, 26; persistence of, 8, 60, 76, 114–16, 118, 152–53, 160; polite racism and, 7, 214, 333–34, 384–85.
Rafael, Vicente, 372
Reagan, Ronald, 220, 236
Reference Materials for the Education of Soldiers from Korea (Chōsen shusshinhei no kyōiku sankō shiryō) (Inspectorate General of Military Training), 54–60
registration and recruitment, 125–62; counterquestions during, 164, 166–175; internee responses to, 111, 163–205; questionnaires and, 27, 78, 109, 127–37, 154–57, 161, 415–16n18
Reischauer, Edwin O., 101–8, 119–20, 220, 222, 230–31; "Reischauer Memo" of, 101–8, 118, 231
"Relocation Center Address," 137, 165
relocation centers, 78, 111, 113, 145, 151, 158, 163, 165–66, 176; as liberal nation-state writ-small, 82, 140. See also internment, Japanese American

women, Japanese American *(continued)* 198–201; registration and, 175; as second order citizens, 229; U.S. liberation of, 192. *See also* Women's Army Auxiliary Corps

women, Korean: abjected, 362; assimilation to Japanese norms and, 341, 348–49, 352–53, 368, 442–43n30; edification of, 287, 289; film viewing and, 304; "ignorance" of, 289–91; image of, 435n68; as laborers, 71; masculinist nationalism and, 373–74; as "modern girls," 355, 355*fig;* as mothers, 289–93, 349, 435n74; as objects of reform and sexual violence, 370–73; opposition to military service and, 289–94; as self-determining, 310; Young Women's Training Centers and, 275, 277. *See also* "comfort women"

Women's Army Auxiliary Corps (WAAC), 133, 173, 192

World War I, 11, 208

World War II: cold war memories of, 384, 445n9; postcolonial imperialism and, 9; similarities of the United States and Japan during, 6, 8–9. *See also* Asia-Pacific War; total war

World War II combat film, 223, 317–18, 334

Wylie, John, 348

Yamashita Tomoyuki (Tiger of Malaya), 295

Yamato race, 11, 51, 156, 333; in *An Investigation of Global Policy with the Yamato Race as Nucleus* (*Yamato minzoku o* *chūkaku to suru sekai seisaku no kentō*), 16–17, 49–51, 268, 398–99n43; Korean relationship to, 327–28; Sun Goddess (Amaterasu) and, 400n62

Yasuda Yojūro, 23

Yasui, Kenny, 218

Yasukuni Shrine, 4, 280, 302, 328

Yata Naoyuki, 350

"yellow and brown peoples," the, 12, 26, 82, 104, 118–19, 220, 231

Yi In-sŏk, 293, 300

Yi Kwang-su, 23, 27, 329, 361, 366–369

Yi Ŭn, 23, 337

Yi Yŏng-il, 304

Yonemitsu, Robert, 217

Yoneyama, Lisa, 192, 445n9

Yoshida Seiji, 290, 435n68

Yoshida Toshiguma, 40, 41, 75–76, 287–89, 291

You and I (K. *Nŏ wan a,* J. *Kimi to boku*), 305, 350, 361–66, 369–70; ethnic cross-dressing and, 365; exchange of women, 365–66; masculinity and, 362–66; overcoming ethnic difference and, 363–64, 366

Young Men's Training Centers, 41

Young Women's Training Centers, 275, 277

Youth Special Training Centers, 273–74, 276*fig*, 277, 288

Yun, Mrs (pseudonym), 296–98

Zacharias, Ellis M., 131–32

Zone of Interior, 83–84, 87

"zones of indifference"

Text:	10/14 Fournier
Display:	Fournier
Compositor:	Integrated Composition Systems
Cartographer:	Bill Nelson